"A DIET THAT TASTES SO GOOD YOU COULD PUT THE WHOLE FAMILY ON IT."
—*Woman's Day*

"A beautiful book . . . more than 500 mouth-watering recipes . . . easy-to-read tips . . . one of the best basic cooking volumes."
—*Health* Magazine

"A good cut above the common run . . . a no-nonsense book, useful for anyone who wants to lose weight."
—*Library Journal*

"After feasting, go straight with *Weight Watchers*® *365-Day Menu Cookbook*—low-cal offerings here don't *taste* like skinny food."
—*Cosmopolitan*

"You can enjoy food and drink you never thought you could on a weight loss program . . . with *Weight Watchers*® *365-Day Menu Cookbook*."
—*Star*

"Full of out-of-the-ordinary menus and recipes, food that even a non-dieter can enjoy."
—*Boston Herald American*

"In our opinion, Weight Watchers, with its emphasis on good nutrition, gradual weight loss, and long-term results, is an excellent diet."
—*Good Housekeeping* Magazine

"The safest and most effective popular weight loss program."
—*McCall's* Magazine

WEIGHT WATCHERS®
365~DAY MENU COOKBOOK

Drawings by Melanie Gaines Arwin

Photographs by Gus Francisco

A PLUME BOOK

NEW AMERICAN LIBRARY

TIMES MIRROR

NEW YORK AND SCARBOROUGH, ONTARIO

WEIGHT WATCHERS *is a registered trademark of*
Weight Watchers International, Inc.

Acknowledgments

No cookbook is the work of one person alone. Preparing *Weight Watchers 365-Day Menu Cookbook* involved many hours creating themes, menus, and recipes, testing and editing, and finally selecting from among the many attractive dishes those to be photographed. Thanks are due primarily to the millions of members who ask, "What should I cook today?" A special thanks to Mrs. Susan O'Reilly, who always yearned: "If only you could tell me what to eat every day of the year."

My personal wholehearted thanks to Patty Barnett, Bianca Brown, John Dietrich, Judy Marshel-Ellner, Carol Gray, Anne Hosansky, Lynette McEvoy, Harriet Pollock, Eileen Pregosin, Nina Procaccini, Judi Rettmer, and Isabel Sobol for their invaluable contributions to this book.

Felice Lippert

FELICE LIPPERT
Vice-President, Food Research
   and Development
Weight Watchers International, Inc.

A hardcover edition was published by The New American Library, Inc., and simultaneously in Canada by The New American Library of Canada Limited.

Ⓟ PLUME TRADEMARK REG. U.S. PAT. OFF. AND FOREIGN COUNTRIES
REGISTERED TRADEMARK—MARCA REGISTRADA
HECHO EN WESTFORD, MASS., U.S.A.

SIGNET, SIGNET CLASSIC, MENTOR, PLUME, MERIDIAN and NAL BOOKS
are published *in the United States* by The New American Library, Inc., 1633 Broadway,
New York, New York 10019, *in Canada* by The New American Library of Canada Limited,
81 Mack Avenue, Scarborough, Ontario M1L 1M8

Library of Congress Cataloging in Publication Data
Main entry under title:

Weight Watchers 365-day menu cookbook.

Includes index.
1. Reducing diets—Recipes. 2. Reducing diets
—Menus. I. Weight Watchers International.
RM222.2.W299   1983   641.5'635   82-18936
ISBN 0-452-25396-9

Weight Watchers and Ⓦ are registered trademarks of Weight Watchers International, Inc.

First Plume Printing, September, 1983

1 2 3 4 5 6 7 8 9

PRINTED IN THE UNITED STATES OF AMERICA

A Note from Jean Nidetch

Are you the type of shopper who casts a careful eye on labels?

There's a "label" on this book that you can be assured stands for Grade-A quality. I refer to the two simple words: Weight and Watchers. Together they stand for the largest weight-control company in the world, and the most respected.

If I may take a nostalgic journey, come with me to the apartment house I lived in, in Little Neck, New York. That's where our first meetings were held, back in 1962. We began with just *six* women . . . and I suppose it's almost legendary how I shared my latest diet with them. It was one I had been jolted into going on by being asked when I was "due" (a reasonable question, but not when you aren't pregnant!). So I ran to the New York City Board of Health Obesity Clinic. The diet they gave me, which was to become the basis of the original Weight Watchers Program, was well balanced. However, I sensed that something more than calorie-counting was needed; the missing ingredient was the "I-know-just-what-you-mean" that only comes from fellow (and sister) "midnight checkers" of refrigerator lights. That's when I phoned my six fat friends.

Although we didn't realize it at the time, our recipe for success was something called *group support*. It was to become the hallmark of the Weight Watchers Organization, for the hands joined together now encircle the globe. The six have multiplied astoundingly into more than *twelve million*. That's how many women, men, and teenagers have come through our doors in search of an answer to the burden of extra pounds that can weigh you down not only physically but mentally and emotionally. So universal was and is the need that today the sun seldom sets on Weight Watchers classes. They can be found in nearly every corner of the world, from major cities to villages scarcely visible on most maps. Our members span the decades (from teens to nineties) and encompass all races, religions, careers, and social levels, for overweight is no respecter of these boundaries. In a multitude of languages, Weight Watchers members share their common problems, their mutual discoveries, their stunning rebirths.

Today's world is not only highly weight-conscious but also attuned to the importance of proper nutrition and physical fitness. So our Program has become multifaceted to include scientifically evolved weight-loss and maintenance plans, behavior modification, and exercise.

But the help we offer extends far beyond the classes. Our "label" appears on best-selling cookbooks, magazines, camps for overweight youngsters and adults, and an ever-increasing array of convenient food products. And wherever the name "Weight Watchers" is seen or heard, you have the satisfaction of knowing it is backed up by the expertise of highly skilled professionals. Many of them have lent their nutritional knowledge and culinary abilities to the making of this cookbook.

And what incredible ingredients they have

poured into it! For just as our tiny group of six is ancient history, so, too, are the days when dieting meant a steady stream of "no-no's." As you'll discover when you turn these pages, our modernized Food Plan includes foods (and drinks) never thought possible on a weight-loss plan. There are, in fact, *three plans*; our members can select "Full Choice," "Limited Choice," or "No Choice," depending on whether their tastes run to abundant variety or the safety of a more restricted menu plan. (There is even a Vegetarian Plan.) Since this book is based on our "Full Choice Plan," it brings you a dazzling range of options.

But you don't have to be on a diet to find this book an invaluable "partner." What it does is take the burden of meal-planning off your shoulders by supplying well-balanced, carefully thought-out menu plans. For the first time, we have divided a cookbook into daily menus—appropriately so, since eating successfully is a day-by-day challenge!

Now *you* have a chance to sample our exciting world for yourself and discover that it is possible to eat healthfully and control your weight without starvation, without boredom, without even having to forfeit many favorites. In a word: *enjoyably!*

Isn't it delicious to know that with this book that "choice" is yours?

Jean Nidetch

JEAN NIDETCH
Founder, Weight Watchers
International, Inc.

Contents

Introduction

Dear Reader,

Congratulations! You've invested in a year's supply of carefully planned, nutritionally balanced, and very tasty menus—all keyed to the updated version of the world's most famous weight-loss plan.

In tune with the life-style of the '80s, the Weight Watchers Program has a new look that offers a greater degree of freedom, flexibility, and fun than ever before, all within the guidelines of good nutrition. The Food Plan now allows foods seldom before given "permits" on a weight-loss plan, plus a new range of "legal" cooking methods, including sautéing and stir-frying.

Who ever heard of a diet that lets you eat peanut butter, dried fruits, crispbreads, graham crackers, popcorn, sweet potatoes, liverwurst, and fruit-flavored gelatin? And that's just the beginning! Imagine flavoring foods with imitation bacon bits, cocoa, shredded coconut, barbecue sauce, ketchup; or being able to enjoy olives, pickle relish, seafood cocktail sauce, sugar, fructose, honey, molasses, syrup, wheat germ—even beer and wine (not only for cooking but as an accompaniment to meals or social occasions).

What do so many additional foods and cooking methods cry out for? A brand-new Weight Watchers cookbook. So, in keeping with the busy lives most of us live these fast-paced days, we've concocted the most helpful cookbook we could think of: *Weight Watchers 365-Day Menu Cookbook*. It's our answer to those cries of "I get bored cooking (or eating) the same things day in and day out," or "I can't decide what to make for dinner," or "I'm not imaginative enough to be creative with meals." Now "imagination" is at your fingertips, for this book does the planning for you. Some of the menus are geared for days when you may not be very hungry; others show you how to make use of salads and vegetables as fillers. There are "entertaining" menus for special days, such as Easter, Passover, Christmas, and New Year's Eve, whether it's a family get-together or a full-scale party.

Each weekly Menu Plan is based on a nutritionally sound seven-day intake of food. For this reason, while you may use the Menu Plan for Week 3 before that for Week 1, you should follow that week's meal plans *exactly* if you want to be assured of proper nutritional balance. By the same token, there is no reason why you cannot reverse Day 1 and Day 7, but you should be sure to use the *entire* day's meals when you make that change.

These nutrition- and appearance-conscious days, learning to prepare well-balanced meals is an essential skill. As the Weight Watchers Organization knows from its more than eighteen years of firsthand experience helping hundreds of thousands of overweight women, men, and youths, a successful diet is one that helps establish a healthy pattern of eating on a *lifelong* basis. Ever since the inception of Weight Watchers—back in 1963—we have been dedicated to the basic principle of weight loss via good nutrition. Over the years, the Program has undergone

1

many changes, but our keystone of healthy eating has remained the same.

In those beginning days, our "food department" was a one-person operation and the Food Plan was a far more typical diet (based on the New York City Board of Health Obesity Clinic Diet). Since that time, an entire Food Research and Development Department has come into existence, one that includes a renowned medical consultant and a large staff of skilled nutritionists, chefs, and home economists. Every recipe in this book was developed and tested in the busy kitchens of Weight Watchers International. And what changes have been blended into those recipes! Weight Watchers constantly keeps in step with the most up-to-date medical and nutritional findings, and incorporates new foods and techniques into the Food Plan whenever possible.

Today, Weight Watchers offers members the option of three weight-loss plans—"Full Choice," "Limited Choice," and "No Choice," depending on whether the individual prefers the fullest degree of personal responsibility, or the discipline of strict guidelines. We've also inaugurated a Vege-tarian Plan to accommodate those who wish to refrain from eating meat, fish, and poultry. And since the real aim of weight loss is to *remain* slim, we have created a Maintenance Plan that guides members as they add foods to their basic diet. All the plans are medically and nutritionally supervised.

The Weight Watchers Program is more than a "diet": it is actually a *four*-way strategy for losing and maintaining weight. It includes not only the Food Plan but also a Personal Action Plan designed to help change behavior in very positive ways, a Personal Exercise Plan for shaping up and trimming down, plus global classes that provide the priceless ingredient of group support.

Whether you are a Weight Watchers member or new to our scene, whether you want to lose weight, maintain it, or simply learn how to prepare well-balanced meals, you will find a year's supply of tasty answers in this book. Just remember: a key aspect of our Food Plan is *portion control*, so weigh and measure all foods with great care.

Bon appétit.

FELICE LIPPERT
Vice-President, Food Research
and Development
Weight Watchers International, Inc.

Successful Menu Planning

Menu planning isn't the exclusive province of caterers and French chefs. Every time you make breakfast, lunch, or dinner, you've planned a menu.

The trick, though, is not to plan for just one meal at a time. Planning for a larger time frame—a whole day or week—is better. That way, you can distribute the intake of protein, carbohydrate, and fat for greater taste appeal, balance, and nutrition. You know instantly, for example, how many servings of bread you'll have on a particular day, how much fruit, or whether you've forgotten to include an important nutrient. No one food is one hundred percent nourishing, so variety is important. Moreover, it alleviates boredom.

When you see your allotted food intake set before you in black and white, you'll be less likely to deviate or binge. If you know you'll be going all-out for a special-occasion dinner, you can arrange an appropriate breakfast and lunch on that day.

And remember, there's no substitute for a good breakfast. It's been proven that those who do not skip this important meal work more efficiently, react faster, and are better equipped to face the day. Always take time for breakfast.

Another advantage of menu planning is that it will help you cut down on waste. You know at a glance what ingredients you need, the quantities, the time you should allot for preparation and cooking, and exactly how much you'll be eating.

Menu planning will help extend your grocery budget by cutting out impulse buying. Why buy something if there's no call for it on your schedule? It will also enable you to incorporate seasonal produce and supermarket specials into your diet.

Never again will that feeling of panic overtake you at four o'clock, the feeling that makes you put your hand to your head and moan, "Oh, no! What will I make for dinner tonight?"

Organization is the key. Organization means making lists: inventories of frozen and canned goods on hand, shopping guides, basic menus, reliable old recipes and interesting new ones that might help inspire you. Always maintain an adequate stock of the staple foods and basic seasonings you and your family enjoy most.

The best place to start to organize is right in your kitchen. Rearrange your storage space for maximum efficiency. Put the things you use most often where they're easiest to reach. Keep the tools for a particular job near your work area. Have enough different shapes and sizes of pots, pans, serving dishes, and utensils to accommodate the quantity and kinds of cooking you do. A kitchen scale is invaluable.

Adapt leftovers. Put them in casseroles or freeze them for future use. If your family balks, tell them you're promoting food ecology by recycling, or that leftovers today may mean steak tomorrow. If *that* fails, tell them the unvarnished truth: Food is simply too expensive to waste.

Compare supermarket ads, and bone up

on nutrition information. Investing a little time now will save time, money, and energy later.

* * *

Successful menu planning is part art and part science. The kitchen is your laboratory; the table, your canvas. But don't worry. You need neither a PhD in chemistry nor Van Gogh's dexterity with a palette knife to create meals that are nourishing both physically and emotionally.

The emotional connotations of food are very important. Do you feel more satisfied after gulping a fast-food hamburger or after a leisurely candlelight dinner? Do you associate the warmth of childhood with the school cafeteria or with special holiday meals?

Eating is definitely a sensory experience, so take the time to enjoy it. Take pleasure from the obvious amenities: pretty china, glassware, table linens, flowers, lighting, music.

But even more, notice how food appeals to all the senses. Is the aroma pleasing? Is the color natural-looking and appealing? Into what shapes has the food been cut and arranged? And in what sorts of containers is it served?

Eat slowly, savoring the taste and texture of everything and you'll realize why the English poet Alexander Pope wrote, ". . . 'tis substantial happiness to eat."

* * *

There is no "right" or "wrong" way to create a dish. Individual, family, and ethnic preferences vary, as do budgets. Often there are medical restrictions to consider as well. The only way to find out whether something works for you is to try it. All you really need are a few common-sense ground rules and a willingness to experiment in the name of creativity.

Remember that contrasts are important. Even babies reach a point where they reject a meal that is completely pureed.

Follow the guidelines of our menu plans by selecting a main dish first. Then look for vegetables that work with it. Keep in mind that a tossed salad goes with almost everything. Include an assortment of uncooked fresh fruits and vegetables for color, texture, and nutrition.

If you're planning a multi-course luncheon or dinner, a good rule of thumb is to serve mildly flavored dishes first, stronger ones later. The greater the number of courses, the fewer number of dishes you need in each.

Try not to serve the same food in the same form twice in one day. And don't repeat a major ingredient in two separate dishes. Potato soup and baked potatoes in the same meal are a gastronomic bore. Too many highly seasoned dishes, on the other hand, are a gastronomic overkill.

Limit the number of mixtures (combinations, or so-called made or composed dishes). One casserole or mixed salad per meal is sufficient.

Let people recognize what it is they're eating. Although socially conscious hostesses in Imperial Rome delighted their guests by serving the outrageous and exotic (like boiled parrot and stuffed dormouse), today's dinner guest is not so adventurous. Too many surprises where their stomachs are concerned can upset people.

* * *

You don't have to be a fancy cook to be a good one. And you don't have to dine lavishly to be well nourished. Skillful flavoring and compatible ingredients—not exotic foods and complex recipes—are what's important.

But you do have to be an informed shopper, especially when you stop to realize that the average American family spends one quarter of its annual income on food.

The four easiest-to-observe shopping tips are:

Make a list and stick to it.
Don't shop on an empty stomach.
Don't shop at the last minute before entertaining.

Use coupons, but only for things you know you'll need.

Other shopping tricks take a little more thought.

Weigh the availability of foods against their cost per serving. The least expensive way to serve asparagus, for instance, depends on the season. Fresh asparagus may be reasonable in the spring, but canned and frozen asparagus may be your best bets at other times of the year.

Consider cost per serving, not cost per pound. Boneless meat can yield up to twice as many servings as the same amount of meat with bones. If you do choose bone-in meat, use the bones to make soup.

Check labels for nutritional information and expiration dates. They're printed for your benefit. Breads labeled "whole grain" and "enriched," for example, are highest in vitamin B and minerals.

Evaporated and dried milk usually cost less than fluid milk but supply equivalent amounts of calcium and protein.

Buy the lowest market grade of canned goods that will give you the results you want. Light meat tuna might be acceptable to you in casseroles, where only white will do in a salad or sandwich. Similarly, lower grade canned tomatoes are usually fine in soups, stews, and casseroles, where their appearance doesn't matter.

Be aware of price differences. Compare the costs of brand-name and generic items. See whether a supermarket or specialty store (fish store, meat market, or cheese shop) has better prices on items of comparable quality.

Buy by weight, not by the size, shape, or color of a package. Ingenious (usually plastic) dispensers generally cost more and add to our already mammoth solid-waste disposal problems. Plain, straightforward packaging is often the most economical.

Compare the costs of prepared or partially prepared foods with foods you make from scratch. If time is a factor, consider whether the added convenience isn't worth a few extra cents. And if you just plain hate to cook, take that into account, too.

See whether it's cheaper to buy in quantity. Stock up at sales, particularly if you have a large freezer. One hint is to cook stewing chickens in quantity (when their price is good), wrap them in portion-sized packages, and label and freeze them for future use.

In the past, people were confined to eating just what grew in their region. If nothing grew, because of drought, flood, insects, blight, war, or worn-out soil, they had nothing to eat. Since they couldn't keep food, they gorged when it was plentiful and starved when it wasn't.

We're fortunate to live in a time and place where transportation and technology make a wide variety of edibles consistently available. But that shouldn't give us license to waste. Make everything count.

Use the trimmed ends or yellowed outer leaves of vegetables in soups, casseroles, and other dishes where looks don't count. That makes nutritional sense too, since the outer leaves of cabbage, broccoli, and lettuce are higher in nutrients than the inner leaves.

Use up leftover meat, fish, chicken, and cheese in salads, casseroles, and omelets. Turn chicken and turkey carcasses into broth. Crumble stale bread for crumbs.

* * *

Once you've selected a menu, shopped for the ingredients and prepared them, it's time to get down to the actual cooking. With practice and a little imagination, you can apply a technique from one recipe to ingredients from another to create a dish that's your very own. We hope the recipes and menu plans in this book will get you started.

But if you still need a little extra incentive to get going, remember the words of the famed gourmet Brillat-Savarin: "The discovery of a new dish does more for human happiness than the discovery of a star."

General Information

1. Each menu plan has been developed to fulfill the requirements of a complete week in accordance with the Weight Watchers Full Choice Food Plan for Women. The amounts indicated are for one serving. When a serving-size range is given, Men should choose the upper end of the range; the entire range is available to Youths (males 11 through 17 and females 11 through 14). Additions for Men and Youths are indicated on each menu plan.

2. Bold type on menu plans indicates that the recipe is included in this book. Menus are based on one serving of each recipe.

3. The menu plans were developed with an eye to seasonal availability of fresh fruits and vegetables. However, if fresh is not available, frozen or canned may be substituted.

4. The weights indicated on the menu plans for poultry, meat, and fish do not include skin or bones. Before eating poultry, remove and discard the skin.

5. Economy- and energy-saving tips are included for broiled and/or roasted poultry and meat. (Where applicable, these tips have been included in the menu plan introductions.) These items may be cooked in larger quantities than necessary for one meal, and the leftovers frozen for future use. To freeze, wrap weighed portions in moisture–vapor resistant material: heavy-duty aluminum foil, freezer paper, or plastic freezer bags. Press as much air as possible out of the package. Be sure to label it, indicating contents, date, and amount. Freeze at 0°F. or lower. Cooked poultry may be frozen for up to 2 months; cooked meat for as long as 3 months. To thaw, place the wrapped food in the refrigerator.

6. For Weight Watchers members who take lunch to work and prefer not to make their own menu substitutions, and for non-members who pack and carry lunch, we have included Midday Meal "Brown-Bag" Substitutions; refer to the Appendix (pp. 313–320) for this section. It is recommended that you pack meals in plastic or insulated vacuum containers, aluminum foil, or plastic wrap. Vacuum containers should be chilled or rinsed with cold water before filling with foods that are to be kept cold, and rinsed with hot water before filling with heated foods.

7. Not every menu includes a beverage. Water, club soda, mineral water, coffee, or tea may be added to any meal. It is recommended that at least 6 to 8 glasses of water be consumed daily.

8. "Snacks, at Planned Times" may be consumed with any of the day's meals instead of being taken as snacks.

9. Wherever ½ cup skim milk has been included in the menu, it may be combined with diet soda to make a creamy, frothy

treat. Here's a recipe to help you get started:

MILK FROTH
Makes 1 serving

1 cup cold diet soda (flavors such as raspberry, orange, black cherry, or cherry-cola)
½ cup cold skim milk

Combine soda and milk in blender container; process at high speed for 3 minutes. Pour into a tall glass over ice; serve immediately.

Per serving: 45 calories; 4 g protein; 0.2 g fat; 6 g carbohydrate; 128 mg sodium

10. Check the menu plan and make a weekly shopping list. Before beginning to prepare a recipe, make certain every item is on hand.

11. Nonstick cookware makes it possible to cook without fat. Use cookware manufactured with a nonstick surface, or spray an ordinary pan with a nonstick cooking spray.

12. For best recipe results, always take time to measure and weigh—don't try to judge portions by eye. We recommend the use of the following items to help you with portion control: a scale for weighing food, measuring cups for both liquid and dry measures, and measuring spoons. All dry measurements should be level. Recipe directions may sometimes look as if they're taking the long way around, but remember, they're all shortcuts to weight control.

13. The herbs used in these recipes are *dried* unless otherwise indicated. If you are substituting fresh herbs, use approximately four times the amount of dried (e.g., 1 teaspoon chopped fresh basil instead of ¼ teaspoon dried basil leaves). If you are substituting ground (powdered) herbs for dried leaves, use approximately half the amount of dried (e.g., ¼ teaspoon ground thyme instead of ½ teaspoon dried thyme leaves).

14. If you are substituting fresh spices for ground, use approximately eight times the amount of ground (e.g., 1 teaspoon minced fresh ginger root instead of ⅛ teaspoon ground ginger).

15. The fruit and juice should be fresh, or frozen or canned with no sugar added. Canned fruit may be packed in its own or another juice, in a juice blend, in water, and with artificial sweetener. Apple cider should be unfermented.

16. The vegetables are fresh unless otherwise indicated. If you substitute frozen or canned vegetables, it may be necessary to adjust cooking times accordingly.

17. Meat should be trimmed of all visible fat.

18. Canned fish should be well drained before weighing.

19. The bagels and hamburger and frankfurter rolls should weigh 2 ounces each; one half should weigh 1 ounce.

20. The graham crackers should each be 2½ inches square.

21. When vegetable oil is called for, oils such as safflower, sunflower, soybean, corn, cottonseed, peanut, or any of these combined may be used. Since olive oil and sesame oil have distinctive flavors, they have been specifically indicated. There are two types of sesame oil: light and dark. The light oil is relatively flavorless and may be used as a substitute for any other vegetable oil. When sesame oil is specified, use the dark variety. This product, made from *toasted* sesame seeds, has a rich amber color and a characteristic sesame flavor.

22. To enhance enjoyment and provide additional variety, we have included some low-calorie and reduced-calorie products. The following is a guide to the products used in this book:

Low-calorie whipped topping
　3 calories per tablespoon
Low-calorie chocolate topping
　16 calories per tablespoon
Low-calorie maple syrup
　12 calories per tablespoon
Reduced-calorie fruit-flavored spreads
　8 calories per teaspoon
Low-calorie Italian dressing
　2 calories per tablespoon

Low-calorie French dressing
6 calories per tablespoon
Flavored low-calorie gelatins
8 calories per ½ cup

When substituting a product with a different caloric value, be sure not to exceed a total of 20 calories daily.

23. We have included recipes for Homemade White and Whole Wheat Bread (see page 258) and Homemade Mayonnaise (see page 288). These may be used whenever bread or mayonnaise is called for in other recipes and menu plans.

24. Some of our recipes call for cooked rice or pasta. The nutrition information has been calculated on the assumption that these items have been cooked without additional salt.

25. We have included recipes for Chicken Broth, Beef Broth, and Vegetable Broth. These broths were developed without the addition of salt and have been used in various other recipes throughout the book. If desired, bouillon (made from cubes or instant broth and seasoning mix) may be substituted for homemade broth. Use 1 cube or packet dissolved in ¾ cup hot water for each ¾ cup broth. Since these products do contain salt, the amount of salt called for in the recipe may have to be adjusted.

26. In any recipe for more than one serving it is important to mix ingredients well and to *divide evenly*, so that each portion will be the same size.

27. It is recommended that chilled foods be served on chilled plates and hot foods on warmed plates. Plates and glassware should be chilled in the refrigerator for approximately five minutes before serving. Plates and platters can be heated by placing them in a warm oven (no more than 200°F.) for five to ten minutes before serving, or in a warmer, or on a warming tray.

Oven Temperatures

Oven thermostats should be checked at least once a year. If your oven does not have a thermostat or regulator, the following chart will give you an idea of the equivalent amount of heat required for each temperature range.

250° to 275°F. Very slow oven
300° to 325°F. Slow oven
350° to 375°F. Moderate oven
400° to 425°F. Hot oven
450° to 475°F. Very hot oven
500° to 525°F. Extremely hot oven

An oven thermometer can be purchased and placed in the oven to help determine the degree of heat.

Since foods bake faster in heat-resistant glass than in shiny metal pans, it is recommended that the temperature be lowered by 25°F. when baking in glass.

Microwave Ovens

Many of our recipes can be cooked in a microwave oven. Since there is no one standard that applies to all ovens, you will have to experiment with your unit and follow the manufacturer's advice for timing. Generally, you should allow about ¼ of the cooking time. This means that if our recipe suggests 20 minutes, allow 5 minutes in your microwave oven (or slightly less, since it's wiser to undercook than overcook). Please note that our roasting procedures for beef, ham, lamb, and pork require the use of a rack so that fat can drain off into the pan. Plastic racks are available for use in microwave ovens.

Slow Cookers

If you enjoy cooking with this appliance, there's no reason why you can't adapt many of our recipes to its use. We're giving you a headstart on Chicken Broth: Combine all ingredients; cook covered on low for 12 hours; strain and proceed as in the basic recipe.

Artificial Sweeteners

The use of artificial sweeteners on the Weight Watchers Food Plan has always been optional. Natural sweetness is available in the form of fruits and honey. You may also use white and brown sugar, fructose, molasses, and syrup. The use of artificial sweeteners is completely optional, and we believe that the decision about using them should be made by you and your physician.

Nutrition Notes

Nutrition is defined as the process by which we utilize foods in order to maintain healthy bodily functions. Foods provide the nutrients necessary for energy, growth, and repair of body tissues, as well as for regulation and control of body processes. You need about forty different nutrients to stay healthy. These include proteins, fats, carbohydrates, vitamins, minerals, and water. It is the *amount* of proteins, carbohydrates, and fats in foods that determines their energy value or caloric content. The objective of daily menu planning is to provide yourself with basic nutrients while staying within your caloric limit.

Proteins are necessary for building and maintaining body tissues. Poultry, meat, fish, eggs, milk, and cheese are the best sources of protein. Fats and carbohydrates provide energy in addition to assisting other body functions. Fruit, vegetables, cereals, and grains are rich in carbohydrates. Margarine, vegetable oils, poultry, meat, and fish supply the fats we need.

Vitamins and minerals are also essential for the body's proper functioning. Sodium is especially important for maintaining body water and therefore has a significant effect on weight control. Sodium occurs naturally in some foods, and additional amounts are often added in processing prepared foods.

Variety is the key to successful menu planning. No single food supplies all the essential nutrients in the amounts needed. The greater the variety of food the less likely you are to develop either a deficiency or an excess of any single nutrient, and the more interesting and attractive your diet will be.

This cookbook contains menu plans and recipes. Approximate nutrient values are provided with each recipe for calories, protein, fat, carbohydrate, and sodium. The menus provide approximately 1,200 calories per day for women, 1,600 calories for men, and 1,700 calories for youths. These daily averages are based on one week's intake. The menus will allow you to plan nutritious meals, expand your choice of selections, help with portion control, and maintain a well-balanced diet.

THE MENU PLANNER

Ambrosia was the legendary food of the gods on Mount Olympus. In the great hall of the Palace of Jupiter, the gods feasted each day, washing down their ambrosia with nectar served by the goddess Hebe.

As they ate and drank they talked over the affairs of heaven and earth and listened to the songs of the Muses, while Apollo, the god of music, played his lyre. At sunset, the gods returned to their respective homes to sleep and refresh themselves for the next day's feasting and talking.

Today, the word "ambrosia" is used to describe an especially delicious food or drink.

To start the year off divinely, try Cereal with Spiced Fruit Ambrosia (Day 1). And best wishes for a healthy, prosperous year!

WEEK 1

DAY 1

MORNING MEAL
Cereal with Spiced Fruit Ambrosia
Coffee or Tea

MIDDAY MEAL
Cauliflower and Zucchini Soup
Shrimp Scampi
½ cup Steamed Broccoli
Green Salad with **Russian Dressing**
Frozen Apple-Banana Dessert
4 fluid ounces Champagne
Coffee or Tea

EVENING MEAL
Reuben Sandwich
Lettuce and Radish Salad
    with **Tarragon Vinaigrette**
½ medium Grapefruit

SNACKS, AT PLANNED TIMES
2 cups Plain Popcorn; Diet Soda; ½ cup Cherry-
    Flavored Low-Calorie Gelatin

Serving Information
Men and Youth: Add 2 slices Rye Bread and ½
    cup Orange Sections
Youth: Add 1 cup Skim Milk

DAY 4

MORNING MEAL
½ cup Grapefruit Juice
1 serving Hot Cereal, ¾ ounce uncooked
1 slice Toasted Whole Wheat Bread
1 teaspoon Margarine
1 cup Skim Milk
Coffee or Tea

MIDDAY MEAL
3–4 ounces Broiled Veal Patty
Lettuce Wedge with Lemon Juice
Carrot-Pumpkin Pudding

EVENING MEAL
Beef and Corn Casserole
Green Salad with **Basic Vinaigrette**
½ cup Canned Sliced Peaches

SNACKS, AT PLANNED TIMES
1 cup Tomato Juice; 10 Oyster Crackers;
    1 cup **Hot Mocha Milk**

Serving Information
Men and Youth: Add 1 Hamburger Roll, 4 medium
    Dried Apricot Halves, and 2 Dates
Youth: Add 1 cup Skim Milk and ½ cup Plain
    Unflavored Yogurt

DAY 5

MORNING MEAL
1 small Orange
Open-Face Grilled Cheese Sandwich I
¼ cup Skim Milk
Coffee or Tea

MIDDAY MEAL
Mushroom Omelet
½ cup Alfalfa or Bean Sprouts
    with **Wine Vinaigrette**
1 ounce Whole Wheat Roll
½ cup Fruit Salad
¼ cup Skim Milk
Coffee or Tea

EVENING MEAL
3–4 ounces Poached Scrod Fillet
2 teaspoons Chili Sauce
Slow-Cooked Vegetable Medley
1 small Apple

SNACKS, AT PLANNED TIMES
½ cup Fruit-Flavored Gelatin; ¾ cup Plain
    Unflavored Yogurt

Serving Information
Men and Youth: Add 1 ounce Whole Wheat Roll,
    ½ medium Banana, sliced, 2 ounces Pita Bread,
    and ½ cup Canned Pineapple Chunks
Youth: Add 1½ cups Skim Milk

DAY 2

MORNING MEAL
1 cup Honeydew or Cantaloupe Balls
1/3 cup Part-Skim Ricotta Cheese
1 slice Raisin Bread
1 cup Skim Milk
Coffee or Tea

MIDDAY MEAL
3–4 ounces Broiled Beef Liver
1/4 cup Sliced Onion sautéed in 1 1/2 teaspoons
    Vegetable Oil
1 cup Cooked Wax Beans with Diced Pimiento
Sparkling Mineral Water

EVENING MEAL
3–4 ounces Broiled Chicken
Cucumber and Tomato Salad
2 Green Olives
1 ounce Enriched Roll
1/2 cup Applesauce with 1 tablespoon Raisins

SNACKS, AT PLANNED TIMES
1/2 cup Plain Unflavored Yogurt with 1 teaspoon
    Reduced-Calorie Apricot Spread; 1/2 cup
    Strawberries

Serving Information
Men and Youth: Add 1 slice Raisin Bread, 1/2
    English Muffin, toasted, 1 large Tangerine, and
    4 medium Dried Apricot Halves
Youth: Add 1 cup Skim Milk

DAY 3

MORNING MEAL
1/3 cup Pineapple Juice
Bread Pudding
Coffee or Tea

MIDDAY MEAL
2/3 cup Cottage Cheese
6 Melba Toast Rounds
1 1/2 teaspoons Margarine
Tossed Salad with Lemon Juice
1/2 cup Orange and Grapefruit Sections

EVENING MEAL
Baked Fish Casserole
Sliced Radishes on Lettuce
    with Cider Vinegar
1 small Pear
1/4 cup Skim Milk
Coffee or Tea

SNACKS, AT PLANNED TIMES
3/4 cup **Chicken Broth**; 3/4 ounce Crispbread;
    1 cup Skim Milk

Serving Information
Men and Youth: Add 1/3 cup Pineapple Juice, 1
    slice Pumpernickel Bread, and 1 small Apple
Youth: Add 2 cups Skim Milk

DAY 6

MORNING MEAL
1/2 medium Banana
3/4 ounce Ready-to-Eat Cereal
1 cup Skim Milk
Coffee or Tea

MIDDAY MEAL
3–4 ounces Sardines
2 teaspoons Mayonnaise
1/4 cup Sliced Onion
1 medium Tomato, sliced
1 slice Pumpernickel Bread
Mineral Water with Lemon Wedge

EVENING MEAL
3–4 ounces Roast Pork
1 cup Cooked Bean Sprouts with 1/4 cup Canned
    Water Chestnuts and 1/2 teaspoon Sesame
    Seeds
Green Salad with **Gingered Vinaigrette**
4 fluid ounces Red Wine
2-inch wedge Honeydew

SNACKS, AT PLANNED TIMES
4 Canned Apricot Halves with 2 tablespoons
    Juice with 1/4 cup Plain Unflavored Yogurt;
    Root Beer Froth; 2 Graham Crackers

Serving Information
Men and Youth: Add 2 tablespoons Raisins, 1
    slice Pumpernickel Bread, 1/2 cup Canned Fruit
    Cocktail, 2-inch wedge Honeydew, and 2 Graham
    Crackers
Youth: Add 1 cup Skim Milk

DAY 7

MORNING MEAL
1/3 cup Prune Juice
1/3 cup Cottage Cheese
1/2 small Enriched Bagel
1 teaspoon Reduced-Calorie Margarine
1/2 cup Skim Milk
Coffee or Tea

MIDDAY MEAL
Sesame Chicken with Green Beans
4 ounces Baked Potato
Watercress and Radish Salad with Lemon Juice
1/2 cup Orange Sections

EVENING MEAL
Fish Balls with Herb Sauce
1/2 cup Steamed Mushrooms
1/2 cup Steamed Red Bell Pepper Slices
Sparkling Mineral Water with Twist of Lime

SNACKS, AT PLANNED TIMES
1 serving Vanilla-Flavored Low-Calorie Milk
    Beverage; 1/2 cup Canned Crushed Pineapple

Serving Information
Men and Youth: Add 1/2 small Enriched Bagel,
    1 slice Cracked Wheat Bread, and 1/2 cup
    Canned Cherries
Youth: Add 1/2 cup Skim Milk and 1/2 cup Plain
    Unflavored Yogurt

Recipes labeled "creole" traditionally contain rice, tomatoes, green pepper, and potent seasonings. One of these seasonings is cumin, a highly aromatic member of the parsley family.

WEEK **2**

Although cumin seeds resemble caraway, beware. They are far stronger and should be used sparingly. You can substitute cumin for caraway in bread recipes—just use half as much. Or try it in eggs, chicken salad, curry, or sprinkled over cookies before baking. And for an interesting appetizer spread, blend cumin seeds to taste with cottage or Cheddar cheese. Beef Liver Creole (Day 1) contains cumin.

Economy Tip—Broiled chicken is on the menu on Day 2. Leftovers may be frozen and used in Curried Chicken Salad recipe (Week 3, Day 6).

Energy-Saving Tip—Broil chicken breast for Cold Chicken Platter recipe (Day 4) while broiling chicken for Day 2. Chill.

DAY **1**

MORNING MEAL
½ medium Grapefruit
1 serving Hot Cereal, ¾ ounce uncooked
½ cup Skim Milk
Coffee or Tea

MIDDAY MEAL
3–4 ounces Tuna on Lettuce Leaves
2 teaspoons Mayonnaise
½ cup Chilled Cooked Asparagus Tips
2 Black Olives
1 ounce Pita Bread
1 teaspoon Margarine
½ cup Skim Milk
Coffee or Tea

EVENING MEAL
¾ cup **Beef Broth**
10 Oyster Crackers
Beef Liver Creole
½ cup Cooked Enriched Rice
½ cup Fruit Salad

SNACKS, AT PLANNED TIMES
½ cup Orange-Flavored Low-Calorie Gelatin;
   ½ cup Orange Sections; **Hot Cocoa** with
   Cinnamon Stick Stirrer

Serving Information
Men and Youth: Add 1 slice Whole Wheat Bread,
   ½ medium Banana, 1 small Apple, and 2
   Graham Crackers
Youth: Add 1½ cups Skim Milk

DAY **4**

MORNING MEAL
⅓ cup Apple Juice
1 Scrambled Egg with Chives
½ small Enriched Bagel
½ cup Skim Milk
Coffee or Tea

MIDDAY MEAL
Cold Chicken Platter
1 slice Oatmeal or Whole Wheat Bread
2-inch wedge Honeydew with Lime Wedge

EVENING MEAL
1 cup Tomato Juice
Grilled Ham Steak with Pineapple
¼ cup Steamed Chinese Pea Pods
½ cup Steamed Cauliflower
Green Salad with **Herb Dressing**
¼ cup Canned Fruit Cocktail with ¼ cup Plain
   Unflavored Yogurt and ½ teaspoon Honey

SNACKS, AT PLANNED TIMES
½ cup Skim Milk; 2 Graham Crackers;
   Marinated Carrots

Serving Information
Men and Youth: Add ⅓ cup Apple Juice and 1
   English Muffin, split and toasted
Men: Add 1 ounce Boned Cooked Ham Steak at
   the Evening Meal
Youth: Add 2 cups Skim Milk

DAY **5**

MORNING MEAL
1 small Orange
1 ounce Swiss Cheese
1 slice Rye Bread
½ cup Skim Milk
Coffee or Tea

MIDDAY MEAL
3 tablespoons Peanut Butter
2 teaspoons Reduced-Calorie Grape Spread
2 slices Raisin Bread
½ cup Skim Milk
Coffee or Tea

EVENING MEAL
3–4 ounces Broiled Veal Chop
½ cup Steamed Broccoli with
   Lemon "Butter" Sauce
Mixed Vegetable Salad
3 ounces Chocolate-Flavored Dietary Frozen
   Dessert

SNACKS, AT PLANNED TIMES
2 Canned Pineapple Slices with 2 tablespoons
   Juice and 1 teaspoon Shredded Coconut;
   Root Beer Froth

Serving Information
Men and Youth: Add 1 small Apple, 1 slice
   Cracked Wheat Bread, and 2 tablespoons
   Raisins
Youth: Add 1½ cups Skim Milk

DAY 2

MORNING MEAL
½ cup Orange Juice
⅓ cup Cottage Cheese
1 slice Raisin Bread
½ cup Skim Milk
Coffee or Tea

MIDDAY MEAL
French Omelet with 1 teaspoon Imitation
    Bacon Bits
1 slice Pumpernickel Bread
1¼ teaspoons Margarine
½ cup Steamed Chopped Kale with ¼ cup
    Sliced Canned Water Chestnuts
½ cup Skim Milk
Coffee or Tea

EVENING MEAL
3–4 ounces Broiled Chicken
½ cup Steamed Zucchini with dash Oregano
½ cup Steamed Wax Beans
Green Salad with **Thousand Island Dressing**
Tropical Treat

SNACKS, AT PLANNED TIMES
½ cup Applesauce with dash Cinnamon;
    Coconut-Coffee Mounds

Serving Information
Men and Youth: Add 1 slice Pumpernickel Bread,
    ¼ small Pineapple, and 1 ounce Whole Wheat
    Roll
Youth: Add 1½ cups Skim Milk

DAY 3   15

MORNING MEAL
½ cup Canned Sliced Peaches
¾ ounce Ready-to-Eat Cereal
½ cup Skim Milk
Coffee or Tea

MIDDAY MEAL
Tomato Stuffed with Herb Cheese
Lettuce Wedge with 1 teaspoon Mayonnaise
4 Melba Toast Slices
1 teaspoon Margarine
1 cup Strawberries

EVENING MEAL
3–4 ounces Broiled Flounder
4 ounces Baked Potato with ¼ cup Plain
    Unflavored Yogurt plus Chives
½ cup Cooked Spinach
Endive Salad with **Garlic Vinaigrette**
½ cup Canned Cherries

SNACKS, AT PLANNED TIMES
1 cup Mixed Vegetable Juice with Celery Sticks;
    ¾ cup Buttermilk

Serving Information
Men and Youth: Add 1 slice Enriched Bread, ¾
    ounce Crispbread, and 1 large Tangerine
Youth: Add 1½ cups Skim Milk

DAY 6

MORNING MEAL
Honey-Stewed Prunes
1 serving Hot Cereal, ¾ ounce uncooked
½ cup Skim Milk
Coffee or Tea

MIDDAY MEAL
Sardine Salad
1 medium Tomato, sliced
¼ cup Sliced Onion
1 ounce Enriched Roll
1 teaspoon Margarine
½ cup Lime-Flavored Gelatin
½ cup Skim Milk
Coffee or Tea

EVENING MEAL
3–4 ounces Broiled Hamburger
1 Hamburger Roll
2 teaspoons Ketchup
1 medium Dill Pickle
Curried Cole Slaw
Green Salad with **Dijon-Herb Dressing**
Apple Compote

SNACKS, AT PLANNED TIMES
½ medium Papaya or ½ medium Grapefruit;
    ½ cup Vanilla-Flavored Low-Calorie Milk
    Pudding

Serving Information
Men and Youth: Add ⅓ cup Pineapple Juice, 1
    slice Toasted Enriched Bread, 1 ounce Enriched
    Roll, and ½ cup Canned Fruit Cocktail
Youth: Add 1 cup Skim Milk

DAY 7

MORNING MEAL
Broiled Grapefruit
1 Poached Egg
½ English Muffin, toasted
¾ teaspoon Margarine
½ cup Skim Milk
Coffee or Tea

MIDDAY MEAL
Bean and Squash Soup
6 Saltines
Hearts of Lettuce with **Green Goddess Salad
    Dressing**
Sparkling Mineral Water with Lemon Wedge

EVENING MEAL
3–4 ounces Broiled Scallops with Lemon Juice
½ cup Cooked Enriched Noodles
Broiled Tomato
Spinach Salad with **Lemon Salad Dressing**
4 fluid ounces White Wine
2 Canned Peach Halves with 2 tablespoons Juice

SNACKS, AT PLANNED TIMES
1 cup Strawberries; **Coffee-Yogurt Shake**

Serving Information
Men and Youth: Add ½ English Muffin, toasted,
    4 Canned Apricot Halves with 2 tablespoons
    Juice, and 2 Canned Peach Halves with 2
    tablespoons Juice
Youth: Add ½ cup Skim Milk and ¾ cup Plain
    Unflavored Yogurt

Eat not to dullness; drink not to elevation.

—Benjamin Franklin
(1706–1790)

The practical virtues of the delicately flavored corn product known as hominy— no-nonsense nutrition, ease of preparation, and low cost—would have appealed to Benjamin Franklin.

Hominy is made from mature kernels of ordinary white or yellow field corn (the white is more expensive) that have been hulled, or shelled. When broken into large fragments, it's called coarse grits, pearl hominy, samp, or groats. A finer grind produces meal or grits.

We put it to good use in Hominy Grits Soufflé (Day 3).

Economy Tip—Roast chicken is on the menu on Day 7. Leftovers may be frozen and used in Chicken Salad Oriental recipe (Week 7, Day 4).

MORNING MEAL
1 cup Strawberries
¾ ounce Ready-to-Eat Cereal
½ cup Skim Milk
Coffee or Tea

MIDDAY MEAL
¾ cup **Beef Broth**
Open-Face Grilled Cheese Sandwich II
Tossed Salad with **Wine Vinaigrette**
½ cup Canned Mandarin Orange Sections with
    1 teaspoon Shredded Coconut

EVENING MEAL
3–4 ounces Broiled Veal Chop
½ cup Cooked Brussels Sprouts
Broiled Tomato
Sliced Belgian Endive on Lettuce with 1 teaspoon
    Mayonnaise
Baked Apple

SNACKS, AT PLANNED TIMES
½ cup Skim Milk; ½ Matzo Board with 1
    teaspoon Margarine and 1 teaspoon Reduced-
    Calorie Apricot Spread; ½ cup Plain
    Unflavored Yogurt

Serving Information
Men and Youth: Add 1 slice Enriched Bread,
    1 slice Whole Wheat Bread, and 4 Canned
    Apricot Halves with 2 tablespoons Juice
Youth: Add 1½ cups Skim Milk

MORNING MEAL
Oven-Stewed Prunes
⅓ cup Cottage Cheese
¾ ounce Crispbread
½ cup Skim Milk
Coffee or Tea

MIDDAY MEAL
½ cup Tomato Juice with Lemon Wedge
Salmon Mousse
Endive and Watercress Salad with Lemon Juice
6 Saltines
Sparkling Mineral Water with Lime Wedge

EVENING MEAL
Mediterranean Stew
½ cup Steamed Broccoli
Green Salad with 1 tablespoon Plain Unflavored
    Yogurt
1 ounce Pita Bread
¾ teaspoon Margarine
½ medium Papaya or ½ medium Grapefruit

SNACKS, AT PLANNED TIMES
½ cup Chocolate-Flavored Low-Calorie Milk
    Pudding; 3 medium Dried Apricot Halves

Serving Information
Men and Youth: Add 1 cup Melon Balls, 1 ounce
    Pita Bread, and 2 Dried Figs
Youth: Add 2 cups Skim Milk

MORNING MEAL
½ cup Grapefruit and Orange Sections
1 serving Hot Cereal, ¾ ounce uncooked
½ cup Skim Milk
Coffee or Tea

MIDDAY MEAL
⅔ cup Cottage Cheese
Alfalfa or Bean Sprouts and Cherry Tomatoes
    on Lettuce
Garlic Bread
Pear Frozen Yogurt

EVENING MEAL
¾ cup Onion Bouillon
3–4 ounces Broiled Chicken Livers
6 medium Cooked Asparagus Spears with
    1 teaspoon Margarine and 1 teaspoon Sesame
    Seeds
Cauliflower Florets and Sliced Radishes on
    Lettuce with **Savory Vinaigrette**
4 fluid ounces Red Wine
Coffee or Tea

SNACKS, AT PLANNED TIMES
½ cup Canned Sliced Peaches; 2 Graham
    Crackers; ½ cup Skim Milk

Serving Information
Men and Youth: Add ½ medium Banana, sliced,
    4 Melba Toast Slices, 2 tablespoons Raisins,
    1 slice Pumpernickel Bread, and ½ cup Fruit
    Salad
Youth: Add 1 cup Skim Milk

DAY 2

MORNING MEAL
1 medium Kiwi Fruit or 1 small Orange
⅓ cup Part-Skim Ricotta Cheese with
    2 teaspoons Reduced-Calorie Strawberry
    Spread
6 Melba Toast Rounds
½ cup Skim Milk
Coffee or Tea

MIDDAY MEAL
3–4 ounces Roast Beef on 1 ounce Enriched Roll
    with **Horseradish-Chili Sauce**
Cucumber Sticks and Cherry Tomatoes
½ cup Vanilla-Flavored Low-Calorie Milk Pudding

EVENING MEAL
Egg Salad
½ cup Steamed Chinese Pea Pods
½ cup Steamed Carrots
Spinach, Mushroom, Radish Salad with
    Basic Vinaigrette
2 Canned Pear Halves with 2 tablespoons Juice

SNACKS, AT PLANNED TIMES
Strawberry Shake; 12 fluid ounces Light Beer;
    10 Oyster Crackers

Serving Information
Men and Youth: Add ½ cup Fruit Salad, 1 ounce
    Enriched Roll, and 1 slice Rye Bread
Youth: Add 1½ cups Skim Milk

DAY 3

MORNING MEAL
1 large Tangerine
¾ ounce Ready-to-Eat Cereal
½ cup Skim Milk
Coffee or Tea

MIDDAY MEAL
Hominy Grits Soufflé
Tossed Salad with **Russian Dressing**
½ cup Grapefruit Sections

EVENING MEAL
3–4 ounces Broiled Scrod
½ cup Steamed Escarole
Zucchini and Carrot Salad with
    Sesame Vinaigrette
1 slice **Homemade White Bread**
¾ teaspoon Margarine
Hot Spiced Tea

SNACKS, AT PLANNED TIMES
2 Graham Crackers; ½ cup **Hot Mocha Milk;**
    ½ cup Plain Unflavored Yogurt with ¼ medium
    Banana, sliced, and 1 tablespoon Raisins

Serving Information
Men and Youth: Add ½ small Enriched Bagel
    with 1 teaspoon Reduced-Calorie Apricot
    Spread, ½ cup Orange Juice, 1 slice **Home-
    made White Bread,** and 1 small Apple
Youth: Add 1½ cups Skim Milk and ½ cup **Hot
    Mocha Milk**

DAY 6

MORNING MEAL
½ cup Orange Juice
Corn Muffins
½ cup Skim Milk
Coffee or Tea

MIDDAY MEAL
Curried Chicken Salad
Chicory and Sliced Red Bell Pepper Salad with
    1 teaspoon Reduced-Calorie Mayonnaise
1 slice Cracked Wheat Bread
½ cup Skim Milk
Coffee or Tea

EVENING MEAL
3–4 ounces Broiled Halibut
½ cup Cooked Sliced Beets
½ cup Steamed Green Beans with Mushrooms
Sliced Tomato on Lettuce with Wine Vinegar
½ cup Cherry-Flavored Low-Calorie Gelatin

SNACKS, AT PLANNED TIMES
3 ounces Dietary Frozen Dessert; ½ cup
    Strawberries with ¼ cup Buttermilk

Serving Information
Men and Youth: Add 2 slices Cracked Wheat
    Bread, 1 small Pear, and ½ cup Canned Man-
    darin Orange Sections
Youth: Add 1 cup Skim Milk

DAY 7

MORNING MEAL
½ medium Grapefruit
⅓ cup Part-Skim Ricotta Cheese with
    1 tablespoon Chopped Scallion
1 small Enriched Bagel
½ cup Skim Milk
Coffee or Tea

MIDDAY MEAL
3 ounces Boiled Ham
¼ cup Steamed Butternut Squash
Cucumber and Radish Slices on Lettuce with
    1¼ teaspoons Mayonnaise
1 slice Rye Bread
1 Canned Pineapple Slice with 1 tablespoon Juice

EVENING MEAL
¾ cup **Chicken Broth**
3–4 ounces Roast Chicken
Orange Broccoli
½ cup Stewed Tomatoes
Hearts of Lettuce with **Gingered Vinaigrette**
Coconut-Honey Shake

SNACKS, AT PLANNED TIMES
½ cup Plain Unflavored Yogurt; ½ cup Canned
    Cherries; 1 cup Mixed Vegetable Juice with
    Celery and Carrot Sticks

Serving Information
Men and Youth: Add 2 Canned Pineapple Slices
    with 2 tablespoons Juice, 1 ounce Whole Wheat
    Roll, and ½ cup Applesauce
Men: Add 1 ounce Boiled Ham at the Midday
    Meal
Youth: Add 1½ cups Skim Milk

Our menus and recipes transport us to Italy this week, so here is a brief glossary of Italian cooking terms: *Arreganata* means made with bread crumbs, parsley, and Parmesan cheese. Our arreganata mixture is paired with hearts of artichokes, but it's also good with fish. *Venetian* dishes contain wine and onions, and our Liver Venetian is no exception. *Florentine* calls for the main ingredient (usually eggs, chicken, or fish) to be set on a bed of spinach.

Your fork is your passport to Italy as you enjoy Zucchini Italian Style (Day 1), Hearts of Artichoke Arreganata (Day 3), Liver Venetian and Romaine with Vinaigrette Parmesan (Day 4), ricotta cheese (Day 6), and Fillet of Sole Florentine (Day 7).

Ready? *Mangia!*

WEEK 4

DAY 1

MORNING MEAL
½ cup Orange Sections
1 Scrambled Egg with 1 teaspoon Imitation
   Bacon Bits
1 slice Toasted Whole Wheat Bread
½ cup Skim Milk
Coffee or Tea

MIDDAY MEAL
2 ounces Sliced Jarlsberg Cheese on 6 Melba
   Toast Rounds
Tomato Slices and 2 Black Olives on Lettuce
Cole Slaw Vinaigrette
1 cup Melon Balls
½ cup Skim Milk
Coffee or Tea

EVENING MEAL
3–4 ounces Broiled Salmon Steak
Zucchini Italian Style
Chicory and Escarole Salad with **Basic Vinaigrette**
2 Canned Pear Halves with 2 tablespoons Juice

SNACKS, AT PLANNED TIMES
½ cup Chocolate-Flavored Low-Calorie Milk
   Pudding; 1 Graham Cracker; ¾ cup **Chicken
   Broth** with 10 Oyster Crackers

Serving Information
Men and Youth: Add 1 slice Rye Bread and 2
   Canned Plums with 2 tablespoons Juice
Youth: Add 1½ cups Skim Milk

DAY 4

MORNING MEAL
½ cup Fruit Salad
⅓ cup Cottage Cheese
½ English Muffin, toasted
¼ cup Skim Milk
Coffee or Tea

MIDDAY MEAL
Liver Venetian
½ cup Cooked Cauliflower Florets
Romaine Lettuce Salad with
   Vinaigrette Parmesan
4 Canned Apricot Halves with 2 tablespoons
   Juice
¾ cup Skim Milk

EVENING MEAL
3–4 ounces Sliced Roast Turkey on 1 slice Whole
   Wheat Bread with Lettuce Leaves, Tomato
   Slices, and 1½ teaspoons Mayonnaise
½ cup Canned Cream-Style Corn
½ cup Cooked Julienne Carrots
1 medium Kiwi Fruit or 1 cup Strawberries

SNACKS, AT PLANNED TIMES
½ cup Strawberry-Flavored Gelatin; 1 cup Skim
   Milk

Serving Information
Men and Youth: Add ½ English Muffin, toasted,
   1 slice Cracked Wheat Bread, 4 Canned Apricot
   Halves with 2 tablespoons Juice, and ½ cup
   Canned Cherries
Youth: Add 1 cup Skim Milk

DAY 5

MORNING MEAL
½ cup Orange Juice
Open-Face Grilled Cheese Sandwich I
½ cup Skim Milk
Coffee or Tea

MIDDAY MEAL
Tuna Boats
Bean Salad
1 ounce Pita Bread
½ cup Plain Unflavored Yogurt
Coffee or Tea

EVENING MEAL
3–4 ounces Broiled Lamb Patty
½ cup Steamed Mushrooms
½ cup Grated Beets on Lettuce with
   Cider Vinegar
4 fluid ounces Red Wine
Coffee or Tea

SNACKS, AT PLANNED TIMES
Hot Spiced Tea; 3 ounces Vanilla-Flavored
   Dietary Frozen Dessert; ½ cup Canned Fruit
   Cocktail

Serving Information
Men and Youth: Add ½ cup Orange Juice and 1
   Hamburger Roll
Youth: Add 1 cup Skim Milk

DAY 2

MORNING MEAL
½ medium Banana, sliced
¾ ounce Ready-to-Eat Cereal
½ cup Skim Milk
Coffee or Tea

MIDDAY MEAL
¾ cup **Vegetable Broth**
Crab Meat Mold
6 Saltines
¼ small Pineapple

EVENING MEAL
3–4 ounces Roast Beef
Baked Yams
½ cup Steamed Red Bell Pepper and Broccoli
Hearts of Lettuce with **Dijon-Herb Dressing**
4 fluid ounces Rosé Wine
1 medium Kiwi Fruit or ½ medium Grapefruit

SNACKS, AT PLANNED TIMES
1 slice Toasted Raisin Bread with 1 teaspoon
    Reduced-Calorie Margarine; ½ cup Plain
    Unflavored Yogurt

Serving Information
Men and Youth: Add 1 slice Pumpernickel Bread,
    2 tablespoons Raisins, 1 small Apple, 1 ounce
    Whole Wheat Roll, and ½ medium Banana
Youth: Add 1½ cups Skim Milk

DAY 3

MORNING MEAL
Broiled Grapefruit
1 Poached Egg
1 slice Rye Bread
1 teaspoon Margarine
½ cup Skim Milk
Coffee or Tea

MIDDAY MEAL
3–4 ounces Broiled Chicken
½ cup Steamed Spinach
Green Salad with **Russian Dressing**
1 ounce Pita Bread
½ cup Lemon-Flavored Low-Calorie Gelatin

EVENING MEAL
Hearts of Artichoke Arreganata
3–4 ounces Broiled Veal Chop
½ cup Cooked Asparagus Tips
Cucumber Slices on Lettuce with
    Garlic Vinaigrette
1 large Tangerine
½ cup Skim Milk
Coffee or Tea

SNACKS, AT PLANNED TIMES
½ medium Papaya or 1 small Orange; 1 serving
    Chocolate-Flavored Low-Calorie Milk Beverage

Serving Information
Men and Youth: Add 1 cup Strawberries, 1 slice
    Enriched Bread, and 2 Graham Crackers
Youth: Add 2 cups Skim Milk

DAY 6

MORNING MEAL
1 cup Honeydew or Cantaloupe Balls
¾ ounce Ready-to-Eat Cereal
1 cup Skim Milk
Coffee or Tea

MIDDAY MEAL
Chicken Greek Style
Green Salad with ¼ cup Sliced Red Onion and
    Basic Vinaigrette
1 ounce Enriched Roll
½ cup Strawberries

EVENING MEAL
⅔ cup Part-Skim Ricotta Cheese mixed with
    Cinnamon and Artificial Sweetener
1 slice Toasted Raisin Bread
½ cup Chilled Blanched Broccoli Spears with
    Pimiento Slices
Hearts of Lettuce with **Russian Dressing**
Baked Apple

SNACKS, AT PLANNED TIMES
2 cups Plain Popcorn; ½ cup Vanilla-Flavored
    Low-Calorie Milk Pudding with 1 Chopped Date

Serving Information
Men and Youth: Add 1 small Enriched Bagel
    with 2 teaspoons Reduced-Calorie Strawberry
    Spread, ½ cup Strawberries, and 1 Chopped
    Date
Youth: Add ½ cup Plain Unflavored Yogurt

DAY 7

MORNING MEAL
1 small Orange, cut into wedges
1 ounce Canadian Bacon
1 slice Rye Bread
½ cup Skim Milk
Coffee or Tea

MIDDAY MEAL
1 cup Tomato Juice
Mushroom Omelet
Tossed Salad with **Sesame Vinaigrette**
¾ ounce Crispbread
1 Canned Peach Half with 1 tablespoon Juice

EVENING MEAL
Fillet of Sole Florentine
½ cup Baked Acorn Squash
½ cup Steamed Carrot Slices
Sliced Radishes and Celery on Shredded Lettuce
    with ¾ teaspoon Mayonnaise sprinkled with
    Chopped Chives
½ cup Lime-Flavored Low-Calorie Gelatin

SNACKS, AT PLANNED TIMES
½ cup Plain Unflavored Yogurt with 1 tablespoon
    Raisins; ½ cup Applesauce; ½ cup Skim Milk

Serving Information
Men and Youth: Add 1 English Muffin, split and
    toasted, 1 Canned Peach Half with 1 tablespoon
    Juice, 1 tablespoon Raisins, and ½ cup Canned
    Mandarin Orange Sections
Youth: Add 2 cups Skim Milk

20 | Ground Hog Day is February 2nd. Only six more weeks of winter if the ground hog sees his shadow. Incidentally, how is your silhouette these days?

While ground hog isn't on the menu, Chili-Cheese Rarebit, also known in food circles as "rabbit," is. And later in the week, you'll find Székely Goulash, a dish discovered as serendipitously as the ground hog discovers his shadow.

In 1846, Székely, the librarian of Pest County, Hungary, arrived at a restaurant too late to order from the dinner menu, so he asked for leftover pork served with sauerkraut. The appeal of this new dish was so immediate that the very next day the poet Petőfi asked for *Székely's gulyás*. For our version of this famous dish (Day 7) we've replaced the sour cream with yogurt.

WEEK 5

DAY 1

MORNING MEAL
½ cup Canned Crushed Pineapple
⅓ cup Part-Skim Ricotta Cheese
1 slice Raisin Bread
½ cup Skim Milk
Coffee or Tea

MIDDAY MEAL
Salmon Salad
Celery Sticks, Cucumber Sticks, and
    2 Green Olives
1 slice Rye Bread
1½ teaspoons Margarine
½ cup Skim Milk
Coffee or Tea

EVENING MEAL
1 cup Mixed Vegetable Juice
3–4 ounces Broiled Calf Liver
½ cup Steamed Zucchini Slices
½ cup Steamed Wax Beans
Radish Salad
½ cup Orange and Grapefruit Sections

SNACKS, AT PLANNED TIMES
1 cup Skim Milk; 2 Graham Crackers; 2 Canned
    Pear Halves with 2 tablespoons Juice

Serving Information
Men and Youth: Add 1 small Apple and 1 slice
    Enriched Bread
Youth: Add 1 cup Skim Milk

DAY 4

MORNING MEAL
1 cup Strawberries
¾ ounce Ready-to-Eat Cereal
½ cup Skim Milk
Coffee or Tea

MIDDAY MEAL
Fish and Tomato Aspic
6 Saltines
1 teaspoon Margarine
2 Canned Plums with 2 tablespoons Juice
½ cup Skim Milk
Coffee or Tea

EVENING MEAL
3–4 ounces Sliced Broiled Steak
4 ounces Baked Potato
½ cup Cooked Broccoli Spears
Lettuce Wedge with **Russian Dressing**
1 large Tangerine

SNACKS, AT PLANNED TIMES
Watercress and Mushroom Salad with **Basic
    Vinaigrette**; 1 serving Chocolate-Flavored
    Low-Calorie Milk Beverage

Serving Information
Men and Youth: Add ½ cup Orange and Grape-
    fruit Juice, 20 Oyster Crackers, and ½ cup
    Canned Cherries
Youth: Add 1 cup Skim Milk

DAY 5

MORNING MEAL
½ cup Grapefruit Sections
1 Poached Egg
½ English Muffin, toasted
1 teaspoon Margarine
½ cup Skim Milk
Coffee or Tea

MIDDAY MEAL
Cream of Cauliflower Soup
3–4 ounces Sliced Roast Turkey
Endive Salad with **Garlic Vinaigrette**
1 medium Dill Pickle
1 ounce Enriched Roll
½ cup Skim Milk
Coffee or Tea

EVENING MEAL
3–4 ounces Broiled Halibut
Green Beans and Tomatoes Hungarian Style
Romaine Lettuce with Cucumber Slices and
    3 tablespoons Plain Unflavored Yogurt
3 ounces Vanilla-Flavored Dietary Frozen Dessert
    with 1 teaspoon Chocolate Syrup

SNACKS, AT PLANNED TIMES
½ cup Raspberry-Flavored Gelatin; 1 medium
    Kiwi Fruit or ½ cup Canned Pineapple Chunks

Serving Information
Men and Youth: Add ½ cup Grapefruit Sections,
    ½ English Muffin, toasted, 2 Canned Pineapple
    Slices with 2 tablespoons Juice, and 1 slice
    Rye Bread
Youth: Add 1 cup Skim Milk and ½ cup Plain
    Unflavored Yogurt

DAY 2

MORNING MEAL
1/3 cup Apple Juice
3/4 ounce Ready-to-Eat Cereal
1/2 cup Skim Milk
Coffee or Tea

MIDDAY MEAL
3/4 cup **Chicken Broth**
Chili-Cheese Rarebit
Romaine Lettuce and Pimiento Salad with
   Tarragon Vinaigrette
Sparkling Mineral Water

EVENING MEAL
3–4 ounces Broiled Bluefish with Lemon Wedge
1 medium Ear Corn with 1 teaspoon Margarine
Broiled Tomato
1/2 cup Cooked Chopped Spinach
12 fluid ounces Light Beer
1 cup Honeydew or Cantaloupe Balls

SNACKS, AT PLANNED TIMES
2 Chopped Dates with 1/4 cup Plain Unflavored
   Yogurt; 1/2 cup Vanilla-Flavored Low-Calorie
   Milk Pudding

Serving Information
Men and Youth: Add 2/3 cup Apple Juice, 1 Eng-
   lish Muffin, split and toasted, and 1/2 medium
   Grapefruit
Youth: Add 1 1/2 cups Skim Milk

DAY 3

MORNING MEAL
1/2 cup Orange Sections
Cinnamon-Cheese Toast
1/2 cup Skim Milk
Coffee or Tea

MIDDAY MEAL
Mushroom-Stuffed Eggs
Sliced Red and Green Bell Pepper Rings
   on Lettuce
1 slice Rye Bread
1/2 cup Skim Milk
Coffee or Tea

EVENING MEAL
3–4 ounces Broiled Chicken
1/2 cup Cooked Carrot Slices with 1/4 cup
   Cooked Peas
Green Salad with 1 teaspoon Mayonnaise
1/2 cup Fruit Salad

SNACKS, AT PLANNED TIMES
2 Canned Peach Halves with 2 tablespoons Juice;
   1 cup Skim Milk

Serving Information
Men and Youth: Add 4 medium Dried Apricot
   Halves, 2 ounces Enriched Roll, and 2 Graham
   Crackers
Youth: Add 1/2 cup Skim Milk and 1/2 cup Plain
   Unflavored Yogurt

DAY 6

MORNING MEAL
1/3 cup Pineapple Juice
1 ounce Smoked Salmon
1/2 small Enriched Bagel
1 teaspoon Reduced-Calorie Margarine
1/2 medium Tomato, sliced
1/2 cup Skim Milk
Coffee or Tea

MIDDAY MEAL
1 ounce Sliced Emmenthal Cheese
1 ounce Sliced Edam Cheese
6 Melba Toast Rounds
Green Salad with Lemon Juice
4 fluid ounces White Wine
Coffee or Tea

EVENING MEAL
3–4 ounces Roast Veal
Millet with Vegetables
Lettuce Wedge with **Herb Dressing**
1/2 cup Vanilla-Flavored Low-Calorie Milk Pudding

SNACKS, AT PLANNED TIMES
1/2 cup Canned Fruit Cocktail with 1/4 cup Plain
   Unflavored Yogurt; 1 small Orange

Serving Information
Men and Youth: Add 1/2 small Enriched Bagel,
   1 cup Melon Balls, and 3/4 ounce Crispbread
Youth: Add 1 1/2 cups Skim Milk

DAY 7

MORNING MEAL
1/2 medium Banana
1 serving Hot Cereal, 3/4 ounce uncooked
3/4 cup Skim Milk
Coffee or Tea

MIDDAY MEAL
1 Scrambled Egg
1/2 cup Alfalfa or Bean Sprouts with Sliced
   Radishes on Lettuce with 1 teaspoon
   Mayonnaise
1 1/2 tablespoons Peanut Butter on 1 slice Whole
   Wheat Bread with 1 teaspoon Reduced-Calorie
   Apricot Spread
1/2 cup Cherry-Flavored Low-Calorie Gelatin

EVENING MEAL
Székely Goulash
Spinach and Mushroom Salad
   with **Tarragon Vinaigrette**
1 cup Strawberries

SNACKS, AT PLANNED TIMES
1/3 cup Grape Juice; 2 Graham Crackers; 1/2 cup
   Plain Unflavored Yogurt with 1 teaspoon Honey
   and 1/4 teaspoon Wheat Germ

Serving Information
Men and Youth: Add 2 tablespoons Raisins, 1
   slice Cracked Wheat Bread, 1/2 cup Canned
   Mandarin Orange Sections, 1/3 cup Grape Juice,
   and 1 ounce Whole Wheat Roll
Youth: Add 1 cup Skim Milk

22

We call to your attention the shapely, shiny eggplant, a relative of the potato. Eggplant, which originated in India, is actually a berry, although we eat it as a vegetable. The first variety known to Europeans may have resembled a hen's egg —hence the name.

Eggplants vary in length from two to twelve inches, and the skin surface may be dark purple, white, red, or yellowish, even striped. They're available all year round.

We'd also like to introduce tofu, or bean curd. It's a soft, cheeselike product made from soybeans. Tofu, an excellent, inexpensive, versatile form of protein, is as important to Oriental culture and cooking as bread is to ours.

Put eggplant on your shopping list this week. It's part of Layered Eggplant-Cheese Bake (Day 1) and Tofu, Beans, and Eggplant (Day 6).

WEEK 6

DAY 1

MORNING MEAL
1/3 cup Pineapple Juice
Bread Pudding
Coffee or Tea

MIDDAY MEAL
Layered Eggplant-Cheese Bake
1/2 cup Sliced Cooked Beets
Lettuce Wedge with **Thousand Island Dressing**
1 slice Oatmeal or Whole Wheat Bread
2 teaspoons Margarine
1/2 cup Strawberry-Flavored Low-Calorie Gelatin

EVENING MEAL
3–4 ounces Steamed Whitefish
1 cup Steamed Carrots
Belgian Endive Salad with **Sesame Vinaigrette**
4 fluid ounces White Wine
3 ounces Chocolate-Flavored Dietary Frozen Dessert

SNACKS, AT PLANNED TIMES
1/2 cup Orange and Grapefruit Sections; 1/2 cup Skim Milk; 3/4 ounce Crispbread

Serving Information
Men and Youth: Add 1/3 cup Pineapple Juice, 1 slice Oatmeal or Whole Wheat Bread, and 3/4 cup Canned Apple Slices
Youth: Add 2 cups Skim Milk

DAY 4

MORNING MEAL
1/2 medium Banana
3/4 ounce Ready-to-Eat Cereal
1 cup Skim Milk
Coffee or Tea

MIDDAY MEAL
Open-Face Grilled Cheese Sandwich II
1/2 cup Carrot Sticks
6 medium Chilled Cooked Asparagus Spears
1 serving Vanilla-Flavored Low-Calorie Milk Beverage

EVENING MEAL
3–4 ounces Broiled Scallops
1/2 cup Cooked Okra
1/2 cup Cooked Red Cabbage with 1 teaspoon Caraway Seeds
1 ounce Whole Wheat Roll
2 teaspoons Margarine
2 Canned Pear Halves with 2 tablespoons Juice

SNACKS, AT PLANNED TIMES
Baked Apple; 1 cup Tomato Juice with 3 Saltines and 1 teaspoon Margarine

Serving Information
Men and Youth: Add 1 slice Whole Wheat Bread, 1/2 cup Canned Pineapple Chunks, and 1 ounce Whole Wheat Roll
Youth: Add 1 cup Skim Milk

DAY 5

MORNING MEAL
Oven-Stewed Prunes
1/3 cup Cottage Cheese
1 slice Pumpernickel Bread
1/2 cup Skim Milk
Coffee or Tea

MIDDAY MEAL
1/3 cup Apple Juice
3–4 ounces Tuna
Green Bell Pepper and Cucumber Slices with 1 1/2 teaspoons Mayonnaise
4 Melba Toast Slices
1/2 cup Skim Milk
Coffee or Tea

EVENING MEAL
3–4 ounces Roast Beef
1/2 cup Cooked Peas
1/2 cup Cooked Diced Carrot
Spinach and Mushroom Salad with **Dill Vinaigrette**
1 cup Honeydew Balls with Lime Wedge

SNACKS, AT PLANNED TIMES
1/2 cup Plain Unflavored Yogurt with 1 teaspoon Reduced-Calorie Grape Spread; 1/2 cup Lime-Flavored Low-Calorie Gelatin

Serving Information
Men and Youth: Add 1 slice Pumpernickel Bread, 1/2 cup Fruit Salad, 2 Dates, and 1 slice Rye Bread
Youth: Add 1/2 cup Skim Milk and 1/2 cup Plain Unflavored Yogurt

DAY **2**

MORNING MEAL
4 medium Dried Apricot Halves
1 serving Hot Cereal, ¾ ounce uncooked, with
   1 teaspoon Margarine
¾ cup Skim Milk
Coffee or Tea

MIDDAY MEAL
3–4 ounces Sliced Roast Turkey with
   Russian Dressing
½ cup Chilled Cooked Artichoke Hearts
Tossed Salad with Lemon Juice
1 slice Rye Bread
1 cup Strawberries

EVENING MEAL
3–4 ounces Broiled Calf Liver
½ cup Steamed Cauliflower
½ cup Cooked Spinach
Hearts of Lettuce and Sliced Radishes with
   ¼ recipe **Yogurt Dressing**
Frozen Apple-Banana Dessert

SNACKS, AT PLANNED TIMES
¾ cup **Chicken Broth** with 6 Melba Toast Rounds
   and 1 teaspoon Margarine; 1 cup Mixed Vegetable Juice

Serving Information
Men and Youth: Add 1 slice Rye Bread, 1 English
   Muffin, split and toasted, and 1 small Pear
Youth: Add 1 cup Skim Milk

DAY **3**   23

MORNING MEAL
½ cup Orange Juice
⅓ cup Part-Skim Ricotta Cheese
1 ounce Pita Bread
1 teaspoon Margarine
¼ cup Skim Milk
Coffee or Tea

MIDDAY MEAL
Scrod-Vegetable Bake
Chicory and Romaine Salad with 2 Green Olives,
   Capers, and **Basic Vinaigrette**
¾ cup Skim Milk

EVENING MEAL
3–4 ounces Broiled Hamburger with 2 teaspoons
   Ketchup mixed with 1 teaspoon Mayonnaise
½ Hamburger Roll
Potato Crisps
½ medium Dill Pickle, sliced
½ medium Tomato, sliced
½ cup Canned Fruit Cocktail

SNACKS, AT PLANNED TIMES
½ cup Plain Unflavored Yogurt with ½ cup
   Canned Sliced Peaches; ½ cup Grape-Flavored
   Low-Calorie Gelatin

Serving Information
Men and Youth: Add 1 slice Enriched Bread, 2
   Canned Plums with 2 tablespoons Juice, ½
   Hamburger Roll, and ½ cup Canned Mandarin
   Orange Sections
Youth: Add 2 cups Skim Milk

DAY **6**

MORNING MEAL
½ medium Grapefruit
1 Poached Egg
½ English Muffin, toasted
1 teaspoon Margarine
½ cup Skim Milk
Coffee or Tea

MIDDAY MEAL
Skewered Marinated Chicken
Escarole and Bean Sprout Salad with 1 teaspoon
   Imitation Bacon Bits and **Dijon-Herb Dressing**
1 large Tangerine

EVENING MEAL
Tofu, Beans, and Eggplant
Tossed Salad with 1½ teaspoons Vegetable Oil
   plus Wine Vinegar
¾ ounce Crispbread
½ cup Skim Milk
Coffee or Tea

SNACKS, AT PLANNED TIMES
½ cup Canned Cherries; ½ cup Chocolate-
   Flavored Low-Calorie Milk Pudding; 2 Graham
   Crackers

Serving Information
Men and Youth: Add ½ English Muffin, toasted,
   1 ounce Enriched Roll, and 4 Canned Apricot
   Halves with 2 tablespoons Juice
Youth: Add 1½ cups Skim Milk

DAY **7**

MORNING MEAL
Applesauce Oatmeal with 1 tablespoon Raisins
½ cup Skim Milk
Coffee or Tea

MIDDAY MEAL
⅔ cup Cottage Cheese with ½ cup Canned
   Crushed Pineapple and 1 teaspoon Shredded
   Coconut on Lettuce Leaves
½ medium Tomato, sliced
6 Melba Toast Rounds
2 teaspoons Margarine
½ cup Skim Milk
Coffee or Tea

EVENING MEAL
1 Scrambled Egg
Spinach-Yam Loaf
Grated Carrot and Alfalfa or Bean Sprouts on Romaine
   Lettuce with 1 teaspoon Mayonnaise
½ cup Skim Milk
Coffee or Tea

SNACKS, AT PLANNED TIMES
8 fluid ounces Beer; ½ cup Orange and
   Grapefruit Sections

Serving Information
Men and Youth: Add ½ cup Orange Juice, 2
   Canned Peach Halves with 2 tablespoons Juice,
   20 Oyster Crackers, 1 slice Cracked Wheat
   Bread, and 1 medium Kiwi Fruit or ½ cup
   Orange and Grapefruit Sections
Youth: Add 1½ cups Skim Milk

WEEK 7

This Valentine's Day, send your sweetie some love apples. Better known—and loved—as tomatoes, they're native to the Andes Mountains of South America.

The Spanish introduced the tomato to Europe in the sixteenth century. The Italians christened it *pomodoro* ("golden apple") because its original color was yellow. Europeans used tomatoes only as ornamental fruits until about the eighteenth century.

Although tomatoes have been a staple of Mexican cooking for centuries, they were spurned in this country until the nineteenth century. Americans thought they were poisonous. The fact that no less a personage than Thomas Jefferson grew and enjoyed them didn't sway public opinion.

For a romantic Valentine's Day dinner serve Chicken Liver Pilaf (Day 3) with sparkling chilled champagne. Add candlelight and soft music. And, of course, broiled love apples.

DAY 1

MORNING MEAL
½ medium Grapefruit
1 Poached Egg
½ English Muffin, toasted
½ cup Skim Milk
Coffee or Tea

MIDDAY MEAL
3–4 ounces Broiled Sole
Creamed Kale and Onions
Green Salad with **Sesame Vinaigrette**
1 large Tangerine

EVENING MEAL
Fennel Pork
⅔ cup Cooked Enriched Spaghetti with ½ cup Tomato Sauce
½ cup Cooked Green Beans
Endive and Pimiento Salad with 1 teaspoon Vegetable Oil plus Cider Vinegar
¼ cup Skim Milk
Coffee or Tea

SNACKS, AT PLANNED TIMES
½ cup Plain Unflavored Yogurt with 2 teaspoons Reduced-Calorie Strawberry Spread; ½ cup Canned Crushed Pineapple

Serving Information
Men and Youth: Add ½ English Muffin, toasted, 1 slice Whole Wheat Bread, 4 Canned Apricot Halves with 2 tablespoons Juice, 1 small Apple, and 2 Graham Crackers
Youth: Add 1¼ cups Skim Milk

DAY 4

MORNING MEAL
¾ cup Canned Apple Slices
1 serving Hot Cereal, ¾ ounce uncooked
1 cup Skim Milk
Coffee or Tea

MIDDAY MEAL
3–4 ounces Tuna
Radishes, Cherry Tomatoes, and 2 Black Olives on Lettuce with 1 teaspoon Mayonnaise
4 Melba Toast Slices
½ cup Canned Fruit Cocktail

EVENING MEAL
Chicken Salad Oriental
Spinach and Mushroom Salad with 1 teaspoon Imitation Bacon Bits, 1 teaspoon Sesame Oil, and Rice Vinegar
Hot Spiced Tea

SNACKS, AT PLANNED TIMES
½ cup Grapefruit Sections; 1 cup Skim Milk; 2 Graham Crackers

Serving Information
Men and Youth: Add ¾ ounce Crispbread, 1 ounce Whole Wheat Roll, and ½ cup Canned Mandarin Orange Sections
Youth: Add 1 cup Skim Milk

DAY 5

MORNING MEAL
⅓ cup Pineapple Juice
1 Scrambled Egg with Chives
¾ ounce Crispbread
½ cup Skim Milk
Coffee or Tea

MIDDAY MEAL
Vegetable Chowder
3–4 ounces Broiled Lamb Chop
½ cup Cooked Chopped Broccoli with Pimiento Strips
½ cup Grape-Flavored Low-Calorie Gelatin

EVENING MEAL
Grilled Cheese Soufflé
Tossed Salad with **Tarragon Vinaigrette**
¼ cup Skim Milk
Coffee or Tea

SNACKS, AT PLANNED TIMES
½ cup Canned Cherries with ½ cup Plain Unflavored Yogurt; 1 medium Kiwi Fruit or 1 small Orange

Serving Information
Men and Youth: Add ⅓ cup Pineapple Juice, 1 slice Rye Bread, and 4 Canned Plums with ¼ cup Juice
Youth: Add 2 cups Skim Milk

MORNING MEAL
¾ ounce Ready-to-Eat Cereal with ¼ medium
   Banana, sliced, and 1 tablespoon Raisins
¾ cup Skim Milk
Coffee or Tea

MIDDAY MEAL
1 cup Mixed Vegetable Juice
Cheese-Salad Sandwich
Carrot and Celery Sticks
1 small Orange

EVENING MEAL
Flounder Véronique
½ cup Steamed Asparagus Tips
Alfalfa or Bean Sprouts on Lettuce
1 ounce Enriched Roll
½ cup Vanilla-Flavored Low-Calorie Milk Pudding

SNACKS, AT PLANNED TIMES
½ cup Lime-Flavored Low-Calorie Gelatin with
   1 tablespoon Low-Calorie Whipped Topping;
   ½ cup Strawberries with 1 tablespoon Plain
   Unflavored Yogurt

Serving Information
Men and Youth: Add 1 tablespoon Raisins, 1 slice
   Toasted Enriched Bread, 1 ounce Enriched Roll,
   and ½ cup Strawberries
Youth: Add 1 cup Skim Milk

MORNING MEAL
Honey-Stewed Prunes
1¼ ounces Cottage Cheese
½ ounce Smoked Salmon
½ small Enriched Bagel
1 teaspoon Reduced-Calorie Margarine
¼ cup Skim Milk
Coffee or Tea

MIDDAY MEAL
3–4 ounces Broiled Hamburger
1 teaspoon Pickle Relish
1 slice Rye Bread
Curried Cole Slaw
Diet Soda or Sparkling Mineral Water

EVENING MEAL
¾ cup **Chicken Broth**
Chicken Liver Pilaf
Broiled Tomato
Romaine Salad with Capers and
   Garlic Vinaigrette
4 fluid ounces Champagne
½ cup Plain Unflavored Yogurt with 4 medium
   Dried Apricot Halves, chopped

SNACKS, AT PLANNED TIMES
¾ cup Skim Milk; 1 cup Honeydew or
   Cantaloupe Balls

Serving Information
 Men and Youth: Add 1 slice Rye Bread, 1 small
   Pear, 6 Melba Toast Rounds, and 2 Dates
Youth: Add 1 cup Skim Milk

MORNING MEAL
½ cup Applesauce
1 tablespoon Peanut Butter
1 slice Raisin Bread
1 cup Skim Milk
Coffee or Tea

MIDDAY MEAL
3–4 ounces Broiled Halibut
Colache
Shredded Lettuce with 2 Green Olives,
   1 teaspoon Grated Parmesan Cheese, and
   1 teaspoon Mayonnaise
Club Soda

EVENING MEAL
3–4 ounces Sliced Roast Turkey
¼ cup Baked Acorn Squash
½ cup Cooked Green Beans
Bean Sprouts and Carrot Salad with
   Sesame Vinaigrette
4 fluid ounces White Wine
Piña Freeze

SNACKS, AT PLANNED TIMES
½ cup Orange and Grapefruit Sections; ¾ cup
   Onion Bouillon with 10 Oyster Crackers

Serving Information
Men and Youth: Add ½ cup Canned Sliced
   Peaches and 2 slices Rye Bread
Youth: Add 1 cup Skim Milk and ½ cup Plain
   Unflavored Yogurt

MORNING MEAL
½ cup Orange Juice
¾ ounce Ready-to-Eat Cereal
1 cup Skim Milk
Coffee or Tea

MIDDAY MEAL
Open-Face Grilled Cheese Sandwich I
1 Hard-Cooked Egg, sliced
Broccoli Salad
1 serving Vanilla-Flavored Low-Calorie Milk
   Beverage

EVENING MEAL
⅓ cup Hot Apple Cider
3–4 ounces Steamed Bass
1 cup Spaghetti Squash
Green Bell Pepper Rings on Lettuce with
   1 teaspoon Mayonnaise
Coffee or Tea

SNACKS, AT PLANNED TIMES
½ cup Canned Mandarin Orange Sections
   sprinkled with 1 teaspoon Shredded Coconut;
   1 cup Tomato Juice with 6 Saltines

Serving Information
Men and Youth: Add 1 slice Toasted Enriched
   Bread, 2 Dates, 1 slice Pumpernickel Bread,
   ⅓ cup Hot Apple Cider, and 2 tablespoons
   Raisins
Youth: Add 1 cup Skim Milk

Fennel, an aromatic plant native to the Mediterranean area, has a long history; the emperor Charlemagne grew it in his garden.

A relative of the carrot, fennel has bright green, feathery foliage and yellow flowers. The stalks taste sweet and are crisp, and the bulb has a flavor reminiscent of anise. Fennel can be used raw in salads or as a cooked vegetable. Fennel seed, available both whole and ground, is used as a seasoning and is especially good with baked fish or sauerkraut.

We'll be using the bulb to make Fennel Parmesan (Day 1). And in case you want to celebrate Washington's Birthday, we have the perfect dessert recipe—Cherry Tarts (Day 4).

WEEK 8

DAY 1

MORNING MEAL
½ cup Grapefruit Sections
⅓ cup Cottage Cheese
½ medium Tomato, sliced
4 Melba Toast Slices
¼ cup Skim Milk
Coffee or Tea

MIDDAY MEAL
3–4 ounces Sliced Cooked Turkey
Fennel Parmesan
Tossed Salad with 1½ teaspoons Vegetable Oil
    plus Wine Vinegar
1 ounce Enriched Roll
1 cup Skim Milk

EVENING MEAL
3–4 ounces Sautéed Calf Liver, using 1½
    teaspoons Vegetable Oil
½ cup Steamed Sliced Onion
½ cup Steamed Green Beans and Julienne Carrot
1 small Pear

SNACKS, AT PLANNED TIMES
½ cup Cherry-Flavored Low-Calorie Gelatin with
    ½ cup Canned Cherries; ¾ cup Skim Milk;
    2 Graham Crackers

Serving Information
Men and Youth: Add 2 Canned Plums with 2
    tablespoons Juice and 1 slice Pumpernickel
    Bread
Youth: Add 1¾ cups Skim Milk

DAY 4

MORNING MEAL
1 small Orange
1 Poached Egg
½ English Muffin, toasted
½ cup Skim Milk
Coffee or Tea

MIDDAY MEAL
3–4 ounces Salmon on Lettuce with Tomato
    Wedges and Cucumber Slices
½ medium Dill Pickle
½ cup Lemon-Flavored Low-Calorie Gelatin
½ cup Skim Milk
Coffee or Tea

EVENING MEAL
Chicken Provençale
4 ounces Baked Potato
Lettuce and Grated Carrot Salad
    with **Wine Vinaigrette**
4 fluid ounces White Wine
Cherry Tarts
Coffee or Tea

SNACKS, AT PLANNED TIMES
½ cup Chocolate-Flavored Low-Calorie Milk
    Pudding; 1 large Tangerine

Serving Information
Men and Youth: Add ½ English Muffin, toasted,
    2 Graham Crackers, ½ cup Applesauce, and
    1 large Tangerine
Youth: Add 1½ cups Skim Milk

DAY 5

MORNING MEAL
½ cup Canned Sliced Peaches
¾ ounce Ready-to-Eat Cereal
1 cup Skim Milk
Coffee or Tea

MIDDAY MEAL
Gypsy Cheese Salad
1 slice Pumpernickel Bread
1 teaspoon Margarine
½ cup Orange Sections

EVENING MEAL
Stewed Tripe
½ cup Steamed Cauliflower with Lemon Wedge
Celery and Carrot Sticks with **Curry Dip** and
    10 Oyster Crackers
¾ cup Strawberries

SNACKS, AT PLANNED TIMES
¾ cup Skim Milk; 4 Melba Toast Slices with
    1 teaspoon Margarine; ¾ cup Onion Bouillon
    sprinkled with 1 teaspoon Grated Parmesan
    Cheese

Serving Information
Men and Youth: Add 3 medium Prunes, 1 slice
    Toasted Enriched Bread, 2 Dates, and 1 ounce
    Whole Wheat Roll
Youth: Add 1 cup Skim Milk

DAY 2

MORNING MEAL
1 cup Strawberries topped with 1 tablespoon
   Plain Unflavored Yogurt
Honey-Coconut Toast
¼ cup Skim Milk
Coffee or Tea

MIDDAY MEAL
3–4 ounces Broiled Fillet of Scrod
½ cup Cooked Chopped Broccoli
½ cup Steamed Red Bell Pepper Slices
½ cup Skim Milk
Coffee or Tea

EVENING MEAL
Stuffed Mushroom Appetizer
3–4 ounces Baked Chicken
1 medium Ear Corn, boiled
1 teaspoon Margarine
Romaine Lettuce with 1 teaspoon Mayonnaise
   mixed with 1 teaspoon Plain Unflavored Yogurt
½ cup Canned Fruit Cocktail

SNACKS, AT PLANNED TIMES
20 small Grapes; ¾ cup Buttermilk; ½ cup
   Strawberry-Flavored Gelatin

Serving Information
Men and Youth: Add 1 small Apple, 1 English
   Muffin, split and toasted, and 4 medium Dried
   Apricot Halves
Youth: Add 2 cups Skim Milk

DAY 3

MORNING MEAL
½ medium Banana
¾ ounce Ready-to-Eat Cereal
¾ cup Skim Milk
Coffee or Tea

MIDDAY MEAL
Lentil and Escarole Soup
⅓ cup Pot Cheese on Lettuce Leaves
½ medium Tomato, sliced, with 1 teaspoon
   Vegetable Oil plus Cider Vinegar
6 Saltines
1 cup Skim Milk

EVENING MEAL
3–4 ounces Baked Veal Chop
½ cup Steamed Spinach with 1 teaspoon
   Imitation Bacon Bits
½ cup Cooked Sliced Summer Squash
1 cup Melon Balls
¼ cup Skim Milk
Coffee or Tea

SNACKS, AT PLANNED TIMES
1 medium Kiwi Fruit or ½ medium Grapefruit;
   1 slice Toasted Rye Bread with 1 teaspoon
   Margarine

Serving Information
Men and Youth: Add ½ medium Banana, ½ cup
   Fruit Salad, 2 ounces Enriched French Bread,
   and 2 tablespoons Raisins
Youth: Add 1¾ cups Skim Milk

DAY 6

MORNING MEAL
½ cup Grapefruit Juice
⅓ cup Part-Skim Ricotta Cheese sprinkled with
   ½ teaspoon Sesame Seeds
1 slice Toasted Rye Bread
1 teaspoon Margarine
½ cup Skim Milk
Coffee or Tea

MIDDAY MEAL
Mushroom Omelet
½ cup Steamed Sliced Zucchini with
   Pimiento Strips
¾ ounce Crispbread
½ cup Cherry-Flavored Low-Calorie Gelatin

EVENING MEAL
3–4 ounces Baked Brook Trout with
   Lemon Wedges
½ cup Cooked Wild or Enriched Rice
Chicory Salad with **Oregano Vinaigrette**
4 fluid ounces Champagne
Coconut-Coffee Mounds
Coffee or Tea

SNACKS, AT PLANNED TIMES
Baked Apple; ½ cup Plain Unflavored Yogurt
   with 2 tablespoons Raisins

Serving Information
Men and Youth: Add 1 small Pear and 2 ounces
   Pita Bread
Youth: Add 1½ cups Skim Milk

DAY 7

MORNING MEAL
3 medium Prunes
1 serving Hot Cereal, ¾ ounce uncooked
½ cup Skim Milk
Coffee or Tea

MIDDAY MEAL
Flounder Meunière
6 medium Steamed Asparagus Spears with
   Lemon Wedge
½ cup Cooked Carrot Slices
1 slice Whole Wheat Bread
1 teaspoon Margarine
Hot Spiced Tea

EVENING MEAL
3–4 ounces Broiled Chopped Beefsteak with
   1 teaspoon Ketchup
½ Hamburger Roll
½ cup Cooked Sliced Beets
½ cup Cooked Wax Beans
Watercress Salad with 1 teaspoon Mayonnaise
½ small Mango or 1 small Orange

SNACKS, AT PLANNED TIMES
½ cup Plain Unflavored Yogurt; ½ medium
   Banana; ½ cup **Hot Mocha Milk**

Serving Information
Men and Youth: Add ½ cup Orange Juice, 1 slice
   Cracked Wheat Bread, ½ cup Canned Pine-
   apple Chunks, ½ Hamburger Roll, and 2
   Graham Crackers
Youth: Add 1½ cups Skim Milk and ½ cup **Hot
   Mocha Milk**

It's easy to confuse endive and escarole. They're very closely related and can be used interchangeably in salads and cooking.

Endive has a cylindrical shape and white leaves with light green tips which press close together, tapering almost to a point. Endive is imported from Belgium and is available from October to May.

Escarole is characterized by broad, wavy, yellowish green leaves and a somewhat bitter flavor. Although it is considered a winter salad green, escarole is generally available all year round. Leaves should be crisp and tender and should snap off easily. Avoid heads with wilted or brown-edged leaves.

Both escarole and endive appear on this week's menu. Endive and Beet Salad (Day 4) provides an excellent color, flavor, and texture contrast. Escarole and Tomato Medley (Day 6) is a tangy combination.

DAY 1

MORNING MEAL
Honey-Stewed Prunes
1 Soft-Cooked Egg
1 slice Toasted Whole Wheat Bread
1 teaspoon Margarine
¼ cup Skim Milk
Coffee or Tea

MIDDAY MEAL
Chick Pea Croquettes (Falafel)
Sliced Tomato on Shredded Lettuce with
   1 teaspoon Reduced-Calorie Mayonnaise
1 ounce Pita Bread
2 Canned Pear Halves with 2 tablespoons Juice

EVENING MEAL
Scrod Greek Style
½ cup Cooked Broccoli Spears with
   Lemon Wedge
Tossed Salad with **Dijon-Herb Dressing**
4 fluid ounces White Wine
Coffee or Tea

SNACKS, AT PLANNED TIMES
½ small Mango or ½ medium Grapefruit; ¾ cup
   Skim Milk; 1 Graham Cracker

Serving Information
Men and Youth: Add ½ cup Grapefruit Juice,
   1 ounce Enriched Roll, ½ cup Canned Fruit
   Cocktail, and 2 Graham Crackers
Men: Add ½ ounce Julienne Swiss Cheese to
   salad at the Midday Meal
Youth: Add 1¾ cups Skim Milk

DAY 4

MORNING MEAL
Cereal with Spiced Fruit Ambrosia
Coffee or Tea

MIDDAY MEAL
3–4 ounces Broiled Calf Liver
½ cup Steamed Cauliflower
Bean Sprouts with 1 teaspoon Sesame Seeds
   and 1 teaspoon Vegetable Oil plus Rice
   Vinegar
1 slice Rye Bread
1 canned Peach Half with 1 tablespoon Juice

EVENING MEAL
1 cup Mixed Vegetable Juice
3–4 ounces Broiled Veal Patty
½ Hamburger Roll
½ cup Cooked Wax Beans
Endive and Beet Salad
½ cup Orange Sections

SNACKS, AT PLANNED TIMES
½ cup Plain Unflavored Yogurt with ¼ cup
   Canned Pineapple Tidbits; ½ English Muffin,
   toasted, with 1 teaspoon Margarine and
   1 teaspoon Reduced-Calorie Grape Spread

Serving Information
Men and Youth: Add 1 slice Pumpernickel Bread,
   3 Canned Peach Halves with 3 tablespoons
   Juice, ¼ cup Canned Pineapple Tidbits, and ½
   English Muffin, toasted
Youth: Add 2 cups Skim Milk

DAY 5

MORNING MEAL
1 cup Honeydew or Cantaloupe Balls
Caraway-Cheese Toast
¼ cup Skim Milk
Coffee or Tea

MIDDAY MEAL
3–4 ounces Sardines
Green Bell Pepper Rings and ¼ cup Red Onion
   Rings on Lettuce with 1 teaspoon Mayonnaise
¾ cup Skim Milk

EVENING MEAL
3–4 ounces Broiled Steak
Chick Peas (Garbanzos) with Tiny Shells
½ cup Steamed Eggplant
Lettuce Wedge with **Savory Vinaigrette**
½ cup Fruit Salad

SNACKS, AT PLANNED TIMES
2 Canned Plums with 2 tablespoons Juice
   sprinkled with 1 teaspoon Shredded Coconut;
   1 serving Vanilla-Flavored Low-Calorie Milk
   Beverage

Serving Information
Men and Youth: Add 1 slice Enriched Bread, 1
   small Orange, 1 ounce Whole Wheat Roll, and
   1 small Pear
Youth: Add 1 cup Skim Milk

MORNING MEAL
1 cup Strawberries
¾ ounce Ready-to-Eat Cereal
1 cup Skim Milk
Coffee or Tea

MIDDAY MEAL
3–4 ounces Tuna
Spinach Salad with Lemon Juice
Garlic Bread
Orange Ambrosia

EVENING MEAL
1 cup Tomato Juice
3–4 ounces Roast Beef
½ cup Cooked Brown Rice
½ cup Steamed Green Beans with 1 teaspoon
    Margarine
Romaine and Chicory Salad with
    Basic Vinaigrette
¼ medium Papaya or ½ cup Melon Balls

SNACKS, AT PLANNED TIMES
½ cup Raspberry-Flavored Low-Calorie Gelatin;
    ½ cup Plain Unflavored Yogurt with ¼ cup
    Canned Sliced Peaches

Serving Information
Men and Youth: Add 1 slice Toasted Whole
    Wheat Bread, ¾ ounce Crispbread, ¼ medium
    Papaya or ½ cup Melon Balls, and ¼ cup
    Canned Sliced Peaches
Youth: Add 1 cup Skim Milk

MORNING MEAL
½ medium Grapefruit, spread with 1 teaspoon
    Reduced-Calorie Orange Marmalade
1 Scrambled Egg
½ small Enriched Bagel
½ cup Skim Milk
Coffee or Tea

MIDDAY MEAL
⅔ cup Cottage Cheese on Lettuce Leaves with
    Pimiento Strips and 1 Green Olive
6 Melba Toast Rounds
1 teaspoon Margarine
2 Dates
½ cup Skim Milk
Coffee or Tea

EVENING MEAL
Cream of Asparagus and Leek Soup
3–4 ounces Broiled Flounder
½ cup Julienne Carrot sautéed in 1 teaspoon
    Margarine
½ cup Applesauce
¾ cup Skim Milk

SNACKS, AT PLANNED TIMES
Sparkling Mineral Water with Twist of Lemon;
    Hot Spiced Tea; 2 Graham Crackers

Serving Information
Men and Youth: Add ½ small Enriched Bagel,
    2 Dates, and 1 slice Rye Bread
Youth: Add 1¼ cups Skim Milk

MORNING MEAL
1 medium Kiwi Fruit or 1 cup Strawberries
¾ ounce Ready-to-Eat Cereal
½ cup Skim Milk
Coffee or Tea

MIDDAY MEAL
Chicken Donna
Escarole and Tomato Medley
6 Melba Toast Rounds
1 teaspoon Margarine
20 small Grapes

EVENING MEAL
Mushroom Loaf
Romaine Lettuce, Sliced Radishes, and
    ½ teaspoon Imitation Bacon Bits with
    ½ recipe **Yogurt Dressing**
1 small Apple

SNACKS, AT PLANNED TIMES
Lime Yogurt Dip with Crudités; 4 fluid ounces
    Red Wine

Serving Information
Men and Youth: Add 1 slice Cracked Wheat
    Bread, ⅔ cup Apple Cider, ½ English Muffin,
    toasted, and 1 Dried Fig
Youth: Add 1½ cups Skim Milk

MORNING MEAL
½ cup Orange and Grapefruit Sections
1 Hard-Cooked Egg, sliced
½ Matzo Board
1 teaspoon Margarine
¼ cup Skim Milk
Coffee or Tea

MIDDAY MEAL
⅓ cup Grape Juice
3–4 ounces Broiled Haddock
½ cup Steamed Mushroom Caps
Watercress and Sliced Cucumber with
    Lemon Salad Dressing
Pineapple-Orange Pudding

EVENING MEAL
Shepherd's Beef Pie
½ cup Steamed Swiss Chard
Belgian Endive Salad with **Sesame Vinaigrette**
8 fluid ounces Beer
20 small Grapes

SNACKS, AT PLANNED TIMES
½ cup Strawberries with 1 tablespoon Plain
    Unflavored Yogurt; 1 cup Skim Milk; 2 Graham
    Crackers

Serving Information
Men and Youth: Add ½ Matzo Board, 1 slice Rye
    Bread, and 20 small Grapes
Youth: Add 1¾ cups Skim Milk

The best ways to prepare vegetables and still retain their color and vitamin content are *blanching* and *steaming*.

Blanching consists of boiling briefly in lightly salted water. The amount of time required varies with the type of vegetable. Certain vegetables, like cabbages and onions, may be blanched to reduce their pungency. Other vegetables and fruits, including tomatoes and peaches, can be blanched (or scalded) to make them easier to peel.

Steaming involves placing prepared vegetables in a perforated container or basket, suspending it in a pot over about an inch of boiling water, and covering the pot tightly. Then reduce the heat just enough to keep the water bubbling. Vegetables cook very quickly this way and require minimal attention. Be sure to avoid overcooking.

WEEK 10

DAY 1

MORNING MEAL
½ cup Canned Fruit Cocktail
¾ ounce Ready-to-Eat Cereal
1 cup Skim Milk
Coffee or Tea

MIDDAY MEAL
⅓ cup Cottage Cheese on Lettuce Leaves
½ cup Chilled Boiled Beets
Green Salad with **Cider Vinaigrette**
1 ounce Pita Bread
Coffee or Tea

EVENING MEAL
3–4 ounces Broiled Hamburger
½ cup Cooked Green Beans
Sliced Tomato, Cucumber, and Mushrooms on
   Lettuce Leaves with 2 teaspoons Mayonnaise
Lady Fingers
1 cup Skim Milk

SNACKS, AT PLANNED TIMES
½ cup Cherry-Flavored Low-Calorie Gelatin;
   ½ cup Grapefruit Sections

Serving Information
Men and Youth: Add ½ cup Canned Cherries,
   1 Hamburger Roll, and ½ cup Canned Mandarin
   Orange Sections
Youth: Add 1 cup Skim Milk

DAY 4

MORNING MEAL
1 small Orange
⅓ cup Pot Cheese
1 slice Toasted Enriched Bread
1 teaspoon Margarine
¼ cup Skim Milk
Coffee or Tea

MIDDAY MEAL
Sweet 'n' Sour Liver
½ cup Steamed Cauliflower
Julienne Zucchini on Lettuce with Lemon Juice
½ cup Vanilla-Flavored Low-Calorie Milk
   Pudding

EVENING MEAL
3–4 ounces Steamed Cod with Lemon Slices
½ cup Steamed Kale with 2 teaspoons Diced
   Pimiento
Lettuce and Sliced Radishes with 1 teaspoon
   Vegetable Oil plus Tarragon Vinegar
½ cup Applesauce with 1 tablespoon Raisins
   and 2 tablespoons Plain Unflavored Yogurt

SNACKS, AT PLANNED TIMES
Coconut-Honey Shake; 1 English Muffin, split
   and toasted, with 1 teaspoon Margarine and
   1 teaspoon Reduced-Calorie Grape Spread

Serving Information
Men and Youth: Add ⅔ cup Apple Juice and
   2 Graham Crackers
Youth: Add 1¼ cups Skim Milk

DAY 5

MORNING MEAL
½ medium Grapefruit sprinkled with 1 teaspoon
   Shredded Coconut
⅓ cup Part-Skim Ricotta Cheese
1 slice Raisin Bread
½ cup Skim Milk
Coffee or Tea

MIDDAY MEAL
Sautéed Chicken and Vegetables
Escarole and Leaf Lettuce with Wine Vinegar
1 serving Chocolate-Flavored Low-Calorie Milk
   Beverage

EVENING MEAL
Potato, Eggs, and Cheese Salad
Spinach Leaves with ¼ cup Sliced Water
   Chestnuts and 1 teaspoon Imitation Bacon Bits
1 ounce Enriched Roll
1 teaspoon Reduced-Calorie Strawberry Spread
½ cup Fruit Salad

SNACKS, AT PLANNED TIMES
4 Canned Apricot Halves with 2 tablespoons
   Juice and ¼ cup Plain Unflavored Yogurt;
   ½ cup Raspberry-Flavored Gelatin with
   1 tablespoon Low-Calorie Whipped Topping

Serving Information
Men and Youth: Add ¾ ounce Crispbread and
   2 Dates
Youth: Add 1½ cups Skim Milk

DAY 2

MORNING MEAL
½ cup Orange Juice
1 Sunnyside-Up Egg cooked in 1 teaspoon
    Reduced-Calorie Margarine
1 slice Pumpernickel Bread
¼ cup Skim Milk
Coffee or Tea

MIDDAY MEAL
2 ounces Sliced Muenster Cheese melted on
    1 slice Whole Wheat Bread
Romaine Lettuce with 1 teaspoon Imitation
    Bacon Bits plus **Russian Dressing**
1 small Apple
¾ cup Skim Milk

EVENING MEAL
1 cup Mixed Vegetable Juice
Mustard-Broiled Flounder
½ cup Cooked Artichoke Hearts
1 cup Steamed Spinach
Tossed Salad with **Dill Vinaigrette**
2 Canned Peach Halves with 2 tablespoons Juice

SNACKS, AT PLANNED TIMES
4 Melba Toast Slices with 2 teaspoons Reduced-
    Calorie Apricot Spread; ¾ cup Buttermilk

Serving Information
Men and Youth: Add 1 slice Whole Wheat Bread,
    ½ cup Orange Juice, 1 ounce Enriched Roll,
    and 2 Canned Plums with 2 tablespoons Juice
Youth: Add 2 cups Skim Milk

DAY 3

MORNING MEAL
½ cup Strawberries
Granola
½ cup Skim Milk
Coffee or Tea

MIDDAY MEAL
3 ounces Sliced Liverwurst
¼ cup Sliced Spanish Onion
Lettuce Leaves and Tomato Slices
1 slice Rye Bread
½ cup Canned Cherries with 2 tablespoons
    Plain Unflavored Yogurt

EVENING MEAL
3–4 ounces Roast Chicken
Herbed Vegetables
Chicory and Bean Sprouts with 2 teaspoons
    Low-Calorie Italian Dressing
4 fluid ounces White Wine
Coffee or Tea

SNACKS, AT PLANNED TIMES
1 cup Cantaloupe Balls; Carrot and Celery Sticks
    with **Curry Dip**

Serving Information
Men and Youth: Add ½ English Muffin, toasted,
    1 slice Rye Bread, and 12 large Grapes
Men: Add 1 ounce Sliced Liverwurst at the
    Midday Meal
Youth: Add 1½ cups Skim Milk

DAY 6

MORNING MEAL
½ medium Banana, sliced
¾ ounce Ready-to-Eat Cereal
1 cup Skim Milk
Coffee or Tea

MIDDAY MEAL
3–4 ounces Broiled Pork Chop
½ cup Sauerkraut
½ cup Stewed Tomatoes
1 slice Rye Bread
1 teaspoon Margarine
½ cup Plain Unflavored Yogurt with 2 teaspoons
    Reduced-Calorie Strawberry Spread

EVENING MEAL
3–4 ounces Boiled Shrimp with 2 teaspoons
    Seafood Cocktail Sauce
6 medium Cooked Asparagus Spears
Lemony Brussels Sprouts and Carrots Salad
¾ ounce Crispbread
1 teaspoon Margarine
1 medium Kiwi Fruit or ½ cup Canned Fruit
    Cocktail

SNACKS, AT PLANNED TIMES
1 cup Tomato Juice; 20 Oyster Crackers;
    1 large Tangerine

Serving Information
Men and Youth: Add 2 tablespoons Raisins, 1
    slice Toasted Whole Wheat Bread, 1 cup
    Strawberries, 1 slice Rye Bread, and ½ cup
    Orange Juice
Youth: Add 1 cup Skim Milk

DAY 7

MORNING MEAL
½ cup Grapefruit Juice
Pancakes
1 teaspoon Reduced-Calorie Margarine
1 teaspoon Reduced-Calorie Peach Spread
¼ cup Skim Milk
Coffee or Tea

MIDDAY MEAL
3–4 ounces Sliced Roast Turkey
½ cup Cooked Okra with ½ cup Tomato Sauce
½ cup Cooked Sliced Mushrooms
¼ small Pineapple

EVENING MEAL
Creamed Cannellini 'n' Pasta
Iceberg Lettuce, Grated Red Cabbage, and
    1½–2 ounces Tuna with ¼ recipe
    Yogurt Dressing
½ cup Lemon-Flavored Low-Calorie Gelatin

SNACKS, AT PLANNED TIMES
½ cup Skim Milk; 2 Graham Crackers; ½ cup
    Canned Fruit Cocktail

Serving Information
Men and Youth: Add 2 ounces Enriched Italian
    Bread and 2 Canned Pear Halves with 2 table-
    spoons Juice
Men: Add ½ ounce Tuna at the Evening Meal
Youth: Add 1¼ cups Skim Milk

Eat no onions nor garlic,
for we are to utter sweet breath.

—WILLIAM SHAKESPEARE,
A Midsummer Night's Dream

Instead, try a sweeter relation: asparagus. Asparagus, like onions and garlic a member of the lily family, comes in white and green varieties. Look for stalks that are straight and fresh-looking. Tips should be compact and pointed. Generally, the thicker the spear, the more tender it's likely to be. Keep asparagus in the coldest part of the refrigerator, wrapped at its base with a damp paper towel.

Asparagus in the supermarket is a sure sign that spring is just around the corner. For a taste of the season to come, we recommend Asparagus Soup (Day 4).

Economy Tip—Roast beef is on the menu on Day 4. Leftovers may be frozen and used in Mushroom-Beef Hash (Day 6).

WEEK 11

DAY 1

MORNING MEAL
½ cup Orange and Grapefruit Juice
⅓ cup Part-Skim Ricotta Cheese
1 slice Raisin Bread
½ cup Skim Milk
Coffee or Tea

MIDDAY MEAL
Crab Meat Salad in Pita Bread
Tomato Slices on Lettuce Leaves
1 small Pear

EVENING MEAL
3–4 ounces Broiled Chicken Livers
Curried Cauliflower
½ cup Cooked Sliced Zucchini
Tossed Salad with Lemon Juice
¼ small Pineapple
4 fluid ounces Rosé Wine
½ cup Skim Milk
Coffee or Tea

SNACKS, AT PLANNED TIMES
½ cup Chocolate-Flavored Low-Calorie Milk
Pudding; 1 slice Whole Wheat Bread with
1 teaspoon each Reduced-Calorie Margarine
and Reduced-Calorie Grape Spread

Serving Information
Men and Youth: Add 6 Melba Toast Rounds and
½ cup Canned Cherries
Youth: Add 2 cups Skim Milk

DAY 4

MORNING MEAL
⅓ cup Apple Juice
1 serving Hot Cereal, ¾ ounce uncooked, with
½ teaspoon Maple Syrup
½ cup Skim Milk
Coffee or Tea

MIDDAY MEAL
2 Eggs scrambled in 1 teaspoon Margarine
½ cup Red Bell Pepper Slices
1 slice Toasted Whole Wheat Bread
1 teaspoon Reduced-Calorie Margarine
1 small Orange
1 cup Skim Milk

EVENING MEAL
Asparagus Soup
3–4 ounces Roast Beef
½ cup Whipped Baked Acorn Squash
½ cup Cooked Wax Beans
Belgian Endive and Radish Salad with
Tarragon Vinegar
½ medium Papaya or ¼ small Pineapple

SNACKS, AT PLANNED TIMES
2 cups Plain Popcorn; 2 Graham Crackers;
½ cup Skim Milk

Serving Information
Men and Youth: Add ⅓ cup Apple Juice and
¾ ounce Crispbread
Youth: Add 1½ cups Skim Milk

DAY 5

MORNING MEAL
½ cup Orange Sections
1 Poached Egg
½ English Muffin, toasted
1 teaspoon Margarine
¼ cup Skim Milk
Coffee or Tea

MIDDAY MEAL
Ginger-Broiled Chicken
½ cup Cooked Chinese Pea Pods
Spinach and Mushroom Salad with
Vinaigrette Parmesan
1 cup Skim Milk

EVENING MEAL
1 cup Mixed Vegetable Juice
3–4 ounces Broiled Swordfish
½ cup Cooked Cut Asparagus
½ cup Stewed Tomatoes
1 slice Pumpernickel Bread
1 teaspoon Margarine
Banana-Prune Pudding

SNACKS, AT PLANNED TIMES
½ cup **Hot Mocha Milk** with 1 tablespoon
Low-Calorie Whipped Topping; ½ cup
Applesauce

Serving Information
Men and Youth: Add ½ English Muffin, toasted,
1 ounce Enriched Roll, 12 large Grapes, and
½ cup Canned Pineapple Chunks
Youth: Add ¾ cup Skim Milk and ½ cup Plain
Unflavored Yogurt

DAY 2

MORNING MEAL
½ medium Banana, sliced
¾ ounce Ready-to-Eat Cereal
½ cup Skim Milk
Coffee or Tea

MIDDAY MEAL
3–4 ounces Sliced Roast Turkey
½ medium Cucumber, sliced
2 slices Rye Bread
1 teaspoon Mayonnaise mixed with 1 teaspoon
    Ketchup
½ cup Plain Unflavored Yogurt with 1 teaspoon
    Honey

EVENING MEAL
Baked Codfish with Lemon
½ cup Cooked Enriched Rice
½ cup Cooked Green Beans
Lettuce Wedge with **Garlic Vinaigrette**
1 small Apple

SNACKS, AT PLANNED TIMES
1 cup Tomato Juice; **Strawberry Shake**

Serving Information
Men and Youth: Add 1 slice Whole Wheat Bread,
    4 Canned Apricot Halves with 2 tablespoons
    Juice, and 6 Saltines
Youth: Add 1½ cups Skim Milk

DAY 3

MORNING MEAL
½ medium Grapefruit, spread with ½ teaspoon
    Honey and broiled
1 ounce Swiss Cheese
1 slice Enriched Bread
¼ cup Skim Milk
Coffee or Tea

MIDDAY MEAL
3–4 ounces Broiled Hamburger
½ Hamburger Roll
1 teaspoon Mustard
Green Bean Confetti Salad
½ cup Canned Sliced Peaches
¾ cup Skim Milk

EVENING MEAL
¾ cup **Chicken Broth**
3–4 ounces Poached Chicken
¼ cup Cooked Peas with 2 tablespoons Cooked
    Pearl Onions and 1 teaspoon Margarine
Green Salad with 1 teaspoon Mayonnaise and
    1 teaspoon Chili Sauce
½ cup Strawberry-Flavored Low-Calorie Gelatin

SNACKS, AT PLANNED TIMES
1 cup Tomato Juice with ½ cup Celery and
    Carrot Sticks; ½ cup Plain Unflavored Yogurt
    with 2 tablespoons Raisins

Serving Information
Men and Youth: Add ½ Hamburger Roll, 1 large
    Tangerine, 20 Oyster Crackers, and 2 table-
    spoons Raisins
Youth: Add 1 cup Skim Milk

DAY 6

MORNING MEAL
1 cup Strawberries, sliced
¾ ounce Ready-to-Eat Cereal
1 cup Skim Milk
Coffee or Tea

MIDDAY MEAL
Creamy Potato Salad
½ cup Mushrooms on Lettuce with 1 tablespoon
    Low-Calorie Italian Dressing
½ cup Canned Fruit Cocktail
1 cup Skim Milk

EVENING MEAL
Mushroom-Beef Hash
½ cup Cooked Cabbage
½ cup Cooked Sliced Carrot
Romaine Lettuce Salad with 1 teaspoon
    Mayonnaise
½ cup Lime-Flavored Low-Calorie Gelatin

SNACKS, AT PLANNED TIMES
1 large Tangerine; 8 fluid ounces Beer

Serving Information
Men and Youth: Add ½ cup Orange Juice, ¾
    ounce Ready-to-Eat Cereal, 1 slice Pumper-
    nickel Bread, 1 medium Kiwi Fruit or ½ cup
    Sliced Peaches, and 1 cup Honeydew Balls
Youth: Add 1 cup Skim Milk

DAY 7

MORNING MEAL
½ small Cantaloupe
1 ounce Muenster Cheese
½ small Enriched Bagel, toasted
¼ cup Skim Milk
Coffee or Tea

MIDDAY MEAL
3–4 ounces Tuna mixed with 2 teaspoons
    Mayonnaise
½ medium Tomato, sliced
½ medium Green Bell Pepper, sliced
1 slice Enriched Bread
¾ cup Skim Milk

EVENING MEAL
Chicken and Cannellini Casserole
½ cup Cooked Spinach
Tossed Salad with **Russian Dressing**
1 slice Toasted Rye Bread
½ cup Canned Pineapple Chunks

SNACKS, AT PLANNED TIMES
¾ cup Buttermilk; 2 Dates; ½ cup Cherry-
    Flavored Gelatin

Serving Information
Men and Youth: Add ½ small Enriched Bagel,
    1 slice Enriched Bread, ½ cup Fruit Salad, and
    2 Dates
Men: Add ½ ounce Tuna at the Midday Meal
Youth: Add 1 cup Skim Milk

Meet the cardoon, a thistlelike, silvery-green prickly plant that's related to the artichoke but resembles a large stalk of celery.

WEEK 12

Cardoons come from the Mediterranean region and are perennials. Their leaves and stalks are edible, but it's the leafy midribs that are prized for their tender flesh. The flavor is delicate, resembling the artichoke and oyster plant (salsify).

We've provided a recipe for Cardoons Milanaise (Day 3). Food cooked à la Milanaise is generally dipped in egg and bread crumbs that have been mixed with grated Parmesan cheese, then fried in clarified butter. For our Cardoons Milanaise, we've used the traditional bread crumb and Parmesan cheese combination, but instead of frying, our recipe calls for baking.

DAY 1

MORNING MEAL
1 cup Strawberries
1/3 cup Cottage Cheese
1 slice Toasted Cracked Wheat Bread
1 cup Skim Milk
Coffee or Tea

MIDDAY MEAL
Egg Foo Yung
Zucchini and Carrot Salad with 1 teaspoon
    Sesame Oil plus Wine Vinegar
4 Canned Apricot Halves with 2 tablespoons
    Juice

EVENING MEAL
3–4 ounces Broiled Halibut
1/2 cup Cooked Sliced Carrot
Hearts of Lettuce with 1 teaspoon Mayonnaise
    and 1 teaspoon Ketchup
1 ounce Whole Wheat Roll
1 teaspoon Margarine
1/2 cup Lime-Flavored Low-Calorie Gelatin with
    1 tablespoon Low-Calorie Whipped Topping

SNACKS, AT PLANNED TIMES
1/2 cup Plain Unflavored Yogurt; 1/2 cup
    Applesauce

Serving Information
Men and Youth: Add 1 slice Rye Bread, 2 table-
    spoons Raisins, and 1 ounce Whole Wheat Roll
Youth: Add 1 cup Skim Milk

DAY 4

MORNING MEAL
1/2 medium Banana, sliced
3/4 ounce Ready-to-Eat Cereal
1 slice Toasted Enriched Bread
1 teaspoon Margarine
1 cup Skim Milk
Coffee or Tea

MIDDAY MEAL
Shredded Iceberg Lettuce, Sliced Mushrooms,
    1 Sliced Hard-Cooked Egg, 1 ounce Shredded
    Swiss Cheese, and Tomato Wedges with
    Oregano Vinaigrette
3/4 ounce Crispbread
Coconut-Orange Gelatin

EVENING MEAL
Seviche
Tossed Salad with **Sesame Vinaigrette**
1 ounce Enriched Roll
1/2 cup Strawberries with 1/2 cup Plain
    Unflavored Yogurt

SNACKS, AT PLANNED TIMES
1/2 medium Grapefruit sprinkled with 1/2 teaspoon
    Shredded Coconut; 12 fluid ounces Light Beer

Serving Information
Men and Youth: Add 4 medium Dried Apricot
    Halves, 1 ounce Enriched Roll, 1/2 cup Straw-
    berries, and 20 Oyster Crackers
Youth: Add 2 cups Skim Milk

DAY 5

MORNING MEAL
1/2 cup Orange Juice
Open-Face Grilled Cheese Sandwich I
1/4 cup Skim Milk
Coffee or Tea

MIDDAY MEAL
3–4 ounces Sardines
1/4 cup Onion Rings
Cucumber-Radish Salad
2 Canned Pineapple Slices with 2 tablespoons
    Juice
3/4 cup Skim Milk

EVENING MEAL
Pepper Steak
1/2 cup Cooked Enriched Rice
1/2 cup Steamed Sliced Zucchini
Hearts of Lettuce with 1/2 teaspoon Olive Oil
    plus Wine Vinegar
1/2 cup Canned Sliced Peaches

SNACKS, AT PLANNED TIMES
1/2 cup Plain Unflavored Yogurt with 2 teaspoons
    Reduced-Calorie Strawberry Spread; 6 Saltines
    with 1 1/2 teaspoons Reduced-Calorie Margarine

Serving Information
Men and Youth: Add 1/2 cup Orange Juice, 1
    English Muffin, split and toasted, 2 Dates, and
    2 Canned Pear Halves with 2 tablespoons Juice
Youth: Add 1 cup Skim Milk

MORNING MEAL
½ small Cantaloupe
¾ ounce Ready-to-Eat Cereal
¾ cup Skim Milk
Coffee or Tea

MIDDAY MEAL
"Calzone"
½ cup Cooked Artichoke Hearts with Lemon
   Wedges
Tomato and Cucumber Slices on Lettuce with
   Wine Vinegar
½ cup Canned Fruit Cocktail

EVENING MEAL
Turkey Florentine
½ cup Cooked Green Beans with ½ cup
   Tomato Sauce
Escarole Salad with 2 teaspoons Low-Calorie
   Italian Dressing
1 ounce Enriched Italian Bread
Sparkling Mineral Water with Twist of Lime

SNACKS, AT PLANNED TIMES
1 small Pear; ¾ cup Buttermilk

Serving Information
Men and Youth: Add 1 slice Pumpernickel Bread,
   1 ounce Enriched Italian Bread, 2 canned Plums
   with 2 tablespoons Juice, and 1 cup Honeydew
   Balls
Youth: Add 1¼ cups Skim Milk

MORNING MEAL
1 cup Tomato Juice
1 Poached Egg
1 slice Toasted Whole Wheat Bread
1½ teaspoons Margarine
¼ cup Skim Milk
Coffee or Tea

MIDDAY MEAL
3–4 ounces Broiled Chicken
½ cup Cooked Peas
Cardoons Milanaise
Mocha Sundae

EVENING MEAL
Broccoli-Shoot Appetizer
3–4 ounces Roast Beef
4 ounces Baked Potato with 2 tablespoons Plain
   Unflavored Yogurt
½ cup Steamed Green Bell Pepper Slices
½ cup Canned Pineapple Chunks

SNACKS, AT PLANNED TIMES
1 small Apple; 1 serving Chocolate-Flavored
   Low-Calorie Milk Beverage

Serving Information
Men and Youth: Add 1 slice Enriched Bread,
   1 small Pear, and 2 Graham Crackers
Youth: Add 1¾ cups Skim Milk

MORNING MEAL
½ medium Banana, sliced
1 serving Hot Cereal, ¾ ounce uncooked
½ cup Skim Milk
Coffee or Tea

MIDDAY MEAL
Curried Kidney Beans
Lettuce and Alfalfa or Bean Sprouts Salad with
   Basic Vinaigrette
1 ounce Pita Bread
Coffee-Yogurt Shake

EVENING MEAL
3–4 ounces Broiled Veal Chop
6 medium Cooked Asparagus Spears
½ cup Cooked Celery
1 ounce Enriched Roll
1 teaspoon Reduced-Calorie Margarine
¼ small Cantaloupe

SNACKS, AT PLANNED TIMES
½ cup Chocolate-Flavored Low-Calorie Milk
   Pudding; 2 Graham Crackers; 1 medium Kiwi
   Fruit or 1 small Orange

Serving Information
Men and Youth: Add 1 Dried Fig, 1 slice Cracked
   Wheat Bread, ¾ cup Canned Apple Slices, ¼
   small Cantaloupe, and ½ Matzo Board
Men: Add 1 ounce Broiled Veal at the Evening
   Meal
Youth: Add 1½ cups Skim Milk

MORNING MEAL
½ cup Orange and Grapefruit Sections
Vegetable Cottage Cheese
½ small Enriched Bagel
¼ cup Skim Milk
Coffee or Tea

MIDDAY MEAL
3–4 ounces Sliced Cooked Chicken
½ medium Tomato, sliced
Lettuce Leaves
2 teaspoons Reduced-Calorie Mayonnaise
1 slice Rye Bread
½ cup Orange-Flavored Gelatin

EVENING MEAL
3–4 ounces Broiled Liver
¼ cup Sliced Onion sautéed in 1 teaspoon
   Margarine
½ cup Steamed Kohlrabi
Watercress and Bibb Lettuce Salad with
   1 teaspoon Vegetable Oil plus Cider Vinegar
Frozen Mango Yogurt

SNACKS, AT PLANNED TIMES
¾ cup Buttermilk; 4 medium Dried Apricot
   Halves

Serving Information
Men and Youth: Add ½ small Enriched Bagel, 1
   slice Rye Bread, and ½ cup Canned Mandarin
   Orange Sections
Youth: Add 1¾ cups Skim Milk

Cooking with wine has glamorous connotations. The delicious anticipation that comes with trying a new wine-flavored recipe is often headier than just drinking the wine would be. But use wine with discretion. It should gently enhance and improve the flavor of the food, not drown it.

The finer the wine you add to a dish, the better that dish will taste. A good rule to follow is, if you wouldn't drink it, don't cook with it. Inferior wines usually overpower any dish. However, save very expensive vintage wines for special occasions. Moderately priced wines are fine for most cooking.

Most of us associate white wine with certain foods and red wine with others. Therefore, it's a good idea to cook with the same type of wine you'd drink with that particular meal.

Chicken Livers Sautéed in Wine (Day 4) emerge succulent and aromatic. Cheers!

WEEK 13

DAY 1

MORNING MEAL
½ medium Grapefruit
¾ ounce Ready-to-Eat Cereal
½ cup Skim Milk
Coffee or Tea

MIDDAY MEAL
Stuffed French Toast
Carrot and Celery Sticks
1 serving Chocolate-Flavored Low-Calorie
  Milk Beverage

EVENING MEAL
3–4 ounces Roast Chicken
½ cup Cooked Peas
½ cup Steamed Red Cabbage
Tossed Salad with **Dill Vinaigrette**
1 ounce Enriched Roll
1 teaspoon Margarine
Stuffed Baked Apple

SNACKS, AT PLANNED TIMES
1 cup Mixed Vegetable Juice; **Root Beer Froth**

Serving Information
Men and Youth: Add 6 Saltines and 1 large
  Tangerine
Youth: Add 1½ cups Skim Milk

DAY 4

MORNING MEAL
½ cup Blueberries
¾ ounce Ready-to-Eat Cereal
1 cup Skim Milk
Coffee or Tea

MIDDAY MEAL
Chicken Livers Sautéed in Wine
Cucumber and Tomato Salad
1 ounce Whole Wheat Roll
½ cup Canned Cherries

EVENING MEAL
3–4 ounces Baked Veal Cutlet
¼ cup Steamed Okra
Zucchini Spaghetti
1 slice Pumpernickel Bread
½ cup Lemon-Flavored Low-Calorie Gelatin

SNACKS, AT PLANNED TIMES
½ cup Chocolate-Flavored Low-Calorie Milk
  Pudding; ½ cup Orange and Grapefruit
  Sections

Serving Information
Men and Youth: Add 1 slice Enriched Bread, ½
  cup Canned Cherries, and 2 Graham Crackers
Youth: Add 1 cup Skim Milk

DAY 5

MORNING MEAL
½ cup Grapefruit Juice
1 Soft-Cooked Egg
1 slice Toasted Enriched Bread
1 teaspoon Margarine
¼ cup Skim Milk
Coffee or Tea

MIDDAY MEAL
1 cup Mixed Vegetable Juice
Curried Scrod
½ cup Cooked Green Beans
Watercress and Boston Lettuce Salad with
  Pesto Dressing
1 slice Whole Wheat Bread
Coffee or Tea

EVENING MEAL
3–4 ounces Roast Fresh Ham
Sweet Potato Tzimmes
½ cup Steamed Chinese Pea Pods
Hearts of Lettuce with 1¼ teaspoons Mayonnaise
¼ medium Papaya, diced, or ½ cup Strawberries,
  with 2 tablespoons Plain Unflavored Yogurt

SNACKS, AT PLANNED TIMES
¾ cup Buttermilk; 1 small Apple

Serving Information
Men and Youth: Add 1 slice Whole Wheat Bread,
  1 small Pear, ¼ medium Papaya, diced, or ½
  cup Strawberries, and 4 Canned Pineapple
  Spears with 2 tablespoons Juice
Youth: Add 1¾ cups Skim Milk

DAY 2

MORNING MEAL
½ cup Orange Juice
1 Poached Egg
1 slice Rye Bread
¼ cup Skim Milk
Coffee or Tea

MIDDAY MEAL
3–4 ounces Tuna
2 teaspoons Mayonnaise
1 slice Enriched Bread
Lettuce Wedge with **Sesame Vinaigrette**
½ cup Strawberry-Flavored Low-Calorie Gelatin
¾ cup Skim Milk

EVENING MEAL
Armenian Lamb Stew
½ cup Cooked Cracked Wheat (Bulgur)
Green and Red Bell Pepper Rings and Cucumber
   Slices on Lettuce with Lemon Juice
4 fluid ounces Red Wine
½ cup Fruit Salad

SNACKS, AT PLANNED TIMES
¾ cup Buttermilk; 2 Canned Pear Halves with
   2 tablespoons Juice

Serving Information
Men and Youth: Add 1 slice Enriched Bread, 2
   Dried Figs, and 1 slice Pumpernickel Bread
Youth: Add 1 cup Skim Milk

DAY 3

MORNING MEAL
2-inch wedge Honeydew
Open-Face Grilled Cheese Sandwich I
¼ cup Skim Milk
Coffee or Tea

MIDDAY MEAL
1½–2 ounces Sliced Cooked Chicken and
   1 Sliced Hard-Cooked Egg on Lettuce with
   1 teaspoon Mayonnaise
Fruit Slaw
1 serving Vanilla-Flavored Low-Calorie Milk
   Beverage

EVENING MEAL
¾ cup **Chicken Broth**
3–4 ounces Broiled Haddock with Lemon Wedges
½ cup Sliced Cooked Beets
½ cup Steamed Spinach
Chicory and Sliced Radish Salad with
   ¾ teaspoon Vegetable Oil plus Tarragon
   Vinegar
½ English Muffin, toasted
1 teaspoon Reduced-Calorie Margarine
½ cup Strawberries

SNACKS, AT PLANNED TIMES
¾ ounce Ready-to-Eat Cereal; ½ cup Skim Milk;
   2 Canned Peach Halves with 2 tablespoons
   Juice

Serving Information
Men and Youth: Add 1 ounce Pita Bread, ½
   medium Papaya or 1 small Apple, 20 Oyster
   Crackers, ½ cup Strawberries, and 4 medium
   Dried Apricot Halves
Youth: Add 1¾ cups Skim Milk

DAY 6

MORNING MEAL
1 small Orange
⅓ cup Part-Skim Ricotta Cheese
1 slice Toasted Raisin Bread
¼ cup Skim Milk
Coffee or Tea

MIDDAY MEAL
Chicken Teriyaki
Mixed Vegetable Salad
¼ small Cantaloupe
¾ cup Skim Milk

EVENING MEAL
3–4 ounces Broiled Fillet of Flounder
Broiled Tomato
½ cup Steamed Broccoli
Cucumber, Radish, and Green Bell Pepper Slices
   on Lettuce with 2 teaspoons Mayonnaise
1 slice Rye Bread with 1 teaspoon Reduced-
   Calorie Margarine
4 fluid ounces White Wine
Coffee or Tea

SNACKS, AT PLANNED TIMES
1 cup Skim Milk with 1 teaspoon Chocolate
   Syrup; ½ small Mango or 1 small Pear

Serving Information
Men and Youth: Add 1 slice Cracked Wheat
   Bread, ¼ small Cantaloupe, ½ cup Canned
   Mandarin Orange Sections, and 6 Melba Toast
   Rounds
Youth: Add 2 cups Skim Milk

DAY 7

MORNING MEAL
½ medium Banana, sliced
¾ ounce Ready-to-Eat Cereal
1 cup Skim Milk
Coffee or Tea

MIDDAY MEAL
Mexican Soup
Alfalfa or Bean Sprouts and 2 tablespoons Diced
   Red Onion on Lettuce with **Herb Dressing**
½ cup Plain Unflavored Yogurt with 1 teaspoon
   Honey

EVENING MEAL
3–4 ounces Broiled Flank Steak
4 ounces Baked Potato with 1½ teaspoons
   Reduced-Calorie Margarine
½ cup Steamed Kale
2 Canned Pear Halves with 2 tablespoons Juice

SNACKS, AT PLANNED TIMES
20 small Grapes; 1 cup Tomato Juice

Serving Information
Men and Youth: Add 2 Dates, chopped, ½
   English Muffin, toasted, ½ cup Applesauce,
   1 ounce Enriched Roll, 20 Oyster Crackers, and
   2 tablespoons Raisins
Men: Add 1 ounce Canned Chick Peas (Garban-
   zos) to Midday Meal Salad
Youth: Add 1 cup Skim Milk

Let onion atoms lurk within
  the bowl
And, half-suspected,
  animate the whole.

    —Recipe for salad, *Lady Holland's
    Memoir*, Vol. I, by Sydney Smith

WEEK 14

Salads figure prominently in our menu
plans. They are easy to prepare, colorful,
and contribute texture, fiber, and nutrients.

    While the advice quoted above is good,
too heavy a reliance on onions might have
an adverse effect on one's love life! For the
sake of variety, we've scattered dozens of
alternatives throughout this book.

    You can put just about anything into a
salad, and it should taste fine when you're
done. Tasty salad choices offered this week
include Grated Red Cabbage and Bean
Sprouts (Day 1), Bacon-Flavored Potato
Salad (Day 3), Relish Salad (Day 5), and
Curried Cole Slaw (Day 7).

DAY 1

MORNING MEAL
½ cup Orange Juice
1 Poached Egg
Cornmeal Pancakes
⅓ cup Skim Milk
Coffee or Tea

MIDDAY MEAL
3–4 ounces Broiled Swordfish
½ cup Cooked Chopped Spinach
½ cup Cooked Diced Carrot
Tossed Salad with Lemon Juice
1 ounce Whole Wheat Roll
1 teaspoon Margarine
½ small Cantaloupe

EVENING MEAL
Jellied Veal Mold
½ cup Steamed Brussels Sprouts
½ cup Steamed Cauliflower
Grated Red Cabbage and Bean Sprouts on
  Lettuce with **Wine Vinaigrette**
1 small Apple

SNACKS, AT PLANNED TIMES
Lemonade; ½ cup Vanilla-Flavored Low-Calorie
  Milk Pudding

Serving Information
Men and Youth: Add ½ cup Orange Juice, 4
  medium Dried Apricot Halves, 1 slice Cracked
  Wheat Bread, and 2 Graham Crackers
Youth: Add 1⅔ cups Skim Milk

DAY 4

MORNING MEAL
⅓ cup Apple Juice
⅓ cup Cottage Cheese
½ small Enriched Bagel
¼ cup Skim Milk
Coffee or Tea

MIDDAY MEAL
French Omelet
Watercress and Sliced Radish Salad with
  Lemon Salad Dressing
1 slice Rye Bread
½ teaspoon Reduced-Calorie Margarine
½ cup Cherry-Flavored Low-Calorie Gelatin

EVENING MEAL
¾ cup **Vegetable Broth**
Savory Pinto Beans
6 medium Steamed Asparagus Spears
Tossed Salad with Wine Vinegar
1 medium Kiwi Fruit or ½ small Cantaloupe

SNACKS, AT PLANNED TIMES
Strawberry-Apple Frost; ½ English Muffin,
  toasted, with 1 teaspoon Reduced-Calorie
  Raspberry Spread; ¾ cup Skim Milk

Serving Information
Men and Youth: Add ⅓ cup Apple Juice, ½ small
  Enriched Bagel, and ½ English Muffin, toasted
Men: Add ½ ounce Diced Cheddar Cheese to
  Salad at the Evening Meal
Youth: Add 1¾ cups Skim Milk

DAY 5

MORNING MEAL
½ cup Grapefruit Sections
¾ ounce Ready-to-Eat Cereal
¾ cup Skim Milk
Coffee or Tea

MIDDAY MEAL
3–4 ounces Boiled Shrimp
2 teaspoons Seafood Cocktail Sauce
½ cup Steamed Green Beans
Relish Salad
1 slice Enriched Bread
1 teaspoon Reduced-Calorie Margarine
½ cup Applesauce

EVENING MEAL
Yogurt-Mushroom Appetizer
3–4 ounces Broiled Fillet of Beef
½ cup Cooked Cauliflower
¼ cup Chilled Cooked Sliced Beets on Lettuce
  with Cider Vinegar
1 ounce Enriched Roll
4 fluid ounces Red Wine
Coffee or Tea

SNACKS, AT PLANNED TIMES
¾ cup Buttermilk; 1 small Pear; 2 cups Plain
  Popcorn

Serving Information
Men and Youth: Add 2 tablespoons Raisins, 6
  Saltines, and 1 ounce Enriched Roll
Youth: Add 1¼ cups Skim Milk

MORNING MEAL
1 cup Tomato Juice
1 ounce Cheddar Cheese
1 slice Toasted Pumpernickel Bread
1 teaspoon Margarine
¼ cup Skim Milk
Coffee or Tea

MIDDAY MEAL
3–4 ounces Sliced Roast Turkey
Tomato and Cucumber Slices on Lettuce with
    1 teaspoon Reduced-Calorie Mayonnaise
1 slice Whole Wheat Bread
2 Canned Peach Halves with 2 tablespoons Juice
¾ cup Skim Milk

EVENING MEAL
Pork and Vegetable Medley
½ cup Cooked Sliced Summer Squash
½ cup Cooked Broccoli
Shredded Lettuce and Sliced Celery with
    1 teaspoon Imitation Bacon Bits and
    2 teaspoons Low-Calorie French Dressing
½ medium Grapefruit

SNACKS, AT PLANNED TIMES
1 cup **Hot Mocha Milk**; 2 Graham Crackers;
    Oven-Stewed Prunes

Serving Information
Men and Youth: Add 2-inch wedge Honeydew
    and 1 slice Whole Wheat Bread
Youth: Add 1 cup Skim Milk

MORNING MEAL
½ medium Banana, sliced
¾ ounce Ready-to-Eat Cereal
½ cup Skim Milk
Coffee or Tea

MIDDAY MEAL
3–4 ounces Poached Chicken Livers
Bacon-Flavored Potato Salad
1 slice Cracked Wheat Bread
1 teaspoon Margarine
½ cup Canned Fruit Cocktail

EVENING MEAL
3–4 ounces Broiled Haddock
¼ cup Cooked Peas
¼ cup Cooked Sliced Mushrooms
Red and Green Bell Pepper Strips on Lettuce
    with 1 teaspoon Vegetable Oil plus Tarragon
    Vinegar
4 fluid ounces White Wine
Coffee or Tea

SNACKS, AT PLANNED TIMES
½ cup Plain Unflavored Yogurt with Vanilla
    Extract and Artificial Sweetener; 1 small
    Orange; ½ cup Skim Milk with 1 teaspoon
    Chocolate Syrup, whipped in blender

Serving Information
Men and Youth: Add 2 tablespoons Raisins, ¾
    cup Canned Apple Slices, 2 ounces Enriched
    Roll, and 2 Canned Pear Halves with 2 table-
    spoons Juice
Youth: Add 1¼ cups Skim Milk

MORNING MEAL
⅓ cup Grape Juice
1 Scrambled Egg
1 slice Toasted Rye Bread
1 teaspoon Margarine
¼ cup Skim Milk
Coffee or Tea

MIDDAY MEAL
Cheese Pizza Pocket
Carrot and Celery Sticks
Romaine Lettuce and Cherry Tomato Salad with
    1 teaspoon Imitation Bacon Bits and
    1 teaspoon Reduced-Calorie Mayonnaise
1 cup Strawberries
¾ cup Skim Milk

EVENING MEAL
Braised Chicken with Vegetables
½ cup Cooked Sliced Zucchini
½ cup Cooked Broccoli Spears
Tropical Treat

SNACKS, AT PLANNED TIMES
½ cup Plain Unflavored Yogurt with 2 teaspoons
    Reduced-Calorie Apricot Spread; 1 cup
    Tomato Juice

Serving Information
Men and Youth: Add ⅓ cup Grape Juice, 4
    Canned Apricot Halves with 2 tablespoons
    Juice, 1 ounce Pita Bread, and 20 Oyster
    Crackers
Youth: Add 2 cups Skim Milk

MORNING MEAL
2 Dates, chopped
¾ ounce Ready-to-Eat Cereal
1 slice Toasted Enriched Bread
1 teaspoon Margarine
1 cup Skim Milk
Coffee or Tea

MIDDAY MEAL
Baked Striped Bass with Vegetables
Curried Cole Slaw
½ cup Cooked Green Beans
1 ounce Enriched Roll
1 teaspoon Margarine
½ cup Strawberry-Flavored Gelatin

EVENING MEAL
Marinated Chuck Steak
½ cup Steamed Eggplant Slices
½ cup Steamed Spinach
Alfalfa or Bean Sprouts and 2 tablespoons Diced
    Onion on Lettuce with 2 teaspoons Low-
    Calorie Italian Dressing
½ cup Butterscotch-Flavored Low-Calorie Milk
    Pudding

SNACKS, AT PLANNED TIMES
½ cup Orange Sections; ¼ small Pineapple

Serving Information
Men and Youth: Add 2 Dates, chopped, and 2
    ounces Enriched Italian Bread
Youth: Add 2 cups Skim Milk

WEEK 15

This menu plan includes meals for two religious holidays rich in symbolic foods: Passover and Easter. Both holidays share one symbol: the egg.

The main course of the Midday Meal on Day 7 is Roast Fillet of Beef with Green Peppercorns, a menu suitable for Easter. Any beef roast can be substituted for the fillet, but use only *green* peppercorns. Their flavor is unique. You can buy them packed in vinegar or brine in most specialty stores.

Matzo Brei (Day 4), made with the traditional unleavened bread, is a Passover treat. Stir-fry it or cook it like a pancake. Traditional "kishka" is a stuffing mixture, bound in beef casings. Our Mock Kishka (Day 3) doesn't use a casing; it's formed into a loaf. And for a delicious holiday dessert try Fruited Matzo Kugel (Day 4).

Economy Tip—Roast chicken is on the menu on Day 3. Leftovers may be frozen and used in Red Chicken with Potatoes recipe (Week 17, Day 6).

DAY 1

MORNING MEAL
½ small Cantaloupe
1 Scrambled Egg
½ English Muffin, toasted
1 teaspoon Margarine
1 cup Skim Milk
Coffee or Tea

MIDDAY MEAL
3–4 ounces Broiled Hamburger
2 teaspoons Ketchup
¼ cup Steamed Onion Slices
½ cup Steamed Mushrooms
Broiled Tomato
Lettuce Wedge
1 slice Rye Bread
1 teaspoon Margarine
Club Soda with Twist of Lime

EVENING MEAL
3–4 ounces Baked Turkey Cutlets
½ cup Cooked Enriched Rice
½ cup Steamed Broccoli
½ cup Steamed Carrot
Bibb and Boston Lettuce Salad with 1 teaspoon
    Vegetable Oil plus Rice Vinegar
Mineral Water with Mint Sprig

SNACKS, AT PLANNED TIMES
Frozen Apple-Banana Dessert; ½ cup Canned
    Sliced Peaches topped with 1 teaspoon
    Shredded Coconut

Serving Information
Men and Youth: Add ½ English Muffin, toasted,
    and 1 small Orange
Youth: Add 2 cups Skim Milk

DAY 4

MORNING MEAL
⅓ cup Apple Juice
Matzo Brei
½ cup Skim Milk
Coffee or Tea

MIDDAY MEAL
1½–2 ounces Broiled Veal Patty
½ cup Steamed Red Bell Pepper Strips
½ cup Steamed Zucchini Sticks
Cherry Tomatoes on Lettuce with Cider Vinegar
Coffee or Tea

EVENING MEAL
3–4 ounces Roast Beef
½ cup Steamed Brussels Sprouts
½ cup Steamed Sliced Carrot
Green Salad with Red Wine Vinegar and
    Seasonings
½ Matzo Board
4 fluid ounces Red Wine
Fruited Matzo Kugel
Coffee or Tea

SNACKS, AT PLANNED TIMES
¾ cup Plain Unflavored Yogurt; 1 small Orange

Serving Information
Men and Youth: Add ⅓ cup Apple Juice, 1 Matzo
    Board, and 2 tablespoons Raisins
Youth: Add 1½ cups Skim Milk

DAY 5

MORNING MEAL
1 cup Cantaloupe Balls
⅓ cup Pot Cheese
½ Matzo Board
½ cup Skim Milk
Coffee or Tea

MIDDAY MEAL
2 ounces Sliced Swiss Cheese
Sliced Tomato, Lettuce Wedge, and Dill Pickle
    Spears topped with 2 teaspoons Mayonnaise
2 Dates
Lemonade

EVENING MEAL
3–4 ounces Broiled Flounder
4 ounces Baked Potato
1 teaspoon Margarine
½ cup Steamed Spinach
½ cup Steamed Diced Carrot
Watercress and Cucumber Salad with
    Lemon Juice
1 small Apple
½ cup Skim Milk
Coffee or Tea

SNACKS, AT PLANNED TIMES
1 cup Skim Milk; **Hot Spiced Tea**

Serving Information
Men and Youth: Add 1 Matzo Board and 2 Dates
Youth: Add 1 cup Skim Milk

MORNING MEAL

DAY 2

MORNING MEAL
½ cup Grapefruit Juice
¾ ounce Ready-to-Eat Cereal
1 slice Toasted Enriched Bread
1 teaspoon Reduced-Calorie Orange Marmalade
1 cup Skim Milk ☐ Coffee or Tea

MIDDAY MEAL
3–4 ounces Tuna
Tomato and Cucumber Slices and 2 Olives on
    Lettuce Leaves topped with 1 teaspoon Grated
    Parmesan Cheese and 2 teaspoons Reduced-
    Calorie Mayonnaise
2 Melba Toast Slices
1 teaspoon Reduced-Calorie Margarine
½ cup Honeydew Balls

EVENING MEAL
3–4 ounces Broiled Beef Liver
Vegetable Medley
Watercress and Radish Salad with **Savory
    Vinaigrette**
1 ounce Whole Wheat Roll
1 teaspoon Reduced-Calorie Margarine
½ cup Cooked Rhubarb Topped with 2 teaspoons
    Low-Calorie Whipped Topping

SNACKS, AT PLANNED TIMES
½ cup Canned Pineapple Chunks; ½ cup Plain
    Unflavored Yogurt

Serving Information
Men and Youth: Add ½ cup Grapefruit Juice, ½
    cup Honeydew Balls, 2 Melba Toast Slices,
    ½ cup Canned Pineapple Chunks, 1 ounce
    Whole Wheat Roll, and ½ cup Cooked Rhubarb
Youth: Add 1 cup Skim Milk

DAY 3

41

MORNING MEAL
½ cup Orange Sections
⅓ cup Cottage Cheese
½ Cinnamon-Raisin English Muffin, toasted
1 cup Skim Milk ☐ Coffee or Tea

MIDDAY MEAL
2 ounces Sliced Muenster Cheese
Grated Carrots, Alfalfa or Bean Sprouts, and
    Chopped Tomato on Shredded Lettuce with
    2½ teaspoons Reduced-Calorie Mayonnaise
2 Dill Pickle Spears
2 Canned Apricot Halves with 2 tablespoons
    Juice

EVENING MEAL
¾ cup **Chicken Broth**
Rutabaga Appetizer
3–4 ounces Roast Chicken
½ cup Steamed Green Beans
Mock Kishka
Tossed Salad with Lemon Juice
½ Matzo Board
4 fluid ounces Red Wine ☐ Coffee or Tea

SNACKS, AT PLANNED TIMES
¾ cup Buttermilk; ½ cup Applesauce sprinkled
    with Cinnamon

Serving Information
Men and Youth: Add ½ cup Orange Sections,
    ½ Cinnamon-Raisin English Muffin, toasted,
    2 Canned Apricot Halves with 2 tablespoons
    Juice, and ½ Matzo Board
Youth: Add 2 cups Skim Milk

DAY 6

MORNING MEAL
1 cup Strawberries
¾ ounce Ready-to-Eat Cereal
1 cup Skim Milk
Coffee or Tea

MIDDAY MEAL
Mushroom Loaf
½ cup Cooked Wax Beans
Green Salad with **Gingered Vinaigrette** and
    1 teaspoon Grated Parmesan Cheese
Mineral Water with Twist of Lemon

EVENING MEAL
3–4 ounces Baked Veal Cutlet
¼ cup Steamed Onion Slices
½ cup Blanched Cauliflower
½ cup Blanched Broccoli
Tossed Salad with 2 teaspoons Vegetable Oil
    plus Cider Vinegar
1 slice Whole Wheat Bread
Club Soda with Mint Sprig

SNACKS, AT PLANNED TIMES
½ cup Canned Fruit Cocktail topped with
    1 teaspoon Shredded Coconut; ¾ cup
    Buttermilk; ¼ small Pineapple

Serving Information
Men and Youth: Add 1 slice Toasted Enriched
    Bread, 1 ounce Enriched Roll, and ½ cup
    Applesauce
Youth: Add 1½ cups Skim Milk

DAY 7

MORNING MEAL
Coffee-Cheese Delight
½ cup Skim Milk
Coffee or Tea

MIDDAY MEAL
Herbed Beef Broth
Roast Fillet of Beef with Green Peppercorns
Vegetable Mold
Holiday Salad
1 ounce Enriched French Bread
1 teaspoon Margarine
4 fluid ounces Champagne
Lime-Orange Ice in Lime Cups

EVENING MEAL
Sea Trout with Mushroom Stuffing
½ cup Steamed Asparagus Tips
Tossed Salad and Tomato Slices with
    Tarragon Vinegar
1 cup Skim Milk

SNACKS, AT PLANNED TIMES
½ medium Banana; **Coconut-Honey Shake**

Serving Information
Men and Youth: Add ½ cup Orange Juice, 1 slice
    Whole Wheat Bread, ½ medium Banana, and 2
    Graham Crackers
Youth: Add 2 cups Skim Milk

42

Olive oil, as much a seasoning as a fat, has a more distinctive flavor and lower smoking point than other edible oils. It is made by crushing tree-ripened olives, then extracting the liquid. Processing produces the first crude olive oil, which is then refined.

Oil from the first pressing of the fruit is referred to as virgin olive oil. It is greenish in color, may be slightly hazy, and is highly prized for its strong olive flavor. The most refined olive oil is straw-yellow in color. As with other vegetable oils, olive oil should be protected from direct sunlight and high temperatures. Cold causes it to cloud and thicken, but this has little effect on its flavor or quality.

A characteristic component of Mediterranean cookery, olive oil is imported from France, Italy, Spain, and Greece. Fine-quality California olive oil is also available.

We'll use olive oil this week to prepare Calf Liver with Tomato (Day 4).

DAY 1

MORNING MEAL
Cereal with Spiced Fruit Ambrosia
1 slice Toasted Enriched Bread
1 teaspoon Reduced-Calorie Cherry Spread
¼ cup Skim Milk
Coffee or Tea

MIDDAY MEAL
Open-Face Grilled Cheese Sandwich II
Lettuce and Grated Carrot Salad with
    1 teaspoon Mayonnaise
1 small Pear
¾ cup Skim Milk

EVENING MEAL
Cauliflower and Zucchini Soup
Fruited Chicken
½ cup Cooked Baby Peas with Diced Pimiento
½ cup Strawberry-Flavored Low-Calorie Gelatin

SNACKS, AT PLANNED TIMES
¾ ounce Crispbread with 2 teaspoons Reduced-
    Calorie Margarine; 1 cup Tomato Juice

Serving Information
Men and Youth: Add ½ cup Orange Juice, 2
    ounces Whole Wheat Roll, and 2 Dates
Youth: Add 2 cups Skim Milk

DAY 4

MORNING MEAL
½ cup Orange Sections
1 ounce Cheddar Cheese
1 slice Pumpernickel Bread
½ cup Skim Milk
Coffee or Tea

MIDDAY MEAL
3–4 ounces Broiled Cod
½ cup Steamed Broccoli
Chicory and Romaine Lettuce Salad with
    Thousand Island Dressing
1 slice Rye Bread
1½ teaspoons Reduced-Calorie Margarine
½ cup Canned Sliced Peaches

EVENING MEAL
Calf Liver with Tomato
½ cup Cooked Wax Beans
½ cup Cooked Collards with Lemon Slices
Lettuce Wedge with 1 teaspoon Reduced-Calorie
    Mayonnaise
10 small Grapes

SNACKS, AT PLANNED TIMES
1 cup Skim Milk; ¼ small Cantaloupe; ½ Matzo
    Board with 1 teaspoon Reduced-Calorie
    Apricot Spread

Serving Information
Men and Youth: Add 2 ounces Pita Bread, ¼
    small Cantaloupe, and 10 small Grapes
Youth: Add 1½ cups Skim Milk

DAY 5

MORNING MEAL
4 medium Dried Apricot Halves
¾ ounce Ready-to-Eat Cereal
¾ cup Skim Milk
Coffee or Tea

MIDDAY MEAL
Mushroom Omelet
Tomato Slices on Lettuce with ¼ recipe
    Yogurt Dressing
1 slice Enriched Bread
½ cup Strawberry-Flavored Low-Calorie Gelatin
    with ¼ cup Strawberries

EVENING MEAL
Chili-Burgers
½ cup Cooked Asparagus Tips
½ cup Cooked Cauliflower
Watercress and Sliced Radish Salad with Cider
    Vinegar
Mandarin Chiffon Pie

SNACKS, AT PLANNED TIMES
1 medium Kiwi Fruit or ½ medium Grapefruit;
    Melba Toast Puffs

Serving Information
Men and Youth: Add 2 tablespoons Raisins,
    1 Hamburger Roll, and 1 small Apple
Youth: Add 1¼ cups Skim Milk

MORNING MEAL
1/3 cup Pineapple Juice
Cinnamon-Cheese Toast
1/4 cup Skim Milk
Coffee or Tea

MIDDAY MEAL
Potato Pie
1/2 cup Cooked Green Beans
Sliced Cucumber and Red Bell Pepper Rings on
   Lettuce with **Cider Vinaigrette**
3/4 cup Skim Milk with 1 teaspoon Chocolate
   Syrup

EVENING MEAL
3–4 ounces Broiled Fillet of Sole
1/4 cup Cooked Brussels Sprouts
1/2 cup Cooked Sliced Summer Squash
Grated Red Cabbage with Bean Sprouts and
   2 teaspoons Mayonnaise
1/2 cup Vanilla-Flavored Low-Calorie Milk Pudding

SNACKS, AT PLANNED TIMES
1 small Orange; 1/2 cup Applesauce; 1/2 cup
   Strawberry-Flavored Gelatin

Serving Information
Men and Youth: Add 1/3 cup Pineapple Juice, 1
   ounce Enriched Roll, and 1 large Tangerine
Youth: Add 1 cup Skim Milk

MORNING MEAL
1/2 medium Grapefruit
3/4 ounce Ready-to-Eat Cereal
1 cup Skim Milk
Coffee or Tea

MIDDAY MEAL
1/3 cup Part-Skim Ricotta Cheese mixed with
   1/4 cup Canned Crushed Pineapple on Lettuce
   Leaves
1/2 small Enriched Bagel
1 teaspoon Margarine
1/2 cup Strawberries with 1 tablespoon Low-
   Calorie Whipped Topping

EVENING MEAL
3–4 ounces Broiled Steak
1/2 cup Steamed Chinese Pea Pods
Green Beans with Peanut Sauce
Tossed Salad with Lemon Juice
1 slice Whole Wheat Bread
1 teaspoon Margarine
4 fluid ounces Red Wine
Coffee or Tea

SNACKS, AT PLANNED TIMES
1/2 cup Plain Unflavored Yogurt; 1/2 medium
   Banana; 1/2 cup Grape-Flavored Low-Calorie
   Gelatin

Serving Information
Men and Youth: Add 2 tablespoons Raisins, 1
   slice Enriched Bread, 1/2 small Enriched Bagel,
   1/2 cup Strawberries, and 2 Canned Pear Halves
   with 2 tablespoons Juice
Youth: Add 2 cups Skim Milk

MORNING MEAL
1/3 cup Apple Juice
1/3 cup Pot Cheese
1 slice Toasted Whole Wheat Bread
1 teaspoon Margarine
1/4 cup Skim Milk
Coffee or Tea

MIDDAY MEAL
3–4 ounces Sliced Roast Turkey
1/2 medium Dill Pickle
1 slice Rye Bread
1 teaspoon Mayonnaise
4 Canned Apricot Halves with 2 tablespoons
   Juice
3/4 cup Skim Milk

EVENING MEAL
Captain's Flounder
1/2 cup Cooked Spinach
Fennel Parmesan
Alfalfa or Bean Sprouts on Lettuce with Lemon
   Juice
4 fluid ounces White Wine
Coffee or Tea

SNACKS, AT PLANNED TIMES
1/2 cup Chocolate-Flavored Low-Calorie Milk
   Pudding; 2-inch wedge Honeydew

Serving Information
Men and Youth: Add 1/3 cup Apple Juice, 1 slice
   Rye Bread, 1 Dried Fig, 1 ounce Whole Wheat
   Roll, and 1/4 small Pineapple
Youth: Add 1 cup Skim Milk

MORNING MEAL
3 medium Prunes, pitted and chopped
3/4 ounce Ready-to-Eat Cereal
1 slice Toasted Whole Wheat Bread
1 teaspoon Margarine
3/4 cup Skim Milk ☐ Coffee or Tea

MIDDAY MEAL
Vegetable Lasagna
Cucumber Spears and Green Bell Pepper Strips
   on Lettuce with 1 teaspoon Olive Oil plus
   Wine Vinegar
1/2 cup Fruit Salad sprinkled with 1/2 teaspoon
   Shredded Coconut

EVENING MEAL
**Steak au Poivre (Peppered Steak) with
   Garlic "Butter"**
1/2 cup Cooked Brown Rice
1/2 cup Whipped Baked Acorn Squash
1/2 cup Cooked Green Beans
Boston Lettuce and Sliced Mushroom Salad with
   2 teaspoons Low-Calorie Italian Dressing
1/4 cup Skim Milk ☐ Coffee or Tea

SNACKS, AT PLANNED TIMES
1 serving Vanilla-Flavored Low-Calorie Milk
   Beverage; 2 Graham Crackers; 1/2 medium
   Papaya or 1/2 small Cantaloupe

Serving Information
Men and Youth: Add 1 slice Pumpernickel Bread,
   1 ounce Enriched French Bread, and 2 Canned
   Peach Halves with 2 tablespoons Juice
Youth: Add 1 cup Skim Milk

The apple, one of nature's oldest and best-known fruits (remember the Garden of Eden?), really belongs to the rose family. In ancient Persia, it was considered the fruit of immortality. Greek and Roman mythology used the apple as a symbol of love and beauty.

Allspice has a misleading name. It's not a combination of spices but the aromatic dried, unripe fruit of a myrtle-like tree. The flavor resembles a mixture of cloves, cinnamon, and nutmeg—hence its name.

Apples appear in this week's menu plan as a Morning Meal dish, a beverage, and a dessert. In Swedish Apple Bake (Day 7), we have combined apples and allspice.

Economy Tip—Broiled sliced steak is on the menu on Day 4. Leftovers may be frozen and used in Oriental Steak Salad recipe (Week 27, Day 5).

WEEK 17

DAY 1

MORNING MEAL
1/3 cup Prune Juice
1 Scrambled Egg with Chives and 1 teaspoon Imitation Bacon Bits
1/2 English Muffin, toasted
1 teaspoon Margarine
1/4 cup Skim Milk
Coffee or Tea

MIDDAY MEAL
3/4 cup **Vegetable Broth**
Pineapple Flounder
1/2 cup Steamed Broccoli
Shredded Red Cabbage topped with Alfalfa or Bean Sprouts and Lemon Juice
Mineral Water with Twist of Lemon

EVENING MEAL
Cheese Pizza Pocket
Carrot, Celery, and Green Bell Pepper Sticks
Tossed Salad with 1 teaspoon Vegetable Oil plus Wine Vinegar
1/2 cup Raspberry-Flavored Low-Calorie Gelatin
3/4 cup Skim Milk

SNACKS, AT PLANNED TIMES
1 serving Vanilla-Flavored Low-Calorie Milk Beverage; 2 medium Dried Apricot Halves; 1 cup Cantaloupe Balls

Serving Information
Men and Youth: Add 1/3 cup Prune Juice, 1/2 English Muffin, toasted, 1 ounce Enriched Roll, 1 small Pear, and 1/2 cup Raspberries
Youth: Add 2 cups Skim Milk

DAY 4

MORNING MEAL
Peaches and Cheese Breakfast
1 slice Raisin Bread
1 teaspoon Margarine
1 cup Skim Milk
Coffee or Tea

MIDDAY MEAL
3–4 ounces Sliced Roast Turkey
1/2 medium Tomato, sliced
Lettuce Leaves
1 slice Whole Wheat Bread
1 teaspoon Mayonnaise
1/2 cup Chocolate-Flavored Low-Calorie Milk Pudding

EVENING MEAL
1 cup Tomato Juice with Lemon Wedge
3–4 ounces Sliced Broiled Steak
3 ounces Baked Yam with 1 teaspoon Margarine
1/4 cup Steamed Onion Slices
1/2 cup Steamed Spinach
Green Salad with Lemon Juice and Herbs
Sparkling Mineral Water with Twist of Lime

SNACKS, AT PLANNED TIMES
1/2 cup Raspberries mixed with 1/2 cup Strawberries topped with 1 tablespoon Low-Calorie Whipped Topping; 1/4 small Cantaloupe

Serving Information
Men and Youth: Add 1/2 cup Orange Juice, 1 slice Whole Wheat Bread, and 1/2 cup Raspberries
Youth: Add 1 cup Skim Milk

DAY 5

MORNING MEAL
1/3 cup Apple Juice
1 ounce Colby Cheese
1/2 small Enriched Bagel
1/2 cup Skim Milk
Coffee or Tea

MIDDAY MEAL
Poached Codfish with Asparagus and Tomatoes
1/2 cup Steamed Zucchini Slices
Shredded Cabbage with Sliced Radishes and 1 teaspoon Mayonnaise
1 slice Enriched Bread
1/2 cup Skim Milk
Coffee or Tea

EVENING MEAL
Tofu Sandwich Sans Bread
1/2 cup Steamed Bean Sprouts
1/2 cup Steamed Broccoli
Sliced Cucumber on Lettuce Leaves with 1 teaspoon Imitation Bacon Bits and Lemon Juice
12 fluid ounces Light Beer

SNACKS, AT PLANNED TIMES
3 ounces Vanilla-Flavored Dietary Frozen Dessert; 1 cup Honeydew Balls topped with 1/4 cup Plain Unflavored Yogurt

Serving Information
Men and Youth: Add 1/3 cup Apple Juice, 1/2 small Enriched Bagel, and 1 ounce Enriched Roll
Youth: Add 2 cups Skim Milk

DAY 2

MORNING MEAL
½ cup Orange Juice
1 serving Hot Cereal, ¾ ounce uncooked
1 teaspoon Reduced-Calorie Margarine
1 cup Skim Milk □ Coffee or Tea

MIDDAY MEAL
3–4 ounces Broiled Chicken
½ cup Steamed Green Beans
½ cup Steamed Mushrooms
Green Salad with Sliced Tomato, **Savory Vinaigrette,** and 1 teaspoon Imitation Bacon Bits
1 slice Whole Wheat Bread
1 teaspoon Reduced-Calorie Margarine
1 small Apple

EVENING MEAL
Ham Strips with Rice and Water Chestnuts
½ cup Cooked Yellow Straightneck Squash
½ cup Cooked Asparagus Tips
Sliced Cucumber and Radishes on Lettuce with Tarragon Vinegar
4 fluid ounces Red Wine □ Coffee or Tea

SNACKS, AT PLANNED TIMES
¾ cup Buttermilk; 2 Graham Crackers; ½ cup Canned Sliced Peaches topped with 1 teaspoon Toasted Shredded Coconut

Serving Information
Men and Youth: Add ½ cup Orange Juice, 1 slice Toasted Enriched Bread, and ½ cup Canned Sliced Peaches
Men: Add 1 ounce Broiled Chicken at the Midday Meal
Youth: Add 2 cups Skim Milk

DAY 3

MORNING MEAL
½ medium Grapefruit
1 Hard-Cooked Egg, sliced
1 slice Toasted Rye Bread
1 teaspoon Margarine
¼ cup Skim Milk
Coffee or Tea

MIDDAY MEAL
Lunch Box Fish and Cheese
½ cup Cauliflower Florets
Curried Cole Slaw
1 small Orange

EVENING MEAL
3–4 ounces Broiled Veal Patty
¼ cup Steamed Chinese Pea Pods
½ medium Tomato, sliced
Tossed Salad with 2 teaspoons Vegetable Oil plus Wine Vinegar
Club Soda with Mint Sprig

SNACKS, AT PLANNED TIMES
Pear Frozen Yogurt; ¾ cup Skim Milk

Serving Information
Men and Youth: Add 1 slice Toasted Rye Bread, 1 ounce Whole Wheat Roll, and ½ cup Canned Pineapple Chunks
Youth: Add 2 cups Skim Milk

DAY 6

MORNING MEAL
½ medium Banana, sliced
¾ ounce Ready-to-Eat Cereal
1 cup Skim Milk
Coffee or Tea

MIDDAY MEAL
Creamed Turnip and Cauliflower Soup
3–4 ounces Broiled Chicken Livers with 1 teaspoon Imitation Bacon Bits
½ cup Steamed Green Beans
Chilled Vegetable Salad
1 ounce Whole Wheat Roll
½ cup Cherry-Flavored Low-Calorie Gelatin

EVENING MEAL
Red Chicken with Potatoes
½ cup Steamed Kale
½ cup Steamed Scallop Squash
Green Salad with **Dijon-Herb Dressing**
Sparkling Mineral Water with Mint Sprig

SNACKS, AT PLANNED TIMES
½ cup Blueberries with 3 tablespoons Plain Unflavored Yogurt; ½ cup Skim Milk; 1 medium Kiwi Fruit or 1 cup Strawberries

Serving Information
Men and Youth: Add ½ medium Banana, 2 ounces Enriched French Bread, ½ cup Blueberries, and 2 Graham Crackers
Youth: Add 1½ cups Skim Milk

DAY 7

MORNING MEAL
Swedish Apple Bake
1 cup Skim Milk
Coffee or Tea

MIDDAY MEAL
3–4 ounces Sliced Roast Beef
Cherry Tomatoes and Green Bell Pepper Strips on Lettuce with 1 teaspoon Mayonnaise
2 Dill Pickle Spears
1 slice Whole Wheat Bread
½ cup Canned Pineapple Chunks

EVENING MEAL
3–4 ounces Broiled Shrimp with Lemon Wedge
Sesame and Ginger Carrots
½ cup Cooked Peas
Tossed Salad with **Garlic Vinaigrette**
4 fluid ounces White Wine
Coffee or Tea

SNACKS, AT PLANNED TIMES
¾ cup Buttermilk; 2 Graham Crackers; ½ medium Papaya or ½ small Cantaloupe

Serving Information
Men and Youth: Add ½ cup Grapefruit Juice, 1 slice Whole Wheat Bread, and ½ medium Papaya or 1 small Pear
Youth: Add 1 cup Skim Milk

Which adaptable little
vegetable can resemble buttons,
an ear, an egg-filled bird's nest, a trumpet,
a cone, a bear's head, a saddle, or coral
formation (though not all at once)? It's the
mushroom, of which some 3,000 varieties are
found in this hemisphere alone—not all of
them edible. Today there's not much room
for confusion, since the cultivated
mushrooms found in supermarkets are of
similar varieties.

When buying mushrooms, consider
freshness, color, and shape. Avoid withered,
brown-looking mushrooms. Withering is a
sign of age. Mushrooms that appear bright
and attractive in the store can be
refrigerated for four or five days with little
damage. Never peel a mushroom. Much of
its flavor and nutritional value is in the skin.

Marinated Mushroom Appetizer (Day 4)
makes a tasty first course. Its rich flavor
whets the appetite without overwhelming
the palate. Its easy, do-ahead preparation
also makes it a great company dish.

WEEK 18

DAY 1

MORNING MEAL
Honey-Stewed Prunes
1 serving Hot Cereal, ¾ ounce uncooked
1 teaspoon Reduced-Calorie Margarine
1 cup Skim Milk
Coffee or Tea

MIDDAY MEAL
3 ounces Smoked Whitefish
2 tablespoons Sliced Onion
½ medium Tomato, sliced
½ small Enriched Bagel
1 teaspoon Mayonnaise
1 small Apple

EVENING MEAL
¾ cup **Chicken Broth**
Greek Salad
6 Melba Toast Rounds
1 teaspoon Reduced-Calorie Margarine
1 cup Strawberries topped with 1 tablespoon
    Low-Calorie Whipped Topping

SNACKS, AT PLANNED TIMES
½ cup Chocolate-Flavored Low-Calorie Milk
    Pudding; 2 Graham Crackers; ½ cup Cherry-
    Flavored Low-Calorie Gelatin

Serving Information
Men and Youth: Add ½ cup Orange Juice, ½
    small Enriched Bagel, 2 Graham Crackers, and
    ½ cup Canned Fruit Cocktail
Men: Add 1 ounce Smoked Whitefish at the
    Midday Meal
Youth: Add 2 cups Skim Milk

DAY 4

MORNING MEAL
½ cup Grapefruit Sections
1 ounce Brie Cheese
¾ ounce Crispbread
½ cup Skim Milk
Coffee or Tea

MIDDAY MEAL
1 cup Mixed Vegetable Juice
3–4 ounces Poached Salmon
½ cup Cooked Zucchini Slices with Diced
    Pimiento
1 slice Enriched Bread
1 teaspoon Margarine
½ cup Vanilla-Flavored Low-Calorie Milk
    Pudding

EVENING MEAL
Marinated Mushroom Appetizer
3–4 ounces Broiled Pork Chop
½ cup Steamed Green Beans with ¼ cup
    Canned Water Chestnuts
Tossed Salad with 1 teaspoon Vegetable Oil
    plus Lemon Juice
½ cup Skim Milk
Coffee or Tea

SNACKS, AT PLANNED TIMES
½ cup Raspberries with 1 teaspoon Shredded
    Coconut; ½ small Cantaloupe

Serving Information
Men and Youth: Add ½ cup Grapefruit Sections,
    ¾ ounce Crispbread, ½ cup Raspberries, and
    1 slice Whole Wheat Bread
Youth: Add 2 cups Skim Milk

DAY 5

MORNING MEAL
⅓ cup Grape Juice
1 serving Hot Cereal, ¾ ounce uncooked
1 cup Skim Milk
Coffee or Tea

MIDDAY MEAL
Egg Foo Yung
½ cup Cooked Bean Sprouts
Spinach Salad with 1 teaspoon Vegetable Oil
    plus Wine Vinegar
1 slice Toasted Pumpernickel Bread
Club Soda with Twist of Lemon

EVENING MEAL
3–4 ounces Roast Veal
¼ cup Cooked Sliced Beets
½ cup Cooked Cauliflower Florets
Shredded Cabbage and Shredded Carrots with
    2 teaspoons Vegetable Oil plus Cider Vinegar
    and Seasonings
1 slice Rye Bread
4 fluid ounces Champagne
Coffee or Tea

SNACKS, AT PLANNED TIMES
½ cup Canned Fruit Cocktail; 1 cup
    Strawberries; ¾ cup Buttermilk

Serving Information
Men and Youth: Add ⅔ cup Grape Juice, 1 slice
    Rye Bread, ½ cup Canned Fruit Cocktail, and
    2 Graham Crackers
Youth: Add 1 cup Skim Milk

MORNING MEAL
1 medium Kiwi Fruit or 2-inch wedge Honeydew
1 Soft-Cooked Egg
½ English Muffin, toasted
¼ cup Skim Milk
Coffee or Tea

MIDDAY MEAL
3 tablespoons Peanut Butter on 1 slice Raisin
    Bread topped with 2 teaspoons Reduced-
    Calorie Strawberry Spread
Carrot and Celery Sticks
½ cup Applesauce
Hot Spiced Tea

EVENING MEAL
Spicy Meat Turnovers
¼ cup Cooked Peas
½ cup Cooked Wax Beans
Tossed Salad with Green Bell Pepper Rings and
    Lemon Juice
6 fluid ounces Light Beer
Fruit "Pie"
Coffee or Tea

SNACKS, AT PLANNED TIMES
Pineapple-Coconut Cookies; ¾ cup Skim Milk

Serving Information
Men and Youth: Add ½ English Muffin, toasted,
    1 slice Raisin Bread, and ½ cup Applesauce
Youth: Add 1 cup Skim Milk

MORNING MEAL
½ medium Banana, sliced
¾ ounce Ready-to-Eat Cereal
1 cup Skim Milk
Coffee or Tea

MIDDAY MEAL
3–4 ounces Broiled Chicken
½ medium Cucumber, sliced
Alfalfa or Bean Sprouts and Radish Slices on
    Lettuce with **Dill Vinaigrette**
1 slice Cracked Wheat Bread
1 teaspoon Margarine
Club Soda with Mint Sprig

EVENING MEAL
1 cup Tomato Juice
3–4 ounces Broiled Calf Liver
Baked Yams
Stir-Fry Pea Pods
Green Salad with Wine Vinegar and Herbs
4 medium Dried Apricot Halves

SNACKS, AT PLANNED TIMES
½ cup Orange-Flavored Low-Calorie Gelatin with
    ½ cup Orange Sections; ½ cup Plain
    Unflavored Yogurt with 1 teaspoon Reduced-
    Calorie Apricot Spread

Serving Information
Men and Youth: Add ½ medium Banana, sliced,
    1 slice Enriched Bread, 1 ounce Whole Wheat
    Roll, and ½ cup Orange Sections
Youth: Add 1 cup Skim Milk

MORNING MEAL
1 cup Cantaloupe Balls
⅓ cup Pot Cheese
2 Graham Crackers
¼ cup Skim Milk
Coffee or Tea

MIDDAY MEAL
Trinidad Snapper
½ cup Steamed Sliced Eggplant
Tossed Salad with **Savory Vinaigrette**
½ cup Canned Pineapple Chunks with Chopped
    Fresh Mint Leaves
¾ cup Skim Milk

EVENING MEAL
3–4 ounces Broiled Lamb Chop
1 cup Steamed Kale
½ cup Steamed Yellow Straightneck Squash
Endive topped with Sliced Radishes and
    1 teaspoon Mayonnaise
1 small Nectarine

SNACKS, AT PLANNED TIMES
½ cup Plain Unflavored Yogurt with ½ teaspoon
    Honey and 1 teaspoon Wheat Germ; ¾ cup
    Beef Broth with 6 Saltines

Serving Information
Men and Youth: Add 1 slice Toasted Pumper-
    nickel Bread, ½ cup Canned Pineapple Chunks,
    1 ounce Whole Wheat Roll, and 1 small
    Nectarine
Youth: Add 2 cups Skim Milk

MORNING MEAL
⅓ cup Pineapple Juice
Bran Waffles
¼ cup Skim Milk
Coffee or Tea

MIDDAY MEAL
⅔ cup Cottage Cheese with Chives
½ medium Tomato, sliced
Carrot and Green Bell Pepper Sticks
3 Melba Toast Rounds
1 teaspoon Margarine
¾ cup Buttermilk

EVENING MEAL
Chicken Cavalfiore
½ cup Cooked Artichoke Hearts
½ cup Cooked Sliced Zucchini
Green Salad with Lemon Juice
¼ cup Skim Milk
Coffee or Tea

SNACKS, AT PLANNED TIMES
1 small Orange; **Raisin-Popcorn Snack;** 8 fluid
    ounces Beer

Serving Information
Men and Youth: Add ⅓ cup Pineapple Juice,
    1 small Pear, and 1 slice Enriched Bread
Youth: Add 1½ cups Skim Milk

M is not just for Mother and the million things she gave you. M is also for Melon Mousse (on the menu for Day 3). Merely macerate honeydew melon balls in lemon juice and salt. (Macerate means to make soft by soaking in liquid.) When making a melon mousse, it's important to use a bowl, beaters, and evaporated skimmed milk that have all been well chilled. Cold hardens the milk fat and aids whipping.

More eminently marvelous menu plans call for Mushroom Loaf (Day 2) and Veal Medley (Day 4). The Morning Meal for Day 7 is a perfect one for Mother's Day. We've planned Cinnamon-Cheese Toast with Hot Spiced Tea. Later in the day, drink to her health with a glass of white wine!

WEEK 19

DAY 1

MORNING MEAL
½ cup Canned Sliced Peaches
⅓ cup Part-Skim Ricotta Cheese with Cinnamon
½ Matzo Board
1 teaspoon Margarine
¼ cup Skim Milk
Coffee or Tea

MIDDAY MEAL
3–4 ounces Canned Salmon
Sliced Tomato and ¼ cup Onion Rings on Lettuce with 1 teaspoon Mayonnaise
1 slice Toasted Rye Bread
½ cup Plain Unflavored Yogurt with 2 teaspoons Reduced-Calorie Strawberry Spread

EVENING MEAL
"Refried" Beans
Celery and Carrot Sticks with **Curry Dip**
1 Corn Tortilla
1 cup Strawberries

SNACKS, AT PLANNED TIMES
1 small Apple; ½ cup **Hot Mocha Milk**

Serving Information
Men and Youth: Add 1 slice Rye Bread, 1 Corn Tortilla, and 10 large Cherries
Men: Add 1 ounce Canned Chick Peas (Garbanzos) to Salad at the Midday Meal
Youth: Add ¾ cup Skim Milk and ½ cup **Hot Mocha Milk**

DAY 4

MORNING MEAL
½ cup Grapefruit Juice
1 ounce Cheddar Cheese melted on 1 slice Pumpernickel Bread
½ cup Skim Milk
Coffee or Tea

MIDDAY MEAL
3 ounces Boiled Knockwurst with 1 teaspoon Prepared Mustard
½ cup Sauerkraut
12 fluid ounces Light Beer

EVENING MEAL
Veal Medley
½ cup Baked Acorn Squash
Tossed Salad with **Dijon-Herb Dressing**
¼ small Cantaloupe
½ cup Skim Milk
Coffee or Tea

SNACKS, AT PLANNED TIMES
2 medium Apricots; ½ cup Plain Unflavored Yogurt with ¼ cup Canned Mandarin Orange Sections

Serving Information
Men and Youth: Add 1 Frankfurter Roll, ¼ small Cantaloupe, and ¼ cup Canned Mandarin Orange Sections
Men: Add 1 ounce Boiled Knockwurst at the Midday Meal
Youth: Add 1 cup Skim Milk

DAY 5

MORNING MEAL
½ medium Banana, sliced
¾ ounce Ready-to-Eat Cereal
1 cup Skim Milk
Coffee or Tea

MIDDAY MEAL
Poached Halibut Parmesan
½ cup Steamed Green Beans
½ cup Steamed Cauliflower
½ small Mango or 1 cup Strawberries

EVENING MEAL
1 cup Tomato Juice with Lemon Wedge
Spinach-Cucumber Egg Salad
1 ounce Pita Bread
1 teaspoon Reduced-Calorie Margarine
½ cup Blueberries

SNACKS, AT PLANNED TIMES
1 serving Chocolate-Flavored Low-Calorie Milk Beverage; 1 slice Rye Bread with 1 teaspoon Margarine

Serving Information
Men and Youth: Add 1 small Enriched Bagel and 2 Dried Figs
Youth: Add 2 cups Skim Milk

DAY 2

MORNING MEAL
½ medium Grapefruit
¾ ounce Ready-to-Eat Cereal
¾ cup Skim Milk
Coffee or Tea

MIDDAY MEAL
Mushroom Loaf
Sliced Cucumber and Grated Carrot on Lettuce
   Leaves with 1 teaspoon Mayonnaise
3-inch x 1½-inch triangle Watermelon

EVENING MEAL
Coffee-Roasted Leg of Lamb
4 ounces Baked Potato with 1 teaspoon Margarine
½ cup Steamed Broccoli
Romaine and Sliced Mushroom Salad with
   Garlic Vinaigrette
1 cup Skim Milk

SNACKS, AT PLANNED TIMES
1 cup Mixed Vegetable Juice; ½ cup Canned
   Fruit Cocktail with 2 tablespoons Plain
   Unflavored Yogurt

Serving Information
Men and Youth: Add 1 slice Whole Wheat Bread,
   6 Saltines, and ½ cup Applesauce
Youth: Add 1½ cups Skim Milk

DAY 3

MORNING MEAL
⅓ cup Apple Juice
1 Scrambled Egg
½ English Muffin, toasted
1 teaspoon Margarine
¼ cup Skim Milk
Coffee or Tea

MIDDAY MEAL
3–4 ounces Roast Chicken
½ cup Cooked Peas
Lettuce Wedge with 1 teaspoon Reduced-Calorie
   Mayonnaise
1 slice Toasted Whole Wheat Bread
1 teaspoon Reduced-Calorie Margarine
½ cup Chocolate-Flavored Low-Calorie Milk
   Pudding

EVENING MEAL
3–4 ounces Broiled Flounder
½ cup Steamed Spinach
½ cup Steamed Sliced Carrot
Tossed Salad with **Russian Dressing**
Melon Mousse
¼ cup Skim Milk
Coffee or Tea

SNACKS, AT PLANNED TIMES
¾ ounce Crispbread with 2 teaspoons Reduced-
   Calorie Grape Spread; 2 medium Plums

Serving Information
Men and Youth: Add ⅓ cup Apple Juice, ½
   English Muffin, toasted, 1 medium Peach, and
   1 ounce Enriched Roll
Youth: Add 1½ cups Skim Milk

DAY 6

MORNING MEAL
1 small Pear
1 ounce Brie Cheese
¾ ounce Crispbread
¼ cup Skim Milk
Coffee or Tea

MIDDAY MEAL
Tofu Casserole
Alfalfa or Bean Sprouts with ¼ cup Sliced
   Canned Water Chestnuts on Lettuce and
   Sesame Vinaigrette
½ cup Strawberry-Flavored Gelatin
1 cup Skim Milk

EVENING MEAL
3–4 ounces Broiled Hamburger
½ Hamburger Roll
2 teaspoons Ketchup
Eggplant and Pepper Salad
½ medium Dill Pickle, sliced
Coffee-Yogurt Shake

SNACKS, AT PLANNED TIMES
1 cup Honeydew Balls; 2 Dates; ¾ cup
   Beef Broth with Carrot Sticks

Serving Information
Men and Youth: Add 1 slice Whole Wheat Bread,
   1 small Apple, ½ Hamburger Roll, 1 small
   Nectarine, and 2 Dates
Men: Add 1 ounce Shredded Tofu (Soybean
   Curd) to Salad at the Midday Meal
Youth: Add 1¾ cups Skim Milk

DAY 7

MORNING MEAL
½ small Cantaloupe
Cinnamon-Cheese Toast
Hot Spiced Tea

MIDDAY MEAL
Tarragon Chicken Livers
½ cup Cooked Sliced Zucchini
Spinach and Mushroom Salad with
   Basic Vinaigrette
½ cup Lemon-Flavored Low-Calorie Gelatin

EVENING MEAL
Fruited Yogurt Soup
3–4 ounces Boiled Shrimp
6 medium Steamed Asparagus Spears
Broiled Tomato
Garlic Bread
4 fluid ounces White Wine
Coffee or Tea

SNACKS, AT PLANNED TIMES
¾ cup Buttermilk; 20 small Grapes

Serving Information
Men and Youth: Add 1 slice Enriched Bread and
   1 small Pear
Youth: Add 1 cup Skim Milk

Long prized for its distinctive flavor and piquant aroma, nutmeg was one of the spices Columbus sought when he sailed west from Spain in search of the East Indies (Indonesia). Later, in Colonial America, nutmegs were used as more than a flavoring: because of their unique shape, they were sold as charms at country fairs!

Nutmeg is the hard kernel of the apricotlike fruit that grows on a variety of nutmeg trees. The intermingled nutmeg fruit and flowers are gathered on long hooked poles. The fruit is carefully split in half to expose its hard seeds. The seed covering is then removed, dried, and used to make mace—a sister spice of nutmeg.

Nutmeg is sold either whole or ground. Its sweet flavor improves many foods, especially creamed dishes and fruit desserts. Try sprinkling nutmeg over spinach, squash, sweet potatoes, or cauliflower. It's also delicious in egg dishes and adds zing to Spinach Frittata (Day 4), an Italian omelet.

WEEK 20

DAY 1

MORNING MEAL
½ small Cantaloupe
¾ ounce Ready-to-Eat Cereal
¾ cup Skim Milk
Coffee or Tea

MIDDAY MEAL
Macaroni-Cheese Mold
¼ cup Cooked Peas
¼ cup Cooked Sliced Carrot
Green Salad with **Dijon-Herb Dressing**
Sparkling Mineral Water with Mint Sprig

EVENING MEAL
3–4 ounces Broiled Hamburger
2 tablespoons Chopped Onion
1 Hamburger Roll with 2 teaspoons Ketchup and
    1 teaspoon Pickle Relish
½ cup Steamed Cauliflower
Cucumber and Tomato Salad
12 fluid ounces Light Beer

SNACKS, AT PLANNED TIMES
1 small Pear; ¾ cup Buttermilk; 1 medium Peach

Serving Information
Men and Youth: Add 2 tablespoons Raisins, 1
    slice Toasted Rye Bread, 1 ounce Enriched
    Roll, 1 small Apple, and 1 small Orange
Youth: Add 2 cups Skim Milk

DAY 4

MORNING MEAL
1 small Orange
1 serving Hot Cereal, ¾ ounce uncooked
1 cup Skim Milk
Coffee or Tea

MIDDAY MEAL
Spinach Frittata
Green Salad with 1 teaspoon Imitation Bacon
    Bits plus Lemon Juice
1 slice Whole Wheat Bread
1 teaspoon Reduced-Calorie Margarine
Club Soda with Twist of Lime

EVENING MEAL
3–4 ounces Baked Halibut
½ cup Cooked Wild or Enriched Rice
½ cup Steamed Zucchini
Tossed Salad with **Garlic Vinaigrette**
4 fluid ounces White Wine
Coffee or Tea

SNACKS, AT PLANNED TIMES
½ cup Vanilla-Flavored Low-Calorie Milk
    Pudding with ¼ medium Banana, sliced, and
    1 teaspoon Shredded Coconut; ¾ cup Canned
    Fruit Cocktail; 2 Graham Crackers

Serving Information
Men and Youth: Add 1 slice Whole Wheat Bread,
    ½ cup Canned Sliced Peaches, and 1 ounce
    Enriched Roll
Youth: Add 2 cups Skim Milk

DAY 5

MORNING MEAL
1 cup Tomato Juice
Caraway-Cheese Toast
½ cup Skim Milk
Coffee or Tea

MIDDAY MEAL
3 tablespoons Peanut Butter
1 slice Raisin Bread
2 teaspoons Reduced-Calorie Orange Marmalade
Carrot and Celery Sticks
½ cup Applesauce sprinkled with Cinnamon

EVENING MEAL
3–4 ounces Broiled Steak
½ cup Steamed Broccoli
Oriental-Style Spinach Salad
Fruit "Pie"
½ cup Skim Milk
Coffee or Tea

SNACKS, AT PLANNED TIMES
Root Beer Froth; ½ cup Strawberries topped
    with ¼ cup Plain Unflavored Yogurt; 1 medium
    Peach

Serving Information
Men and Youth: Add 1 slice Raisin Bread, ½ cup
    Applesauce, 1 ounce Enriched Roll, and ½
    cup Strawberries
Youth: Add 1 cup Skim Milk and ¼ cup Plain
    Unflavored Yogurt

DAY 2

MORNING MEAL
½ cup Orange Juice
1 Poached Egg
1 slice Toasted Whole Wheat Bread
1 teaspoon Reduced-Calorie Margarine
¼ cup Skim Milk
Coffee or Tea

MIDDAY MEAL
2¼–3 ounces Sliced Cooked Chicken on Lettuce
   Leaves with 1 teaspoon Mayonnaise
Stuffed Cherry Tomatoes
1 slice Rye Bread
½ cup Lime-Flavored Low-Calorie Gelatin
¾ cup Skim Milk

EVENING MEAL
3–4 ounces Broiled Haddock
¼ cup Baked Acorn Squash
½ cup Steamed Green Beans
Tossed Salad with Tarragon Vinegar
20 small Grapes

SNACKS, AT PLANNED TIMES
½ medium Banana, sliced, with ½ cup Plain
   Unflavored Yogurt; 1 cup Tomato Juice

Serving Information
Men and Youth: Add ½ cup Orange Juice, 1 slice
   Rye Bread, ½ medium Banana, sliced, and 6
   Saltines
Men: Add 1 ounce Sliced Cooked Chicken at the
   Midday Meal
Youth: Add 1 cup Skim Milk

DAY 3

MORNING MEAL
½ medium Grapefruit
Cinnamon-Cheese Toast
½ cup Skim Milk
Coffee or Tea

MIDDAY MEAL
Shrimp on Toast
Green Salad with 1 ounce Shredded Colby
   Cheese and **Tarragon Vinaigrette**
4 Canned Pineapple Spears with 2 tablespoons
   Juice

EVENING MEAL
3–4 ounces Broiled Beef Liver
½ cup Steamed Sliced Onion
½ cup Steamed Sliced Mushrooms
6 medium Cooked Asparagus Spears
1 small Apple

SNACKS, AT PLANNED TIMES
¾ cup Buttermilk; ½ English Muffin, toasted,
   with 1 teaspoon Margarine and 2 teaspoons
   Reduced-Calorie Apricot Spread

Serving Information
Men and Youth: Add 1 slice Enriched Bread, 4
   Canned Pineapple Spears with 2 tablespoons
   Juice, and 2 Graham Crackers
Youth: Add 1½ cups Skim Milk

DAY 6

MORNING MEAL
⅓ cup Grape Juice
¾ ounce Ready-to-Eat Cereal
1 cup Skim Milk
Coffee or Tea

MIDDAY MEAL
Glazed Turkey Mold
¼ cup Cooked Green Beans
¼ cup Cooked Cauliflower Florets
Tomato Slices on Lettuce
¼ cup Skim Milk
Coffee or Tea

EVENING MEAL
Swordfish Kebabs
¼ cup Cooked Beets
½ cup Cooked Kale
Green Salad with Wine Vinegar
1 slice Enriched Bread
12 fluid ounces Light Beer

SNACKS, AT PLANNED TIMES
1 medium Kiwi Fruit or 1 small Orange;
   2 Graham Crackers; 3 ounces Dietary Frozen
   Dessert with 1 tablespoon Low-Calorie
   Chocolate Topping

Serving Information
Men and Youth: Add ⅓ cup Grape Juice, 1 slice
   Rye Bread, and ½ cup Canned Pineapple
   Chunks
Youth: Add 1¼ cups Skim Milk

DAY 7

MORNING MEAL
½ medium Grapefruit
1 ounce Smoked Salmon
½ small Enriched Bagel
1 teaspoon Reduced-Calorie Margarine
¼ cup Skim Milk □ Coffee or Tea

MIDDAY MEAL
1 cup Mixed Vegetable Juice
Crispy-Crunchy Salad with 1½ ounces Canned
   Chick Peas (Garbanzos)
"Fallen" Strawberry Cheesecake
Hot Spiced Tea

EVENING MEAL
Chilled Cucumber Soup
2¼–3 ounces Roast Beef
Broccoli Medley
½ cup Wax Beans
Tossed Salad with Radish Slices, 3 tablespoons
   Sliced Canned Water Chestnuts, and Lemon
   Juice
3 Melba Toast Slices
½ cup Skim Milk □ Coffee or Tea

SNACKS, AT PLANNED TIMES
2 Canned Pear Halves with 2 tablespoons Juice;
   ¼ small Cantaloupe

Serving Information
Men and Youth: Add 1 slice Whole Wheat Bread,
   2 Canned Pear Halves with 2 tablespoons Juice,
   1 ounce Enriched Roll, and ¼ small Cantaloupe
Men: Add ½ ounce Chick Peas (Garbanzos) at
   the Midday Meal
Youth: Add 2 cups Skim Milk

As the days get longer and warmer, you'll want to plan ahead so you can spend less time in the kitchen and more outdoors.

Minted Carrots (Day 1) are a great help. You can make them as much as *one week* ahead of serving time. Just keep them well covered in the refrigerator.

Broccoli Quiche (Day 3) is another time-saver. Leftovers can be refrigerated and reheated for another meal. Or make two and freeze one.

Calamari with Spaghetti (Day 6) is a must-do-ahead. Calamari—six-inch-long, pen-shaped squid—should be cleaned the day before serving and allowed to "rest" for at least twelve hours. This helps them to become firm and flavorful.

Our Broccoli Quiche is a variation of Quiche Lorraine, a savory baked custard tart. The word "quiche" comes from the French-German dialect spoken in Alsace-Lorraine, where the dish originated.

WEEK 21

DAY 1

MORNING MEAL
½ cup Fruit Salad
¾ ounce Ready-to-Eat Cereal
1 cup Skim Milk
Coffee or Tea

MIDDAY MEAL
Egg Foo Yung
½ cup Steamed Green Beans
1 ounce Enriched Roll
1 teaspoon Margarine
1 small Orange

EVENING MEAL
1 cup Mixed Vegetable Juice
3–4 ounces Broiled Veal Chop
¼ cup Cooked Peas with 2 tablespoons Cooked
    Sliced Mushrooms
Minted Carrots
Lettuce Wedge with 2 teaspoons Mayonnaise
½ cup Watermelon Balls

SNACKS, AT PLANNED TIMES
¾ cup Buttermilk; ½ Matzo Board with
    1 teaspoon Reduced-Calorie Apricot Spread

Serving Information
Men and Youth: Add ½ cup Fruit Salad, 1 slice
    Toasted Enriched Bread, 1 slice Cracked Wheat
    Bread, and ½ cup Blueberries
Youth: Add 2 cups Skim Milk

DAY 4

MORNING MEAL
1 cup Tomato Juice
⅓ cup Part-Skim Ricotta Cheese with Cinnamon
½ small Enriched Bagel
¼ cup Skim Milk
Coffee or Tea

MIDDAY MEAL
Layered Baked Flounder
½ cup Cooked Brussels Sprouts
Tossed Salad with 1 teaspoon Vegetable Oil
    plus Cider Vinegar
½ cup Blueberries

EVENING MEAL
Chicken Sorrentino
½ cup Cooked Cauliflower
½ cup Cooked Italian Green Beans
Escarole and Red Bell Pepper Salad with
    1½ teaspoons Mayonnaise
½ cup Strawberry-Flavored Low-Calorie Gelatin

SNACKS, AT PLANNED TIMES
½ cup Skim Milk; ½ medium Papaya or 1 small
    Nectarine; 2 medium Apricots

Serving Information
Men and Youth: Add 1 medium Banana and 2
    ounces Enriched Italian Bread
Youth: Add 1¼ cups Skim Milk

DAY 5

MORNING MEAL
Cereal with Spiced Fruit Ambrosia
Coffee or Tea

MIDDAY MEAL
3 tablespoons Peanut Butter on 1 slice Raisin
    Bread with 2 teaspoons Reduced-Calorie
    Grape Spread
1 medium Peach
1 cup Skim Milk

EVENING MEAL
Middle Eastern Burgers
½ cup Steamed Sliced Zucchini
Green Salad with Wine Vinegar
Sparkling Mineral Water with Lemon Wedge

SNACKS, AT PLANNED TIMES
½ small Mango or 2-inch wedge Honeydew;
    ½ cup Tomato Juice mixed with ½ cup Clam
    Juice; Celery and Carrot Sticks

Serving Information
Men and Youth: Add 1 slice Raisin Bread, 6
    Saltines, 10 large Cherries, and 2 Dates
Youth: Add 2 cups Skim Milk

MORNING MEAL
Coffee-Cheese Delight
¼ cup Skim Milk
Coffee or Tea

MIDDAY MEAL
3–4 ounces Pan-Broiled Calf Liver
Bean Salad
1 slice Whole Wheat Bread
1 teaspoon Margarine
½ cup Chocolate-Flavored Low-Calorie Milk
Pudding

EVENING MEAL
3–4 ounces Baked Red Snapper
½ cup Baked Acorn Squash
Curried Cole Slaw
Sliced Cucumber and Tomato Salad with
Vinaigrette Parmesan
2-inch wedge Honeydew

SNACKS, AT PLANNED TIMES
½ cup Applesauce; ¾ cup Skim Milk; 4 fluid
ounces Red Wine

Serving Information
Men and Youth: Add 2 ounces Whole Wheat Roll,
2-inch wedge Honeydew, and 2 medium Plums
Youth: Add 1 cup Skim Milk

MORNING MEAL
½ cup Grapefruit Juice
1 serving Hot Cereal, ¾ ounce uncooked
½ cup Skim Milk
Coffee or Tea

MIDDAY MEAL
Broccoli Quiche
Watercress Salad with ½ Hard-Cooked Egg,
sliced, and 2 teaspoons Low-Calorie French
Dressing
3 Melba Toast Rounds
½ cup Strawberries topped with 1 tablespoon
Plain Unflavored Yogurt

EVENING MEAL
¼ small Cantaloupe
3–4 ounces Roast Beef
4 ounces Baked Potato with 1 teaspoon
Margarine
6 medium Steamed Asparagus Spears
Romaine and Sliced Radish Salad with 1½
teaspoons Plain Unflavored Yogurt mixed with
1 teaspoon Mayonnaise
½ cup Canned Fruit Cocktail

SNACKS, AT PLANNED TIMES
¾ cup **Chicken Broth** with 10 Oyster Crackers;
1 cup Skim Milk

Serving Information
Men and Youth: Add ½ cup Grapefruit Juice, ½
English Muffin, toasted, 3 Melba Toast Rounds,
½ cup Strawberries, 10 Oyster Crackers, 1
small Pear, and ¼ small Cantaloupe
Youth: Add 1½ cups Skim Milk

MORNING MEAL
½ cup Orange Sections
1 Scrambled Egg
1 slice Toasted Rye Bread
Coffee or Tea

MIDDAY MEAL
Cream of Broccoli Soup
3–4 ounces Sliced Roast Turkey
1 slice Enriched Bread
1 teaspoon Mayonnaise
½ cup Cherry-Flavored Gelatin

EVENING MEAL
Calamari with Spaghetti
½ cup Steamed Wax Beans
Green Bell Pepper Slices on Lettuce with
1 teaspoon Low-Calorie Italian Dressing
1 small Pear
⅔ cup Skim Milk

SNACKS, AT PLANNED TIMES
½ small Cantaloupe; ¾ cup Buttermilk

Serving Information
Men and Youth: Add 1 slice Enriched Bread and
1 cup Strawberries
Youth: Add 1⅓ cups Skim Milk

MORNING MEAL
½ cup Orange and Grapefruit Juice
⅓ cup Cottage Cheese with ½ teaspoon
Caraway Seeds
1 slice Pumpernickel Bread
¼ cup Skim Milk □ Coffee or Tea

MIDDAY MEAL
3 ounces Sliced Liverwurst
Tomato Slices on Lettuce with 1½ teaspoons
Plain Unflavored Yogurt mixed with 1 teaspoon
Mayonnaise
1 small Apple
¼ cup Skim Milk
Coffee or Tea

EVENING MEAL
3–4 ounces Roast Veal
½ cup Cooked Green Beans
½ cup Cooked Sliced Carrot
Green Goddess Salad
4 fluid ounces Champagne
Fruited Custard Pie □ Coffee or Tea

SNACKS, AT PLANNED TIMES
1 Canned Pineapple Slice with 1 tablespoon Juice
and 3 tablespoons Plain Unflavored Yogurt;
2 Graham Crackers

Serving Information
Men and Youth: Add ½ cup Orange and Grape-
fruit Juice, 1 ounce Enriched Roll, and 1
Graham Cracker
Men: Add 1 ounce Sliced Liverwurst at the
Midday Meal
Youth: Add 1½ cups Skim Milk

Mark Memorial Day and the unofficial start of summer with your first cookout of the year. Try our picnic menu on Day 1.

Tangy Oyster-Vegetable Medley heads our menu on Day 7. Oysters are a bother, but their sea-taste tripping on the tongue is worth it! Oysters must be perfectly fresh, their shells firmly closed. Store them at a temperature of 41° to 48°F. If you buy them already shucked, their liquor should be clear, not milky.

One of the sure signs of summer on the menu this week is cantaloupe, a perennial favorite.

Economy Tip—Baked ham is on the menu on Day 6. Leftovers may be frozen and used in Ham and Vegetables with Paprika Yogurt (Week 25, Day 6).

Energy-Saving Tip—Poach chicken for Chicken and Eggplant Bake recipe (Week 25, Day 2) and chilled chicken platter (Week 25, Day 5) while poaching chicken for Day 7; freeze.

WEEK 22

DAY 1

MORNING MEAL
½ small Cantaloupe
1 Poached Egg
½ English Muffin, toasted
¼ cup Skim Milk
Coffee or Tea

MIDDAY MEAL
3–4 ounces Grilled Hamburger *or*
   3 ounces Grilled Frankfurter
1 Hamburger *or* Frankfurter Roll
2 teaspoons Reduced-Calorie Ketchup
Mustard
¼ cup Onion Rings
1 medium Dill Pickle
Cole Slaw Vinaigrette
12 fluid ounces Light Beer
3-inch x 1½-inch triangle Watermelon

EVENING MEAL
3–4 ounces Broiled Salmon Steak
Eggplant and Zucchini Casserole
Lettuce Wedge with **Green Goddess Salad Dressing**
½ cup Orange-Flavored Low-Calorie Gelatin

SNACKS, AT PLANNED TIMES
¾ cup Skim Milk with 1 teaspoon Chocolate Syrup; **Stewed Dried Apricots**

Serving Information
Men and Youth: Add ½ English Muffin, toasted, and ½ cup Canned Mandarin Orange Sections
Men: Add 1 ounce Grilled Frankfurter at the Midday Meal if Frankfurter is chosen
Youth: Add 1¼ cups Skim Milk

DAY 4

MORNING MEAL
½ cup Grapefruit Juice
¾ ounce Ready-to-Eat Cereal
1 cup Skim Milk
Coffee or Tea

MIDDAY MEAL
Spinach-Cucumber Egg Salad
1 slice Pumpernickel Bread
1 teaspoon Margarine
1 small Apple

EVENING MEAL
Texas Barbecued Pork Chops
1 cup Steamed Cauliflower
Romaine and Watercress Salad with
   Garlic Vinaigrette
1 ounce Whole Wheat Roll
1 teaspoon Margarine
Lemonade

SNACKS, AT PLANNED TIMES
3 ounces Vanilla-Flavored Dietary Frozen Dessert; Zucchini and Carrot Sticks with ½ recipe **Yogurt Dip**

Serving Information
Men and Youth: Add ½ cup Grapefruit Juice, 1 small Enriched Bagel, 2 Graham Crackers, and ¼ small Pineapple
Youth: Add 1 cup Skim Milk

DAY 5

MORNING MEAL
1 small Pear
1 ounce Brie Cheese
¾ ounce Crispbread
¼ cup Skim Milk
Coffee or Tea

MIDDAY MEAL
3 ounces Canned Chick Pea (Garbanzos) with ½ teaspoon Sesame Seeds, toasted, on Lettuce
Cherry Tomatoes and Zucchini Spears
Marinated Carrots
Fruit 'n' Nut Candy
¾ cup Skim Milk

EVENING MEAL
3–4 ounces Roast Turkey
Curried Pasta with Gingered Peas
½ cup Steamed Whole Green Beans
Red and Green Bell Pepper Rings on Lettuce with 1 teaspoon Vegetable Oil plus Cider Vinegar
½ medium Papaya or 1 cup Strawberries

SNACKS, AT PLANNED TIMES
3 Melba Toast Rounds with 2 teaspoons Reduced-Calorie Peach Spread; ½ cup Raspberry-Flavored Gelatin with 1 tablespoon Low-Calorie Whipped Topping

Serving Information
Men and Youth: Add 1 slice Whole Wheat Bread, 3 Melba Toast Rounds, and ½ cup Raspberries
Men: Add 1 ounce Canned Chick Peas at the Midday Meal
Youth: Add 1 cup Skim Milk

DAY 2

MORNING MEAL
1/3 cup Grape Juice
Cinnamon-Cheese Toast
1/4 cup Skim Milk
Coffee or Tea

MIDDAY MEAL
Vegetable-Stuffed Chicken Breasts
Cucumber Slices on Lettuce with
   Dill Vinaigrette
1/2 cup Plain Unflavored Yogurt with 2 teaspoons
   Reduced-Calorie Cherry Spread

EVENING MEAL
3–4 ounces Roast Veal
1/2 cup Cooked Spaghetti Squash
Mixed Vegetable Salad
1 ounce Enriched Roll
1 teaspoon Margarine
1/2 cup Fruit Salad

SNACKS, AT PLANNED TIMES
3/4 cup Skim Milk; 2 Graham Crackers; 1 small
   Orange

Serving Information
Men and Youth: Add 1/3 cup Grape Juice and 1
   slice Cracked Wheat Bread
Youth: Add 2 cups Skim Milk

DAY 3

MORNING MEAL
Applesauce Oatmeal with 1 tablespoon Raisins
1/4 cup Skim Milk
Coffee or Tea

MIDDAY MEAL
Curried Seafood Salad
1 ounce Pita Bread
10 large Cherries

EVENING MEAL
Cheese and Rice-Stuffed Mushrooms
1/2 cup Cooked Peas
Tomato Slices on Lettuce with 2 teaspoons
   Mayonnaise
1 medium Peach

SNACKS, AT PLANNED TIMES
1/2 cup Butterscotch-Flavored Low-Calorie Milk
   Pudding; 1 cup Tomato Juice

Serving Information
Men and Youth: Add 2 tablespoons Raisins, 10
   large Cherries, 1 ounce Whole Wheat Roll, and
   20 Oyster Crackers
Youth: Add 1 3/4 cups Skim Milk

DAY 6

MORNING MEAL
1/2 cup Orange Sections
3/4 ounce Ready-to-Eat Cereal
1/2 cup Skim Milk
Coffee or Tea

MIDDAY MEAL
Sautéed Liver with Mustard Cauliflower
6 medium Cooked Asparagus Spears with
   Lemon "Butter" Sauce
1 slice Cracked Wheat Bread
1 serving Chocolate-Flavored Low-Calorie Milk
   Beverage

EVENING MEAL
3 ounces Baked Ham
1/2 cup Baked Acorn Squash
1/2 cup Cooked Wax Beans
Tossed Salad with 1 teaspoon Mayonnaise
1 slice Rye Bread
4 fluid ounces Red Wine
1/4 small Pineapple

SNACKS, AT PLANNED TIMES
12 large Grapes; 1/2 cup Lime-Flavored Low-
   Calorie Gelatin with 1/4 cup Plain Unflavored
   Yogurt

Serving Information
Men and Youth: Add 1 slice Rye Bread, 3/4 ounce
   Crispbread, and 12 large Grapes
Men: Add 1 ounce Baked Ham at the Evening
   Meal
Youth: Add 2 cups Skim Milk

DAY 7

MORNING MEAL
1/3 cup Apple Juice
Baked Corn and Tomato Omelet
1 slice Toasted Enriched Bread
1 teaspoon Margarine
1/2 cup Skim Milk
Coffee or Tea

MIDDAY MEAL
3–4 ounces Poached Chicken
1/2 cup Steamed Rutabaga
Spinach and Mushroom Salad with Lemon Juice
1/2 small Mango or 1/2 small Cantaloupe

EVENING MEAL
Tangy Oyster-Vegetable Medley
Alfalfa or Bean Sprouts on Lettuce with **Herb
   Dressing**
1/2 English Muffin, toasted
1 teaspoon Reduced-Calorie Margarine
2 medium Plums

SNACKS, AT PLANNED TIMES
1 cup Plain Popcorn; 1 cup Skim Milk;
   Coconut-Honey Shake

Serving Information
Men and Youth: Add 2/3 cup Apple Juice, 1 ounce
   Whole Wheat Roll, 1/2 English Muffin, toasted,
   and 2 Dates
Youth: Add 2 cups Skim Milk

June 10th is Children's Day, a good time to remember that it's never too early to encourage good eating habits.

Teenagers should learn that there's life beyond pizza and burgers. Experimenting in the kitchen will broaden their culinary horizons, although getting them to clean up after themselves may be a little more difficult.

Encourage children to help with meal preparation. It's a painless way for them to learn the fundamentals of cooking, nutrition, and menu planning. "Magically" transforming an assortment of ingredients into a fragrant, attractive finished product may also give picky eaters the incentive to taste a wider variety of foods.

Raito is the soothing milk-based accompaniment to a fiery curry. Tomato-Cucumber Raito (Day 2) is a delicious salad from India, redolent with eastern spices and cooled with yogurt.

WEEK 23

DAY 1

MORNING MEAL
½ medium Grapefruit
¾ ounce Ready-to-Eat Cereal
1 cup Skim Milk
Coffee or Tea

MIDDAY MEAL
¾ cup **Herbed Beef Broth**
Grilled Cheese Soufflé
Green Salad with **Cider Vinaigrette**
2 Pimiento-Stuffed Olives
2 Melba Toast Slices
¾ cup Honeydew Balls mixed with ½ cup
    Watermelon Balls

EVENING MEAL
Ginger-Broiled Chicken
½ cup Steamed Chinese Pea Pods
½ cup Steamed Carrot
Tossed Salad with **Dijon-Herb Dressing**
1 ounce Enriched Roll
1 teaspoon Reduced-Calorie Margarine
4 fluid ounces White Wine
Coffee or Tea

SNACKS, AT PLANNED TIMES
¾ cup Skim Milk; **Open-Face "Ice Cream"
    Sandwich**

Serving Information
Men and Youth: Add 2 tablespoons Raisins, 2
    Melba Toast Slices, and 1 ounce Enriched Roll
Youth: Add 1¼ cups Skim Milk

DAY 4

MORNING MEAL
½ small Cantaloupe
¾ ounce Ready-to-Eat Cereal
1 cup Skim Milk
Coffee or Tea

MIDDAY MEAL
3–4 ounces Broiled Calf Liver
½ cup Steamed Spinach
½ cup Steamed Sliced Mushrooms
Bibb and Boston Lettuce Salad with 1 teaspoon
    Vegetable Oil plus Cider Vinegar
1 ounce Enriched Roll
1 teaspoon Reduced-Calorie Margarine
Club Soda with Twist of Lime

EVENING MEAL
1 cup Tomato Juice
3–4 ounces Roast Leg of Lamb
½ cup Cooked Sliced Carrot
½ cup Cooked Wax Beans
Braised Leek Salad
½ cup Raspberries with 1 tablespoon Low-
    Calorie Whipped Topping and 1 teaspoon
    Shredded Coconut, toasted

SNACKS, AT PLANNED TIMES
2 Graham Crackers; ½ cup Skim Milk;
    Strawberry Shake

Serving Information
Men and Youth: Add 2 tablespoons Raisins, 1
    ounce Enriched Roll, ½ cup Raspberries, and
    2 Graham Crackers
Youth: Add 1½ cups Skim Milk

DAY 5

MORNING MEAL
⅓ cup Prune Juice
1 Scrambled Egg with Chives
½ small Enriched Bagel
1 teaspoon Margarine
¼ cup Skim Milk
Coffee or Tea

MIDDAY MEAL
Iceberg-Tomato Ring
Carrot and Green Bell Pepper Sticks
½ cup Chocolate-Flavored Low-Calorie Milk
    Pudding

EVENING MEAL
Crisp "Oven-Fried" Chicken
3 ounces Baked Yam
¼ cup Cooked Peas
½ cup Cooked Yellow Straightneck Squash
Tossed Salad with 1 teaspoon Reduced-Calorie
    Mayonnaise
6 fluid ounces Light Beer

SNACKS, AT PLANNED TIMES
Orange Ambrosia; ½ cup Grapefruit Sections;
    ¾ cup Skim Milk

Serving Information
Men and Youth: Add ⅓ cup Prune Juice, ½ small
    Enriched Bagel, 1 slice Whole Wheat Bread,
    and 1 small Apple
Youth: Add 2 cups Skim Milk

DAY 2

MORNING MEAL
½ cup Orange Juice
1 ounce Colby Cheese
1 slice Toasted Whole Wheat Bread
1 teaspoon Reduced-Calorie Margarine
½ cup Skim Milk
Coffee or Tea

MIDDAY MEAL
Fillet of Sole Florentine
½ cup Cooked Green Beans
Tomato-Cucumber Raito
Root Beer Froth

EVENING MEAL
Bean Curd Soup
Spinach Salad with 1½ teaspoons Vegetable Oil
   plus Wine Vinegar
6 Saltines
2 medium Apricots

SNACKS, AT PLANNED TIMES
½ cup Canned Fruit Cocktail; 1 cup Mixed
   Vegetable Juice

Serving Information
Men and Youth: Add ½ cup Orange Juice, 1 slice
   Toasted Whole Wheat Bread, 1 slice Enriched
   Bread, 2 medium Apricots, and ½ cup Canned
   Fruit Cocktail
Men: Add 1 ounce each Canned Chick Peas and
   Shredded Tofu to the Evening Meal Salad
Youth: Add 1½ cups Skim Milk

DAY 3

MORNING MEAL
⅓ cup Grape Juice
1 Soft-Cooked Egg
1 slice Toasted Enriched Bread
1 teaspoon Margarine
¼ cup Skim Milk
Coffee or Tea

MIDDAY MEAL
3–4 ounces Sliced Roast Turkey Breast
Tomato Slices and Green Bell Pepper Rings on
   Lettuce
1 ounce Pita Bread
1 teaspoon Mayonnaise
½ medium Banana
¾ cup Skim Milk

EVENING MEAL
3–4 ounces Broiled Veal Patty
4 ounces Baked Potato with 1 teaspoon each
   Margarine and Imitation Bacon Bits
½ cup Steamed Broccoli
Curried Cole Slaw
4 fluid ounces White Wine
Coffee or Tea

SNACKS, AT PLANNED TIMES
1 medium Kiwi Fruit or ½ medium Grapefruit;
   ½ cup Plain Unflavored Yogurt; ½ cup Cherry-
   Flavored Low-Calorie Gelatin

Serving Information
Men and Youth: Add ⅓ cup Grape Juice, ½
   medium Banana, and 2 ounces Whole Wheat
   Roll
Youth: Add 2 cups Skim Milk

DAY 6

MORNING MEAL
⅓ cup Apple Juice
1 ounce Cheddar Cheese
½ English Muffin, toasted
½ cup Skim Milk
Coffee or Tea

MIDDAY MEAL
Mushroom Loaf
½ cup Cooked Artichoke Hearts
Endive and Watercress topped with Radish Slices
   and 1 teaspoon Vegetable Oil plus Tarragon
   Vinegar
Mineral Water with Mint Sprig

EVENING MEAL
1 cup Mixed Vegetable Juice
Oyster Stew
Cucumber and Tomato Slices on Lettuce with
   Lemon Juice
Pear Frozen Yogurt

SNACKS, AT PLANNED TIMES
½ small Mango or 1 cup Strawberries; ½ cup
   Orange-Flavored Low-Calorie Gelatin

Serving Information
Men and Youth: Add ⅔ cup Apple Juice, ½
   English Muffin, toasted, 1 slice Rye Bread, and
   ½ cup Orange Sections
Youth: Add 1 cup Skim Milk

DAY 7

MORNING MEAL
⅓ cup Pineapple Juice
¾ ounce Ready-to-Eat Cereal
1 teaspoon Shredded Coconut
1 cup Skim Milk
Coffee or Tea

MIDDAY MEAL
Sautéed Chick Peas Italian Style
½ cup Cooked Brown Rice
½ cup Cooked Spinach
Green Salad with 1 teaspoon Mayonnaise
Club Soda

EVENING MEAL
Piquant Hamburgers
1 Hamburger Roll
¼ cup Onion Rings
½ medium Tomato, sliced
2 Dill Pickle Spears
1 cup Honeydew Balls

SNACKS, AT PLANNED TIMES
½ cup Vanilla-Flavored Low-Calorie Milk Pudding;
   10 large Cherries

Serving Information
Men and Youth: 1 slice Pumpernickel Bread and
   10 large Cherries
Men: Add ½ ounce Shredded Swiss Cheese to
   Salad at the Midday Meal
Youth: Add 2 cups Skim Milk

Several flavor combinations that have stood the test of time appear here. Build a meal around any of them and you'll never go wrong.

Salmon Chowder (Day 2) is teamed with Green Salad and Dill Vinaigrette. Salmon and dill are a traditional pair with a long history.

Broiled Calf Liver with Pearl Onions and Sliced Mushrooms (Day 4) is another combination long popular for its harmonious taste, color, and texture. And grilled Canadian bacon with Buttermilk Pancakes (Day 6) is a morning meal duo no one can refuse!

The mention of certain foods automatically calls to mind an association with many others, like lettuce and tomatoes, peanut butter and jelly, or peaches and cream. At one time, though, all three were novel combinations.

WEEK 24

DAY 1

MORNING MEAL
½ cup Orange Juice
1 Sunnyside-Up Egg
1 slice Toasted Whole Wheat Bread
1 teaspoon Margarine
½ cup Skim Milk
Coffee or Tea

MIDDAY MEAL
Layered Eggplant-Cheese Bake
Sliced Tomato on Bed of Endive topped with Alfalfa or Bean Sprouts and Wine Vinegar
1 ounce Whole Wheat Roll
2 Canned Pear Halves with 2 tablespoons Juice
½ cup Skim Milk □ Coffee or Tea

EVENING MEAL
Shrimp Scampi
½ cup Cooked Beets
½ cup Cooked Spinach
Tossed Salad with Green Bell Pepper Rings and **Russian Dressing**
4 fluid ounces White Wine
Coffee or Tea

SNACKS, AT PLANNED TIMES
½ cup Lemon-Flavored Low-Calorie Gelatin with ¼ cup Plain Unflavored Yogurt; **Pineapple-Banana Milk Shake**

Serving Information
Men and Youth: Add ½ cup Orange Juice, 1 slice Toasted Whole Wheat Bread, 2 Canned Pear Halves with 2 tablespoons Juice, and 1 ounce Whole Wheat Roll
Youth: Add 2 cups Skim Milk

DAY 4

MORNING MEAL
½ cup Grapefruit Juice
1 serving Hot Cereal, ¾ ounce uncooked
1 teaspoon Reduced-Calorie Margarine
½ cup Skim Milk
Coffee or Tea

MIDDAY MEAL
3–4 ounces Broiled Calf Liver
¼ cup Steamed Pearl Onions
½ cup Steamed Sliced Mushrooms
1 slice Enriched Bread
1 teaspoon Margarine
Mineral Water with Twist of Lime

EVENING MEAL
Chicken Indienne
½ cup Cooked Asparagus Tips
Tossed Salad with **Gingered Vinaigrette**
1 ounce Enriched Roll
4 fluid ounces White Wine
Coffee or Tea

SNACKS, AT PLANNED TIMES
Red, White, and Blue Parfait; ½ cup Cooked Rhubarb; 1 cup Skim Milk

Serving Information
Men and Youth: Add ½ cup Grapefruit Juice, 1 slice Toasted Raisin Bread, and ½ cup Cooked Rhubarb
Youth: Add 1½ cups Skim Milk

DAY 5

MORNING MEAL
½ cup Orange Sections
1 ounce Swiss Cheese
½ small Enriched Bagel
¼ cup Skim Milk
Coffee or Tea

MIDDAY MEAL
3–4 ounces Baked Halibut
Baked Eggplant Slices
Green Salad with **Dijon-Herb Dressing**
6 Melba Toast Rounds
½ cup Canned Fruit Cocktail topped with 1 teaspoon Shredded Coconut, toasted
¾ cup Skim Milk

EVENING MEAL
Swiss Steak
¼ cup Cooked Peas
½ cup Cooked Cauliflower
Shredded Lettuce topped with Sliced Radishes and 1 teaspoon Mayonnaise
Club Soda with Mint Sprig

SNACKS, AT PLANNED TIMES
½ cup Raspberries; 1 serving Chocolate-Flavored Low-Calorie Milk Beverage

Serving Information
Men and Youth: Add ½ small Enriched Bagel, 1 slice Whole Wheat Bread, and ½ cup Raspberries
Youth: Add 1 cup Skim Milk

DAY 2

MORNING MEAL
⅓ cup Prune Juice
¾ ounce Ready-to-Eat Cereal
1 cup Skim Milk
Coffee or Tea

MIDDAY MEAL
Salmon Chowder
Green Salad with **Dill Vinaigrette**
15 Oyster Crackers
Sparkling Mineral Water with Mint Sprig

EVENING MEAL
Curried Meat Hash
½ cup Steamed Green Beans
¼ cup Steamed Diced Carrot
Sliced Cucumber and Radishes on Lettuce with
    Lemon Juice
1 ounce Pita Bread
½ cup Strawberry-Flavored Low-Calorie Gelatin
    with ¼ cup Strawberries

SNACKS, AT PLANNED TIMES
¾ cup Buttermilk; 1 cup Tomato Juice; 1 small
    Apple

Serving Information
Men and Youth: Add ⅓ cup Prune Juice, 1 Eng-
    lish Muffin, split and toasted, with 1 teaspoon
    Reduced-Calorie Grape Spread, and 1 small
    Nectarine
Youth: Add 1 cup Skim Milk

DAY 3

MORNING MEAL
½ medium Papaya or ½ small Cantaloupe
1 Poached Egg
1 slice Toasted Enriched Bread
1 teaspoon Margarine
½ cup Skim Milk
Coffee or Tea

MIDDAY MEAL
Tofu-Sesame Appetizer
2¼–3 ounces Sliced Roast Turkey Breast
½ medium Tomato, sliced
1 slice Whole Wheat Bread
1 teaspoon Mayonnaise
½ cup Applesauce

EVENING MEAL
3–4 ounces Broiled Flounder
½ cup Steamed Broccoli
½ cup Steamed Yellow Straightneck Squash
Green Salad with Red Bell Pepper Rings and
    1 teaspoon Vegetable Oil plus Cider Vinegar
½ cup Skim Milk
Coffee or Tea

SNACKS, AT PLANNED TIMES
½ cup Vanilla-Flavored Low-Calorie Milk
    Pudding; 3-inch x 1½-inch triangle Watermelon

Serving Information
Men and Youth: Add 1 slice Toasted Enriched
    Bread, ½ cup Applesauce, and 2 Graham
    Crackers
Men: Add 1 ounce Sliced Roast Turkey at the
    Midday Meal
Youth: Add 2 cups Skim Milk

DAY 6

MORNING MEAL
⅓ cup Grape Juice
1 ounce Grilled Canadian Bacon
Buttermilk Pancakes
⅓ cup Skim Milk
Coffee or Tea

MIDDAY MEAL
¾ cup **Chicken Broth**
Pinto Bean Salad
1 ounce Whole Wheat Roll
½ small Cantaloupe

EVENING MEAL
1 cup Mixed Vegetable Juice
Stuffed Eggs
Tomato, Cucumber, Zucchini, and Radish Slices
    with 1 teaspoon Vegetable Oil plus Cider
    Vinegar
⅓ cup Skim Milk
Coffee or Tea

SNACKS, AT PLANNED TIMES
1 cup Plain Popcorn with 2 tablespoons Raisins;
    ¾ cup Buttermilk; 1 Graham Cracker

Serving Information
Men and Youth: Add ⅓ cup Grape Juice, 1 ounce
    Whole Wheat Roll, and 1 slice Rye Bread
Men: Add ½ ounce Shredded Colby Cheese to
    Salad at the Evening Meal
Youth: Add 1½ cups Skim Milk

DAY 7

MORNING MEAL
1 small Nectarine, sliced
1 serving Hot Cereal, ¾ ounce uncooked
1 cup Skim Milk
Coffee or Tea

MIDDAY MEAL
Cheese Pizza Pocket
Carrot, Celery, and Green Bell Pepper Sticks on
    Lettuce with 2 teaspoons Mayonnaise
Baked Apple

EVENING MEAL
3–4 ounces Broiled Veal Chop
½ cup Cooked Sliced Beets
½ cup Cooked Broccoli
Green Salad with **Savory Vinaigrette**
1 slice Pumpernickel Bread
4 fluid ounces Champagne
Coffee or Tea

SNACKS, AT PLANNED TIMES
Orange-Strawberry Cups; ½ cup Vanilla-Flavored
    Low-Calorie Milk Pudding

Serving Information
Men and Youth: Add ⅓ cup Apple Juice, 2
    Graham Crackers, and 1 slice Pumpernickel
    Bread
Youth: Add 2 cups Skim Milk

Classic pâtés are savory mixtures of liver and other meat, poultry, or game. Perhaps the best known is pâté de foie gras, which is made from the livers of specially fattened geese or ducks. Certain pâtés are known as terrines, after the glazed earthenware casseroles in which they are cooked.

Pâtés can be smooth and velvety or coarse in texture. Smooth pâtés are served from their dish with a knife or spoon, then spread on toast or crackers. More solid mixtures are cut in thin slices and eaten either on crackers or with a knife and fork. Substantial pâtés are generally served as a main dish, accompanied by a salad.

The meats for both pâtés and terrines should be well seasoned. Since they must be prepared well ahead of serving time, they're excellent buffet dishes.

Liver-Yam Pâté (Day 1) is made of chicken livers and yams, with a nice blend of seasonings and should be served spread on crackers.

DAY 1

MORNING MEAL
1 medium Peach, sliced
¾ ounce Ready-to-Eat Cereal
1 slice Toasted Raisin Bread with 1 teaspoon Reduced-Calorie Strawberry Spread
1 cup Skim Milk
Coffee or Tea

MIDDAY MEAL
3–4 ounces Broiled Cod with 1 teaspoon Margarine and Lemon Wedges
½ cup Steamed Zucchini Slices
Shredded Lettuce and Pimiento Strips with **Dill Vinaigrette**
½ cup Skim Milk
Coffee or Tea

EVENING MEAL
¾ cup **Chicken Broth**
Liver-Yam Pâté
Cucumber and Tomato Slices on Lettuce with **Dijon-Herb Dressing**
½ cup Blueberries with ¼ cup Plain Unflavored Yogurt

SNACKS, AT PLANNED TIMES
1 cup Plain Popcorn; 8 fluid ounces Beer; ½ small Mango or ½ small Cantaloupe

Serving Information
Men and Youth: Add 1 slice Toasted Raisin Bread, 1 slice Toasted Rye Bread, ½ cup Blueberries, and ½ small Mango or 1 small Apple
Youth: Add 1½ cups Skim Milk

DAY 4

MORNING MEAL
½ cup Orange Juice
1 Poached Egg
½ English Muffin, toasted
½ cup Skim Milk
Coffee or Tea

MIDDAY MEAL
Cucumber-Liverwurst Sandwich
Julienne Carrot on Chicory with **Savory Vinaigrette**
½ cup Skim Milk
Coffee or Tea

EVENING MEAL
¾ cup **Vegetable Broth**
3–4 ounces Broiled Veal Chop
6 medium Cooked Asparagus Spears with Lemon Juice and 2 teaspoons Margarine
½ cup Cooked Sliced Carrot
½ cup Lime-Flavored Low-Calorie Gelatin with 1 tablespoon Low-Calorie Whipped Topping

SNACKS, AT PLANNED TIMES
1 small Nectarine; 1 cup Skim Milk; 10 large Cherries

Serving Information
Men and Youth: Add ½ English Muffin, toasted, 1 ounce Enriched Roll, and 10 large Cherries
Men: Add 1 ounce Broiled Veal Chop at the Evening Meal
Youth: Add 1 cup Skim Milk

DAY 5

MORNING MEAL
1 small Apple
1 ounce Cheddar Cheese
1 slice Toasted Rye Bread
1 teaspoon Reduced-Calorie Raspberry Spread
¼ cup Skim Milk
Coffee or Tea

MIDDAY MEAL
Chilled Chicken Platter (3 ounces Sliced Cooked Chicken, ½ cup Cooked Green Beans, Tomato and Cucumber Slices on Lettuce Leaves with Lemon Juice)
3 Melba Toast Rounds
Banana and Raisin Pudding Cake
¾ cup Skim Milk

EVENING MEAL
Tuna Ratatouille
Tossed Salad with **Oregano Vinaigrette**
Garlic Bread
½ cup Skim Milk
Coffee or Tea

SNACKS, AT PLANNED TIMES
1 cup Strawberries with 1 tablespoon Plain Unflavored Yogurt; ½ cup Orange-Flavored Low-Calorie Gelatin

Serving Information
Men and Youth: Add 1 slice Toasted Rye Bread, 1 slice Pumpernickel Bread, and ½ cup Canned Mandarin Orange Sections
Youth: Add 1½ cups Skim Milk

MORNING MEAL
2-inch wedge Honeydew
Open-Face Grilled Cheese Sandwich I
¼ cup Skim Milk
Coffee or Tea

MIDDAY MEAL
1½ ounces Broiled Canadian Bacon
1 Egg scrambled in 1 teaspoon Margarine
Baked Broccoli with Mustard Sauce
Green Bell Pepper Rings on Lettuce with
    2 teaspoons Low-Calorie Italian Dressing
1 cup Skim Milk

EVENING MEAL
Chicken and Eggplant Bake
½ cup Cooked Wax Beans
¼ cup Cooked Artichoke Hearts, chilled, on
    Bibb Lettuce
1 ounce Enriched Roll
1 teaspoon Reduced-Calorie Margarine
2 medium Apricots

SNACKS, AT PLANNED TIMES
3 ounces Vanilla-Flavored Dietary Frozen
    Dessert; **Hot Spiced Tea**

Serving Information
Men and Youth: Add 2-inch wedge Honeydew,
    1 slice Whole Wheat Bread, 1 small Apple, and
    2 Graham Crackers
Men: Add ½ ounce Broiled Canadian Bacon at
    the Midday Meal
Youth: Add 1¾ cups Skim Milk

MORNING MEAL
½ medium Banana, sliced
¾ ounce Ready-to-Eat Cereal
1 cup Skim Milk
Coffee or Tea

MIDDAY MEAL
Tomato-Cheese-Stuffed Pitas
Green Salad with 1 teaspoon Imitation Bacon
    Bits and 1 teaspoon Vegetable Oil plus Wine
    Vinegar
½ cup Fruit Salad

EVENING MEAL
Cauliflower and Zucchini Soup
3–4 ounces Poached Salmon
1 medium Ear Corn, boiled
1 teaspoon Margarine
Spinach and Mushroom Salad with **Tarragon
    Vinaigrette**
4 fluid ounces White Wine
Coffee or Tea

SNACKS, AT PLANNED TIMES
½ medium Papaya or 1 cup Strawberries;
    1 serving Chocolate-Flavored Low-Calorie Milk
    Beverage

Serving Information
Men and Youth: Add ½ medium Banana, 2 ounces
    Enriched Roll, ½ cup Fruit Salad, and ½ cup
    Raspberries
Youth: Add ½ cup Plain Unflavored Yogurt and
    1 cup Skim Milk

MORNING MEAL
Broiled Grapefruit
1 serving Hot Cereal, ¾ ounce uncooked, with
    1 teaspoon Maple Syrup and ½ teaspoon
    Margarine
1 cup Skim Milk
Coffee or Tea

MIDDAY MEAL
⅔ cup Cottage Cheese with 2 tablespoons
    Chopped Scallion
½ medium Tomato, sliced
1 slice Pumpernickel Bread
1 teaspoon Margarine
Club Soda with Twist of Lemon

EVENING MEAL
Ham and Vegetables with Paprika Yogurt
½ cup Cooked Sliced Mushrooms
Sliced Belgian Endive with **Herb Dressing**
4 fluid ounces Red Wine
Coffee or Tea

SNACKS, AT PLANNED TIMES
½ cup Orange Sections; 3-inch x 1½-inch
    triangle Watermelon

Serving Information
Men and Youth: Add 1 slice Toasted Raisin
    Bread, 1 small Pear, 1 ounce Whole Wheat Roll,
    and ½ cup Orange Sections
Youth: Add 2 cups Skim Milk

MORNING MEAL
⅓ cup Prune Juice
Bread Pudding
¼ cup Skim Milk
Coffee or Tea

MIDDAY MEAL
3 ounces Cooked Dried Soybeans with ½ cup
    Tomato Sauce and 1 ounce Grated Swiss
    Cheese
Green Salad with 1 teaspoon Sesame Oil plus
    Rice Vinegar
4 Melba Toast Slices
¾ cup Skim Milk

EVENING MEAL
3–4 ounces Broiled Shrimp with
    Lemon "Butter" Sauce
½ cup Cooked Brussels Sprouts
Crispy-Crunchy Salad
1 slice Enriched Bread
Sparkling Mineral Water with Mint Sprig

SNACKS, AT PLANNED TIMES
1 medium Kiwi Fruit or 2-inch wedge Honeydew;
    Root Beer Froth; ¼ small Pineapple

Serving Information
Men and Youth: Add ¼ small Pineapple and 2
    Graham Crackers
Men: Add 1 ounce Cooked Dried Soybeans at
    the Midday Meal
Youth: Add 1 cup Skim Milk

Mackerel isn't exactly the Cary Grant of fishes. In fact, it has a definite image problem. But give mackerel a good press agent and that will change. Our Mackerel Patties (Day 7) is a whale of a dish. Other seafood delights we've scheduled include broiled trout (Day 2), poached salmon (Day 3), and broiled sea bass (Day 4).

Economy Tip—Roast beef is on the menu on Day 5. Leftovers may be frozen and used at the Midday Meal (Week 29, Day 3), in Potato-Beef Hash recipe (Week 29, Day 5), and in Marinated Julienne Beef recipe (Week 30, Day 3).

Energy-Saving Tip—While roasting chicken for Day 2, also roast chicken for Sesame Chicken with Green Beans recipe (Day 7 and Week 32, Day 2), the Midday Meal (Week 28, Day 4), Polynesian Chicken recipe (Week 30, Day 2), Crêpes Divan recipe (Week 31, Day 6), and Japanese Chicken Salad recipe (Week 33, Day 4); freeze.

DAY 1

MORNING MEAL
1 small Orange
¾ ounce Ready-to-Eat Cereal
1 cup Skim Milk
Coffee or Tea

MIDDAY MEAL
¾ cup **Chicken Broth**
Tomato Stuffed with Herb Cheese
1 slice Rye Bread
1 teaspoon Margarine
½ cup Lemon-Flavored Low-Calorie Gelatin

EVENING MEAL
3–4 ounces Baked Lamb Chop
¼ cup Baked Acorn Squash
½ cup Cooked Broccoli
Tossed Salad with **Wine Vinaigrette**
1 ounce Enriched Roll
1 teaspoon Margarine
½ cup Canned Fruit Cocktail with 1 teaspoon Shredded Coconut

SNACKS, AT PLANNED TIMES
¾ cup Buttermilk; **Tropical Treat**

Serving Information
Men and Youth: Add 2 tablespoons Raisins, 1 slice Rye Bread, ½ cup Canned Fruit Cocktail, and 2 Graham Crackers
Youth: Add 1 cup Skim Milk

DAY 4

MORNING MEAL
½ medium Banana, sliced
¾ ounce Ready-to-Eat Cereal
1 cup Skim Milk
Coffee or Tea

MIDDAY MEAL
3–4 ounces Broiled Calf Liver
¼ cup Steamed Chopped Onion
½ cup Steamed Cauliflower Florets
Green Salad with **Garlic Vinaigrette**
1 cup Honeydew Balls

EVENING MEAL
Fresh Mushroom Soup with 6 Saltines
3–4 ounces Broiled Sea Bass
1 medium Ear Corn, boiled
1 teaspoon Margarine
½ cup Cooked Kale
Hearts of Lettuce with 1 teaspoon Mayonnaise
½ cup Cherry-Flavored Gelatin with 1 tablespoon Low-Calorie Whipped Topping

SNACKS, AT PLANNED TIMES
½ cup Chocolate-Flavored Low-Calorie Milk Pudding; 2 Graham Crackers; 1 small Apple

Serving Information
Men and Youth: Add ½ medium Banana, sliced, and 2 ounces Whole Wheat Roll
Youth: Add 2 cups Skim Milk

DAY 5

MORNING MEAL
½ cup Orange Juice
Bread Pudding
¼ cup Skim Milk
Coffee or Tea

MIDDAY MEAL
Cheese Pizza Pocket
Sliced Radishes and Cucumbers on Lettuce with **Tarragon Vinaigrette**
1 medium Peach

EVENING MEAL
3–4 ounces Sliced Roast Beef with **Horseradish-Chili Sauce**
½ cup Steamed Butternut Squash
½ cup Steamed Broccoli
Green Salad with 2 teaspoons Vegetable Oil plus Cider Vinegar
4 fluid ounces Red Wine
¼ cup Skim Milk
Coffee or Tea

SNACKS, AT PLANNED TIMES
½ cup Fruit Salad; ½ cup Plain Unflavored Yogurt with ½ teaspoon Honey

Serving Information
Men and Youth: Add ½ cup Orange Juice, ½ cup Fruit Salad, 2 ounces Whole Wheat Roll, and ½ cup Raspberries
Youth: Add 1¾ cups Skim Milk

MORNING MEAL
1/3 cup Prune Juice
Scramble 'n' Spinach
1 slice Toasted Whole Wheat Bread
1 teaspoon Margarine
1/4 cup Skim Milk
Coffee or Tea

MIDDAY MEAL
3–4 ounces Roast Chicken Breast
1/2 cup Steamed Asparagus Tips
Green Salad with **Russian Dressing**
1 slice Enriched Bread
1/2 cup Vanilla-Flavored Low-Calorie Milk
   Pudding

EVENING MEAL
3–4 ounces Broiled Trout
1/2 cup Cooked Enriched Noodles
1/4 cup Steamed Chinese Pea Pods
Shredded Cabbage topped with Alfalfa or Bean
   Sprouts and 1 teaspoon Vegetable Oil plus
   Wine Vinegar
1/2 small Cantaloupe
3/4 cup Skim Milk

SNACKS, AT PLANNED TIMES
1 cup Mixed Vegetable Juice; **Honey-Glazed
   Pears**

Serving Information
Men and Youth: Add 1/3 cup Prune Juice, 1 slice
   Toasted Whole Wheat Bread, 10 large Cherries,
   and 6 Saltines
Youth: Add 2 cups Skim Milk

MORNING MEAL
1/2 medium Grapefruit
1/3 cup Part-Skim Ricotta Cheese
1/2 small Enriched Bagel
1/2 cup Skim Milk
Coffee or Tea

MIDDAY MEAL
3–4 ounces Poached Salmon
1 cup Cooked Baby Carrots
Cucumber and Tomato Salad
1/2 cup Applesauce
1/2 cup Skim Milk
Coffee or Tea

EVENING MEAL
Mexican Beef Patty
1/4 cup Steamed Beets
1/2 cup Steamed Green Beans
Tossed Salad with 1 1/2 teaspoons Vegetable Oil
   plus Tarragon Vinegar
1 ounce Pita Bread
Club Soda with Twist of Lemon

SNACKS, AT PLANNED TIMES
1/2 cup Blackberries; 1/2 cup Plain Unflavored
   Yogurt; 1 cup Tomato Juice with Green Bell
   Pepper Sticks

Serving Information
Men and Youth: Add 1/2 small Enriched Bagel,
   1/2 cup Applesauce, and 1 ounce Pita Bread
Youth: Add 1 cup Skim Milk

MORNING MEAL
1 cup Strawberries
3/4 ounce Ready-to-Eat Cereal
1 cup Skim Milk
Coffee or Tea

MIDDAY MEAL
Mushroom Omelet
Tossed Salad with Green Bell Pepper Rings and
   Cider Vinaigrette
1/2 English Muffin, toasted
1 1/2 teaspoons Reduced-Calorie Margarine
1/2 cup Canned Mandarin Orange Sections

EVENING MEAL
3–4 ounces Roast Veal
1/2 cup Steamed Okra with 1/4 cup **Marinara Sauce**
Broiled Tomato
Green Salad with Bean Sprouts and Lemon Juice
1 ounce Enriched Roll
Lime Cooler

SNACKS, AT PLANNED TIMES
3/4 cup Buttermilk; 2 Graham Crackers; 3-inch x
   1 1/2-inch triangle Watermelon

Serving Information
Men and Youth: Add 1/2 cup Canned Mandarin
   Orange Sections and 2 Graham Crackers
Youth: Add 2 cups Skim Milk

MORNING MEAL
1/3 cup Apple Juice
Open-Face Grilled Cheese Sandwich I
1/4 cup Skim Milk
Coffee or Tea

MIDDAY MEAL
Mackerel Patties
1/2 cup Cooked Sliced Zucchini
Curried Cole Slaw
3 Melba Toast Rounds
1 teaspoon Reduced-Calorie Margarine
Sparkling Mineral Water with Twist of Lemon

EVENING MEAL
Sesame Chicken with Green Beans
1/4 cup Cooked Artichoke Hearts
1/4 cup Cooked Carrot Slices
Shredded Lettuce topped with Green Bell Pepper
   Rings and Rice Vinegar
1/2 cup Blueberries with 1/2 cup Plain Unflavored
   Yogurt

SNACKS, AT PLANNED TIMES
1 cup Plain Popcorn; 12 fluid ounces Light Beer;
   1 medium Kiwi Fruit or 1/2 small Cantaloupe;
   3/4 cup Skim Milk

Serving Information
Men and Youth: Add 1/3 cup Apple Juice, 3
   Melba Toast Rounds, 1 slice Rye Bread, and
   1/2 cup Blueberries
Youth: Add 1 3/4 cups Skim Milk

WEEK 27

Strange to see how a good dinner and feasting reconciles everybody.

> —Samuel Pepys's
> *Diary* for November 9, 1665

The Declaration of Independence might never have been written if the representatives of the British government and American colonies had taken Pepys's advice.

But we all know how history turned out. And we also know how a July 4th barbecue seems to improve dispositions and get the summer rolling.

The Evening Meal for Day 3 includes a number of dishes that can be prepared in advance, a real plus if you want to make the most of a holiday like the Fourth of July.

In Canada, Dominion Day is celebrated on July 1st. We suggest that our friends across the border use our Day 3 menu.

Energy-Saving Tip—While broiling chicken for Day 6, broil chicken breast for Cold Chicken Platter recipe (Week 30, Day 5); freeze.

DAY 1

MORNING MEAL
⅓ cup Pineapple Juice
1 Scrambled Egg
1 slice Toasted Rye Bread
1 teaspoon Reduced-Calorie Margarine
½ cup Skim Milk
Coffee or Tea

MIDDAY MEAL
⅔ cup Cottage Cheese
1 medium Tomato, sliced
Sliced Cucumber on Lettuce with Lemon Juice
    and Seasonings
1 slice Whole Wheat Bread
½ small Cantaloupe

EVENING MEAL
Tuna Casserole Parmesan
Tossed Salad with 1 teaspoon Vegetable Oil
    plus Wine Vinegar and Herbs
1 ounce Enriched Roll
Sparkling Mineral Water with Lemon Wedge

SNACKS, AT PLANNED TIMES
½ cup Cherry-Flavored Low-Calorie Gelatin;
    ½ cup Raspberries; 1 cup Skim Milk

Serving Information
Men and Youth: Add ⅓ cup Pineapple Juice,
    1 slice Toasted Rye Bread, 10 large Cherries,
    1 ounce Whole Wheat Roll, and ½ cup Rasp-
    berries
Youth: Add 2 cups Skim Milk

DAY 4

MORNING MEAL
½ medium Banana, sliced
¾ ounce Ready-to-Eat Cereal
1 cup Skim Milk
Coffee or Tea

MIDDAY MEAL
Mushroom Pizza
Carrot, Celery, and Red Bell Pepper Sticks on
    Lettuce with 1 teaspoon Vegetable Oil plus
    Cider Vinegar
½ cup Orange-Flavored Low-Calorie Gelatin
    with ½ cup Orange Sections

EVENING MEAL
3–4 ounces Broiled Flounder
½ cup Steamed Brussels Sprouts
½ cup Steamed Cauliflower
Tossed Salad with 1 teaspoon Mayonnaise
1 slice Whole Wheat Bread
Sparkling Mineral Water with Twist of Lemon

SNACKS, AT PLANNED TIMES
3 ounces Chocolate-Flavored Dietary Frozen
    Dessert; **Coconut-Honey Shake**

Serving Information
Men and Youth: Add ½ medium Banana, sliced,
    1½ ounces Crispbread, and ½ cup Orange
    Sections
Youth: Add 2 cups Skim Milk

DAY 5

MORNING MEAL
⅓ cup Grape Juice
⅓ cup Part-Skim Ricotta Cheese
½ small Enriched Bagel, toasted
¼ cup Skim Milk
Coffee or Tea

MIDDAY MEAL
Danish Apple Soup
3–4 ounces Broiled Fillet of Sole with
    Lemon Wedge
¼ cup Cooked Peas
Shredded Cabbage topped with Alfalfa or Bean
    Sprouts and 1 teaspoon Vegetable Oil plus
    Tarragon Vinegar
1 slice Pumpernickel Bread
1 teaspoon Reduced-Calorie Margarine
¾ cup Skim Milk

EVENING MEAL
1 cup Tomato Juice
Oriental Steak Salad
1 ounce Enriched Roll
1 teaspoon Reduced-Calorie Margarine
½ cup Lime-Flavored Low-Calorie Gelatin

SNACKS, AT PLANNED TIMES
1 cup Strawberries with ½ cup Plain Unflavored
    Yogurt; ¾ cup **Beef Broth**

Serving Information
Men and Youth: Add ⅓ cup Grape Juice, ½ small
    Enriched Bagel, toasted, and 6 Saltines
Youth: Add 1 cup Skim Milk

DAY 2

MORNING MEAL
1 small Orange
1 serving Hot Cereal, ¾ ounce uncooked
1 cup Skim Milk
Coffee or Tea

MIDDAY MEAL
Turkey Kiev
6 medium Steamed Asparagus Spears
Tossed Salad with Green Bell Pepper Rings and
    Lemon Juice
3-inch x 1½-inch triangle Watermelon

EVENING MEAL
3–4 ounces Broiled Chicken Livers
½ cup Steamed Onion Slices
½ cup Steamed Wax Beans
Green Salad with 1 tablespoon Low-Calorie
    Italian Dressing
3 Melba Toast Rounds
Club Soda with Mint Sprig

SNACKS, AT PLANNED TIMES
½ cup Plain Unflavored Yogurt; 10 large
    Cherries; **Hot Spiced Tea**

Serving Information
Men and Youth: Add 2 ounces Enriched Roll and
    10 large Cherries
Youth: Add 1 cup Skim Milk

DAY 3

MORNING MEAL
½ medium Grapefruit
1 ounce Swiss Cheese
½ English Muffin, toasted
1½ teaspoons Margarine
½ cup Skim Milk
Coffee or Tea

MIDDAY MEAL
Shrimp Scampi
1 cup Cooked Sliced Carrots
Tossed Salad with **Dijon-Herb Dressing**
½ cup Cooked Rhubarb with 1 tablespoon
    Low-Calorie Whipped Topping

EVENING MEAL
Marinated Chuck Steak
¼ cup Chilled Cooked Beets
½ cup Chilled Cooked Green Beans with
    1 teaspoon Imitation Bacon Bits
Curried Cole Slaw
8 fluid ounces Beer
½ cup Fruit Salad

SNACKS, AT PLANNED TIMES
Pineapple-Yogurt Pudding; 2 Graham Crackers;
    ¾ cup Buttermilk

Serving Information
Men and Youth: Add ½ English Muffin, toasted,
    and ½ cup Fruit Salad
Youth: Add 1½ cups Skim Milk

DAY 6

MORNING MEAL
1 medium Peach, sliced
1 serving Hot Cereal, ¾ ounce uncooked
1 cup Skim Milk
Coffee or Tea

MIDDAY MEAL
3–4 ounces Sliced Broiled Chicken Breast
Linguine Primavera
1 cup Honeydew or Cantaloupe Balls

EVENING MEAL
¾ cup **Vegetable Broth**
Pinto Bean Salad
½ cup Cooked Bean Sprouts
½ cup Cherry-Flavored Gelatin

SNACKS, AT PLANNED TIMES
½ cup Vanilla-Flavored Low-Calorie Milk
    Pudding; ½ cup Canned Fruit Cocktail;
    2 Graham Crackers

Serving Information
Men and Youth: Add 2 tablespoons Raisins, 2
    ounces Whole Wheat Roll, and ½ cup Canned
    Fruit Cocktail
Men: Add 1 ounce Sliced Broiled Chicken at the
    Midday Meal
Youth: Add 2 cups Skim Milk

DAY 7

MORNING MEAL
Stewed Dried Apricots
1 ounce Grilled Canadian Bacon
½ English Muffin, toasted
1 teaspoon Mayonnaise
¼ cup Skim Milk
Coffee or Tea

MIDDAY MEAL
Open-Face Grilled Cheese Sandwich II
Tossed Salad with **Savory Vinaigrette**
½ cup Strawberry-Flavored Low-Calorie Gelatin
¾ cup Skim Milk

EVENING MEAL
½ medium Grapefruit
Mushroom Omelet
½ cup Cooked Sliced Zucchini
Melba Toast Parmesan
Green Salad with Lemon Juice
4 fluid ounces White Wine
Coffee or Tea

SNACKS, AT PLANNED TIMES
½ medium Banana; 1 serving Chocolate-Flavored
    Low-Calorie Milk Beverage

Serving Information
Men and Youth: Add ½ English Muffin, toasted,
    and 1 cup Strawberries
Youth: Add 1 cup Skim Milk

The bean sprout is a popular, nourishing vegetable. Its pleasant, mild flavor complements salads, stews, soups, and even sandwiches. Bean sprouts are an essential ingredient in chop suey, chow mein, and other Oriental dishes.

They are available canned or fresh, or you can grow your own. Just layer one-quarter inch of seeds at the bottom of a one-quart jar; add an inch of water, cover the jar with gauze, and soak overnight. Drain, rinse, and repeat this procedure three times a day for two more days. Your sprouts should be ready to eat.

Bean sprouts appear on the menu twice this week, in Bean Sprouts with Muenster Julienne (Day 2) and Ginger-Spiced Bean Sprouts and Onions (Day 5). If you're using canned bean sprouts, remember to rinse and drain them well.

WEEK 28

DAY 1

MORNING MEAL
½ cup Orange Juice
⅓ cup Cottage Cheese
½ small Enriched Bagel
¼ cup Skim Milk
Coffee or Tea

MIDDAY MEAL
3–4 ounces Broiled Cod with **Lemon "Butter" Sauce**
½ cup Steamed Cauliflower
Mock Hummus with Vegetable Dippers
1 ounce Pita Bread
½ cup Canned Sliced Peaches with ¼ cup Plain Unflavored Yogurt

EVENING MEAL
Chicken Livers Florentine
½ cup Red Bell Pepper Slices sautéed in 1 teaspoon Margarine
Bibb Lettuce and Grated Carrot Salad with 2 teaspoons Low-Calorie Italian Dressing
4 fluid ounces Red Wine
¼ cup Skim Milk
Coffee or Tea

SNACKS, AT PLANNED TIMES
Honey-Stewed Prunes; ½ cup Chocolate-Flavored Low-Calorie Milk Pudding

Serving Information
Men and Youth: Add ½ cup Orange Juice and ½ small Enriched Bagel
Youth: Add 1½ cups Skim Milk

DAY 4

MORNING MEAL
1 cup Strawberries
¾ ounce Ready-to-Eat Cereal
½ cup Skim Milk
Coffee or Tea

MIDDAY MEAL
3–4 ounces Sliced Cooked Chicken
White Salad
4 Melba Toast Slices
1 teaspoon Margarine
1 small Nectarine

EVENING MEAL
1 cup Tomato Juice
Chili-Burgers
½ Hamburger Roll
¼ cup Cooked Peas
½ cup Cooked Sliced Carrot
Shredded Lettuce with 2 teaspoons Mayonnaise
Lemonade

SNACKS, AT PLANNED TIMES
½ cup Skim Milk; 1 Graham Cracker; **Mocha Sundae**

Serving Information
Men and Youth: Add 1 slice Enriched Bread, ½ Hamburger Roll, 1 Graham Cracker, and 1 small Apple
Youth: Add 2 cups Skim Milk

DAY 5

MORNING MEAL
2-inch wedge Honeydew
1 Scrambled Egg
1 slice Toasted Rye Bread
1 teaspoon Margarine
¼ cup Skim Milk
Coffee or Tea

MIDDAY MEAL
3–4 ounces Broiled Veal Chop
Ginger-Spiced Bean Sprouts and Onions
Cucumber and Radish Salad with **Tarragon Vinaigrette**
½ cup Applesauce with ¼ cup Plain Unflavored Yogurt

EVENING MEAL
Curried Scrod
6 medium Cooked Asparagus Spears
Watercress Salad with Cider Vinegar
1 ounce Enriched Roll
4 fluid ounces White Wine
¼ cup Skim Milk
Coffee or Tea

SNACKS, AT PLANNED TIMES
1 serving Vanilla-Flavored Low-Calorie Milk Beverage; 3-inch x 1½-inch triangle Watermelon

Serving Information
Men and Youth: Add 2 ounces Enriched Italian Bread, 2 Dates, and 1 ounce Enriched Roll
Youth: Add 1½ cups Skim Milk

MORNING MEAL
1 cup Tomato Juice
Knockwurst Breakfast
1 slice Toasted Whole Wheat Bread
¼ cup Skim Milk
Coffee or Tea

MIDDAY MEAL
Bean Sprouts with Muenster Julienne
Cherry Tomatoes on Lettuce with
   Russian Dressing
¼ small Cantaloupe
¾ cup Skim Milk

EVENING MEAL
Artichoke Hearts Español
Pineapple Flounder
½ cup Cooked Diced Carrot
½ cup Cooked Broccoli Florets
Tossed Salad with Lemon Juice
½ cup Blueberries

SNACKS, AT PLANNED TIMES
1 cup Skim Milk; 2 Graham Crackers; 2 medium
   Plums

Serving Information
Men and Youth: Add 2 ounces Whole Wheat Roll,
   ¼ small Cantaloupe, and 1 medium Peach
Youth: Add 2 cups Skim Milk

MORNING MEAL
⅓ cup Grape Juice
⅓ cup Part-Skim Ricotta Cheese
¾ ounce Crispbread
¼ cup Skim Milk
Coffee or Tea

MIDDAY MEAL
Egg Salad
½ medium Dill Pickle
1 slice Rye Bread
Yogurt-Banana Shake

EVENING MEAL
Turkey Breast with Cream of Corn Sauce
½ cup Cooked Brussels Sprouts
Spinach and Mushroom Salad with 1 teaspoon
   Imitation Bacon Bits and **Wine Vinaigrette**
½ cup Strawberry-Flavored Low-Calorie Gelatin
½ cup Skim Milk
Coffee or Tea

SNACKS, AT PLANNED TIMES
½ cup Grapefruit Sections; Celery and Zucchini
   Sticks with **Curry Dip**

Serving Information
Men and Youth: Add ⅔ cup Grape Juice, 1 slice
   Rye Bread, and ½ cup Raspberries
Youth: Add 1¼ cups Skim Milk

MORNING MEAL
½ medium Banana, sliced
¾ ounce Ready-to-Eat Cereal
1 cup Skim Milk
Coffee or Tea

MIDDAY MEAL
Potato-Cheddar Broil
½ cup Cooked Sliced Zucchini
Hearts of Lettuce with 1 teaspoon Mayonnaise
½ small Mango or 1 cup Strawberries

EVENING MEAL
Crisp "Oven-Fried" Chicken
½ cup Cooked Green Beans with ½ teaspoon
   Sesame Seeds
Alfalfa or Bean Sprouts on Lettuce with
   2 teaspoons Vegetable Oil plus Cider Vinegar
Cherry Cobbler

SNACKS, AT PLANNED TIMES
½ cup Plain Unflavored Yogurt with 2 teaspoons
   Reduced-Calorie Apricot Spread; 1 cup Mixed
   Vegetable Juice with 3 Melba Toast Rounds

Serving Information
Men and Youth: Add 2 tablespoons Raisins, 1
   English Muffin, split and toasted, and 4 Canned
   Apricot Halves with 2 tablespoons Juice
Youth: Add 2 cups Skim Milk

MORNING MEAL
½ cup Grapefruit Juice
Bread Pudding
¼ cup Skim Milk
Coffee or Tea

MIDDAY MEAL
3–4 ounces Boiled Shrimp with Lemon Wedges
Broiled Tomato
Chicory and Romaine Salad with **Herb Dressing**
½ cup Vanilla-Flavored Low-Calorie Milk
   Pudding

EVENING MEAL
Roast Pork Tenderloin
½ cup Steamed Chinese Pea Pods
½ cup Baked Eggplant
Tossed Salad with 1½ teaspoons Mayonnaise
2 Canned Pear Halves with 2 tablespoons Juice
   and 2 tablespoons Plain Unflavored Yogurt

SNACKS, AT PLANNED TIMES
12 fluid ounces Light Beer; 20 Oyster Crackers;
   ½ cup Lemon-Flavored Low-Calorie Gelatin
   with 1 tablespoon Low-Calorie Whipped
   Topping

Serving Information
Men and Youth: Add ½ cup Grapefruit Juice,
   6 Melba Toast Rounds, 1 slice Whole Wheat
   Bread, and 1 medium Peach
Youth: Add 1¾ cups Skim Milk

To be hard-boiled is to be tough, right? Well, tough is okay for characters in gangster movies, but it isn't too good for eggs. Cooking an egg might seem like child's play, but it does take some skill to turn out a firm egg that's not rubbery.

Here's how. Put the eggs in a pan, then cover them with *cold* water. Cover the pan and *slowly* heat the water to a simmer. For soft-cooked eggs, remove the pan from heat and let stand for 3 to 5 minutes. For hard-cooked eggs, keep simmering for 20 to 25 minutes. Place in cold water at once to prevent the yolks from discoloring.

Try our method for hard-cooking eggs when you make the Egg and Green Goddess Platter (Day 6).

Economy Tip—Roast turkey is on the menu on Day 2. Leftovers may be frozen and used at Midday Meals (Week 31, Day 3 and Week 32, Day 1) and in Honeyed Turkey with Broccoli recipe (Week 32, Day 4).

WEEK 29

DAY 1

MORNING MEAL
1 cup Strawberries
1 ounce Smoked Whitefish
½ small Enriched Bagel
¼ cup Skim Milk
Coffee or Tea

MIDDAY MEAL
Ginger-Broiled Chicken
Mandarin Rice Salad
½ cup Plain Unflavored Yogurt with 1 tablespoon Raisins

EVENING MEAL
3–4 ounces Broiled Beef Liver
½ cup Sliced Onion sautéed in 1 teaspoon Margarine
½ cup Cooked Broccoli with Lemon Wedge
Lettuce and Sliced Bell Pepper Salad with 1 teaspoon Imitation Bacon Bits and
Savory Vinaigrette
¼ small Pineapple

SNACKS, AT PLANNED TIMES
¾ cup Skim Milk; 2 Graham Crackers; 1 cup Mixed Vegetable Juice

Serving Information
Men and Youth: Add ½ small Enriched Bagel, 2 tablespoons Raisins, and 4 Melba Toast Slices
Youth: Add 1 cup Skim Milk

DAY 4

MORNING MEAL
2-inch wedge Honeydew with Lemon Slice
Pancakes with 1 teaspoon Maple Syrup
¼ cup Skim Milk
Coffee or Tea

MIDDAY MEAL
3–4 ounces Poached Haddock
½ cup Cooked Peas with Pimiento Strips
Tossed Salad with Wine Vinegar
½ cup Lime-Flavored Gelatin

EVENING MEAL
Turkey Piccata
½ cup Cooked Broccoli Spears
½ cup Cooked Mushrooms
Cucumber Spears on Shredded Lettuce with ¼ recipe **Yogurt Dressing**
2 ounces Enriched Italian Bread
½ cup Fruit Salad

SNACKS, AT PLANNED TIMES
½ cup Plain Unflavored Yogurt; ½ medium Banana; **Lemonade**

Serving Information
Men and Youth: Add 1 slice Enriched Bread, ½ cup Fruit Salad, and 20 Oyster Crackers
Youth: Add 1¾ cups Skim Milk

DAY 5

MORNING MEAL
½ cup Blueberries
¾ ounce Ready-to-Eat Cereal
½ cup Skim Milk
Coffee or Tea

MIDDAY MEAL
Tomato Stuffed with Herb Cheese
Celery and Carrot Sticks
6 Melba Toast Rounds
½ cup Vanilla-Flavored Low-Calorie Milk Pudding

EVENING MEAL
Potato-Beef Hash
½ cup Cooked Diced Carrot with 3 tablespoons Cooked Pearl Onions
Lettuce Wedge with **Dill Vinaigrette**
Bittersweet Chocolate "Cream"

SNACKS, AT PLANNED TIMES
1 small Orange; 1 small Pear

Serving Information
Men and Youth: Add ⅔ cup Apple Juice, 12 large Grapes, and 2 ounces Enriched Roll
Youth: Add 2 cups Skim Milk

MORNING MEAL
1/3 cup Prune Juice
1 Poached Egg
1/2 English Muffin, toasted
1 teaspoon Margarine
1/4 cup Skim Milk
Coffee or Tea

MIDDAY MEAL
1/2 small Cantaloupe filled with 1/3 cup Cottage
   Cheese
Tofu Salad
1 ounce Enriched Roll
1 teaspoon Margarine
1/2 cup Cherry-Flavored Low-Calorie Gelatin

EVENING MEAL
3–4 ounces Roast Turkey
1/2 cup Steamed Spinach
1/2 cup Steamed Sliced Carrot
Radish Salad
4 fluid ounces White Wine
Coffee or Tea

SNACKS, AT PLANNED TIMES
12 large Grapes; 1/2 cup Chocolate-Flavored
   Low-Calorie Milk Pudding; 3/4 cup Skim Milk

Serving Information
Men and Youth: Add 1/3 cup Prune Juice, 1/2
   English Muffin, toasted, 10 large Cherries, and
   1 slice Cracked Wheat Bread
Men: Add 1 ounce Cubed Tofu (Soybean Curd)
   to **Tofu Salad**
Youth: Add 2 cups Skim Milk

MORNING MEAL
1/2 medium Grapefruit
3/4 ounce Ready-to-Eat Cereal
1 cup Skim Milk
Coffee or Tea

MIDDAY MEAL
Vegetable Soup
3–4 ounces Sliced Roast Beef
Tomato Slices on Lettuce with 1 teaspoon
   Reduced-Calorie Mayonnaise
1 slice Rye Bread
1/4 medium Papaya or 1/2 cup Strawberries

EVENING MEAL
Flounder Fillet Rolls with Vegetables
1/2 cup Cooked Enriched Noodles with 1 teaspoon
   Reduced-Calorie Margarine
1/2 cup Cooked Green Beans
Lime Cooler

SNACKS, AT PLANNED TIMES
6 Saltines with 2 teaspoons Reduced-Calorie
   Strawberry Spread; 1 cup Skim Milk;
   1 medium Peach

Serving Information
Men and Youth: Add 1 slice Rye Bread, 1/4
   medium Papaya or 1/2 cup Strawberries, and
   1 small Apple
Youth: Add 2 cups Skim Milk

MORNING MEAL
1/2 cup Grapefruit Juice
1/3 cup Part-Skim Ricotta Cheese
1 slice Toasted Raisin Bread
1/4 cup Skim Milk
Coffee or Tea

MIDDAY MEAL
Egg and Green Goddess Platter
1 slice Toasted Enriched Bread
1 teaspoon Margarine
1/2 cup Raspberry-Flavored Low-Calorie Gelatin

EVENING MEAL
3–4 ounces Baked Cod
1/2 cup Cooked Green Beans
1/2 cup Cooked Sliced Beets
Cole Slaw Vinaigrette
4 fluid ounces White Wine
3-inch x 1 1/2-inch triangle Watermelon

SNACKS, AT PLANNED TIMES
3/4 cup Skim Milk; 2 Graham Crackers; 2 medium
   Plums

Serving Information
Men and Youth: Add 1/2 cup Grapefruit Juice,
   1 slice Toasted Enriched Bread, and 1/2 cup
   Raspberries
Youth: Add 1 3/4 cups Skim Milk

MORNING MEAL
1/2 cup Canned Sliced Peaches
3/4 ounce Ready-to-Eat Cereal
1 cup Skim Milk
Coffee or Tea

MIDDAY MEAL
Salmon Salad
1/4 cup Sliced Onion
1 ounce Pita Bread
1/2 cup Plain Unflavored Yogurt with 1/2 cup
   Strawberries

EVENING MEAL
3–4 ounces Broiled Steak
1/2 cup Cooked Wax Beans
Cauliflower Salad
1 ounce Whole Wheat Roll
1 teaspoon Margarine
1/2 medium Papaya or 1/2 small Cantaloupe

SNACKS, AT PLANNED TIMES
Coconut-Orange Gelatin; 1 cup Tomato Juice

Serving Information
Men and Youth: Add 4 medium Dried Apricot
   Halves, 1 slice Toasted Cracked Wheat Bread,
   1/2 cup Strawberries, and 1 ounce Whole Wheat
   Roll
Youth: Add 2 cups Skim Milk

Garlic is no dim bulb. A modest amount imparts a pungent background flavor, lighting up dishes served round the world.

Its magical properties are legendary. Worn around one's neck, garlic is reputed to keep demons, witches, and vampires at bay. Hung in one's home, it's said to make the evil eye look for trouble elsewhere.

Three types of garlic are marketed. They are the strong white Creole, the large Tahitian, and the small pink Italian. Look for unblemished bulbs that feel heavy for their size.

Sweet and Tangy Scrod (Day 4), Cheese-Stuffed Zucchini (Day 4), Marinated Julienne Beef (Day 3), and Garlic Bread (Day 5) use garlic in four different ways. If you're worried about being kissing-sweet after all that, try chewing fresh parsley or mint leaves.

WEEK 30

DAY 1

MORNING MEAL
½ small Mango or 2-inch wedge Honeydew
1 Egg mixed with 1 teaspoon Imitation Bacon Bits and scrambled in 1 teaspoon Margarine
1 slice Toasted Whole Wheat Bread
¼ cup Skim Milk
Coffee or Tea

MIDDAY MEAL
Cheese Pizza Pocket
Oriental Salad
1 medium Peach
¾ cup Skim Milk

EVENING MEAL
Marinated Broccoli Appetizer
3–4 ounces Baked Flounder
½ cup Steamed Green Beans
½ cup Steamed Julienne Carrot
4 fluid ounces White Wine
Coffee or Tea

SNACKS, AT PLANNED TIMES
½ cup Plain Unflavored Yogurt with 3 medium Dried Apricot Halves; 2 cups Plain Popcorn

Serving Information
Men and Youth: Add 1 slice Whole Wheat Bread and 2 Dates
Youth: Add 2 cups Skim Milk

DAY 4

MORNING MEAL
⅓ cup Grape Juice
1 Poached Egg
½ English Muffin, toasted
1 teaspoon Margarine
¼ cup Skim Milk
Coffee or Tea

MIDDAY MEAL
Cheese-Stuffed Zucchini
Tossed Salad with 2 teaspoons Low-Calorie Italian Dressing
1 ounce Whole Wheat Roll
½ cup Vanilla-Flavored Low-Calorie Milk Pudding

EVENING MEAL
Sweet and Tangy Scrod
¼ cup Cooked Brussels Sprouts
Lettuce and Sliced Radish Salad with Lemon Juice
¼ medium Papaya or ¼ small Cantaloupe

SNACKS, AT PLANNED TIMES
¾ cup Honeydew Balls; ¾ cup Skim Milk; 10 small Grapes

Serving Information
Men and Youth: Add ⅓ cup Grape Juice, ½ English Muffin, toasted, 1 slice Enriched Bread, ¼ medium Papaya or ¼ small Cantaloupe, and 10 small Grapes
Youth: Add 1 cup Skim Milk

DAY 5

MORNING MEAL
½ medium Banana, sliced
¾ ounce Ready-to-Eat Cereal
½ cup Skim Milk
Coffee or Tea

MIDDAY MEAL
Cold Chicken Platter
½ cup Chilled Green Beans
1 ounce Pita Bread
1 teaspoon Reduced-Calorie Mayonnaise
½ cup Strawberry-Flavored Low-Calorie Gelatin

EVENING MEAL
3–4 ounces Broiled Steak
¼ cup Steamed Sliced Onion
½ cup Steamed Mushroom Caps
Tossed Salad with Lemon Juice
Garlic Bread
½ cup Orange and Grapefruit Sections

SNACKS, AT PLANNED TIMES
1 cup Tomato Juice with 10 Oyster Crackers;
Strawberry-Apple Frost

Serving Information
Men and Youth: Add ½ medium Banana, 2 ounces Whole Wheat Roll, and 1 small Nectarine
Youth: Add 1½ cups Skim Milk

DAY 2

MORNING MEAL
1 small Nectarine, sliced
¾ ounce Ready-to-Eat Cereal
1 cup Skim Milk
Coffee or Tea

MIDDAY MEAL
Polynesian Chicken
1 ounce Enriched Roll
1 teaspoon Reduced-Calorie Margarine
½ cup Cherry-Flavored Low-Calorie Gelatin with
   1 tablespoon Low-Calorie Whipped Topping

EVENING MEAL
3–4 ounces Pan-Broiled Beef Liver
½ cup Baked Spaghetti Squash
Cucumber and Tomato Salad
1 slice Rye Bread
Lime Cooler

SNACKS, AT PLANNED TIMES
2-inch wedge Honeydew; 1 serving Chocolate-
   Flavored Low-Calorie Milk Beverage

Serving Information
Men and Youth: Add 1 slice Rye Bread, ½ cup
   Applesauce with 2 tablespoons Raisins, and
   2 Graham Crackers
Youth: Add 2 cups Skim Milk

DAY 3

MORNING MEAL
½ cup Orange Juice
⅓ cup Part-Skim Ricotta Cheese
½ small Enriched Bagel
½ cup Skim Milk
Coffee or Tea

MIDDAY MEAL
3–4 ounces Broiled Turkey Patty
½ Hamburger Roll
2 teaspoons Ketchup mixed with 1 teaspoon
   Reduced-Calorie Mayonnaise
Potato Crisps
Curried Cole Slaw
½ cup Skim Milk
Coffee or Tea

EVENING MEAL
Gazpacho
Marinated Julienne Beef
6 medium Cooked Asparagus Spears, chilled,
   with Lemon Juice
3-inch x 1½-inch triangle Watermelon
Iced Tea

SNACKS, AT PLANNED TIMES
½ cup Plain Unflavored Yogurt with 2 teaspoons
   Reduced-Calorie Raspberry Spread; 1 small
   Apple

Serving Information
Men and Youth: Add ½ cup Orange Juice, ½
   small Enriched Bagel, ½ Hamburger Roll, and
   ½ cup Raspberries
Youth: Add 1 cup Skim Milk

DAY 6

MORNING MEAL
Fruited Bread Pudding
¼ cup Skim Milk
Coffee or Tea

MIDDAY MEAL
3–4 ounces Tuna
Tomato Slices with 2 tablespoons Chopped
   Scallion and 2 teaspoons Reduced-Calorie
   Mayonnaise
1 slice Pumpernickel Bread
Banana-Prune Pudding

EVENING MEAL
3–4 ounces Broiled Veal Chop
Cauliflower with Mushroom Sauce
Romaine and Cucumber Salad with **Savory
   Vinaigrette**
1 slice Enriched Bread
½ cup Orange-Flavored Gelatin

SNACKS, AT PLANNED TIMES
Celery and Carrot Sticks with **Curry Dip;**
   ½ small Cantaloupe

Serving Information
Men and Youth: Add ⅔ cup Apple Juice, 1 slice
   Pumpernickel Bread, 20 Oyster Crackers, and
   1 cup Strawberries
Youth: Add 1¾ cups Skim Milk

DAY 7

MORNING MEAL
1 medium Kiwi Fruit or 2 tablespoons Raisins
¾ ounce Ready-to-Eat Cereal
½ cup Skim Milk
Coffee or Tea

MIDDAY MEAL
⅔ cup Cottage Cheese and 2 Canned Pineapple
   Slices on Lettuce topped with 2 tablespoons
   Juice
3 Melba Toast Rounds
Iced Coffee with 3 tablespoons Skim Milk

EVENING MEAL
½ medium Grapefruit
Broccoli Quiche
Watercress and Bibb Lettuce Salad with
   2 teaspoons Low-Calorie French Dressing
1 ounce Enriched French Bread
1 teaspoon Margarine
Spiced Pumpkin Cake
Coffee or Tea

SNACKS, AT PLANNED TIMES
½ cup Butterscotch-Flavored Low-Calorie Milk
   Pudding; 8 fluid ounces Beer

Serving Information
Men and Youth: Add 10 large Cherries and 6
   Saltines
Youth: Add 1½ cups Skim Milk

Two ingredients whose origins are lost in the mists of history appear in this week's menu plan: parsley and honey.

Parsley comes to us from the ancient Greek *petrose linon,* or "celery growing among rocks." This hardy biennial herb originated in the Mediterranean area, where it had symbolic as well as culinary uses.

Ancient Egyptians sprinkled it over the graves of their dead. In ancient Greece and Rome, the bodies of the deceased were strewn with parsley. In Old England, when one was said to be "in need of parsley," one was breathing his last.

Honey is the oldest sweetener known to man. Until sugarcane was discovered in the New World, honey was the only sweet substance available. In literature, from the Bible to Winnie the Pooh, honey is equated with happiness.

Parsley appears in Canadian Parsley Soup (Day 3). Honey flavors Honey-Stewed Prunes (Day 7).

WEEK 31

DAY 1

MORNING MEAL
½ medium Grapefruit, spread with ½ teaspoon Honey and broiled
1 Poached Egg
1 slice Toasted Cracked Wheat Bread
1 teaspoon Margarine
¼ cup Skim Milk
Coffee or Tea

MIDDAY MEAL
Chick Pea Croquettes (Falafel)
½ medium Tomato, sliced
Tossed Salad with Green Bell Pepper Rings and 1 teaspoon Vegetable Oil plus Wine Vinegar
1 ounce Pita Bread
½ cup Fruit Salad

EVENING MEAL
1 cup Tomato Juice
3–4 ounces Baked Sea Bass
½ cup Baked Acorn Squash
½ cup Steamed Spinach
Green Salad with **Cider Vinaigrette**
½ cup Cherry-Flavored Low-Calorie Gelatin

SNACKS, AT PLANNED TIMES
1 small Nectarine; 1 Graham Cracker; ¾ cup Skim Milk

Serving Information
Men and Youth: Add ½ cup Fruit Salad, 1 ounce Enriched Roll, and 2 Graham Crackers
Men: Add ½ ounce Shredded Swiss Cheese to Salad at the Midday Meal
Youth: Add 2 cups Skim Milk

DAY 4

MORNING MEAL
Cereal with Spiced Fruit Ambrosia
1 slice Toasted Whole Wheat Bread
1 teaspoon Reduced-Calorie Margarine
¼ cup Skim Milk
Coffee or Tea

MIDDAY MEAL
3–4 ounces Broiled Chicken Livers
½ cup Steamed Mushrooms
Sliced Cucumber and Radishes on Lettuce with **Dijon-Herb Dressing**
2 Canned Pear Halves with 2 tablespoons Juice

EVENING MEAL
3–4 ounces Broiled Veal Chop
½ cup Cooked Artichoke Hearts
½ cup Cooked Wax Beans
Cole Slaw Vinaigrette
1 slice Pumpernickel Bread
1 cup Honeydew or Cantaloupe Balls

SNACKS, AT PLANNED TIMES
1 cup Mixed Vegetable Juice with 10 Oyster Crackers; ¾ cup Skim Milk; 1 Graham Cracker

Serving Information
Men and Youth: Add ½ cup Orange Juice, 1 slice Enriched Bread, and 2 Canned Pear Halves with 2 tablespoons Juice
Youth: Add 1¼ cups Skim Milk

DAY 5

MORNING MEAL
⅓ cup Apple Juice
Open-Face Grilled Cheese Sandwich I
½ cup Skim Milk
Coffee or Tea

MIDDAY MEAL
¾ cup **Vegetable Broth**
Salmon Salad on Lettuce
Rice Crisps
Carrot, Zucchini, and Red Bell Pepper Sticks
½ cup Raspberry-Flavored Low-Calorie Gelatin with ¼ cup Plain Unflavored Yogurt

EVENING MEAL
Steak Pizzaiola
1 cup Steamed Broccoli
Tossed Salad with **Savory Vinaigrette**
8 fluid ounces Beer

SNACKS, AT PLANNED TIMES
½ small Mango or ½ medium Grapefruit; 10 large Cherries; ¾ cup Buttermilk

Serving Information
Men and Youth: Add ⅓ cup Apple Juice, 2 ounces Whole Wheat Roll, and 10 large Cherries
Youth: Add 1 cup Skim Milk

DAY 2

MORNING MEAL
½ medium Banana, sliced
¾ ounce Ready-to-Eat Cereal
¾ cup Skim Milk
Coffee or Tea

MIDDAY MEAL
Peach and Cottage Cheese Mold
Alfalfa or Bean Sprouts on Lettuce with
    Basic Vinaigrette
1 ounce Enriched Roll
1 teaspoon Reduced-Calorie Margarine
Lemonade

EVENING MEAL
3–4 ounces Broiled Lamb Chop
½ cup Cooked Beets
½ cup Cooked Asparagus Tips
Shredded Cabbage with Grated Carrot and
    1 teaspoon Mayonnaise
1 slice Rye Bread
1 teaspoon Reduced-Calorie Margarine
Sparkling Mineral Water with Twist of Lime

SNACKS, AT PLANNED TIMES
1 cup Mixed Vegetable Juice; 1 cup
    Strawberries; 1 serving Vanilla-Flavored
    Low-Calorie Milk Beverage

Serving Information
Men and Youth: Add ½ medium Banana, sliced,
    1 ounce Enriched Roll, 1 small Orange, and 6
    Saltines
Youth: Add 2 cups Skim Milk

DAY 3

MORNING MEAL
½ cup Orange Sections
1 Scrambled Egg with Chives
½ English Muffin, toasted
1 teaspoon Margarine
1 teaspoon Reduced-Calorie Apricot Spread
¼ cup Skim Milk
Coffee or Tea

MIDDAY MEAL
Canadian Parsley Soup
3–4 ounces Sliced Roast Turkey Breast
Tossed Salad with 1 teaspoon Vegetable Oil
    plus Cider Vinegar
1 slice Enriched Bread
¾ cup Skim Milk

EVENING MEAL
3–4 ounces Baked Perch
Broiled Tomato
½ cup Steamed Cauliflower
Green Salad with **Russian Dressing**
4 fluid ounces White Wine
3-inch x 1½-inch triangle Watermelon

SNACKS, AT PLANNED TIMES
½ cup Blueberries; ½ cup Plain Unflavored
    Yogurt; 1 cup Plain Popcorn; Diet Soda

Serving Information
Men and Youth: Add ½ cup Orange Sections,
    ½ English Muffin, toasted, 1 slice Rye Bread,
    ½ cup Blueberries, and 1 small Apple
Youth: Add 1 cup Skim Milk

DAY 6

MORNING MEAL
1 medium Peach, sliced
¾ ounce Ready-to-Eat Cereal
1 cup Skim Milk
Coffee or Tea

MIDDAY MEAL
3 tablespoons Peanut Butter on 1 slice Enriched
    Bread with 2 teaspoons Reduced-Calorie
    Strawberry Spread
Green Salad with Lemon Juice
Club Soda with Twist of Lemon

EVENING MEAL
Crêpes Divan
½ cup Steamed Chinese Pea Pods
Sliced Tomato and Bean Sprouts on Lettuce
Sparkling Mineral Water with Mint Sprig

SNACKS, AT PLANNED TIMES
1 small Orange; **Baked Apple**; ¾ cup Skim Milk

Serving Information
Men and Youth: Add ½ cup Grapefruit Juice, 1
    slice Toasted Rye Bread, and 2 Graham Crackers
Youth: Add 2 cups Skim Milk

DAY 7

MORNING MEAL
Honey-Stewed Prunes
1 Sunnyside-Up Egg
½ English Muffin, toasted
1 teaspoon Margarine
½ teaspoon Honey
½ cup Skim Milk
Coffee or Tea

MIDDAY MEAL
3–4 ounces Poached Fillet of Sole
½ cup Cooked Green Beans
Tossed Salad with 1 teaspoon Vegetable Oil plus
    Wine Vinegar and Herbs
½ cup Lemon-Flavored Low-Calorie Gelatin
½ cup Skim Milk
Coffee or Tea

EVENING MEAL
3–4 ounces Roast Beef
4 ounces Baked Potato
1 teaspoon Margarine
½ cup Steamed Brussels Sprouts
Green Salad with Lemon Juice
4 fluid ounces Red Wine
Coffee or Tea

SNACKS, AT PLANNED TIMES
1 medium Kiwi Fruit or 1 small Orange;
    Pear Frozen Yogurt

Serving Information
Men and Youth: Add ½ English Muffin, toasted,
    ½ small Cantaloupe, and 1 ounce Whole Wheat
    Roll
Youth: Add 1 cup Skim Milk

The sunchoke is the root of a variety of sunflower plant. It is commonly known as the Jerusalem artichoke, which is somewhat inaccurate since it has no connection with either Jerusalem or artichokes.

When cooked, this native North American tuber tastes slightly like an artichoke. Perhaps that, in combination with its sunflower genealogy, is how the name "sunchoke" originated. Broiled, sautéed, or mashed, the sunchoke makes an interesting substitute for potatoes.

Eaten raw, its texture is crisp and crunchy, its flavor delicately nutty. Raw sunchokes may be sliced and used in salads, as a garnish for soups, or as crudités.

When buying sunchokes, look for unblemished vegetables that resemble knotty potatoes or fresh ginger root. If you grow them in your garden, note that they can be harvested all winter!

Try sunchokes in Sunchoke and Kraut Salad (Day 4).

WEEK 32

DAY 1

MORNING MEAL
½ cup Grapefruit Juice
Cornmeal-Swiss Bake
¼ cup Skim Milk
Coffee or Tea

MIDDAY MEAL
3–4 ounces Sliced Roast Turkey
½ medium Tomato, sliced
Lettuce Leaves
1 ounce Pita Bread
1 teaspoon Mayonnaise
Sparkling Mineral Water with Twist of Lemon

EVENING MEAL
3–4 ounces Sautéed Chicken Livers, using
    1 teaspoon Margarine
¼ cup Steamed Onion Rings
½ cup Steamed Sliced Carrot
Tossed Salad with 1 teaspoon Vegetable Oil
    plus Wine Vinegar
½ cup Fruit Salad

SNACKS, AT PLANNED TIMES
¾ cup Skim Milk; 2 Graham Crackers;
    Banana "Cream"

Serving Information
Men and Youth: Add ½ cup Grapefruit Juice,
    1 ounce Pita Bread, and ½ cup Fruit Salad
Youth: Add 2 cups Skim Milk

DAY 4

MORNING MEAL
½ small Cantaloupe
1 Scrambled Egg with 1 teaspoon Imitation
    Bacon Bits
1 slice Toasted Enriched Bread
1 teaspoon Margarine
½ cup Skim Milk
Coffee or Tea

MIDDAY MEAL
3–4 ounces Tuna with 2 teaspoons Reduced-
    Calorie Mayonnaise
Sunchoke and Kraut Salad
1 slice Pumpernickel Bread
¾ cup Buttermilk

EVENING MEAL
Honeyed Turkey with Broccoli
½ cup Cooked Yellow Straightneck Squash
Green Salad with Wine Vinegar and Garlic
½ cup Skim Milk
Coffee or Tea

SNACKS, AT PLANNED TIMES
½ cup Canned Fruit Cocktail; ½ cup Watermelon
    Balls; 1 cup Mixed Vegetable Juice with
    Carrot Sticks

Serving Information
Men and Youth: Add 1 slice Toasted Enriched
    Bread, 1 slice Rye Bread, 1 medium Peach, and
    ½ cup Canned Fruit Cocktail
Youth: Add 1 cup Skim Milk

DAY 5

MORNING MEAL
½ medium Banana, sliced
¾ ounce Ready-to-Eat Cereal
1 cup Skim Milk
Coffee or Tea

MIDDAY MEAL
Two-Cheese Herbed Pasta
Tossed Salad with 1½–2 ounces Diced Cooked
    Chicken, 1 teaspoon Sesame Seeds, and 1
    teaspoon Vegetable Oil plus Tarragon Vinegar
1 ounce Enriched Italian Bread
1 teaspoon Reduced-Calorie Margarine
½ cup Cherry-Flavored Low-Calorie Gelatin

EVENING MEAL
Baked Oat-Burgers
¼ cup Cooked Peas
½ cup Cooked Carrot Slices
2 Melba Toast Slices
1 teaspoon Reduced-Calorie Margarine
4 fluid ounces Red Wine
Coffee or Tea

SNACKS, AT PLANNED TIMES
1 cup Strawberries with ¼ cup Plain Unflavored
    Yogurt; 3 ounces Chocolate-Flavored Dietary
    Frozen Dessert

Serving Information
Men and Youth: Add ½ medium Banana, sliced,
    1 ounce Enriched Italian Bread, 2 Melba Toast
    Slices, and 1 small Orange
Youth: Add 1 cup Skim Milk

MORNING MEAL
1/3 cup Pineapple Juice
1 Soft-Cooked Egg
1 slice Toasted Whole Wheat Bread
1 teaspoon Margarine
1/2 cup Skim Milk
Coffee or Tea

MIDDAY MEAL
1 cup Tomato Juice with Lemon Wedge
3–4 ounces Broiled Flounder Fillet
1/2 cup Cooked Sliced Eggplant
Green Salad with **Wine Vinaigrette**
1 cup Honeydew or Cantaloupe Balls

EVENING MEAL
Sesame Chicken with Green Beans
1/2 cup Cooked Beets
Tomato, Cucumber, and Green Bell Pepper Slices
    on Lettuce with Cider Vinegar plus Seasonings
1 ounce Enriched Roll
1/2 cup Skim Milk
Coffee or Tea

SNACKS, AT PLANNED TIMES
1/2 cup Butterscotch-Flavored Low-Calorie Milk
    Pudding; 1/2 cup Canned Sliced Peaches with
    1 teaspoon Shredded Coconut

Serving Information
Men and Youth: Add 1/3 cup Pineapple Juice, 2
    ounces Whole Wheat Roll, and 1/2 cup Canned
    Sliced Peaches
Youth: Add 2 cups Skim Milk

MORNING MEAL
1 small Orange
Cinnamon-Cheese Toast
1/4 cup Skim Milk
Coffee or Tea

MIDDAY MEAL
3–4 ounces Sliced Roast Beef
2 Dill Pickle Spears
Lettuce Leaves
1 slice Rye Bread
1 1/2 teaspoons Mayonnaise
Mineral Water with Twist of Lime

EVENING MEAL
3–4 ounces Broiled Shrimp
1/4 cup Canned Water Chestnuts
1/4 cup Steamed Chinese Pea Pods
Watercress Salad with **Herb Dressing**
4 fluid ounces White Wine
1/4 small Pineapple

SNACKS, AT PLANNED TIMES
Fruited Yogurt Mold; 3/4 cup Skim Milk; 3/4 ounce
    Crispbread with 2 teaspoons Reduced-Calorie
    Apricot Spread

Serving Information
Men and Youth: Add 1 slice Rye Bread, 1 ounce
    Enriched Roll, and 1/4 small Pineapple
Youth: Add 1 cup Skim Milk

MORNING MEAL
1 cup Tomato Juice
1/3 cup Cottage Cheese
1/2 small Enriched Bagel
1/4 cup Skim Milk
Coffee or Tea

MIDDAY MEAL
Egg Salad
1/2 English Muffin, toasted
Green Salad with Lemon Juice
1 small Nectarine
3/4 cup Skim Milk

EVENING MEAL
Green Bean and Red Cabbage Appetizer
3–4 ounces Roast Veal
1/2 cup Brussels Sprouts
Romaine and Chicory Salad with Cider Vinegar
Coffee-Yogurt Shake

SNACKS, AT PLANNED TIMES
2-inch wedge Honeydew; **Mocha Sundae**

Serving Information
Men and Youth: Add 1/2 small Enriched Bagel, 1/2
    English Muffin, toasted, and 1 small Nectarine
Youth: Add 2 cups Skim Milk

MORNING MEAL
1/2 cup Grapefruit Sections
1 serving Hot Cereal, 3/4 ounce uncooked
1 cup Skim Milk
Coffee or Tea

MIDDAY MEAL
Chilled Fish and Rice Salad
Sliced Cucumber and Radishes on Lettuce with
    1 teaspoon Vegetable Oil plus Wine Vinegar
6 Saltines
1 cup Cooked Rhubarb

EVENING MEAL
3–4 ounces Broiled Flank Steak
Vegetable-Stuffed Cabbage Leaves
Tossed Salad with **Dijon-Herb Dressing**
1 ounce Enriched Roll
1 teaspoon Reduced-Calorie Margarine
6 fluid ounces Light Beer

SNACKS, AT PLANNED TIMES
1/2 cup Vanilla-Flavored Low-Calorie Milk Pudding
    sprinkled with 1 teaspoon Shredded Coconut;
    1 small Pear

Serving Information
Men and Youth: Add 1/2 cup Grapefruit Sections
    and 1 ounce Enriched Roll
Youth: Add 1 cup Skim Milk and 3/4 cup Buttermilk

| Gazpacho calls itself vegetable soup, but it's so brimming with summer's bounty that it could be called a liquid salad.

The most widely duplicated gazpacho recipe comes from the Andalusian region of Spain. It's made by thickening a puree of cucumbers, tomatoes, and green peppers with bread crumbs.

In southern Spain, chopped raw onions are a pungent addition. Near Córdoba, gazpacho contains olive oil, vinegar, water, garlic, and almonds. This version is white.

Icy-cold gazpacho is a refreshing antidote to the oppressive heat of summer.

Gazpacho is part of the menu plan for Day 5. Try serving it in soup bowls with frosted rims.

MORNING MEAL
2-inch wedge Honeydew
Caraway-Cheese Toast
½ cup Skim Milk
Coffee or Tea

MIDDAY MEAL
Ginger-Broiled Chicken
¼ cup Cooked Peas
¼ cup Cooked Wax Beans
Tossed Salad with Red Bell Pepper Rings and
    ½ recipe **Yogurt Dressing**
½ cup Cherry-Flavored Low-Calorie Gelatin

EVENING MEAL
Tortilla Bake
½ cup Cooked Spinach
Green Salad with 1¾ teaspoons Vegetable Oil
    plus Tarragon Vinegar
1 ounce Whole Wheat Roll
1 teaspoon Margarine
½ cup Fruit Salad
¼ cup Skim Milk
Coffee or Tea

SNACKS, AT PLANNED TIMES
3 ounces Chocolate-Flavored Dietary Frozen
    Dessert; ¾ cup **Beef Broth**

Serving Information
Men and Youth: Add 10 large Cherries, 2 Graham
    Crackers, 1 ounce Whole Wheat Roll, and ½
    cup Fruit Salad
Youth: Add 1¼ cups Skim Milk

MORNING MEAL
1 small Orange
⅓ cup Part-Skim Ricotta Cheese with 1 teaspoon
    Sesame Seeds
1 slice Pumpernickel Bread
¼ cup Skim Milk
Coffee or Tea

MIDDAY MEAL
3–4 ounces Broiled Calf Liver
¼ cup Onion Rings sautéed in 1 teaspoon
    Margarine
½ cup Steamed Sliced Mushrooms
Tossed Salad with **Cider Vinaigrette**
1 ounce Whole Wheat Roll
¾ cup Skim Milk

EVENING MEAL
Japanese Chicken Salad
½ cup Chilled Cauliflower Florets
½ cup Chilled Blanched Green Beans
Sliced Tomato and Bean Sprouts on Lettuce with
    Lemon Juice
Baked Apple

SNACKS, AT PLANNED TIMES
1 cup Mixed Vegetable Juice with 6 Saltines;
    Pineapple-Yogurt Shake

Serving Information
Men and Youth: Add 1 slice Pumpernickel Bread,
    6 Melba Toast Rounds, and 1 small Pear
Youth: Add 2 cups Skim Milk

MORNING MEAL
⅓ cup Grape Juice
1 ounce Cheddar Cheese
1 slice Toasted Rye Bread
½ cup Skim Milk
Coffee or Tea

MIDDAY MEAL
Gazpacho
3–4 ounces Broiled Fillet of Sole with
    Lemon Wedge
Shredded Cabbage with Grated Carrot and
    1 teaspoon Reduced-Calorie Mayonnaise
½ cup Grapefruit Sections

EVENING MEAL
3–4 ounces Roast Beef
½ cup Cooked Enriched Noodles
½ cup Cooked Kale
Endive and Boston Lettuce Salad with 1 teaspoon
    Vegetable Oil plus Cider Vinegar
½ cup Skim Milk
Coffee or Tea

SNACKS, AT PLANNED TIMES
½ cup Raspberries; ½ cup Plain Unflavored
    Yogurt; ½ cup Orange-Flavored Low-Calorie
    Gelatin

Serving Information
Men and Youth: Add ⅔ cup Grape Juice, 1 slice
    Enriched Bread, 1 ounce Whole Wheat Roll, and
    ½ cup Raspberries
Youth: Add 1 cup Skim Milk

DAY 2

MORNING MEAL
½ medium Grapefruit
¾ ounce Ready-to-Eat Cereal
1 cup Skim Milk
Coffee or Tea

MIDDAY MEAL
⅔ cup Cottage Cheese
½ medium Tomato, sliced
Sliced Cucumber and Radishes on Lettuce with
  Wine Vinaigrette and 1 teaspoon Imitation
  Bacon Bits
1 slice Enriched Bread
1 teaspoon Margarine
Coffee or Tea

EVENING MEAL
Frankfurter Stir-Fry
½ cup Steamed Sliced Zucchini
Tossed Salad with **Dijon-Herb Dressing**
1 slice Rye Bread
Club Soda with Mint Sprig

SNACKS, AT PLANNED TIMES
Frozen Mango Yogurt; Root Beer Froth

Serving Information
Men and Youth: Add 2 tablespoons Raisins, ½
  English Muffin, toasted, 1 slice Enriched Bread,
  and 4 medium Dried Apricot Halves
Men: Add 8 teaspoons Cottage Cheese at the
  Midday Meal
Youth: Add 2 cups Skim Milk

DAY 3

MORNING MEAL
1 cup Strawberries with 2 teaspoons Shredded
  Coconut
1 serving Hot Cereal, ¾ ounce uncooked
1 cup Skim Milk
Coffee or Tea

MIDDAY MEAL
Egg and Prosciutto Melt
Green Salad with 1½ teaspoons Vegetable Oil
  plus Wine Vinegar
1 small Apple

EVENING MEAL
3–4 ounces Broiled Scallops with Lemon Juice
½ cup Cooked Brown Rice
½ cup Cooked Broccoli Florets
Cucumber and Tomato Salad
4 fluid ounces White Wine
Coffee or Tea

SNACKS, AT PLANNED TIMES
½ cup Vanilla-Flavored Low-Calorie Milk
  Pudding; 3-inch x 1½-inch triangle Watermelon

Serving Information
Men and Youth: Add 1 slice Toasted Rye Bread,
  1 ounce Whole Wheat Roll, and ½ cup Canned
  Sliced Peaches
Men: Add ¼ ounce Prosciutto to **Egg and
  Prosciutto Melt**
Youth: Add 1 cup Skim Milk

DAY 6

MORNING MEAL
½ medium Banana, sliced
¾ ounce Ready-to-Eat Cereal
1 cup Skim Milk
Coffee or Tea

MIDDAY MEAL
3–4 ounces Sliced Roast Turkey Breast
Zucchini Sticks
Green Salad with Alfalfa or Bean Sprouts and
  Wine Vinaigrette
2 Melba Toast Slices
1 teaspoon Reduced-Calorie Margarine
½ cup Lemon-Flavored Gelatin

EVENING MEAL
3–4 ounces Broiled Veal Chop
½ cup Steamed Brussels Sprouts
½ cup Steamed Eggplant
Sliced Cucumber on Shredded Red Cabbage
  with 1 teaspoon Mayonnaise
1 slice Enriched Bread
1 teaspoon Reduced-Calorie Margarine
½ small Cantaloupe

SNACKS, AT PLANNED TIMES
1 small Pear; ¾ cup Buttermilk; 2 Graham
  Crackers

Serving Information
Men and Youth: Add ½ medium Banana, 1 slice
  Toasted Whole Wheat Bread, 2 Melba Toast
  Slices, and ½ cup Canned Mandarin Orange
  Sections
Youth: Add 2 cups Skim Milk

DAY 7

MORNING MEAL
⅓ cup Apple Juice
1 ounce Smoked Salmon
½ English Muffin, toasted
1½ teaspoons Reduced-Calorie Margarine
½ cup Skim Milk
Coffee or Tea

MIDDAY MEAL
Mediterranean Eggs in Nest
Tossed Salad with Green Bell Pepper Rings and
  Sesame Vinaigrette
½ cup Skim Milk
Coffee or Tea

EVENING MEAL
Broiled Soft-Shell Crabs
¼ cup Cooked Artichoke Hearts
½ cup Cooked Scallop Squash
Green Salad with Pimiento Strips and Tarragon
  Vinegar
4 fluid ounces White Wine
Coffee or Tea

SNACKS, AT PLANNED TIMES
3 ounces Vanilla-Flavored Dietary Frozen
  Dessert; 1 cup Strawberries with ¼ cup Plain
  Unflavored Yogurt

Serving Information
Men and Youth: Add ⅓ cup Apple Juice, ½
  English Muffin, toasted, ½ cup Orange Sec-
  tions, and 2 Graham Crackers
Youth: Add 1 cup Skim Milk and ¼ cup Plain
  Unflavored Yogurt

The fragrant magic that pesto weaves belies its easy preparation. In Genoa, where pesto originated, fresh basil, garlic, cheese, and olive oil are ground by hand into a paste.

Pesto, which means "pounded," keeps well. Just place it in a jar, but make sure a thin layer of oil has risen to the top before you seal it. Use it in soup, on broiled fish or steak, over green beans, or as a zesty topping for baked potatoes. Team it with spaghetti squash as we do (Day 7), or make pesto bread instead of garlic bread to perk up an Italian dinner.

Spaghetti squash, incidentally, is another culinary misnomer. Neither spaghetti nor squash, the cooked pulp of this eminently edible gourd assumes the appearance of spaghetti. It's equally delicious when topped with other sauces usually used on pasta.

Economy Tip—Baked ham steak is on the menu on Day 2. Leftovers may be frozen and used in Ham 'n' Vegetable Burgers recipe (Week 37, Day 7).

WEEK 34

DAY 1

MORNING MEAL
½ cup Blueberries
¾ ounce Ready-to-Eat Cereal
1 cup Skim Milk
Coffee or Tea

MIDDAY MEAL
⅔ cup Cottage Cheese
½ medium Tomato, diced
¼ cup Grated Carrot
2 Green Olives
1 slice Toasted Rye Bread
1 teaspoon Margarine
Mineral Water with Slice of Lime

EVENING MEAL
¾ cup Tomato Juice with Lemon Wedge
Veal à la Fontina
⅔ cup Cooked Enriched Spaghetti
½ cup Steamed Green Beans
Tossed Salad with **Garlic Vinaigrette**
½ cup Lime-Flavored Low-Calorie Gelatin

SNACKS, AT PLANNED TIMES
½ cup Plain Unflavored Yogurt with 2 tablespoons Raisins; 1 small Orange

Serving Information
Men and Youth: Add ½ cup Blueberries, 1 slice Rye Bread, 1 ounce Enriched Italian Bread, 2 tablespoons Raisins, and ½ cup Canned Fruit Cocktail
Youth: Add 1 cup Skim Milk

DAY 4

MORNING MEAL
1 cup Strawberries
1 serving Hot Cereal, ¾ ounce uncooked
1 teaspoon Margarine
1 cup Skim Milk
Coffee or Tea

MIDDAY MEAL
Liver Manfredi
½ cup Cooked Sliced Zucchini
Green Salad with **Gingered Vinaigrette**
Mineral Water with Slice of Lemon

EVENING MEAL
¾ cup **Vegetable Broth**
3–4 ounces Sliced Roast Turkey
½ cup Cooked Cauliflower Florets
Potato and Green Bean Salad
1 slice Whole Wheat Bread
Lemonade

SNACKS, AT PLANNED TIMES
½ cup Blueberries; ½ cup Plain Unflavored Yogurt; 1 cup Cooked Rhubarb

Serving Information
Men and Youth: Add 1 small Apple and 1 slice Whole Wheat Bread
Youth: Add 2 cups Skim Milk

DAY 5

MORNING MEAL
⅓ cup Pineapple Juice
1 Scrambled Egg with Chives
½ small Enriched Bagel
1 teaspoon Margarine
½ cup Skim Milk
Coffee or Tea

MIDDAY MEAL
3–4 ounces Tuna with 2 teaspoons Reduced-Calorie Mayonnaise and 1 teaspoon Pickle Relish
Sliced Tomato
Lettuce Leaves
1 slice Enriched Bread
½ small Mango or 1 small Nectarine

EVENING MEAL
Chili-Burgers
½ cup Steamed Asparagus Tips
Tossed Salad with 1 teaspoon Vegetable Oil plus Cider Vinegar
½ cup Skim Milk
Coffee or Tea

SNACKS, AT PLANNED TIMES
1 cup Tomato Juice; ½ cup Raspberries with ¼ cup Plain Unflavored Yogurt; 2 Graham Crackers

Serving Information
Men and Youth: Add ⅓ cup Pineapple Juice, ½ small Enriched Bagel, 1 slice Enriched Bread, and ½ cup Raspberries
Youth: Add 1 cup Skim Milk

DAY 2

MORNING MEAL
½ cup Grapefruit Juice
1 Poached Egg
½ English Muffin, toasted
¼ cup Skim Milk □ Coffee or Tea

MIDDAY MEAL
1 cup Mixed Vegetable Juice
Baked Red Snapper
¼ cup Cooked Peas
Sliced Cucumber and Radishes on Lettuce with
    1 teaspoon Vegetable Oil plus Wine Vinegar
1 slice Enriched Bread
¾ cup Skim Milk

EVENING MEAL
3 ounces Baked Ham Steak
½ cup Steamed Sliced Carrot
Sautéed Caraway Cabbage
Green Salad with Green Bell Pepper Rings and
    Cider Vinegar
1 ounce Enriched Roll
Sparkling Mineral Water with Mint Sprig

SNACKS, AT PLANNED TIMES
½ cup Vanilla-Flavored Low-Calorie Milk
    Pudding; 10 large Cherries; 1 cup Watermelon
    Balls

Serving Information
Men and Youth: Add ½ cup Grapefruit Juice, ½
    English Muffin, toasted, 1 ounce Enriched Roll,
    and 10 large Cherries
Men: Add 1 ounce Baked Ham Steak at the
    Evening Meal
Youth: Add 1 cup Skim Milk

DAY 3

MORNING MEAL
½ cup Orange Sections
⅓ cup Part-Skim Ricotta Cheese
1 slice Toasted Raisin Bread
½ cup Skim Milk
Coffee or Tea

MIDDAY MEAL
Mushroom Omelet
Tossed Salad with Bean Sprouts and 1 tablespoon
    Low-Calorie French Dressing
1 ounce Whole Wheat Roll
1 teaspoon Margarine
½ cup Cherry-Flavored Low-Calorie Gelatin
½ cup Skim Milk
Coffee or Tea

EVENING MEAL
Frogs' Legs Meunière
½ cup Steamed Broccoli
½ cup Steamed Wax Beans
Sliced Tomato on Lettuce with Lemon Juice
4 fluid ounces White Wine
Coffee or Tea

SNACKS, AT PLANNED TIMES
1 small Pear; ¾ cup Buttermilk; ½ cup Fruit
    Salad with 1 teaspoon Shredded Coconut

Serving Information
Men and Youth: Add 1 slice Toasted Raisin Bread,
    ½ medium Banana, sliced, ½ cup Fruit Salad,
    and 2 Graham Crackers
Youth: Add 2 cups Skim Milk

DAY 6

MORNING MEAL
½ cup Applesauce
1 ounce Cheddar Cheese
1 slice Toasted Pumpernickel Bread
¼ cup Skim Milk
Coffee or Tea

MIDDAY MEAL
3–4 ounces Broiled Chicken Breast
½ cup Cooked Spinach
Romaine Lettuce Salad with **Dill Vinaigrette**
Sparkling Mineral Water

EVENING MEAL
Sea Trout with Mushroom Stuffing
1 medium Ear Corn, boiled
¼ cup Cooked Sliced Beets
Endive with 5 Cherry Tomatoes, halved, and
    1 teaspoon Reduced-Calorie Mayonnaise
½ cup Strawberry-Flavored Gelatin
¾ cup Skim Milk

SNACKS, AT PLANNED TIMES
¾ cup Buttermilk; ½ medium Banana; 1 cup
    Honeydew or Cantaloupe Balls

Serving Information
Men and Youth: Add ½ cup Applesauce, 1 slice
    Toasted Pumpernickel Bread, 1 ounce Whole
    Wheat Roll, and ½ medium Banana
Youth: Add 2 cups Skim Milk

DAY 7

MORNING MEAL
2 tablespoons Raisins or ½ cup Fruit Salad
¾ ounce Ready-to-Eat Cereal
1 cup Skim Milk
Coffee or Tea

MIDDAY MEAL
Tossed Salad with 3 ounces Canned Chick Peas
    (Garbanzos) and **Dijon-Herb Dressing**
1 ounce Enriched Roll
Peanut Butter Fudge

EVENING MEAL
3–4 ounces Broiled Steak
Spaghetti Squash Pesto
½ cup Cooked Cauliflower
Green Salad with **Sesame Vinaigrette**
1 slice Rye Bread
8 fluid ounces Beer

SNACKS, AT PLANNED TIMES
3 medium Dried Apricot Halves; ½ cup Skim
    Milk; ½ medium Papaya or ½ small
    Cantaloupe

Serving Information
Men and Youth: Add 2 tablespoons Raisins, 1
    ounce Enriched Roll, and 1 slice Rye Bread
Men: Add 1 ounce Chick Peas (Garbanzos) at the
    Midday Meal
Youth: Add 1½ cups Skim Milk

Stir-frying, the main method of preparing Chinese dishes, has become popular in the United States. It involves constant stirring, turning, and tossing of foods in a little bit of oil over high heat.

You can use a traditional wok or a flat-bottomed skillet. The shape of the wok, however, makes it ideal for serious stir-frying. It needs less oil than a skillet, has a larger surface area so foods cook more quickly, withstands very high heat, and is unlikely to overflow.

To stir-fry, have all the ingredients specified in the recipe set out and prepared. Solid ingredients should be cut to similar sizes and shapes so they will cook evenly. Vegetables should be stir-fried just until their natural color intensifies.

Practice your stir-frying technique with Stir-Fried Cabbage 'n' Squash (Day 5). Remember that most stir-fried dishes should not be rewarmed. To preserve their crisp texture, serve them immediately.

MORNING MEAL
½ cup Grapefruit Sections
Open-Face Grilled Cheese Sandwich I
¼ cup Skim Milk
Coffee or Tea

MIDDAY MEAL
Celery-Ricotta Bake
Lettuce and Red Bell Pepper Salad with
  Savory Vinaigrette
Oatmeal-Raisin Loaf
Coffee or Tea

EVENING MEAL
Blueberry Soup
3–4 ounces Broiled Chicken
½ cup Cooked Brussels Sprouts
Bean Salad
¼ small Cantaloupe
¼ cup Skim Milk
Coffee or Tea

SNACKS, AT PLANNED TIMES
½ English Muffin, toasted, with 1 teaspoon
  Margarine; ½ cup Cherry-Flavored Low-
  Calorie Gelatin with ¼ cup Plain Unflavored
  Yogurt

Serving Information
Men and Youth: Add 1 ounce Enriched Roll, 1
  slice Pumpernickel Bread, ¼ small Cantaloupe,
  and ½ cup Fruit Salad
Youth: Add 1½ cups Skim Milk

MORNING MEAL
⅓ cup Pineapple Juice
Applesauce Oatmeal
1 slice Toasted Whole Wheat Bread
1 teaspoon Margarine
¼ cup Skim Milk ☐ Coffee or Tea

MIDDAY MEAL
3–4 ounces Broiled Beef Liver
¼ cup Cooked Sliced Onion
Zucchini Spaghetti
Watercress and Bibb Lettuce Salad with
  Lemon Salad Dressing
2-inch wedge Honeydew
¼ cup Skim Milk ☐ Coffee or Tea

EVENING MEAL
3–4 ounces Roast Veal
Eggplant Stuffing
½ cup Cooked Broccoli Spears
Romaine and Sliced Radish Salad with
  1 teaspoon Reduced-Calorie Mayonnaise
½ cup Chocolate-Flavored Low-Calorie Milk
  Pudding

SNACKS, AT PLANNED TIMES
½ cup Orange-Flavored Gelatin with ¼ cup
  Canned Mandarin Orange Sections; 1 cup
  Plain Popcorn

Serving Information
Men and Youth: Add ⅓ cup Pineapple Juice,
  2-inch wedge Honeydew, 2 ounces Enriched
  French Bread, and ¼ cup Canned Mandarin
  Orange Sections
Youth: Add 2 cups Skim Milk

MORNING MEAL
½ cup Orange Sections
1 Poached Egg
1 slice Toasted Rye Bread
1 teaspoon Margarine
¼ cup Skim Milk
Coffee or Tea

MIDDAY MEAL
3–4 ounces Sliced Roast Turkey
Stir-Fried Cabbage 'n' Squash
6 medium Cooked Asparagus Spears
1 ounce Enriched Roll
1 teaspoon Reduced-Calorie Margarine
1 cup Watermelon Chunks

EVENING MEAL
1 cup Tomato Juice
Marinated Chuck Steak
¼ cup Cooked Artichoke Hearts
½ cup Cooked Celery
Escarole with 2 tablespoons Sliced Canned
  Water Chestnuts and **Wine Vinaigrette**
3 ounces Vanilla-Flavored Dietary Frozen Dessert

SNACKS, AT PLANNED TIMES
1 cup Skim Milk; 2 Graham Crackers;
  Mushrooms and Cauliflower Florets with
  Curry Dip

Serving Information
Men and Youth: Add ⅔ cup Grape Juice, 1 ounce
  Enriched Roll, and 10 large Cherries
Youth: Add 1¾ cups Skim Milk

DAY 2

MORNING MEAL
1 cup Strawberries
¾ ounce Ready-to-Eat Cereal
½ cup Skim Milk
Coffee or Tea

MIDDAY MEAL
Pan-Broiled Snappers
4 ounces Baked Potato
½ cup Cooked Sliced Zucchini
Tomato Slices on Lettuce with 1½ teaspoons
    Mayonnaise
3 Melba Toast Rounds
½ cup Applesauce with 3 tablespoons Plain
    Unflavored Yogurt

EVENING MEAL
Cucumber-Ham Bake
½ cup Cooked Spaghetti Squash
½ cup Cooked Green Beans
1 ounce Enriched Roll
1 teaspoon Margarine
1 small Pear

SNACKS, AT PLANNED TIMES
½ cup Vanilla-Flavored Low-Calorie Milk
    Pudding; 4 fluid ounces Red Wine

Serving Information
Men and Youth: Add 1 slice Enriched Bread, 2
    Graham Crackers, and 4 Dates
Men: Add 4 teaspoons Cottage Cheese to Salad
    at the Midday Meal
Youth: Add 1½ cups Skim Milk

DAY 3

MORNING MEAL
½ cup Orange Juice
Cinnamon-Cheese Toast
¼ cup Skim Milk
Coffee or Tea

MIDDAY MEAL
2 Eggs scrambled in 1 teaspoon Margarine
Tossed Salad with ¼ recipe **Yogurt Dressing**
½ small Enriched Bagel with 1 teaspoon
    Reduced-Calorie Grape Spread
Pineapple-Mango "Ice Cream"

EVENING MEAL
Broiled Soft-Shell Crabs
½ cup Steamed Chinese Pea Pods
½ cup Steamed Cauliflower
Alfalfa or Bean Sprouts on Lettuce with **Oregano
    Vinaigrette**
½ cup Plain Unflavored Yogurt with 1 teaspoon
    Honey

SNACKS, AT PLANNED TIMES
1 cup Mixed Vegetable Juice; 1 medium Peach

Serving Information
Men and Youth: Add ½ small Enriched Bagel, 6
    Saltines, and 2 tablespoons Raisins
Youth: Add 1¾ cups Skim Milk

DAY 6

MORNING MEAL
½ small Cantaloupe
⅓ cup Part-Skim Ricotta Cheese
½ English Muffin, toasted
1 teaspoon Margarine
¼ cup Skim Milk
Coffee or Tea

MIDDAY MEAL
Creamed Shrimp Pasta
Red and Green Bell Pepper Strips on Lettuce with
    Cider Vinegar
1 small Apple
Lime Cooler

EVENING MEAL
Chili-Cheese Rarebit
¼ cup Cooked Peas with 2 tablespoons Cooked
    Pearl Onions
½ cup Steamed Summer Squash Slices
½ cup Fruit Salad
¼ cup Skim Milk
Coffee or Tea

SNACKS, AT PLANNED TIMES
¾ cup Buttermilk; ½ cup Cherry-Flavored
    Low-Calorie Gelatin

Serving Information
Men and Youth: Add ½ English Muffin, toasted,
    1 slice Whole Wheat Bread, and ½ cup Canned
    Sliced Peaches
Youth: Add 1½ cups Skim Milk

DAY 7

MORNING MEAL
½ medium Banana, sliced
¾ ounce Ready-to-Eat Cereal
½ cup Skim Milk
Coffee or Tea

MIDDAY MEAL
Chilled Cucumber Soup with 20 Oyster Crackers
Tomato Slices sprinkled with 1 tablespoon
    Chopped Scallion on Lettuce with **Tarragon
    Vinaigrette**
Peanut Butter Custard Cups

EVENING MEAL
3–4 ounces Broiled Lamb Chop
¼ cup Baked Butternut Squash
Minted Carrots
1 slice Enriched Bread
1 teaspoon Margarine
Sparkling Mineral Water with Twist of Lemon

SNACKS, AT PLANNED TIMES
12 fluid ounces Light Beer; ½ medium Papaya
    or 1 small Orange

Serving Information
Men and Youth: Add ½ cup Grapefruit Juice,
    1 slice Pumpernickel Bread, 6 Melba Toast
    Rounds, and ½ cup Canned Fruit Cocktail
Youth: Add 2 cups Skim Milk

Although Labor Day is on the horizon, fresh summer produce is still abundant. Your shopping list for this week should include apples, beets, and rutabagas, as well as cantaloupe, lettuce, tomatoes, and cucumbers.

Two unusual and delicious combinations this week are Apple-Beet Relish (Day 6) and Ham and Rutabaga Dice (Day 3).

Economy Tip—Broiled chicken breast is on the menu on Day 2 and roast chicken on Day 4. Since chicken breasts are generally more expensive per pound than whole chickens, buy chickens whole and cut them up yourself. Freeze the uncooked necks and backs for Chicken and Legumes Casserole recipe (Week 43, Day 1 and Week 46, Day 1). For this week, broil the breast portions for Day 2, and roast the remaining pieces for Day 4. Leftovers may be frozen and used in Crêpes Divan recipe (Week 37, Day 1) and in Lunch Box Chick Pea Sandwich recipe (Week 38, Day 1).

WEEK 36

DAY 1

MORNING MEAL
½ small Cantaloupe
⅓ cup Cottage Cheese sprinkled with Cinnamon
6 Melba Toast Rounds
1 teaspoon Reduced-Calorie Margarine
¼ cup Skim Milk
Coffee or Tea

MIDDAY MEAL
Reuben Sandwich
½ medium Tomato, sliced
Lettuce Leaves
1 teaspoon Mayonnaise
1 small Pear
¾ cup Skim Milk

EVENING MEAL
3–4 ounces Broiled Flounder Fillet with Lemon Wedge
4 ounces Baked Potato
1½ teaspoons Margarine
6 medium Steamed Asparagus Spears
Curried Cole Slaw
8 fluid ounces Beer

SNACKS, AT PLANNED TIMES
½ cup Plain Unflavored Yogurt; 1 cup Strawberries; ½ cup Orange-Flavored Low-Calorie Gelatin

Serving Information
Men and Youth: Add 2 ounces Whole Wheat Roll and ½ cup Orange Sections
Youth: Add 1 cup Skim Milk

DAY 4

MORNING MEAL
⅓ cup Apple Juice
Scramble 'n' Spinach
½ English Muffin, toasted
1 teaspoon Reduced-Calorie Margarine
½ cup Skim Milk
Coffee or Tea

MIDDAY MEAL
Lunch Box Veal
Tossed Salad with **Dijon-Herb Dressing**
1 slice Pumpernickel Bread
1 cup Honeydew Balls

EVENING MEAL
3–4 ounces Roast Chicken
½ cup Cooked Enriched Rice
½ cup Steamed Green Beans
Sliced Tomato and Radishes on Lettuce with **Garlic Vinaigrette**
Club Soda with Mint Sprig

SNACKS, AT PLANNED TIMES
3 ounces Chocolate-Flavored Dietary Frozen Dessert; **Root Beer Froth**

Serving Information
Men and Youth: Add ⅓ cup Apple Juice, ½ English Muffin, toasted, and 1 small Apple
Youth: Add 1½ cups Skim Milk

DAY 5

MORNING MEAL
1 cup Strawberries
1 serving Hot Cereal, ¾ ounce uncooked, with 1 teaspoon Maple Syrup
1 cup Skim Milk
Coffee or Tea

MIDDAY MEAL
⅔ cup Cottage Cheese in 1 medium Green Bell Pepper
Red Bell Pepper and Zucchini Sticks
2 Green Olives
1 slice Rye Bread
1 teaspoon Margarine
Mineral Water with Slice of Lime

EVENING MEAL
3–4 ounces Sautéed Chicken Livers, using 1 teaspoon Margarine
¼ cup Steamed Onion Rings
½ cup Steamed Mushrooms
Green Salad with 1 teaspoon Vegetable Oil plus Cider Vinegar
½ cup Grapefruit Sections

SNACKS, AT PLANNED TIMES
1 cup Cooked Rhubarb; 2 Graham Crackers; **Lime Yogurt Dip with Crudités**

Serving Information
Men and Youth: Add ½ cup Orange Juice, 1 slice Rye Bread, 2 ounces Whole Wheat Roll, and ½ cup Grapefruit Sections
Youth: Add 2 cups Skim Milk

DAY 2

MORNING MEAL
½ cup Orange Juice
Pancakes
1 teaspoon Low-Calorie Maple Syrup
¼ cup Skim Milk
Coffee or Tea

MIDDAY MEAL
3–4 ounces Sardines
¼ cup Onion Rings
Sliced Cucumber on Lettuce with
   Sesame Vinaigrette
1 slice Enriched Bread
2 medium Plums

EVENING MEAL
3–4 ounces Broiled Chicken Breast
Baked Broccoli with Mustard Sauce
Tossed Salad with **Lemon Salad Dressing**
1 slice Whole Wheat Bread
Sparkling Mineral Water with Twist of Lemon

SNACKS, AT PLANNED TIMES
1 cup Mixed Vegetable Juice with 10 Oyster
   Crackers; ½ cup Fruit Salad; ¾ cup
   Buttermilk

Serving Information
Men and Youth: Add ½ cup Orange Juice, 1 slice
   Enriched Bread, and ½ cup Fruit Salad
Youth: Add 1¾ cups Skim Milk

DAY 3

MORNING MEAL
½ medium Grapefruit
¾ ounce Ready-to-Eat Cereal
1 cup Skim Milk
Coffee or Tea

MIDDAY MEAL
Ham and Rutabaga Dice
Endive and Watercress Salad with 1 teaspoon
   Vegetable Oil plus Wine Vinegar
1 ounce Enriched Roll
½ cup Lime-Flavored Low-Calorie Gelatin

EVENING MEAL
3–4 ounces Baked Scallops
½ cup Steamed Kale
½ cup Steamed Sliced Carrot
Green Salad with Lemon Juice
Garlic Bread
4 fluid ounces White Wine
Coffee or Tea

SNACKS, AT PLANNED TIMES
½ cup Vanilla-Flavored Low-Calorie Milk
   Pudding; ½ cup Canned Sliced Peaches;
   ¼ small Pineapple

Serving Information
Men and Youth: Add 2 tablespoons Raisins, ½
   English Muffin, toasted, 1 ounce Enriched Roll,
   ½ cup Canned Mandarin Orange Sections, and
   ½ cup Canned Sliced Peaches
Men: Add 1 ounce Baked Scallops at the Evening
   Meal
Youth: Add 1 cup Skim Milk

DAY 6

MORNING MEAL
1 medium Kiwi Fruit or ½ medium Grapefruit
1 tablespoon Peanut Butter
2 teaspoons Reduced-Calorie Strawberry Spread
½ Matzo Board
¼ cup Skim Milk
Coffee or Tea

MIDDAY MEAL
French Omelet
½ medium Tomato, sliced
Tossed Salad with Lemon Juice
½ small Enriched Bagel
½ cup Melon Balls

EVENING MEAL
3–4 ounces Baked Bluefish
½ cup Baked Sliced Eggplant
½ cup Cooked Spinach
Apple-Beet Relish
½ cup Chocolate-Flavored Low-Calorie Milk
   Pudding

SNACKS, AT PLANNED TIMES
½ cup Canned Fruit Cocktail with 1 teaspoon
   Shredded Coconut; ¾ cup Skim Milk

Serving Information
Men and Youth: Add ½ Matzo Board, ½ small
   Enriched Bagel, and ½ cup Canned Fruit
   Cocktail
Youth: Add 2 cups Skim Milk

DAY 7

MORNING MEAL
½ small Mango or 1 cup Strawberries
¾ ounce Ready-to-Eat Cereal
1 cup Skim Milk
Coffee or Tea

MIDDAY MEAL
3–4 ounces Tuna with ¼ cup Diced Celery and
   2 teaspoons Reduced-Calorie Mayonnaise
Lettuce Leaves
2 Dill Pickle Spears
1 slice Whole Wheat Bread
Sparkling Mineral Water with Twist of Lemon

EVENING MEAL
3–4 ounces Broiled Steak
½ cup Cooked Enriched Noodles with 1 teaspoon
   Reduced-Calorie Margarine
½ cup Steamed Mushroom Caps
½ cup Steamed Broccoli
Sliced Green Bell Pepper and Radishes on
   Lettuce with **Dill Vinaigrette**
4 fluid ounces Red Wine
Spiced Pineapple Pumpkin

SNACKS, AT PLANNED TIMES
2 Graham Crackers; ½ cup Plain Unflavored
   Yogurt with ¼ cup Blueberries

Serving Information
Men and Youth: Add 1 slice Whole Wheat Bread,
   2 medium Plums, and 1 ounce Enriched Roll
Youth: Add 2 cups Skim Milk

Kasha (buckwheat groats) is similar to grits (see Week 3). Both are coarsely ground cereal grains. But where grits is a staple of American Southern cooking, kasha is a traditionally Russian dish.

Kasha is also found in the diets of the Germans, English, Scandinavians, and Slavs. Folklore has it that this unrefined, nutritious cereal contributes to good health.

Because it's an old-fashioned, unrefined, unglamorous product, kasha was unpopular for a number of years. Now, that old-fashioned has been redefined as "hearty," unrefined as "healthy," and unglamorous as "economical," kasha is being rediscovered. Try it and draw your own conclusions.

Groats (for Kasha Mix, Day 6) can be found in grocery and health food stores, or at local mills that specialize in grinding "old-fashioned" cereals.

DAY 1

MORNING MEAL
Coffee-Cheese Delight
¼ cup Skim Milk
Coffee or Tea

MIDDAY MEAL
Tomato Soup
Crêpes Divan
Watercress and Alfalfa or Bean Sprout Salad
  with **Wine Vinaigrette**
¼ small Cantaloupe

EVENING MEAL
Papaya Shrimp
½ cup Cooked Broccoli
½ cup Cooked Sliced Carrot
Romaine and Sliced Cucumber Salad with
  1 teaspoon Olive Oil plus Cider Vinegar
½ cup Orange Sections

SNACKS, AT PLANNED TIMES
1 serving Chocolate-Flavored Low-Calorie Milk
  Beverage; Celery and Zucchini Sticks with
  ½ recipe **Yogurt Dip**

Serving Information
Men and Youth: Add 1 cup Strawberries, ¼ small
  Cantaloupe, 2 Graham Crackers, and 1 slice
  Enriched Bread
Youth: Add 1¾ cups Skim Milk

DAY 4

MORNING MEAL
½ medium Grapefruit
¾ ounce Ready-to-Eat Cereal
½ cup Skim Milk
Coffee or Tea

MIDDAY MEAL
Tuna-Potato Cakes
¼ cup Cooked Peas with ¼ cup Cooked Sliced
  Mushrooms
Tomato and Green Bell Pepper Slices on Lettuce
  with 1 teaspoon Mayonnaise
Baked Apple
¼ cup Skim Milk
Coffee or Tea

EVENING MEAL
Chilled Tomato Appetizer
Crisp "Oven-Fried" Chicken
½ cup Steamed Whole Green Beans
Cole Slaw Vinaigrette
1 ounce Enriched Roll
½ cup Cherry-Flavored Low-Calorie Gelatin

SNACKS, AT PLANNED TIMES
½ cup Blueberries with 2 tablespoons Plain
  Unflavored Yogurt; ½ cup Vanilla-Flavored
  Low-Calorie Milk Pudding

Serving Information
Men and Youth: Add ½ medium Banana, 1 Ham-
  burger Roll, and 10 large Cherries
Youth: Add 2 cups Skim Milk

DAY 5

MORNING MEAL
⅓ cup Grape Juice
Cinnamon-Cheese Toast
¼ cup Skim Milk
Coffee or Tea

MIDDAY MEAL
Curried Meat Hash
Lettuce and Sliced Radish Salad with
  Vinaigrette Parmesan
1 ounce Pita Bread
½ cup Plain Unflavored Yogurt with 2
  tablespoons Canned Crushed Pineapple

EVENING MEAL
Fillet of Sole Florentine
¼ cup Baked Acorn Squash
½ cup Steamed French-Style Green Beans
1 ounce Enriched Italian Bread
1 teaspoon Reduced-Calorie Margarine
4 fluid ounces White Wine
¼ cup Skim Milk
Coffee or Tea

SNACKS, AT PLANNED TIMES
½ small Cantaloupe; ½ cup **Hot Mocha Milk**

Serving Information
Men and Youth: Add ⅓ cup Grape Juice, 1 ounce
  Pita Bread, and 2 medium Plums
Youth: Add 1½ cups Skim Milk

DAY 2

MORNING MEAL
½ cup Grapefruit Juice
1 serving Hot Cereal, ¾ ounce uncooked
½ cup Skim Milk
Coffee or Tea

MIDDAY MEAL
Liver Venetian
½ cup Cooked Wax Beans
Lettuce and Red Bell Pepper Salad with
    1½ teaspoons Mayonnaise
1 slice Whole Wheat Bread
1 medium Peach

EVENING MEAL
Turkey-Cheese Strata
6 medium Cooked Asparagus Spears
½ cup Cooked Spaghetti Squash
1 ounce Enriched Roll
1 teaspoon Margarine
3 ounces Chocolate-Flavored Dietary Frozen
    Dessert with 1 teaspoon Chocolate Syrup and
    1 tablespoon Low-Calorie Whipped Topping

SNACKS, AT PLANNED TIMES
1 cup Plain Popcorn; ½ cup Raspberry-Flavored
    Gelatin; 1 cup Skim Milk

Serving Information
Men and Youth: Add ½ cup Grapefruit Juice,
    1 small Enriched Bagel, 2 tablespoons Raisins,
    and ½ cup Raspberries
Youth: Add 1½ cups Skim Milk

DAY 3

MORNING MEAL
½ cup Fruit Salad
1 tablespoon Peanut Butter
1 teaspoon Reduced-Calorie Strawberry Spread
½ English Muffin, toasted
¼ cup Skim Milk
Coffee or Tea

MIDDAY MEAL
Split Pea Soup with 20 Oyster Crackers
Tossed Salad with **Green Goddess Salad Dressing**
1 small Apple

EVENING MEAL
3–4 ounces Broiled Pork Chop
½ cup Cooked Celery
½ cup Cooked Sliced Turnips
Chilled Vegetable Salad
2-inch wedge Casaba or Honeydew Melon

SNACKS, AT PLANNED TIMES
Coconut-Coffee Mounds; 1 cup Mixed Vegetable
    Juice

Serving Information
Men and Youth: Add ½ English Muffin, toasted,
    1 slice Whole Wheat Bread, 2-inch wedge
    Casaba or Honeydew Melon, and 2 Graham
    Crackers
Men: Add 2 ounces Canned Chick Peas (Gar-
    banzos) to Salad at the Midday Meal
Youth: Add 1¾ cups Skim Milk

DAY 6

MORNING MEAL
2-inch wedge Honeydew
1 Poached Egg
1 slice Toasted Whole Wheat Bread
¼ cup Skim Milk
Coffee or Tea

MIDDAY MEAL
3–4 ounces Pan-Broiled Veal Cutlet
Kasha Mix
½ cup Cooked Cauliflower
Escarole and Bibb Lettuce Salad with
    Herb Dressing
½ cup Butterscotch-Flavored Low-Calorie Milk
    Pudding

EVENING MEAL
Cheese-Stuffed Zucchini
Creamed Rutabaga
½ cup Cooked Eggplant Slices
Tossed Salad with 2 teaspoons Low-Calorie
    Italian Dressing
4 Canned Apricot Halves with 2 tablespoons
    Juice topped with 1 tablespoon Plain
    Unflavored Yogurt

SNACKS, AT PLANNED TIMES
1 small Pear; ½ cup Skim Milk; 2 Graham
    Crackers

Serving Information
Men and Youth: Add ¾ ounce Crispbread and
    ¼ small Pineapple
Youth: Add 1¼ cups Skim Milk

DAY 7

MORNING MEAL
Honey-Stewed Prunes
¾ ounce Ready-to-Eat Cereal
1 slice Toasted Enriched Bread
1 teaspoon Margarine
1 cup Skim Milk
Coffee or Tea

MIDDAY MEAL
3–4 ounces Baked Cod
Vegetable-Stuffed Grape Leaves
Lettuce and Bean Sprout Salad with 1 teaspoon
    Vegetable Oil plus Cider Vinegar
Lemonade

EVENING MEAL
Ham 'n' Vegetable Burgers
½ Hamburger Roll
¼ cup Sliced Onion
½ medium Dill Pickle
Grated Cabbage and Carrot Salad with
    1 teaspoon Mayonnaise
½ small Mango or ¼ small Pineapple

SNACKS, AT PLANNED TIMES
1 small Orange; ½ cup Plain Unflavored Yogurt
    with 2 teaspoons Reduced-Calorie Strawberry
    Spread

Serving Information
Men and Youth: Add 1 serving **Honey-Stewed
    Prunes,** 1 slice Cracked Wheat Bread, ½ cup
    Applesauce, and ½ Hamburger Roll
Men: Add ½ ounce Diced Cooked Ham to Salad
    at the Evening Meal
Youth: Add 2 cups Skim Milk

Acorn squash is a native American gourd. The first Europeans who sailed here were introduced to the vegetable by the Massachusetts Indians, who gave it its name. They called it *asquash*, meaning "eaten green."

Select heavy, shiny, dark green acorn squash that are free of cuts and bruises. The rind should have distinct ridges. Avoid squash whose outsides are mottled with large orange areas; they're overripe.

Squash is an efficient addition to oven-cooked meals, since it will bake at almost any temperature. Baked Spiced Acorn Squash appears on the menu for Day 2.

Economy Tip—Roast turkey is on the menu on Day 6. Leftovers may be frozen and used at the Midday Meal (Week 40, Day 3), in Turkey-Barley Soup recipe (Week 41, Day 3), Turkey Island Style recipe (Week 42, Day 2), and Turkey Pockets recipe (Week 43, Day 3).

WEEK 38

DAY 1

MORNING MEAL
1 cup Strawberries
1 serving Hot Cereal, ¾ ounce uncooked
1 cup Skim Milk
Coffee or Tea

MIDDAY MEAL
Lunch Box Chick Pea Sandwich
Sliced Tomatoes and Cucumbers on Lettuce
   with **Dijon-Herb Dressing**
½ medium Banana

EVENING MEAL
3–4 ounces Broiled Scallops
½ cup Steamed Peas
½ cup Steamed Carrot Slices
Tossed Salad with **Dill Vinaigrette**
½ cup Lime-Flavored Low-Calorie Gelatin

SNACKS, AT PLANNED TIMES
1 small Apple; ¾ cup Buttermilk; 2 cups Plain
   Popcorn; 8 fluid ounces Beer

Serving Information
Men and Youth: Add ½ medium Banana and
   1 slice Whole Wheat Bread
Men: Add ½ ounce Shredded Cheddar Cheese
   to Salad at the Evening Meal
Youth: Add 2 cups Skim Milk

DAY 4

MORNING MEAL
½ medium Banana, sliced
¾ ounce Ready-to-Eat Cereal
½ cup Skim Milk
Coffee or Tea

MIDDAY MEAL
3–4 ounces Broiled Chicken Livers
½ cup Steamed Sliced Mushrooms with
   ½ teaspoon Sesame Seeds, toasted
½ cup Steamed Broccoli Florets
1 slice Rye Bread
Garlic "Butter"
2 medium Plums

EVENING MEAL
3–4 ounces Roast Cornish Hen
Potato-Rice Casserole
¼ cup Steamed Chinese Pea Pods
½ cup Steamed Spinach
Tossed Salad with Lemon Juice
1 slice Enriched Bread
1 teaspoon Reduced-Calorie Margarine
4 fluid ounces White Wine
Coffee or Tea

SNACKS, AT PLANNED TIMES
¾ cup Buttermilk; ½ small Cantaloupe; ¾ cup
   Vegetable Broth

Serving Information
Men and Youth: Add ½ medium Banana, sliced,
   1 slice Rye Bread, 1 ounce Whole Wheat Roll,
   and ½ cup Applesauce
Youth: Add 1½ cups Skim Milk

DAY 5

MORNING MEAL
1 medium Kiwi Fruit or 2-inch wedge Honeydew
Open-Face Grilled Cheese Sandwich I
½ cup Skim Milk
Coffee or Tea

MIDDAY MEAL
Tuna Tomato Flowers
Celery and Carrot Sticks
1 slice Pumpernickel Bread
1 teaspoon Margarine
½ cup Fruit Salad

EVENING MEAL
1 cup Mixed Vegetable Juice
3–4 ounces Broiled Hamburger
½ cup Steamed Onion Slices
½ cup Steamed Asparagus Tips
Green Salad with **Vinaigrette Parmesan**
1 ounce Whole Wheat Roll
Sparkling Mineral Water with Mint Sprig

SNACKS, AT PLANNED TIMES
½ cup Blueberries; ½ cup Plain Unflavored
   Yogurt; **Root Beer Froth**

Serving Information
Men and Youth: Add ½ cup Fruit Salad, 1 ounce
   Whole Wheat Roll, ½ cup Blueberries, and 2
   Dates
Youth: Add 1 cup Skim Milk and ¼ cup Plain
   Unflavored Yogurt

DAY 2

MORNING MEAL
1 small Orange
¾ ounce Ready-to-Eat Cereal
1 cup Skim Milk
Coffee or Tea

MIDDAY MEAL
Egg Salad
Sliced Radishes and Bean Sprouts on Lettuce
1 slice Toasted Rye Bread
Sparkling Mineral Water with Twist of Lemon

EVENING MEAL
3–4 ounces Broiled Steak
Baked Spiced Acorn Squash
½ cup Steamed Asparagus Tips
Romaine Lettuce topped with Alfalfa or Bean
   Sprouts and 1 teaspoon Reduced-Calorie
   Mayonnaise
1 ounce Enriched Roll
1 teaspoon Reduced-Calorie Margarine
Lime Cooler

SNACKS, AT PLANNED TIMES
Strawberry Shake; 1 medium Peach, sliced, with
   ¼ cup Plain Unflavored Yogurt

Serving Information
Men and Youth: Add 1 slice Enriched Bread, ½
   cup Canned Fruit Cocktail, and 2 Graham
   Crackers
Youth: Add 1 cup Skim Milk and ¼ cup Plain
   Unflavored Yogurt

DAY 3

MORNING MEAL
½ medium Grapefruit
1 Scrambled Egg
½ English Muffin, toasted
1 teaspoon Margarine
1 teaspoon Reduced-Calorie Strawberry Spread
½ cup Skim Milk □ Coffee or Tea

MIDDAY MEAL
Ginger-Broiled Chicken
½ cup Steamed Sliced Zucchini
¼ cup Steamed Red Bell Pepper Strips
Green Salad with Lemon Juice
1 slice Whole Wheat Bread
1 teaspoon Margarine
Club Soda with Mint Sprig

EVENING MEAL
1 cup Tomato Juice
3–4 ounces Broiled Scrod
½ cup Steamed Rutabaga
½ cup Steamed Kale
Tossed Salad with 1 teaspoon Vegetable Oil plus
   Wine Vinegar
1 small Pear
½ cup Skim Milk □ Coffee or Tea

SNACKS, AT PLANNED TIMES
2 medium Dried Apricot Halves; 1 cup Skim Milk;
   Coconut-Orange Gelatin

Serving Information
Men and Youth: Add ½ English Muffin, toasted,
   1 small Apple, 1 ounce Enriched Roll, and 2
   medium Dried Apricot Halves
Youth: Add 1 cup Skim Milk

DAY 6

MORNING MEAL
⅓ cup Grape Juice
1 serving Hot Cereal, ¾ ounce uncooked
½ cup Skim Milk
Coffee or Tea

MIDDAY MEAL
1½ tablespoons Peanut Butter on 1 slice Whole
   Wheat Bread with 1 teaspoon Reduced-Calorie
   Apricot Spread
Green Bell Pepper and Zucchini Sticks
½ cup Skim Milk
Coffee or Tea

EVENING MEAL
¾ cup **Turkey Broth**
Artichoke Hearts Español
3¾–5 ounces Roast Turkey
Holiday Noodle Pudding
½ cup Steamed Green Beans with ¼ cup
   Steamed Mushroom Caps
½ cup Steamed Sliced Carrot
Tossed Salad with **Savory Vinaigrette**
1 ounce Enriched Roll
4 fluid ounces White Wine
½ cup Cherry-Flavored Low-Calorie Gelatin
Coffee or Tea

SNACKS, AT PLANNED TIMES
1 cup Cantaloupe Balls; 1 cup Skim Milk

Serving Information
Men and Youth: Add ⅓ cup Grape Juice, 1 slice
   Whole Wheat Bread, 10 large Cherries, and 1
   ounce Enriched Roll
Youth: Add 1 cup Skim Milk

DAY 7

MORNING MEAL
1 small Pear, cut into wedges
1 ounce Muenster Cheese
½ small Enriched Bagel
1 teaspoon Reduced-Calorie Margarine
Coffee or Tea

MIDDAY MEAL
Baked Codfish with Lemon
½ cup Steamed Spinach
Green Salad with Lemon Juice
1 slice Rye Bread
1 teaspoon Reduced-Calorie Margarine
½ cup Skim Milk
Coffee or Tea

EVENING MEAL
¾ cup **Beef Broth**
Lamb Rosé
½ cup Steamed Cauliflower Florets
Broiled Tomato
Bean Sprouts on Romaine Lettuce with
   Lemon Juice
Apple Compote
Hot Spiced Tea

SNACKS, AT PLANNED TIMES
½ cup Plain Unflavored Yogurt; 1 cup
   Strawberries

Serving Information
Men and Youth: Add ½ small Enriched Bagel,
   2 medium Plums, and 1 slice Rye Bread
Youth: Add 2 cups Skim Milk

Many good cooks are wary of working with yeast dough. But yeast is hardy and can withstand a lot of abuse. With practice, you'll find a kneading rhythm that is pleasant and relaxing. The finished product should prove that your worst fears are unfounded. The only caution necessary is to check the expiration date on the yeast packet since outdated yeast can't do much.

No food is more basic—or more symbolic of sustenance than bread, and very few cooking experiences are as rewarding as feeling a loaf of bread take shape in your hands. Saying "I made that" gives an incomparable sense of accomplishment.

Homemade White Bread is planned for Day 5. Roast Shoulder of Veal, later in the week, calls for a bouquet garni; remember to remove it before serving time.

Economy Tip—Roast chicken is on the menu on Day 6. Leftovers may be frozen and used in Sesame Chicken with Green Beans recipe (Week 45, Day 3).

WEEK 39

DAY 1

MORNING MEAL
4 Canned Pineapple Spears with 2 tablespoons Juice
1 Sunnyside-Up Egg
1 slice Toasted **Homemade Whole Wheat Bread**
1 teaspoon Margarine
½ cup Skim Milk
Coffee or Tea

MIDDAY MEAL
⅔ cup Part-Skim Ricotta Cheese with 1 Black Olive, sliced, and ½ medium Tomato, diced, on Escarole
Celery Sticks
¾ ounce Crispbread
1 teaspoon Margarine
Sparkling Mineral Water with Slice of Lemon

EVENING MEAL
Fresh Mushroom Soup
Curried Seafood Salad
1 ounce Enriched Roll
2-inch wedge Honeydew
¼ cup Skim Milk
Coffee or Tea

SNACKS, AT PLANNED TIMES
½ cup Plain Unflavored Yogurt; ½ cup Blueberries; 1 cup Mixed Vegetable Juice

Serving Information
Men and Youth: Add 4 Canned Pineapple Spears with 2 tablespoons Juice, ¾ ounce Crispbread, ½ cup Blueberries, and 6 Saltines
Youth: Add 1¼ cups Skim Milk

DAY 4

MORNING MEAL
½ cup Orange Juice
1 serving Hot Cereal, ¾ ounce uncooked
1 cup Skim Milk
Coffee or Tea

MIDDAY MEAL
Vegetable-Cheese Platter
6 Melba Toast Rounds
1 teaspoon Margarine
½ cup Applesauce sprinkled with Cinnamon

EVENING MEAL
Baked Veal Loaves
¼ cup Cooked Peas
½ cup Cooked Wax Beans
Green Salad with **Garlic Vinaigrette**
1 ounce Enriched Roll
Mineral Water with Twist of Lime

SNACKS, AT PLANNED TIMES
1 cup Tomato Juice with Green Bell Pepper and Zucchini Sticks; ¾ cup Skim Milk; 1 small Pear

Serving Information
Men and Youth: Add ½ cup Orange Juice, 2 tablespoons Raisins, 3 Melba Toast Rounds, ½ cup Applesauce, and 1 ounce Enriched Roll
Youth: Add 1¼ cups Skim Milk

DAY 5

MORNING MEAL
⅓ cup Apple Juice
1 ounce Cheddar Cheese
½ small Enriched Bagel
½ cup Skim Milk
Coffee or Tea

MIDDAY MEAL
Salmon Salad
Sliced Tomato and Cucumber on Lettuce with 1 teaspoon Vegetable Oil plus Cider Vinegar
1 slice **Homemade White Bread**
2 medium Plums

EVENING MEAL
¾ cup **Beef Broth**
Tangy Pork and Rice
½ cup Baked Yellow Straightneck Squash
Sliced Radishes and Bean Sprouts on Shredded Cabbage with 1 teaspoon Reduced-Calorie Mayonnaise
Sparkling Mineral Water with Mint Sprig

SNACKS, AT PLANNED TIMES
½ cup Plain Unflavored Yogurt; 1 cup Strawberries; **Coconut-Coffee Mounds**

Serving Information
Men and Youth: Add ⅓ cup Apple Juice, ½ small Enriched Bagel, and 1 slice **Homemade White Bread**
Youth: Add 1½ cups Skim Milk

MORNING MEAL
½ medium Grapefruit
¾ ounce Ready-to-Eat Cereal
1 cup Skim Milk
Coffee or Tea

MIDDAY MEAL
Grilled Cheese Soufflé
½ cup Steamed Green Beans
Sliced Radishes and Cucumbers on Lettuce with
   Dijon-Herb Dressing
½ cup Orange Sections with 1 teaspoon
   Shredded Coconut

EVENING MEAL
3–4 ounces Broiled Steak
Sautéed Mushrooms and Onions
½ cup Steamed Spinach
Green Salad with 2 teaspoons Reduced-Calorie
   Mayonnaise
1 slice Rye Bread
4 fluid ounces Red Wine
Coffee or Tea

SNACKS, AT PLANNED TIMES
½ cup Strawberry-Flavored Low-Calorie Gelatin;
   Frozen Apple-Banana Dessert

Serving Information
Men and Youth: Add 1 ounce Whole Wheat Roll,
   ½ cup Orange Sections, ½ cup Strawberries,
   and 2 Graham Crackers
Youth: Add 2 cups Skim Milk

MORNING MEAL
1 medium Peach, sliced
⅓ cup Cottage Cheese
1 slice Toasted Raisin Bread
¼ cup Skim Milk
Coffee or Tea

MIDDAY MEAL
3–4 ounces Broiled Fillet of Sole with
   Lemon Wedge
½ cup Cooked Cauliflower
Shredded Cabbage and Carrot with 2 teaspoons
   Reduced-Calorie Mayonnaise
½ cup Canned Fruit Cocktail

EVENING MEAL
¾ cup **Chicken Broth**
Spaghetti with Chicken Liver Sauce
¼ cup Cooked Chinese Pea Pods
Tossed Salad with 1 teaspoon Vegetable Oil plus
   Wine Vinegar
1 slice Pumpernickel Bread
¾ cup Skim Milk

SNACKS, AT PLANNED TIMES
½ cup Butterscotch-Flavored Low-Calorie Milk
   Pudding; 1 cup Honeydew or Cantaloupe Balls

Serving Information
Men and Youth: Add 1 cup Grapefruit Juice, 1
   slice Toasted Raisin Bread, and ½ cup Canned
   Fruit Cocktail
Youth: Add 1 cup Skim Milk

MORNING MEAL
½ small Cantaloupe
1 Soft-Cooked Egg
½ English Muffin, toasted
1 teaspoon Reduced-Calorie Margarine
¼ cup Skim Milk □ Coffee or Tea

MIDDAY MEAL
Vegetable Soup
Chilled Squash and Chick Pea Salad
2 Dill Pickle Spears
½ medium Tomato, sliced
1 slice **Homemade Whole Wheat Bread** with
   ½ teaspoon Honey
¾ cup Skim Milk

EVENING MEAL
4½–6 ounces Roast Chicken
½ cup Steamed Zucchini
½ cup Steamed Red Bell Pepper Strips
Alfalfa or Bean Sprouts on Watercress with 1
   teaspoon Reduced-Calorie Mayonnaise
4 fluid ounces White Wine □ Coffee or Tea

SNACKS, AT PLANNED TIMES
3 ounces Chocolate-Flavored Dietary Frozen
   Dessert; ½ cup Blackberries with ¼ cup Plain
   Unflavored Yogurt

Serving Information
Men and Youth: Add ½ English Muffin, toasted,
   1 slice **Homemade Whole Wheat Bread,** 1 small
   Apple, and ½ cup Blueberries
Men: Add ½ ounce Roast Chicken at the Evening
   Meal
Youth: Add 2 cups Skim Milk

MORNING MEAL
½ medium Banana, sliced
¾ ounce Ready-to-Eat Cereal
1 cup Skim Milk
Coffee or Tea

MIDDAY MEAL
3 tablespoons Peanut Butter on 1 slice
   Homemade White Bread with 2 teaspoons
   Reduced-Calorie Grape Spread
Carrot and Celery Sticks
1 small Orange

EVENING MEAL
Roast Shoulder of Veal
4 ounces Baked Potato
1½ teaspoons Reduced-Calorie Margarine
¼ cup Cooked Brussels Sprouts
Baked Eggplant Slices
Green Salad with **Sesame Vinaigrette**
Sparkling Mineral Water

SNACKS, AT PLANNED TIMES
1 cup Tomato Juice with 10 Oyster Crackers;
   Hot Cocoa; 20 small Grapes

Serving Information
Men and Youth: Add ½ medium Banana, sliced,
   1 slice **Homemade White Bread,** and 10 Oyster
   Crackers
Youth: Add 2 cups Skim Milk

Trivia buffs may remember Buttermilk as Dale Evans's horse. But the buttermilk we use is the liquid that's left behind after butter has been churned. It contains very little fat, since most of the milkfat has gone into the butter.

Buttermilk varies, depending on whether the milk and cream it was made from were fresh or slightly soured. Most of today's buttermilk is made from freshly skimmed milk that has been pasteurized, cooled, and inoculated with a special culture, then allowed to ferment under suitable conditions. The concentration of butterfat and other milk solids is the same as in skim milk. Salt is sometimes added for flavor.

When buttermilk is used in a recipe, use baking soda for leavening instead of baking powder. Honey-Wheat Muffins (Day 6) are made with buttermilk batter.

WEEK 40

DAY 1

MORNING MEAL
½ cup Orange Juice
1 Poached Egg
½ English Muffin, toasted
1 teaspoon Reduced-Calorie Margarine
¼ cup Skim Milk
Coffee or Tea

MIDDAY MEAL
Fillet of Sole Florentine
½ medium Tomato, sliced
Sliced Radishes and Cucumber on Lettuce with Lemon Juice and 1 teaspoon Imitation Bacon Bits
1 small Apple
¾ cup Skim Milk

EVENING MEAL
Ginger-Broiled Chicken
½ cup Cooked Beets
½ cup Cooked Green Beans
Green Salad with **Dijon-Herb Dressing**
1 ounce Enriched Roll
1 teaspoon Margarine
4 fluid ounces White Wine
Coffee or Tea

SNACKS, AT PLANNED TIMES
½ cup Vanilla-Flavored Low-Calorie Milk Pudding; 10 large Cherries; **Hot Spiced Tea;** 2 Graham Crackers

Serving Information
Men and Youth: Add ½ cup Orange Juice, ½ English Muffin, toasted, and 10 large Cherries
Youth: Add 2 cups Skim Milk

DAY 4

MORNING MEAL
⅓ cup Grape Juice
1 ounce Colby Cheese
½ English Muffin, toasted
½ cup Skim Milk
Coffee or Tea

MIDDAY MEAL
3–4 ounces Roast Beef
2 Dill Pickle Spears
Curried Cole Slaw
1 slice Rye Bread
1 teaspoon Mayonnaise
Sparkling Mineral Water with Slice of Lemon

EVENING MEAL
¾ cup **Chicken Broth**
Apricot Chicken
Seasoned Cucumber Bake
Tossed Salad with Lemon Juice
1 ounce Enriched Roll
½ cup Skim Milk
Coffee or Tea

SNACKS, AT PLANNED TIMES
1 cup Strawberries; ¾ cup Buttermilk; 1 cup Mixed Vegetable Juice with Carrot Sticks

Serving Information
Men and Youth: Add ⅔ cup Grape Juice, ½ English Muffin, toasted, 1 slice Rye Bread, and 1 small Apple
Youth: Add 1 cup Skim Milk

DAY 5

MORNING MEAL
1 medium Persimmon or ½ medium Grapefruit
¾ ounce Ready-to-Eat Cereal
1 cup Skim Milk
Coffee or Tea

MIDDAY MEAL
Mustard-Broiled Flounder
½ cup Cooked Broccoli
Green Salad with 1 teaspoon Vegetable Oil plus Wine Vinegar and Herbs
1 slice Enriched Bread
1 teaspoon Reduced-Calorie Margarine
½ cup Skim Milk
Coffee or Tea

EVENING MEAL
Cornmeal-Swiss Bake
½ cup Steamed Spinach
Sliced Tomato on Lettuce with 1 teaspoon Reduced-Calorie Mayonnaise
Carob Soufflé

SNACKS, AT PLANNED TIMES
3 ounces Chocolate-Flavored Dietary Frozen Dessert; 1 cup Melon Balls

Serving Information
Men and Youth: Add ½ medium Banana and 2 Graham Crackers
Youth: Add 1½ cups Skim Milk

DAY 2

MORNING MEAL
½ medium Banana, sliced
1 serving Hot Cereal, ¾ ounce uncooked
1 cup Skim Milk
Coffee or Tea

MIDDAY MEAL
2 ounces Julienne Swiss Cheese
Tossed Salad with 2 Green Olives, sliced, and
    1 teaspoon Vegetable Oil plus Wine Vinegar
1 slice Rye Bread
1 teaspoon Margarine
½ medium Grapefruit

EVENING MEAL
¾ cup **Beef Broth**
3–4 ounces Broiled Hamburger
Spaghetti Squash with Tomato Sauce
Green Salad with Lemon Juice
1 slice Whole Wheat Bread
Club Soda with Twist of Lime

SNACKS, AT PLANNED TIMES
¾ cup Buttermilk; ½ cup Fruit Salad; ½ cup
    Cherry-Flavored Low-Calorie Gelatin

Serving Information
Men and Youth: Add ½ medium Banana, sliced,
    1 slice Rye Bread, 6 Saltines, and ½ cup Fruit
    Salad
Youth: Add 2 cups Skim Milk

DAY 3

MORNING MEAL
Banana Bread Pudding
½ cup Skim Milk
Coffee or Tea

MIDDAY MEAL
3–4 ounces Sliced Roast Turkey
½ medium Tomato, sliced, and Green Bell Pepper
    Rings on Shredded Cabbage with 1 teaspoon
    Mayonnaise
½ cup Orange-Flavored Low-Calorie Gelatin

EVENING MEAL
Shrimp Scampi
½ cup Cooked Wild or Enriched Rice
½ cup Cooked Artichoke Hearts
½ cup Steamed Spinach
Cherry Tomato Halves on Lettuce with 1
    teaspoon Vegetable Oil plus Cider Vinegar
8 fluid ounces Beer

SNACKS, AT PLANNED TIMES
1 medium Kiwi Fruit or 1 small Orange; ½ cup
    Plain Unflavored Yogurt; ½ cup Raspberries

Serving Information
Men and Youth: Add 1 slice Rye Bread, ½ cup
    Orange Sections, 1 ounce Whole Wheat Roll,
    and ½ cup Raspberries
Youth: Add 1½ cups Skim Milk

DAY 6

MORNING MEAL
⅓ cup Apple Juice
1 Scrambled Egg with Chives
Honey-Wheat Muffins
2 teaspoons Reduced-Calorie Margarine
⅔ cup Skim Milk
Coffee or Tea

MIDDAY MEAL
⅔ cup Cottage Cheese stuffed in Green Bell
    Pepper topped with Chopped Pimiento
3 Melba Toast Rounds
1 small Pear

EVENING MEAL
Potted Shoulder Lamb Chops
½ cup Steamed Kale
Green Salad topped with Alfalfa or Bean Sprouts
    and 1 teaspoon Imitation Bacon Bits plus Cider
    Vinegar
Sparkling Mineral Water with Slice of Lime

SNACKS, AT PLANNED TIMES
½ cup Cherry-Flavored Low-Calorie Gelatin;
    ½ cup Orange Sections; ¾ cup Buttermilk

Serving Information
Men and Youth: Add ⅓ cup Apple Juice, 2
    ounces Whole Wheat Roll, and ½ cup Canned
    Fruit Cocktail
Youth: Add 1⅓ cups Skim Milk

DAY 7

MORNING MEAL
½ cup Grapefruit Juice
Cinnamon-Cheese Toast
½ cup Skim Milk
Coffee or Tea

MIDDAY MEAL
Chicken Livers "Stroganoff"
¼ cup Steamed Peas
Sliced Radishes and Red Bell Pepper Rings on
    Watercress with **Creamy Oriental Dressing**
Club Soda with Twist of Lemon

EVENING MEAL
3–4 ounces Broiled Veal Chop
4 ounces Baked Potato
1 teaspoon Margarine
½ cup Cooked Asparagus Tips
Tossed Salad with **Sesame Vinaigrette**
4 fluid ounces Red Wine
Coffee or Tea

SNACKS, AT PLANNED TIMES
½ cup Blueberries with ¼ cup Plain Unflavored
    Yogurt; ¼ small Pineapple

Serving Information
Men and Youth: Add ½ cup Grapefruit Juice, 2
    ounces Enriched Roll, and 1 slice Rye Bread
Youth: Add 1½ cups Skim Milk

Barley, one of the oldest food plants used by man, has a nutty flavor and a stick-to-the-ribs texture that have made it popular for over thirty centuries. This cereal grass is also referred to as John Barleycorn because it can be fermented to make beer or Scotch.

The Lake Dwellers in Switzerland grew three varieties of barley 3,000 years ago and, according to the Bible, it was one of the crops destroyed by the plagues of Egypt. Barley was used extensively by the ancient Greeks and Romans, and also in Victorian England to make barley water.

Until the sixteenth century, barley was also used to make bread. Its low gluten content makes it a poor bread flour, however, so when wheat flour was found to make a lighter loaf, barley lost one of its traditional uses.

Today, barley is used in soups. It's also an excellent side dish with hearty meat meals.

We've added barley to Turkey-Barley Soup (Day 3), good on a chilly autumn day.

WEEK 41

DAY 1

MORNING MEAL
½ cup Orange Juice
1 Scrambled Egg
1 slice Toasted Whole Wheat Bread
1 teaspoon Margarine
2 teaspoons Grape-Flavored Reduced-Calorie Spread
½ cup Skim Milk
Coffee or Tea

MIDDAY MEAL
¾ cup **Chicken Broth**
Open-Face Grilled Cheese Sandwich I
Garbanzo-Stuffed Peppers
1 medium Peach

EVENING MEAL
Shrimp Oregano
½ cup Cooked Enriched Rice
½ cup Steamed Green Beans
Green Salad with **Wine Vinaigrette**
4 fluid ounces White Wine
Coffee or Tea

SNACKS, AT PLANNED TIMES
¾ cup Buttermilk; ½ cup Canned Fruit Cocktail with 1 teaspoon Shredded Coconut; **Root Beer Froth**

Serving Information
Men and Youth: Add ½ cup Orange Juice, 1 ounce Enriched Roll, and ½ cup Canned Fruit Cocktail
Men: Add ¼ ounce Shredded Swiss Cheese to Salad at the Evening Meal
Youth: Add 1½ cups Skim Milk

DAY 4

MORNING MEAL
½ medium Papaya or 2-inch wedge Honeydew
1 serving Hot Cereal, ¾ ounce uncooked
½ Cinnamon-Raisin English Muffin, toasted
1 teaspoon Margarine
1 cup Skim Milk
Coffee or Tea

MIDDAY MEAL
3–4 ounces Broiled Calf Liver
¼ cup Sliced Onion sautéed in 1 teaspoon Margarine
½ cup Steamed Broccoli
Tossed Salad with Tarragon Vinegar and Herbs
½ cup Raspberries

EVENING MEAL
3–4 ounces Broiled Veal Chop
Squash Parmesan
½ cup Cooked Asparagus Tips
Green Salad with Lemon Juice
1 ounce Enriched Roll
4 fluid ounces Red Wine
Coffee or Tea

SNACKS, AT PLANNED TIMES
½ cup Chocolate-Flavored Low-Calorie Milk Pudding; **Orange Ambrosia**

Serving Information
Men and Youth: Add ½ medium Papaya or 2-inch wedge Honeydew, ½ Cinnamon-Raisin English Muffin, toasted, 1 slice Rye Bread, and ½ cup Raspberries
Youth: Add 2 cups Skim Milk

DAY 5

MORNING MEAL
1 cup Mixed Vegetable Juice
1 ounce Cheddar Cheese
½ small Enriched Bagel
½ cup Skim Milk
Coffee or Tea

MIDDAY MEAL
Seafood Garden Salad
1 slice Enriched Bread
1 teaspoon Reduced-Calorie Margarine
½ cup Fruit Salad

EVENING MEAL
3–4 ounces Broiled Steak
½ cup Cooked Wax Beans
½ cup Cooked Spinach
Tossed Salad with 1½ teaspoons Reduced-Calorie Mayonnaise
1 slice Whole Wheat Bread
Sparkling Mineral Water with Slice of Lime

SNACKS, AT PLANNED TIMES
Orange-Strawberry Cups; 2 Canned Pear Halves with 2 tablespoons Juice; ½ cup Plain Unflavored Yogurt

Serving Information
Men and Youth: Add ½ small Enriched Bagel, 1 slice Enriched Bread, and ½ cup Fruit Salad
Youth: Add 1½ cups Skim Milk

DAY 2

MORNING MEAL
⅓ cup Grape Juice
¾ ounce Ready-to-Eat Cereal
1 cup Skim Milk
Coffee or Tea

MIDDAY MEAL
¾ cup **Vegetable Broth**
Tomato-Cheese-Stuffed Pitas
Carrot and Celery Sticks
Sliced Cucumber on Lettuce with 1 teaspoon
   Mayonnaise and 1 teaspoon Imitation Bacon
   Bits
Mineral Water with Twist of Lemon

EVENING MEAL
1 cup Tomato Juice
3–4 ounces Broiled Beef Tenderloin
Artichoke Hearts Español
½ cup Baked Summer Squash Slices
Tossed Salad with 1 teaspoon Vegetable Oil
   plus Cider Vinegar
1 slice Enriched Bread
1 teaspoon Margarine
Iced Tea

SNACKS, AT PLANNED TIMES
Pineapple-Banana Milk Shake; 1 cup Strawberries
   with ¼ cup Plain Unflavored Yogurt

Serving Information
Men and Youth: Add ⅓ cup Grape Juice, 1 slice
   Enriched Bread, 1 small Apple, and 2 Graham
   Crackers
Youth: Add 2 cups Skim Milk

DAY 3

MORNING MEAL
½ medium Grapefruit
1 Poached Egg
1 slice Toasted Whole Wheat Bread
1 teaspoon Margarine
½ cup Skim Milk
Coffee or Tea

MIDDAY MEAL
Turkey-Barley Soup with 6 Saltines
Red Cabbage topped with Bean Sprouts, 2 ounces
   Shredded Tofu, and **Wine Vinaigrette**
½ cup Skim Milk
Coffee or Tea

EVENING MEAL
3–4 ounces Baked Fillet of Flounder
Green Beans and Tomatoes Hungarian Style
Green Salad with Lemon Juice
Sparkling Mineral Water with Twist of Lemon

SNACKS, AT PLANNED TIMES
Baked Apple with 1 teaspoon Honey; ¾ cup
   Buttermilk; ½ medium Banana

Serving Information
Men and Youth: Add 1 ounce Enriched Roll and
   ½ medium Banana
Men: Add ½ ounce Shredded Tofu at the Mid-
   day Meal
Youth: Add 1 cup Skim Milk

DAY 6

MORNING MEAL
1 medium Kiwi Fruit or ½ cup Blueberries
¾ ounce Ready-to-Eat Cereal
1 slice Toasted Rye Bread
1 teaspoon Margarine
1 cup Skim Milk
Coffee or Tea

MIDDAY MEAL
Chicken Breasts with Raisin Sauce
½ cup Cooked Sliced Carrot
½ cup Cooked Kale
Green Salad with Lemon Juice
1 ounce Enriched Roll
¾ cup Cooked Rhubarb with 1 tablespoon Low-
   Calorie Whipped Topping

EVENING MEAL
1 cup Tomato Juice
Mushroom Loaf
½ medium Tomato, sliced
Tossed Salad with **Oregano Vinaigrette**
Hot Spiced Tea

SNACKS, AT PLANNED TIMES
½ cup Cherry-Flavored Low-Calorie Gelatin;
   Yogurt-Banana Shake

Serving Information
Men and Youth: Add 2 tablespoons Raisins, 6
   Saltines, and ½ cup Canned Fruit Cocktail
Youth: Add 2 cups Skim Milk

DAY 7

MORNING MEAL
½ cup Grapefruit Juice
Creamed Egg 'n' Muffin
½ cup Skim Milk
Coffee or Tea

MIDDAY MEAL
¾ cup **Vegetable Broth**
3–4 ounces Poached Salmon
½ cup Steamed Chopped Celery
½ cup Steamed Spinach
4 fluid ounces White Wine
Coffee or Tea

EVENING MEAL
Cauliflower and Zucchini Soup
Stuffed Cucumber
Potato and Green Bean Salad
½ cup Canned Sliced Peaches

SNACKS, AT PLANNED TIMES
1 serving Vanilla-Flavored Low-Calorie Milk
   Beverage; 1 small Apple

Serving Information
Men and Youth: Add ½ cup Grapefruit Juice and
   2 ounces Enriched Roll
Men: Add 1 ounce Poached Salmon at the Midday
   Meal
Youth: Add 1½ cups Skim Milk

WEEK 42

Fall foliage marks the season for apple cider. Cider, the juice of apples that have been ground to a pulp and then pressed, is available in both sweet (nonfermented) and hard (fermented) forms. Commercial cider is often treated to resist spoilage. Check the labels before you buy to be sure you are getting the kind you want.

The taste of sweet cider, a beverage that originated in New England, depends on the kind and quality of apples used.

The alcohol content of hard cider varies. It is very popular in Europe, especially in England and northern France, where it's called *cidre*. Cider is also used to make applejack (apple brandy) and vinegar.

Apple cider gives an old favorite a new seasonal twist in Apple Cider Slaw (Day 4).

In Canada, Thanksgiving is celebrated on the second Monday in October. We suggest that our Canadian friends switch this week with Week 47, which includes our special Thanksgiving Day menu.

DAY 1

MORNING MEAL
1 cup Strawberries, sliced
⅓ cup Cottage Cheese
1 slice Toasted Raisin Bread
1 teaspoon Margarine
1 teaspoon Reduced-Calorie Apricot Spread
½ cup Skim Milk ☐ Coffee or Tea

MIDDAY MEAL
3–4 ounces Roast Chicken
Honey-Glazed Yams
½ cup Steamed Broccoli
Watercress and Cucumber Salad with
    Vinaigrette Parmesan
½ cup Lemon-Flavored Low-Calorie Gelatin

EVENING MEAL
3–4 ounces Broiled Chicken Livers
½ cup Steamed Onion Rings
½ cup Steamed Green Beans
Tossed Salad with 1 teaspoon Vegetable Oil plus
    Wine Vinegar
¾ ounce Crispbread
1 cup Cantaloupe Balls
½ cup Skim Milk ☐ Coffee or Tea

SNACKS, AT PLANNED TIMES
½ cup Canned Crushed Pineapple topped with
    1 teaspoon Shredded Coconut; ½ cup Vanilla-
    Flavored Low-Calorie Milk Pudding

Serving Information
Men and Youth: Add 1 slice Toasted Raisin Bread,
    ½ cup Canned Mandarin Orange Sections, ¾
    ounce Crispbread, and ½ cup Canned Crushed
    Pineapple
Youth: Add 1 cup Skim Milk

DAY 4

MORNING MEAL
½ small Cantaloupe
1 serving Hot Cereal, ¾ ounce uncooked
1 teaspoon Reduced-Calorie Margarine
½ cup Skim Milk
Coffee or Tea

MIDDAY MEAL
3–4 ounces Broiled Flounder with Lemon Wedge
¼ cup Steamed Beets
Apple Cider Slaw
1 slice Rye Bread
1 teaspoon Reduced-Calorie Margarine
3 medium Dried Apricot Halves

EVENING MEAL
1 cup Tomato Juice
Chicken and Egg Salad (1½–2 ounces Diced
    Cooked Chicken and 1 Diced Hard-Cooked
    Egg on Tossed Salad with 1 teaspoon Sesame
    Oil plus Rice Vinegar)
Tomato and Cucumber Slices
2 ounces Whole Wheat Roll
½ cup Skim Milk
Coffee or Tea

SNACKS, AT PLANNED TIMES
½ cup Canned Fruit Cocktail; 1 serving
    Chocolate-Flavored Low-Calorie Milk Beverage

Serving Information
Men and Youth: Add 2 tablespoons Raisins, 1
    slice Rye Bread, and ½ cup Canned Fruit
    Cocktail
Youth: Add 2 cups Skim Milk

DAY 5

MORNING MEAL
⅓ cup Apple Juice
1 Scrambled Egg
½ small Enriched Bagel
1 teaspoon Margarine
1 teaspoon Reduced-Calorie Strawberry Spread
½ cup Skim Milk
Coffee or Tea

MIDDAY MEAL
Peanut Soup
1½ ounces Julienne Swiss Cheese with Sliced
    Cucumber, Radishes, and Green Bell Pepper
    on Lettuce
2 teaspoons Reduced-Calorie Mayonnaise
3 Saltines
½ cup Orange Sections

EVENING MEAL
Ham 'n' Turkey Casserole
½ cup Cooked Brussels Sprouts
½ cup Cooked Wax Beans
Green Salad with **Dijon-Herb Dressing**
8 fluid ounces Beer

SNACKS, AT PLANNED TIMES
½ medium Banana; 1 cup Skim Milk; ½ cup
    Cherry-Flavored Low-Calorie Gelatin

Serving Information
Men and Youth: Add ⅓ cup Apple Juice, ½
    small Enriched Bagel, ½ cup Orange Sections,
    1 slice Rye Bread, and ½ medium Banana
Men: Add ¼ ounce Julienne Swiss Cheese at
    the Midday Meal
Youth: Add 1½ cups Skim Milk

DAY **2**

MORNING MEAL
1 small Orange
1 Poached Egg
½ English Muffin, toasted
1 teaspoon Margarine
¼ cup Skim Milk
Coffee or Tea

MIDDAY MEAL
3–4 ounces Baked Scrod
½ cup Steamed Zucchini Slices
Herb-Stuffed Tomatoes
Bean Sprouts on Lettuce with 1 tablespoon Low-
   Calorie Italian Dressing
Lemonade

EVENING MEAL
Turkey Island Style
½ cup Steamed Spaghetti Squash
Romaine Lettuce topped with Shredded Carrot
   and **Gingered Vinaigrette**
1 ounce Whole Wheat Roll
1 teaspoon Margarine
Mineral Water with Twist of Lemon

SNACKS, AT PLANNED TIMES
Root Beer Froth; ½ cup Blackberries; ½ cup
   Plain Unflavored Yogurt with ½ teaspoon
   Honey

Serving Information
Men and Youth: Add ½ English Muffin, toasted,
   1 small Apple, 2 Graham Crackers, and ½ cup
   Blackberries
Youth: Add 1¾ cups Skim Milk

DAY **3**

MORNING MEAL
½ medium Banana, sliced
¾ ounce Ready-to-Eat Cereal
1 cup Skim Milk
Coffee or Tea

MIDDAY MEAL
3–4 ounces Broiled Hamburger
1 Hamburger Roll
½ medium Tomato, sliced
2 Dill Pickle Spears
Carrot and Celery Sticks
1 teaspoon Mayonnaise
½ cup Orange-Flavored Low-Calorie Gelatin

EVENING MEAL
3–4 ounces Broiled Scallops
4 ounces Baked Potato topped with 2 tablespoons
   Plain Unflavored Yogurt and 1 teaspoon
   Imitation Bacon Bits
Creamed Spinach
Green Salad with 1½ teaspoons Vegetable Oil
   plus Cider Vinegar
4 fluid ounces White Wine
Coffee or Tea

SNACKS, AT PLANNED TIMES
1 medium Kiwi Fruit or 2-inch wedge Honeydew;
   3 ounces Vanilla-Flavored Dietary Frozen
   Dessert

Serving Information
Men and Youth: Add ½ medium Banana, sliced,
   and 1 slice Enriched Bread
Youth: Add 1 cup Skim Milk

DAY **6**

MORNING MEAL
½ medium Grapefruit
Cinnamon-Cheese Toast
¼ cup Skim Milk
Coffee or Tea

MIDDAY MEAL
3–4 ounces Baked Veal Chop
½ cup Steamed Carrot Slices
Sliced Tomato and Bean Sprouts on Bibb
   Lettuce with 1½ teaspoons Vegetable Oil plus
   Cider Vinegar
1 slice Pumpernickel Bread
1 small Pear

EVENING MEAL
Mussel Stew with 20 Oyster Crackers
Tossed Salad with 1 teaspoon Reduced-Calorie
   Mayonnaise mixed with 2 tablespoons Plain
   Unflavored Yogurt
½ cup Skim Milk
Coffee or Tea

SNACKS, AT PLANNED TIMES
1 cup Mixed Vegetable Juice; ½ cup
   Butterscotch-Flavored Low-Calorie Milk
   Pudding; ½ cup Canned Sliced Peaches

Serving Information
Men and Youth: Add 2 ounces Whole Wheat Roll
   and ½ cup Canned Sliced Peaches
Youth: Add 1¼ cups Skim Milk

DAY **7**

MORNING MEAL
½ cup Orange Juice
1 Sunnyside-Up Egg
½ English Muffin, toasted
¼ cup Skim Milk
Coffee or Tea

MIDDAY MEAL
3 tablespoons Peanut Butter on 1 slice Raisin
   Bread with 1 teaspoon Reduced-Calorie Apple
   Spread
¾ cup Skim Milk

EVENING MEAL
Lemon-Minted Lamb
½ cup Cooked Artichoke Hearts
½ cup Steamed Mushrooms
Endive and Watercress Salad with Lemon Juice
4 fluid ounces Champagne
Coffee or Tea

SNACKS, AT PLANNED TIMES
Pineapple-Banana Milk Shake; Mocha Sundae

Serving Information
Men and Youth: Add ½ cup Orange Juice, 1 slice
   Raisin Bread, and 2 Graham Crackers
Youth: Add 2 cups Skim Milk

96 | Pilaf is typically a rice dish native to the Near and Middle East and Greece. In India, it's called *pilau*, but westerners have adopted the Turkish pronunciation, pilaf.

Traditional pilaf is made of well-seasoned rice sautéed in oil or butter (we use margarine), then cooked in broth. Slow simmering allows the rice to soak up flavoring, and each grain emerges fluffy and well cooked. Fish, vegetables, meat, and fruit combinations are tossed with cooked rice, herbs, and spices. Incidentally, pilaf is a good way to use up frozen chicken giblets.

In our version, Vegetable Pilaf (Day 3), the vegetables are mixed with lemon rind and raisins for added taste, texture, and color. Although in most pilaf recipes you start with raw rice, we've shortened things a bit by using cooked enriched rice.

WEEK 43

DAY 1

MORNING MEAL
½ medium Banana, sliced
1 serving Hot Cereal, ¾ ounce uncooked
1 cup Skim Milk
Coffee or Tea

MIDDAY MEAL
Chicken and Legumes Casserole
½ cup Steamed Green Beans
Sliced Tomato and Cucumber on Lettuce with 1 teaspoon Sesame Oil plus Rice Vinegar
Mineral Water

EVENING MEAL
Salmon-Zucchini Kebobs
½ cup Cooked Enriched Noodles
¼ cup Cooked Peas
Tossed Salad with 1 tablespoon Low-Calorie French Dressing
1 slice Whole Wheat Bread
1 teaspoon Margarine
Honey-Glazed Pears

SNACKS, AT PLANNED TIMES
¾ cup Buttermilk; ½ medium Grapefruit

Serving Information
Men and Youth: Add ½ medium Banana, 1 slice Enriched Bread, and 1 slice Whole Wheat Bread
Men: Add ½ ounce Shredded Tofu and ½ ounce Canned Chick Peas to Salad at the Evening Meal
Youth: Add 2 cups Skim Milk

DAY 4

MORNING MEAL
⅓ cup Grape Juice
¾ ounce Ready-to-Eat Cereal
1 cup Skim Milk
Coffee or Tea

MIDDAY MEAL
1 cup Mixed Vegetable Juice
3–4 ounces Broiled Calf Liver
½ cup Steamed Onion Rings
½ cup Steamed Mushroom Caps
Cherry Tomatoes on Lettuce with **Dill Vinaigrette**
1 slice Rye Bread
Mineral Water

EVENING MEAL
¾ cup **Chicken Broth**
3–4 ounces Broiled Chicken Breast
½ cup Steamed Sliced Celery with ½ teaspoon Caraway Seeds
Marinated Carrots
Tossed Salad with 1 teaspoon Vegetable Oil plus Red Wine Vinegar
1 ounce Enriched Roll
1 teaspoon Reduced-Calorie Margarine
Iced Tea

SNACKS, AT PLANNED TIMES
½ cup Orange Sections; **Fruited Yogurt Mold**

Serving Information
Men and Youth: Add ⅓ cup Grape Juice, 1 ounce Enriched Roll, ½ cup Orange Sections, and 2 Graham Crackers
Youth: Add 1 cup Skim Milk

DAY 5

MORNING MEAL
1 medium Kiwi Fruit or ½ medium Grapefruit
1 ounce Swiss Cheese
½ small Enriched Bagel
¼ cup Skim Milk
Coffee or Tea

MIDDAY MEAL
Garbanzo-Stuffed Peppers
Crispy-Crunchy Salad
1 slice Pumpernickel Bread
1 teaspoon Reduced-Calorie Margarine
½ cup Canned Pineapple Chunks
½ cup Skim Milk
Coffee or Tea

EVENING MEAL
3–4 ounces Roast Leg of Lamb
¼ cup Baked Acorn Squash mashed with Cinnamon and Artificial Sweetener
½ cup Cooked Wax Beans
Green Salad with **Wine Vinaigrette**
4 fluid ounces Red Wine
Carrot-Apple Pudding

SNACKS, AT PLANNED TIMES
Crudités with **Curry Dip**; ¼ cup Strawberries with ½ cup Plain Unflavored Yogurt

Serving Information
Men and Youth: Add ½ small Enriched Bagel, ½ cup Canned Pineapple Chunks, 1 ounce Enriched Roll, and ¾ cup Strawberries
Men: Add 1¼ ounces Shredded Tofu to **Crispy-Crunchy Salad**
Youth: Add 1¼ cups Skim Milk

MORNING MEAL
½ cup Orange Juice
1 Soft-Cooked Egg
½ English Muffin, toasted
1 teaspoon Reduced-Calorie Margarine
½ cup Skim Milk
Coffee or Tea

MIDDAY MEAL
Feta Cheese Salad
1 ounce Pita Bread
1 teaspoon Margarine
½ cup Orange-Flavored Low-Calorie Gelatin

EVENING MEAL
1 cup Tomato Juice with Lemon Wedge
3–4 ounces Roast Beef with 2 teaspoons
   Barbecue Sauce
½ cup Steamed Broccoli Florets
Sweet and Sour Cabbage
Boston Lettuce Salad with **Dijon-Herb Dressing**
1 ounce Enriched Roll
½ cup Skim Milk
Coffee or Tea

SNACKS, AT PLANNED TIMES
½ cup Canned Fruit Cocktail; ½ cup Plain
   Unflavored Yogurt with 1 tablespoon Raisins
   and 1 teaspoon Wheat Germ

Serving Information
Men and Youth: Add ½ cup Orange Juice, ½
   English Muffin, toasted, 1 ounce Pita Bread,
   ½ cup Canned Fruit Cocktail, and 1 tablespoon
   Raisins
Youth: Add 1 cup Skim Milk

MORNING MEAL
⅓ cup Pineapple Juice
⅓ cup Pot Cheese
1 slice Toasted Raisin Bread
¼ cup Skim Milk
Coffee or Tea

MIDDAY MEAL
Turkey Pockets
Green Salad with 1 teaspoon Vegetable Oil plus
   Rice Vinegar
1 cup Honeydew or Cantaloupe Balls topped
   with 1 teaspoon Shredded Coconut

EVENING MEAL
3–4 ounces Broiled Scrod
Vegetable Pilaf
½ cup Steamed Spinach
Watercress and Sliced Cucumber Salad with
   1 teaspoon Reduced-Calorie Mayonnaise
4 fluid ounces White Wine
Coffee or Tea

SNACKS, AT PLANNED TIMES
¾ cup Skim Milk; Green Bell Pepper Sticks and
   Cauliflower Florets; ½ cup Chocolate-Flavored
   Low-Calorie Milk Pudding

Serving Information
Men and Youth: Add ⅓ cup Pineapple Juice, 1
   slice Raisin Bread, and 1 small Apple
Youth: Add 1¾ cups Skim Milk

MORNING MEAL
⅓ cup Apple Juice
1 serving Hot Cereal, ¾ ounce uncooked
1 teaspoon Margarine
1 cup Skim Milk
Coffee or Tea

MIDDAY MEAL
Stuffed French Toast
Tossed Salad with Lemon Juice
Hot Spiced Tea with 1 teaspoon Honey

EVENING MEAL
1 cup Tomato Juice
3–4 ounces Roast Veal
4 ounces Baked Potato
½ cup Steamed Artichoke Hearts
½ cup Steamed Crookneck Squash Slices
Sliced Tomato and Alfalfa or Bean Sprouts on
   Romaine Lettuce with **Herb Dressing**
Sparkling Mineral Water with Twist of Lime

SNACKS, AT PLANNED TIMES
½ cup Cooked Rhubarb; 1 cup Cantaloupe
   Chunks; ¾ cup Buttermilk

Serving Information
Men and Youth: Add ⅓ cup Apple Juice, 2
   tablespoons Raisins, 1 small Orange, and 1
   ounce Enriched Roll
Youth: Add 2 cups Skim Milk

MORNING MEAL
1 small Orange
1 Scrambled Egg
1 slice Toasted Enriched Bread
¼ cup Skim Milk
Coffee or Tea

MIDDAY MEAL
Flounder Italiano
¼ cup Cooked Beets
½ cup Cooked Green Beans
Grated Radishes and Carrot on Shredded
   Cabbage
1 teaspoon Mayonnaise
1 medium Persimmon or 1 small Pear
¾ cup Skim Milk

EVENING MEAL
3–4 ounces Broiled Steak
Baked Eggplant Slices
½ cup Steamed Asparagus Tips
Green Salad with 1 teaspoon Mayonnaise
4 fluid ounces Red Wine
Coffee or Tea

SNACKS, AT PLANNED TIMES
½ cup Plain Unflavored Yogurt with
   2 tablespoons Applesauce plus Cinnamon;
   Fruit Mélange; 1 Graham Cracker

Serving Information
Men and Youth: Add 1 slice Rye Bread, ½
   medium Banana, and 1 ounce Whole Wheat Roll
Youth: Add 2 cups Skim Milk

Halloween brings thoughts of witches. Witches conjure potions. As do good cooks.

In the days before medicine and botany were exact sciences, there were probably some bad-tempered "witches" who understood the psychedelic effects of herbs such as hemp, henbane, and belladonna. But other people who were labeled as witches might have been no more than herbal healers.

If Halloween still has you spooked, try some old-fashioned remedies handed down from the days of poultices and infusions. Place a sprig of rosemary, fennel, or dill on your lapel or under your pillow. All three are said to protect against the evil eye.

Carry a piece of angelica root, reputed to stop witches in mid-spell. Or take bay leaves trick-or-treating with you. They have a reputation for counteracting evil spirits.

Some potions play tricks. Others, like our Autumn Treat (Day 3), are pleasantly bewitching.

WEEK 44

DAY 1

MORNING MEAL
½ medium Banana, sliced
¾ ounce Ready-to-Eat Cereal
1 cup Skim Milk
Coffee or Tea

MIDDAY MEAL
3 tablespoons Peanut Butter on 1 slice Raisin Bread with 1½ teaspoons Reduced-Calorie Apricot Spread
Green Bell Pepper and Zucchini Sticks
1 small Apple

EVENING MEAL
¾ cup **Chicken Broth**
Lemon-Broiled Snappers (Baby Bluefish)
4 ounces Baked Potato
¼ cup Steamed Peas
Green Salad with Cider Vinegar and Herbs
¾ ounce Crispbread
½ cup Lime-Flavored Low-Calorie Gelatin

SNACKS, AT PLANNED TIMES
1 serving Vanilla-Flavored Low-Calorie Milk Beverage; 1 cup Strawberries

Serving Information
Men and Youth: Add ½ medium Banana, sliced, 1 slice Raisin Bread, ½ cup Canned Sliced Peaches, and ¾ cup Canned Apple Slices
Youth: Add 1 cup Skim Milk

DAY 4

MORNING MEAL
1 small Orange
1 serving Hot Cereal, ¾ ounce uncooked
1 teaspoon Margarine
1 cup Skim Milk
Coffee or Tea

MIDDAY MEAL
3–4 ounces Broiled Beef Liver
¼ cup Steamed Onion Rings
½ cup Steamed Asparagus Tips
Tossed Salad with **Tarragon Vinaigrette** and 1 teaspoon Grated Parmesan Cheese
1 ounce Enriched Roll
½ cup Canned Pineapple Chunks

EVENING MEAL
Chilled Tomato Appetizer
3–4 ounces Roast Beef
½ cup Steamed Sliced Carrot
½ cup Steamed Sliced Eggplant
Bean Sprouts on Lettuce with Lemon Juice
1 slice Rye Bread
1 teaspoon Margarine
Iced Tea

SNACKS, AT PLANNED TIMES
½ cup Chocolate-Flavored Low-Calorie Milk Pudding; 1 small Pear

Serving Information
Men and Youth: Add 2 tablespoons Raisins, 1 slice Toasted Whole Wheat Bread, ½ cup Canned Pineapple Chunks, and 2 Graham Crackers
Youth: Add 1 cup Skim Milk

DAY 5

MORNING MEAL
⅓ cup Apple Juice
⅓ cup Part-Skim Ricotta Cheese
1 slice Raisin Bread
¼ cup Skim Milk
Coffee or Tea

MIDDAY MEAL
Broccoli "Meatballs"
½ cup Steamed Scallop Squash
Salad with Sliced Egg
½ cup Strawberry-Flavored Gelatin

EVENING MEAL
Salmon Salad
Green Bell Pepper Rings and 1 ounce Julienne Fontina Cheese on Lettuce with 1 teaspoon Mayonnaise
1 ounce Whole Wheat Roll
1 medium Kiwi Fruit or ½ medium Grapefruit
¾ cup Skim Milk

SNACKS, AT PLANNED TIMES
½ cup **Hot Mocha Milk;** 3 ounces Vanilla-Flavored Dietary Frozen Dessert

Serving Information
Men and Youth: Add ⅓ cup Apple Juice, 1 slice Raisin Bread, 1 ounce Enriched Roll, and 1 cup Strawberries
Youth: Add 1 cup Skim Milk and ½ cup **Hot Mocha Milk**

DAY 2

MORNING MEAL
½ cup Orange Juice
1 Scrambled Egg
½ English Muffin, toasted
1 teaspoon Margarine
½ cup Skim Milk
Coffee or Tea

MIDDAY MEAL
Fruited Cheese Delight
Watercress Salad with 1 teaspoon Reduced-
    Calorie Mayonnaise
1 slice Rye Bread
1 teaspoon Reduced-Calorie Margarine
1 cup Skim Milk

EVENING MEAL
3–4 ounces Broiled Hamburger
½ Hamburger Roll
½ cup Cooked Green Beans
½ medium Tomato, sliced
Shredded Cabbage with Sliced Radishes and
    1 teaspoon Vegetable Oil plus Wine Vinegar
8 fluid ounces Beer

SNACKS, AT PLANNED TIMES
Coffee-Yogurt Shake; ½ cup Blueberries

Serving Information
Men and Youth: Add ½ cup Orange Juice, ½
    English Muffin, toasted, ½ Hamburger Roll, and
    ½ cup Blueberries
Youth: Add 2 cups Skim Milk

DAY 3

MORNING MEAL
1 cup Cantaloupe Balls
1 ounce Swiss Cheese
½ small Enriched Bagel
¼ cup Skim Milk
Coffee or Tea

MIDDAY MEAL
Scallop Bisque
Green Salad with **Sesame Vinaigrette**
Peanut Butter "Ice Cream" Sandwich

EVENING MEAL
3–4 ounces Baked Chicken Breast
½ cup Steamed Wax Beans
½ cup Steamed Cauliflower Florets
Romaine and Bibb Salad with **Pesto Dressing**
½ cup Skim Milk
Coffee or Tea

SNACKS, AT PLANNED TIMES
1 medium Peach; **Autumn Treat;** 1 cup Plain
    Popcorn

Serving Information
Men and Youth: Add 1 small Apple and 1 ounce
    Enriched Roll
Youth: Add 2 cups Skim Milk

DAY 6

MORNING MEAL
½ medium Papaya or 1 cup Strawberries
¾ ounce Ready-to-Eat Cereal
¾ cup Skim Milk
Coffee or Tea

MIDDAY MEAL
Pasta Kugel
Tossed Salad with **Herb Dressing**
½ cup Cherry-Flavored Low-Calorie Gelatin with
    ¼ cup Canned Fruit Cocktail

EVENING MEAL
1 cup Mixed Vegetable Juice
Rabbit Bourguignon
Green Salad with Lemon Juice
1 ounce Enriched Roll
Sparkling Mineral Water with Mint Sprig

SNACKS, AT PLANNED TIMES
¾ cup Buttermilk; ½ cup Melon Balls; ½ cup
    Cooked Rhubarb

Serving Information
Men and Youth: Add 2 tablespoons Raisins, 4
    Melba Toast Slices, ¼ cup Canned Fruit Cock-
    tail, 1 ounce Enriched Roll, and ½ cup Melon
    Balls
Youth: Add 1¼ cups Skim Milk

DAY 7

MORNING MEAL
⅓ cup Pineapple Juice
1 Poached Egg
½ English Muffin, toasted
1 teaspoon Reduced-Calorie Margarine
¼ cup Skim Milk
Coffee or Tea

MIDDAY MEAL
3–4 ounces Broiled Flounder
½ cup Cooked Broccoli
Sliced Cucumber on Lettuce with 1 teaspoon
    Savory Vinaigrette
1 slice Enriched Bread
¾ cup Skim Milk

EVENING MEAL
3–4 ounces Broiled Steak
½ cup Steamed Beets
½ cup Steamed Cabbage
Sliced Tomato and Radishes on Bibb Lettuce
    with 1 teaspoon Mayonnaise
1 ounce Whole Wheat Roll
1 teaspoon Reduced-Calorie Margarine
4 fluid ounces Red Wine
Coffee or Tea

SNACKS, AT PLANNED TIMES
½ cup Vanilla-Flavored Low-Calorie Milk
    Pudding; 10 large Cherries; ½ cup Grapefruit
    Sections

Serving Information
Men and Youth: Add 1 ounce Whole Wheat Roll,
    10 large Cherries, and 2 Graham Crackers
Youth: Add 2 cups Skim Milk

Mussels are delicious and easy to prepare. Clean each mussel thoroughly with a wire brush or plastic pot scrubber, removing any mud and grass that cling to the shells. Be sure to remove the "beard."

The shells of live mussels are usually tightly closed and open when cooked; you should discard any mussels whose shells are unopened after cooking, on the off chance that you overlooked a dead one.

Mussels can be either served plain on the half-shell in their own cooking liquid after they've been steamed for four or five minutes, or eaten lukewarm or cold topped with a mayonnaise or vinaigrette dressing. Try them in Mussel-Rice Casserole (Day 3).

Economy Tip—Baked ham is on the menu on Day 5. Leftovers may be frozen and used in Creamed Cabbage and Ham recipe (Week 51, Day 2).

MORNING MEAL
½ cup Orange Juice
1 Soft-Cooked Egg
1 slice Toasted Whole Wheat Bread
1 teaspoon Margarine
½ cup Skim Milk
Coffee or Tea

MIDDAY MEAL
Chick Pea Croquettes (Falafel)
Green Salad with 1 teaspoon Vegetable Oil plus Wine Vinegar
2 Melba Toast Slices
¼ small Pineapple

EVENING MEAL
3–4 ounces Broiled Haddock
½ cup Cooked Enriched Noodles
½ cup Cooked Green Beans
Vegetable Salad with Relish Dressing
Club Soda with Twist of Lemon

SNACKS, AT PLANNED TIMES
1 cup Mixed Vegetable Juice; 3 ounces Dietary Frozen Dessert with ½ teaspoon Chocolate Syrup

Serving Information
Men and Youth: Add 1 slice Rye Bread, ¼ small Pineapple, and 1 slice Whole Wheat Bread
Men: Add 1 ounce Broiled Haddock at the Evening Meal
Youth: Add 1½ cups Skim Milk

MORNING MEAL
½ cup Orange Sections
¾ ounce Ready-to-Eat Cereal
¾ cup Skim Milk
Coffee or Tea

MIDDAY MEAL
3–4 ounces Broiled Liver
2 tablespoons Sliced Onion sautéed in 1 teaspoon Margarine
½ cup Cooked Spinach
Red Cabbage topped with Bean Sprouts and sprinkled with Lemon Juice
1 slice Pumpernickel Bread
1 teaspoon Margarine
½ cup Applesauce

EVENING MEAL
Veal Patties and Mushrooms
½ Hamburger Roll
½ cup Cooked Carrot Slices
½ cup Cooked Cauliflower
Green Salad with 1 teaspoon Mayonnaise
¼ cup Skim Milk
Coffee or Tea

SNACKS, AT PLANNED TIMES
½ cup Cherry-Flavored Gelatin; **Pear Frozen Yogurt**

Serving Information
Men and Youth: Add 1 slice Rye Bread, ½ cup Applesauce, ½ Hamburger Roll, and 1 small Orange
Youth: Add 1½ cups Skim Milk

MORNING MEAL
½ cup Grapefruit Juice
1 Poached Egg
½ English Muffin, toasted
1 teaspoon Margarine
½ cup Skim Milk
Coffee or Tea

MIDDAY MEAL
Potato Soup
Open-Face Grilled Cheese Sandwich II
Dill Pickle Spears
4 medium Dried Apricot Halves

EVENING MEAL
3 ounces Baked Ham
Broiled Tomato
½ cup Steamed Broccoli
Watercress and Alfalfa or Bean Sprouts Salad with 1 teaspoon Vegetable Oil plus Wine Vinegar and Herbs
½ cup Skim Milk
Coffee or Tea

SNACKS, AT PLANNED TIMES
1 cup Mixed Vegetable Juice; **Coconut-Honey Shake**; 1 medium Persimmon or 1 small Apple

Serving Information
Men and Youth: Add ½ English Muffin, toasted, ½ cup Grapefruit Juice, 1 slice Whole Wheat Bread, and 1 small Apple
Men: Add 1 ounce Baked Ham at the Evening Meal
Youth: Add 2 cups Skim Milk

MORNING MEAL
½ cup Strawberries
Applesauce Oatmeal
1 slice Toasted Rye Bread
1 teaspoon Margarine
¼ cup Skim Milk
Coffee or Tea

MIDDAY MEAL
Cheese Pizza Pocket
Carrot and Celery Sticks
Tossed Salad with 1 teaspoon Imitation Bacon
  Bits and 1 teaspoon Mayonnaise
½ cup Skim Milk
Coffee or Tea

EVENING MEAL
3–4 ounces Broiled Steak
Creamy Broccoli
½ cup Cooked Wax Beans
Lettuce with Tomato and Cucumber Slices
4 fluid ounces Red Wine
Coffee or Tea

SNACKS, AT PLANNED TIMES
Strawberry Shake; ½ medium Papaya or 1 small
  Pear; 2 Graham Crackers

Serving Information
Men and Youth: Add ½ cup Strawberries, 2
  ounces Whole Wheat Roll, and ½ medium
  Papaya or 1 small Apple
Youth: Add 1¼ cups Skim Milk

MORNING MEAL
1 cup Tomato Juice
1 Scrambled Egg
1 ounce Enriched Roll
1 teaspoon Reduced-Calorie Strawberry Spread
½ cup Skim Milk
Coffee or Tea

MIDDAY MEAL
Sesame Chicken with Green Beans
½ cup Cooked Asparagus Tips
Green Salad with Lemon Juice
1 slice Cracked Wheat Bread
½ cup Canned Sliced Peaches

EVENING MEAL
Mussel-Rice Casserole
½ cup Cooked Sliced Zucchini
½ medium Tomato, sliced
Tossed Salad with **Tarragon Vinaigrette**
½ cup Skim Milk
Coffee or Tea

SNACKS, AT PLANNED TIMES
¾ cup Buttermilk; ½ medium Banana

Serving Information
Men and Youth: Add 1 ounce Enriched Roll, 6
  Saltines, and ½ medium Banana
Youth: Add 1 cup Skim Milk

MORNING MEAL
1 small Orange
1 serving Hot Cereal, ¾ ounce uncooked
¾ cup Skim Milk
Coffee or Tea

MIDDAY MEAL
Mushroom Caps Soufflé
Celery-Ricotta Bake
Green Salad with 1½ teaspoons Vegetable Oil
  plus Cider Vinegar
1 slice Rye Bread
12 large Grapes

EVENING MEAL
3–4 ounces Roast Turkey
¼ cup Baked Acorn Squash with Cinnamon
½ cup Cooked Wax Beans
Radish Salad
Lime Cooler

SNACKS, AT PLANNED TIMES
½ cup Raspberries; ¾ cup Buttermilk; 2 Graham
  Crackers

Serving Information
Men and Youth: Add 2 tablespoons Raisins and
  2 ounces Enriched French Bread
Youth: Add 1¾ cups Skim Milk

MORNING MEAL
⅓ cup Apple Juice
Peanut-Cheese Muffin
½ cup Skim Milk
Coffee or Tea

MIDDAY MEAL
3–4 ounces Broiled Scrod
½ medium Tomato, sliced
6 medium Cooked Asparagus Spears
Lettuce with Zucchini Slices and Green Bell
  Pepper Rings
1 teaspoon Reduced-Calorie Mayonnaise
3 Melba Toast Rounds
1 cup Skim Milk

EVENING MEAL
Hot Mushroom Turnovers
3–4 ounces Roast Beef
½ cup Cooked Green Beans
Tossed Salad with 1 teaspoon Imitation Bacon
  Bits and **Basic Vinaigrette**
4 fluid ounces Champagne
Coffee or Tea

SNACKS, AT PLANNED TIMES
1 cup Cantaloupe Balls; 1 cup Strawberries with
  3½ tablespoons Plain Unflavored Yogurt

Serving Information
Men and Youth: Add ⅔ cup Apple Juice and 2
  ounces Enriched Roll
Youth: Add 1½ cups Skim Milk

With the holidays fast approaching, many cooks seek innovative ways to make their tables look more festive. An old Danish proverb says, "When serving, first put out the flowers, then bring out the food."

Flowers are always lovely, but this year why not try an edible centerpiece? A decorative basket filled with fresh fruit, each variety glowing with ripe perfection, is a feast for the eyes during dinner, and afterward it can serve as dessert.

Baskets of artfully arranged crudités, cut up and ready to dip or munch, add visual spice. A large, fragrant loaf of home-baked bread sitting atop a wooden cutting board is a sure conversation starter, and it will also make your guests feel that you went to special effort for them.

With a little imagination, each platter or bowl you bring to the table can be garnished attractively.

WEEK 46

DAY 1

MORNING MEAL
½ medium Banana, sliced
¾ ounce Ready-to-Eat Cereal
¾ cup Skim Milk □ Coffee or Tea

MIDDAY MEAL
⅔ cup Part-Skim Ricotta Cheese with
   2 tablespoons Scallion, chopped
Cucumber and Pimiento Slices on Romaine
   Lettuce with 2 Sliced Green Olives
6 Melba Toast Rounds □ 1 teaspoon Margarine
¼ cup Skim Milk □ Coffee or Tea

EVENING MEAL
1 cup Tomato Juice
Chicken and Legumes Casserole
½ cup Steamed Sliced Carrot
½ cup Steamed Broccoli
Boston and Bibb Lettuce Salad with Alfalfa or
   Bean Sprouts and 1 tablespoon Low-Calorie
   Italian Dressing
1 ounce Whole Wheat Roll □ 1 teaspoon Margarine
Coffee or Tea

SNACKS, AT PLANNED TIMES
1 cup Honeydew Balls; ½ cup Plain Unflavored
   Yogurt with 2 tablespoons Raisins and
   ½ teaspoon Shredded Coconut

Serving Information
Men and Youth: Add ½ medium Banana, sliced,
   1 ounce Whole Wheat Roll, 2 tablespoons
   Raisins, and 2 Graham Crackers
Men: Add ½ ounce Diced Tofu and ½ ounce
   Canned Chick Peas to Salad at the Evening
   Meal
Youth: Add 2 cups Skim Milk

DAY 4

MORNING MEAL
½ cup Canned Fruit Cocktail
¾ ounce Ready-to-Eat Cereal
¾ cup Skim Milk
Coffee or Tea

MIDDAY MEAL
Liver Loaf Pâté
Green Salad with **Basic Vinaigrette**
3 each Melba Toast Rounds and Saltines
Club Soda with Lemon Wedge

EVENING MEAL
3–4 ounces Roast Pork
¼ cup Steamed Sliced Onion
½ cup Steamed Mushrooms
½ cup Steamed Sliced Zucchini
Tossed Salad with **Vinaigrette Parmesan**
½ cup Canned Crushed Pineapple

SNACKS, AT PLANNED TIMES
1 medium Ugli Fruit or ½ medium Grapefruit;
   1 serving Vanilla-Flavored Low-Calorie Milk
   Beverage; 1 cup Mixed Vegetable Juice with
   ¾ ounce Crispbread

Serving Information
Men and Youth: Add 4 medium Dried Apricot
   Halves, 1 slice Rye Bread, 1 slice Whole Wheat
   Bread, and 1 small Apple
Youth: Add 1¾ cups Skim Milk

DAY 5

MORNING MEAL
1 small Orange
⅓ cup Cottage Cheese
½ English Muffin, toasted
1 teaspoon Reduced-Calorie Grape Spread
¼ cup Skim Milk □ Coffee or Tea

MIDDAY MEAL
3–4 ounces Sardines
2 tablespoons Red Onion Rings
Carrot and Celery Sticks
Lettuce Wedge with 2 teaspoons Reduced-
   Calorie Mayonnaise
1 slice Toasted Whole Wheat Bread
1 small Apple
¾ cup Skim Milk

EVENING MEAL
3–4 ounces Broiled Veal Patty
2 teaspoons Ketchup
½ cup Cooked Spinach
½ cup Baked Eggplant Slices
Green Salad with 2 teaspoons Vegetable Oil plus
   Wine Vinegar and Herbs
8 fluid ounces Beer

SNACKS, AT PLANNED TIMES
Honey-Glazed Pears; Lime Cooler;
   ½ cup Cherry-Flavored Low-Calorie
   Gelatin; 1 cup Skim Milk

Serving Information
Men and Youth: Add ½ English Muffin, toasted,
   ½ Hamburger Roll, and ½ cup Canned Sliced
   Peaches
Youth: Add 1 cup Skim Milk

DAY 2

MORNING MEAL
½ medium Grapefruit
1 Poached Egg
½ Matzo Board
1 teaspoon Reduced-Calorie Margarine
½ cup Skim Milk ☐ Coffee or Tea

MIDDAY MEAL
1 cup Mixed Vegetable Juice
3–4 ounces Canned Salmon with ¼ cup Diced
    Celery, 2 tablespoons Diced Onion, and
    2 teaspoons Reduced-Calorie Mayonnaise
Tomato Slices on Lettuce Leaves
1 slice Pumpernickel Bread
½ cup Lemon-Flavored Low-Calorie Gelatin

EVENING MEAL
3–4 ounces Roast Beef
Horseradish-Chili Sauce
3 ounces Baked Yam with Cinnamon, Artificial
    Sweetener, and 1 teaspoon Reduced-Calorie
    Margarine
¼ cup Steamed Mushroom Caps
6 medium Steamed Asparagus Spears
Watercress and Sliced Radish Salad with
    1 teaspoon Sesame Oil plus Rice Vinegar
½ cup Skim Milk ☐ Coffee or Tea

SNACKS, AT PLANNED TIMES
¾ cup Buttermilk; 20 small Grapes; ½ cup
    Canned Sliced Peaches

Serving Information
Men and Youth: Add ½ Matzo Board, ½ cup
    Canned Fruit Cocktail, and 1 ounce Enriched
    Roll
Youth: Add 1 cup Skim Milk

DAY 3

MORNING MEAL
1 small Pear, quartered
1 ounce Camembert Cheese
1 slice Toasted Rye Bread
½ cup Skim Milk
Coffee or Tea

MIDDAY MEAL
2 sliced Hard-Cooked Eggs
½ cup Grated Carrot with 1 tablespoon Raisins,
    ½ teaspoon Sunflower Seeds, and 2 teaspoons
    Mayonnaise
Romaine Lettuce Leaves
1 slice Toasted Whole Wheat Bread
½ cup Skim Milk
Coffee or Tea

EVENING MEAL
3–4 ounces Broiled Scallops
½ cup Steamed Brussels Sprouts
½ cup Steamed Wax Beans
Cucumber Slices and Red Bell Pepper Rings on
    Lettuce with 1 teaspoon Vegetable Oil plus
    Cider Vinegar and Herbs
4 fluid ounces White Wine
Coffee or Tea

SNACKS, AT PLANNED TIMES
Berries with Lemon-Cinnamon Yogurt; 1 cup
    Cantaloupe Balls

Serving Information
Men and Youth: Add ½ medium Grapefruit, 1
    tablespoon Raisins, and 2 ounces Enriched
    French Bread
Youth: Add 2 cups Skim Milk

DAY 6

MORNING MEAL
⅓ cup Apple Juice
Grilled Tortillas
½ cup Skim Milk
Coffee or Tea

MIDDAY MEAL
3–4 ounces Sliced Cooked Chicken
Romaine Lettuce with Cherry Tomatoes, Sliced
    Cucumber, and Green Bell Pepper Rings
2 teaspoons Reduced-Calorie Mayonnaise
Dill Pickle Spears
4 Melba Toast Slices
½ medium Grapefruit

EVENING MEAL
Sautéed Shrimp and Corn
½ cup Cooked Broccoli with ¼ cup Diced
    Pimiento
Watercress and Bibb Lettuce Salad with
    1 teaspoon Vegetable Oil plus Tarragon
    Vinegar
½ cup Skim Milk
Coffee or Tea

SNACKS, AT PLANNED TIMES
1 medium Persimmon or 1 small Pear; 1 serving
    Chocolate-Flavored Low-Calorie Milk Beverage

Serving Information
Men and Youth: Add ⅔ cup Apple Juice and 1
    ounce Enriched Roll
Youth: Add 1 cup Skim Milk

DAY 7

MORNING MEAL
⅓ cup Pineapple Juice
1 serving Hot Cereal, ¾ ounce uncooked
1 cup Skim Milk
Coffee or Tea

MIDDAY MEAL
Cheese Omelet I
Green Salad with 2 sliced Black Olives and
    1½ teaspoons Olive Oil plus Wine Vinegar
1 slice Rye Bread
1 small Orange

EVENING MEAL
Radish Pinwheels
3–4 ounces Broiled Steak
½ cup Cooked Artichoke Hearts
½ cup Cooked Sliced Carrot
Escarole and Boston Lettuce Salad with
    Lemon Juice
1 ounce Whole Wheat Roll
4 fluid ounces Red Wine
Coffee or Tea

SNACKS, AT PLANNED TIMES
¾ cup Buttermilk; ½ cup Applesauce sprinkled
    with 1 teaspoon Wheat Germ; ½ cup
    Strawberry-Flavored Low-Calorie Gelatin with
    1 tablespoon Low-Calorie Whipped Topping

Serving Information
Men and Youth: Add ⅓ cup Pineapple Juice, 1
    slice Rye Bread, and 2 Graham Crackers
Youth: Add 1 cup Skim Milk

WEEK 47

Thanksgiving was the first American holiday. The Pilgrims invited their Indian neighbors, who brought maize to the feast.

The Thanksgiving holiday gained acceptance a lot sooner than one of its now customary dishes—potatoes. Legend has it that the humble tuber we know and appreciate today had to make *seven* trips across the Atlantic before finding favor on American shores, sometime during the sixteenth century. And although the potato was well liked in England, Ireland, and many parts of the Continent, it remained suspect in France until a famed botanist extolled its virtues in 1771.

Potatoes are versatile and lend themselves to a variety of cooking techniques. Today potato dishes are as traditionally American as the fourth Thursday in November. We include Potato-Pumpkin Puffs as part of our Thanksgiving meal (Day 4).

DAY 1

MORNING MEAL
½ cup Orange Sections
⅓ cup Cottage Cheese with ½ teaspoon Caraway Seeds
1 slice Whole Wheat Bread with 1 teaspoon Reduced-Calorie Strawberry Spread
½ cup Skim Milk ☐ Coffee or Tea

MIDDAY MEAL
3–4 ounces Canned Salmon mixed with 1 tablespoon Reduced-Calorie Mayonnaise and 1 teaspoon Pickle Relish
Lettuce Wedges ☐ Carrot and Celery Sticks
1 slice Rye Bread
½ cup Skim Milk ☐ Coffee or Tea

EVENING MEAL
3–4 ounces Baked Chicken Cutlet with ¼ cup Steamed Sliced Onion
½ cup Baked Spaghetti Squash with ½ cup Tomato Sauce and 1 teaspoon Grated Parmesan Cheese
½ cup Steamed Broccoli with Chopped Pimiento
Tossed Salad with **Dill Vinaigrette**
1 small Apple

SNACKS, AT PLANNED TIMES
½ cup Cherry-Flavored Low-Calorie Gelatin; ½ cup Canned Crushed Pineapple; ½ cup Plain Unflavored Yogurt

Serving Information
Men and Youth: Add 1 slice Whole Wheat Bread, 1 ounce Enriched Roll, and 4 medium Dried Apricot Halves
Youth: Add 1 cup Skim Milk

DAY 4

MORNING MEAL
1 cup Strawberries
¾ ounce Ready-to-Eat Cereal
¾ cup Skim Milk
Coffee or Tea

MIDDAY MEAL
Cauliflower and Zucchini Soup
Roast Turkey with Mushroom Gravy
Potato-Pumpkin Puffs
Asparagus Pimiento
Red Leaf Salad
4 fluid ounces Champagne
Fruit "Pie"
Hot Spiced Tea

EVENING MEAL
3–4 ounces Broiled Flounder Fillet
½ cup Steamed Spinach
½ cup Steamed Wax Beans
1 ounce Enriched Roll
1¼ teaspoons Margarine
¼ cup Skim Milk
Coffee or Tea

SNACKS, AT PLANNED TIMES
¾ cup Buttermilk; 10 small Grapes; 1 small Apple

Serving Information
Men and Youth: Add 1 slice Rye Bread, 1 ounce Enriched Roll, ½ cup Canned Crushed Pineapple, and 10 small Grapes
Youth: Add 1¼ cups Skim Milk

DAY 5

MORNING MEAL
⅓ cup Pineapple Juice
1 Scrambled Egg with 1 teaspoon Imitation Bacon Bits
1 slice Toasted Pumpernickel Bread
1 teaspoon Margarine
½ cup Skim Milk
Coffee or Tea

MIDDAY MEAL
2 ounces Brie Cheese on Lettuce Leaves with Tomato Wedges and Celery and Carrot Sticks
2 Black Olives
6 Melba Toast Rounds
1 teaspoon Margarine
1 small Pear

EVENING MEAL
3–4 ounces Broiled Lamb Chop with 1 teaspoon Prepared Horseradish
½ cup Steamed Broccoli
½ cup Steamed Cauliflower
Tossed Salad with Diced Pimiento and **Vinaigrette Parmesan**
½ cup Skim Milk
Coffee or Tea

SNACKS, AT PLANNED TIMES
½ cup Plain Unflavored Yogurt with 2 teaspoons Reduced-Calorie Apricot Spread; 1 cup Honeydew or Cantaloupe Balls

Serving Information
Men and Youth: Add ⅓ cup Pineapple Juice, 2 ounces Enriched Roll, and 2 tablespoons Raisins
Youth: Add 2 cups Skim Milk

DAY 2

MORNING MEAL
Creamy Apple-Raisin Oatmeal
½ cup Skim Milk
Coffee or Tea

MIDDAY MEAL
¾ cup **Beef Broth**
⅔ cup Part-Skim Ricotta Cheese with
    1 tablespoon Chopped Scallion
Romaine Lettuce with Cucumber Slices, Cherry
    Tomatoes, and 1 Sliced Black Olive
6 Melba Toast Rounds
1 small Orange

EVENING MEAL
Liver-Noodle Casserole
½ cup Steamed Green Beans
½ cup Steamed Sliced Carrot
Green Salad with 1 tablespoon Reduced-Calorie
    Mayonnaise
½ cup Skim Milk
Coffee or Tea

SNACKS, AT PLANNED TIMES
½ cup Lemon-Flavored Low-Calorie Gelatin with
    ½ medium Banana, sliced; 2 Graham Crackers

Serving Information
Men and Youth: Add ⅔ cup Apple Juice, 2 ounces
    Enriched Italian Bread, and ½ medium Banana
Youth: Add 2 cups Skim Milk

DAY 3

MORNING MEAL
½ cup Applesauce
1 Poached Egg
½ English Muffin, toasted
1 teaspoon Margarine
½ cup Skim Milk
Coffee or Tea

MIDDAY MEAL
3–4 ounces Tuna mixed with ¼ cup Diced Celery,
    2 tablespoons Minced Scallion, and 2
    teaspoons Reduced-Calorie Mayonnaise
Lettuce with Alfalfa or Bean Sprouts, Grated
    Carrot, and ½ teaspoon Sunflower Seeds
Dill Pickle Spears
½ cup Canned Fruit Cocktail

EVENING MEAL
3–4 ounces Broiled Hamburger
½ Hamburger Roll
2 teaspoons Ketchup
½ cup Steamed Mushrooms
Tossed Salad with **Savory Vinaigrette**
½ cup Skim Milk
Coffee or Tea

SNACKS, AT PLANNED TIMES
½ cup Plain Unflavored Yogurt with 2 teaspoons
    Reduced-Calorie Strawberry Spread; 1 medium
    Kiwi Fruit or 1 small Orange; 1 cup Mixed
    Vegetable Juice

Serving Information
Men and Youth: Add ½ English Muffin, toasted,
    ½ Hamburger Roll, and 2 Dates
Youth: Add 1 cup Skim Milk

DAY 6

MORNING MEAL
½ cup Canned Fruit Cocktail
¾ ounce Ready-to-Eat Cereal
1 cup Skim Milk
Coffee or Tea

MIDDAY MEAL
French Omelet
Spinach and Mushroom Salad with 1 teaspoon
    Sesame Oil plus Rice Vinegar
1 slice Toasted Rye Bread
Sparkling Mineral Water with Twist of Lemon

EVENING MEAL
Split Pea-Mushroom Stew
20 Oyster Crackers
Green Salad with 2 teaspoons Reduced-Calorie
    Mayonnaise
½ medium Grapefruit

SNACKS, AT PLANNED TIMES
¼ small Pineapple; ¾ cup Buttermilk; 1 cup
    Plain Popcorn

Serving Information
Men and Youth: Add 1 slice Toasted Rye Bread,
    20 small Grapes, and 2 Graham Crackers
Men: Add ½ ounce Shredded Cheddar Cheese to
    Salad at the Midday Meal
Youth: Add 1 cup Skim Milk

DAY 7

MORNING MEAL
½ cup Orange Sections sprinkled with
    1 teaspoon Shredded Coconut
⅓ cup Cottage Cheese
½ Matzo Board with 1 teaspoon Reduced-Calorie
    Grape Spread
½ cup Skim Milk □ Coffee or Tea

MIDDAY MEAL
3–4 ounces Sliced Cooked Turkey
Romaine Lettuce, Cherry Tomatoes, Cucumber
    Slices, and Green Bell Pepper Rings with
    2 teaspoons Olive Oil plus Tarragon Vinegar
    and Seasonings
2 Canned Plums with 2 tablespoons Juice

EVENING MEAL
3 ounces Cooked Knockwurst with 1 teaspoon
    Prepared Mustard
1 Frankfurter Roll
Sautéed Caraway Cabbage
½ cup Cooked Green Beans
Tossed Salad with 2 teaspoons Low-Calorie
    Italian Dressing
8 fluid ounces Beer

SNACKS, AT PLANNED TIMES
3 ounces Dietary Frozen Dessert; ½ cup Plain
    Unflavored Yogurt with ¾ teaspoon Honey

Serving Information
Men and Youth: Add ½ Matzo Board, 1 slice Rye
    Bread, 2 Canned Plums with 2 tablespoons
    Juice, 1 small Apple, and 2 Dates
Men: Add 1 ounce Cooked Knockwurst at the
    Evening Meal
Youth: Add 1½ cups Skim Milk

106 | You enjoy having your home look festive for the holidays. Take a few extra seconds to make the meals you serve seem special.

Use a pastry bag to create a multitude of easy special effects. Try piping mashed potatoes around a turkey or roast, or fill mushroom caps, tomato cups, squash halves, or eggplant boats with purees of other vegetables.

Top dark-colored soups with a spoonful of plain unflavored yogurt. When you see how good that looks, take it one step further. Sprinkle the yogurt with chili or curry powder, or with turmeric.

Another decorating trick is to fill a noodle, rice, or gelatin ring with vegetables. It creates visual interest and at the same time saves using two separate serving dishes.

Use scooped-out melons, orange cups, or grapefruit halves to hold fruit or fish salads.

And top the meal off with our delicious and elegant Crêpes à l'Orange (Day 6).

WEEK 48

DAY 1

MORNING MEAL
½ cup Grapefruit Juice
1 Poached Egg
1 slice Toasted Rye Bread
1 teaspoon Margarine
½ cup Skim Milk
Coffee or Tea

MIDDAY MEAL
2¼–3 ounces Broiled Chicken
½ cup Cooked Asparagus Tips
Tofu-Vegetable Salad
½ cup Canned Sliced Peaches

EVENING MEAL
Layered Baked Flounder
¼ cup Cooked Peas
½ cup Cooked Wax Beans
Tossed Salad with 1 teaspoon Imitation Bacon Bits plus **Tarragon Vinaigrette**
Hot Spiced Tea

SNACKS, AT PLANNED TIMES
Lemonade; 2 Graham Crackers with ½ teaspoon Honey; ½ cup Blueberries with 2 tablespoons Plain Unflavored Yogurt

Serving Information
Men and Youth: Add 1 slice Rye Bread, 2 Graham Crackers, and ½ cup Applesauce
Men: Add 1 ounce Broiled Chicken at the Midday Meal
Youth: Add 1½ cups Skim Milk

DAY 4

MORNING MEAL
½ cup Fruit Salad
1 serving Hot Cereal, ¾ ounce uncooked
1 cup Skim Milk
Coffee or Tea

MIDDAY MEAL
¾ cup **Vegetable Broth** with 10 Oyster Crackers
3–4 ounces Broiled Beef Liver with 2 teaspoons Steak Sauce
¼ cup Steamed Sliced Onion
½ cup Steamed Cauliflower
1 slice Enriched Bread
1 teaspoon Margarine
½ cup Orange Sections

EVENING MEAL
3–4 ounces Broiled Veal Chop
¼ cup Cooked Sliced Beets
½ cup Cooked Green Beans
Green Salad with Cucumber Slices and 2 teaspoons Sesame Oil plus Rice Vinegar
1 ounce Enriched Roll
Coffee or Tea

SNACKS, AT PLANNED TIMES
½ cup Vanilla-Flavored Low-Calorie Milk Pudding; ½ cup Applesauce

Serving Information
Men and Youth: Add 2 tablespoons Raisins, 10 Oyster Crackers, and 2 Graham Crackers
Youth: Add 2 cups Skim Milk

DAY 5

MORNING MEAL
⅓ cup Grape Juice
⅓ cup Pot Cheese
1 slice Raisin Bread
½ cup Skim Milk
Coffee or Tea

MIDDAY MEAL
3–4 ounces Broiled Scrod with **Lemon "Butter" Sauce**
½ cup Steamed Sliced Zucchini
½ cup Steamed Wax Beans
1 small Apple

EVENING MEAL
3–4 ounces Broiled Steak
3 ounces Baked Yam
½ cup Cooked Brussels Sprouts
Tossed Salad with Diced Tomato, Green Bell Pepper Rings, and 2 teaspoons Mayonnaise
½ cup Skim Milk
Coffee or Tea

SNACKS, AT PLANNED TIMES
¾ cup Buttermilk; ½ cup Canned Fruit Cocktail; 1 cup Tomato Juice with 2 Melba Toast Slices

Serving Information
Men and Youth: Add ⅓ cup Grape Juice, 1 slice Raisin Bread, 1 slice Whole Wheat Bread, and 1 cup Melon Balls
Youth: Add 1 cup Skim Milk

DAY 2

MORNING MEAL
1/3 cup Apple Juice
3/4 ounce Ready-to-Eat Cereal
1 cup Skim Milk
Coffee or Tea

MIDDAY MEAL
Tomato Stuffed with Herb Cheese
4 Melba Toast Slices
1 teaspoon Margarine
1/2 cup Chocolate-Flavored Low-Calorie Milk
   Pudding with 1 teaspoon Shredded Coconut

EVENING MEAL
Easy Beef Soup
Green Salad with 1 teaspoon Vegetable Oil plus
   Wine Vinegar
1 ounce Enriched Roll
1 teaspoon Margarine
Honey-Stewed Prunes

SNACKS, AT PLANNED TIMES
1/2 cup Cherry-Flavored Low-Calorie Gelatin;
   1 cup Strawberries

Serving Information
Men and Youth: Add 2/3 cup Apple Juice, 1 slice
   Toasted Whole Wheat Bread with 1 teaspoon
   Reduced-Calorie Apricot Spread, 1 ounce En-
   riched Roll, and 1/2 cup Canned Fruit Cocktail
Youth: Add 1 cup Skim Milk

DAY 3

MORNING MEAL
1 cup Honeydew or Cantaloupe Balls
1 ounce Cheddar Cheese
1/2 English Muffin, toasted
1 cup **Hot Mocha Milk**

MIDDAY MEAL
1 1/2–2 ounces Sliced Cooked Turkey
Potato-Spinach Combo
Carrot and Celery Sticks on Lettuce
2 Canned Pear Halves with 2 tablespoons Juice

EVENING MEAL
Tuna "Newburg"
1/4 cup Baked Acorn Squash
1/2 cup Steamed Broccoli with 1/2 teaspoon
   Margarine
Tossed Salad with 1 teaspoon Mayonnaise
4 fluid ounces White Wine
Coffee or Tea

SNACKS, AT PLANNED TIMES
1/2 medium Banana, sliced, with 2 tablespoons
   Plain Unflavored Yogurt; Zucchini Sticks and
   Red Bell Pepper Rings

Serving Information
Men and Youth: Add 1/2 English Muffin, toasted,
   1/4 small Pineapple, and 1/2 medium Banana,
   sliced
Youth: Add 2 cups Skim Milk

DAY 6

MORNING MEAL
1/2 cup Orange Juice
3/4 ounce Ready-to-Eat Cereal
3/4 cup Skim Milk
Coffee or Tea

MIDDAY MEAL
3/4 cup **Chicken Broth**
3–4 ounces Roast Chicken
Baked Eggplant Slices
1/2 cup Cooked Kale
Tossed Salad with Lemon Juice and Herbs
Lemonade

EVENING MEAL
2 ounces Cooked Shrimp with 1 teaspoon
   Seafood Cocktail Sauce
1/2 cup Cooked Artichoke Hearts with 2 teaspoons
   Margarine
1/2 cup Cooked Sliced Carrot
Green Salad with **Wine Vinaigrette**
4 fluid ounces White Wine
Crêpes à l'Orange
Coffee or Tea

SNACKS, AT PLANNED TIMES
3 ounces Dietary Frozen Dessert; 1/2 cup Skim
   Milk; 2 Graham Crackers

Serving Information
Men and Youth: Add 1 ounce Enriched Roll, 2
   Canned Pear Halves with 2 tablespoons Juice,
   and 1 slice Rye Bread
Youth: Add 1 3/4 cups Skim Milk

DAY 7

MORNING MEAL
1/2 medium Grapefruit
1 Scrambled Egg with Chives
1 slice Toasted Whole Wheat Bread
1/2 cup Skim Milk
Coffee or Tea

MIDDAY MEAL
Chilled Fish Salad with Cucumber Slices and
   Dill Pickle Spears
6 Saltines
2 Canned Pineapple Slices with 2 tablespoons
   Juice

EVENING MEAL
Spiced Tomato Appetizer
3–4 ounces Sliced Roast Beef
1/2 cup Cooked Enriched Noodles with 1 teaspoon
   Margarine and 1/2 teaspoon Sugar
1/2 cup Steamed Spinach
Tossed Salad with Lemon Juice and Seasonings
1/2 cup Skim Milk
Coffee or Tea

SNACKS, AT PLANNED TIMES
1/2 cup Applesauce; 1/2 cup Plain Unflavored
   Yogurt with 2 teaspoons Reduced-Calorie
   Apricot Spread

Serving Information
Men and Youth: Add 2/3 cup Apple Juice, 2
   ounces Enriched French Bread, and 1/2 cup
   Canned Sliced Peaches
Youth: Add 1 cup Skim Milk

Homemade Mayonnaise is really not a luxury. The taste is so superior to commercial brands that the initial loss of convenience becomes secondary.

The origin of the word is a subject of dispute. Some food historians say the Duke of Richelieu (1696–1788) invented the creamy sauce, naming it *mahonnaise* in honor of his military victory in the battle of Mahón. Other food experts say the word comes from the Old French *moyeu*, meaning "egg yolk."

Whatever its etymology, certain facts about mayonnaise are indisputable. It's *very* important to add the oil *slowly*, so the emulsion doesn't separate; and to have all the ingredients at the same temperature so they bind more thoroughly.

Homemade Mayonnaise appears on our menu plan twice this week (Day 2 and Day 4). Since it will keep under refrigeration for about six or seven days, you'll only need to make it once.

MORNING MEAL
4 Canned Apricots with 2 tablespoons Juice
1 serving Hot Cereal, ¾ ounce uncooked
¾ cup Skim Milk
Coffee or Tea

MIDDAY MEAL
Open-Face Grilled Cheese Sandwich II
½ medium Dill Pickle
Carrot and Celery Sticks
½ cup Chocolate-Flavored Low-Calorie Milk
    Pudding

EVENING MEAL
Veal Ragout
½ cup Cooked Enriched Rice
½ cup Cooked Brussels Sprouts
Green Salad with 1 teaspoon Vegetable Oil plus
    Lemon Juice
4 fluid ounces Red Wine
½ cup Applesauce
¼ cup Skim Milk
Coffee or Tea

SNACKS, AT PLANNED TIMES
1 slice Toasted Whole Wheat Bread with
    1 teaspoon Reduced-Calorie Apricot Spread;
    ½ cup Strawberry-Flavored Low-Calorie
    Gelatin; 1 cup Strawberries

Serving Information
Men and Youth: Add 2 tablespoons Raisins, 1
    Dried Fig, and 1 slice Rye Bread
Youth: Add 1¼ cups Skim Milk

MORNING MEAL
½ medium Grapefruit
Cinnamon-Cheese Toast
½ cup Skim Milk
Coffee or Tea

MIDDAY MEAL
3–4 ounces Broiled Calf Liver
2 tablespoons Cooked Sliced Onion
½ cup Cooked Enriched Noodles
½ cup Steamed Asparagus Tips
Tossed Salad with **Chili Vinaigrette**
Sparkling Mineral Water with Twist of Lime

EVENING MEAL
Onion Soup with 1 ounce Enriched French Bread
3–4 ounces Broiled Scrod
½ cup Cooked Spinach
Bean Sprouts with Shredded Red Cabbage,
    ¾ teaspoon Imitation Bacon Bits, and
    1 teaspoon **Homemade Mayonnaise**
½ cup Skim Milk
Coffee or Tea

SNACKS, AT PLANNED TIMES
½ cup Plain Unflavored Yogurt; ½ cup Canned
    Mandarin Orange Sections; 1 small Apple

Serving Information
Men and Youth: Add 1 ounce Enriched French
    Bread and 1 small Pear
Youth: Add 1 cup Skim Milk

MORNING MEAL
⅓ cup Grape Juice
1 tablespoon Peanut Butter
1 teaspoon Reduced-Calorie Strawberry Spread
1 slice Toasted Enriched Bread
¼ cup Skim Milk
Coffee or Tea

MIDDAY MEAL
1 cup Tomato Juice
Mushroom Omelet
Green Salad with Cucumber Slices, Bean
    Sprouts, and Lemon Juice
½ cup Canned Pineapple Chunks

EVENING MEAL
¾ cup **Beef Broth**
Veal Tongue with Onion Sauce
½ cup Steamed Cauliflower
½ cup Cooked Kale
Tossed Salad with Tomato Wedges, Wine
    Vinegar, and Herbs
¼ cup Skim Milk
Coffee or Tea

SNACKS, AT PLANNED TIMES
¾ cup Buttermilk; ¾ ounce Crispbread;
    3 ounces Dietary Frozen Dessert

Serving Information
Men and Youth: Add ⅔ cup Grape Juice, 1 slice
    Toasted Enriched Bread, and 4 Melba Toast
    Slices
Youth: Add 1½ cups Skim Milk

DAY 2

MORNING MEAL
1 cup Tomato Juice
⅓ cup Cottage Cheese
½ English Muffin, toasted
½ cup Skim Milk
Coffee or Tea

MIDDAY MEAL
1½–2 ounces Sliced Cooked Chicken on Lettuce
   with Tomato and Cucumber Slices
2 teaspoons **Homemade Mayonnaise**
Orange Soufflé

EVENING MEAL
Tuna-Cheese Burgers
½ cup Cooked Zucchini Slices
½ cup Cooked Wax Beans
Tossed Salad with **Cider Vinaigrette**
2 Canned Peach Halves with 2 tablespoons Juice
¼ cup Skim Milk
Coffee or Tea

SNACKS, AT PLANNED TIMES
½ medium Banana; ¾ cup Buttermilk; ½ cup
   Blueberries

Serving Information
Men and Youth: Add ½ English Muffin, toasted,
   ½ Hamburger Roll, 10 small Grapes, and ½
   medium Banana
Youth: Add 2 cups Skim Milk

DAY 3

MORNING MEAL
½ cup Orange Juice
¾ ounce Ready-to-Eat Cereal
1 ounce Enriched Roll
½ teaspoon Honey
¾ cup Skim Milk
Coffee or Tea

MIDDAY MEAL
Salmon Salad
Shredded Lettuce with Radish Slices and Diced
   Pimiento
1 ounce Pita Bread
½ cup Cherry-Flavored Low-Calorie Gelatin with
   ½ cup Canned Fruit Cocktail

EVENING MEAL
3–4 ounces Broiled Steak
2 teaspoons Steak Sauce
Sautéed Mushrooms and Onions
¾ cup Cooked Green Beans
Green Salad with 1½ teaspoons Vegetable Oil
   plus Wine Vinegar
4 fluid ounces Red Wine
¼ cup Skim Milk
Coffee or Tea

SNACKS, AT PLANNED TIMES
½ cup Skim Milk; 2 Graham Crackers; 3 ounces
   Dietary Frozen Dessert

Serving Information
Men and Youth: Add 2 slices Enriched Bread and
   ½ cup Canned Pineapple Chunks
Youth: Add 1 cup Skim Milk

DAY 6

MORNING MEAL
½ cup Orange Sections
¾ ounce Ready-to-Eat Cereal
½ cup Skim Milk
Coffee or Tea

MIDDAY MEAL
Stir-Cooked Turkey
4 ounces Baked Potato with 1 teaspoon Reduced-
   Calorie Margarine
¼ cup Cooked Chinese Pea Pods with 1 teaspoon
   Sesame Seeds, toasted
Tossed Salad with Radish Slices and
   Vinaigrette Parmesan
Sparkling Mineral Water or Diet Soda

EVENING MEAL
Layered Baked Flounder
½ cup Cooked Green Beans
½ cup Baked Spaghetti Squash with ¼ cup
   Tomato Sauce
Green Salad with 2 tablespoons Slivered Water
   Chestnuts and 1½ teaspoons Sesame Oil plus
   Rice Vinegar
Coffee or Tea

SNACKS, AT PLANNED TIMES
2 Canned Pear Halves with 2 tablespoons Juice;
   ½ cup Blackberries with 2 tablespoons Plain
   Unflavored Yogurt

Serving Information
Men and Youth: Add 2 ounces Enriched French
   Bread and 1 cup Strawberries
Youth: Add ½ cup Skim Milk and ½ cup
   Chocolate-Flavored Low-Calorie Milk Pudding

DAY 7

MORNING MEAL
½ cup Grapefruit Juice
1 Scrambled Egg with Chives and 2 teaspoons
   Ketchup
1 slice Toasted Rye Bread
1 teaspoon Margarine
½ cup Skim Milk □ Coffee or Tea

MIDDAY MEAL
Broiled Bologna-Cheese Muffin
½ cup Chilled Cooked Sliced Beets
Celery and Zucchini Sticks on Lettuce
¼ cup Skim Milk □ Coffee or Tea

EVENING MEAL
3–4 ounces Roast Chicken
½ cup Cooked Broccoli
½ cup Cooked Diced Carrot
Tossed Salad with Red Bell Pepper Rings and
   1½ teaspoons Vegetable Oil plus Wine
   Vinegar and Seasonings
½ small Cantaloupe with Lemon Wedge
¼ cup Skim Milk □ Coffee or Tea

SNACKS, AT PLANNED TIMES
2 Canned Peach Halves with 2 tablespoons Juice;
   ¾ cup Buttermilk; 1 cup Mixed Vegetable
   Juice

Serving Information
Men and Youth: Add ⅔ cup Pineapple Juice, 1
   small Apple, 1 ounce Enriched Roll, and 6
   Saltines
Men: Add ½ ounce Roast Chicken at the Eve-
   ning Meal
Youth: Add 2 cups Skim Milk

| You may have noticed that liver appears regularly, once a week. Be it pork, beef, lamb, calf, or poultry liver, all are high in nutrition and provide the single richest food source of iron available.

You may have noticed that liver appears regularly, once a week. Be it pork, beef, lamb, calf, or poultry liver, all are high in nutrition and provide the single richest food source of iron available.

Liver is also a good buy. Properly prepared, it emerges moist and tender.

This organ is more perishable than other cuts of meat, so make sure it's fresh. If you plan to freeze the liver you buy, ask if it was previously frozen. Don't refreeze it.

The thin, opaque outer membrane of all but poultry liver should be peeled or trimmed before cooking. It has a tendency to shrivel when cooked, causing the meat to curl. Large veins also should be removed.

Cook liver at moderate temperatures. You'll have a tastier, juicier, more tender meal.

Our menu for Day 1 calls for broiled liver as part of the Midday Meal. Take into account the size and thickness of the meat so that you do not overcook it.

DAY 1

MORNING MEAL
⅓ cup Apple Juice
½ small Enriched Bagel
⅓ cup Pot Cheese
½ cup Skim Milk □ Coffee or Tea

MIDDAY MEAL
3–4 ounces Broiled Liver
¼ cup Sliced Onion sautéed in 1½ teaspoons Reduced-Calorie Margarine
½ cup Steamed Green Beans
Green Salad with Lemon Juice and 1 teaspoon Imitation Bacon Bits
1 slice Enriched Bread
1 teaspoon Reduced-Calorie Margarine
Coffee or Tea

EVENING MEAL
1 cup Tomato Juice
Flounder in Orange Sauce
½ cup Steamed Asparagus Tips
½ cup Steamed Sliced Carrot
Tossed Salad with **Gingered Vinaigrette**
½ cup Skim Milk
Coffee or Tea

SNACKS, AT PLANNED TIMES
½ cup Plain Unflavored Yogurt with ¼ cup Strawberries; 2 Graham Crackers; ½ cup Canned Fruit Cocktail

Serving Information
Men and Youth: Add ⅓ cup Apple Juice, ½ small Enriched Bagel, ¼ cup Strawberries, 1 small Apple, and 2 Graham Crackers
Youth: Add 2 cups Skim Milk

DAY 4

MORNING MEAL
½ cup Canned Sliced Peaches
1 serving Hot Cereal, ¾ ounce uncooked
1 ounce Enriched Roll
1 teaspoon Reduced-Calorie Margarine
1 teaspoon Reduced-Calorie Strawberry Spread
½ cup Skim Milk
Coffee or Tea

MIDDAY MEAL
Cheese Soufflé
½ cup Cooked Green Beans
Green Salad with **Dijon-Herb Dressing**
½ cup Orange-Flavored Low-Calorie Gelatin with ½ cup Canned Mandarin Orange Sections

EVENING MEAL
Chicken and Pork Meatballs
½ cup Cooked Kale
½ cup Steamed Cauliflower
Curried Cole Slaw
1 slice Whole Wheat Bread
4 fluid ounces Rosé Wine
Coffee or Tea

SNACKS, AT PLANNED TIMES
¾ cup Buttermilk; 1 cup Plain Popcorn; **Lime-Orange Ice in Lime Cups**

Serving Information
Men and Youth: Add ¾ ounce Crispbread and ½ cup Applesauce
Youth: Add 1½ cups Skim Milk

DAY 5

MORNING MEAL
1 cup Tomato Juice
1 ounce Swiss Cheese
½ small Enriched Bagel
½ cup Skim Milk
Coffee or Tea

MIDDAY MEAL
Creamy Tuna Salad on Lettuce Leaves with Green Bell Pepper Rings and 1 Green Olive
1 slice Enriched Bread
1 teaspoon Margarine
½ cup Grapefruit Sections

EVENING MEAL
3–4 ounces Roast Turkey Breast
Fennel Parmesan
¼ cup Steamed Carrot Slices mixed with ¼ cup Steamed Chinese Pea Pods
Green Salad with 2 teaspoons Vegetable Oil plus Cider Vinegar
Coffee or Tea

SNACKS, AT PLANNED TIMES
Pineapple-Banana Milk Shake; Raspberry-Grape Yogurt

Serving Information
Men and Youth: Add ½ small Enriched Bagel, 10 small Grapes, and 4 medium Dried Apricot Halves
Youth: Add 1½ cups Skim Milk

DAY 2

MORNING MEAL
½ cup Grapefruit Juice
¾ ounce Ready-to-Eat Cereal
½ cup Skim Milk
Coffee or Tea

MIDDAY MEAL
Stuffed Rigatoni
Baked Eggplant Slices
½ cup Cooked Peas
Cucumber and Radish Slices on Lettuce with
   ½ teaspoon Sunflower Seeds and 1 teaspoon
   Reduced-Calorie Mayonnaise
2 Canned Peach Halves with 2 tablespoons Juice

EVENING MEAL
3 ounces Baked Ham
Vegetable-Stuffed Grape Leaves
½ cup Cooked Wax Beans
Green Salad with Tomato Slices and
   Wine Vinaigrette
Piña Freeze

SNACKS, AT PLANNED TIMES
1 slice Toasted Whole Wheat Bread with 1
   teaspoon Margarine; **Coffee-Yogurt Shake**

Serving Information
Men and Youth: Add 2 tablespoons Raisins, 2
   Canned Peach Halves with 2 tablespoons Juice,
   and 2 ounces Enriched Roll with 2 teaspoons
   Reduced-Calorie Grape Spread
Men: Add 1 ounce Baked Ham at the Evening
   Meal
Youth: Add 1½ cups Skim Milk

DAY 3

MORNING MEAL
⅓ cup Prune Juice
1 ounce Cheddar Cheese
½ English Muffin, toasted
¼ cup Skim Milk
Coffee or Tea

MIDDAY MEAL
3–4 ounces Baked Scrod
Broiled Onion-Topped Tomatoes
½ cup Cooked Broccoli
Tossed Salad with **Tarragon Vinaigrette**
1 slice Toasted Rye Bread
1 teaspoon Margarine
¾ cup Skim Milk

EVENING MEAL
Veal Soup with 10 Oyster Crackers
Bean Sprouts and Green Bell Pepper Rings on
   Lettuce with 1 teaspoon Vegetable Oil plus
   Wine Vinegar and Herbs
½ cup Chocolate-Flavored Low-Calorie Milk
   Pudding
Coffee or Tea

SNACKS, AT PLANNED TIMES
1 small Apple; 1 cup Cantaloupe Balls

Serving Information
Men and Youth: Add ½ English Muffin, toasted,
   1 slice Rye Bread, 5 Oyster Crackers, and 1
   small Pear
Youth: Add 1 cup Skim Milk

DAY 6

MORNING MEAL
¾ cup Canned Apple Slices
¾ ounce Ready-to-Eat Cereal
½ cup Skim Milk
Hot Spiced Tea

MIDDAY MEAL
1½–2 ounces Sliced Cooked Chicken
Tomato and Cucumber Slices on Lettuce with
   2 teaspoons Mayonnaise
6 Melba Toast Rounds
1 Graham Cracker
½ cup Skim Milk
Coffee or Tea

EVENING MEAL
Herbed Beef Broth
3–4 ounces Roast Beef
Potato Pancakes with ½ cup Applesauce
½ cup Cooked Spinach
½ cup Cooked Sliced Carrot
Tossed Salad with Lemon Juice and Herbs
4 fluid ounces Red Wine
Autumn Treat
Coffee or Tea

SNACKS, AT PLANNED TIMES
½ cup Plain Unflavored Yogurt with ½ teaspoon
   Honey; 1 medium Kiwi Fruit or ½ medium
   Grapefruit

Serving Information
Men and Youth: Add 1 ounce Enriched Roll, 2
   Graham Crackers, and 2 Dates
Youth: Add 2 cups Skim Milk

DAY 7

MORNING MEAL
1 cup Cantaloupe Balls
⅓ cup Cottage Cheese
1 slice Toasted Raisin Bread
¼ cup Skim Milk
Coffee or Tea

MIDDAY MEAL
Stuffed Eggs
Green Bell Pepper Rings and Tomato Wedges
½ medium Dill Pickle
1 slice Pumpernickel Bread
1 teaspoon Margarine
¾ cup Skim Milk

EVENING MEAL
3–4 ounces Baked Haddock
½ cup Steamed Mushroom Caps
½ cup Steamed Asparagus Tips with ¾ teaspoon
   Margarine
Cucumber-Radish Salad
4 fluid ounces Champagne
Coffee or Tea

SNACKS, AT PLANNED TIMES
½ cup Canned Fruit Cocktail sprinkled with 1
   teaspoon Shredded Coconut; ¾ cup
   Buttermilk; ½ medium Banana

Serving Information
Men and Youth: Add 1 slice Toasted Raisin
   Bread, ⅔ cup Grape Juice, 1 slice Rye Bread,
   and ½ medium Banana
Youth: Add 1¼ cups Skim Milk

WEEK 51

The true origins of macaroni are as enigmatic as the Mona Lisa's smile.

According to one legend, a Chinese maiden was lured away from her breadmaking by her lover, a member of Marco Polo's expedition to the Orient. Leaves blew into the neglected dough, and, in an attempt to salvage it, she forced the dough through a wicker basket. It emerged, leafless, in thin strands which dried in the sun. She presented it to her lover and he cooked it aboard his ship on the return trip to Italy, and found it delicious.

True or not, it's a historical fact that by the fourteenth century, Italy was the only European country in which macaroni was made. The method of manufacture was an Italian secret. A statesman of the time was credited with naming it. When served some, he reportedly announced, *"Ma caroni"* ("How very dear").

Basil, the herb the French call *l'herbe royale*, makes Basil Macaroni (Day 7) a dish fit for a king.

DAY 1

MORNING MEAL
½ cup Blueberries
¾ ounce Ready-to-Eat Cereal
½ small Enriched Bagel
1 teaspoon Reduced-Calorie Orange Marmalade
1 cup Skim Milk
Coffee or Tea

MIDDAY MEAL
Open-Face Grilled Cheese Sandwich II
Cucumber Slices, Radish Slices, and Pimiento Strips on Romaine Lettuce with **Tarragon Vinaigrette**
Dill Pickle Spears
½ cup Skim Milk
Coffee or Tea

EVENING MEAL
Chicken and Peppers
½ cup Steamed Broccoli
½ cup Steamed Sliced Carrot
Alfalfa or Bean Sprouts and Cherry Tomatoes on Escarole
2 teaspoons Reduced-Calorie Mayonnaise
12 large Grapes
½ cup Skim Milk
Coffee or Tea

SNACKS, AT PLANNED TIMES
1 cup Tomato Juice with 6 Saltines; 1 small Orange

Serving Information
Men and Youth: Add 2 Dates, ½ small Enriched Bagel, and 1 small Apple
Youth: Add 1½ cups Skim Milk

DAY 4

MORNING MEAL
½ medium Banana, sliced
¾ ounce Ready-to-Eat Cereal
1 cup Skim Milk ☐ Coffee or Tea

MIDDAY MEAL
3–4 ounces Sautéed Chicken Livers, using 2 teaspoons Reduced-Calorie Margarine
¼ cup Steamed Onion Slices
½ cup Steamed Mushrooms
Watercress and Romaine Salad with Radish and Cucumber Slices
2 teaspoons Low-Calorie Thousand Island Dressing
1 slice Enriched Bread
¼ cup Skim Milk ☐ Coffee or Tea

EVENING MEAL
Sautéed Curried Veal and Eggplant
½ cup Cooked Spaghetti Squash with ½ cup Tomato Sauce
Green Salad with 2 teaspoons Reduced-Calorie Mayonnaise
1 ounce Enriched French Bread
Sparkling Mineral Water with Twist of Lime

SNACKS, AT PLANNED TIMES
4 medium Dried Apricot Halves; ¾ cup Skim Milk; 1 cup Strawberries

Serving Information
Men and Youth: Add ½ medium Banana, sliced, ¾ ounce Crispbread, and 1 ounce Enriched French Bread
Youth: Add 1 cup Skim Milk

DAY 5

MORNING MEAL
½ small Cantaloupe
⅓ cup Cottage Cheese
½ Matzo Board
1 teaspoon Reduced-Calorie Apricot Spread
½ cup Skim Milk
Coffee or Tea

MIDDAY MEAL
3–4 ounces Roast Chicken
½ cup Steamed Sliced Carrot
½ cup Cooked Chopped Spinach
Fruit and Yam Salad with Honeyed Yogurt Dressing
4 Melba Toast Slices
Coffee or Tea

EVENING MEAL
3–4 ounces Broiled Lamb Chop
½ cup Cooked Brussels Sprouts
½ cup Steamed Mushroom Caps
Romaine Lettuce and Alfalfa or Bean Sprouts with **Savory Vinaigrette**
8 fluid ounces Beer

SNACKS, AT PLANNED TIMES
1 small Apple; ¾ cup Buttermilk; Crudités with **Yogurt-Chive Dip**; 1 cup Plain Popcorn with 2 teaspoons Margarine, melted

Serving Information
Men and Youth: Add ½ Matzo Board, 1 slice Pumpernickel Bread, ½ cup Canned Fruit Cocktail, and ⅔ cup Apple Juice
Youth: Add 2 cups Skim Milk

DAY 2

MORNING MEAL
½ medium Grapefruit
1 Soft-Cooked Egg
½ English Muffin, toasted
1 teaspoon Reduced-Calorie Grape Spread
¼ cup Skim Milk □ Coffee or Tea

MIDDAY MEAL
3–4 ounces Broiled Flounder Fillet
½ cup Cooked Green Beans
Grated Carrot and Celery Sticks on Shredded
    Lettuce
2 teaspoons Reduced-Calorie Mayonnaise
½ cup Skim Milk
Coffee or Tea

EVENING MEAL
Creamed Cabbage and Ham
Lettuce Wedge and Tomato Slices with
    Cider Vinaigrette
1 ounce Enriched Roll
½ cup Plain Unflavored Yogurt with 1 tablespoon
    Raisins and 1 teaspoon Shredded Coconut

SNACKS, AT PLANNED TIMES
Pineapple-Strawberry Whip; 1 Graham Cracker;
    1 cup Mixed Vegetable Juice

Serving Information
Men and Youth: Add ½ English Muffin, toasted,
    1 slice Rye Bread, 1 tablespoon Raisins, and
    1 small Pear
Men: Add 1 ounce Broiled Flounder Fillet at the
    Midday Meal
Youth: Add 1¼ cups Skim Milk

DAY 3   113

MORNING MEAL
½ cup Applesauce with Cinnamon
⅓ cup Part-Skim Ricotta Cheese
1 slice Toasted Whole Wheat Bread
½ cup Skim Milk
Coffee or Tea

MIDDAY MEAL
French Omelet
Spinach and Mushroom Salad with 1 tablespoon
    Diced Onion, 1 teaspoon Imitation Bacon Bits,
    and Lemon Juice
½ cup Strawberry-Flavored Low-Calorie Gelatin
    with 2 tablespoons Plain Unflavored Yogurt

EVENING MEAL
⅓ cup Pineapple Juice
Far East Scallops
½ cup Cooked Enriched Rice
Tossed Salad with 1 teaspoon Sesame Oil plus
    Rice Vinegar
4 fluid ounces White Wine
¼ cup Skim Milk
Coffee or Tea

SNACKS, AT PLANNED TIMES
1 cup Skim Milk; 1 cup Cantaloupe Balls

Serving Information
Men and Youth: Add 1 slice Toasted Whole
    Wheat Bread, 4 Melba Toast Slices, and ⅓
    cup Pineappple Juice
Youth: Add 1¼ cups Skim Milk

DAY 6

MORNING MEAL
½ cup Orange Juice
1 Scrambled Egg with 1 teaspoon Imitation
    Bacon Bits
1 slice Toasted Rye Bread
1 teaspoon Margarine
½ cup Skim Milk
Coffee or Tea

MIDDAY MEAL
3 tablespoons Peanut Butter
1 teaspoon Reduced-Calorie Strawberry Spread
1 slice Whole Wheat Bread
½ cup Lemon-Flavored Low-Calorie Gelatin
¼ cup Skim Milk
Coffee or Tea

EVENING MEAL
1 cup Mixed Vegetable Juice
Poached Swordfish
¼ cup Cooked Sliced Beets
½ cup Cooked Cauliflower
Green Salad with Lemon Juice
½ cup Canned Fruit Cocktail
¼ cup Skim Milk
Coffee or Tea

SNACKS, AT PLANNED TIMES
1 small Pear; ½ cup Vanilla-Flavored Low-Calorie
    Milk Pudding

Serving Information
Men and Youth: Add 1 slice Whole Wheat Bread,
    6 Saltines, and 4 medium Dried Apricot Halves
Youth: Add 2 cups Skim Milk

DAY 7

MORNING MEAL
½ medium Banana
1 serving Hot Cereal, ¾ ounce uncooked
1 cup Skim Milk
Coffee or Tea

MIDDAY MEAL
Bean Sprouts with Muenster Julienne
Tomato Wedges and Red Bell Pepper Rings on
    Lettuce with **Garlic Vinaigrette**
1 slice Toasted Rye Bread
1 teaspoon Margarine
Club Soda with Lemon Wedge

EVENING MEAL
3 ounces Cooked Beef Sausage
Basil Macaroni
½ cup Cooked Green Beans with Pimiento Strips
Tossed Salad with **Oregano Vinaigrette**
4 fluid ounces Red Wine
Coffee or Tea

SNACKS, AT PLANNED TIMES
1 cup Strawberries; ½ cup Plain Unflavored
    Yogurt; ½ cup Canned Sliced Peaches

Serving Information
Men and Youth: Add ½ medium Banana and 2
    ounces Enriched Roll
Men: Add 1 ounce Cooked Beef Sausage at the
    Evening Meal
Youth: Add 1 cup Skim Milk

The Christmas week menu includes scallops, the only bivalve to have a patron saint. The apostle St. James wore a scallop shell as his personal emblem.

Scallops also figure in the legends of Greek mythology. The goddess Aphrodite skimmed the Aegean waves on a scallop shell drawn by a team of six seahorses.

Although the scallop is symbolic of faith, grace, and beauty, it has a practical side as well. The tender adductor muscle of the scallop is surprisingly firm and has a delicately sweet and succulent taste.

There are two varieties—bay scallops and sea scallops. Bay scallops range in size from two to three inches. Sea scallops, which are about two inches larger, are more abundant and therefore less expensive. You can use either type to make Bacon-Scallop Kebabs (Day 6).

For Christmas we've scheduled a special meal (Day 2) that features Cream Puffs with Strawberry Sauce and champagne.

MORNING MEAL
½ cup Orange Juice
⅓ cup Pot Cheese
½ small Enriched Bagel
1 teaspoon Reduced-Calorie Apricot Spread
Coffee or Tea

MIDDAY MEAL
3–4 ounces Sliced Cooked Chicken
Boston and Bibb Lettuce Salad with Cherry
    Tomatoes and Pimiento Strips □ Coffee or Tea

COCKTAIL PARTY
Hot Mushroom Turnovers
Radish Pinwheels
Cucumber Spears, Zucchini Sticks, and Broccoli
    and Cauliflower Florets with **Curry Dip**
Strawberry-Apple Frost

DINNER
¾ cup **Vegetable Broth**
Lobster in Creamy Sauce
½ cup Steamed Spinach
½ cup Steamed Sliced Carrot
Tossed Salad with **Dijon-Herb Dressing**
3½ fluid ounces White Wine
½ cup Orange-Flavored Low-Calorie Gelatin
Coffee or Tea

SNACKS, AT PLANNED TIMES
½ cup Blueberries with 1½ tablespoons Plain
    Unflavored Yogurt

Serving Information
Men and Youth: Add ½ small Enriched Bagel,
    1 slice Rye Bread, and 1 small Apple
Youth: Add 1¾ cups Skim Milk

MORNING MEAL
1 cup Tomato Juice
1 Poached Egg
½ English Muffin, toasted
1 teaspoon Margarine
½ cup Skim Milk
Coffee or Tea

MIDDAY MEAL
3–4 ounces Roast Beef
Sautéed Salsify
½ cup Steamed Asparagus Tips
Sliced Radishes on Lettuce with Lemon Juice
    and Herbs
½ cup Canned Fruit Cocktail

EVENING MEAL
3–4 ounces Roast Cornish Hen
½ cup Cooked Wild or Enriched Rice with
    ¼ cup Steamed Mushroom Caps
½ cup Cooked Sliced Zucchini
Green Salad with **Russian Dressing** and
    1 teaspoon Grated Parmesan Cheese
1 medium Persimmon or 1 small Apple

SNACKS, AT PLANNED TIMES
½ medium Banana, sliced, with ¼ cup Plain
    Unflavored Yogurt; ¾ cup Buttermilk;
    2 Graham Crackers

Serving Information
Men and Youth: Add ½ medium Banana, sliced,
    and 2 Graham Crackers
Youth: Add 1½ cups Skim Milk and ¼ cup Plain
    Unflavored Yogurt

MORNING MEAL
½ medium Grapefruit
¾ ounce Ready-to-Eat Cereal
1 cup Skim Milk
Coffee or Tea

MIDDAY MEAL
Shrimp Scampi
½ cup Cooked Brussels Sprouts
½ medium Tomato, sliced
Bibb Lettuce Salad with **Basic Vinaigrette**
½ cup Lemon-Flavored Low-Calorie Gelatin

EVENING MEAL
Tomato Soup with 10 Oyster Crackers
Mushroom Omelet
½ cup Cooked Broccoli
1 ounce Enriched Roll
1 teaspoon Reduced-Calorie Orange Marmalade
½ cup Skim Milk
Coffee or Tea

SNACKS, AT PLANNED TIMES
1 small Pear; 3 ounces Dietary Frozen Dessert

Serving Information
Men and Youth: Add ⅔ cup Apple Juice, 1 slice
    Rye Bread, 1 ounce Enriched Roll, and 4 me-
    dium Dried Apricot Halves
Youth: Add 1 cup Skim Milk

MORNING MEAL
½ medium Papaya or 1 small Orange
1 serving Hot Cereal, ¾ ounce uncooked
½ cup Skim Milk
Coffee or Tea

MIDDAY MEAL
Artichoke and Eggplant Appetizer
Roast Loin of Pork with **Orange-Apricot Sauce**
Bulgur Pilaf
Pimiento-Topped Steamed Broccoli
Green Salad with **Gingered Vinaigrette**
4 fluid ounces Champagne
Cream Puffs with Strawberry Sauce
Hot Spiced Tea

EVENING MEAL
Garbanzo-Stuffed Peppers
Tomato and Cucumber Slices with ½ Hard-
    Cooked Egg, sliced, and ¼ teaspoon Imitation
    Bacon Bits
2 Melba Toast Slices
¼ cup Skim Milk
Coffee or Tea

SNACKS, AT PLANNED TIMES
¾ cup **Beef Broth** with Carrot and Celery Sticks;
    ¾ cup Skim Milk; 2 Graham Crackers

Serving Information
Men and Youth: Add 2 tablespoons Raisins, 2
    ounces Whole Wheat Roll, and 1 small Pear
Men: Add ¼ ounce Grated Swiss Cheese to
    Salad at the Evening Meal
Youth: Add 1¾ cups Skim Milk

MORNING MEAL
1 medium Kiwi Fruit or 1 cup Strawberries
Cinnamon-Cheese Toast
½ cup Skim Milk
Coffee or Tea

MIDDAY MEAL
Sesame Chicken with Green Beans
½ cup Steamed Cauliflower Florets
Tossed Salad with **Creamy Oriental Dressing**
Sparkling Mineral Water with Twist of Lime

EVENING MEAL
1 cup Mixed Vegetable Juice
3–4 ounces Broiled Fillet of Sole with
    Lemon Wedge
½ cup Cooked Peas
½ cup Cooked Sliced Crookneck Squash
Watercress and Endive Salad with **Lemon Salad
    Dressing**
1 slice Rye Bread
1 teaspoon Reduced-Calorie Margarine
½ cup Strawberry-Flavored Low-Calorie Gelatin

SNACKS, AT PLANNED TIMES
Pear Frozen Yogurt; 2 Canned Peach Halves with
    2 tablespoons Juice

Serving Information
Men and Youth: Add 2 ounces Whole Wheat Roll
    and ½ cup Canned Fruit Cocktail
Youth: Add 1½ cups Skim Milk

MORNING MEAL
½ cup Orange Sections
1 tablespoon Peanut Butter
2 teaspoons Reduced-Calorie Strawberry Spread
1 slice Toasted Raisin Bread
¼ cup Skim Milk
Coffee or Tea

MIDDAY MEAL
¼ cup Canned Pineapple Chunks on Lettuce
    topped with ⅓ cup Part-Skim Ricotta Cheese
Cauliflower-Cheese Crisp
¼ cup Skim Milk
Coffee or Tea

EVENING MEAL
Chilled Tomato Appetizer with 3 Melba Toast
    Slices
Bacon-Scallop Kebabs
Parsley Potatoes
¼ cup Cooked Peas with 1¼ teaspoons
    Margarine
Tossed Salad with **Pesto Dressing**
½ cup Melon Balls

SNACKS, AT PLANNED TIMES
1 cup Skim Milk; 4 medium Dried Apricot Halves

Serving Information
Men and Youth: Add ½ cup Orange Sections,
    1 slice Toasted Raisin Bread, 1 slice Enriched
    Bread, and ½ cup Melon Balls
Men: Add 4 teaspoons Part-Skim Ricotta Cheese
    at the Midday Meal
Youth: Add 1¾ cups Skim Milk

MORNING MEAL
Cereal with Spiced Fruit Ambrosia
Coffee or Tea

MIDDAY MEAL
Liver Venetian
½ cup Cooked Spinach
Tossed Salad with 1½ teaspoons Vegetable Oil
    plus Cider Vinegar and Seasonings
1 slice Enriched Bread
Coffee or Tea

EVENING MEAL
3–4 ounces Roast Veal
½ cup Cooked Sliced Carrot
½ cup Cooked Sliced Turnips
Sweet and Sour Cabbage
1 ounce Enriched French Bread
4 fluid ounces Red Wine
¼ medium Papaya or 10 small Grapes
Coffee or Tea

SNACKS, AT PLANNED TIMES
¾ cup Buttermilk; 1 cup Strawberries

Serving Information
Men and Youth: Add ⅔ cup Pineapple Juice, 1
    slice Enriched Bread, and 1 ounce Enriched
    French Bread
Youth: Add 2 cups Skim Milk

THE LAST DAY OF THE YEAR

A partridge in a pear tree, the song tells us, is appropriate for the first day of Christmas, but Swiss-Stuffed Pears could become a December 31st tradition.

The pear, now grown in temperate zones all over the world, originated in the area stretching from central Europe to Asia. In the Middle Ages, pears were grown exclusively in the orchards of castles and monasteries. Today France leads the world in pear production.

The pear is one of the few fruits that improves in flavor and texture when allowed to ripen off the tree. Therefore, it is picked when mature but still hard.

Buy pears that are firm but not too hard. They should yield to gentle pressure at the stem end.

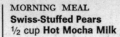

MORNING MEAL
Swiss-Stuffed Pears
½ cup **Hot Mocha Milk**

MIDDAY MEAL
⅓ cup Cottage Cheese
Watercress and Endive Salad with Sliced Radishes, Lemon Juice, and Seasonings
½ cup Cherry-Flavored Low-Calorie Gelatin

COCKTAIL PARTY
Steak Tartare
½ recipe **Yogurt Dip** with Mushrooms, Tomato Wedges, Broccoli and Cauliflower Florets, Green Bell Pepper Strips, and Carrot and Celery Sticks
Sparkling Mineral Water with Twist of Lime or Lemon

DINNER
Cauliflower and Zucchini Soup
Chicken Breasts with Raisin Sauce
Baked Yams
½ cup Steamed Spinach
Sliced Tomato and Cucumber Salad with **Tarragon Vinaigrette**
Banana-Apple Soft "Ice Cream"

MIDNIGHT SNACK
½ English Muffin, toasted, *or* ½ small Enriched Bagel, *or* ¾ ounce Crispbread, with 1 teaspoon each Margarine and Reduced-Calorie Apricot Spread; 1 cup Strawberries with 1 tablespoon Low-Calorie Whipped Topping; 4 fluid ounces Champagne

Serving Information
Men and Youth: Add ½ English Muffin, toasted, ½ cup Canned Fruit Cocktail, 4 medium Dried Apricot Halves, 2 Graham Crackers, and 12 large Grapes
Youth: Add 2 cups Skim Milk

We'll end this section and our year as we began them, by wishing you a happy, healthy, thoroughly delicious new year to come!

RECIPES

Starters

What the overture is to an opera, the starter is to a meal: a foretaste of the delights to come. Whether you select Stuffed Mushroom Appetizer, Blueberry Soup, or any of the other starter recipes, your meal will begin on a high note that makes adherence to your weight-loss program easy. And the delicious inspirations in this section can be music to your palate.

ARTICHOKE AND EGGPLANT APPETIZER
See Menu Plan for Week 52.
Makes 6 servings

1 cup diced eggplant, parboiled 5 minutes
1 cup frozen artichoke hearts, cooked
    5 minutes
1 cup sliced mushrooms
6 cherry tomatoes, cut into halves
½ cup diced celery, parboiled 5 minutes
2 tablespoons plus 2 teaspoons wine vinegar
1 teaspoon minced fresh basil
1 small garlic clove, minced
Dash each salt and pepper
6 lettuce leaves, formed into cups

Combine all ingredients except lettuce in medium bowl and toss. Serve in lettuce leaf cups.

Per serving: 26 calories; 2 g protein; 0.2 g fat;
7 g carbohydrate; 51 mg sodium

ARTICHOKE HEARTS ESPAÑOL
See Menu Plans for Weeks 28, 38, and 41.
Makes 4 servings

2 black olives, pitted
2 green olives, pitted
1 cup water
1-inch piece lemon rind
¼ teaspoon salt
1 cup frozen artichoke hearts, about 8
1 tablespoon lemon juice
1 tablespoon pimiento strips
1 teaspoon chopped fresh parsley
1 teaspoon small capers
Dash pepper

Cut olives into thin slices and set aside. In small saucepan combine water, lemon rind, and salt. Bring to a boil and add artichoke hearts. Reduce heat to medium and cook until artichokes are fork-tender. Drain and discard lemon rind. In small bowl combine artichoke hearts, lemon juice, pimiento strips, olives, parsley, capers, and pepper. Cover and chill, tossing occasionally.

Per serving: 22 calories; 1 g protein; 1 g fat;
6 g carbohydrate; 189 mg sodium

BROCCOLI-SHOOT APPETIZER
See Menu Plan for Week 12.
Makes 2 servings

2 cups broccoli florets, blanched
½ cup alfalfa sprouts
½ cup drained canned sliced bamboo
    shoots
¼ cup rice vinegar
2 tablespoons water
1 teaspoon soy sauce
1 teaspoon sesame oil
1 garlic clove, minced
1 medium tomato, cut into 8 wedges

Combine broccoli, alfalfa sprouts, and bamboo shoots in salad bowl. In measuring cup mix vinegar with water, soy sauce, sesame oil, and garlic until well blended. Pour over vegetables and toss to coat. Garnish with tomato wedges.

Per serving: 114 calories; 9 g protein; 3 g fat;
16 g carbohydrate; 221 mg sodium

CHILLED TOMATO APPETIZER
See Menu Plans for Weeks 37 and 52.
Makes 2 servings

2 cups tomato juice
1 cup pared, seeded, and diced cucumber
¼ teaspoon Worcestershire sauce
Dash each salt, pepper, ground mace, and
    ground cumin
1 scored cucumber slice

Combine all ingredients except cucumber slice in blender container and process until smooth. Chill. Garnish with cucumber slice.

Per serving: 57 calories; 3 g protein; 0.4 g fat;
13 g carbohydrate; 578 mg sodium

GREEN BEAN AND RED CABBAGE APPETIZER
See Menu Plan for Week 32.
Makes 2 servings

2 teaspoons olive oil
½ cup diagonally sliced green beans,
    ½-inch pieces
½ garlic clove, chopped with ½ teaspoon
    salt
½ teaspoon minced fresh ginger root
2 cups thinly sliced red cabbage
¼ teaspoon salt
⅛ teaspoon celery seeds
Dash ground marjoram
½ teaspoon lemon juice

Heat oil in medium skillet. Add green beans, garlic, and ginger. Sauté over medium heat until beans are just tender-crisp, about 2 to 3 minutes. *Do not overcook.* Remove beans from pan and keep warm. Add cabbage, salt, celery seeds, and marjoram to skillet. Cook, stirring occasionally, until cabbage is tender. Stir in lemon juice. Return beans to skillet and stir to combine with cabbage.

Per serving: 81 calories; 2 g protein; 5 g fat;
9 g carbohydrate; 906 mg sodium

HOT MUSHROOM TURNOVERS
See Menu Plans for Weeks 45 and 52.
Makes 8 servings, about 3 turnovers each

½ cup plus 2 tablespoons enriched flour
¼ teaspoon salt
2 tablespoons plus 2 teaspoons margarine
¼ cup plain unflavored yogurt
1½ cups minced mushrooms
1 tablespoon dehydrated onion flakes
1 tablespoon chopped fresh parsley
¼ teaspoon Worcestershire sauce
1 garlic clove, minced
Dash each thyme leaves, salt, and pepper

Combine flour and salt in mixing bowl. Cut in margarine until mixture resembles a coarse meal. Add yogurt and mix thoroughly. Form dough into a ball and chill about 1 hour.

Combine remaining ingredients in nonstick skillet; cook until mushrooms are soft and all of the moisture has evaporated.

Preheat oven to 375°F. Roll out dough to about ⅛-inch thickness. With a pastry wheel, cut lengthwise strips 2½ inches apart; then cut crosswise, making 2½-inch squares. Reroll scraps of dough and continue cutting until all dough is used. Place an equal amount of mushroom mixture on each square (about 1 teaspoon) and fold in half to enclose filling and form a triangle; seal well by pressing edges together with prongs of a fork. Bake on ungreased baking sheet 20 to 25 minutes or until lightly browned.

Per serving: 77 calories; 2 g protein; 4 g fat;
8 g carbohydrate; 148 mg sodium

MARINATED BROCCOLI APPETIZER
See Menu Plan for Week 30.
Makes 2 servings

1 cup broccoli florets, blanched
¼ cup grapefruit juice
1 tablespoon chopped scallion
2 teaspoons vegetable oil
½ teaspoon salt
Dash each artificial sweetener and pepper
2 large lettuce leaves, formed into cups

Combine all ingredients except lettuce in a small bowl; toss. Cover and refrigerate at least 2 hours or overnight. Serve in lettuce cups.

Per serving: 86 calories; 3 g protein; 5 g fat;
9 g carbohydrate; 604 mg sodium

MARINATED MUSHROOM APPETIZER
See Menu Plan for Week 18.
Makes 2 servings

2 cups small mushroom caps
2 tablespoons lemon juice
1 tablespoon minced shallots
2 teaspoons sesame oil
½ teaspoon minced fresh garlic
¼ cup tarragon vinegar
½ teaspoon salt
Dash pepper
Artificial sweetener to equal 1 teaspoon
  sugar
2 parsley sprigs
Leaves from 1 celery rib
2 large lettuce leaves, formed into cups

Place mushrooms in small bowl; sprinkle with lemon juice. Combine shallots, oil, and garlic in saucepan and heat. Add vinegar, salt, and pepper. Simmer 5 minutes. Remove from heat. Add mushrooms, sweetener, parsley, and celery leaves; toss to combine. Cover and marinate in refrigerator overnight. Serve in lettuce leaf cups.

Per serving: 86 calories; 3 g protein; 5 g fat;
10 g carbohydrate; 612 mg sodium

RADISH PINWHEELS
See Menu Plans for Weeks 46 and 52.
Makes 8 servings

¾ cup finely chopped radishes
¼ cup finely chopped green bell pepper
¼ teaspoon salt
2 tablespoons plus 2 teaspoons reduced-
  calorie mayonnaise
2 teaspoons finely chopped chives
1 teaspoon Dijon-style mustard
Dash white pepper
3 slices enriched white bread

Combine radishes, green pepper, and salt in a bowl; let stand 15 minutes. Place on piece of cloth and squeeze out excess moisture. In bowl combine mayonnaise with chives, mustard, and pepper; add radish-pepper mixture and mix well. Using a rolling pin, roll out each slice of bread until very thin. Spread ⅓ of radish mixture over each slice and roll up, jelly-roll fashion. Wrap each roll in plastic wrap and chill 3 hours. Using a serrated knife, cut each roll crosswise into 8 slices.

Per serving: 39 calories; 1 g protein; 2 g fat;
6 g carbohydrate; 164 mg sodium

RUTABAGA APPETIZER
See Menu Plan for Week 15.
Makes 1 serving

¼ cup pared and grated rutabaga
1 teaspoon vegetable oil
½ teaspoon sugar
½ teaspoon red wine vinegar
⅛ teaspoon salt
Dash white pepper
½ cup lettuce leaves
1 parsley sprig
1 cherry tomato, cut in half

In bowl combine all ingredients except lettuce leaves, parsley, and tomato. Line a salad plate with lettuce leaves; top with rutabaga mixture. Garnish with parsley and tomato halves.

Per serving: 74 calories; 1 g protein; 5 g fat;
8 g carbohydrate; 311 mg sodium

SPICED TOMATO APPETIZER
See Menu Plan for Week 48.
Makes 2 servings

2 medium tomatoes, peeled and quartered
¼ cup tarragon vinegar
1 tablespoon chopped onion
2 teaspoons olive oil
1 teaspoon sugar
½ garlic clove, minced
Dash each powdered mustard and ground
   red pepper
1 tablespoon chopped parsley stems
Lettuce leaves
Chopped fresh basil to garnish

Place tomatoes in bowl and set aside. Combine next 6 ingredients in blender container and process. Pour over tomatoes. Sprinkle with parsley stems; cover and refrigerate overnight.

Arrange bed of lettuce on salad plate; top with tomato mixture and garnish with basil.

Per serving: 85 calories; 2 g protein; 5 g fat;
10 g carbohydrate; 7 mg sodium

STEAK TARTARE
See Menu Plan for the Last Day of the Year.
Makes 4 servings

8 ounces twice-ground lean sirloin
1 tablespoon plus 1 teaspoon minced
   shallots
1 tablespoon minced fresh parsley
1 tablespoon ice water
1 teaspoon Worcestershire sauce
1 teaspoon lemon juice
¼ teaspoon Dijon-style mustard
Dash each salt and pepper
Capers and pimiento strips to garnish
4 slices enriched white bread, toasted and
   cut into triangles

In a small glass or stainless-steel bowl combine all ingredients except capers, pimientos, and toast; toss lightly. Chill for not more than 1 hour. Garnish with capers and pimientos. Serve on toast triangles.

Per serving: 181 calories; 14 g protein; 7 g fat;
15 g carbohydrate; 250 mg sodium

STUFFED MUSHROOM APPETIZER
These can be made ahead of time and refrigerated until ready to bake. A food processor can be used to mince the peppers, celery, scallions, garlic, and mushroom stems. It can also be used to grate the Parmesan cheese and chop the parsley.
See Menu Plan for Week 8.
Makes 4 servings

12 large mushrooms
2 tablespoons lemon juice
½ cup minced green and red bell peppers
½ cup minced celery
½ cup minced scallions
1 teaspoon minced fresh garlic
Dash each salt and pepper
¾ cup Chicken Broth (see page 127)
1 tablespoon grated Parmesan cheese
2 teaspoons chopped fresh parsley
Italian parsley sprigs to garnish

Wash mushrooms and sprinkle with lemon juice. Remove and mince stems. Combine stems, peppers, celery, scallions, and garlic in nonstick pan. Cook, stirring occasionally, until tender; add salt and pepper. Fill each mushroom cap with an equal amount of stuffing; place in shallow casserole. Add broth to casserole and sprinkle mushrooms with Parmesan cheese. Bake at 400°F. for 20 to 25 minutes. Garnish with chopped parsley and parsley sprigs and serve immediately.

Per serving: 44 calories; 3 g protein; 1 g fat;
6 g carbohydrate; 140 mg sodium

TOFU-SESAME APPETIZER
See Menu Plan for Week 24.
Makes 2 servings

4 ounces tofu (soybean curd)
3 tablespoons water
1 teaspoon cornstarch
1 tablespoon soy sauce
2 teaspoons white wine
½ teaspoon honey
¼ teaspoon grated fresh ginger root
Dash powdered mustard
1 teaspoon sesame seeds, toasted

Brown tofu on both sides in heated non-stick skillet. Remove to a dish and let cool.

In small saucepan combine water with cornstarch; stir to dissolve cornstarch. Add soy sauce, wine, honey, ginger, and mustard. Stirring constantly bring mixture to a boil and cook until thickened; let cool.

Cut tofu into ½-inch pieces. Pour sauce over tofu, cover, and marinate for ½ hour; turn pieces and spoon sauce over other side. Just before serving sprinkle with sesame seeds.

Per serving: 69 calories; 5 g protein; 3 g fat; 5 g carbohydrate; 559 mg sodium

YOGURT-MUSHROOM APPETIZER
See Menu Plan for Week 14.
Makes 2 servings

1 tablespoon margarine
½ cup minced onion
1 small garlic clove, minced
4½ cups chopped mushrooms
⅛ teaspoon salt
Dash pepper
2 teaspoons chopped chives
1½ teaspoons lemon juice
1 teaspoon chopped fresh parsley
¼ cup plain unflavored yogurt
Lettuce leaves
2 parsley sprigs

Melt margarine in skillet; add onion and garlic and sauté until lightly browned. Add mushrooms, salt, and pepper; cook over low heat, stirring occasionally, for 10 minutes or until mushrooms are soft and all of the liquid has evaporated. Stir in chives, lemon juice, and parsley. Spoon the mixture into a small bowl and cool. Stir in yogurt; cover and chill. Line 2 small plates with lettuce leaves; top each with ½ of the mushroom appetizer and garnish with a parsley sprig.

Per serving: 152 calories; 8 g protein; 7 g fat; 16 g carbohydrate; 272 mg sodium

BLUEBERRY SOUP
See Menu Plan for Week 35.
Makes 4 servings

1 cup blueberries
1 cup water, divided
⅔ cup grape juice, no sugar added
1 teaspoon honey
2 teaspoons cornstarch
Artificial sweetener to equal 2 teaspoons
  sugar

Combine blueberries, ¾ cup water, grape juice, and honey in medium saucepan; cover and simmer over low heat until berries are soft, about 5 minutes. *Do not overcook.* Dissolve cornstarch in remaining ¼ cup water; stir dissolved cornstarch and sweetener into soup and cook, stirring occasionally, until mixture thickens enough to coat back of spoon. Remove from heat; cool and refrigerate, covered, until well chilled.

Per serving: 55 calories; 0.3 g protein; 0.2 g fat; 14 g carbohydrate; 1 mg sodium

DANISH APPLE SOUP
See Menu Plan for Week 27.
Makes 4 servings

4 small apples
3 cups water, divided
1 tablespoon grated lemon rind
¾ teaspoon ground cinnamon
1 teaspoon sugar
½ teaspoon salt
1 tablespoon cornstarch, dissolved in
   1 tablespoon water
1 tablespoon plus 1 teaspoon red Burgundy
   wine

Pare and core 3 apples and cut each into eighths. In saucepan combine sliced apples, 2 cups water, the lemon rind, and cinnamon. Bring to a boil; reduce heat and simmer for 15 minutes. Add sugar and salt. Transfer to blender container; process until pureed. Return to saucepan. Add remaining water; bring to a boil. Stirring constantly, gradually add dissolved cornstarch. Continue to stir and cook until slightly thickened; stir in Burgundy. Core remaining apple; cut into small dice and stir into soup. Serve hot or chilled.

Per serving: 83 calories; 0.3 g protein; 1 g fat;
21 g carbohydrate; 325 mg sodium

FRUITED YOGURT SOUP
See Menu Plan for Week 19.
Makes 4 servings

2 cups plain unflavored yogurt
2 medium peaches, peeled, pitted, and
   diced
1 cup strawberries, sliced
½ cup orange juice
½ cup water
Artificial sweetener to equal 4 teaspoons
   sugar
2 teaspoons honey
Mint leaves to garnish

Combine all ingredients except mint leaves in blender container; process until smooth. Transfer to 1-quart serving dish. Chill at least 2 hours. Garnish with mint leaves.

Per serving: 129 calories; 5 g protein; 4 g fat;
20 g carbohydrate; 53 mg sodium

CHILLED CUCUMBER SOUP
The longer this soup chills, the stronger the curry flavor will become.
See Menu Plans for Weeks 20 and 35.
Makes 1 serving

1 medium cucumber, pared, seeded, and
   sliced
¾ cup buttermilk
½ cup peeled and chopped tomato
1 teaspoon chopped scallion
1 small garlic clove
¼ teaspoon curry powder
¼ teaspoon salt
Dash pepper
1½ teaspoons chopped fresh parsley

In blender container combine cucumber, buttermilk, tomato, scallion, and garlic. Process until mixture is smooth. Add curry powder, salt, and pepper; process until combined. Pour into a bowl; cover and chill about 1 hour. Sprinkle with chopped parsley before serving.

Per serving: 135 calories; 9 g protein; 2 g fat;
22 g carbohydrate; 747 mg sodium

GAZPACHO
See Menu Plans for Weeks 30 and 33.
Makes 4 servings

2 cups tomato juice
½ cup pared, seeded, and diced cucumber
½ cup diced celery
½ cup diced green bell pepper
¼ cup sliced scallions
2 tablespoons olive oil
1 teaspoon Worcestershire sauce
1 teaspoon chopped fresh parsley
½ teaspoon salt
¼ teaspoon freshly ground pepper
1 garlic clove, minced

Combine all ingredients in medium bowl. Cover and chill overnight. Stir just before serving.

Per serving: 100 calories; 2 g protein; 7 g fat;
8 g carbohydrate; 554 mg sodium

BEEF BROTH

This can be prepared and then frozen for use when needed. Freeze in ¼-cup portions and defrost only the amount that is required for a recipe. This can be done in ice cube trays; once frozen, store the cubes in a plastic bag. Using our trays, 2 ice cubes yield about ¼ cup.

See Menu Plan for Week 3 and various other weeks.
Makes about 2 quarts

4 pounds beef bones, sawed into pieces
1 cup sliced celery
1 cup sliced carrots
1 medium onion, studded with 1 whole
   clove
1 gallon water
5 parsley stems
5 peppercorns
¼ teaspoon thyme leaves
1 small bay leaf

Place bones on rack in roasting pan. Roast at 400°F. for 1 hour. While bones are roasting, cook celery, carrots, and clove-studded onion in separate baking pan in oven for 30 minutes. Transfer bones and vegetables to a kettle; add remaining ingredients. Bring to a boil; reduce heat and remove scum from surface, partially cover, and simmer 3 hours or until reduced by ½. Strain liquid to remove solids. Refrigerate broth until fat congeals on surface. Remove and discard fat.

Note: Nutrition data are not available for homemade Beef Broth. Therefore, we are using the nutrition information for commercial broth and seasoning mix. A ¾-cup serving contains 12 calories, 1 g protein, and 2 g carbohydrate.

HERBED BEEF BROTH

See Menu Plans for Weeks 15, 23, and 50.
Makes 4 servings

3 cups Beef Broth (see above)
2 teaspoons chopped fresh parsley
2 teaspoons chopped fresh or freeze-dried
   chives

Pour ¾ cup heated Beef Broth into each of 4 soup bowls. Sprinkle each serving with ½ teaspoon each parsley and chives.

Per serving: 13 calories; 1 g protein; 0.1 g fat; 1 g carbohydrate; 1 mg sodium

CHICKEN BROTH

It's a good idea to always have this in the freezer. Freeze in ¼-cup portions so you can defrost only what you need for a recipe. A convenient method of doing this is to freeze the broth in ice cube trays and then store the cubes in a plastic bag. Using our trays, 2 ice cubes yield about ¼ cup.

See Menu Plan for Week 4 and various other weeks.
Makes about 2 quarts

2 pounds chicken necks and backs, skinned
3 quarts water
1 large onion
¾ cup sliced carrots
¾ cup sliced celery
5 parsley stems
3 peppercorns
⅛ teaspoon thyme leaves

Combine all ingredients in kettle. Bring to a boil; reduce heat, remove scum from surface, partially cover, and simmer 2½ hours or until reduced by about ⅓. Strain liquid to remove solids. Refrigerate broth until fat congeals on surface. Remove and discard fat.

Note: Nutrition data are not available for homemade Chicken Broth. Therefore, we are using the nutrition information for commercial broth and seasoning mix. A ¾-cup serving contains 12 calories, 1 g protein, and 2 g carbohydrate.

TURKEY BROTH

This broth can be made in advance and frozen, in measured portions, until needed.
See Menu Plan for Week 38.
Makes about 3 cups

Turkey neck, heart, and gizzard, trimmed
    of all fat
1¼ quarts water
1 teaspoon salt
1 celery rib, cut in half
3 parsley sprigs
1 small bay leaf
¼ teaspoon thyme leaves
3 peppercorns
1 carrot, scraped and cut into pieces

Cut turkey neck into 3 pieces and place in saucepan with heart and gizzard. Add water and salt. Make a bouquet garni by tying celery, parsley, bay leaf, thyme, and peppercorns in a piece of cheesecloth. Add bouquet garni and carrot to pot. Bring to a boil and skim scum from surface. Reduce heat and simmer, partially covered, for 2 hours. Strain broth, discarding solids. Refrigerate until fat congeals on surface; remove and discard fat.

Per serving: 11 calories; 0.4 g protein; 0.1 g fat;
3 g carbohydrate; 576 mg sodium

VEGETABLE BROTH

This broth can be prepared in advance, measured, and frozen for use at a later date.
See Menu Plan for Week 48 and various other weeks.
Makes about 1 quart

1½ cups thickly sliced onions
1 cup cut-up carrots, large chunks
1 cup cut-up celery, large chunks
2 medium tomatoes, cut into wedges
6 parsley sprigs
2 bay leaves
2 garlic cloves, crushed
5 peppercorns
Dash salt
1½ quarts water, divided

Combine all ingredients except water in roasting pan. Bake at 400°F. for 35 minutes.

Transfer vegetable mixture to large saucepan. Add 1 cup water to hot roasting pan, scraping browned particles from bottom and sides of pan; place over moderate heat and bring to a boil. Transfer mixture to saucepan containing vegetables; add remaining water. Simmer about 1 hour. Strain liquid, discarding solids.

Note: Nutrition data are not available for homemade Vegetable Broth. Therefore, we are using the nutrition information for commercial broth and seasoning mix. A ¾-cup serving contains 12 calories, 1 g protein, 2 g carbohydrate, and 25 mg sodium.

ASPARAGUS SOUP

Asparagus is one of the most perishable vegetables available in the marketplace. To store, wrap base of stalks with a damp paper towel and keep in coldest part of your refrigerator.
See Menu Plan for Week 11.
Makes 2 servings

½ pound asparagus spears
1 tablespoon margarine
1 tablespoon enriched flour
2 cups heated water
¾ teaspoon salt
Dash each ground nutmeg and white
    pepper

Cut asparagus into 1-inch pieces; reserve tips and set aside. Melt margarine in saucepan. Stir in flour and cook over low heat, stirring constantly, for 3 minutes. Remove from heat; gradually add heated water, stirring constantly. Return to heat; add asparagus (not including tips) and salt. Bring mixture to a boil over high heat. Reduce heat to moderate, cover, and cook 20 minutes or until asparagus are tender. Pour mixture, ½ at a time, into blender container and process until smooth. Return to saucepan. Add reserved asparagus tips, nutmeg, and pepper; simmer 5 minutes or until tips are tender.

Per serving: 94 calories; 3 g protein; 6 g fat;
9 g carbohydrate; 948 mg sodium

CAULIFLOWER AND ZUCCHINI SOUP

See Menu Plan for Week 25 and various other weeks.
Makes 4 servings

1 medium head cauliflower, about 1½
   pounds
3 cups water
1 cup sliced carrots
1 cup sliced celery
½ bay leaf
1 medium zucchini, about 5 ounces, halved
   and cut into 1-inch chunks
2 teaspoons lemon juice
¾ teaspoon salt
¼ teaspoon thyme leaves
Dash each ground allspice and ground
   nutmeg

Chop ⅔ of the cauliflower; break remainder of head into florets and reserve. In medium saucepan combine chopped cauliflower, water, carrots, celery, and bay leaf. Cover and bring to a boil. Reduce heat and simmer 30 minutes. Remove from heat and remove bay leaf. Transfer mixture to blender container and process until smooth; return to saucepan. Add reserved florets and remaining ingredients; simmer uncovered, stirring occasionally, 20 to 25 minutes or until florets and zucchini are tender-crisp.

Per serving: 69 calories; 6 g protein; 0.5 g fat;
14 g carbohydrate; 507 mg sodium

FRESH MUSHROOM SOUP

See Menu Plans for Weeks 26 and 39.
Makes 2 servings

⅓ cup plus 2 teaspoons diced onion
1 tablespoon plus 1 teaspoon enriched flour
2 cups sliced mushrooms
2 cups water
1 packet instant chicken broth and
   seasoning mix
⅛ teaspoon ground thyme
Dash each salt and pepper
2 teaspoons chopped fresh parsley

Spray saucepan with nonstick cooking spray.

Add onion; cook, stirring occasionally, about 5 minutes or until softened. Stir in flour and cook until mixture is lightly browned. Add mushrooms; cook 5 minutes. Stir in water, broth mix, and thyme. Bring mixture to a boil; reduce heat and simmer 10 minutes or until slightly thickened. Season with salt and pepper. Just before serving, sprinkle with parsley.

Per serving: 63 calories; 4 g protein; 0.4 g fat;
12 g carbohydrate; 529 mg sodium

ONION SOUP

See Menu Plan for Week 49.
Makes 4 servings

1 tablespoon plus 1 teaspoon margarine
1½ cups sliced onions
3 cups Beef Broth (see page 127)
1 whole clove
Dash freshly ground pepper

Melt margarine in medium saucepan. Add onions and sauté over low heat until very soft and golden brown, about 20 minutes. Add broth, clove, and pepper; simmer 30 minutes.

Per serving: 70 calories; 2 g protein; 4 g fat;
8 g carbohydrate; 60 mg sodium

Variation:
Onion Soup Gratinée—Follow directions for Onion Soup; divide soup into 4 individual flameproof crocks or bowls. Float a 1-ounce slice toasted enriched French bread on each portion of soup. Top each slice of toast with 2 ounces sliced Swiss cheese. Broil 1 to 2 minutes or until cheese is lightly browned. Serve immediately.

Per serving: 346 calories; 20 g protein; 20 g fat;
21 g carbohydrate; 326 mg sodium

TOMATO SOUP

See Menu Plan for Week 37.
Makes 2 servings

4 cups canned whole tomatoes
4 medium celery ribs, cut into 1-inch pieces
½ cup diced onion
¼ garlic clove, minced
1 teaspoon honey
¼ teaspoon salt
Dash white pepper

Place tomatoes in blender container or work bowl of food processor and process until smooth, about 5 seconds. Pour into large saucepan; add celery, cover, and bring to a boil. Uncover, reduce heat to low, and simmer for 1 hour. Strain mixture through sieve and return liquid to saucepan; discard solids. Add onion and garlic to liquid in saucepan; cover and simmer 30 to 40 minutes. Strain through sieve again, discarding solids. Stir in honey, salt, and pepper.

Per serving: 143 calories; 6 g protein; 1 g fat;
31 g carbohydrate; 1,023 mg sodium

VEGETABLE SOUP

See Menu Plans for Weeks 29 and 39.
Makes 2 servings

¾ cup quartered small mushrooms
¼ cup diced celery
¼ cup diced carrot
¼ cup diced parsnip
1 packet instant chicken broth and
   seasoning mix
2 cups water
2 teaspoons margarine
1 tablespoon enriched flour
⅛ teaspoon thyme leaves
Dash pepper
2 teaspoons chopped fresh parsley

In saucepan combine mushrooms, celery, carrot, parsnip, and broth mix; add water and bring to a boil. Reduce heat and simmer 15 minutes. Melt margarine in skillet. Stir in flour and cook over low heat, stirring constantly, for 3 minutes. Remove from heat. Measure ½ cup liquid from cooked vegetables and gradually add to flour, stirring constantly until mixture is smooth.

Add to soup remaining in saucepan along with thyme and pepper; simmer 15 minutes longer. Just before serving sprinkle with parsley.

Per serving: 87 calories; 3 g protein; 4 g fat;
11 g carbohydrate; 492 mg sodium

CREAM OF ASPARAGUS AND LEEK SOUP

See Menu Plan for Week 9.
Makes 6 servings

6 medium frozen asparagus spears, cooked
2 tablespoons margarine
2 cups chopped leeks, white portion only
1 tablespoon enriched flour
2¼ cups Chicken Broth (see page 127)
¾ cup evaporated skimmed milk
Dash each salt, white pepper, and ground
   nutmeg
Chopped fresh parsley to garnish

Cut off stems of asparagus, reserving tips. Puree stems in blender container or work bowl of food processor. Melt margarine in small saucepan; add leeks and sauté until soft. Add flour, stirring constantly. Stir in broth and pureed asparagus. Simmer for 10 minutes. Add asparagus tips, milk, and seasonings. Heat but *do not allow to boil*. Garnish with chopped fresh parsley.

Per serving: 110 calories; 5 g protein; 4 g fat;
15 g carbohydrate; 120 mg sodium

CREAM OF BROCCOLI SOUP

See Menu Plan for Week 21.
Makes 6 servings

2 cups cooked broccoli
2 tablespoons margarine
½ cup minced scallions
2 tablespoons enriched flour
2¼ cups Chicken Broth (see page 127)
   or chicken bouillon
Dash each salt, pepper, and ground nutmeg
1 cup cauliflower, cooked and pureed
1 cup evaporated skimmed milk

Remove stems from broccoli and puree; reserve florets for garnish. Melt margarine in medium saucepan; sauté scallions until soft. Add flour, stirring constantly. Add broth, salt, pepper, and nutmeg. Bring to a boil; add pureed vegetables. Reduce heat and gradually stir in milk. Heat thoroughly, *but do not boil*. Serve garnished with broccoli florets.

Per serving: 104 calories; 6 g protein; 4 g fat; 12 g carbohydrate; 135 mg sodium

CREAM OF CAULIFLOWER SOUP

This soup freezes well.
See Menu Plan for Week 5.
Makes 4 servings

4 cups cauliflower florets
4¾ cups water
1 packet instant chicken broth and
    seasoning mix
2 teaspoons arrowroot
½ cup skim milk
2 tablespoons chopped fresh parsley
Dash white pepper

Place cauliflower in saucepan. Add water and broth mix; bring to a boil. Reduce heat to moderate and simmer for 15 to 20 minutes or until cauliflower is soft. Transfer mixture in 3 batches to blender container and puree. Return puree to saucepan and heat. In small bowl combine arrowroot with milk and pour into cauliflower mixture; cook, stirring constantly, until thickened. Stir in parsley and pepper and serve.

Per serving: 45 calories; 4 g protein; 0.3 g fat; 8 g carbohydrate; 217 mg sodium

CREAMED TURNIP AND CAULIFLOWER SOUP

See Menu Plan for Week 17.
Makes 4 servings

3 cups Chicken Broth (see page 127)
1 cup pared and diced white turnips
1 cup chopped cauliflower
¼ cup chopped fresh parsley
½ garlic clove
½ teaspoon salt, divided
Dash each pepper and ground nutmeg
2 teaspoons margarine
2 teaspoons enriched flour
½ cup skim milk

In large saucepan combine broth, turnips, cauliflower, and parsley. Cover and bring to a boil. Chop garlic with ¼ teaspoon salt and add to vegetables. Reduce heat and simmer until turnips are very tender, at least 30 minutes. Transfer to blender container; add remaining salt, pepper, and nutmeg, and process until smooth. Pour back into saucepan; keep hot. Melt margarine in small saucepan over low heat. Stirring constantly, add flour and cook for 1 minute. Gradually add milk, stirring briskly with a wire whisk until flour and margarine are well blended. Cook, stirring constantly, until sauce begins to thicken; *do not boil*. Add sauce to soup and increase heat to medium. Cook soup, stirring constantly, 5 minutes longer to develop a creamy consistency.

Per serving: 62 calories; 3 g protein; 2 g fat; 8 g carbohydrate; 512 mg sodium

VEGETABLE CHOWDER

See Menu Plan for Week 7.
Makes 4 servings

1 tablespoon plus 1 teaspoon vegetable oil
2 cups diced zucchini
1 cup mushrooms, cut into quarters
1 cup cut green beans, 2-inch pieces
1 cup sliced carrots
1 cup diced onions
½ cup diced celery
1 medium green bell pepper, seeded and
    diced
2 cups Chicken Broth (see page 127)
1 cup tomato sauce
1 to 2 teaspoons Worcestershire sauce
½ teaspoon ground thyme
Dash hot sauce (optional)
1 cup skim milk
1 tablespoon chopped fresh parsley

Heat oil in large pot; add next 7 ingredients and sauté, stirring occasionally, for 10 minutes. Add remaining ingredients except milk and parsley; simmer 30 to 40 minutes, stirring occasionally. Stir in milk; heat *but do not boil*. Garnish with parsley.

Per serving: 156 calories; 7 g protein; 6 g fat; 23 g carbohydrate; 375 mg sodium

Eggs and Cheese

Eggs and cheese may be two of the most versatile foods around.
Each can stand on its own as the basis for a meal or do a delicious
disappearing act in conjunction with other ingredients. Cold
cheese dishes such as Cheese-Salad Sandwich and Tomato
Stuffed with Herb Cheese will help you beat the heat on a hot
day. Used together, cheese and eggs are a winning combination
in omelets and quiches, while fluffy beaten egg whites help your
soufflés rise to new heights.

SCRAMBLE 'N' SPINACH
See Menu Plans for Weeks 26 and 36.
Makes 2 servings

1 tablespoon minced onion
1 tablespoon minced celery
2 eggs, beaten
½ teaspoon salt
Dash white pepper
1 cup hot, cooked and well-drained chopped
    spinach, seasoned with dash each salt,
    pepper, and ground nutmeg
½ teaspoon chopped fresh parsley

Spray a nonstick skillet with nonstick cooking spray. Add onion and celery; cover and cook until tender, stirring occasionally. Add eggs, salt, and pepper; scramble lightly. Place hot spinach on plate, spreading to make a well in center. Fill center with eggs. Sprinkle with parsley.

Per serving: 104 calories; 9 g protein; 6 g fat;
5 g carbohydrate; 800 mg sodium

BAKED CORN AND TOMATO OMELET
See Menu Plan for Week 22.
Makes 2 servings

½ cup tomato sauce
½ cup diced celery
¼ cup diced red bell pepper
1 teaspoon prepared mustard
1 teaspoon lemon juice
⅛ teaspoon salt
Dash each oregano leaves and pepper
2 eggs
½ cup canned cream-style corn
1 teaspoon chopped fresh parsley

Combine tomato sauce, celery, red pepper, mustard, lemon juice, salt, oregano, and pepper in small skillet. Cook over low heat, stirring occasionally, about 10 minutes or until mixture has thickened; set aside.

In bowl combine eggs with corn and beat. Spray an 8-inch skillet that has an ovenproof or removable handle with nonstick cooking spray; heat. Pour egg mixture into skillet. Cook, stirring slightly as eggs begin to set.

When bottom is set but surface is still creamy, spread tomato sauce mixture over eggs, leaving a 1-inch edge uncovered all the way around. Sprinkle egg border with parsley. Preheat oven to 350°F.

Transfer skillet to oven and bake 10 to 12 minutes or until eggs are completely set. Slide onto serving platter.

Per serving: 164 calories; 9 g protein; 6 g fat;
20 g carbohydrate; 718 mg sodium

CHEESE OMELET I
See Menu Plan for Week 46.
Makes 1 serving

1 teaspoon margarine
1 egg
1 tablespoon water
Dash salt
1 ounce grated Swiss cheese

Melt margarine until hot in a 6½-inch nonstick skillet or omelet pan that has a flame-proof handle. Combine egg, water, and salt in small bowl and beat with wire whisk. Pour egg mixture into skillet and cook until bottom is lightly browned and firm. Sprinkle grated cheese over egg. Place under broiler as close to heat source as possible; broil until top puffs and turns light brown. Remove from broiler and fold omelet in half. Roll out of pan onto heated plate.

Per serving: 219 calories; 14 g protein; 17 g fat;
2 g carbohydrate; 375 mg sodium

Variation:
Cheese Omelet II—Omit margarine. Heat skillet and proceed as directed.

Per serving: 185 calories; 14 g protein; 13 g fat;
2 g carbohydrate; 329 mg sodium

EGG FOO YUNG
Chinese-style pancakes.
See Menu Plans for Weeks 12, 18, and 21.
Makes 2 servings

1½ cups shredded cabbage
1 cup cooked brown rice
½ cup grated carrot
½ cup sliced scallions, divided
1 teaspoon sesame seeds, toasted
1 garlic clove, minced
¼ teaspoon minced fresh ginger root
¼ teaspoon pepper
4 eggs, beaten
1 tablespoon plus 1 teaspoon soy sauce,
    divided
¾ cup Chicken Broth (see page 127)
2 teaspoons cornstarch, dissolved in
    1 tablespoon water

In bowl combine cabbage, rice, carrot, ¼
cup scallions, sesame seeds, garlic, ginger,
and pepper. In separate bowl beat eggs with
1 tablespoon soy sauce; stir into vegetable
mixture. Spray nonstick skillet with nonstick cooking spray and heat. Drop ¼ cup
of batter for each pancake into heated skillet; cook, turning once, until brown on each
side. Repeat until all batter is used. In small
saucepan combine broth, remaining 1 teaspoon soy sauce, and ¼ cup scallions. Bring
to a boil; stir in dissolved cornstarch and
cook, stirring constantly, until thickened.
Serve sauce over pancakes.

Per serving: 337 calories; 17 g protein; 13 g fat;
38 g carbohydrate; 910 mg sodium

FRENCH OMELET
*See Menu Plan for Week 2 and various other
weeks.*
Makes 1 serving

2 eggs
1 tablespoon plus 1 teaspoon water
¼ teaspoon salt
Dash pepper
1 teaspoon margarine

In bowl, using a wire whisk or fork, combine all ingredients except margarine. Melt
margarine in a 7-inch nonstick omelet pan
or skillet. When pan is hot, add egg mixture.
Using a rubber spatula or a fork, carefully
lift cooked edges of egg mixture and tilt
pan, so that uncooked portion flows underneath. When bottom of omelet is lightly
browned and top surface is still moist, fold
omelet in half; invert onto a warm plate
and serve.

Per serving: 192 calories; 12 g protein; 15 g fat;
1 g carbohydrate; 768 mg sodium

MATZO BREI
See Menu Plan for Week 15.
Makes 2 servings

2 eggs
¼ cup water
¼ teaspoon ground cinnamon
¼ teaspoon salt
1 matzo board, broken into pieces
2 teaspoons margarine

In a medium bowl beat eggs slightly. Stir
in water, cinnamon, and salt; add matzo and
let stand 15 minutes. Melt margarine in a
nonstick skillet; add matzo mixture, cover,
and cook over medium heat until browned
on bottom. With a spatula loosen sides of
matzo mixture, slide onto a dish, and invert
into skillet to brown other side.

Per serving: 183 calories; 8 g protein; 10 g fat;
15 g carbohydrate; 407 mg sodium

MUSHROOM OMELET
*See Menu Plan for Week 4 and various other
weeks.*
Makes 1 serving

2 cups sliced mushrooms
¼ cup minced celery with leaves
½ teaspoon salt
2 eggs
Dash freshly ground pepper
1 teaspoon margarine

Heat nonstick skillet over medium heat; add
mushrooms, celery, and salt. Cover and cook

until mushrooms are tender. Set aside. In a small bowl beat together eggs and pepper. Melt margarine until hot in nonstick skillet. Pour eggs into skillet and cook over medium heat. As eggs begin to set, lift cooked edges of omelet and tilt pan so that uncooked portion flows underneath. When bottom of omelet is lightly browned and top surface is still moist, spread mushroom mixture over ½ of omelet. Fold other ½ of omelet over mushroom mixture. Invert omelet onto plate.

Per serving: 250 calories; 18 g protein; 16 g fat; 11 g carbohydrate; 1,416 mg sodium

SPINACH FRITTATA

Nutmeg adds something special to eggs and spinach.
See Menu Plan for Week 20.
Makes 2 servings

4 eggs, well beaten
¾ cup cooked frozen chopped spinach, squeezed (10-ounce package)
¼ cup chopped fresh parsley
¼ teaspoon salt
⅛ teaspoon minced fresh garlic
Dash each pepper and ground nutmeg
1 tablespoon margarine
¼ cup chopped scallions
1 teaspoon sesame seeds, lightly toasted

In bowl combine eggs, spinach, parsley, salt, garlic, pepper, and nutmeg. Melt margarine in 12-inch nonstick skillet that has a removable or flameproof handle. Add scallions and sauté 2 minutes. Pour in egg-spinach mixture. Cook over moderately high heat, briskly shaking pan back and forth to prevent sticking. When underside is lightly browned, broil for a few minutes until frittata is set. Sprinkle with sesame seeds.

Per serving: 263 calories; 18 g protein; 18 g fat; 10 g carbohydrate; 583 mg sodium

CAROB SOUFFLÉ

For best results eggs should be at room temperature, about 70°F. The whites will then beat to maximum volume.
See Menu Plan for Week 40.
Makes 2 servings

2 eggs, separated
2 teaspoons margarine
1 teaspoon sugar
1 tablespoon plus 1 teaspoon unsweetened carob powder
Artificial sweetener to equal 4 teaspoons sugar
⅛ teaspoon vanilla extract
2 slices raisin bread, lightly toasted and made into fine crumbs
Dash salt

Preheat oven to 350°F. In medium bowl beat egg yolks with margarine and sugar until fluffy. Beat in carob, sweetener, and vanilla, then bread crumbs. In a separate bowl beat egg whites with salt until stiff peaks form; fold whites into yolk mixture. Pour into a 3-cup soufflé dish that has been sprayed with nonstick cooking spray. Bake for 30 minutes. Serve immediately.

Per serving: 199 calories; 8 g protein; 11 g fat; 19 g carbohydrate; 268 mg sodium

CHEESE SOUFFLÉ

Soufflés are easy to manage if the egg whites are handled properly. For best results eggs should be at room temperature, about 70°F. Be sure to separate eggs carefully so that no yolk mixes with the whites. Whites should be beaten in a clean dry bowl and gently folded into yolks.
See Menu Plan for Week 50.
Makes 2 servings

1 tablespoon margarine
1 tablespoon minced onion
2 tablespoons enriched flour
¾ cup buttermilk
2 ounces coarsely grated sharp Cheddar cheese
¼ teaspoon each powdered mustard and salt
2 eggs, separated
Dash ground red pepper
⅛ teaspoon cream of tartar
2 teaspoons chopped chives

Preheat oven to 375°F. Melt margarine in saucepan; add onion and sauté until softened. Add flour and cook, stirring constantly, for 2 minutes. Remove pan from heat and stir in buttermilk. Return to heat and bring to a boil, stirring constantly. Add cheese, mustard, and salt; stir until cheese is melted. Remove from heat. Beat in egg yolks, 1 at a time; add red pepper. In bowl beat whites until foamy; add cream of tartar and beat until stiff peaks form. Gently fold whites and chives into yolk mixture. Turn soufflé into a 4- or 5-cup soufflé dish that has been sprayed with nonstick cooking spray. Bake 25 minutes. Serve immediately.
Per serving: 312 calories; 17 g protein; 22 g fat; 12 g carbohydrate; 688 mg sodium

GRILLED CHEESE SOUFFLÉ

See Menu Plans for Weeks 7, 23, and 39.
Makes 4 servings

4 eggs, separated
2 tablespoons plus 2 teaspoons reduced-calorie mayonnaise
2 teaspoons grated Parmesan cheese
Dash each salt and pepper
4 slices enriched bread, toasted
4 ounces sliced white Cheddar cheese
12 medium frozen asparagus spears, cooked

Preheat oven to 350°F. In medium bowl, using an electric mixer, beat egg yolks for 3 to 4 minutes or until thick and lemon-colored. Beat in mayonnaise, Parmesan cheese, salt, and pepper. In large bowl, using clean beaters, beat egg whites until stiff but not dry. Carefully stir ⅓ of the egg whites into the yolk mixture; then fold yolk mixture into remaining egg whites. Arrange toast on bottom of shallow 8 x 8 x 2-inch casserole that has been sprayed with non-stick cooking spray; top with cheese, then asparagus. Gently spoon egg mixture over asparagus. Bake for 20 minutes.
Per serving: 299 calories; 17 g protein; 18 g fat; 16 g carbohydrate; 503 mg sodium

HOMINY GRITS SOUFFLÉ

See Menu Plan for Week 3.
Makes 4 servings

4 ounces uncooked enriched hominy grits
3 cups boiling water
1 teaspoon salt
1 tablespoon plus 1 teaspoon margarine
½ cup chopped onion
1 garlic clove, minced
⅓ cup seeded and diced canned jalapeño peppers
4 ounces grated sharp Cheddar cheese
4 eggs, separated
1 teaspoon Worcestershire sauce
Dash hot sauce

Preheat oven to 350°F. In saucepan stir grits into boiling salted water; cook, stirring until soft. Melt margarine in small skillet; add onion and garlic and sauté until soft. In bowl combine cooked grits, onion mixture, and peppers; add cheese, egg yolks, Worcestershire and hot sauces. In separate bowl beat egg whites until stiff; gradually fold into grits mixture. Transfer to 2-quart casserole and bake 30 to 35 minutes or until a thin-bladed knife, when inserted in center, comes out clean.

Per serving: 345 calories; 16 g protein; 19 g fat; 27 g carbohydrate; 879 mg sodium

MUSHROOM CAPS SOUFFLÉ

See Menu Plan for Week 45.
Makes 2 servings

12 large mushrooms, about 2-inch diameter each
2 teaspoons sesame oil
½ cup skim milk
1 tablespoon plus ¾ teaspoon whole wheat flour
2 eggs, separated
¾ cup drained and diced pimientos
¼ cup thinly sliced scallions, green portion only
2 tablespoons chopped fresh parsley
¼ teaspoon garlic powder
⅛ teaspoon white pepper
⅛ teaspoon salt (optional)
Parsley sprigs to garnish

Wash mushrooms and dry with paper towels. Remove stems and reserve for another use. Brush each cap with an equal amount of sesame oil; arrange on baking sheet, stem-side up, and set aside.

Pour milk into small saucepan. Place over medium heat and gradually add flour, stirring constantly with wire whisk. Continue to stir and cook until thickened. Set aside to cool. Preheat oven to 400°F.

Beat egg yolks in medium bowl; stir in vegetables and seasonings. Add yolk mixture to cooled milk. In clean bowl beat whites until stiff peaks form. Gently fold whites into yolk mixture. Spoon an equal amount of mixture into each mushroom cap. Bake 20 to 25 minutes. Garnish with parsley sprigs and serve immediately.

Per serving: 232 calories; 14 g protein; 11 g fat; 20 g carbohydrate; 146 mg sodium

ORANGE SOUFFLÉ

See Menu Plan for Week 49.
Makes 4 servings

4 eggs, separated
Artificial sweetener to equal 9 teaspoons sugar
2 teaspoons sugar
2 tablespoons plus 1½ teaspoons enriched flour
1 cup skim milk, heated
2 tablespoons plus 2 teaspoons reduced-calorie orange marmalade
Rind of 1 small orange, blanched and shredded
⅛ teaspoon orange extract
Dash salt

In small saucepan combine egg yolks, sweetener, and sugar; mix until thick. Add flour and mix well. Briskly stir in milk. Stirring constantly, cook over medium heat until thickened. Continue to stir and simmer gently 2 minutes to form a custard. Remove from heat and allow to cool. Preheat oven to 400°F. Add marmalade, rind, and extract to cooled custard. Beat egg whites with salt until stiff peaks form; gently fold into yolk mixture. Spoon into a 1½-quart soufflé dish that has been sprayed with nonstick cooking spray. Bake 5 minutes. Reduce oven temperature to 350°F. and bake until golden brown, about 35 minutes. Serve immediately.

Per serving: 148 calories; 9 g protein; 6 g fat; 15 g carbohydrate; 135 mg sodium

EGG AND GREEN GODDESS PLATTER
See Menu Plan for Week 29.
Makes 1 serving

1 cup shredded lettuce
2 eggs, hard-cooked and cut lengthwise into halves
Green Goddess Salad Dressing (see page 289)
5 cherry tomatoes, cut into halves
Parsley or dill sprigs to garnish

Arrange lettuce on small oval dish. Top with egg halves, cut-side down; pour dressing over eggs. Arrange tomato halves around eggs and garnish with parsley or dill.

Per serving: 264 calories; 20 g protein; 11 g fat; 19 g carbohydrate; 440 mg sodium

EGG SALAD
See Menu Plans for Weeks 3, 28, 32, and 38.
Makes 1 serving

2 eggs, hard-cooked and chopped
1 tablespoon plus 1 teaspoon reduced-calorie mayonnaise
¼ teaspoon Dijon-style mustard
2 tablespoons minced celery
2 tablespoons diced green or red bell pepper
Dash each salt and white pepper

In a bowl combine eggs with mayonnaise and mustard. Add celery, diced pepper, salt, and pepper, and combine.

Per serving: 213 calories; 13 g protein; 15 g fat; 6 g carbohydrate; 482 mg sodium

FETA CHEESE SALAD
See Menu Plan for Week 43.
Makes 2 servings

4 cups shredded iceberg lettuce
1 cup grated carrots
1 medium cucumber, scored and sliced
1 cup sliced radishes
½ cup alfalfa sprouts
4 ounces feta cheese, cut into 1-inch cubes
4 black olives, pitted and sliced

Arrange a bed of 2 cups lettuce on each of 2 salad plates; top each with ½ cup grated carrots. Surround each portion of carrots with ½ of the cucumber slices and ½ of the sliced radishes. Top each salad with ¼ cup alfalfa sprouts, then 2 ounces feta cheese. Garnish each with ½ of the sliced olives.

Per serving: 239 calories; 13 g protein; 14 g fat; 17 g carbohydrate; 747 mg sodium

GREEK SALAD
Lettuce, tomatoes, green pepper, and cucumber should be well chilled before preparing.
See Menu Plan for Week 18.
Makes 2 servings

3 cups torn romaine lettuce
1 cup halved cherry tomatoes
1 medium cucumber, pared and cut into large dice
½ medium green bell pepper, seeded and thinly sliced
½ cup thinly sliced red onion
4 ounces feta cheese, cut into large dice
4 black olives
2 tablespoons wine vinegar
1 tablespoon minced fresh parsley
2 teaspoons olive oil
1 teaspoon grated lemon rind
¼ teaspoon mashed fresh garlic
Dash each salt and freshly ground pepper

Combine all ingredients in a salad bowl; toss well and serve.

Per serving: 258 calories; 11 g protein; 19 g fat; 13 g carbohydrate; 993 mg sodium

GYPSY CHEESE SALAD
See Menu Plan for Week 8.
Makes 2 servings

1⅓ cups cottage cheese
¼ cup diced red bell pepper
¼ cup grated carrot
½ small apple, cored, diced, and sprinkled
    with lemon juice
2 tablespoons chopped fresh parsley
4 drops hot sauce
1 teaspoon Worcestershire sauce
4 large lettuce leaves
1 medium tomato, cut into wedges
1 medium cucumber, sliced

Combine all ingredients except lettuce, tomato, and cucumber in small bowl. Serve on
lettuce leaves, surrounded by tomato wedges
and cucumber slices.

Per serving: 211 calories; 21 g protein; 7 g fat;
17 g carbohydrate; 623 mg sodium

POTATO, EGGS, AND CHEESE SALAD
See Menu Plan for Week 10.
Makes 2 servings

1 tablespoon plus 2 teaspoons tarragon
    vinegar
1½ teaspoons lemon juice
¼ teaspoon salt
Dash pepper
8 ounces peeled cooked potatoes, diced
2 eggs, hard-cooked and chopped
2 ounces Swiss cheese, cubed
1 tablespoon plus 1 teaspoon reduced-
    calorie mayonnaise
1 teaspoon chopped fresh parsley

In bowl combine vinegar, lemon juice, salt,
and pepper. Add potatoes; toss and refrigerate 1 hour. Add eggs, cheese, mayonnaise,
and parsley to potato mixture; toss to combine. Chill again before serving.

Per serving: 287 calories; 16 g protein; 15 g fat;
21 g carbohydrate; 516 mg sodium

SALAD WITH SLICED EGG
See Menu Plan for Week 44.
Makes 2 servings

1 cup torn lettuce leaves
1 medium tomato, diced
1 medium cucumber, pared, seeded, and
    diced
½ recipe (2 servings) Basic Vinaigrette
    Dressing (see page 286)
1 egg, hard-cooked and sliced

Combine lettuce, tomato, and cucumber in
salad bowl; chill. When ready to serve, pour
dressing over salad and toss to coat. Garnish
with egg slices.

Per serving: 110 calories; 5 g protein; 8 g fat;
7 g carbohydrate; 121 mg sodium

SPINACH-CUCUMBER EGG SALAD
See Menu Plans for Weeks 19 and 22.
Makes 2 servings

4 eggs, hard-cooked and chopped
½ cup well-squeezed cooked chopped
    spinach
½ cup seeded and diced pared cucumber
2 teaspoons sweet pickle relish
1 teaspoon each lemon juice and lime juice
½ teaspoon salt
Dash each ground nutmeg and pepper
Lettuce leaves

Combine all ingredients except lettuce in
medium bowl; stir well. Cover and chill ½
to 1 hour. Serve on bed of lettuce leaves.

Per serving: 189 calories; 15 g protein; 11 g fat;
7 g carbohydrate; 793 mg sodium

CARAWAY-CHEESE TOAST

Whole wheat toast can be substituted for the pitas.
See Menu Plans for Weeks 9, 20, and 33.
Makes 2 servings

Prepared mustard (optional)
2 pita breads, 1 ounce each
2 ounces grated Swiss cheese
½ teaspoon caraway seeds

Spread small amount of mustard on each pita, if desired. Sprinkle each with 1 ounce Swiss cheese and ¼ teaspoon caraway seeds. Place in broiler pan or on aluminum foil and broil until cheese is thoroughly melted.

Per serving: 184 calories; 11 g protein; 9 g fat;
15 g carbohydrate; 207 mg sodium

CINNAMON-CHEESE TOAST

See Menu Plan for Week 5 and various other weeks.
Makes 1 serving

⅓ cup cottage cheese
Artificial sweetener to equal 1 teaspoon
    sugar
⅛ teaspoon ground cinnamon
1 slice raisin bread, toasted
1 teaspoon shredded coconut

In a small bowl mix cottage cheese with sweetener and cinnamon. Spread on toast. Sprinkle with coconut; broil for 2 to 3 minutes or until bubbly.

Per serving: 149 calories; 11 g protein; 5 g fat;
16 g carbohydrate; 388 mg sodium

COFFEE-CHEESE DELIGHT

See Menu Plans for Weeks 15, 21, and 37.
Makes 2 servings

⅔ cup part-skim ricotta cheese
2 large prunes, pitted and chopped
1 teaspoon instant coffee
¼ teaspoon chocolate extract
2 canned pear halves with 2 tablespoons
    juice, no sugar added
2 slices enriched bread, toasted and cut into
    wedges

Combine first 4 ingredients in a bowl. Place each pear half in a small dish; top each with ½ of the cheese mixture and sprinkle with 1 tablespoon juice. Serve with toast wedges.

Per serving: 241 calories; 12 g protein; 8 g fat;
32 g carbohydrate; 222 mg sodium

HONEY-COCONUT TOAST

See Menu Plan for Week 8.
Makes 2 servings

2 eggs, beaten
2 tablespoons buttermilk
Artificial sweetener to equal 2 teaspoons
    sugar (optional)
½ teaspoon vanilla extract
⅛ teaspoon ground cinnamon
2 slices raisin bread
2 teaspoons margarine
1 teaspoon honey, heated
2 teaspoons shredded coconut

In shallow bowl combine eggs with buttermilk, sweetener if desired, vanilla, and cinnamon. Dip bread into egg mixture, turning on both sides. Let stand until most of the liquid is absorbed. Heat margarine in nonstick skillet and add bread; pour any remaining egg mixture over bread. Cook, turning to brown both sides. Transfer to nonstick baking sheet; spread each slice with ½ teaspoon honey and sprinkle each with 1 teaspoon coconut. Broil 5 minutes. Serve immediately.

Per serving: 204 calories; 8 g protein; 11 g fat;
18 g carbohydrate; 214 mg sodium

GRILLED TORTILLAS

See Menu Plan for Week 46.
Makes 2 servings

2 corn tortillas, 6-inch diameter each
2 ounces hard cheese (Swiss, Muenster,
    Cheddar, etc.), grated
1 to 2 tablespoons drained and chopped
    pimiento
2 teaspoons imitation bacon bits

Place tortillas on nonstick baking sheet; top each with 1 ounce cheese, ½ of the chopped pimiento, and 1 teaspoon bacon bits. Bake at 350°F. for 10 to 15 minutes or until cheese is melted.

Per serving: 160 calories; 10 g protein; 9 g fat; 11 g carbohydrate; 171 mg sodium

MUSHROOM PIZZA
See Menu Plan for Week 27.
Makes 2 servings

2 teaspoons olive oil
1 garlic clove, minced
2 cups sliced mushrooms
1 tablespoon chopped fresh parsley
1 cup cooked enriched rice
2 eggs, beaten
1 cup tomato sauce
2 teaspoons grated Parmesan cheese
2 ounces grated Mozzarella cheese

Heat oil in small skillet; add garlic and sauté for 2 minutes. Add mushrooms and parsley and cook, stirring occasionally, until mushrooms are tender; set aside.

In bowl combine rice and eggs. Spray a 9-inch springform pan with nonstick cooking spray. Spread rice-egg mixture evenly over bottom of pan and bake at 425°F. for 10 minutes or until set. Remove from oven.

Pour tomato sauce evenly over rice crust. Top with mushroom mixture. Sprinkle with Parmesan cheese and top with Mozzarella cheese. Bake for 10 minutes longer or until cheese melts. Remove sides of pan and serve.

Per serving: 382 calories; 19 g protein; 19 g fat; 35 g carbohydrate; 867 mg sodium

OPEN-FACE GRILLED CHEESE SANDWICH I
See Menu Plan for Week 31 and various other weeks.
Makes 2 servings

2 ounces sliced American, Cheddar, Muenster, or Swiss cheese
2 slices enriched white, whole wheat, rye, pumpernickel, or cracked wheat bread, toasted
½ medium tomato, sliced (optional)

Preheat broiler. Place 1 ounce of cheese on each slice of toast. Top each with ½ of the tomato slices, if desired. Place in broiler pan or on aluminum foil; broil 3 to 4 minutes or until cheese melts.

Per serving: 168 calories; 8 g protein; 10 g fat; 12 g carbohydrate; 347 mg sodium

OPEN-FACE GRILLED CHEESE SANDWICH II
See Menu Plan for Week 3 and various other weeks.
Makes 2 servings

4 ounces sliced American, Cheddar, Muenster, or Swiss cheese
2 slices enriched white, whole wheat, rye, pumpernickel, or cracked wheat bread, toasted
½ medium tomato, sliced (optional)

Preheat broiler. Place 2 ounces of cheese on each slice of bread. Top each with half of the tomato slices, if desired. Place in broiling pan or on aluminum foil and broil for 3 to 4 minutes or until cheese melts.

Per serving: 275 calories; 15 g protein; 18 g fat; 13 g carbohydrate; 428 mg sodium

REUBEN SANDWICH
See Menu Plans for Weeks 1 and 36.
Makes 1 serving

½ cup drained sauerkraut
1 slice rye bread
2 ounces skinned and boned cooked turkey, sliced
1 ounce Swiss cheese

Place sauerkraut on rye bread; top with turkey and Swiss cheese. Place in broiling pan or on aluminum foil and broil until cheese melts.

Per serving: 283 calories; 28 g protein; 11 g fat; 19 g carbohydrate; 1,121 mg sodium

PANCAKES
See Menu Plans for Weeks 10, 29, and 36.
Makes 2 servings

⅓ cup nonfat dry milk powder
2 tablespoons plus 1½ teaspoons enriched
   flour
¼ teaspoon ground cinnamon
⅛ teaspoon salt
1 tablespoon margarine, melted
2 eggs, separated
2 teaspoons sugar

Sift together dry milk, flour, cinnamon, and salt. Set aside. Combine margarine and egg yolks. In a medium bowl beat egg whites with sugar until stiff. Lightly fold yolk mixture into whites; then gradually fold in sifted ingredients. Let stand 5 minutes. Heat nonstick skillet over medium heat. Drop batter, 1 tablespoon at a time, into skillet. Lightly spread with back of spoon to form pancakes. Cook until underside is browned; turn pancakes and cook 1 minute longer. Serve hot.
Per serving: 221 calories; 11 g protein; 11 g fat;
18 g carbohydrate; 345 mg sodium

STUFFED FRENCH TOAST
See Menu Plans for Weeks 13 and 43.
Makes 1 serving

⅓ cup cottage cheese
1 tablespoon raisins
¼ teaspoon vanilla extract
¼ teaspoon brown sugar
2 slices oatmeal or whole wheat bread
1 egg
1 tablespoon water
1 teaspoon reduced-calorie margarine
2 teaspoons reduced-calorie strawberry
   spread

Combine first 4 ingredients in small bowl; spread on 1 slice of bread and top with remaining bread to form a sandwich. In small bowl beat egg with water; transfer to small shallow pan and soak sandwich, turning occasionally, for 10 minutes or until all egg is absorbed. Melt margarine in small skillet; add sandwich. Cook until bottom is golden brown; turn and brown other side. Top with strawberry spread and serve.
Per serving: 356 calories; 21 g protein; 13 g fat;
40 g carbohydrate; 418 mg sodium

MUSHROOM-STUFFED EGGS
See Menu Plan for Week 5.
Makes 2 servings

2 teaspoons margarine
1 tablespoon plus 1 teaspoon minced
   scallion
1 cup finely chopped mushrooms
Dash each salt, pepper, and thyme leaves
4 eggs, hard-cooked
1 tablespoon plus 1 teaspoon reduced-
   calorie mayonnaise
1½ teaspoons lemon juice
8 parsley sprigs

Melt margarine in nonstick skillet; add scallion and sauté for 2 minutes. Add mushrooms, salt, pepper, and thyme and cook 3 to 5 minutes or until all liquid has evaporated; cool. Cut each egg in half lengthwise; remove yolks and reserve whites. Push yolks through a sieve into a bowl. Add mushroom mixture, mayonnaise, and lemon juice; stir to combine. Fill each egg white with an equal amount of mixture and garnish with a parsley sprig.
Per serving: 234 calories; 14 g protein; 17 g fat;
6 g carbohydrate; 335 mg sodium

STUFFED EGGS
See Menu Plans for Weeks 24 and 50.
Makes 2 servings

4 eggs, hard-cooked
¼ cup chopped peeled tomato
2 teaspoons mayonnaise
¼ teaspoon salt
⅛ teaspoon lemon juice
Dash pepper
Lettuce leaves

Cut thin piece off narrow end of each egg and set aside. Carefully scoop out yolks, reserving whites. Press yolks through sieve into small bowl; add tomato, mayonnaise, salt, lemon juice, and pepper to yolks and mix to combine. Stuff ¼ of yolk mixture into each reserved egg white, mounding stuffing on top. Arrange lettuce leaves on serving plate; stand stuffed eggs on leaves. Chop reserved egg white pieces and sprinkle over lettuce and eggs. Chill before serving.

Per serving: 199 calories; 13 g protein; 15 g fat; 3 g carbohydrate; 444 mg sodium

BROCCOLI QUICHE

This quiche may be prepared in advance, refrigerated, and reheated when ready to use.
See Menu Plans for Weeks 21 and 30.
Makes 8 servings

½ cup plus 2 tablespoons enriched flour
¾ teaspoon salt, divided
2 tablespoons plus 2 teaspoons margarine
¼ cup plain unflavored yogurt
1 cup well-drained cooked chopped broccoli
¼ cup finely chopped scallions
1 tablespoon plus 1 teaspoon imitation
   bacon bits
8 ounces Swiss cheese, shredded, divided
4 eggs, slightly beaten
1 cup evaporated skimmed milk
⅛ teaspoon pepper

Combine flour and ¼ teaspoon salt in mixing bowl. Cut in margarine until mixture resembles a coarse meal. Add yogurt and mix thoroughly; form into a ball. Roll dough out to approximately ⅛-inch thickness. Fit into a 9-inch pie pan or quiche dish; flute or crimp edges and set aside. Combine vegetables and bacon bits. Cover bottom of pastry shell with 4 ounces cheese; add entire vegetable mixture. Combine eggs, milk, ½ teaspoon salt, and pepper. Pour egg mixture over vegetables; top evenly with remaining cheese. Bake at 325°F. for 50 to 60 minutes or till knife, when inserted in center, comes out clean. Remove from oven and let stand 10 minutes before serving.

Per serving: 252 calories; 16 g protein; 15 g fat; 13 g carbohydrate; 463 mg sodium

CELERY-RICOTTA BAKE

See Menu Plans for Weeks 35 and 45.
Makes 2 servings

1½ cups pared celery sticks, 2 x ½ inches each
¾ cup Chicken Broth (see page 127) or chicken bouillon
½ teaspoon chopped fresh parsley
Dash each salt and pepper
⅔ cup part-skim ricotta cheese

Combine celery sticks and broth in 1-quart baking pan. Cover and bake at 350°F. for 50 minutes. Remove from oven and drain; broth may be reserved for use at another time.

Combine celery, parsley, salt, and pepper in small flameproof baking pan. Spread cheese over celery mixture; broil until slightly browned.

Per serving: 132 calories; 10 g protein; 7 g fat; 8 g carbohydrate; 298 mg sodium

CHEESE-STUFFED ZUCCHINI
See Menu Plans for Weeks 30 and 37.
Makes 2 servings

2 medium zucchini, about 5 ounces each
2 teaspoons olive oil
1 cup sliced mushrooms
1 teaspoon minced fresh garlic
4 ounces Mozzarella cheese, diced
1 tablespoon chopped fresh basil, or
   1 teaspoon dried
1 tablespoon chopped fresh parsley
Dash each salt, pepper, and ground nutmeg
2 teaspoons grated Parmesan cheese

Trim ends off each zucchini; slice each in half lengthwise and scoop out pulp, reserving shells. Heat oil in small saucepan; add zucchini pulp, mushrooms, and garlic. Sauté until all ingredients are soft. Transfer mixture to a bowl. Add Mozzarella cheese, basil, parsley, and seasonings; toss well. Spoon ¼ of mixture into each zucchini shell and arrange shells, side by side, in a casserole. Sprinkle each with ½ teaspoon Parmesan cheese. Cover and bake 30 minutes at 350°F.; remove cover and continue baking 15 minutes longer.

Per serving: 266 calories; 16 g protein; 19 g fat; 10 g carbohydrate; 403 mg sodium

CORNMEAL-SWISS BAKE
See Menu Plans for Weeks 32 and 40.
Makes 2 servings

2 cups chopped cauliflower
1½ cups water
2 ounces uncooked enriched yellow
   cornmeal
¾ teaspoon salt
1 teaspoon prepared mustard
⅛ teaspoon ground celery seed
Dash each ground sage and pepper
2 ounces grated Swiss cheese
¼ teaspoon sweet Hungarian paprika

Steam cauliflower until tender yet firm, about 5 minutes; set aside.

In saucepan bring water to a boil; briskly stir in cornmeal and salt. Reduce heat and cook, stirring occasionally, until mixture begins to thicken. Stir in mustard, celery seed, sage, and pepper; continue cooking 2 to 3 minutes longer or until cornmeal is quite thick. Stir in cauliflower. Spread mixture evenly over bottom of an 8-inch square nonstick baking pan. Cover and refrigerate overnight.

Preheat oven to 350°F. Combine cheese and paprika and sprinkle over cornmeal mixture. Bake 25 to 30 minutes. Cut into 4 squares and serve.

Per serving: 238 calories; 13 g protein; 8 g fat; 29 g carbohydrate; 981 mg sodium

LAYERED EGGPLANT-CHEESE BAKE
See Menu Plans for Weeks 6 and 24.
Makes 2 servings

1 small eggplant, about 10 ounces
1 teaspoon salt
2 ounces Swiss cheese, shredded
2 ounces Mozzarella cheese, shredded
½ teaspoon oregano leaves
½ teaspoon chopped fresh parsley
Dash white pepper

With vegetable peeler, pare skin of eggplant lengthwise at 1-inch intervals to produce a striped effect. Cut eggplant crosswise into 8 slices, about ¼ inch each. Sprinkle with salt on both sides. Place slices on a rack over a pan. Let stand 30 minutes. Pat slices dry with paper towels.

In bowl combine the cheeses, oregano, parsley, and pepper. Spray a nonstick 8-inch square baking pan with nonstick cooking spray. Place 2 slices of eggplant in bottom of pan; top with ¼ of the cheese mixture. Repeat procedure 3 more times, ending with cheese on top. Insert 2 toothpicks into each stack. Cover and bake at 350°F. for 25 minutes. Remove toothpicks before serving.

Per serving: 223 calories; 15 g protein; 14 g fat; 10 g carbohydrate; 1,355 mg sodium

MUSHROOM LOAF
See Menu Plan for Week 19 and various other weeks.
Makes 2 servings

4 cups chopped mushrooms
1 cup chopped celery, about 4 ribs
¼ cup chopped fresh parsley
⅔ cup cottage cheese
2 eggs
⅓ cup plus 2 teaspoons plain dried bread crumbs
¼ teaspoon basil leaves
¼ teaspoon oregano leaves
Dash salt
1 medium zucchini, about 5 ounces, scrubbed and trimmed
Parsley sprigs to garnish

Combine mushrooms, celery, and chopped parsley in work bowl of food processor; process until almost pureed. Add remaining ingredients except zucchini and garnish; continue to process until well combined. Transfer ½ of mixture to a 7⅜ x 3⅝ x 2¼-inch loaf pan that has been sprayed with nonstick cooking spray. Place zucchini in center of mixture; top with remaining mixture. Cover with foil. Place loaf pan in larger pan that contains about 1 inch water; bake at 350°F., adding more water as needed, for 1½ hours or until a knife, when inserted in center, comes out clean. Cool. Unmold, cover, and chill for at least 3 hours. Garnish with parsley sprigs.

Per serving: 300 calories; 24 g protein; 10 g fat; 29 g carbohydrate; 684 mg sodium

STUFFED RIGATONI
See Menu Plan for Week 50.
Makes 4 servings

2⅔ cups part-skim ricotta cheese
2 tablespoons chopped fresh parsley
1 tablespoon plus 1 teaspoon grated Parmesan cheese
Dash each salt and freshly ground pepper
2⅔ cups cooked enriched rigatoni (macaroni tubes)

2 cups Marinara Sauce (see page 285)
Chopped fresh parsley to garnish

In small bowl combine ricotta cheese, 2 tablespoons parsley, Parmesan cheese, salt, and pepper; mix until thoroughly blended. Fill each macaroni tube with an equal amount of cheese mixture. Arrange side by side in oblong casserole. Pour sauce evenly over stuffed rigatoni. Bake at 375°F. for 35 minutes. Garnish with chopped parsley just before serving.

Per serving: 416 calories; 26 g protein; 18 g fat; 39 g carbohydrate; 928 mg sodium

TORTILLA BAKE
See Menu Plan for Week 33.
Makes 4 servings

4 corn tortillas, 6-inch diameter each, heated
4 ounces Monterey Jack cheese, grated and divided
4 eggs, beaten
1 cup skim milk
1 teaspoon chopped jalapeño pepper
½ teaspoon chili powder
¼ teaspoon powdered mustard
1 teaspoon olive oil
1 garlic clove, minced
½ cup tomato sauce
⅛ teaspoon ground cumin
1 medium tomato, cut into 8 slices
1 tablespoon plus 1 teaspoon chopped onion
Parsley sprigs to garnish

Place 1 tortilla in each of 4 round individual casseroles that have been sprayed with nonstick cooking spray. Top each with ½ ounce grated cheese. In bowl combine eggs, milk, jalapeño pepper, chili powder, and mustard. Pour ¼ of egg mixture into each casserole and sprinkle with ½ ounce cheese. Bake at 350°F. for 30 minutes.

Heat olive oil in small saucepan. Add garlic and sauté until tender. Stir in tomato sauce and cumin; cook 2 minutes. Spoon ¼ of sauce over each tortilla. Garnish each portion with 2 tomato slices, 1 teaspoon chopped onion, and parsley.

Per serving: 279 calories; 17 g protein; 16 g fat; 17 g carbohydrate; 405 mg sodium

VEGETABLE LASAGNA
See Menu Plan for Week 16.
Makes 4 servings

2 medium zucchini, 5 to 6 ounces each,
    sliced lengthwise into ¼-inch thick slices
1⅓ cups part-skim ricotta cheese
½ cup cooked, drained, and chopped
    spinach
1 tablespoon minced fresh parsley
2 teaspoons grated Parmesan cheese
1 teaspoon salt
Dash pepper
1 cup cooked cauliflower, pureed
1 cup sliced mushrooms
4 ounces part-skim Mozzarella cheese, sliced
½ cup crushed canned plum tomatoes
½ teaspoon garlic powder

Place zucchini on nonstick baking sheet. Bake at 400°F., turning once, until lightly browned, about 20 minutes.

In small bowl combine ricotta, spinach, parsley, Parmesan cheese, salt, and pepper. Set aside.

Spray a shallow 1½-quart casserole with nonstick cooking spray; line bottom with zucchini, covering entire surface. Add ricotta mixture and spread evenly. Layer cauliflower, mushrooms, Mozzarella cheese, and tomatoes over ricotta mixture; sprinkle with garlic powder. Bake at 375°F. until cheese melts, about 40 minutes. Remove and let set before cutting.

Per serving: 236 calories; 21 g protein; 12 g fat; 13 g carbohydrate; 923 mg sodium

CHILI-CHEESE RAREBIT
See Menu Plans for Weeks 5 and 35.
Makes 2 servings

2 teaspoons margarine
1 tablespoon diced onion
2 tablespoons diced green bell pepper
1 cup canned tomatoes, chopped
¾ teaspoon chili powder, or to taste
4 ounces sharp Cheddar cheese, shredded
1 teaspoon cornstarch, dissolved in
    1 tablespoon water
2 slices rye bread, toasted

Melt margarine in saucepan; add onion and sauté until softened. Add green pepper and sauté about 3 minutes longer. Add tomatoes and chili powder and simmer mixture 10 minutes or until some of the liquid has evaporated. Add cheese and cook over low heat, stirring constantly, until cheese is melted. Stir in dissolved cornstarch and simmer, stirring constantly, until thickened. Serve over toast.

Per serving: 356 calories; 18 g protein; 23 g fat; 21 g carbohydrate; 693 mg sodium

CREAMED EGG 'N' MUFFIN
See Menu Plan for Week 41.
Makes 2 servings

2 eggs, hard-cooked and cut into halves
1 tablespoon plus 1 teaspoon reduced-
    calorie margarine
1¼ teaspoons enriched flour
½ cup evaporated skimmed milk
1 teaspoon chopped chives
½ teaspoon Worcestershire sauce
2 whole wheat English muffins, split and
    toasted
Dash paprika
1 teaspoon minced fresh parsley

Finely chop egg whites. In a bowl crumble yolks and set aside. Melt margarine in small saucepan. Add flour and combine thoroughly. Slowly pour in milk and cook over medium heat, stirring constantly with wire whisk until sauce bubbles and thickens. Add chives, Worcestershire, and chopped egg whites; stir to combine. Spoon ¼ of mixture over each muffin half, then ¼ of the crumbled yolks. Sprinkle each with paprika and then with ¼ teaspoon minced parsley.

Per serving: 300 calories; 15 g protein; 11 g fat; 35 g carbohydrate; 527 mg sodium

EGG AND PROSCIUTTO MELT

The spiciness of prosciutto (spiced Italian ham) contrasts well with the sweet flavor of fruit. Traditionally it's served with melon wedges, but for a different taste treat, try it with apples.

See Menu Plan for Week 33.
Makes 4 servings

4 English muffins, split and toasted
3 ounces thinly sliced prosciutto
24 medium cooked asparagus spears, hot
4 eggs, poached
2 ounces Gruyère cheese, grated

Place 2 muffin halves in each of 4 individual casseroles. Top muffins in each casserole with ¼ of the prosciutto, then 6 asparagus spears, and 1 poached egg. Sprinkle each portion with ½ ounce grated cheese. Broil until cheese melts.

Per serving: 322 calories; 21 g protein; 13 g fat;
30 g carbohydrate; 672 mg sodium

MEDITERRANEAN EGGS IN NEST

See Menu Plan for Week 33.
Makes 2 servings

8 ounces pared potatoes, boiled and mashed
2 teaspoons margarine
2 teaspoons grated Parmesan cheese
1 teaspoon chopped chives
1 medium tomato, peeled, seeded, and chopped
½ cup chopped onion
Dash each salt and pepper
4 eggs, poached
4 black olives, pitted and sliced

In bowl combine mashed potatoes, margarine, cheese, and chives. Divide mixture into 4 equal balls; flatten and shape each ball into an 8-inch round. Place on nonstick baking sheet and bake at 375°F. for 15 minutes or until lightly browned. With a broad spatula, transfer potato nests to serving platter and keep warm.

In saucepan cook tomato and onion until soft; add salt and pepper. Place a poached egg on each potato round and top with ¼ of the tomato mixture. Garnish with olive slices.

Per serving: 324 calories; 17 g protein; 18 g fat;
25 g carbohydrate; 293 mg sodium

"CALZONE"

See Menu Plan for Week 12.
Makes 2 servings

2 teaspoons margarine
2 cups sliced mushrooms
⅔ cup part-skim ricotta cheese
2 ounces Mozzarella cheese, diced
Dash each salt and pepper
2 pita breads, 1 ounce each

Melt margarine in skillet; add mushrooms and sauté until tender. In bowl combine mushrooms with ricotta and Mozzarella cheeses. Season with salt and pepper. Divide mixture into 2 portions. Cut opening at edge of each pita to form pocket. Spoon 1 portion cheese mixture into each pita pocket. Wrap each stuffed pita in foil and bake at 350°F. for 15 minutes.

Per serving: 322 calories; 21 g protein; 16 g fat;
23 g carbohydrate; 387 mg sodium

CHEESE PIZZA POCKET

See Menu Plan for Week 26 and various other weeks.
Makes 2 servings

1⅓ cups part skim-ricotta cheese
½ cup peeled, seeded, and diced tomato
2 tablespoons minced fresh parsley
1 tablespoon minced green bell pepper
2 teaspoons grated Parmesan cheese
Dash each oregano leaves, garlic powder, salt, and pepper
2 pita breads, 1 ounce each

In small bowl combine all ingredients except bread. Slice pita breads horizontally, halfway around and open to form pocket; stuff with ricotta mixture. Stand upright in small pan; bake at 400°F. for 15 minutes or until cheese is melted.

Per serving: 338 calories; 24 g protein; 16 g fat;
26 g carbohydrate; 391 mg sodium

CHEESE-SALAD SANDWICH
See Menu Plan for Week 7.
Makes 2 servings

1 tablespoon vegetable oil
1 tablespoon wine vinegar
1 tablespoon water
⅛ teaspoon dill weed
⅛ teaspoon oregano leaves
Dash pepper
4 ounces Swiss cheese, cut into strips
½ cup sliced cucumber
¼ cup sliced radishes
1 tablespoon chopped scallion
2 pita breads, 1 ounce each

Combine first 6 ingredients in bowl. Add remaining ingredients except pita breads; stir to coat cheese and vegetables. Cover and marinate in refrigerator for at least 1 hour. Cut each pita bread halfway around edge and open to form a pocket. Spoon ½ of salad mixture into each pita pocket.

Per serving: 363 calories; 19 g protein; 24 g fat; 18 g carbohydrate; 154 mg sodium

TOMATO-CHEESE-STUFFED PITAS
See Menu Plans for Weeks 25 and 41.
Makes 2 servings

2 pita breads, 1 ounce each
2 thin tomato slices
⅔ cup part-skim ricotta cheese
1 ounce grated Mozzarella cheese
1 ounce grated Swiss cheese
¼ teaspoon oregano leaves
¼ teaspoon salt
Dash each thyme leaves and ground nutmeg

Preheat oven to 350°F. Slice pita breads horizontally, halfway around, and open each to form a pocket. Slide 1 tomato slice into each pocket. Combine remaining ingredients in a small bowl. Stuff ½ of mixture into each pocket. Transfer to small baking pan. Bake 15 minutes or until cheese is melted.

Per serving: 288 calories; 19 g protein; 15 g fat; 20 g carbohydrate; 487 mg sodium

MACARONI-CHEESE MOLD
See Menu Plan for Week 20.
Makes 2 servings

1⅓ cups hot cooked enriched elbow macaroni
4 ounces sharp Cheddar cheese, coarsely grated, divided
¼ cup plain unflavored yogurt
1 tablespoon plus 1 teaspoon reduced-calorie mayonnaise
1 teaspoon Dijon-style mustard
¼ cup diced celery
2 tablespoons diced pimiento
2 tablespoons diced green bell pepper
4 green bell pepper strips
3 pimiento strips

In bowl combine elbow macaroni with ½ of the cheese; toss until cheese is melted. In a small bowl combine remaining cheese with yogurt, mayonnaise, and mustard; add to macaroni mixture and stir to combine. Add celery, diced pimiento, and diced green pepper. Toss well; cool.

Line a 6¼ x 3½ x 2-inch loaf pan with foil. Pack cooled mixture firmly into pan. Cover with foil and weight with 2 small cans (e.g., tomato paste). Refrigerate overnight.

Remove weight and foil. With sharp knife loosen loaf around edges and unmold onto serving plate. Garnish top with vegetable strips, alternating pepper and pimiento.

Per serving: 388 calories; 19 g protein; 22 g fat; 28 g carbohydrate; 513 mg sodium

TOMATO STUFFED WITH HERB CHEESE
See Menu Plans for Weeks 2, 26, 29, and 48.
Makes 2 servings

1⅓ cups cottage cheese
2 tablespoons minced scallion
1 tablespoon chopped fresh parsley
1 tablespoon chopped fresh dill
1 small garlic clove, minced
Dash each salt and white pepper
2 medium tomatoes
2 parsley sprigs

In bowl combine cottage cheese with scallion, parsley, dill, garlic, salt, and pepper. With pointed knife remove stem end of each tomato. Make 4 vertical intersecting cuts through top of each tomato, almost to the base, dividing tomatoes into eighths; spread tomatoes open. Fill center of each tomato with half of herb cheese; garnish each with 1 parsley sprig.

Per serving: 185 calories; 20 g protein; 7 g fat; 11 g carbohydrate; 705 mg sodium

VEGETABLE-CHEESE PLATTER

Cottage cheese may be substituted for the ricotta cheese in this recipe.
See Menu Plan for Week 39.
Makes 2 servings

⅔ cup part-skim ricotta cheese
¼ cup plain unflavored yogurt
½ teaspoon Dijon-style mustard
¼ teaspoon salt
⅛ teaspoon mashed fresh garlic
Dash white pepper
¼ cup grated carrot
¼ cup minced green bell pepper
¼ cup minced celery
1 medium cucumber, pared and cut lengthwise into quarters
2 eggs, hard-cooked and cut lengthwise into quarters
8 small celery ribs
1 medium tomato, cut into 8 wedges
Chopped fresh parsley to garnish

In bowl combine cheese with yogurt, mustard, salt, garlic, and pepper. Add carrot, green pepper, and minced celery; mix well and chill for 1 hour.

Spoon cheese mixture onto center of serving platter. Cut each cucumber quarter in half crosswise. Arrange cucumber spears, eggs, celery ribs, and tomato wedges alternately around edge of platter. Garnish with parsley.

Per serving: 260 calories; 19 g protein; 15 g fat; 17 g carbohydrate; 647 mg sodium

VEGETABLE COTTAGE CHEESE
See Menu Plan for Week 12.
Makes 1 serving

⅓ cup cottage cheese
2 tablespoons minced red bell pepper
2 tablespoons grated carrot
2 tablespoons plain unflavored yogurt
1 tablespoon chopped scallion
1 tablespoon alfalfa sprouts
Dash pepper

Combine all ingredients in a bowl. Chill.

Per serving: 112 calories; 11 g protein; 4 g fat; 7 g carbohydrate; 322 mg sodium

BEAN SPROUTS WITH MUENSTER JULIENNE
See Menu Plans for Weeks 28 and 51.
Makes 2 servings

2 cups bean sprouts
¼ cup diced carrot
¼ cup diced red bell pepper
1 teaspoon chopped fresh ginger root
1 teaspoon chopped fresh parsley
¼ medium garlic clove, minced with ½ teaspoon salt
Dash pepper
4 ounces Muenster cheese, sliced into thin strips

Heat nonstick skillet over medium heat. Add all ingredients except cheese and toss to combine. Cover, reduce heat to low, and cook until sprouts are just wilted but still slightly crisp, 3 to 5 minutes. Remove from heat and gently stir in cheese. Cook 1 to 2 minutes to just heat but not melt cheese.

Per serving: 252 calories; 17 g protein; 17 g fat; 9 g carbohydrate; 982 mg sodium

BROCCOLI "MEATBALLS"
See Menu Plan for Week 44.
Makes 4 servings

1 cup cooked and pureed broccoli
½ cup plus 1 tablespoon plain dried bread
    crumbs
2 eggs
1 tablespoon plus 1 teaspoon grated
    Parmesan cheese
½ teaspoon salt
1 garlic clove, mashed, or ¼ teaspoon garlic
    powder
Dash each onion powder and freshly ground
    pepper
¾ ounce cornflakes, made into crumbs

Combine all ingredients except cornflakes
in medium bowl. Form mixture into sixteen
1½-inch balls; roll each in cornflake crumbs,
coating evenly. Place balls on nonstick baking sheet that has been sprayed with nonstick cooking spray. Bake at 400°F., turning
once, for 40 minutes or until nicely browned.

Per serving: 142 calories; 8 g protein; 5 g fat;
16 g carbohydrate; 566 mg sodium

CAULIFLOWER-CHEESE CRISP
See Menu Plan for Week 52.
Makes 2 servings

1 cup cooked large cauliflower florets, cut
    into ¼-inch thick slices
2 ounces Mozzarella cheese, shredded
1 tablespoon plus 1½ teaspoons plain dried
    bread crumbs
⅛ teaspoon salt
Dash each pepper and minced fresh garlic

Preheat oven to 350°F. Combine all ingredients in small bowl. Spray a 6- or 8-inch
skillet* that has a flameproof or removable
handle with nonstick cooking spray. Turn
cauliflower mixture into skillet; press in
lightly. Bake 5 minutes; then broil until
lightly browned.

Per serving: 109 calories; 7 g protein; 6 g fat;
6 g carbohydrate; 286 mg sodium

* A 1-quart flameproof casserole may be substituted for the skillet in this recipe.

CHEESE AND RICE-STUFFED MUSHROOMS

Green peppercorns add a unique flavor.
They can usually be purchased in specialty
food stores or the gourmet section of your
supermarket.

See Menu Plan for Week 22.
Makes 2 servings

8 large mushrooms, about 2½ cups
1 cup cooked short-grain brown rice
4 ounces Cheddar cheese, grated
2 teaspoons prepared horseradish
2 teaspoons Dijon-style mustard
1 teaspoon minced green peppercorns
1 teaspoon lemon juice
Dash each salt and pepper
1 large green bell pepper, seeded and cut
    into 8 rings
1½ cups cooked chopped spinach
1½ teaspoons chopped fresh parsley
4 watercress sprigs
2 cherry tomatoes

Preheat oven to 350°F. Remove stems from
mushrooms.* In saucepan steam mushroom
caps until just tender, about 5 minutes. Cool
in cold water, drain, and set aside.

In bowl combine rice, cheese, horseradish,
mustard, peppercorns, lemon juice, salt, and
pepper; mix well. Pressing firmly, stuff each
mushroom cap with ⅛ of the rice mixture.
Place stuffed caps in 9 x 13 x 2-inch nonstick
baking pan; bake 20 to 25 minutes.

Arrange 4 pepper rings on each of 2
plates. Spoon ⅛ of spinach into center of
each ring; top each with 1 mushroom cap.
Sprinkle caps with parsley and garnish each
plate with 2 watercress sprigs and 1 cherry
tomato.

Per serving: 423 calories; 25 g protein; 21 g fat;
37 g carbohydrate; 695 mg sodium

* Mushroom stems can be chopped and reserved for use later in the week.

Oriental
Steak
Salad

Clockwise:
Bean Curd Soup;
Onion Soup;
French bread;
Vegetable Chowder

Frankfurter
Stir-Fry

Left:
Coconut-Coffee
Mounds;
Fruit 'n' Nut Candy

Right:
Peanut Butter
Fudge

Crêpes à l'Orange

*Yogurt Dip
or Dressing with
vegetable dippers;
mineral water with
lemon slices;
Steak Tartare with
bread triangles*

Fruited Yogurt Mold

Left:
Chicken Provençale
Right:
Turkey Piccata

*Saltine crackers
and melba
toast rounds;
Liver Loaf Pâté*

Crêpes Divan

Baked Corn and
Tomato Omelet

Clockwise: Homemade
White Bread;
Homemade Whole
Wheat Bread;
peanut butter;
honey; Honey-Wheat
Muffins;
Corn Muffins;
reduced-calorie
strawberry spread

Calamari
with Spaghetti

Above:
Thousand Island
Dressing; Seafood Garden
Salad

Left: Mussels-Rice
Casserole

Clockwise:
Chilled Tomato Appetizer;
Stuffed Mushroom Appetizer;
Radish Pinwheels

Stuffed Rigatoni

POTATO-CHEDDAR BROIL
The potato skin adds an attractive border to this delicious combo.
See Menu Plan for Week 28.
Makes 2 servings

8 ounces sliced potatoes, ¼-inch thick
   slices
Dash each salt and pepper
4 ounces sharp Cheddar cheese, cut into
   thin strips
2 medium tomatoes, sliced

Line baking sheet with foil. Spray with non-stick cooking spray. Sprinkle both sides of potato slices with salt and pepper; arrange on prepared baking sheet. Broil approximately 2 to 3 minutes or until slices are well browned. Turn and broil other side. Remove from broiler and top with cheese. Broil until cheese melts thoroughly. Serve with sliced tomatoes.

Per serving: 337 calories; 18 g protein; 19 g fat;
25 g carbohydrate; 452 mg sodium

Variation:
Before adding cheese, sprinkle potato slices with a few drops Worcestershire sauce.

TWO-CHEESE HERBED PASTA
See Menu Plan for Week 32.
Makes 2 servings

2 teaspoons margarine
½ garlic clove, minced with ¼ teaspoon salt
1⅓ cups cooked enriched spaghetti
½ teaspoon chopped fresh parsley
¼ teaspoon oregano leaves
⅛ teaspoon thyme leaves
1 ounce crumbled Bleu cheese, room
   temperature
⅓ cup pot cheese, room temperature

Melt margarine in medium skillet. Add garlic and sauté 1 minute. Add spaghetti, parsley, oregano, and thyme; sauté over low heat, stirring occasionally, about 5 minutes or until spaghetti is heated through. Transfer pasta to serving plate. Sprinkle Bleu cheese over center of pasta. Mound pot cheese over Bleu.

Per serving: 219 calories; 11 g protein; 9 g fat;
24 g carbohydrate; 687 mg sodium

Note: Cheese-topped pasta can be placed in 300°F. oven to warm cheese.

CRÊPES À L'ORANGE
The filling for these crêpes can be prepared while the batter is standing (see crêpe method).
   The batter can be mixed in a blender container, food processor, or with a wire whisk.
See Menu Plan for Week 48.
Makes 2 servings

Crêpes
¼ cup plus 1 tablespoon enriched flour
1 egg
1 teaspoon vanilla extract
½ cup water

Filling
1 egg, separated
Artificial sweetener to equal 4 teaspoons
   sugar
2 teaspoons enriched flour
½ cup skim milk, heated
1 teaspoon grated orange rind, blanched
⅛ teaspoon orange extract
Dash salt

Orange Sauce
1 cup orange juice
1 tablespoon plus 1 teaspoon reduced-
   calorie orange marmalade

Garnish
1 tablespoon slivered orange rind, blanched

To Prepare Crêpes: Place flour, egg, and extract in blender container; add water and process until smooth. Let batter stand 20 minutes. Heat a 6- to 7-inch nonstick omelet pan. Pour in ¼ of batter (about ¼ cup), quickly tilting pan to coat entire bottom. When underside of crêpe is dry, turn and briefly cook other side. Slide onto plate. Repeat 3 more times, making 4 crêpes.

To Prepare Filling: Combine egg yolk and sweetener in small nonstick saucepan; stir briskly to blend well. Beat in flour. Gradually pour in milk, stirring constantly until smooth. Cook over medium heat, beating constantly with wire whisk, about 2 minutes or until thickened. (As sauce comes to a boil it will get lumpy but will become smooth as soon as beaten.) Stir in orange rind and extract and remove from heat. Beat egg white with salt until stiff peaks form; gently fold into yolk mixture.

To Prepare Orange Sauce: Combine juice and marmalade in 9-inch skillet; cook, stirring constantly, until reduced by half.

To Serve: Spoon ¼ of filling onto center of each crêpe; fold over both sides of crêpe to enclose filling. Pour Orange Sauce over crêpes and sprinkle with slivered orange rind.

Per serving: 267 calories; 11 g protein; 6 g fat; 39 g carbohydrate; 170 mg sodium

CRÊPES DIVAN
See Menu Plans for Weeks 31 and 37.
Makes 2 servings

Crêpes
2 eggs
¼ cup plus 1 tablespoon enriched flour
¼ cup water
Dash salt

Filling
4 ounces skinned and boned cooked
   chicken, cut into cubes
½ cup cooked chopped broccoli
½ cup cooked sliced mushrooms
½ teaspoon onion powder
Dash pepper

Sauce
2 teaspoons margarine
2 teaspoons enriched flour
¾ cup chicken bouillon, heated
½ cup skim milk, heated
Dash each salt, pepper, and ground nutmeg

Garnish
Parsley sprigs

To Prepare Crêpes: Combine first 4 ingredients in blender container; process until smooth. Let stand 10 minutes. Heat nonstick omelet pan. Pour ¼ of batter (about 3 tablespoons) into pan; quickly tilt pan to spread batter evenly over surface. Cook until underside is dry; turn crêpe and cook a few seconds longer. Repeat process 3 more times to make 4 crêpes.

To Prepare Filling: Place chicken, broccoli, and mushrooms in bowl; add onion powder and pepper and toss to combine.

To Prepare Sauce: Melt margarine in small saucepan; stir in flour. Stirring constantly, add bouillon and milk; continue to stir and cook until thickened. *Do not boil.* Season with salt, pepper, and nutmeg.

To Serve: Spoon ¼ of filling onto center of each crêpe; roll crêpes to enclose filling. Place seam-side down in shallow small flame-proof casserole; top with sauce. Bake at 400°F. about 20 minutes or until heated through; then broil just until lightly browned, about 2 minutes. Garnish with parsley.

Per serving: 343 calories; 30 g protein; 14 g fat; 24 g carbohydrate; 1,053 mg sodium

FRUITED CHEESE DELIGHT
See Menu Plan for Week 44.
Makes 2 servings

1⅓ cups cottage cheese
1 teaspoon each honey and lemon juice
Artificial sweetener to equal 1 teaspoon
   sugar
⅛ teaspoon vanilla extract
Dash salt
¾ teaspoon unflavored gelatin
⅓ cup apple juice, no sugar added
12 large grapes, cut into halves
¼ cup diced carrot, ¼-inch cubes

Combine cheese, honey, lemon juice, sweetener, vanilla, and salt in blender container or work bowl of food processor; process about 2 minutes, occasionally scraping mixture from sides. Mixture should be very smooth. Transfer to bowl.

In small glass measuring cup sprinkle gelatin over apple juice and let stand to soften. Set cup into pan of heated water and stir juice until gelatin is dissolved; cool slightly. Add dissolved gelatin, grapes, and diced carrot to cheese mixture and stir to combine. Spoon into 2 individual dishes; cover and refrigerate until firm, about 3 to 4 hours.

Per serving: 225 calories; 20 g protein; 7 g fat; 20 g carbohydrate; 679 mg sodium

PEACH AND COTTAGE CHEESE MOLD
See Menu Plan for Week 31.
Makes 2 servings

1 envelope unflavored gelatin
¼ cup cold water
1 cup canned sliced peaches, no sugar added
1⅓ cups cottage cheese
¼ cup plain unflavored yogurt
2 teaspoons honey
1 teaspoon lemon juice
Artificial sweetener to equal 1 teaspoon
    sugar
⅛ teaspoon ground cinnamon
Lettuce leaves to garnish

In small ovenproof cup sprinkle gelatin over water and let stand to soften. Set cup in saucepan containing enough hot water to reach halfway up side of cup. Heat, stirring constantly, until gelatin is dissolved. Drain juice from 1 cup sliced peaches into dissolved gelatin; stir to combine. Pour a thin layer of juice mixture (about ¼ inch) into 1-quart soufflé dish or cake pan that has been rinsed with cold water. Chill about 10 minutes or until gelatin is almost set. Arrange a few peach slices decoratively over the gelatin layer; chill. Cut remaining peaches into ¼-inch pieces and place in bowl. Add remaining gelatin mixture, cottage cheese,

yogurt, honey, lemon juice, sweetener, and cinnamon; stir to combine. Spoon over peaches in soufflé dish. Cover and chill at least 6 hours. With a pointed knife loosen mold around edges. Dip dish into hot water for a few seconds to loosen mold, then unmold onto serving plate. Garnish with lettuce leaves.

Per serving: 268 calories; 25 g protein; 8 g fat; 26 g carbohydrate; 624 mg sodium

PEACHES AND CHEESE BREAKFAST
See Menu Plan for Week 17.
Makes 2 servings

⅔ cup part-skim ricotta cheese
1 cup canned sliced peaches, no sugar added
½ teaspoon unflavored gelatin
2 teaspoons honey
Artificial sweetener to equal 4 teaspoons
    sugar
Dash salt

In blender container or work bowl of food processor process cheese until smooth and lump-free. Set aside. Drain juice from 1 cup sliced peaches into small bowl; sprinkle gelatin over juice and let stand to soften. Add honey and set bowl into pan of hot water; stir until gelatin is dissolved. Remove from water; add cheese, artificial sweetener, and salt. Divide peaches into 2 bowls. Pour ½ of cheese mixture over each portion of peaches. Refrigerate at least 1 hour.

Per serving: 197 calories; 11 g protein; 7 g fat; 25 g carbohydrate; 200 mg sodium

SWISS-STUFFED PEARS
See Menu Plan for the Last Day of the Year.
Makes 2 servings

2 small pears, pared and stems removed
Lemon juice
2 ounces grated Swiss cheese

Preheat oven to 350°F. Cut each pear in half lengthwise; using a melon-baller or small spoon remove and discard seeds. Scoop out chunks of pear to create a hollow in each pear half; reserve chunks. Rub pear halves with lemon juice and set aside.

In a small bowl combine pear chunks, ¼ teaspoon lemon juice, and cheese. Spoon ¼ of mixture into each pear half; place stuffed pears in 8-inch square nonstick baking pan. Cover pan with foil and bake 20 to 25 minutes; uncover and bake until cheese is lightly browned, about 5 minutes longer.

Per serving: 192 calories; 9 g protein; 8 g fat; 22 g carbohydrate; 77 mg sodium

Poultry, Veal, and Wild Game

The delicate flavors of chicken, veal, and wild game lend themselves to a variety of sauces, seasonings, and accompaniments. Capitalizing on this, the experts in our test kitchens have created some delicious recipes with an international flair. Chicken Cavalfiore, Polynesian Chicken, Chicken Greek Style, Veal à la Fontina, and Rabbit Bourguignon are some of the marvelous recipes you will find in this section.

CHICKEN CAVALFIORE
See Menu Plan for Week 18.
Makes 2 servings

12 ounces skinned and boned chicken
    breasts
2 teaspoons enriched flour
1 teaspoon margarine
1 teaspoon olive oil
1 cup sliced mushrooms
2 tablespoons lemon juice
1 teaspoon minced fresh garlic
¾ cup Chicken Broth (see page 127)
1 cup cauliflower florets, parboiled
2 teaspoons white wine
2 tablespoons chopped fresh parsley

Lightly coat chicken with flour. Heat margarine and oil in skillet; sauté chicken until lightly browned. Remove chicken from pan and set aside; add mushrooms, lemon juice, and garlic. Sauté, stirring occasionally, until mushrooms are just tender. Add broth; cook, stirring constantly, until mixture comes to a boil. Add chicken, cauliflower, and wine; turn to coat with heated sauce. Sprinkle with parsley just before serving.

Per serving: 275 calories; 38 g protein; 9 g fat;
9 g carbohydrate; 125 mg sodium

CHICKEN DONNA
See Menu Plan for Week 9.
Makes 2 servings

2 teaspoons margarine
1½ pounds skinned chicken parts,
    preferably leg, thigh, and breast*
½ cup small white onions, cut into quarters
2 garlic cloves, minced
2 cups sliced zucchini, ½-inch thick slices
2 cups quartered mushrooms
2 tablespoons lemon juice
¾ cup Chicken Broth (see page 127)
2 teaspoons enriched flour
Dash each salt and pepper
2 teaspoons white wine
Chopped fresh parsley to garnish

* 1½ pounds chicken parts will yield about
8 ounces skinned and boned cooked meat.

Melt margarine in skillet; add chicken parts and sauté until browned. Remove and keep warm. In same pan sauté onions and garlic until onions are translucent. Add zucchini and mushrooms and sprinkle with lemon juice; cook, stirring occasionally, until just tender. In small bowl gradually add broth to flour, stirring constantly until combined; add to vegetable mixture and cook, stirring constantly, until thickened. Add chicken, salt, and pepper. Cover and simmer for 15 minutes. Add white wine and parsley and serve immediately.

Per serving: 343 calories; 38 g protein; 13 g fat;
18 g carbohydrate; 255 mg sodium

CHICKEN GREEK STYLE
See Menu Plan for Week 4.
Makes 2 servings

¾ cup Chicken Broth (see page 127)
2 tablespoons lemon juice
2 skinned chicken breasts, 8 ounces each
2 teaspoons olive oil
½ teaspoon salt
½ teaspoon oregano leaves
Dash each garlic powder and white pepper

Preheat oven to 350°F. Pour broth and lemon juice into small baking pan. Rub each chicken breast with 1 teaspoon oil and place in pan. Sprinkle with seasonings and bake for 20 minutes.

Per serving: 238 calories; 35 g protein; 9 g fat;
2 g carbohydrate; 640 mg sodium

CHICKEN INDIENNE
Chicken is always a favorite standby! Now dress it up India-style with curry, raisins, and coconut.
See Menu Plan for Week 24.
Makes 2 servings

1 teaspoon vegetable oil
½ cup chopped onion
1 garlic clove, minced
1½ pounds skinned chicken legs and thighs*
¾ teaspoon curry powder
2 whole cloves
1-inch cinnamon stick
⅛ teaspoon salt
1 cup Chicken Broth (see page 127)
2 ounces uncooked enriched rice
2 tablespoons raisins
2 teaspoons shredded coconut, lightly toasted

Heat oil in flameproof casserole; add onion and garlic and sauté until softened. Add chicken and sauté until lightly browned on all sides. Stir in curry powder; add cloves, cinnamon, and salt. Stir in broth and rice; bring to a boil. Remove from heat and add raisins.

Cover and transfer casserole to oven. Bake at 350°F. 25 minutes or until rice is tender. Fluff rice with fork. Just before serving remove cloves and cinnamon stick and sprinkle with coconut.

Per serving: 408 calories; 36 g protein; 13 g fat; 38 g carbohydrate; 273 mg sodium

* See footnote page 159.

CHICKEN PROVENÇALE
See Menu Plan for Week 8.
Makes 2 servings

2 teaspoons olive oil
1½ pounds skinned chicken parts, preferably breast, leg, and thigh*
2 cups sliced mushrooms
2 medium tomatoes, peeled, seeded, and chopped
2 cups sliced green or red bell peppers
1 cup sliced onion
1 teaspoon minced fresh garlic
1 teaspoon oregano leaves
Dash salt and pepper

1 tablespoon plus 1 teaspoon white wine
4 black olives, pitted and sliced
1 tablespoon chopped fresh parsley

Heat oil in nonstick skillet; add chicken parts and sauté until lightly browned. Remove chicken and set aside. In same pan sauté all vegetables with garlic until tender. Add oregano, salt, and pepper. Arrange chicken and vegetables in small casserole; add wine. Bake at 375°F. for 25 minutes. Garnish with black olives and parsley.

Per serving: 386 calories; 39 g protein; 16 g fat; 22 g carbohydrate; 284 mg sodium

* See footnote page 159.

CHICKEN SORRENTINO
See Menu Plan for Week 21.
Makes 2 servings

1 cup pared and sliced eggplant
⅓ cup plus 2 teaspoons plain dried bread crumbs
1 tablespoon chopped fresh parsley
½ teaspoon each garlic powder and onion powder
6 ounces skinned and boned chicken breasts
⅓ cup plus 2 teaspoons Chicken Broth (see page 127) or chicken bouillon
1 cup Marinara Sauce (see page 285)
2 ounces Mozzarella cheese, grated
2 teaspoons grated Parmesan cheese

Place eggplant slices on nonstick baking sheet; bake at 375°F. for about 20 minutes or until tender.

While eggplant is baking combine bread crumbs, parsley, garlic, and onion powder on a flat plate. Dip chicken breasts in broth, then coat with crumb mixture. Place on nonstick baking sheet; sprinkle any remaining crumbs evenly over chicken. Bake in oven with eggplant about 15 minutes or until lightly browned.

Pour ½ cup Marinara Sauce into small casserole. Layer chicken, eggplant, and Mozzarella cheese over sauce; pour remaining sauce over cheese. Sprinkle evenly with Parmesan cheese and bake at 400°F. for 20 minutes.

Per serving: 344 calories; 32 g protein; 13 g fat; 25 g carbohydrate; 798 mg sodium

CHICKEN TERIYAKI
See Menu Plan for Week 13.
Makes 2 servings

⅓ cup apple juice, no sugar added
2 tablespoons soy sauce
1 tablespoon rice vinegar
1 teaspoon honey
½ teaspoon grated orange rind
¼ teaspoon minced fresh ginger root
12 ounces skinned and boned chicken
    breasts, cut into ½-inch dice
1 teaspoon vegetable oil

Combine first 6 ingredients in medium bowl; add chicken. Cover and refrigerate overnight or at least 6 hours, stirring occasionally. Heat oil in medium saucepan; remove chicken from marinade and sauté in heated oil 8 minutes, stirring often. Add marinade; cook 2 minutes longer.

Per serving: 257 calories; 40 g protein; 5 g fat;
10 g carbohydrate; 1,224 mg sodium

POLYNESIAN CHICKEN
Teriyaki and soy, combined with pineapple, give leftover chicken the flavor of the Islands. This dish is easy to prepare on a warm summer day!
See Menu Plan for Week 30.
Makes 2 servings

2 teaspoons vegetable oil
1 garlic clove, minced
½ cup thinly sliced carrot
½ cup thinly sliced green bell pepper
½ cup thinly sliced mushrooms
½ cup trimmed Chinese pea pods (stem
    ends and strings removed)
8 ounces skinned and boned cooked
    chicken, sliced
½ cup chopped scallions
1 teaspoon teriyaki sauce
1 teaspoon soy sauce
¾ cup Chicken Broth (see page 127) or
    chicken bouillon
1 cup canned pineapple chunks, no sugar
    added, drain and reserve juice
2 teaspoons cornstarch
Dash each salt and pepper

Heat oil in skillet; add garlic and sauté. Add carrot, green pepper, mushrooms, and pea pods; stir-fry 3 to 5 minutes. Add chicken, scallions, teriyaki and soy sauces; cook just until heated through. Add broth and bring to a boil; stir in pineapple. Dissolve cornstarch in reserved juice; add to skillet and cook, stirring constantly, until mixture is thickened. Season with salt and pepper.

Per serving: 410 calories; 37 g protein; 14 g fat;
36 g carbohydrate; 497 mg sodium

CHICKEN AND CANNELLINI CASSEROLE
See Menu Plan for Week 11.
Makes 4 servings

1½ pounds chicken parts (legs and thighs)*
2 tablespoons diced onion
1 garlic clove, minced
⅓ cup diced celery
2 tablespoons tomato paste
1 cup canned tomatoes, chopped, reserve
    juice
¼ teaspoon each oregano leaves and salt
⅛ teaspoon pepper
12 ounces drained canned cannellini beans
2 teaspoons chopped fresh parsley

Preheat oven to 350°F. Dry chicken with paper towels. Bake on rack in roasting pan 15 minutes, turning once. Remove and discard skin. Spray a saucepan that has an ovenproof handle, or a 1½-quart flameproof casserole, with nonstick cooking spray. Add onion and garlic to pan and cook until softened; add celery. Stir in tomato paste; add tomatoes with reserved juice, oregano, salt, and pepper. Bring mixture to a boil; reduce heat and simmer 5 minutes. Add chicken and beans; stir to combine. Cover and bake 15 minutes. Remove cover and bake 5 minutes longer or until some of the liquid has evaporated and chicken is tender. Sprinkle with parsley.

Per serving: 204 calories; 21 g protein; 5 g fat;
17 g carbohydrate; 342 mg sodium

* See footnote page 159.

CHICKEN AND EGGPLANT BAKE

Paprika is the Hungarian name given to the spice made by grinding the ripe dried pods of red bell pepper. Sweet paprika is made from the choicest pepper, which has a rich red color and sweet, distinctive flavor and aroma. Hungarian paprikas are known for their excellence. This is not surprising since paprika is an essential element in Hungarian cuisine.

See Menu Plan for Week 25.
Makes 4 servings

4 cups cubed eggplant, ¼-inch cubes
½ teaspoon salt
1 tablespoon plus 1 teaspoon margarine
1 cup thickly sliced onions
1 small garlic clove, chopped with
    ½ teaspoon salt
12 ounces skinned and boned cooked
    chicken, cut into ½-inch pieces
2 eggs, beaten
½ cup tomato sauce
2 teaspoons chopped fresh parsley
¼ teaspoon sweet Hungarian paprika
Dash each ground thyme and pepper

Place eggplant in a colander; sprinkle with salt. Let stand 30 minutes. Pat dry with paper towels and set aside.

Preheat oven to 350°F. In small skillet melt margarine. Add onions and garlic. Sauté over medium heat until onions are tender.

In medium bowl combine eggplant, sautéed onion mixture, and remaining ingredients. Transfer to 9-inch glass pie plate and bake for 40 minutes.

Per serving: 307 calories; 30 g protein; 13 g fat; 17 g carbohydrate; 1,120 mg sodium

RED CHICKEN WITH POTATOES

See Menu Plan for Week 17.
Makes 2 servings

2 teaspoons margarine
½ medium red bell pepper, seeded and
    cut into 1-inch pieces
8 ounces cooked and peeled potatoes, cut
    into large dice

8 ounces diced skinned cooked chicken,
    large dice
¼ medium garlic clove
¼ teaspoon salt
1 cup tomato puree
½ teaspoon oregano leaves
¼ teaspoon basil leaves
⅛ teaspoon thyme leaves

Melt margarine in small skillet. Add red pepper; cover and cook over low heat about 5 minutes. Peppers should still be crisp. Combine peppers, potatoes, and chicken in deep 1½-quart casserole. Chop garlic with salt. Using flat side of knife mash garlic and salt together to form a paste. In small bowl combine garlic paste with tomato puree, oregano, basil, and thyme. Add to casserole and stir to combine. Cover and bake 25 to 30 minutes at 350°F. or until heated through.

Per serving: 394 calories; 38 g protein; 13 g fat; 33 g carbohydrate; 990 mg sodium

VEGETABLE-STUFFED CHICKEN BREASTS

The moisture from iceberg lettuce will keep the chicken moist and juicy during cooking.
See Menu Plan for Week 22.
Makes 2 servings

3 skinned and boned chicken breasts,
    4 ounces each
Dash each salt and pepper
1 teaspoon olive oil
½ cup well-squeezed cooked chopped
    spinach
¼ cup diced celery
⅓ garlic clove, chopped with ¼ teaspoon
    salt
3 medium carrots, pared
Iceberg lettuce leaves
¾ cup diced zucchini
½ teaspoon sesame seeds, toasted and
    chopped
½ teaspoon chopped fresh parsley

Pound chicken breasts between 2 sheets of wax paper until slightly flattened. Sprinkle both sides of chicken with salt and pepper; set aside.

Heat oil in small skillet. Add spinach, celery, and chopped garlic; sauté over medium heat 3 to 5 minutes. Remove from heat.

Spread ⅓ of spinach mixture over boned side of each chicken breast. Top each portion of spinach with 1 carrot, placing carrot on a diagonal, about 1 inch from edge of chicken breast; fold breast over carrot and roll up tightly.

Cover bottom of an 8-inch square baking pan with lettuce leaves; top with rolled chicken breasts. Combine zucchini and sesame seeds and sprinkle over chicken. Cover pan with foil and bake at 350°F. 50 to 60 minutes. Transfer chicken breasts to serving platter; discard lettuce leaves and garnish chicken with parsley.

Per serving: 298 calories; 44 g protein; 6 g fat; 17 g carbohydrate; 704 mg sodium

CRISP "OVEN-FRIED" CHICKEN
See Menu Plans for Weeks 23, 28, and 37.
Makes 2 servings

1½ ounces cornflakes, crumbled
1 teaspoon oregano leaves
Dash each salt, pepper, and garlic powder
12 ounces skinned and boned chicken
    breasts, cut into 1-inch wide strips

In small bowl combine cornflakes, oregano, salt, pepper, and garlic powder. Dip chicken strips in water and then in cornflake crumbs, pressing the crumbs to make sure they stick. Place chicken on nonstick baking sheet that has been sprayed with nonstick cooking spray. If any crumbs remain, sprinkle evenly over chicken. Bake at 350°F. for 20 minutes or until done.

Per serving: 279 calories; 41 g protein; 3 g fat; 19 g carbohydrate; 423 mg sodium

BRAISED CHICKEN WITH VEGETABLES
See Menu Plan for Week 14.
Makes 2 servings

1 tablespoon vegetable oil
1½ pounds skinned chicken parts*
¼ teaspoon salt
⅛ teaspoon pepper
½ cup chopped onion
1 garlic clove, minced
1 medium green bell pepper, seeded and
    coarsely chopped
½ medium tomato, peeled and chopped
½ cup sliced mushrooms
½ cup water
1 tablespoon chopped fresh parsley

Heat vegetable oil in a medium saucepan. Add chicken and sauté, turning as necessary, until lightly browned. Sprinkle with salt and pepper. Using a slotted spoon remove chicken to dish. Sauté onion and garlic in same pan until onion is lightly browned. Add green pepper and sauté 2 minutes longer. Add chicken, tomato, mushrooms, water, and parsley; bring to a boil. Reduce heat, cover, and simmer 25 minutes. Remove cover and simmer 5 minutes longer or until chicken is tender.

Per serving: 322 calories; 35 g protein; 16 g fat; 9 g carbohydrate; 391 mg sodium

* See footnote page 159.

CHICKEN AND PEPPERS
See Menu Plan for Week 51.
Makes 2 servings

1½ pounds skinned chicken parts*
Dash each salt and pepper
2 teaspoons margarine
1 cup diced onions
1 garlic clove, minced
1 cup chopped green bell pepper
1 cup seeded and chopped tomatoes
⅛ teaspoon thyme leaves
½ cup heated water

Spray with nonstick cooking spray a skillet large enough to hold chicken parts in 1 layer. Add chicken and cook over high heat until browned on all sides; sprinkle with salt and pepper and set aside. Melt margarine in saucepan; add onions and garlic and sauté until lightly browned. Add chicken, green pepper, tomatoes, and thyme. Pour in water; cover and simmer for 30 minutes. Remove cover and cook 15 minutes longer or until chicken is tender and some of the liquid has evaporated.

Per serving: 323 calories; 36 g protein; 13 g fat; 16 g carbohydrate; 231 mg sodium

* See footnote page 159.

SAUTÉED CHICKEN AND VEGETABLES
See Menu Plan for Week 10.
Makes 2 servings

2 teaspoons vegetable oil
12 ounces skinned and boned chicken, cut into 1-inch pieces
2 cups sliced mushrooms
1 cup sliced zucchini, ⅛-inch thick slices
3 tablespoons diced red bell pepper
½ teaspoon salt
1 teaspoon chopped fresh parsley
1 teaspoon lemon juice

Heat oil in skillet. Add chicken and sauté over medium heat until cooked through and slightly browned. *Do not overcook.* Remove chicken and keep warm. In same skillet combine mushrooms, zucchini, red pepper, and salt. Cover and cook over low heat, stirring occasionally, until vegetables are just tender. Add chicken, parsley, and lemon juice to vegetables. Toss and serve.

Per serving: 287 calories; 40 g protein; 10 g fat; 8 g carbohydrate; 734 mg sodium

SESAME CHICKEN WITH GREEN BEANS
See Menu Plans for Weeks 1, 26, 32, and 45.
Makes 2 servings

2 teaspoons olive oil
½ teaspoon sesame seeds
8 ounces skinned and boned cooked chicken, cut into ¼-inch strips
2 teaspoons shredded coconut, toasted
½ teaspoon salt
Dash pepper
2 cups cooked whole green beans

Heat nonstick skillet. Add olive oil and sesame seeds; cook over medium heat, stirring frequently, until seeds turn light brown. Add chicken and sauté until pieces are heated. Stir in coconut, salt, and pepper. Serve over hot green beans.

Per serving: 301 calories; 35 g protein; 14 g fat; 8 g carbohydrate; 685 mg sodium

GINGER-BROILED CHICKEN
See Menu Plan for Week 11 and various other weeks.
Makes 2 servings

2 teaspoons soy sauce
1 teaspoon grated fresh ginger root
1 garlic clove, minced
2 chicken breasts, 8 ounces each

In small dish combine soy sauce, ginger, and garlic. Lift skin and brush chicken with soy mixture; turn and brush underside. Cover and let stand at room temperature 1 hour. Broil chicken on rack, skin-side down, 10 minutes. Turn and broil 8 to 10 minutes longer or until chicken is tender. Remove and discard skin before serving.

Per serving: 193 calories; 36 g protein; 4 g fat; 1 g carbohydrate; 453 mg sodium

SKEWERED MARINATED CHICKEN
See Menu Plan for Week 6.
Makes 2 servings

½ cup sliced onion

¼ cup cider vinegar
1 teaspoon soy sauce
5 peppercorns, crushed
1 garlic clove, split
1 bay leaf
1 cup water
12 ounces skinned and boned chicken
   breasts, cut into large pieces
1 onion, 4 ounces, cut into 4 wedges (1 cup)
1 medium green bell pepper, seeded and
   cut into 4 pieces
6 cherry tomatoes
¼ teaspoon salt
Dash coarsely ground pepper

Combine first 6 ingredients in bowl; add water and stir to combine. Add the chicken, cover, and refrigerate overnight.

Remove chicken and discard marinade. Thread each of two 12-inch skewers with 6 ounces chicken pieces, 2 onion wedges, 2 green pepper pieces, and 3 cherry tomatoes, alternating chicken with vegetables. Sprinkle with salt and pepper. Place on rack in broiler pan and broil about 8 minutes; turn and broil 5 to 8 minutes longer or until chicken is tender.

Per serving: 259 calories; 42 g protein; 3 g fat;
15 g carbohydrate; 612 mg sodium

APRICOT CHICKEN
See Menu Plan for Week 40.
Makes 2 servings

2 teaspoons vegetable oil
1½ pounds skinned chicken parts*
½ teaspoon salt
⅛ teaspoon ground cinnamon
Dash ground cloves
⅓ cup water
8 canned apricot halves with ¼ cup juice,
   no sugar added
2 teaspoons cornstarch
Fresh mint leaves to garnish

Heat oil in medium skillet; add chicken and sauté over moderately high heat until lightly browned and tender. Sprinkle with salt, cinnamon, and cloves; add water, reduce heat, cover, and cook about 30 minutes. Add apricots, reserving juice. Dissolve cornstarch in apricot juice and add to chicken mixture;

cook, stirring constantly, until thickened. Garnish with mint leaves.

Per serving: 337 calories; 34 g protein; 13 g fat;
20 g carbohydrate; 653 mg sodium

* See footnote page 159.

CHICKEN BREASTS WITH RAISIN SAUCE
See Menu Plans for Weeks 41 and the Last Day of the Year.
Makes 4 servings

4 skinned and boned chicken breasts,
   6 ounces each, reserve skin
Salt
Dash onion powder
1 tablespoon plus 1 teaspoon margarine
1 tablespoon enriched flour
1½ cups Beef Broth (see page 127)
2 tablespoons golden raisins, soaked in
   ½ cup warm water and drained,
   reserve liquid
1 whole clove
Dash each white pepper, ground cinnamon,
   sherry extract, and rum extract
Coarsely grated orange rind, blanched, to
   garnish

Season chicken with dash each salt and onion powder. Tuck ends of each breast under to form rounded mound; cover with skin and place in nonstick baking pan. Bake at 350°F. until done, about 25 minutes. Remove and discard skin. While chicken is baking, prepare fruit sauce.

To prepare sauce, melt margarine in saucepan; add flour and stir, making a roux. Stir over low heat until raw flour taste is "cooked-out," about 5 minutes. Stir in broth; bring to a boil. Add raisins, clove, dash salt, pepper, cinnamon, and extracts. Cook, stirring constantly, about 10 minutes or until thickened. If necessary, adjust consistency with reserved raisin liquid. Remove and discard clove.

Serve each chicken breast topped with ¼ of the sauce and garnished with blanched orange rind.

Per serving: 255 calories; 40 g protein; 7 g fat;
6 g carbohydrate; 232 mg sodium

FRUITED CHICKEN
See Menu Plan for Week 16.
Makes 2 servings

1½ pounds skinned chicken parts*
2 teaspoons enriched flour
2 teaspoons margarine
½ cup orange juice
¼ cup canned crushed pineapple, no sugar added
1 tablespoon raisins
Artificial sweetener to equal 3 teaspoons sugar
2 teaspoons white wine
½ teaspoon Dijon-style mustard
¼ teaspoon ground cinnamon
⅛ teaspoon ground cloves

Dredge chicken in 2 teaspoons flour; set aside. Melt margarine in medium skillet; add chicken and sauté until lightly browned on all sides. Transfer chicken to shallow baking pan. Combine remaining ingredients and pour over chicken. Bake 35 minutes at 350° F., basting often. Broil a few minutes to brown top slightly.

Per serving: 330 calories; 34 g protein; 12 g fat; 19 g carbohydrate; 182 mg sodium

* See footnote page 159.

CHICKEN SALAD ORIENTAL
See Menu Plan for Week 7.
Makes 1 serving

1 tablespoon rice vinegar
1 teaspoon sesame oil
1 teaspoon soy sauce
1 teaspoon water
1 teaspoon lemon juice
4 ounces skinned and boned cooked chicken, cut into 1-inch pieces
¼ cup blanched and chilled Chinese pea pods
2 tablespoons diced canned water chestnuts
2 tablespoons grated carrot
1 tablespoon chopped green bell pepper

Combine first 5 ingredients in bowl. Add remaining ingredients and toss to combine.

Per serving: 293 calories; 35 g protein; 13 g fat; 9 g carbohydrate; 477 mg sodium

COLD CHICKEN PLATTER
See Menu Plans for Weeks 2 and 30.
Makes 2 servings

8 ounces skinned and boned cooked chicken breast
½ cup plain unflavored yogurt
1 tablespoon plus 1 teaspoon ketchup
1 tablespoon mayonnaise
⅓ cup diced dill pickle
⅓ cup diced green bell pepper
1 tablespoon chopped scallion
1 tablespoon chopped capers
Dash artificial sweetener
Dash each salt and pepper
1 cup shredded lettuce
⅔ cup sliced mushrooms, tossed with lemon juice
2 tablespoons pimiento strips

Thinly slice chicken breast and set aside. In a bowl combine yogurt, ketchup, and mayonnaise. Add dill pickle, green pepper, scallion, capers, sweetener, salt, and pepper. Arrange lettuce on a small platter; top with chicken slices and spread with dressing. Arrange sliced mushrooms on lettuce. Garnish chicken with pimiento strips.

Per serving: 320 calories; 39 g protein; 13 g fat; 11 g carbohydrate; 856 mg sodium

CURRIED CHICKEN SALAD
See Menu Plan for Week 3.
Makes 2 servings

¼ cup canned crushed pineapple, no sugar added
1 tablespoon plus 1 teaspoon reduced-calorie mayonnaise
1 teaspoon lemon juice
¼ teaspoon curry powder
Dash each salt and white pepper
8 ounces skinned and boned cooked chicken, cut into 1-inch pieces
½ medium cucumber, pared, seeded, and diced
½ small apple, cored and diced
2 medium green bell peppers, cut into halves lengthwise and seeded
Lettuce leaves

In bowl combine first 5 ingredients. Add chicken, cucumber, and apple; toss to combine. Divide mixture into 4 equal portions and place 1 portion in each pepper half. Serve each person 2 stuffed pepper halves on lettuce leaves.

Per serving: 287 calories; 37 g protein; 8 g fat; 18 g carbohydrate; 249 mg sodium

JAPANESE CHICKEN SALAD

Transform leftover chicken into an Oriental treat.
See Menu Plan for Week 33.
Makes 1 serving

4 ounces skinned and diced cooked chicken
2 teaspoons sliced scallion
1 teaspoon slivered radishes
2 teaspoons rice vinegar
1 teaspoon sesame oil
1 teaspoon soy sauce
¼ teaspoon minced fresh ginger root

In bowl combine chicken, scallion, and radishes. Combine remaining ingredients in small bowl; mix well. Add to chicken mixture and toss to combine.

Per serving: 263 calories; 33 g protein; 13 g fat; 2 g carbohydrate; 468 mg sodium

ROAST TURKEY

Freeze any leftovers and use in Week 48, Day 3 and Week 50, Day 5.
   Serve with Mushroom Gravy (see page 286).
See Menu Plan for Week 47.
Makes about 8 servings

8-pound turkey
2 teaspoons salt
¼ teaspoon thyme leaves
1 cup celery tops
6 parsley sprigs
1 small onion
1 cup Turkey Broth (see page 128)

Remove any loose fat from inside cavity. Dry turkey inside and out with paper towels. Sprinkle salt in cavity and all over skin of turkey. Sprinkle cavity with thyme leaves. Put ½ cup celery tops, 3 parsley sprigs, and the whole onion into large cavity; put remaining parsley sprigs and celery tops into neck cavity. Close neck cavity with skewer and truss turkey. Set turkey on its side on rack that has been sprayed with nonstick cooking spray, in shallow roasting pan. Roast for 30 minutes at 350°F.; turn on other side and roast for 30 minutes more. Reduce heat to 325°F. If meat thermometer is used, insert at this point. If turkey is browning too fast, cover loosely with piece of foil. Continue roasting, basting occasionally with broth, 1½ hours more or until meat thermometer registers 180°F. Remove vegetables from cavities and discard. Let turkey stand for 15 minutes before carving. Remove skin and weigh portions. Serve 4 ounces sliced turkey per portion.

Per serving: 199 calories; 34 g protein; 5 g fat; 2 g carbohydrate; 468 mg sodium

TURKEY-BARLEY SOUP

See Menu Plan for Week 41.
Makes 4 servings

3 cups Chicken Broth (see page 127)
2 cups cooked barley
1 cup sliced mushrooms
1 cup diced onion
1 cup diced celery
1 cup diced carrots
½ cup canned crushed tomatoes
1 bay leaf
½ teaspoon thyme leaves
12 ounces skinned and boned cooked
   turkey, cubed
1 teaspoon salt
Dash pepper
Chopped fresh parsley to garnish

Heat broth in medium saucepan. Add next 8 ingredients to broth and simmer until vegetables are tender. Add turkey, salt, and pepper, and cook 5 to 10 minutes. Remove bay leaf and sprinkle soup with parsley before serving.

Per serving: 288 calories; 30 g protein; 5 g fat; 32 g carbohydrate; 717 mg sodium

GLAZED TURKEY MOLD

A whole turkey need not be roasted for this recipe; turkey parts can be purchased separately. If there is leftover turkey, freeze and use at Midday Meal (Week 21, Day 6).
See Menu Plan for Week 20.
Makes 4 servings

1 pound skinned and boned cooked turkey, cut into 1-inch cubes
1 pound cooked and peeled potatoes, cut into 1-inch cubes
½ cup diced dill pickle, ¼-inch dice
½ cup diced celery, ¼-inch dice
¼ cup chopped scallions
½ cup reduced-calorie mayonnaise, divided
2 to 3 tablespoons lemon juice
2 tablespoons tarragon vinegar
¼ teaspoon salt
⅛ teaspoon white pepper
1 envelope unflavored gelatin
¼ cup water
½ cup evaporated skimmed milk
2 teaspoons Dijon-style mustard
½ cup pimientos, cut into triangles
Green bell pepper strips to garnish
4 black olives, pitted and cut into quarters

In large bowl combine turkey with potatoes, pickle, celery, and scallions. Add ¼ cup mayonnaise, lemon juice, vinegar, salt, and pepper; toss to combine. On an oblong platter shape mixture into a 10 x 6-inch oval; cover and refrigerate for 2 hours.

To prepare glaze, in a small bowl sprinkle gelatin over water to soften. Set bowl in pan with hot water; stir until gelatin is completely dissolved. Remove bowl from pan and stir in milk, mustard, and remaining mayonnaise. Refrigerate, covered, for about 20 minutes or until consistency of unbeaten egg whites.

Place strips of wax paper on platter around turkey mold to keep platter clean. Spoon some of the glaze over the entire mold to make a thin coating; refrigerate until set, about 5 minutes. Repeat procedure until all glaze has been used. If glaze becomes too thick, set it in bowl of warm water and stir until egg white consistency.

To garnish arrange pimiento triangles, pepper strips, and olives on slightly set glaze so that they form a flower. Refrigerate for at least 2 hours after glazing. Carefully remove paper strips from around mold.

Per serving: 396 calories; 41 g protein; 12 g fat; 30 g carbohydrate; 820 mg sodium

HONEYED TURKEY WITH BROCCOLI

This is an excellent recipe for using up leftover turkey.
See Menu Plan for Week 32.
Makes 2 servings

2 teaspoons vegetable oil
8 ounces shredded cooked turkey
Salt and pepper
½ cup canned crushed pineapple, no sugar added
1 teaspoon honey
1 teaspoon lemon juice
2 teaspoons chopped pimiento (optional)
2 cups cooked broccoli florets, warm

Heat oil in medium skillet. Add turkey, ½ teaspoon salt, and dash pepper. Sauté over high heat, stirring occasionally, until turkey begins to brown. Combine pineapple and honey; add to turkey and sauté 3 minutes more. Remove pan from heat and stir in lemon juice; sprinkle with pimiento if desired. Arrange turkey to one side of serving platter. Toss broccoli with dash each salt and pepper. Serve alongside turkey.

Per serving: 320 calories; 38 g protein; 11 g fat; 20 g carbohydrate; 716 mg sodium

STIR-COOKED TURKEY

Serve with baked potato.
See Menu Plan for Week 49.
Makes 2 servings

½ small garlic clove, chopped with ¾ teaspoon salt
12 ounces skinned and boned turkey (from thigh if possible), cut into ¼-inch dice

⅓ cup plus 2 teaspoons plain dried bread crumbs
½ teaspoon basil leaves
Dash white pepper
¼ cup water

Using the flat side of knife, mash garlic-salt mixture to form a paste. In bowl combine diced turkey with garlic paste, bread crumbs, basil, and pepper; stir in water. Spread turkey mixture between 2 pieces of wax paper. Pound mixture until flattened to about ⅛-inch thickness. Heat nonstick skillet. Peel wax paper from meat mixture. Add meat to skillet along with any crumbs that may adhere to paper. Stir-cook over medium heat until meat is browned and cooked through, 2 to 5 minutes.

Per serving: 276 calories; 36 g protein; 8 g fat; 13 g carbohydrate; 1,089 mg sodium

TURKEY BREAST WITH CREAM OF CORN SAUCE
See Menu Plan for Week 28.
Makes 2 servings

1 cup canned cream-style corn
¼ teaspoon lemon juice
Dash each ground nutmeg and pepper
12 ounces skinned and boned turkey breast, cut into 1½ x 1-inch chunks
1 cup pared and diced turnip, ¼-inch dice
½ cup diced carrot, ¼-inch dice
¼ teaspoon salt
1 tablespoon each minced celery and carrot
¼ teaspoon chopped fresh parsley

In blender container combine corn, lemon juice, nutmeg, and pepper. Process until smooth; set aside. Heat medium nonstick skillet; add turkey and brown slightly on all sides over medium heat. Add turnip, diced carrot, salt, and corn mixture. Cover and simmer over low heat, stirring occasionally, 20 to 25 minutes or until vegetables are tender. Remove from heat. Combine minced celery and carrot with parsley and sprinkle over turkey mixture.

Per serving: 332 calories; 44 g protein; 4 g fat; 33 g carbohydrate; 758 mg sodium

TURKEY ISLAND STYLE
This dish is delicious served alone or with rice.
See Menu Plan for Week 42.
Makes 2 servings

1 cup canned pineapple chunks, no sugar added, drain and reserve juice
½ cup tomato juice
1 tablespoon cornstarch
1 tablespoon soy sauce
8 ounces skinned and boned cooked turkey, cut into 2-inch strips
10 cherry tomatoes, cut into halves
1 medium green bell pepper, seeded and cut into 1-inch pieces
½ cup drained canned water chestnuts, thinly sliced
½ cup Chinese snow peas

In large skillet combine reserved pineapple juice, tomato juice, cornstarch, and soy sauce. Cook over low heat, stirring constantly with wire whisk, until mixture thickens. Add pineapple chunks, turkey, and vegetables, and cook until heated (green pepper should be tender-crisp).

Per serving: 355 calories; 37 g protein; 6 g fat; 40 g carbohydrate; 772 mg sodium

TURKEY PICCATA

This dish is usually made with veal. Try this less expensive but just as delicious version. *See Menu Plan for Week 29.*
Makes 2 servings

1 tablespoon plus ¾ teaspoon enriched flour
¼ teaspoon salt
⅛ teaspoon pepper
12 ounces thinly sliced turkey cutlets
1½ teaspoons olive oil
1½ teaspoons margarine
⅓ cup plus 2 teaspoons Chicken Broth (see page 127)
1 tablespoon lemon juice
4 thin lemon slices
1 tablespoon chopped fresh parsley

Mix together flour, salt, and pepper. Dredge cutlets with flour mixture. Heat oil and margarine in skillet that is large enough to hold cutlets in 1 layer. Add cutlets and sauté until browned and cooked, about 2 minutes; remove to a dish and keep warm. Add broth, lemon juice, and lemon slices to skillet; bring to a boil. Return cutlets to skillet, reduce heat, and simmer 3 minutes. Just before serving sprinkle with parsley.

Per serving: 275 calories; 41 g protein; 9 g fat; 6 g carbohydrate; 443 mg sodium

TURKEY-CHEESE STRATA

See Menu Plan for Week 37.
Makes 4 servings

12 ounces skinned and boned turkey breast, cut into 3 equal pieces
4 cups sliced mushrooms
½ cup diced green bell pepper
½ teaspoon salt, divided
½ teaspoon dehydrated orange peel
Generous dash pepper
4 ounces Mozzarella cheese, shredded
8 ounces pared potatoes, cut into ⅛-inch thick slices

Place turkey between sheets of wax paper and pound until very thin, about 1/16 inch thick. Set aside.

Heat 12-inch skillet; add mushrooms, green pepper, and dash of salt. Cook over medium heat, stirring occasionally, until mushrooms are tender and moisture evaporated. Set aside.

Preheat oven to 350°F. Place 4 ounces turkey in bottom of 10 x 6½ x 2-inch nonstick baking pan. In small cup combine remaining salt, orange peel, and pepper; sprinkle ⅓ of mixture over turkey. Top with a layer of ⅓ of the cheese, then ⅓ of the potatoes, then ⅓ of the mushroom mixture. Repeat turkey, cheese, and potato layers, seasoning turkey as before. Top potatoes with remaining turkey and sprinkle with remaining seasonings. Stand remaining potato slices upright along sides of baking dish. Spread remaining mushroom mixture over turkey and top evenly with remaining cheese. Cover with aluminum foil; punch hole in center of foil to vent and bake 40 minutes. Remove foil and bake until cheese browns, about 10 minutes longer.

Per serving: 251 calories; 29 g protein; 8 g fat; 16 g carbohydrate; 452 mg sodium

TURKEY FLORENTINE

See Menu Plan for Week 12.
Makes 2 servings

1 tablespoon vegetable oil
1 garlic clove, minced
4 cups chopped spinach, steamed and drained
Dash pepper
12 ounces turkey cutlets
2 teaspoons reduced-calorie margarine
2 teaspoons enriched flour
½ cup skim milk
2 teaspoons white wine
2 teaspoons grated Parmesan cheese
Dash ground nutmeg

Combine oil and garlic in skillet and heat; add spinach and sauté for 1 to 2 minutes. Stir in pepper and set aside.

Spray a nonstick skillet with nonstick cooking spray; cook turkey cutlets until browned on each side.

Melt margarine in small saucepan; stir in flour. Gradually stir in milk, wine, and cheese; continue to cook, stirring constantly with wire whisk, until thickened. Season with nutmeg.

Line a 1-quart casserole with cooked spinach mixture. Top with turkey and pour sauce evenly over cutlets. Bake at 350°F. for 20 minutes or until heated.

Per serving: 344 calories; 46 g protein; 13 g fat; 8 g carbohydrate; 315 mg sodium

TURKEY KIEV
See Menu Plan for Week 27.
Makes 2 servings

2 turkey cutlets, 6 ounces each
¼ cup reduced-calorie margarine
1 teaspoon imitation bacon bits, crumbled
1 teaspoon chopped chives
¾ ounce cornflakes, made into crumbs
1 cup cooked short-grain brown rice, hot

Pound turkey cutlets to ⅛-inch thickness. In small bowl combine margarine, bacon bits, and chives. Divide margarine mixture in half and shape each half into a log. Place 1 margarine log in center of each turkey cutlet. Wrap turkey cutlets around margarine, tucking in sides to enclose. Roll each cutlet in ½ of the cornflake crumbs and place in an individual casserole that has been sprayed with nonstick cooking spray. Bake at 350°F. for 20 minutes. Serve each portion with ½ cup hot rice.

Per serving: 445 calories; 43 g protein; 15 g fat; 32 g carbohydrate; 547 mg sodium

TURKEY POCKETS
See Menu Plan for Week 43.
Makes 2 servings

8 ounces skinned and boned cooked turkey, diced
½ cup diced celery
¼ cup diced red onion
2 teaspoons mayonnaise
1 teaspoon lime or lemon juice

⅛ teaspoon each salt and ground red pepper
2 whole wheat pita breads, 1 ounce each
Alfalfa sprouts to garnish

In bowl combine all ingredients except pitas and garnish; refrigerate for ½ hour. Slice each pita halfway around edge and open to form pocket. Stuff ½ of turkey mixture into each pocket and garnish with alfalfa sprouts.

Per serving: 314 calories; 36 g protein; 10 g fat; 18 g carbohydrate; 298 mg sodium

VEAL SOUP
See Menu Plan for Week 50.
Makes 2 servings

12 ounces boneless veal, cut into ½-inch cubes
1 medium zucchini, about 5 ounces
2 tablespoons minced onion
¼ teaspoon salt
Generous dash each thyme leaves and pepper
3 cups Beef Broth (see page 127)
2 tablespoons tomato paste
1½ cups sliced celery, cut into ¼-inch thick slices

Heat nonstick skillet over high heat. Cook veal until browned on all sides. Remove veal and set aside.

Cut zucchini into ¼-inch thick slices and cut each slice into quarters. Add zucchini, onion, salt, thyme, and pepper to skillet in which veal was browned. Cover and cook, stirring occasionally, until zucchini is tender-crisp. Set aside.

In medium saucepan combine veal, broth, and tomato paste. Bring to a boil; reduce heat and simmer until veal is tender, about 30 minutes. During last 10 minutes, stir in celery and zucchini mixture.

Per serving: 327 calories; 35 g protein; 15 g fat; 13 g carbohydrate; 577 mg sodium

ROAST SHOULDER OF VEAL

If serving fewer than 8, freeze any leftovers and use in Week 43, Day 6.

See Menu Plan for Week 39.
Makes 8 servings

3 pounds boneless veal shoulder, rolled and tied
¼ teaspoon salt
⅛ teaspoon pepper
¾ cup chopped onions
½ cup chopped carrot
¼ cup chopped celery
¼ cup chopped scallions
Bouquet garni (3 parsley sprigs, 1 bay leaf, 6 peppercorns, and ¼ teaspoon thyme leaves, tied in cheesecloth)
2 tablespoons plus 2 teaspoons white wine
1½ cups Chicken Broth (see page 127), divided
Parsley sprigs to garnish

Brown veal on all sides in nonstick skillet. Sprinkle with salt and pepper. Make a layer of onions, carrot, celery, scallions, and bouquet garni in bottom of medium roasting pan. Transfer veal to rack that has been set over vegetables. Roast at 325°F., turning twice, for 1½ hours or until meat thermometer, which has been inserted in center, registers 160°F. Remove veal and keep warm.

Remove rack from pan and stir wine into vegetables, scraping down brown particles from sides of pan. Stir in ¾ cup broth; place over moderate heat and bring to a boil. Boil 5 minutes. Remove and discard bouquet garni. Pour mixture into blender container; process until smooth. Transfer to saucepan and add remaining broth. Simmer 5 minutes.

Slice veal and arrange on heated serving platter. Spoon some of the sauce over veal and serve remainder in gravy boat. Garnish platter with parsley.

Per serving: 285 calories; 32 g protein; 15 g fat; 4 g carbohydrate; 140 mg sodium

BAKED VEAL LOAVES

See Menu Plan for Week 39.
Makes 2 servings

2 teaspoons margarine
¼ cup chopped onion
12 ounces boneless veal shoulder, cut into cubes
½ cup sliced carrot
1 slice enriched white bread, torn into pieces and soaked in 2 tablespoons water
1 tablespoon plus 2 teaspoons chopped fresh parsley, divided
1 garlic clove
¼ teaspoon salt
Dash each ground sage and white pepper
½ teaspoon arrowroot
2 tablespoons water
1 teaspoon lemon juice

Melt margarine in small skillet; add onion and sauté until softened. Transfer to work bowl of food processor. Add veal and carrot and process until finely chopped. Add bread, 1 tablespoon parsley, garlic, salt, sage, and pepper; process until mixture is smooth and has a pastelike consistency. Divide mixture into two 4½ x 2½ x 1½-inch nonstick loaf pans that have been sprayed with nonstick cooking spray. Smooth tops and bake at 350°F. for 25 to 30 minutes.

In small bowl dissolve arrowroot in water. Drain pan juices from veal loaves into small saucepan. Stirring constantly, add dissolved arrowroot and bring to a boil. Add lemon juice and cook until thickened. Unmold each veal loaf onto a heated plate. Spoon ½ of sauce over each loaf and garnish each with 1 teaspoon chopped parsley.

Per serving: 355 calories; 33 g protein; 19 g fat; 12 g carbohydrate; 467 mg sodium

JELLIED VEAL MOLD

Allow plenty of time for the preparation of this recipe. Its attractiveness and taste make it worth the effort.

See Menu Plan for Week 14.
Makes 4 servings

1½ pounds boned shoulder of veal
1 pound veal bones
1 cup cut-up carrots, 2-inch pieces
2 small onions
3 parsley sprigs
6 peppercorns
3 whole allspice

1 small bay leaf
1 garlic clove, crushed
1½ quarts water
1½ teaspoons salt
1 envelope unflavored gelatin
1 tablespoon lemon juice
Dash white pepper
3 tablespoons chopped fresh parsley,
    divided

Combine first 9 ingredients in a kettle; add water and bring to a boil. Remove scum from surface. Add salt; reduce heat and simmer, partially covered, for 1½ to 2 hours or until veal is very tender. Using a slotted spoon remove veal and carrots to a bowl. Cool; cover and refrigerate. Strain veal broth through a fine sieve into a bowl; discard solids. Cool; cover and refrigerate overnight or until fat congeals on surface.

Remove and discard congealed fat. Spoon jellied broth into a saucepan and cook over low heat just until liquid. Measure 2 cups; remaining broth may be refrigerated or frozen for use at another time. Sprinkle gelatin over broth and let stand 3 minutes to soften. Cook over moderate heat, stirring constantly, until gelatin is dissolved. Stir in lemon juice and pepper. Rinse a 1-quart bowl in cold water. Pour ¼ cup gelatin mixture into bowl; chill until set. Refrigerate remaining gelatin mixture until consistency of unbeaten egg whites.

Thinly slice about ½ of the carrots; dice remaining carrots into ¼-inch cubes and set aside. Arrange some of the carrot slices in a circle over set gelatin, about ⅓ inch from edge of bowl. Measure 1½ tablespoons chopped parsley; reserve remaining parsley. Arrange some of the measured parsley in a circle next to carrots. Arrange remaining carrot slices in a circle inside parsley circle; sprinkle remaining measured parsley in center. Carefully pour about ¼ cup of syrupy gelatin mixture over vegetables; refrigerate until set.

Cut veal into ¼-inch pieces. Combine veal, diced carrots, remaining parsley, and 1 cup syrupy gelatin mixture in a bowl. Spoon veal mixture over set gelatin; add remaining gelatin mixture. Cover bowl tightly with plastic wrap and chill overnight.

To unmold, use a small pointed knife to loosen mold from edge of bowl. Dip bowl into warm water for about 30 seconds. Top bowl with serving platter and invert.

Per serving: 295 calories; 35 g protein; 15 g fat; 4 g carbohydrate; 955 mg sodium

VEAL PATTIES AND MUSHROOMS
See Menu Plan for Week 45.
Makes 2 servings

12 ounces boned shoulder of veal, cut
    into pieces
¾ cup chopped onions, divided
2 tablespoons ice water
1 tablespoon chopped fresh parsley
2 teaspoons cornstarch, divided
¾ teaspoon salt
¼ teaspoon thyme leaves
⅛ teaspoon white pepper
2 cups sliced mushrooms
½ cup water
½ packet instant chicken broth and
    seasoning mix, dissolved in ⅓ cup water
Chopped fresh parsley to garnish

Grind veal with ¼ cup onion, in meat grinder or food processor, until very fine. Add ice water, parsley, 1 teaspoon cornstarch, salt, thyme, and pepper; mix until well combined. Form meat mixture into 4 equal patties. Transfer to rack that has been sprayed with nonstick cooking spray; place in baking pan and bake at 350°F. for 10 minutes; turn and bake 10 minutes longer or until meat is done.

Spray a skillet with nonstick cooking spray; add remaining ½ cup onion and cook until lightly browned. Add mushrooms and cook until softened. Stir in water and simmer for 5 minutes. Add patties and simmer 5 to 10 minutes longer. Combine dissolved broth mix and remaining teaspoon cornstarch; stir into mushroom mixture and simmer 5 more minutes or until thickened. Just before serving sprinkle patties with parsley.

Per serving: 330 calories; 35 g protein; 15 g fat; 13 g carbohydrate; 1,115 mg sodium

VEAL RAGOUT
See Menu Plan for Week 49.
Makes 2 servings

12 ounces boneless shoulder of veal, cut
  into 1½-inch cubes
1 small carrot, scraped and quartered
1 small onion, studded with 1 whole clove
½ celery rib, cut in half
1-inch piece lemon rind
2 parsley sprigs
2½ cups water
Salt
1 tablespoon plus 1 teaspoon margarine
1 tablespoon plus 1 teaspoon enriched flour
1½ cups cooked cauliflower florets, hot
Dash white pepper
2 teaspoons chopped fresh parsley

In saucepan combine veal with enough
water to cover; bring to a boil and cook 2
minutes. Drain in colander.

Tie carrot, clove-studded onion, celery rib,
lemon rind, and parsley sprigs in piece of
cheesecloth and combine in saucepan with
veal, 2½ cups water, and ¼ teaspoon salt.
Bring to a boil; reduce heat to moderate and
remove scum from surface. Cover and cook
45 minutes or until veal is tender. Remove
and discard cheesecloth bag. Allow veal and
liquid to cool in saucepan; cover and refrigerate until fat congeals on top.

Remove congealed fat from surface and
discard. Heat until broth becomes liquid.
Drain veal in colander or sieve, reserving
broth; measure 1½ cups (any remaining
broth can be frozen for use at a future date).
Set veal aside.

Melt margarine in saucepan. Stirring constantly, add flour and cook 2 to 3 minutes.
Remove from heat and gradually stir in
measured veal broth. Return to heat and
cook, stirring constantly, until thickened.
Add veal to sauce and cook until heated.
Stir in cauliflower and dash each salt and
pepper; sprinkle with parsley just before
serving.
Per serving: 397 calories; 35 g protein; 22 g fat;
14 g carbohydrate; 461 mg sodium

SAUTÉED CURRIED VEAL AND EGGPLANT
See Menu Plan for Week 51.
Makes 2 servings

2 cups pared and diced eggplant, ½-inch
  dice
¾ teaspoon salt, divided
12 ounces ground veal
½ cup sliced onion
2 teaspoons olive oil
¾ teaspoon curry powder
⅛ teaspoon chili powder

In colander combine eggplant with ¼ teaspoon salt; toss and let stand 30 minutes.
Pat dry with paper towels.

Pan-broil veal in nonstick skillet over high
heat, breaking veal apart into pieces, until
slightly browned but not cooked through.
Reduce heat to medium; add onion and oil
and sauté 3 to 5 minutes. Add eggplant and
continue sautéeing, stirring occasionally, until eggplant starts to brown. Stir in remaining ½ teaspoon salt and curry and chili
powders; continue cooking until mixture is
well browned and moisture has evaporated.
Per serving: 350 calories; 33 g protein; 19 g fat;
10 g carbohydrate; 894 mg sodium

VEAL À LA FONTINA
See Menu Plan for Week 34.
Makes 4 servings

4 veal scallops or cutlets, 3 ounces each
4 slices Fontina cheese, 1 ounce each
1 tablespoon plus 1 teaspoon enriched flour
1 tablespoon plus 1 teaspoon margarine
1 cup thinly sliced mushrooms
1 tablespoon minced shallots
¾ cup Beef Broth (see page 127)
1 teaspoon tomato paste
1 teaspoon salt
¼ teaspoon ground sage
Dash pepper
1 tablespoon plus 1 teaspoon white wine
Chopped fresh parsley to garnish

Pound veal until flattened. Top each scallop
with a slice of cheese and fold veal to en-

close. Using a meat mallet, seal opening by pounding lightly around edges. Dust each veal "bird" with flour. Melt margarine in nonstick skillet. Add veal and brown quickly on both sides; remove to platter. In same skillet sauté mushrooms and shallots until tender. Add broth, tomato paste, salt, sage, and pepper. Simmer for 5 minutes. Return veal to skillet and simmer a few minutes longer, basting "birds" with sauce. Add wine and sprinkle with parsley.

Per serving: 301 calories; 25 g protein; 19 g fat;
5 g carbohydrate; 709 mg sodium

VEAL MEDLEY

Heart of palm lends an interesting touch to this delicious dish. It is the heart of a tropical palmetto bush and is widely available canned. Its most common usage is in salads; here we've given it a different twist!

See Menu Plan for Week 19.
Makes 2 servings

12 ounces veal cutlets, pounded and cut into 1-inch strips
⅛ teaspoon white pepper
Dash salt
1 tablespoon plus 2 teaspoons margarine, divided
2 cups sliced mushrooms
1 tablespoon enriched flour
¾ cup Chicken Broth (see page 127)
2 teaspoons grated Parmesan cheese
⅛ teaspoon ground thyme
1 cup sliced drained canned hearts of palm, 1-inch pieces
1 cup hot cooked enriched spinach noodles

Season veal with white pepper and salt. Melt 1 teaspoon margarine in small nonstick skillet; add veal and sauté for 3 minutes or until tender, stirring often. Remove veal and set aside. Add 1 teaspoon margarine to skillet and melt; add mushrooms and sauté until tender. Set aside. Melt 1 tablespoon margarine in saucepan; stir in flour. Stirring constantly with a wire whisk, gradually add broth; cook, stirring often, until thickened. Stir in Parmesan cheese and thyme. Stir in

veal, mushrooms, and hearts of palm and cook 5 minutes. Add cooked noodles and toss.

Per serving: 526 calories; 42 g protein; 26 g fat;
30 g carbohydrate; 331 mg sodium

LUNCH BOX VEAL

Prepare the day before, then "brown-bag it" in style!

See Menu Plan for Week 36.
Makes 2 servings

2 teaspoons margarine
½ cup diced onion
12 ounces boneless veal, cut into 1-inch cubes
1 cup skim milk
2 teaspoons chopped fresh parsley
¼ teaspoon salt
¼ teaspoon thyme leaves
Dash pepper

Preheat oven to 350°F. Melt margarine in skillet. Add onion, cover, and cook over low heat about 5 to 8 minutes or until soft; set aside.

Combine veal and milk in work bowl of food processor; process until veal is finely chopped and smooth. Transfer mixture to bowl and add onion mixture, parsley, salt, thyme, and pepper; mix well. Spoon into small loaf pan; tap pan on counter to eliminate all air pockets. Cover with aluminum foil and bake 45 to 50 minutes or until a knife, when inserted in center, comes out clean. Remove loaf from pan and let cool. Refrigerate overnight.

Per serving: 356 calories; 38 g protein; 17 g fat;
10 g carbohydrate; 567 mg sodium

RABBIT BOURGUIGNON
See Menu Plan for Week 44.
Makes 2 servings

1 tablespoon vegetable oil
1 pound rabbit, cut into pieces
½ cup sliced onion
2 teaspoons minced fresh garlic
1 cup sliced mushrooms
1 cup sliced carrots
2 cups canned crushed tomatoes
1 tablespoon plus 1 teaspoon red Burgundy
    wine
½ teaspoon salt
Dash freshly ground pepper
Chopped fresh parsley to garnish

Heat oil in large skillet; add rabbit and brown evenly on all sides. Remove rabbit from pan and set aside. In same pan combine onion and garlic and sauté until soft. Stir in mushrooms and carrots and continue to sauté until vegetables are tender-crisp. Stir in tomatoes and bring to a boil. Reduce heat and simmer several minutes. Add rabbit, wine, salt, and pepper; cover and cook for 45 minutes. If mixture becomes too dry, adjust consistency by adding water. Garnish with parsley.

Per serving: 424 calories; 38 g protein; 19 g fat;
23 g carbohydrate; 949 mg sodium

Meats

Looking for something more interesting than plain old hamburgers? Give ho-hum meat dishes the heave-ho! Recipes like Cucumber-Ham Bake, Potted Shoulder Lamb Chops, Frankfurter Stir-Fry, Liver-Noodle Casserole, and Marinated Chuck Steak suggest the variety of meats and the range of cooking techniques that are at your fingertips.

EASY BEEF SOUP
See Menu Plan for Week 48.
Makes 2 servings

12 ounces boneless beef, from top rib or
   chuck, cut into ½-inch cubes
1½ cups Beef Broth (see page 127) or beef
   bouillon
½ cup water
½ medium onion, about 1½ ounces
1 celery rib, cut in half
⅛ teaspoon oregano leaves
⅛ teaspoon thyme leaves
½ bay leaf
¾ cup sliced carrots, ⅛-inch thick slices
¾ cup sliced celery, ⅛-inch thick slices
1 teaspoon chopped fresh parsley
Dash salt

Broil beef on rack in broiling pan until
browned on all sides and rare.

In medium saucepan combine beef, broth,
water, onion, celery rib, oregano, thyme, and
bay leaf. Cover and simmer about 1 hour or
until meat is tender. Remove and discard
onion, celery, and bay leaf. Add carrots and
sliced celery; cover and simmer until vegetables are tender, about 10 to 15 minutes.
Stir in parsley and salt and serve.

Per serving: 292 calories; 36 g protein; 11 g fat;
10 g carbohydrate; 258 mg sodium

BAKED OAT-BURGERS
Diced green pepper adds a special touch to
this recipe; the burgers are festive-looking as
well as delicious.
See Menu Plan for Week 32.
Makes 2 servings

12 ounces ground beef
½ cup minced onion
½ cup diced green bell pepper
¾ ounce uncooked quick oats
¾ teaspoon salt
⅛ teaspoon prepared horseradish
⅛ teaspoon oregano leaves
Dash pepper

Preheat oven to 350°F. Combine all ingredients in large bowl; mix well. Form mixture into 4 equal patties. Transfer patties to
rack that has been sprayed with nonstick
cooking spray; place rack in baking pan and
bake 25 minutes.

Per serving: 347 calories; 38 g protein; 15 g fat;
13 g carbohydrate; 975 mg sodium

CHILI-BURGERS
Cilantro is the Spanish name for coriander,
an herb native to southern Europe and the
Orient. Sometimes called Chinese parsley
or Mexican parsley, it is the parsleylike leaf
of the coriander plant. These leaves are
much more tender than parsley and have a
zesty flavor that lingers on the tongue. Use
less of this than you would parsley, as a little
bit goes a long way.
See Menu Plans for Weeks 16, 28, and 34.
Makes 2 servings

12 ounces ground beef
½ cup minced onion
½ cup minced green bell pepper
1 tablespoon plus 1 teaspoon ketchup
1 teaspoon chili powder
1 garlic clove, minced
½ teaspoon salt
Dash pepper
½ cup plain unflavored yogurt
Cilantro leaves or parsley sprigs to garnish

In bowl combine beef with next 7 ingredients; mix well. Shape mixture into 4 patties.
Broil on rack, 6 inches from source of heat,
about 5 minutes on each side or until done
to taste. Top each burger with 2 tablespoons
yogurt and garnish with cilantro or parsley.

Per serving: 357 calories; 39 g protein; 17 g fat;
13 g carbohydrate; 839 mg sodium

MEXICAN BEEF PATTY
See Menu Plan for Week 26.
Makes 2 servings

1 cup sliced mushrooms
1 teaspoon minced scallion
1 teaspoon minced celery
1 teaspoon minced pimiento
6 ounces ground beef
2 ounces grated Cheddar cheese
2 tablespoons chopped fresh parsley
2 teaspoons Worcestershire sauce
1 teaspoon salt
Dash pepper

In small nonstick skillet cook mushrooms, scallion, celery, and pimiento until vegetables are soft and accumulated liquid evaporates. Transfer to bowl and combine with remaining ingredients. Form into 2 patties; broil on rack in broiler pan, turning once, until done to taste.

Per serving: 274 calories; 26 g protein; 17 g fat; 3 g carbohydrate; 1,401 mg sodium

MIDDLE EASTERN BURGERS
See Menu Plan for Week 21.
Makes 2 servings

8 ounces lean ground beef
4 ounces lean ground lamb
1 tablespoon minced fresh parsley
½ teaspoon minced fresh garlic
½ teaspoon salt
Dash oregano leaves
2 teaspoons olive oil
½ cup sliced onion
1 medium red bell pepper, roasted,* peeled, seeded, and cut into strips
1 medium tomato, peeled, seeded, and chopped
2 pita breads, 1 ounce each, heated
Prepared mustard to taste

In bowl combine beef, lamb, parsley, garlic, salt, and oregano. Moisten hands with warm water and roll mixture into "sausages," each approximately 2 inches long. Place on rack in broiler pan; broil on all sides until evenly browned. Keep warm. Heat oil in skillet; sauté onion until soft. Add pepper strips and tomato; sauté 1 minute longer. Slice each pita ⅓ of the way around edge to form a pocket. Stuff each pocket with ½ of the "sausages" and top meat with ½ of the vegetable mixture. Serve with mustard.

Per serving: 410 calories; 36 g protein; 19 g fat; 25 g carbohydrate; 676 mg sodium

* To roast pepper, place on broiler pan and broil 6 inches from source of heat, turning to char all sides.

PIQUANT HAMBURGERS
See Menu Plan for Week 23.
Makes 2 servings

12 ounces ground beef
¼ cup plus 1 tablespoon chopped scallions, divided
2 teaspoons teriyaki sauce
Dash pepper
1 teaspoon olive oil
1 garlic clove, minced
1 medium tomato, peeled, seeded, and chopped
4 black olives, pitted and sliced
¼ teaspoon basil leaves
Dash each salt and white pepper
2 tablespoons wine vinegar

In small bowl combine ground beef, ¼ cup scallions, teriyaki sauce, and pepper. Divide into 2 equal portions and form each portion into an oval patty. Broil patties on a rack until done to taste, turning once. While burgers are broiling, heat oil in small saucepan. Add garlic and sauté for 2 minutes. Add tomato, remaining scallions, olives, basil, salt, and white pepper; stir-fry for 1 minute. Add vinegar and cook for 5 minutes longer, stirring frequently. Serve each hamburger with ½ of the sauce.

Per serving: 344 calories; 36 g protein; 19 g fat; 6 g carbohydrate; 425 mg sodium

SPICY MEAT TURNOVERS
See Menu Plan for Week 18.
Makes 2 servings

2 teaspoons margarine
½ cup thinly sliced onion
1 cup beer, divided
¼ teaspoon salt
12 ounces lean ground beef
¾ cup water
1 teaspoon teriyaki sauce
1 teaspoon Dijon-style mustard
½ teaspoon browning sauce
1 tablespoon minced fresh parsley

Melt margarine in skillet; add onion and sauté until soft. Add ½ cup beer; cook until most of the liquid evaporates. Stir in salt and set aside. Divide beef into 2 equal balls. Roll out each between 2 sheets of wax paper, forming two 6-inch circles. Place ½ of onion mixture on each circle. Fold over, pressing seams to form half-moon effect. Remove from paper and broil on rack until browned on both sides, carefully turning once with a spatula. In same skillet combine water, teriyaki sauce, mustard, browning sauce, and remaining beer. Simmer until slightly thickened. Add beef turnovers and serve with sauce. Sprinkle with parsley.

Per serving: 390 calories; 36 g protein; 18 g fat; 10 g carbohydrate; 612 mg sodium

BEEF AND CORN CASSEROLE
See Menu Plan for Week 1.
Makes 2 servings

1 medium red bell pepper, seeded and cut into thin strips
8 ounces cooked ground beef, broken into small pieces
1 cup drained canned whole-kernel corn
½ teaspoon salt
Dash pepper
2 cups hot cooked broccoli florets

In nonstick skillet that has been sprayed with nonstick cooking spray cook red pepper strips until softened. In a 1½-quart casserole combine beef, corn, red pepper strips, salt, and pepper; toss well. Bake 30 minutes at 350°F. Serve over hot broccoli.

Per serving: 410 calories; 39 g protein; 14 g fat; 37 g carbohydrate; 994 mg sodium

CURRIED MEAT HASH
See Menu Plans for Weeks 24 and 37.
Makes 2 servings

12 ounces ground beef
1 teaspoon vegetable oil
½ cup diced onion
½ small tart apple, pared, cored, and chopped
2 tablespoons raisins
2 to 3 teaspoons lemon juice, divided
1 teaspoon curry powder
⅛ teaspoon salt
¾ cup plus 2 tablespoons water, divided
1 teaspoon arrowroot

Place meat on rack in broiler pan. Broil 3 to 4 inches from heat source, turning occasionally, 5 minutes or until thoroughly browned.

Heat oil in saucepan; add onion and sauté until softened. Stir in broiled meat, apple, raisins, 2 teaspoons lemon juice, curry powder, and salt. Add ¾ cup water and stir to combine. Simmer partially covered, stirring occasionally, for 45 minutes or until meat is tender.

In small bowl combine arrowroot with 2 tablespoons water; stir into meat mixture and cook, stirring constantly, until thickened. Add additional lemon juice to taste.

Per serving: 371 calories; 36 g protein; 17 g fat; 18 g carbohydrate; 246 mg sodium

MUSHROOM-BEEF HASH
See Menu Plan for Week 11.
Makes 2 servings

8 ounces boned cooked beef
2 teaspoons margarine
½ cup finely chopped onion
1 teaspoon enriched flour
1 cup sliced mushrooms
¾ cup Beef Broth (see page 127)
¼ teaspoon Worcestershire sauce
2 slices whole wheat bread, toasted
Chopped fresh parsley to garnish

Grind beef in a meat grinder or food processor. In skillet melt margarine; add onion and sauté, stirring occasionally, until onion is lightly browned. Stir in flour. Add mushrooms and beef; cook until mushrooms are softened. Add Beef Broth and Worcestershire; simmer 10 to 15 minutes, stirring occasionally. Spoon over toast and sprinkle with parsley.

Per serving: 372 calories; 39 g protein; 16 g fat; 19 g carbohydrate; 239 mg sodium

POTATO-BEEF HASH
A delicious way to use up leftover beef.
See Menu Plan for Week 29.
Makes 2 servings

1 tablespoon vegetable oil
½ cup diced onion
¼ cup diced green bell pepper
8 ounces chopped cooked beef
8 ounces cooked pared potatoes, diced
1 cup chopped tomatoes
¼ teaspoon salt
⅛ teaspoon thyme leaves
Dash pepper
2 teaspoons chopped fresh parsley

Preheat oven to 350°F. Heat oil in 9-inch nonstick skillet that has a flameproof or removable handle. Add onion and green pepper and sauté until softened. Add beef and potatoes; sauté until potatoes are lightly browned. Add tomatoes, salt, thyme, and pepper. Cook over low heat for 3 minutes, stirring frequently. Press mixture together with back of spoon. Transfer skillet to oven and bake 6 to 8 minutes or until underside is browned. Transfer skillet to broiler and broil 2 minutes or until top is lightly browned. Sprinkle with parsley.

Per serving: 393 calories; 40 g protein; 14 g fat; 26 g carbohydrate; 393 mg sodium

MEDITERRANEAN STEW
If you only need 2 servings, freeze the other 2 for a quick, tasty midday or evening meal.
See Menu Plan for Week 3.
Makes 4 servings

1½ pounds boneless lean beef for stew, cut into 1-inch cubes
2 tablespoons reduced-calorie margarine
1 cup sliced onions
2 cups water
½ cup tomato paste
2 tablespoons raisins
2 tablespoons wine vinegar
2 teaspoons red wine
1 teaspoon honey
1 garlic clove
1 bay leaf
1 cinnamon stick
¼ teaspoon each ground cloves and ground cumin

Broil beef on rack about 20 minutes or until rare, turning once. Melt margarine in medium saucepan. Add onions and beef; cook 5 minutes, stirring occasionally. Add remaining ingredients and stir to combine. Cover and simmer 2 to 2½ hours, stirring occasionally. Remove garlic, bay leaf, and cinnamon stick before serving.

Per serving: 339 calories; 36 g protein; 14 g fat; 16 g carbohydrate; 391 mg sodium

SHEPHERD'S BEEF PIE
This dish freezes well.
See Menu Plan for Week 9.
Makes 4 servings

12 ounces cubed sirloin of beef
1½ cups Beef Broth (see page 127), divided

1 teaspoon salt
2 bay leaves
2 whole cloves
Dash thyme leaves
1 cup sliced carrots
1 cup sliced mushrooms
1 cup diced celery
1 cup diced onions
1 tablespoon plus 1 teaspoon enriched flour
1 pound peeled cooked potatoes, mashed
1 tablespoon plus 1 teaspoon margarine
½ cup skim milk
4 ounces grated Cheddar cheese
1 tablespoon chopped chives

Place beef cubes on rack in broiler pan; broil until browned on all sides.

Transfer beef to medium saucepan; add 1 cup broth, salt, bay leaves, cloves, and thyme. Cover and simmer for approximately 1½ hours or until beef is tender. Add carrots, mushrooms, celery, and onions. Simmer until vegetables are just tender. In small bowl gradually add remaining broth to flour, stirring constantly to form a smooth paste; add to beef and vegetables. Simmer 5 minutes longer.

Spoon equal amounts of mixture into each of 4 casseroles. In small bowl combine potatoes with margarine; stir in skim milk, cheese, and chives. Using a pastry bag fitted with a pastry tube, squeeze ¼ of potato mixture around edge of each casserole. Bake at 375°F. for 10 minutes or until heated through, then broil 6 inches from source of heat 1 to 2 minutes or until potatoes are lightly browned.

Per serving: 373 calories; 26 g protein; 17 g fat;
30 g carbohydrate; 916 mg sodium

MARINATED CHUCK STEAK
See Menu Plans for Weeks 14, 27, and 35.
Makes 2 servings

2 teaspoons teriyaki sauce
1 teaspoon honey
1 teaspoon red Burgundy wine
Dash ground ginger
12 ounces boneless chuck steak
1 teaspoon slivered scallion

In small bowl combine teriyaki sauce, honey, Burgundy, and ginger. Place steak in shallow casserole; pour marinade over steak and marinate in refrigerator for 30 minutes, turning once.

Transfer steak to rack in broiling pan; discard marinade. Broil 5 minutes on each side or until done to desired taste. Slice steak and place on serving plate; garnish with slivered scallion.

Per serving: 259 calories; 34 g protein; 11 g fat;
4 g carbohydrate; 445 mg sodium

MARINATED JULIENNE BEEF
Turn leftover beef into a taste treat for two.
See Menu Plan for Week 30.
Makes 2 servings

8 ounces boneless cooked beef, cut into thin strips
½ cup sliced red onion
3 tablespoons tarragon or red wine vinegar
1 tablespoon chopped fresh basil, or ½ teaspoon dried
2 teaspoons olive oil
½ teaspoon Dijon-style mustard
¼ teaspoon salt
1 small garlic clove, mashed
Dash each artificial sweetener and pepper
Lettuce leaves
Parsley sprigs to garnish

Combine all ingredients except lettuce and parsley in small bowl; toss well. Cover and marinate in refrigerator at least 2 hours or overnight. Serve on bed of lettuce garnished with parsley.

Per serving: 286 calories; 37 g protein; 13 g fat;
7 g carbohydrate; 504 mg sodium

ORIENTAL STEAK SALAD
See Menu Plan for Week 27.
Makes 1 serving

2 cups broccoli florets, blanched
4 ounces sliced cooked steak
½ medium tomato, seeded and diced
2 tablespoons sliced scallion
2 teaspoons rice vinegar
1 teaspoon sesame oil
1 teaspoon soy sauce
1 teaspoon water
⅛ teaspoon minced fresh ginger root

In medium bowl combine broccoli, steak, tomato, and scallion. In small bowl combine remaining ingredients. Add to broccoli mixture and toss to combine.

Per serving: 387 calories; 49 g protein; 13 g fat;
25 g carbohydrate; 524 mg sodium

PEPPER STEAK
See Menu Plan for Week 12.
Makes 2 servings

12 ounces boneless chuck steak
1 tablespoon vegetable oil
1 medium red bell pepper, seeded and cut
    into thin strips
¾ cup Beef Broth (see page 127)
1 teaspoon soy sauce
2 teaspoons cornstarch, dissolved in
    1 tablespoon water
Dash pepper

Broil steak on a rack until rare; cut into thin strips. Heat oil in skillet; add red pepper strips and sauté until tender. Add steak, broth, and soy sauce and cook for 3 minutes. Gradually stir in dissolved cornstarch and cook until sauce thickens. Season with pepper.

Per serving: 348 calories; 36 g protein; 18 g fat;
9 g carbohydrate; 262 mg sodium

STEAK AU POIVRE (PEPPERED STEAK) WITH GARLIC "BUTTER"
See Menu Plan for Week 16.
Makes 2 servings

1 tablespoon crushed black peppercorns

2 boneless club steaks, 6 ounces each
2 tablespoons lemon juice
½ teaspoon Worcestershire sauce
Dash hot sauce
1 tablespoon chopped fresh parsley
2 teaspoons margarine
2 garlic cloves, minced

Press 1½ teaspoons crushed pepper into each steak with heel of hand. In small bowl combine lemon juice, Worcestershire, and hot sauce; set aside. In another bowl combine parsley, margarine, and garlic, and form into 2 equal balls; refrigerate until well chilled. Place steaks on rack in broiler pan and broil about 5 minutes on each side for rare, 7 to 8 minutes for medium. Drizzle lemon juice mixture over steaks while broiling. Serve each steak topped with a garlic "butter" ball.

Per serving: 361 calories; 36 g protein; 21 g fat;
4 g carbohydrate; 173 mg sodium

STEAK PIZZAIOLA
To peel tomatoes, scratch an X in bottom of each tomato; immerse in simmering water for a few seconds or until skin begins to peel at X. Remove from liquid, cool slightly, and peel. This method is also excellent for removing skin from peaches.
See Menu Plan for Week 31.
Makes 2 servings

2 teaspoons olive oil
¼ cup minced onion
2 small garlic cloves, minced
1 cup peeled and chopped tomatoes
¼ teaspoon oregano leaves
Dash salt
Pepper
2 teaspoons chopped fresh parsley
4 black olives, pitted and sliced, divided
12 ounces boneless sirloin steak, cut in half

Heat oil in saucepan; add onion and garlic and sauté until onion is tender. Add tomatoes, oregano, salt, and dash pepper and simmer 10 minutes, stirring occasionally. Stir in parsley and ½ of the sliced olives; keep warm. Sprinkle steaks with dash pepper and place on rack in broiler pan. Broil 2 to 3 minutes on each side or until done to taste. Transfer steaks to serving platter. Spoon tomato mixture over meat and garnish with remaining olives.

Per serving: 312 calories; 37 g protein; 14 g fat; 9 g carbohydrate; 290 mg sodium

SWISS STEAK
See Menu Plan for Week 24.
Makes 2 servings

2 teaspoons enriched flour
¼ teaspoon salt
⅛ teaspoon pepper
2 boneless round steaks, 6 ounces each
1 tablespoon vegetable oil
½ cup chopped onion
½ cup chopped celery
½ cup quartered mushrooms
1 cup canned tomatoes
¾ cup water
2 teaspoons chopped fresh parsley

Combine flour, salt, and pepper. Sprinkle each steak with ¼ of flour mixture; using rim of saucer pound mixture into steaks. Pound ½ of remaining mixture into other side of each steak. Broil steaks on rack in broiler pan 10 minutes, turning once.

Heat oil in saucepan; add onion and sauté until softened. Add steaks, celery, and mushrooms; sauté 3 minutes. Stir in tomatoes and water; bring to a boil. Reduce heat, cover, and simmer 1¾ hours; remove cover and simmer 15 minutes longer or until steaks are tender and sauce is thickened. Sprinkle with parsley just before serving.

Per serving: 316 calories; 35 g protein; 14 g fat; 13 g carbohydrate; 568 mg sodium

ROAST FILLET OF BEEF WITH GREEN PEPPERCORNS
Any beef roast that's on special can be substituted for the fillet. Green peppercorns add an interesting flavor, but if they are not available this will still be delicious.
See Menu Plan for Week 15.
Makes about 4 servings

2 to 3 pounds fillet of beef
1 tablespoon Dijon-style mustard
1 tablespoon green peppercorns, rinsed and chopped
Parsley sprigs to garnish

Preheat oven to 450°F. Coat beef with mustard and green peppercorns; roast on rack in shallow roasting pan for 15 minutes. Turn beef and insert meat thermometer, if desired. Roast for 15 to 20 minutes more or until thermometer registers 140°F. for rare; 160°F. for medium; or 170°F. for well done. Garnish with parsley. Slice and weigh portions, 4 ounces fillet per serving.

Per serving: 279 calories; 32 g protein; 15 g fat; 0.4 g carbohydrate; 191 mg sodium

COFFEE-ROASTED LEG OF LAMB
See Menu Plan for Week 19.
Makes about 6 servings

6-pound leg of lamb
6 garlic cloves, cut into halves
1 teaspoon salt
¼ teaspoon pepper
2 cups black coffee
1 tablespoon Worcestershire sauce
1 tablespoon lemon juice
½ teaspoon ground allspice
½ teaspoon ground cinnamon

Using point of knife, cut slits in lamb and insert garlic halves. Place lamb on rack in roasting pan. Sprinkle with salt and pepper. In bowl combine remaining ingredients. Pour ½ of mixture over lamb. Insert meat thermometer in center of largest muscle, not touching bone. Roast at 325°F. for 45 minutes. Pour remaining coffee mixture over lamb. Continue to roast until tender, about 45 minutes to 1¼ hours longer. Thermometer should register 150°F. for rare; 160°F. to 170°F. for medium; or 175°F. to 180°F. for well done. Remove garlic pieces. Slice and weigh portions, 4 ounces per serving.

Per serving: 219 calories; 33 g protein; 8 g fat; 2 g carbohydrate; 472 mg sodium

LAMB ROSÉ
See Menu Plan for Week 38.
Makes 2 servings

2 teaspoons olive oil
1 cup sliced mushrooms
½ cup chopped onion
2 teaspoons lemon juice
1 garlic clove, minced
½ cup frozen artichoke hearts, thawed
1 teaspoon marjoram leaves
½ teaspoon salt
Dash freshly ground pepper
¾ cup Chicken Broth (see page 127)
1 tablespoon plus 1 teaspoon dry rosé wine
2 teaspoons tomato paste
2 lamb chops, 8 ounces each
Chopped fresh parsley to garnish

Heat oil in medium skillet; add mushrooms, onion, lemon juice, and garlic and sauté until onion is translucent. Add artichoke hearts, marjoram, salt, and pepper and cook briefly. Stir in broth, wine, and tomato paste; simmer over low heat about 10 minutes. While sauce is simmering, broil chops on rack in broiler pan, 6 inches from heat source, about 4 minutes on each side or until done to taste. Transfer chops to serving dish and top with sauce. Garnish with parsley.

Per serving: 321 calories; 36 g protein; 14 g fat; 15 g carbohydrate; 711 mg sodium

LEMON-MINTED LAMB
See Menu Plan for Week 42.
Makes 2 servings

2 teaspoons olive oil
2 small garlic cloves, minced
½ cup water
1 tablespoon lemon juice
½ teaspoon salt
Dash freshly ground pepper
2 tablespoons chopped fresh mint leaves
2 lamb chops, 8 ounces each

Heat oil in small skillet; add garlic and sauté. Stir in water, lemon juice, salt, and pepper; sprinkle mint over mixture and simmer about 10 minutes. Place chops on rack in broiler pan about 6 inches from heat source. Broil 4 minutes on each side or until done to taste. Transfer chops to serving dish and pour lemon-mint sauce over meat.

Per serving: 259 calories; 32 g protein; 13 g fat; 1 g carbohydrate; 632 mg sodium

POTTED SHOULDER LAMB CHOPS
See Menu Plan for Week 40.
Makes 2 servings

2 shoulder lamb chops, 8 ounces each
Salt and pepper
2 teaspoons vegetable oil
¼ cup diced onion
1 garlic clove, minced
1 teaspoon soy sauce
Dash sherry extract
½ cup water
½ cup sliced celery
½ cup sliced green bell pepper
½ cup sliced mushrooms
½ cup sliced drained canned water chestnuts

Place chops on rack in broiling pan; broil 5 minutes on each side. Sprinkle with dash each salt and pepper.

Heat oil in large skillet; add onion and garlic and sauté until lightly browned. Add chops, soy sauce, and extract; then add water and bring liquid to a boil. Reduce heat, cover, and simmer 25 minutes, turning chops once. Add vegetables and dash each salt and pepper. Cook, stirring occasionally, for 5 minutes or until vegetables are tender-crisp.

Per serving: 298 calories; 29 g protein; 15 g fat; 11 g carbohydrate; 430 mg sodium

ARMENIAN LAMB STEW
See Menu Plan for Week 13.
Makes 4 servings

1½ pounds boned lean lamb for stew, cut into 1-inch cubes
1 tablespoon vegetable oil
½ cup diced onion
1 garlic clove, minced
2 cups canned tomatoes

1 cup sliced carrots, ¼-inch thick slices
1 medium red bell pepper, seeded and cut into 1-inch pieces
5 cups cubed eggplant, 1-inch cubes
2 medium zucchini, about 5 ounces each, cut into halves lengthwise, then into ¼-inch thick slices
½ teaspoon each paprika and ground cumin
¼ teaspoon each salt and pepper

Place lamb on rack in broiling pan. Broil 10 minutes. Turn and broil 5 minutes longer; set aside. Heat oil in large saucepan; add onion and garlic and sauté until softened. Add lamb, tomatoes, carrots, and red bell pepper and cook 15 minutes, stirring occasionally. Add remaining ingredients, cover, and simmer, stirring occasionally, 1 hour longer or until lamb is tender.

Per serving: 314 calories; 28 g protein; 13 g fat; 22 g carbohydrate; 384 mg sodium

ROAST LOIN OF PORK
Serve with Orange-Apricot Sauce (see page 286).
See Menu Plan for Week 52.
Makes about 6 servings

1 boneless pork loin roast (2½ to 3 pounds)
1 teaspoon powdered mustard
1 teaspoon marjoram leaves
1 teaspoon salt

Place roast on a rack in a shallow baking pan. Combine remaining ingredients and rub over surface of roast. Insert a meat thermometer. Roast at 350°F. for 30 to 35 minutes per pound or until thermometer reads 170°F. Slice and weigh 4 ounces roast pork per portion.

Per serving: 291 calories; 34 g protein; 16 g fat; 0.3 g carbohydrate; 451 mg sodium

ROAST PORK TENDERLOIN
See Menu Plan for Week 28.
Makes 4 servings

1½ teaspoons salt
½ teaspoon ground sage
¼ teaspoon freshly ground pepper
¼ teaspoon minced bay leaf

½ garlic clove, minced
Dash ground allspice
1½-pound pork tenderloin
12 medium prunes, pitted and cut into halves

In small bowl combine all ingredients except pork and prunes; thoroughly rub mixture into tenderloin. Place on plate, cover, and refrigerate 24 hours.

Preheat oven to 325°F. Brush tenderloin to remove excess seasonings. Place on a rack, insert meat thermometer, and roast about 1 hour or until thermometer registers 170°F. Heat prunes in oven during last 5 minutes of roasting.

To serve, slice tenderloin into ⅛-inch slices. Arrange slices in 2 rows on serving platter and arrange prunes in 1 row, down center of platter, between rows of pork.

Per serving: 330 calories; 33 g protein; 16 g fat; 13 g carbohydrate; 947 mg sodium

FENNEL PORK
Thin oval slices of pork tenderloin are referred to as medallions.
See Menu Plan for Week 7.
Makes 2 servings

12 ounces pork tenderloin, cut into ¾-inch thick medallions
1 tablespoon fennel seeds, ground in blender
1 tablespoon reduced-calorie margarine
1 garlic clove, minced
1 tablespoon enriched flour
¾ cup beef bouillon
Dash white pepper

Roll pork medallions in ground fennel seeds. Place on rack and broil 10 minutes, turning once. Heat margarine with garlic in small saucepan; stir in flour. Gradually add beef bouillon, stirring with a wire whisk. Cook, stirring constantly, until sauce is smooth and thickened; add white pepper. Transfer pork medallions to small nonstick skillet; top with sauce, cover, and simmer 15 to 20 minutes.

Per serving: 281 calories; 29 g protein; 16 g fat; 4 g carbohydrate; 354 mg sodium

TEXAS BARBECUED PORK CHOPS
See Menu Plan for Week 22.
Makes 4 servings

2 pounds rib pork chops
1 cup tomato sauce
2 tablespoons plus 2 teaspoons chili sauce
1 tablespoon plus 1 teaspoon
    Worcestershire sauce
1 tablespoon plus 1 teaspoon lemon juice
2 teaspoons prepared mustard
½ teaspoon sweet Hungarian paprika
⅛ teaspoon each pepper, ground cumin,
    and salt

Arrange pork chops in 9 x 13 x 2-inch baking pan. Combine remaining ingredients in small bowl, mixing well. Pour over chops; cover and refrigerate overnight.

Remove chops from pan and scrape off sauce. Transfer remaining sauce to small saucepan and set aside. Place chops on rack in baking pan; bake at 325°F. for 1¼ hours. While chops are baking, bring sauce to a boil; reduce heat and simmer 15 minutes. Transfer chops to serving platter and top with sauce.

Per serving: 286 calories; 30 g protein; 14 g fat;
8 g carbohydrate; 609 mg sodium

CHICKEN AND PORK MEATBALLS
See Menu Plan for Week 50.
Makes 2 servings

6 ounces boned pork, cut into pieces
6 ounces skinned and boned chicken, cut
    into pieces
¾ teaspoon salt
½ teaspoon minced fresh garlic
¼ teaspoon tarragon leaves
⅛ teaspoon pepper
4 ounces cooked and peeled potatoes, diced
1 teaspoon margarine

Preheat oven to 350°F. In work bowl of food processor, or meat grinder, combine pork, chicken, salt, garlic, tarragon, and pepper; process until meat is finely chopped or ground. Do not over-process. Using a spoon, mash potatoes into meat mixture.

Shape mixture into 6 or 8 equal balls; transfer to rack on baking sheet and bake 35 minutes or until well done. Melt margarine in medium skillet; add meatballs and brown, turning frequently.

Per serving: 274 calories; 33 g protein; 11 g fat;
9 g carbohydrate; 953 mg sodium

PORK AND VEGETABLE MEDLEY
Quick and easy! A delicious way to use up leftover pork roast.
See Menu Plan for Week 14.
Makes 2 servings

1 tablespoon sesame oil
¼ cup diced onion
1 garlic clove, minced
8 ounces boneless cooked pork, cut into
    thin strips
1 tablespoon soy sauce
1 cup broccoli florets
½ cup sliced celery, diagonal slices
½ cup frozen peas
¼ cup drained canned water chestnuts, cut
    into thin strips
½ cup Chicken Broth (see page 127)
Dash pepper

Heat oil in skillet. Add onion and garlic; sauté until softened. Add pork and sauté 5 minutes; sprinkle with soy sauce. Add broccoli, celery, peas, and water chestnuts; toss to combine. Add broth, cover, and simmer 5 to 10 minutes or until vegetables are tender-crisp. Add pepper and stir.

Per serving: 307 calories; 25 g protein; 16 g fat;
17 g carbohydrate; 706 mg sodium

SZÉKELY GOULASH
See Menu Plan for Week 5.
Makes 4 servings

1½ pounds boneless pork butt, cut into
    1½-inch cubes
2 cups sliced onions
1 tablespoon sweet Hungarian paprika
3 tablespoons tomato puree
½ cup water (optional)

1 pound sauerkraut, rinsed and drained (about 2 cups)
½ teaspoon salt
Dash ground red pepper (optional)
½ cup plain unflavored yogurt
1 tablespoon enriched flour

Broil pork on rack in broiling pan for 10 minutes, turning to brown evenly. Cook onions in nonstick saucepan until lightly browned. Stir in paprika. Add tomato puree and pork; cover and simmer for 5 minutes, stirring occasionally. If necessary add ½ cup water, or just enough to keep moist. Simmer 15 minutes longer. Place sauerkraut in saucepan with water to cover; bring to a boil. Boil 5 minutes; drain and add to pork mixture with salt, and pepper if desired. Stir well. Simmer covered, stirring occasionally, for 1 hour or until pork is tender. In small bowl mix yogurt with flour; stir into pork mixture and cook, stirring constantly, until just thickened.

Per serving: 312 calories; 29 g protein; 15 g fat; 17 g carbohydrate; 1,289 mg sodium

TANGY PORK AND RICE
See Menu Plan for Week 39.
Makes 2 servings

1 teaspoon margarine
½ cup minced onion
1 cup mixed vegetable juice
½ cup tomato puree
2 teaspoons red Burgundy wine
½ teaspoon lemon juice
⅛ teaspoon Worcestershire sauce
Salt and pepper
12 ounces boned pork, cut into 2 x ¼-inch strips
1 cup cooked brown rice

Melt margarine in small skillet; add onion. Cover and cook, stirring occasionally, until onion is translucent and very soft, about 5 to 8 minutes.

In small saucepan combine onion, vegetable juice, tomato puree, wine, lemon juice, Worcestershire sauce, and dash each salt and pepper. Set aside.

Place pork on rack in broiler pan and sprinkle with dash each salt and pepper. Broil, turning occasionally, until well browned.

Stir pork into tomato puree mixture; cover and simmer over very low heat for 45 minutes or until tender. Serve over rice.

Per serving: 420 calories; 32 g protein; 16 g fat; 37 g carbohydrate; 750 mg sodium

GRILLED HAM STEAK WITH PINEAPPLE
See Menu Plan for Week 2.
Makes 2 servings

2 canned pineapple slices with 2 tablespoons juice, no sugar added
1 teaspoon Dijon-style mustard
1 teaspoon honey
6 ounces cooked boned ham steak

In a small bowl mix pineapple juice with mustard and honey. Place ham steak on rack in broiling pan and spread with ½ of mustard mixture. Broil 3 to 4 minutes. Turn steak, top with pineapple slices, and spoon remaining mustard mixture over pineapple. Broil 3 to 4 minutes longer or until pineapple is lightly browned and steak is hot.

Per serving: 206 calories; 22 g protein; 8 g fat; 12 g carbohydrate; 846 mg sodium

CREAMED CABBAGE AND HAM
See Menu Plan for Week 51.
Makes 2 servings

2 teaspoons margarine
1 cup sliced onions
1 garlic clove, minced
1 cup julienne carrots
3 cups thinly sliced cabbage
6 ounces boned cooked ham, cut into thin
    strips
2 tablespoons plus 1½ teaspoons enriched
    flour
¾ cup Chicken Broth (see page 127)
½ cup skim milk
⅛ teaspoon ground nutmeg
Dash freshly ground pepper

Melt margarine in medium skillet. Add
onions and garlic and sauté until translucent.
Add carrots and stir-fry 3 minutes. Add cabbage and cook until wilted, about 10 minutes; stir in ham. Place flour in bowl and
gradually add broth, stirring until smooth;
stir into ham mixture. Add milk, nutmeg,
and pepper. Cook, stirring constantly, about
3 minutes or until thickened.

Per serving: 349 calories; 29 g protein; 12 g fat;
33 g carbohydrate; 916 mg sodium

CUCUMBER-HAM BAKE
See Menu Plan for Week 35.
Makes 4 servings

2¼ cups pared, seeded, and sliced
    cucumbers, 2-inch thick slices
1 tablespoon wine vinegar
½ teaspoon salt
6 ounces boned cooked ham, cut into 1-inch
    pieces
2 teaspoons margarine
¼ cup minced onion
2 teaspoons enriched flour
⅛ teaspoon basil leaves
½ cup skim milk
4 ounces shredded Swiss cheese
Dash pepper

In medium bowl combine cucumbers, vinegar, and salt; let stand 30 minutes, stirring
occasionally.

Preheat oven to 375°F. Strain cucumbers
and place in glass or ceramic baking dish.
Bake 15 minutes; stir and continue to bake 15
minutes longer. Remove from oven; reduce
oven heat to 350°F. Combine ham with
cucumbers and set aside.
    Melt margarine in small saucepan; add
onion and sauté until onion is soft. Stirring
constantly, add flour and basil and cook 1
minute. Add milk gradually, stirring briskly
with a wire whisk; continue to stir and cook
until smooth and thick. Add cheese and
pepper and stir until cheese is melted. Combine cheese sauce with cucumber mixture;
bake 20 minutes.

Per serving: 237 calories; 21 g protein; 14 g fat;
7 g carbohydrate; 798 mg sodium

HAM AND RUTABAGA DICE
See Menu Plan for Week 36.
Makes 2 servings

2 teaspoons vegetable oil
2 cups shredded cabbage
1 cup halved and thinly sliced carrots
6 ounces boned cooked ham, cut into 1-inch
    cubes
1 cup cubed rutabaga, 1-inch cubes, steamed
    and cooled
2½ teaspoons water
2 teaspoons prepared mustard
½ teaspoon lemon juice
Dash white pepper

Heat oil in nonstick skillet over medium-low
heat. Add cabbage and carrots, cover, and
cook until vegetables are almost tender. Stir
in ham and rutabaga. In small bowl mix
together water, mustard, lemon juice, and
pepper. Add to vegetables and stir to coat
evenly. Continue to cook, uncovered, until
ham and rutabaga begin to brown slightly.

Per serving: 278 calories; 24 g protein; 13 g fat;
18 g carbohydrate; 848 mg sodium

HAM AND VEGETABLES WITH PAPRIKA YOGURT

Flavor tip—starting potatoes in cold water will make them more flavorful.

See Menu Plan for Week 25.
Makes 2 servings

8 ounces diced pared potatoes, ½-inch dice
2 cups chopped cabbage, ½-inch pieces
½ cup water
½ teaspoon salt, divided
1 cup plain unflavored yogurt
¼ cup plus 1 tablespoon chopped broccoli florets, divided
½ teaspoon sweet Hungarian paprika
¼ teaspoon celery seeds
Dash each ground nutmeg and pepper
6 ounces boneless cooked ham, diced
2 teaspoons cornstarch, dissolved in 2 teaspoons water

Place potatoes in saucepan with cold salted water to cover. Bring to a boil; cover and cook until just tender, about 5 to 7 minutes. Drain and set aside.

In small skillet combine cabbage, water, and ¼ teaspoon salt. Simmer until cabbage is tender, about 3 minutes. Drain and set aside.

In small bowl combine yogurt, ¼ cup chopped broccoli, paprika, celery seeds, remaining ¼ teaspoon salt, nutmeg, and pepper.

In large nonstick skillet combine cooked cabbage, yogurt mixture, ham, and potatoes. Cook over medium heat 5 minutes, stirring often. Stir in dissolved cornstarch and cook, stirring constantly, until mixture thickens. Garnish with remaining 1 tablespoon chopped broccoli.

Per serving: 360 calories; 30 g protein; 12 g fat; 35 g carbohydrate; 1,438 mg sodium

HAM 'N' TURKEY CASSEROLE

Here's a recipe that lets you create a new dish out of leftovers.

See Menu Plan for Week 42.
Makes 2 servings

4 ounces skinned and boned cooked turkey, diced
3 ounces diced cooked ham
1 cup cooked enriched noodles, medium width
½ cup diced green bell pepper
⅓ cup nonfat dry milk powder
1 tablespoon chopped fresh parsley
2 teaspoons grated Parmesan cheese
⅛ teaspoon pepper

Preheat oven to 400°F. In bowl combine all ingredients; mix thoroughly. Transfer to 7 x 5½ x 2-inch casserole that has been sprayed with nonstick cooking spray. Bake until thoroughly heated, about 25 to 30 minutes.

Per serving: 348 calories; 37 g protein; 9 g fat; 27 g carbohydrate; 587 mg sodium

HAM 'N' VEGETABLE BURGERS

See Menu Plan for Week 37.
Makes 2 servings

½ cup pared and diced broccoli stems*
¼ cup minced carrot
3 ounces chopped cooked ham
2 eggs, beaten
¾ ounce uncooked quick oats
1 teaspoon dehydrated onion flakes, dissolved in 2 teaspoons hot water
¼ teaspoon salt
Dash pepper

Steam broccoli and carrot until tender, about 5 to 8 minutes. Combine all ingredients in medium bowl. Shape mixture into 2 equal patties. Spray skillet with nonstick cooking spray and heat; add patties to skillet and cook until firmly set and slightly browned on 1 side; turn and brown other side.

Per serving: 249 calories; 24 g protein; 12 g fat; 12 g carbohydrate; 889 mg sodium

* Reserve broccoli florets for use in other recipes or tossed salads.

HAM STRIPS WITH RICE AND WATER CHESTNUTS
See Menu Plan for Week 17.
Makes 2 servings

2 teaspoons sesame oil
6 ounces boneless cooked ham, cut into thin
   strips
½ cup drained canned water chestnuts, cut
   into slivers
¼ teaspoon salt, divided
Dash white pepper
1 cup cooked brown rice
¾ teaspoon chopped fresh parsley
⅛ teaspoon thyme leaves

Heat oil in large nonstick skillet. Add ham,
water chestnuts, ⅛ teaspoon salt, and pepper. Cook over medium heat, stirring occasionally, until ham is browned and slightly
crisp, about 20 to 30 minutes. In a small
bowl combine rice, parsley, remaining salt,
and thyme. Add to ham mixture. Continue
cooking until rice is heated through.

Per serving: 324 calories; 24 g protein; 13 g fat;
27 g carbohydrate; 1,121 mg sodium

BROILED BOLOGNA-CHEESE MUFFIN
See Menu Plan for Week 49.
Makes 2 servings

1 teaspoon margarine
3 ounces thinly sliced bologna
1 English muffin, split and toasted
2 ounces grated Swiss or Mozzarella cheese

Melt margarine in small skillet. Starting
from edge of each bologna slice, make 4
evenly spaced 1- to 2-inch cuts. Sauté each
slice briefly, just until it begins to shrink
and brown slightly. Top each muffin half
with ½ ounce cheese, then with ½ of the
bologna. Sprinkle each portion of bologna
with ½ of the remaining cheese. Broil until
cheese is melted and browned.

Per serving: 318 calories; 15 g protein; 22 g fat;
14 g carbohydrate; 794 mg sodium

CUCUMBER-LIVERWURST SANDWICH
See Menu Plan for Week 25.
Makes 2 servings

½ cup pared and thinly sliced cucumber
⅓ cup red wine vinegar
6 ounces liverwurst, sliced
4 slices whole wheat bread, toasted
2 teaspoons imitation bacon bits

In a small bowl combine cucumber and
vinegar. Let stand 10 minutes. Place 3
ounces liverwurst on each of 2 slices toast.
Sprinkle each with 1 teaspoon bacon bits.
Drain cucumber slices and place ½ over
each portion of liverwurst. Top each with 1
of the remaining slices of toast.

Per serving: 390 calories; 19 g protein; 24 g fat;
25 g carbohydrate; 1,277 mg sodium

STUFFED CUCUMBER
See Menu Plan for Week 41.
Makes 2 servings

6 ounces liverwurst, mashed
1 tablespoon diced red onion
2 teaspoons imitation bacon bits
2 teaspoons mayonnaise
½ teaspoon prepared mustard
1 medium cucumber, pared, cut in half
   lengthwise, and seeded

In a small bowl combine all ingredients except cucumber. Fill each cucumber cavity
with ½ of mixture. Place stuffed sides of
cucumber halves together and roll tightly in
plastic wrap. Refrigerate until ready to use.
Slice horizontally.

Per serving: 319 calories; 15 g protein; 26 g fat;
6 g carbohydrate; 1,070 mg sodium

KNOCKWURST BREAKFAST
See Menu Plan for Week 28.
Makes 2 servings

2 teaspoons olive oil, divided
½ cup thinly sliced carrot
¼ cup diced green bell pepper

¼ teaspoon salt
¼ teaspoon each minced fresh ginger root
   and garlic
2 ounces knockwurst, cut into ¼-inch thick
   slices
Dash pepper

Heat 1 teaspoon oil in skillet; add carrot, green pepper, and salt. Cover and cook over medium heat, stirring occasionally, until vegetables are tender-crisp. Remove vegetables from skillet and set aside. Heat remaining 1 teaspoon oil in skillet. Add ginger and garlic; sauté 30 seconds. Add knockwurst and pepper; continue to sauté, stirring occasionally, until knockwurst slices are slightly browned on both sides. Return vegetables to skillet and heat through.

Per serving: 136 calories; 5 g protein; 11 g fat;
4 g carbohydrate; 620 mg sodium

FRANKFURTER STIR-FRY
See Menu Plan for Week 33.
Makes 2 servings

1 teaspoon vegetable oil
½ cup sliced onion
6 ounces frankfurters, cut diagonally into
   1-inch pieces
½ cup snow peas, blanched
½ cup julienne carrot, blanched
¼ cup diagonally sliced celery, blanched
1 cup canned pineapple chunks, no sugar
   added
1 teaspoon soy sauce
1 teaspoon cornstarch, dissolved in
   3 tablespoons water

Heat oil in skillet; add onion and sauté until tender. Add frankfurters, snow peas, carrot, and celery, and cook, stirring constantly, for 5 minutes. Add pineapple chunks and soy sauce; cook 2 minutes longer. Stirring constantly, add dissolved cornstarch and cook until sauce thickens.

Per serving: 412 calories; 14 g protein; 26 g fat;
33 g carbohydrate; 1,084 mg sodium

BACON-SCALLOP KEBABS
See Menu Plan for Week 52.
Makes 2 servings

6 ounces scallops, cut into halves
3 ounces Canadian bacon, cut into 8 equal
   pieces
½ cup drained canned water chestnuts, cut
   into halves
¼ cup soy sauce
2 tablespoons rice vinegar
1 garlic clove, minced
½ teaspoon minced fresh ginger root
Dash sherry extract

Combine all ingredients in bowl; toss until well coated. Marinate in refrigerator for about 3 hours, turning frequently. Thread 3 ounces scallops, 1½ ounces bacon, and ½ of the water chestnuts onto each of 2 bamboo or metal skewers, alternating ingredients. Grill over hot coals or broil 6 inches from heat source about 3 minutes on each side. Serve on skewers.

Per serving: 213 calories; 25 g protein; 8 g fat;
9 g carbohydrate; 1,294 mg sodium

STEWED TRIPE
See Menu Plan for Week 8.
Makes 2 servings

1 pound honeycomb tripe,* washed well
1½ quarts water
2 teaspoons olive oil
1 cup sliced onion
1 teaspoon minced fresh garlic
1 cup tomato puree
½ cup sliced celery
½ teaspoon fennel seeds
1 cup sliced carrots
1 tablespoon chopped fresh parsley
Dash each salt and ground red pepper
1 tablespoon plus 1 teaspoon red Burgundy
  wine

Cut tripe into bite-size pieces. Place in pot; add 1 quart water and bring to a boil. Reduce heat and simmer for approximately ½ hour. Drain and set aside.

Heat oil in medium saucepan; add onion and garlic and sauté until translucent. Add tomato puree, celery, and fennel seeds; simmer for a few minutes. Add 2 cups water and tripe. Simmer for approximately 2½ hours. Add carrots, parsley, salt, and pepper; cook ½ hour longer. Stir in wine.

Per serving: 383 calories; 48 g protein; 10 g fat; 26 g carbohydrate; 881 mg sodium

* One pound uncooked tripe will yield about 8 ounces cooked.

VEAL TONGUE WITH ONION SAUCE
See Menu Plan for Week 49.
Makes 2 servings

Tongue
1 medium fresh veal tongue, about 1 pound
2 small carrots, cut into chunks
1 small onion, cut in half
1 small celery rib, cut into chunks
2 parsley sprigs
6 peppercorns, crushed
½ bay leaf

Onion Sauce
2 teaspoons margarine
1 cup sliced onions
Dash each salt, pepper, thyme leaves, and
  basil leaves
2 teaspoons enriched flour
¾ cup Beef Broth (see page 127) or beef
  bouillon
¼ teaspoon lemon juice

To Prepare Tongue: In medium saucepan combine first 7 ingredients with water to cover. Bring to a boil; reduce heat and simmer until tongue is tender, about 1½ hours. Remove tongue from liquid. If desired, liquid may be reserved for use as broth.* Cut and peel away tough skin from tongue; remove large root portion from underside. Trim and remove any ligaments. Weigh 8 ounces; set aside and keep warm.

To Prepare Onion Sauce: Melt margarine in small saucepan. Add onions, salt, pepper, thyme, and basil; sauté over medium heat until onions are soft. Stirring constantly, add flour and cook 1 minute. Using a wire whisk briskly stir in broth, stirring until flour is absorbed. (Sauce will be thin.) Stir in lemon juice.

To Serve: Cutting on an angle, thinly slice tongue. Arrange slices on serving platter and top with sauce.

Per serving: 389 calories; 27 g protein; 23 g fat; 18 g carbohydrate; 242 mg sodium

* To use cooking liquid from tongue as broth, strain liquid and discard solids. Refrigerate until fat congeals on top; remove and discard fat. Broth may be refrigerated or frozen for use in the future.

CHICKEN LIVERS SAUTÉED IN WINE
See Menu Plan for Week 13.
Makes 2 servings

1 tablespoon reduced-calorie margarine
½ cup sliced onion
1 garlic clove, minced
12 ounces chicken livers
1 tablespoon red wine
Dash each salt and pepper

Melt margarine in medium skillet; add onion and garlic and sauté until tender. Add chicken livers and cook, stirring occasionally, for 5 minutes or until livers are done. Add remaining ingredients. Heat and serve.

Per serving: 264 calories; 35 g protein; 9 g fat; 9 g carbohydrate; 288 mg sodium

TARRAGON CHICKEN LIVERS
See Menu Plan for Week 19.
Makes 2 servings

1 tablespoon plus 1 teaspoon reduced-calorie margarine
½ cup chopped onion
12 ounces chicken livers
¼ cup sliced scallions, 1-inch pieces
2 teaspoons red wine
½ teaspoon tarragon leaves
2 slices enriched white bread, toasted and cut into triangles
1 tablespoon chopped fresh parsley

Melt margarine in medium skillet; add onion and sauté until tender. Add chicken livers and sauté until firm, about 7 minutes. Add scallions, red wine, and tarragon; cook 2 minutes longer. Place toast triangles on plate; top with liver mixture. Garnish with parsley.

Per serving: 348 calories; 37 g protein; 11 g fat; 23 g carbohydrate; 338 mg sodium

CHICKEN LIVERS FLORENTINE
See Menu Plan for Week 28.
Makes 2 servings

2 teaspons olive oil
1 cup sliced red onion
Dash each salt and pepper
12 ounces chicken livers
½ cup pared and thinly sliced broccoli stems*
½ garlic clove, minced with ¼ teaspoon salt
1 cup well-drained cooked chopped spinach

Heat oil in medium skillet. Add onion, salt, and pepper; sauté over high heat until onion

slices are soft. Remove onion from skillet and set aside. Preheat oven to 350°F. Add livers, broccoli stems, and garlic to skillet and sauté until livers are firm but still pink inside. Combine cooked onion and spinach with liver mixture. Transfer mixture to 9 x 5 x 2½-inch nonstick loaf pan and bake 10 minutes.

Per serving: 334 calories; 40 g protein; 12 g fat; 19 g carbohydrate; 568 mg sodium

* Reserve broccoli florets for use in other recipes and tossed salads.

CHICKEN LIVERS "STROGANOFF"
See Menu Plan for Week 40.
Makes 2 servings

12 ounces chicken livers
2 teaspoons enriched flour, divided
2 teaspoons margarine
½ cup diced onion
1 cup sliced mushrooms
1 tablespoon plus 1 teaspoon Worcestershire sauce
1 tablespoon plus 1 teaspoon chili sauce
⅛ teaspoon thyme leaves
Dash pepper
½ cup plain unflavored yogurt
2 teaspoons chopped fresh parsley

Dry livers with paper towels and sprinkle with 1 teaspoon flour. Melt margarine in skillet; add diced onion and sauté until softened but not browned. Add livers and sauté about 3 minutes or until just browned. Add mushrooms, Worcestershire, chili sauce, thyme, and pepper; sauté 5 minutes. Combine yogurt and remaining teaspoon flour; stir into liver mixture and heat just to boiling. Sprinkle with parsley and serve.

Per serving: 348 calories; 38 g protein; 12 g fat; 19 g carbohydrate; 355 mg sodium

CHICKEN LIVER PILAF
See Menu Plan for Week 7.
Makes 2 servings

1 tablespoon vegetable oil
1 cup chopped onions
2 cups sliced mushrooms
1 cup sliced celery
12 ounces chicken livers
1 cup cooked brown rice
1 teaspoon each salt and basil leaves
Dash ground nutmeg

Heat oil in skillet; add onions and sauté until softened; add mushrooms and celery and sauté for 5 to 8 minutes or until tender. Spray separate nonstick skillet with nonstick cooking spray; add livers and cook until firm. Add livers and remaining ingredients to vegetable mixture and cook, stirring often, until heated.

Per serving: 460 calories; 40 g protein; 14 g fat; 42 g carbohydrate; 1,381 mg sodium

SPAGHETTI WITH CHICKEN LIVER SAUCE
See Menu Plan for Week 39.
Makes 2 servings

12 ounces chicken livers
2 cups water
1 packet instant chicken broth and
   seasoning mix
2 teaspoons margarine
⅓ cup chopped scallions
1 small garlic clove, minced
2 cups sliced mushrooms
1 teaspoon Worcestershire sauce
⅛ teaspoon thyme leaves
2 teaspoons tomato paste
Dash each salt and pepper
1⅓ cups cooked enriched spaghetti

Cut each liver in half; set aside. Combine water and broth mix in saucepan and bring to a boil. Add livers and boil 3 minutes. Drain, reserving ⅓ cup liquid. Keep livers warm.

Melt margarine in skillet; add scallions and garlic and sauté until softened. Stir in mushrooms, Worcestershire, and thyme; sauté 3 minutes. Combine tomato paste with reserved cooking liquid and stir into vegetable mixture. Bring to a boil; reduce heat and simmer 3 minutes. Add livers and heat; season with salt and pepper. Spoon liver sauce over hot spaghetti.

Per serving: 407 calories; 40 g protein; 11 g fat; 36 g carbohydrate; 733 mg sodium

LIVER-YAM PÂTÉ
See Menu Plan for Week 25.
Makes 2 servings

12 ounces chicken livers
½ garlic clove, chopped with ¼ teaspoon
   salt
⅛ teaspoon ground thyme
3 ounces cooked and peeled yams, mashed
2 teaspoons grated Parmesan cheese
1½ teaspoons lemon juice
1 teaspoon chopped fresh parsley
12 saltines

In a medium nonstick skillet combine chicken livers, garlic, and thyme. Cook over medium heat until livers are firm and cooked throughout. Press liver mixture, including pan juices, through a food mill or a sieve into a small bowl. Finely chop any fibers that do not press through and add to bowl. Add yams, Parmesan cheese, lemon juice, and parsley; stir to combine. Spread on crackers.

Per serving: 367 calories; 38 g protein; 10 g fat; 29 g carbohydrate; 772 mg sodium

LIVER LOAF PÂTÉ
See Menu Plan for Week 46.
Makes 2 servings

12 ounces chicken livers
1 packet instant chicken broth and
   seasoning mix
1 tablespoon plus 1 teaspoon dry sherry
8 ounces boiled and peeled potatoes
¼ cup minced shallots
¼ cup evaporated skimmed milk

2 teaspoons margarine
¼ teaspoon each salt and ground nutmeg
Dash ground red pepper
Parsley sprigs, carrot curls, and radish roses
   to garnish

In nonstick skillet cook chicken livers with broth mix until browned and no longer pink, about 5 minutes. Add sherry and set aside.

Combine remaining ingredients in work bowl of food processor and process until smooth. Add livers and pan juices. Using an on-off motion, process until just blended. Pour into a 3-cup nonstick loaf pan. Chill at least 3 hours, or overnight.

Using a knife or spatula, loosen edges of pâté around sides of pan and invert onto serving plate. Garnish with parsley, carrot curls, and radish roses.

Per serving: 386 calories; 39 g protein; 10 g fat;
30 g carbohydrate; 915 mg sodium

BEEF LIVER CREOLE
See Menu Plan for Week 2.
Makes 2 servings

¾ cup diced onions
½ cup chopped green bell pepper
1½ cups canned tomatoes
¼ teaspoon salt
⅛ teaspoon ground cumin
1 to 2 tablespoons water (optional)
12 ounces beef liver, 1 thick slice

Cook onions in medium saucepan that has been sprayed with nonstick cooking spray until lightly browned. Add green pepper; cook 2 minutes. Add tomatoes, salt, and cumin; cover and simmer for 10 minutes. Add 1 to 2 tablespoons water, if needed, to thin sauce. Spray rack of broiling pan with nonstick cooking spray. Broil liver about 3 minutes or until top is browned; turn and broil for 3 minutes more. Slice liver very thin and add to tomato mixture. Heat 2 minutes and serve.

Per serving: 311 calories; 37 g protein; 7 g fat;
25 g carbohydrate; 770 mg sodium

LIVER-NOODLE CASSEROLE
See Menu Plan for Week 47.
Makes 2 servings

1 tablespoon olive oil
¼ cup diced onion
1 garlic clove, minced
12 ounces sliced beef liver, cut into 1-inch
   strips
1 cup tomato sauce
¼ teaspoon oregano leaves
Dash each salt and pepper
1 cup cooked enriched bow-tie noodles
1 teaspoon grated Parmesan cheese

Heat oil in skillet; add onion and garlic and sauté until onion is softened. Add liver and sauté over high heat for 2 minutes. Stir in tomato sauce, oregano, salt, and pepper; reduce heat to moderate and cook, stirring occasionally, for 2 minutes.

Preheat oven to 350°F. Spray a 1-quart flame proof casserole with nonstick cooking spray. Add liver mixture and noodles and stir to combine; bake 8 minutes. Sprinkle with Parmesan cheese and broil about 1 minute.

Per serving: 462 calories; 40 g protein; 16 g fat;
39 g carbohydrate; 963 mg sodium

SWEET 'N' SOUR LIVER

Scallion may be substituted for the leek in this recipe.

See Menu Plan for Week 10.

Makes 2 servings

⅓ cup pineapple juice, no sugar added
2 teaspoons rice vinegar
1½ teaspoons soy sauce
Dash each ground ginger and ground allspice
1 teaspoon cornstarch, dissolved in 2 teaspoons water
2 tablespoons minced onion and leek
12 ounces beef liver, cut into ¼-inch thick slices
2 teaspoons chopped fresh parsley
Salt and pepper

In small saucepan combine pineapple juice, vinegar, soy sauce, ginger, and allspice. Heat mixture until hot. Stir in dissolved cornstarch. Cook over medium heat, stirring constantly, until sauce comes just to a boil and begins to thicken. Keep warm.

Spray nonstick skillet with nonstick cooking spray and heat. Sprinkle onion-leek combination over bottom of skillet. Place liver slices over onions and sprinkle with parsley and dash each salt and pepper. Cook about 1 to 2 minutes, then turn slices over. Sprinkle with dash each salt and pepper and cook about 1 minute longer or until liver is slightly pink inside when cut with a knife. Transfer slices to serving plate and spoon sauce over liver.

Per serving: 273 calories; 34 g protein; 7 g fat; 17 g carbohydrate; 604 mg sodium

LIVER MANFREDI

To prepare the liver for cooking, remove the thin outer skin and any veins; then weigh.

See Menu Plan for Week 34.

Makes 2 servings

12 ounces sliced calf liver
3 tablespoons soy sauce
½ teaspoon garlic powder
⅓ cup plus 2 teaspoons plain dried bread crumbs

2 tablespoons chopped fresh parsley
2 teaspoons imitation bacon bits, crushed
1 teaspoon sesame seeds, toasted
Lemon slices to garnish

In a bowl combine liver, soy sauce, and garlic powder; set aside. In a separate bowl combine remaining ingredients except lemon. Remove liver from marinade and dip each slice into crumb mixture, coating well. Place liver on nonstick baking sheet that has been sprayed with nonstick cooking spray; sprinkle with any remaining crumbs. Broil 6 inches from source of heat about 5 minutes on each side. Transfer to serving platter; garnish with lemon slices.

Per serving: 326 calories; 36 g protein; 10 g fat; 21 g carbohydrate; 850 mg sodium

CALF LIVER WITH TOMATO

See Menu Plan for Week 16.

Makes 2 servings

2 teaspoons olive oil
1 teaspooon minced fresh garlic
1 cup peeled, seeded, and crushed tomato
¾ cup Chicken Broth (see page 127)
1 teaspoon basil leaves
12 ounces calf liver, cut into bite-size pieces
1 tablespoon plus 1 teaspoon red wine
½ teaspoon salt
Dash pepper

Heat oil in skillet; add garlic and sauté but do not allow to brown. Add tomato, broth, and basil; simmer 5 minutes. In a separate nonstick skillet pan-broil liver until just pink inside. Add liver, wine, salt, and pepper to sauce and heat.

Per serving: 322 calories; 34 g protein; 13 g fat; 14 g carbohydrate; 711 mg sodium

LIVER VENETIAN

See Menu Plans for Weeks 4 and 37.

Makes 2 servings

1 teaspoon olive oil
½ cup thinly sliced onion
1 garlic clove, minced

1 cup sliced mushrooms
12 ounces calf liver, cut into bite-size pieces
2 teaspoons white wine or dry vermouth
Dash each salt and pepper
1 tablespoon minced fresh parsley

Heat oil in small skillet; add onion and gar-lic and sauté until onion is translucent. Add mushrooms and cook briefly. Add liver and sauté just until pink disappears. Add white wine, salt, and pepper. Sprinkle with parsley and serve.

Per serving: 297 calories; 35 g protein; 11 g fat;
14 g carbohydrate; 231 mg sodium

SAUTÉED LIVER WITH MUSTARD CAULIFLOWER

In this recipe we suggest using a glass bowl. Ceramic or stainless steel may also be used, but avoid aluminum as this will react with the acid in the lemon juice and vinegar.

See Menu Plan for Week 22.

Makes 2 servings

2 teabags rose hips tea (optional)
1½ cups boiling water
½ cup sliced onion
1 tablespoon plus 1 teaspoon prepared
    mustard, divided
1 tablespoon lemon juice, divided
2 teaspoons steak sauce
2 teaspoons tarragon vinegar
1 garlic clove, split
12 ounces beef or calf liver, cut into
    1 x 2-inch pieces
2 cups cauliflower florets
¼ teaspoon salt
Dash pepper
2 teaspoons sesame oil

In glass bowl steep teabags, if desired, in water 5 minutes;* remove and discard tea-bags. Add onion, 2 teaspoons mustard, 2 teaspoons lemon juice, steak sauce, vinegar, and garlic; stir well and cool. Add liver; cover and marinate in refrigerator for 2 hours.

Steam cauliflower until tender, about 3 to 5 minutes. Heat medium nonstick skillet. In small container mix remaining mustard with

1 teaspoon lemon juice, salt, and pepper. Add steamed cauliflower and mustard mix-ture to skillet. Cook until cauliflower is slightly browned, stirring frequently; set aside and keep warm.

Heat oil in large skillet over medium heat. Transfer liver to skillet, discarding marinade; sauté until liver is light pink when cut with a knife. Transfer liver and cauliflower to serving platter.

Per serving: 318 calories; 37 g protein; 12 g fat;
15 g carbohydrate; 690 mg sodium

* If preferred, teabags may be eliminated from marinade. Use water and remaining marinade ingredients.

Fish

Fish dishes range from the delicate to the hardy. You can be as
creative as your imagination allows. Use fish in casseroles, aspics,
salads, and soups, in fish cakes, or as kebabs. Fish can be poached,
broiled, baked, or sautéed, and goes equally as well with fruit
as with vegetables. Reel in any of our taste-tempting suggestions
and you won't have to "fish" for compliments.

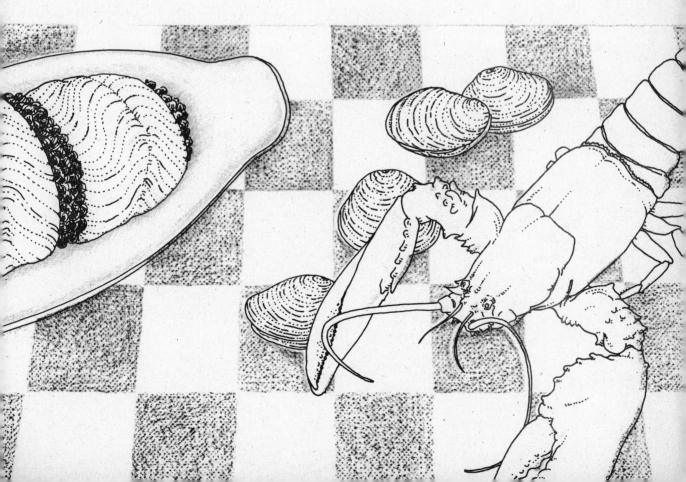

BAKED CODFISH WITH LEMON
See Menu Plans for Weeks 11 and 38.
Makes 2 servings

2 codfish fillets, 6 ounces each
⅛ teaspoon salt
Dash each white pepper and paprika
4 lemon slices
1 tablespoon small capers
2 teaspoons margarine, softened
2 teaspoons chopped fresh parsley

Preheat oven to 375°F. Spray flameproof baking pan, just large enough to hold fish in 1 layer, with nonstick cooking spray. Place fish in pan; sprinkle with salt, pepper, and paprika. Top each fillet with 2 lemon slices and sprinkle with capers. Bake 8 to 10 minutes. Transfer to preheated broiler; broil for 3 minutes or until lemon is lightly browned at the edges. Top each serving with 1 teaspoon margarine; allow to melt. Sprinkle each with 1 teaspoon chopped parsley.

Per serving: 218 calories; 31 g protein; 10 g fat; 1 g carbohydrate; 311 mg sodium

FISH AND TOMATO ASPIC
See Menu Plan for Week 5.
Makes 2 servings

2 cups tomato juice
1 small onion
1 celery rib
1 lemon slice, 1½ inches thick
3 peppercorns
1 envelope unflavored gelatin
¼ cup water
8 ounces cooked cod or flounder fillets, flaked
½ cup finely chopped celery
¼ cup finely chopped dill pickle
Dash each hot sauce, salt, and pepper
Lettuce leaves
6 thin dill pickle slices

In saucepan combine tomato juice, onion, celery rib, lemon slice, and peppercorns. Simmer mixture 10 minutes. In bowl sprinkle gelatin over water and let stand about 5 minutes to soften; strain tomato juice into bowl containing gelatin, discarding solids. Stir until gelatin is dissolved. Chill mixture until slightly thickened. Transfer ¼ cup gelatin mixture to a 4-cup mold that has been rinsed with cold water; chill until set. Fold fish and chopped celery and pickle into remaining gelatin mixture; add hot sauce, salt, and pepper and pour over chilled gelatin in mold. Chill about 6 hours. Unmold onto a platter lined with lettuce leaves and garnish with pickle slices.

Per serving: 286 calories; 40 g protein; 6 g fat; 17 g carbohydrate; 1,195 mg sodium

FISH BALLS WITH HERB SAUCE
See Menu Plan for Week 1.
Makes 2 servings

Fish Balls
4 ounces flaked cooked cod
1 egg, beaten
12 saltines, made into crumbs
2 tablespoons water
1 teaspoon lemon juice
1 teaspoon chopped fresh parsley
¼ teaspoon sweet Hungarian paprika
Dash pepper

Herb Sauce
1 tablespoon margarine
1 tablespoon enriched flour
1 cup skim milk
1 egg, hard-cooked and chopped
½ teaspoon each salt and chopped fresh parsley
¼ teaspoon dill weed
Dash white pepper

To Prepare Fish Balls: In bowl combine first 8 ingredients. Spray a 9-inch pie pan or shallow casserole with nonstick cooking spray. Shape fish mixture into 16 balls. Arrange in pie pan, cover with foil, and bake 30 minutes at 350°F. Remove from oven, uncover, and set aside.

To Prepare Herb Sauce: Melt margarine in small saucepan. Remove from heat and stir in flour. Cook 2 minutes over low heat, stirring occasionally. Gradually add milk, stirring briskly with a wire whisk until flour, margarine, and milk are blended. Continue cooking, stirring constantly with a wooden spoon, until sauce thickens. Add chopped egg, salt, parsley, dill, and pepper; stir to combine. Pour sauce over fish balls and serve.

Per serving: 363 calories; 29 g protein; 17 g fat; 23 g carbohydrate; 1,047 mg sodium

LUNCH BOX FISH 'N' CHEESE
See Menu Plan for Week 17.
Makes 2 servings

2 pita breads, 1 ounce each
1 cup chopped lettuce
4 ounces cooked and boned fish (cod, flounder, etc.), flaked
2 ounces mild Cheddar cheese, broken into pea-size pieces
1 teaspoon lemon juice
1 teaspoon chopped fresh parsley
¼ teaspoon salt

Cut each pita bread ⅓ of the way around edge to create pocket. Set aside. Combine all remaining ingredients in a bowl; toss well. Fill each pocket with ½ of fish mixture.

Per serving: 292 calories; 26 g protein; 13 g fat; 16 g carbohydrate; 534 mg sodium

POACHED CODFISH WITH ASPARAGUS AND TOMATOES
See Menu Plan for Week 17.
Makes 2 servings

½ carrot, chopped
½ celery rib, chopped
2 tablespoons plus 2½ teaspoons lemon juice, divided
4 parsley stems
4 peppercorns, crushed
12 ounces cod fillets
2 teaspoons olive oil
½ cup sliced onion
¼ teaspoon each oregano leaves and basil leaves

Dash thyme leaves
12 medium asparagus spears, blanched and cut into 1½-inch pieces
Salt and pepper
½ cup cherry tomatoes

In medium skillet combine carrot, celery, 2 tablespoons lemon juice, parsley stems, and peppercorns. Add fish to skillet and enough water to barely cover fillets. Cover with vented sheet of foil and bring to a slow simmer. Do not allow poaching liquid to boil. Simmer fish until *almost* completely cooked through, about 3 to 5 minutes, depending on thickness of fillets. Transfer fish to platter and set aside. Discard poaching liquid and wipe skillet dry.

Heat oil in skillet and add onion, oregano, basil, and thyme. Cover and cook over low heat until onion slices are soft. Add asparagus and continue cooking until tender.

Cut fish into large chunks and sprinkle with dash each salt and pepper. Add fish and tomatoes to skillet; cook until fish is cooked through, about 3 to 5 minutes, occasionally stirring gently. *Do not overcook.* Sprinkle with 2½ teaspoons lemon juice and dash each salt and pepper just before serving.

Per serving: 233 calories; 33 g protein; 6 g fat; 13 g carbohydrate; 242 mg sodium

CAPTAIN'S FLOUNDER
See Menu Plan for Week 16.
Makes 2 servings

1 teaspoon margarine
1 cup minced mushrooms
½ cup minced scallions
½ cup minced celery
¼ cup minced red bell pepper
2 ounces cooked or drained canned crab meat
1 slice enriched white bread, made into crumbs
2 tablespoons lemon juice
1 tablespoon chopped fresh parsley
1 teaspoon mayonnaise
½ teaspoon Dijon-style mustard
½ teaspoon salt

Dash white pepper
10 ounces flounder fillets
¾ cup Chicken Broth (see page 127)
2 teaspoons white wine
Dash paprika
Parsley sprigs and lemon wedges to garnish

Preheat oven to 400°F. Melt margarine in nonstick skillet; add mushrooms, scallions, celery, and red pepper. Sauté until vegetables are soft. Transfer mixture to bowl; add crab meat, bread crumbs, lemon juice, parsley, mayonnaise, mustard, salt, and pepper. Mix thoroughly. Spoon mixture into a shallow 1-quart casserole.* Top with fillets, tucking ends under. Pour in Chicken Broth and wine. Sprinkle with paprika. Bake for 12 to 15 minutes or until fish flakes easily when tested with a fork. Garnish with parsley and lemon.

Per serving: 254 calories; 32 g protein; 6 g fat; 16 g carbohydrate; 936 mg sodium

* This dish can also be made in two 2-cup casseroles. Use ½ of the crab meat mixture, 5 ounces flounder, 6 tablespoons broth, and 1 teaspoon wine for each casserole. Proceed as directed.

CHILLED FISH SALAD

An excellent recipe for using up any leftover white fish.
See Menu Plan for Week 48.
Makes 2 servings

8 ounces cooked, skinned, and boned
    flounder (or any other white fish),
    chilled and flaked
½ cup diced celery
2 tablespoons diced onion
2 tablespoons lemon juice
2 teaspoons pickle relish
2 teaspoons mayonnaise
Dash each salt and white pepper
Lettuce leaves

Combine all ingredients except lettuce in bowl; mix well. Serve on bed of lettuce leaves.

Per serving: 284 calories; 35 g protein; 13 g fat; 5 g carbohydrate; 456 mg sodium

FLOUNDER FILLET ROLLS WITH VEGETABLES

See Menu Plan for Week 29.
Makes 2 servings

2 teaspoons margarine
2 tablespoons chopped scallion
¼ cup diced carrot
¼ cup diced celery
⅓ cup apple juice, no sugar added
¼ cup water
1 tablespoon lemon juice
4 flounder fillets, 3 ounces each
⅛ teaspoon salt
⅛ teaspoon thyme leaves
Dash pepper
1 teaspoon cornstarch, dissolved in
    1 tablespoon water

Preheat oven to 350°F. Melt margarine in shallow flameproof casserole; add scallions, carrot, and celery; sauté until vegetables are softened. Add apple juice, water, and lemon juice; bring to a boil. Reduce heat and simmer 5 minutes. Sprinkle fish with salt, thyme, and pepper. Roll each fillet and secure with a toothpick. Carefully place rolls in apple juice mixture; bring to a boil. Cover casserole and transfer to oven; bake for 10 minutes. Using a slotted spoon transfer fish rolls to serving platter; remove toothpicks and keep fish warm. Stir dissolved cornstarch into juice mixture. Stirring constantly, bring to a boil and cook 2 to 3 minutes or until sauce thickens. Pour sauce over fish rolls.

Per serving: 273 calories; 34 g protein; 10 g fat; 9 g carbohydrate; 308 mg sodium

FLOUNDER IN ORANGE SAUCE
See Menu Plan for Week 50.
Makes 2 servings

1 tablespoon reduced-calorie margarine,
    divided
¼ cup chopped onion
¼ cup chopped celery
12 ounces flounder fillets
¼ cup sliced mushrooms
¼ teaspoon salt
Dash pepper
½ cup orange juice
¼ cup chopped fresh parsley
1½ teaspoons enriched flour
½ small orange, thinly sliced
2 parsley sprigs

Melt 1½ teaspoons margarine in large nonstick skillet; add onion and celery and cook
until tender. Place fillets over vegetables; top
with mushrooms and sprinkle with salt and
pepper. Add orange juice and bring to a boil.
Reduce heat to low, cover, and simmer for
10 minutes. Add chopped parsley and simmer 5 minutes longer or until fish flakes
easily. Transfer fish to warmed serving platter. Remove remaining vegetables from skillet with slotted spoon and arrange over fish;
reserve cooking liquid.

   Melt remaining margarine in small saucepan over medium heat; stirring constantly,
add flour and cook until mixture reaches
boiling point. Reduce heat and add reserved
liquid; cook, stirring, until thickened. Pour
sauce over fish and vegetables. Garnish with
orange slices and parsley sprigs.

Per serving: 290 calories; 34 g protein; 10 g fat;
16 g carbohydrate; 505 mg sodium

FLOUNDER ITALIANO
See Menu Plan for Week 43.
Makes 2 servings

½ cup crushed tomatoes
¼ cup diced onion
¼ cup white wine
¼ teaspoon oregano leaves
¼ teaspoon salt
Dash pepper

1 tablespoon plus 1 teaspoon reduced-
    calorie margarine
12 ounces flounder fillets
2 tablespoons plus 1½ teaspoons enriched
    flour
Parsley sprigs to garnish

In large nonstick skillet combine tomatoes,
onion, wine, oregano, salt, and pepper; cook
over medium heat until vegetables are tender. Remove vegetables from skillet and keep
warm. Using same skillet, melt margarine.
Coat fish with flour; place in skillet and
brown over medium heat about 5 minutes
on each side or until fish flakes easily. Transfer fish to serving plate and top with vegetables. Garnish with parsley sprigs.

Per serving: 245 calories; 30 g protein; 5 g fat;
12 g carbohydrate; 508 mg sodium

FLOUNDER MEUNIÈRE
See Menu Plan for Week 8.
Makes 2 servings

12 ounces flounder fillets
2 teaspoons enriched flour
2 teaspoons margarine
½ cup Chicken Broth (see page 127)
2 teaspoons lemon juice
2 teaspoons white wine
1 teaspoon chopped fresh parsley
Dash each salt and white pepper

Dust flounder lightly with flour; set aside.
Heat margarine in nonstick skillet; add
flounder to pan and brown lightly on both
sides. Add broth, lemon juice, and wine.
Simmer briefly, about 3 minutes; sprinkle
with parsley, salt, and pepper.

Per serving: 186 calories; 28 g protein; 5 g fat;
3 g carbohydrate; 273 mg sodium

FLOUNDER VÉRONIQUE
See Menu Plan for Week 7.
Makes 2 servings

1 teaspoon lemon juice
Salt
½ bay leaf

3 peppercorns
1 cup water
12 ounces flounder fillets
1 tablespoon margarine
1 tablespoon enriched flour
¼ cup skim milk
1 tablespoon plus 1¼ teaspoons white wine
20 small white grapes, cut into halves
Dash white pepper

Combine lemon juice, ⅛ teaspoon salt, bay leaf, and peppercorns in medium skillet; add water and bring to a boil. Add fillets; reduce heat, cover, and simmer 5 minutes. Using a slotted spatula, remove fillets and set aside. Strain liquid and reserve ¼ cup.

Melt margarine in saucepan over medium heat. Stir in flour and cook, stirring constantly, for 2 minutes. Gradually add milk and reserved liquid. Stirring constantly with a wire whisk, bring to a boil and cook until smooth and thick. Stir in wine, then grapes and dash each salt and white pepper.

Transfer fillets to a shallow, 12-inch long, 2½-cup oval casserole. Top with sauce and bake at 350°F. for 10 minutes or until heated.

Per serving: 235 calories; 30 g protein; 7 g fat; 8 g carbohydrate; 452 mg sodium

LAYERED BAKED FLOUNDER
See Menu Plans for Weeks 21, 48, and 49.
Makes 2 servings

⅔ cup nonfat dry milk powder, divided
½ cup skim milk
⅓ cup plus 2 teaspoons plain dried bread crumbs
½ teaspoon salt
¼ teaspoon chervil leaves
Dash pepper
½ cup shredded carrot
12 ounces flounder fillets
¾ cup diced celery

Preheat oven to 350°F. Combine ⅓ cup milk powder and the skim milk and set aside. Combine remaining milk powder with bread crumbs, salt, chervil, and pepper; set aside.

Arrange shredded carrot over bottom of small casserole; top with ⅓ of the fillets. Sprinkle with ¼ cup celery, then ⅓ of the crumb mixture. Repeat layers 2 more times. Slowly pour milk mixture over all. Bake for approximately 40 minutes or until milk is bubbling around edges of casserole.

Per serving: 325 calories; 42 g protein; 3 g fat; 32 g carbohydrate; 1,033 mg sodium

MUSTARD-BROILED FLOUNDER
See Menu Plans for Weeks 10 and 40.
Makes 2 servings

½ garlic clove, minced
¼ teaspoon salt
1½ teaspoons prepared mustard
½ teaspoon lemon juice
¼ teaspoon prepared horseradish
12 ounces flounder fillets
Dash pepper

Using the flat side of a knife, mash garlic and salt together to form a paste. In bowl combine garlic paste, mustard, lemon juice, and horseradish. Sprinkle both sides of fillets with pepper. Transfer fillets to a broiler rack that has been sprayed with nonstick cooking spray. Using a pastry brush, brush mustard mixture evenly over one side of fillets. Broil approximately 5 minutes or until fish flakes easily at the touch of a fork.

Per serving: 137 calories; 29 g protein; 1 g fat; 0.1 g carbohydrate; 449 mg sodium

PINEAPPLE FLOUNDER
See Menu Plans for Weeks 17 and 28.
Makes 2 servings

2 teaspoons olive oil
12 ounces flounder fillets
Dash each salt and pepper
½ teaspoon lemon juice
¼ small pineapple, pared and coarsely
    chopped

Heat oil in a medium skillet. Sprinkle both sides of fillets with salt and pepper. Add fillets to skillet and sauté over medium heat about 3 minutes. (If fillets are very thin, sauté 1 minute.) Turn, sprinkle with lemon juice, and spread pineapple over fish. Cover skillet and cook another 3 to 5 minutes (2 to 3 minutes for thin fillets).

Per serving: 209 calories; 29 g protein; 6 g fat; 9 g carbohydrate; 227 mg sodium

BAKED FISH CASSEROLE
See Menu Plan for Week 1.
Makes 4 servings

4 cups shredded cabbage
1 cup sliced onions
½ cup thinly sliced carrot
1 garlic clove, finely chopped with
    ½ teaspoon salt
12 ounces boned cooked halibut, in chunks
2 tablespoons margarine
2 tablespoons enriched flour
1 cup skim milk
2 ounces sharp Cheddar cheese
½ teaspoon salt
Dash each white pepper and ground allspice
1 teaspoon chopped fresh parsley

Spray skillet with nonstick cooking spray; add cabbage, onions, carrot slices, and garlic. Cover and cook over low heat until cabbage is wilted and carrot is tender. Transfer vegetables to a 2-quart casserole that has been sprayed with nonstick cooking spray. Add fish and stir gently to combine.

Preheat oven to 350°F. Melt margarine in small saucepan; add flour and cook over low heat 2 to 3 minutes, stirring constantly.

Add milk gradually, stirring briskly with wire whisk; continue to stir briskly until sauce is a smooth consistency. Add Cheddar cheese, salt, pepper, and allspice. Continue to cook, stirring constantly, until sauce has thickened and cheese is melted.

Combine sauce with vegetables and fish in casserole; sprinkle with parsley. Cover and bake 30 minutes.

Per serving: 337 calories; 30 g protein; 17 g fat; 17 g carbohydrate; 919 mg sodium

CHILLED FISH AND RICE SALAD
See Menu Plan for Week 32.
Makes 2 servings

8 ounces cooked halibut, cod, or flounder
    fillets
1 cup cooked short-grain brown rice
¼ cup diced red bell pepper
2 teaspoons olive oil
½ teaspoon lime juice
½ teaspoon lemon juice
½ teaspoon salt
⅛ teaspoon thyme leaves
Dash pepper

Place fish, rice, and red pepper in medium bowl. Do not combine.

In a small bowl combine oil, lime juice, lemon juice, salt, thyme, and pepper. Pour over fish, rice, and red pepper. Toss gently to combine, breaking fish into large chunks; chill.

Per serving: 348 calories; 31 g protein; 13 g fat; 24 g carbohydrate; 741 mg sodium

POACHED HALIBUT PARMESAN
See Menu Plan for Week 19.
Makes 1 serving

1 tablespoon plus 1½ teaspoons lemon
    juice
Dash each salt and pepper
¾ cup water
6 ounces boneless halibut steak
1 tablespoon reduced-calorie margarine
½ teaspoon chopped fresh parsley

¼ teaspoon minced fresh garlic
1 teaspoon grated Parmesan cheese

In saucepan combine lemon juice, salt, and pepper; add water and bring to a boil. Add fish to liquid and poach for 8 to 10 minutes or until fish flakes easily with a fork. Melt margarine in small saucepan; add parsley and garlic and sauté until garlic is tender. Place fish on plate and top with margarine mixture. Sprinkle with Parmesan cheese.

Per serving: 249 calories; 38 g protein; 9 g fat;
2 g carbohydrate; 508 mg sodium

CURRIED SCROD
See Menu Plans for Weeks 13 and 28.
Makes 2 servings

1 tablespoon Dijon-style mustard
2 teaspoons honey
2 teaspoons lemon juice
Dash each curry powder and salt
12 ounces scrod fillets, ¾ inch thick
1 teaspoon chopped fresh parsley

Combine first 4 ingredients in small bowl. Place scrod in small casserole; pour mustard mixture over fish. Bake at 350°F. for about 25 minutes; broil for 2 minutes. Garnish with parsley.

Per serving: 165 calories; 30 g protein; 1 g fat;
6 g carbohydrate; 438 mg sodium

SCROD GREEK STYLE
See Menu Plan for Week 9.
Makes 2 servings

12 ounces scrod fillets
2 teaspoons olive oil
1 cup sliced onions
1 teaspoon minced fresh garlic
1 cup sliced mushrooms
1 medium tomato, peeled, seeded, and chopped
¾ cup Chicken Broth (see page 127)
Dash each oregano leaves, salt, and white pepper
1 tablespoon plus 1 teaspoon white wine
1 tablespoon chopped fresh parsley
4 black olives, pitted and sliced lengthwise

Wipe scrod fillets with paper towels and set aside. Heat oil in small skillet; add onions and garlic and sauté until translucent; add mushrooms and tomato and cook, stirring constantly, until mushrooms are just tender. Add broth, oregano, salt, and pepper, and simmer a few minutes. Arrange fillets in a shallow 3-cup casserole or baking pan; pour vegetable mixture over fish. Add wine. Bake at 400°F. for approximately 15 to 20 minutes or until fish flakes easily. Remove from oven; garnish with parsley and olives. Serve immediately.

Per serving: 265 calories; 34 g protein; 7 g fat;
15 g carbohydrate; 296 mg sodium

SCROD-VEGETABLE BAKE
See Menu Plan for Week 6.
Makes 2 servings

2 cups sliced zucchini, ¼-inch thick slices
1 cup tomato sauce
1 small garlic clove, minced with dash salt
Dash summer savory leaves
Thyme leaves and pepper
12 ounces scrod fillets
1 cup blanched broccoli florets (optional)
1 teaspoon lemon juice
Dash salt

Blanch zucchini for 2 minutes in boiling salted water until tender-crisp. Drain; rinse with cold water and set aside.

In small saucepan combine tomato sauce, garlic, summer savory, and dash each thyme leaves and pepper. Bring to a boil; reduce heat and simmer 5 minutes. Set aside.

Preheat oven to 350°F. Place fillets in bottom of baking dish (not aluminum). If desired, place broccoli florets alongside fillets. Sprinkle fillets with lemon juice and dash each thyme, pepper, and salt. Arrange zucchini slices over fish in an overlapping pattern. Be sure fish is completely covered. Spoon tomato sauce mixture around edge of fish and vegetables. Cover with foil, vent, and bake for 20 to 25 minutes or until fish flakes easily. When serving, spoon tomato sauce over vegetables.

Per serving: 199 calories; 33 g protein; 1 g fat;
14 g carbohydrate; 843 mg sodium

SWEET AND TANGY SCROD
See Menu Plan for Week 30.
Makes 2 servings

12 ounces scrod fillets
2 teaspoons vegetable oil
¼ cup chopped scallions
1 garlic clove, minced
¼ cup grapefruit juice
1 teaspoon sugar
2 teaspoons cornstarch
½ cup water
½ teaspoon salt
Dash ground ginger
4 green bell pepper rings
4 tomato slices

Arrange fillets in shallow 1-quart baking pan; set aside. Heat oil in small skillet; add scallions and garlic and sauté briefly. Add juice and sugar. Dissolve cornstarch in water and pour into skillet. Cook, stirring constantly, until slightly thickened. Add salt and ginger and stir to combine. Pour sauce over fish; top with pepper rings and tomato slices, arranged attractively. Bake at 400°F. for 15 to 20 minutes or until fish flakes easily when tested with a fork.

Per serving: 223 calories; 31 g protein; 5 g fat;
11 g carbohydrate; 710 mg sodium

LEMON-BROILED SNAPPERS (BABY BLUEFISH)
It's not difficult to pan-dress freshly caught snappers. See Pan-Broiled Snappers recipe for directions.
See Menu Plan for Week 44.
Makes 1 serving

3 snappers, about 4 ounces each,*
   pan-dressed
1 tablespoon lemon juice
1 tablespoon minced onion
1 teaspoon chopped fresh parsley
¼ teaspoon minced fresh garlic
⅛ teaspoon salt
Dash pepper
2 teaspoons reduced-calorie margarine

Arrange fish in nonstick flameproof baking pan. In small bowl combine next 6 ingredients; spread mixture evenly over fish. Broil 5 minutes; turn fish, spread with margarine, and broil 1 minute longer.

Per serving: 202 calories; 34 g protein; 5 g fat;
3 g carbohydrate; 477 mg sodium

* Three whole 4-ounce snappers will yield about 4 ounces cooked meat.

PAN-BROILED SNAPPERS
Snappers are baby bluefish. If you enjoy getting out and catching your own, the best season for snapper fishing is August through September. Three whole 4-ounce snappers will yield about 4 ounces cooked meat.
See Menu Plan for Week 35.
Makes 1 serving

1 tablespoon plus ¾ teaspoon enriched
   flour
⅛ teaspoon each salt and pepper
3 snappers, about 4 ounces each,
   pan-dressed*
Lemon wedge and parsley sprig to garnish

In bowl combine flour, salt, and pepper. Dredge snappers in flour mixture. Transfer to nonstick skillet and cook, over low to medium heat, about 5 minutes on each side or until fish flakes easily at the touch of a fork. Serve garnished with lemon wedge and parsley.

Per serving: 165 calories; 29 g protein; 1 g fat;
7 g carbohydrate; 383 mg sodium

Variation:
Substitute 1 tablespoon plus 1½ teaspoons plain dried bread crumbs for the flour. Proceed as directed.

Per serving: 165 calories; 29 g protein; 2 g fat;
6 g carbohydrate; 444 mg sodium

* It's not difficult to prepare your catch for the pan. Using a sharp knife and starting just behind the side fins, cut off head and remove viscera (internal organs). Holding fish by the tail remove scales from both sides, scraping from tail toward head. Wash fish in cold water.

BAKED RED SNAPPER
See Menu Plan for Week 34.
Makes 2 servings

12 ounces red snapper fillets
2 teaspoons mayonnaise
1 teaspoon Dijon-style mustard
1 teaspoon lemon juice
1 teaspoon each chopped chives and
   chopped fresh parsley
Dash each salt and freshly ground pepper
2 teaspoons grated Parmesan cheese

Arrange fillets in shallow 1-quart flameproof baking dish that has been sprayed with non-stick cooking spray. In bowl combine remaining ingredients except cheese; stir well. Spread mixture over fish and sprinkle with cheese. Bake at 400°F. for 20 minutes. Transfer to preheated broiler and broil for 1 minute.

Per serving: 218 calories; 36 g protein; 10 g fat; 1 g carbohydrate; 398 mg sodium

TRINIDAD SNAPPER
See Menu Plan for Week 18.
Makes 2 servings

2 teaspoons vegetable oil
½ cup sliced onion
1 cup peeled, seeded, and crushed tomatoes
12 ounces red snapper fillets
½ cup Green Chili Sauce (see page 285)

Heat oil in small skillet; add onion and sauté until soft. Add tomatoes; simmer 5 minutes. Set aside. Place fish in oval casserole just large enough to hold fillets in 1 layer. Spread chili sauce over fish and top with tomato mixture. Bake at 400°F. for about 15 minutes or until fish flakes when tested with a fork.

Per serving: 273 calories; 37 g protein; 7 g fat; 17 g carbohydrate; 638 mg sodium

POACHED SWORDFISH
See Menu Plan for Week 51.
Makes 2 servings

1 small onion, studded with 1 whole clove
¼ cup each diced celery and carrot
¼ cup tarragon vinegar
3 parsley stems
½ bay leaf
½ teaspoon salt
1 quart water
12 ounces skinned and boned swordfish
1½ cups cooked spaghetti squash,*
   kept warm

Combine first 6 ingredients in medium saucepan. Add water and bring to a boil; reduce heat and simmer 20 minutes. Remove from heat; cool until lukewarm. Drain and reserve celery, carrots, and liquid; discard onion, parsley stems, and bay leaf. Set aside vegetables and keep warm.

Place fish in small skillet; add reserved liquid to almost cover fish. Cover skillet with aluminum foil; punch hole in center of foil to vent. Bring to a simmer and cook about 5 minutes or until fish flakes easily.

Arrange squash on serving plate; top with fish and surround with carrots and celery.

Per serving: 244 calories; 34 g protein; 7 g fat; 10 g carbohydrate; 672 mg sodium

* See Spaghetti Squash Pesto recipe (page 249) for cooking instructions.

SWORDFISH KEBABS
See Menu Plan for Week 20.
Makes 2 servings

1 tablespoon lemon juice
1 teaspoon steak sauce
¼ teaspoon minced fresh garlic
⅛ teaspoon chervil leaves
12 ounces skinned and boned swordfish,
    cut into 1¼-inch cubes
2 medium green bell peppers, seeded and
    cut into 1¼-inch squares
10 cherry tomatoes

In bowl combine lemon juice, steak sauce, garlic, and chervil. Add swordfish cubes; toss to coat. Cover and marinate in refrigerator for 1 hour, turning pieces once or twice. Divide fish, peppers, and tomatoes into 2 equal portions; thread each portion onto 2 skewers, alternating ingredients. Set skewers on rack on grill or in broiler pan; grill over hot coals or broil about 4 inches from source of heat for 5 minutes, brushing occasionally with remaining marinade. Turn and cook 3 to 4 minutes longer or until fish is done.

Per serving: 235 calories; 34 g protein; 7 g fat;
8 g carbohydrate; 152 mg sodium

BAKED STRIPED BASS WITH VEGETABLES
See Menu Plan for Week 14.
Makes 2 servings

2 teaspoons olive oil
½ cup chopped onion
1 garlic clove, minced
1 cup canned tomatoes
2 tablespoons plus 1½ teaspoons chopped
    fresh parsley, divided
2 tablespoons chopped fresh dill
½ teaspoon salt, divided
Pepper
12 ounces striped bass fillets
1½ teaspoons lemon juice
2 cups spinach leaves
1 tablespoon plus 1 teaspoon white wine

Heat oil in saucepan. Add onion and garlic and sauté until onion is soft. Add tomatoes, 2 tablespoons parsley, the dill, ¼ teaspoon salt, and ⅛ teaspoon pepper; simmer 15 minutes.

Sprinkle fish with lemon juice, ⅛ teaspoon salt, and dash pepper. Spread tomato mixture in a shallow baking pan just large enough to hold fish in 1 layer; top with fillets. Arrange spinach leaves around fish; sprinkle with ⅛ teaspoon salt and dash pepper. Add wine.

Cover dish with foil and bake at 350°F. for 20 minutes or until fish flakes easily when tested with fork. Sprinkle with remaining parsley.

Per serving: 291 calories; 36 g protein; 10 g fat;
14 g carbohydrate; 889 mg sodium

FILLET OF SOLE FLORENTINE
See Menu Plans for Weeks 4, 23, 37, and 40.
Makes 2 servings

2 teaspoons margarine
1 tablespoon lemon juice
½ teaspoon salt, divided
½ teaspoon cornstarch, dissolved in
    2 tablespoons water
½ cup cooked and well-drained chopped
    spinach
¼ cup cooked sliced mushrooms
12 ounces fillet of sole
Dash each white pepper, garlic powder,
    and paprika
Thin lemon slices and chopped fresh
    parsley to garnish

Preheat oven to 400°F. Melt margarine in small saucepan; add lemon juice, ¼ teaspoon salt, and dissolved cornstarch. Cook, stirring constantly, until thickened. Spread spinach over bottom of shallow, oval-shaped, 3-cup casserole. Sprinkle with ¼ teaspoon salt. Spread mushrooms over spinach; place fish over vegetables and pour lemon sauce over fish. Sprinkle with seasonings and bake 15 minutes or until fish flakes when touched with a fork; then broil for 1 minute. Garnish with slices of lemon and chopped parsley.

Per serving: 189 calories; 30 g protein; 5 g fat;
4 g carbohydrate; 910 mg sodium

MACKEREL PATTIES
See Menu Plan for Week 26.
Makes 2 servings

1 tablespoon margarine
2 tablespoons minced onion
¼ cup minced celery
8 ounces cooked mackerel fillets, flaked
4 ounces pared and cooked potatoes,
   mashed
1 teaspoon chopped fresh parsley
⅛ teaspoon each salt and pepper
1 slice enriched white bread, lightly toasted
   and made into crumbs

Melt margarine in skillet; add onion and
sauté for 2 minutes. Add celery and cook
until softened. In bowl combine flaked
mackerel, mashed potatoes, onion-celery mixture, parsley, salt, and pepper. Form into 4
patties and coat with bread crumbs. Place
patties on nonstick baking sheet; bake at
350°F. for 8 minutes or until crumbs are
golden. Turn and bake patties for 8 to 10
minutes more.

Per serving: 397 calories; 29 g protein; 23 g fat;
16 g carbohydrate; 402 mg sodium

SALMON-ZUCCHINI KEBABS
See Menu Plan for Week 43.
Makes 2 servings

12 ounces boned salmon
2 tablespoons water
1 tablespoon plus 1 teaspoon white wine
1 tablespoon lemon juice
1 teaspoon chopped onion
1 garlic clove, chopped
½ teaspoon each salt and ground oregano
1½ cups sliced zucchini, ½-inch thick
   slices
2 medium tomatoes, each cut into 8 wedges

Cut fish into 2-inch squares. Combine water,
wine, lemon juice, onion, garlic, and seasonings in ceramic or glass bowl; stir well.
Add salmon, cover, and refrigerate for 3
hours, turning fish occasionally.
   Thread equal amounts of fish, zucchini,
and tomatoes onto each of 4 skewers,
alternating ingredients. Transfer skewers to
rack on grill or in broiler pan; spoon remaining marinade over kebabs. Grill over hot
coals or broil 6 inches from source of heat,
turning occasionally, 10 to 15 minutes or
until fish flakes easily.

Per serving: 294 calories; 37 g protein; 10 g fat;
10 g carbohydrate; 1,249 mg sodium

SEA TROUT WITH MUSHROOM STUFFING
See Menu Plans for Weeks 15 and 34.
Makes 2 servings

1 teaspoon margarine
1 tablespoon minced shallots
½ cup chopped mushrooms
2 tablespoons minced celery
1 tablespoon chopped pimiento
1 teaspoon lemon juice
¼ teaspoon salt
1 tablespoon chopped fresh parsley
2 teaspoons reduced-calorie mayonnaise
½ teaspoon prepared mustard
12 ounces sea trout fillets

Melt margarine in small nonstick skillet;
add shallots and sauté briefly, being careful
not to burn. Add mushrooms, celery, pimiento, lemon juice, and salt; sauté until
tender. Remove from heat and stir in parsley, mayonnaise, and mustard.
   Arrange fish fillets in baking pan. Spread
vegetable mixture over fillets and bake at
400°F. for about 20 minutes or until fish
flakes easily when tested with a fork.

Per serving: 249 calories; 29 g protein; 13 g fat;
4 g carbohydrate; 490 mg sodium

CALAMARI WITH SPAGHETTI

The word "calamari" is derived from the Latin *calamus*, which means pen. Calamari are squid with pen-shaped skeletal structures.

See Menu Plan for Week 21.
Makes 2 servings

2 teaspoons olive oil
½ cup sliced onion
3 garlic cloves, minced
12 ounces cut-up cleaned calamari
1 cup canned crushed plum tomatoes
1 teaspoon salt
Dash pepper
1⅓ cups hot cooked enriched spaghetti
1 tablespoon chopped fresh parsley

Heat oil in a small to medium saucepan. Add onion and garlic; sauté until translucent. Add squid; cook, stirring occasionally, until moisture evaporates. Add tomatoes, salt, and pepper. Simmer until squid are tender, approximately 45 minutes to 1 hour. Pour squid and sauce over spaghetti and sprinkle with parsley.

Per serving: 325 calories; 32 g protein; 7 g fat;
34 g carbohydrate; 1,635 mg sodium

FROGS' LEGS MEUNIÈRE

The French word *meunière* means miller. Appropriately enough, fish meunière is a classic French dish in which the fish has been dredged in flour, sautéed, cooked with lemon juice, and garnished with parsley. The flour thickens the natural juices of the fish, thus forming the meunière sauce. Frogs' Legs Meunière is a popular dish with those who enjoy French cuisine.

See Menu Plan for Week 34.
Makes 2 servings

1 pound frogs' legs
2 tablespoons plus 1½ teaspoons enriched flour
2 teaspoons margarine
1 garlic clove, minced
¾ cup Chicken Broth (see page 127)
2 tablespoons lemon juice
½ teaspoon salt

Dash white pepper
Chopped fresh parsley to garnish

Rinse frogs' legs in cold water; drain and dry. Dredge legs in flour; set aside. Melt margarine in nonstick skillet; add frogs' legs and sauté until golden brown on all sides. Add garlic and sauté briefly. Add broth, lemon juice, salt, and pepper; simmer 5 minutes. Sprinkle with chopped fresh parsley.

Per serving: 185 calories; 26 g protein; 4 g fat;
10 g carbohydrate; 720 mg sodium

SALMON CHOWDER

A quick and easy meal in less than 30 minutes. Since the ingredients can be kept on hand, this delicious chowder can be prepared at the end of any busy day.

See Menu Plan for Week 24.
Makes 2 servings

2 teaspoons margarine
½ cup diced onion
1 garlic clove, minced
½ cup chopped green bell pepper
1 tablespoon plus ¾ teaspoon enriched flour
2 cups water
1 cup canned tomatoes
¼ teaspoon thyme leaves
¼ teaspoon salt
Dash pepper
1 cup frozen or fresh whole-kernel corn
8 ounces drained, skinned, and boned canned salmon

Melt margarine in saucepan; add onion and garlic and sauté until onion is soft. Add green pepper and sauté a few minutes longer. Stir in flour and cook over low heat, stirring constantly, a few more minutes. Add water, tomatoes, thyme, salt, and pepper. Bring to a boil; reduce heat and simmer 15 minutes, stirring occasionally. Add corn and salmon, and simmer 5 minutes longer or until heated through.

Per serving: 332 calories; 29 g protein; 11 g fat;
32 g carbohydrate; 943 mg sodium

SALMON MOUSSE

This is a good dish to serve for a buffet meal.
See Menu Plan for Week 3.
Makes 2 servings

1½ teaspoons unflavored gelatin
¼ cup boiling water
2 tablespoons lemon juice
1 tablespoon minced onion
8 ounces drained, skinned, and boned
   canned salmon
½ cup skim milk
2 tablespoons plain unflavored yogurt
2 tablespoons reduced-calorie mayonnaise
2 teaspoons chopped fresh dill, or
   ½ teaspoon dill weed
½ teaspoon each white pepper and salt

Place gelatin in blender container. Add next 3 ingredients; process 30 seconds. Add remaining ingredients; process until smooth. Pour mixture into a 1-quart mold that has been rinsed in cold water. Chill for at least 4 hours. Unmold before serving.

Per serving: 242 calories; 28 g protein; 10 g fat;
8 g carbohydrate; 1,142 mg sodium

SALMON SALAD

See Menu Plan for Week 5 and various other weeks.
Makes 2 servings

1½ teaspoons dehydrated onion flakes
2 teaspoons hot water
½ teaspoon lemon juice
8 ounces drained, skinned, and boned
   canned salmon
¼ cup diced celery
¼ cup pared, seeded, and diced cucumber
¼ cup finely chopped carrot
1 tablespoon plus 1 teaspoon reduced-
   calorie mayonnaise
¼ teaspoon salt
Dash white pepper

Place onion flakes in small bowl; add hot water and lemon juice and let stand about 10 minutes. In a medium bowl combine all remaining ingredients. Add reconstituted onion flakes and stir to combine. Chill and serve.

Per serving: 196 calories; 24 g protein; 9 g fat;
5 g carbohydrate; 806 mg sodium

SARDINE SALAD

See Menu Plan for Week 2.
Makes 1 serving

4 ounces drained canned skinless and
   boneless sardines
1 tablespoon minced scallion
1 tablespoon reduced-calorie mayonnaise
½ teaspoon Dijon-style mustard
1 teaspoon lemon juice
Lettuce leaves

In a bowl mash sardines. Add scallion, mayonnaise, mustard, and lemon juice. Serve on a plate lined with lettuce leaves.

Per serving: 278 calories; 28 g protein; 16 g fat;
5 g carbohydrate; 1,086 mg sodium

CREAMY TUNA SALAD

See Menu Plan for Week 50.
Makes 2 servings

⅔ cup cottage cheese
½ teaspoon lemon juice
½ teaspoon Dijon-style mustard
Dash each salt and pepper
4 ounces drained canned tuna
¼ cup chopped celery heart with leaves

In blender container or work bowl of food processor combine cheese, lemon juice, mustard, salt, and pepper. Process until smooth. In small bowl combine cheese mixture, tuna, and celery. Chill before serving.

Per serving: 192 calories; 26 g protein; 9 g fat;
3 g carbohydrate; 873 mg sodium

ICEBERG-TOMATO RING
See Menu Plan for Week 23.
Makes 4 servings

1 envelope unflavored gelatin
¼ cup water
2 cups tomato juice
1 tablespoon Worcestershire sauce
Dash thyme leaves
1 cup chopped iceberg lettuce
¼ cup sliced scallions
1 pound drained canned tuna
1 medium cucumber, pared, seeded, and
   diced
¼ cup reduced-calorie mayonnaise
1 tablespoon drained capers, chopped
1 tablespoon lemon juice
Dash each salt and pepper
Parsley sprigs to garnish

In small saucepan sprinkle gelatin over water
and let stand 5 minutes to soften. Add tomato juice and heat, stirring constantly, until gelatin is dissolved. Stir in Worcestershire
and thyme. Arrange lettuce and scallions in
a 3-cup ring mold; pour in gelatin mixture.
Chill at least 4 hours or until set.
   Combine remaining ingredients except
parsley in bowl. Unmold gelatin onto serving
platter. Mound tuna mixture in center of
ring and garnish with parsley sprigs.

Per serving: 305 calories; 37 g protein; 12 g fat;
11 g carbohydrate; 1,275 mg sodium

TUNA BOATS
See Menu Plan for Week 4.
Makes 2 servings

8 ounces drained canned tuna
1 tablespoon plus 1 teaspoon mayonnaise
2 tablespoons diced pimiento
4 pitted green olives, finely sliced
2 teaspoons lemon juice
1 teaspoon pickle relish
2 celery ribs

In small bowl combine tuna and mayonnaise; add pimiento, olives, lemon juice, and
relish. Stuff each celery rib with ½ of mix-

ture. Wrap in plastic wrap and chill until
ready to use.

Per serving: 314 calories; 33 g protein; 18 g fat;
4 g carbohydrate; 1,222 mg sodium

TUNA CASSEROLE PARMESAN
See Menu Plan for Week 27.
Makes 4 servings

4 cups blanched broccoli florets
2 cups blanched sliced carrots
1 pound drained canned tuna
2 tablespoons margarine
2 tablespoons enriched flour
1 cup evaporated skimmed milk
¼ teaspoon marjoram leaves
Dash each garlic powder, salt, and white
   pepper
2 teaspoons grated Parmesan cheese

Combine broccoli, carrots, and tuna in a
2½-quart casserole. Melt margarine in small
saucepan over low heat; stirring constantly,
add flour. Using a wire whisk, gradually stir
in milk; continue to stir and cook until sauce
thickens. Stir in marjoram, garlic powder,
salt, and pepper. Pour sauce over broccoli-
tuna mixture. Sprinkle with Parmesan
cheese. Bake at 350°F. for 30 minutes.

Per serving: 426 calories; 45 g protein; 16 g fat;
25 g carbohydrate; 968 mg sodium

TUNA-CHEESE BURGERS
These burgers can be prepared in advance
and frozen for a quick and easy meal.
See Menu Plan for Week 49.
Makes 4 servings

1½ cups grated carrots
½ cup minced celery
½ cup minced onion
¼ cup diced green bell pepper, small dice
¼ cup chopped fresh parsley
2 packets instant chicken broth and
   seasoning mix
8 ounces drained canned tuna, flaked
2 whole wheat and bran matzo boards,
   made into crumbs

4 ounces hard cheese (Swiss, Cheddar, American, etc.), sliced
¼ cup ketchup

Combine first 6 ingredients in nonstick skillet; cook over medium heat, stirring occasionally, until vegetables are tender. Combine vegetables, tuna, and matzo crumbs in large mixing bowl; mix thoroughly. Divide into 8 equal portions. Form each portion into a patty and place on nonstick baking sheet. Bake at 400°F. for 15 minutes; turn and bake 5 minutes longer. Top each patty with ½ ounce cheese and bake 5 more minutes. Serve with ketchup.

Per serving: 343 calories; 29 g protein; 13 g fat; 28 g carbohydrate; 1,162 mg sodium

TUNA "NEWBURG"
See Menu Plan for Week 48.
Makes 2 servings

2 tablespoons minced onion
1 cup sliced mushrooms
1 teaspoon margarine
1 tablespoon enriched flour
½ cup each skim and evaporated skimmed milk
1 tablespoon lemon juice
2 teaspoons paprika
¼ teaspoon ground thyme
⅛ teaspoon each salt and white pepper
8 ounces drained canned white meat tuna, flaked
2 slices whole wheat bread, toasted and cut into 2 triangles each
Chopped fresh parsley to garnish

In a nonstick skillet cook onion until translucent. Add mushrooms and cook 2 to 3 minutes. Set aside.

Melt margarine in a skillet and stir flour into the margarine; cook, stirring with a wire whisk (to make a roux) 2 to 3 minutes.

Combine skim and evaporated skimmed milks in a small saucepan and scald over medium heat; add to the roux, stirring constantly, until mixture thickens. Reduce heat and stir in cooked vegetables. Add lemon juice and seasonings and stir to combine.

Stir in tuna and cook 3 to 5 minutes or until thoroughly heated. Divide into 2 portions and serve each with 2 toast triangles; garnish with parsley.

Per serving: 407 calories; 44 g protein; 13 g fat; 29 g carbohydrate; 1,316 mg sodium

TUNA-POTATO CAKES
See Menu Plan for Week 37.
Makes 2 servings

8 ounces pared potatoes, finely grated and squeezed to remove excess moisture
½ cup minced onion
2 teaspoons enriched flour
1 teaspoon honey (optional)
1 teaspoon lemon juice
4 ounces drained canned tuna
2 eggs, beaten
¼ teaspoon salt
¼ teaspoon ground allspice
Dash pepper

In medium bowl combine potatoes, onion, flour, honey if desired, and lemon juice; stir in tuna, eggs, salt, allspice, and pepper. Do not overmix (tuna should remain in small chunks). Heat medium nonstick skillet over medium heat. Spoon ½ of potato batter into skillet, making 2 equal pancakes. Spread each with back of spoon to form an even cake and brown on both sides. Repeat with remaining batter.

Per serving: 304 calories; 26 g protein; 10 g fat; 26 g carbohydrate; 877 mg sodium
With honey: 315 calories; 26 g protein; 10 g fat; 29 g carbohydrate; 877 mg sodium

TUNA RATATOUILLE

This dish is excellent hot or at room temperature. It can be prepared ahead and used as a quick and easy meal on a busy day.
See Menu Plan for Week 25.
Makes 2 servings

3 cups diced eggplant, ½-inch dice
1½ cups sliced zucchini, ¼-inch thick slices
¼ teaspoon salt
2 teaspoons olive oil
1 cup sliced onions
¼ cup diced celery with leaves
1 garlic clove, chopped
¼ teaspoon each oregano leaves and thyme leaves
Dash pepper
2 cups canned whole tomatoes, cut into chunks
8 ounces drained canned tuna

Place eggplant and zucchini in a single layer on paper towels; sprinkle with salt. Let stand 30 minutes; pat dry and set aside. In medium skillet heat oil. Add onions, celery, garlic, oregano, thyme, and pepper. Sauté over medium heat until onions are tender. Add tomatoes, eggplant, and zucchini. Cover and bring to a boil. Reduce heat and simmer, stirring occasionally, 30 to 40 minutes or until eggplant is tender; uncover and cook 10 minutes longer. Stir in tuna and cook 5 minutes longer.

Per serving: 411 calories; 40 g protein; 15 g fat; 30 g carbohydrate; 1,622 mg sodium

TUNA TOMATO FLOWERS

See Menu Plan for Week 38.
Makes 2 servings

2 medium tomatoes
Lettuce leaves
8 ounces drained canned tuna, flaked
1 cup diced celery
2 teaspoons mayonnaise
Chopped fresh parsley to garnish

Remove core from each tomato. Place core-side down and, slicing ¾ of the way down, cut each tomato into eighths; press wedges out to resemble a flower. Arrange a bed of lettuce leaves on each of 2 salad plates; top each with a tomato flower.

In bowl combine tuna, celery, and mayonnaise, mixing thoroughly. Spoon ½ of mixture into center of each tomato and garnish with parsley.

Per serving: 290 calories; 34 g protein; 13 g fat; 7 g carbohydrate; 1,004 mg sodium

BROILED SOFT-SHELL CRABS

See Menu Plans for Weeks 33 and 35.
Makes 2 servings

12 ounces cleaned soft-shell crabs (about 4 medium)
2 teaspoons margarine
½ teaspoon chopped fresh parsley
Dash each salt and pepper
Parsley sprigs to garnish

Broil crabs on rack in broiler pan, 4 inches from heat, 8 to 10 minutes, turning once; set aside. Melt margarine in large skillet; stir in parsley. Add crabs, sprinkle with salt and pepper, and sauté briefly, about 1 to 2 minutes. Serve garnished with parsley sprigs.

Per serving: 140 calories; 20 g protein; 6 g fat; 1 g carbohydrate; 349 mg sodium

CRAB MEAT MOLD

Lump crab meat is solid pieces of white meat from the body of the crab. This form of crab meat is preferable for this recipe and is also excellent for salads and cocktails.
See Menu Plan for Week 4.
Makes 2 servings

1 envelope unflavored gelatin
¼ cup water
½ cup boiling water
8 ounces cooked fresh or drained canned lump crab meat
½ cup plain unflavored yogurt
¼ cup minced onion
¼ cup thinly sliced celery
¼ cup minced green or red bell pepper
2 tablespoons lemon juice

1 tablespoon plus 1 teaspoon mayonnaise
1 teaspoon prepared mustard
Dash each Worcestershire sauce and hot
   sauce
1 medium tomato, sliced
2 teaspoons minced fresh parsley

In bowl sprinkle gelatin over ¼ cup water
and let stand to soften. Add boiling water
and stir constantly until gelatin is dissolved.
In another bowl combine remaining ingredients except tomato and parsley; stir in gelatin mixture. Pour into 2½-cup mold that has
been rinsed in cold water. Chill until firm,
at least 3 hours. Unmold onto serving plate.
Garnish with tomato slices and sprinkle with
parsley.

Per serving: 264 calories; 28 g protein; 12 g fat;
11 g carbohydrate; 1,257 mg sodium

CRAB MEAT SALAD
IN PITA BREAD
See Menu Plan for Week 11.
Makes 1 serving

4 ounces flaked cooked crab meat
2 tablespoons minced celery
2 tablespoons minced red bell pepper
1 tablespoon minced scallion
1 teaspoon minced fresh parsley
1 tablespoon reduced-calorie mayonnaise
2 teaspoons chili sauce
1 teaspoon lemon juice
Dash white pepper
1-ounce pita bread
Lettuce leaves

In bowl combine crab meat, celery, red pepper, scallion, and parsley. In small bowl stir
together mayonnaise, chili sauce, lemon
juice, and pepper; combine with crab meat
mixture. Split pita bread to form pocket;
line with lettuce leaves and fill with Crab
Meat Salad.

Per serving: 246 calories; 23 g protein; 6 g fat;
24 g carbohydrate; 488 mg sodium

SEAFOOD GARDEN SALAD
See Menu Plan for Week 41.
Makes 4 servings

2 cups fresh bean sprouts
1 cup shredded iceberg lettuce
1 cup shredded romaine lettuce
1 cup sliced zucchini, ¼-inch thick slices
1 cup diagonally sliced celery, thin slices
1 cup thinly sliced mushrooms, tossed with
   lemon juice
1 medium red bell pepper, seeded and cut
   into thin strips
1 medium tomato, cut into thin wedges
¼ cup thinly sliced red onion, separated
   into rings
1 tablespoon rice vinegar
8 ounces drained canned solid white tuna,
   separated into chunks
8 ounces cooked crab meat chunks
Thousand Island Dressing (see page 288)

Combine first 9 ingredients in serving bowl;
add rice vinegar and toss. Add tuna and crab
meat and toss gently to combine. Serve with
Thousand Island Dressing.

Per serving: 291 calories; 33 g protein; 11 g fat;
17 g carbohydrate; 750 mg sodium

CURRIED SEAFOOD SALAD
See Menu Plans for Weeks 22 and 39.
Makes 2 servings

8 ounces drained canned lobster or crab
   meat
½ cup thinly sliced mushrooms
¼ cup diced green bell pepper
1 tablespoon lemon juice, divided
Dash each salt and white pepper
¼ cup plain unflavored yogurt
2 teaspoons mayonnaise
½ to ¾ teaspoon curry powder
1 tablespoon chopped fresh parsley, divided
1 teaspoon chopped chives
1 medium tomato, cut into thin wedges
½ medium cucumber, scored and cut
   into 8 slices
Parsley sprigs to garnish

Set aside 3 or 4 pieces of seafood for garnish.

In bowl combine remaining seafood, mushrooms, green pepper, 2 teaspoons lemon juice, salt, and pepper. In small bowl mix yogurt with mayonnaise, curry powder, 2 teaspoons chopped parsley, chives, and remaining teaspoon of lemon juice. Pour over seafood mixture and toss gently to combine. Cover and chill 1 hour.

Spoon seafood salad onto center of serving platter. Surround with tomato wedges and cucumber slices, alternating vegetables. Sprinkle vegetables with remaining chopped parsley and garnish seafood with reserved pieces and parsley sprigs.

Per serving: 192 calories; 24 g protein; 7 g fat;
9 g carbohydrate; 383 mg sodium

LOBSTER IN CREAMY SAUCE
See Menu Plan for Week 52.
Makes 2 servings

2 teaspoons margarine
2 tablespoons chopped onion
1 tablespoon plus ¾ teaspoon enriched
   flour
1 cup skim milk, scalded
1 tablespoon plus 1 teaspoon white wine
1 tablespoon tomato paste
½ teaspoon Worcestershire sauce
⅛ teaspoon salt
Dash each white and ground red pepper
8 ounces cooked lobster meat
⅓ cup plus 2 teaspoons peas
1 slice enriched white bread, toasted and
   cut into 4 triangles
1 tablespoon chopped fresh parsley

Melt margarine in medium saucepan over low heat. Add onion and sauté until translucent; add flour and cook, stirring constantly, 2 to 3 minutes. Gradually pour in milk, stirring constantly with a wire whisk; continue to stir and cook until mixture thickens. Stir in wine, tomato paste, Worcestershire, salt, and peppers. Stir in lobster meat and peas; heat thoroughly. Arrange bread triangles on serving plate; spoon lobster mixture over bread and sprinkle with parsley.

Per serving: 276 calories; 29 g protein; 6 g fat;
23 g carbohydrate; 654 mg sodium

MUSSEL-RICE CASSEROLE
See Menu Plan for Week 45.
Makes 2 servings

2 teaspoons margarine
½ cup chopped onion
1 cup sliced mushrooms
½ cup minced celery
¼ cup raisins
2 tablespoons chopped fresh parsley
2 teaspoons lemon juice
½ teaspoon salt
Dash pepper
2 teaspoons cornstarch
¾ cup Chicken Broth (see page 127),
   at room temperature
8 ounces cleaned, steamed, and shucked
   mussels,* approximately 40
1 cup cooked enriched rice
Lemon slices and parsley sprigs to garnish

In large nonstick skillet melt margarine. Add onion and sauté until onion is just translucent; add next 7 ingredients. In small bowl or measuring cup dissolve cornstarch in broth; add to vegetable mixture and cook, stirring constantly, until slightly thickened. Add mussels and rice. Transfer mixture to

2-quart casserole that has been sprayed with nonstick cooking spray; bake at 375°F. for 20 minutes. Serve garnished with lemon slices and parsley sprigs.

Per serving: 366 calories; 25 g protein; 8 g fat; 49 g carbohydrate; 981 mg sodium

To test mussels for freshness: Hold mussel between thumb and index finger and press laterally, as if sliding the shells across one another. If the shells move, the mussel isn't fresh; a live mussel will remain rigid.

To clean mussels: Scrub mussels with a stiff brush under cold water. Pull off the "beard" and scrape away small barnacles on shells. Discard any shells that are not tightly closed.

To steam mussels: Place mussels in large pot with about 1 inch boiling water. Cover and steam over moderate heat 3 minutes or just until shells open, discarding any that do not open. Drain and remove meat from shells. Weigh 8 ounces.

MUSSEL STEW
See Menu Plan for Week 42.
Makes 2 servings

2 teaspoons olive oil
1 cup chopped onions
2 teaspoons minced fresh garlic
2 cups canned crushed tomatoes
2 tablespoons chopped fresh basil, or 2 teaspoons dried
1 tablespoon plus 1 teaspoon dry white wine
½ teaspoon salt
Dash freshly ground pepper
8 ounces cleaned, steamed, and shucked mussels (about 40),* strain and reserve 1 cup cooking liquid
Chopped fresh parsley to garnish

Heat oil in large skillet; add onions and garlic and sauté briefly. Add tomatoes and basil; simmer for 20 minutes. Stir in wine, salt, and pepper. Add mussels and reserved cooking liquid to sauce. Simmer about 3 minutes. Garnish with parsley.

Per serving: 273 calories; 25 g protein; 9 g fat; 22 g carbohydrate; 1,204 mg sodium

* See Mussel-Rice Casserole (page 220) for cleaning and steaming directions.

OYSTER STEW
See Menu Plan for Week 23.
Makes 2 servings

1 tablespoon plus 1 teaspoon margarine
1 tablespoon plus 1 teaspoon enriched flour
1 tablespoon Worcestershire sauce
1 cup skim milk
8 ounces drained canned oysters
Dash each hot sauce, ground thyme, and salt
1 tablespoon chopped fresh parsley

Melt margarine in medium saucepan; stir in flour and Worcestershire sauce. Stirring constantly with a wire whisk, gradually add milk; cook, stirring constantly, until thickened. Add oysters and cook, stirring gently, for 2 minutes or until hot. Add remaining ingredients and serve immediately.

Per serving: 221 calories; 15 g protein; 10 g fat; 16 g carbohydrate; 680 mg sodium

TANGY OYSTER-VEGETABLE MEDLEY
See Menu Plan for Week 22.
Makes 2 servings

12 ounces shucked oysters*
1 cup clam juice
1 cup whole green beans, steamed
1 cup sliced zucchini, ¼-inch thick slices, steamed
1 tablespoon plus 1 teaspoon chili sauce
1 teaspoon prepared mustard
1 teaspoon prepared horseradish
1 teaspoon lemon juice
Dash each salt and pepper
10 cherry tomatoes

Combine oysters and clam juice in saucepan; bring to a simmer and cook until edges start to curl, about 3 minutes. Remove from heat and set aside.

In 10-inch nonstick skillet combine green beans, zucchini, chili sauce, mustard, horseradish, and lemon juice. Cook over medium heat, stirring occasionally, 3 to 5 minutes. Drain oysters, discarding juice. Combine salt and pepper with vegetables and cook 3 minutes longer. Stir in oysters. Transfer to serving platter and surround with cherry tomatoes.

Per serving: 189 calories; 20 g protein; 4 g fat; 20 g carbohydrate; 963 mg sodium

* To shuck an oyster, hold it firmly with the hinged end of the shell in the palm of your hand. Push the blade of a thick, round-nosed oyster knife between the shells near the hinge. Run it around until you cut through the muscle holding both valves together.

FAR EAST SCALLOPS
A delicious meal in less than 30 minutes.
See Menu Plan for Week 51.
Makes 2 servings

2 teaspoons vegetable oil
½ cup sliced onion
½ teaspoon minced fresh garlic
1 cup sliced mushrooms
1 cup broccoli florets, blanched
½ cup drained canned sliced bamboo shoots
2 teaspoons soy sauce
Dash sherry extract
12 ounces scallops
1 packet instant beef broth and seasoning mix, dissolved in ¾ cup hot water
2 teaspoons cornstarch
1 tablespoon water

Heat oil in wok or skillet. Add onion and garlic and sauté about 1 minute. Add mushrooms, broccoli, and bamboo shoots; stir-fry over high heat about 3 minutes. Stir in soy sauce and extract. Add scallops and stir-fry 3 minutes. Pour in dissolved broth mix. Dissolve cornstarch in water and add to scallop mixture. Cook, stirring constantly, about 3 minutes or until thickened.

Per serving: 259 calories; 32 g protein; 6 g fat; 21 g carbohydrate; 1,201 mg sodium

SCALLOP BISQUE
See Menu Plan for Week 44.
Makes 4 servings

1 tablespoon plus 1 teaspoon margarine
2 medium tomatoes, peeled, seeded, and diced
1½ cups thinly sliced mushrooms
1 cup chopped onions
½ cup chopped leeks, white portion only
½ cup diced celery
1 cup each clam juice and water
1 teaspoon salt
½ teaspoon each freshly ground pepper and thyme leaves
8 ounces pared and diced potatoes
12 ounces scallops, sliced
1 tablespoon plus 1 teaspoon enriched flour
1 cup skim milk
Chopped fresh parsley to garnish

Melt margarine in medium saucepan. Add next 5 ingredients and cook over low heat for about 5 minutes, stirring frequently. Add clam juice, water, salt, pepper, and thyme. Cook 15 minutes longer. Add potatoes and cook an additional 20 minutes. Stir in scallops. Dissolve flour in milk; pour into soup mixture and cook, stirring constantly, until thickened and thoroughly heated. *Do not boil.* Pour into soup bowls and garnish with parsley.

Per serving: 244 calories; 21 g protein; 5 g fat; 30 g carbohydrate; 1,151 mg sodium

SEVICHE

Seviche's flavor is improved the longer it marinates.
See Menu Plan for Week 12.
Makes 4 servings

¾ cup freshly squeezed lime juice
   (from about 6 limes)
1 pound bay scallops
¼ cup sliced onion
¼ cup drained canned green chili peppers,
   seeded
1 tablespoon vegetable oil
1 teaspoon ground coriander
Dash each salt and freshly ground pepper

Pour lime juice over scallops in glass or ceramic bowl. Refrigerate 4 hours, stirring occasionally. Add remaining ingredients; toss to combine. Refrigerate at least 2 hours longer.

Per serving: 144 calories; 18 g protein; 4 g fat; 10 g carbohydrate; 338 mg sodium

CREAMED SHRIMP PASTA
See Menu Plan for Week 35.
Makes 2 servings

2 cups sliced mushrooms
¼ garlic clove, minced
Salt
2 teaspoons margarine
1 tablespoon enriched flour
1 cup skim milk
8 ounces peeled and deveined cooked
   shrimp, cut into ½-inch pieces
½ teaspoon lemon juice
⅛ teaspoon grated lemon rind
Pepper

1⅓ cups cooked enriched margherite*
   or spaghetti, hot
¼ teaspoon chopped fresh parsley

Combine mushrooms, garlic, and ¼ teaspoon salt in medium nonstick skillet; cook over medium heat until mushrooms are tender and moisture evaporated.

Melt margarine in medium saucepan; stirring constantly, add flour and cook over medium heat for 1 minute. Add milk gradually, stirring briskly with a wire whisk; cook, stirring continually, until sauce begins to thicken. Add mushroom mixture, ¼ teaspoon salt, shrimp, lemon juice, lemon rind, and dash pepper; cook until shrimp is thoroughly heated.

On serving platter toss pasta with parsley and dash each salt and pepper; top with shrimp sauce.

Per serving: 356 calories; 38 g protein; 6 g fat; 36 g carbohydrate; 891 mg sodium

* Margherite is *coiled* spaghetti; it adds an interesting texture to this dish.

PAPAYA SHRIMP
See Menu Plan for Week 37.
Makes 4 servings

1½ pounds peeled and deveined medium
    shrimp, reserve shells
1 quart plus 1 cup water
1 celery rib, cut into pieces
½ medium onion
3 parsley stems
5 peppercorns
⅛ teaspoon each basil leaves and thyme
    leaves
1 cup julienne celery
1 cup julienne carrots
1 medium papaya, pared, seeded, and cut
    into ⅛-inch thick slices
¼ teaspoon salt
2 teaspoons lemon juice

In large saucepan combine reserved shells, water, celery rib, onion, parsley, peppercorns, basil, and thyme; cover and bring to a boil. Reduce heat and simmer 1 to 1½ hours. Strain liquid, reserving shells and vegetables; return liquid to saucepan. Place shells and vegetables in double layer of cheesecloth; twist and squeeze juices into liquid. Discard solids. Boil shrimp broth down to 1½ cups; skim scum periodically.

Pour reduced broth into 12-inch skillet; cover and bring to a simmer. Add julienne vegetables; cover and cook 2 to 3 minutes. Add papaya and salt; carefully stir shrimp into mixture, cover, and simmer until shrimp is just cooked through, 3 to 4 minutes. *Do not overcook.* Sprinkle with lemon juice and serve.

Per serving: 208 calories; 32 g protein; 2 g fat;
16 g carbohydrate; 493 mg sodium

SAUTÉED SHRIMP AND CORN
See Menu Plan for Week 46.
Makes 2 servings

1½ teaspoons margarine
½ teaspoon sesame oil
1 cup chopped scallions
1 garlic clove, minced
1 cup drained canned whole-kernel corn
1 teaspoon each brown sugar and salt
Dash freshly ground pepper
12 ounces peeled and deveined shrimp
2 teaspoons cornstarch, dissolved in
    ¼ cup water
Chopped fresh parsley to garnish

Heat margarine and oil in medium skillet. Add scallions and garlic and sauté briefly. Stir in corn, sugar, salt, and pepper; cook about 3 minutes. Add shrimp and sauté 3 minutes longer. Add dissolved cornstarch and cook, stirring constantly, until thickened. Serve garnished with chopped parsley.

Per serving: 321 calories; 34 g protein; 6 g fat;
35 g carbohydrates; 1,693 mg sodium

SHRIMP ON TOAST
See Menu Plan for Week 20.
Makes 2 servings

2 teaspoons margarine
1 tablespoon enriched flour
1 cup skim milk, scalded
1 teaspoon tomato paste
⅛ teaspoon each salt, paprika, and
    powdered mustard
Dash hot sauce
4 ounces cooked, peeled, and deveined
    shrimp, cut into ½-inch pieces
2 slices whole wheat bread, toasted
2 small parsley sprigs

Melt margarine in saucepan; stir in flour and cook, stirring constantly, for 2 minutes. Remove from heat. Gradually add milk. Stir in tomato paste, salt, paprika, mustard, and hot sauce. Cook, stirring constantly, for 5 minutes or until sauce is thickened and smooth. Add shrimp and heat 2 minutes. Spoon ½ of mixture over each slice of toast and garnish with a parsley sprig.

Per serving: 215 calories; 21 g protein; 5 g fat;
21 g carbohydrate; 483 mg sodium

SHRIMP OREGANO
See Menu Plan for Week 41.
Makes 2 servings

1 tablespoon lemon juice
1 tablespoon chopped fresh parsley
2 teaspoons mayonnaise
2 teaspoons enriched flour
½ teaspoon Dijon-style mustard
½ teaspoon minced fresh garlic
¼ teaspoon oregano leaves
1 pound large shrimp
½ teaspoon salt

Combine all ingredients except shrimp and salt in small bowl. Remove shell from underside of shrimp, leaving back and tail intact. To remove vein, hold shrimp so that underside is up and slice down its length. Do not slice through back of shell. Wash under cold running water. Spread shrimp open. Sprinkle each with salt and fill each with an equal amount of mayonnaise mixture. Transfer to shallow nonstick baking pan. Bake at 400°F. for 15 to 20 minutes.

Per serving: 191 calories; 29 g protein; 6 g fat;
5 g carbohydrate; 871 mg sodium

SHRIMP SCAMPI
See Menu Plans for Weeks 1, 24, 27, and 40.
Makes 4 servings

1 tablespoon plus 1 teaspoon margarine
¼ cup diced red bell pepper
1 small garlic clove, finely chopped with
    ½ teaspoon salt
1½ pounds peeled and deveined medium
    or jumbo shrimp
⅓ cup plus 2 teaspoons plain dried
    bread crumbs
1 teaspoon chopped fresh parsley

Melt margarine in 12-inch skillet; add pepper and garlic and sauté over medium heat 1 minute. Add shrimp and sauté, turning occasionally, until shrimp are cooked, about 4 minutes. Be careful not to overcook or shrimp will be dry and tough. Using a slotted spoon, remove shrimp; keep warm. Stir bread crumbs into margarine mixture in skillet; cook, stirring occasionally, until bread crumbs are well toasted. Stir in parsley. Divide shrimp onto 4 plates. Top each portion of shrimp with an equal amount of bread-crumb mixture.

Per serving: 207 calories; 30 g protein; 5 g fat;
8 g carbohydrate; 564 mg sodium

Legumes and Peanut Butter

Legumes are food plants whose pods open along two seams when
the seeds within are ripe. The seeds are usually the edible part of
the legume. Peas, chick peas (garbanzos), lima beans, soybeans,
and lentils are the best known. High in nutrition, easy to prepare,
and very economical, legumes are also delicious. That is probably
why they have been cultivated and consumed for over 8,000 years.

CHICK PEA CROQUETTES (FALAFEL)
See Menu Plans for Weeks 9, 31, and 45.
Makes 2 servings

12 ounces drained canned chick peas (garbanzos)
3 tablespoons plain dried bread crumbs
½ garlic clove, finely chopped with ½ teaspoon salt
¼ teaspoon each basil leaves, ground marjoram, and thyme leaves
¼ teaspoon hot sauce
Dash ground red pepper
Cilantro to garnish
1 cup plain unflavored yogurt

Preheat oven to 350°F. In blender container or work bowl of food processor process chick peas until finely chopped. Transfer to bowl. Add remaining ingredients except yogurt; mix well, making sure seasonings are well distributed. Spray baking sheet with nonstick cooking spray. Shape mixture into 10 balls. Place on baking sheet and bake 13 minutes. Garnish with cilantro and serve with yogurt.

Per serving: 308 calories; 17 g protein; 7 g fat; 46 g carbohydrate; 675 mg sodium (sodium data unavailable for chick peas)

CHILLED SQUASH AND CHICK PEA SALAD
See Menu Plan for Week 39.
Makes 2 servings

3 cups cooked spaghetti squash*
6 ounces drained canned chick peas (garbanzos)
¼ cup minced carrot
1 tablespoon plus 1 teaspoon lemon juice
2 teaspoons olive oil
1 teaspoon chopped fresh parsley
½ teaspoon salt
Dash pepper

In medium bowl combine squash, peas, and carrot. Whisk remaining ingredients together in small bowl and combine with squash mixture. Cover and refrigerate at least 1 hour. Toss before serving.

Per serving: 189 calories; 7 g protein; 7 g fat; 28 g carbohydrate; 560 mg sodium (sodium data unavailable for chick peas)

* See Spaghetti Squash Pesto recipe (page 249) for cooking directions.

GARBANZO-STUFFED PEPPERS
If you're serving only two, remaining peppers may be frozen for use at another meal.
See Menu Plans for Weeks 41, 43, and 52.
Makes 4 servings

4 medium green bell peppers
1 cup diced celery
½ cup diced onion
12 ounces drained canned chick peas (garbanzos), mashed
1 cup canned crushed tomatoes
1 tablespoon basil leaves
⅛ teaspoon each salt and pepper

Cut tops from peppers and remove seeds. Remove stem from top portion, leaving a hole in the top. Parboil peppers and tops 5 minutes; drain and set aside. Preheat oven to 375°F.

Combine celery and onion in nonstick skillet and cook until tender. Transfer to a bowl; add remaining ingredients and mix thoroughly. Spoon ¼ of mixture into each pepper. Replace tops, pressing down gently so that some of mixture comes through hole in center of pepper top.

Place stuffed peppers in nonstick baking pan just large enough to hold peppers tightly. Bake 40 to 50 minutes or until lightly browned.

Per serving: 102 calories; 5 g protein; 1 g fat; 20 g carbohydrate; 173 mg sodium (sodium data unavailable for chick peas)

LUNCH BOX CHICK PEA SANDWICH
See Menu Plan for Week 38.
Makes 2 servings

6 ounces drained canned chick peas (garbanzos), mashed
4 ounces skinned and boned cooked chicken, cut into small dice
½ cup minced carrot
2 teaspoons mayonnaise
1 teaspoon sesame seeds, toasted and minced
¼ teaspoon salt
Dash each pepper, ground sage, and ground allspice
4 slices rye bread

Combine all ingredients except bread in medium bowl; mix well. Spread each of 2 slices of bread with ½ of the mixture and top with 1 of the remaining bread slices.

Per serving: 384 calories; 27 g protein; 11 g fat; 46 g carbohydrate; 644 mg sodium (sodium data unavailable for chick peas)

SAUTÉED CHICK PEAS ITALIAN STYLE
See Menu Plan for Week 23.
Makes 2 servings

1 tablespoon olive oil
2 garlic cloves, minced
12 ounces drained canned chick peas (garbanzos)
½ cup tomato sauce
¼ cup water
½ teaspoon oregano leaves
Dash each salt and pepper
2 teaspoons chopped fresh parsley
1 teaspoon grated Parmesan cheese

Heat oil in medium saucepan; add garlic and sauté 2 minutes. Add remaining ingredients except parsley and cheese and cook 20 minutes, stirring frequently. Sprinkle evenly with parsley and Parmesan cheese.

Per serving: 303 calories; 14 g protein; 11 g fat; 40 g carbohydrate; 428 mg sodium (sodium data unavailable for chick peas)

SPLIT PEA-MUSHROOM STEW
See Menu Plan for Week 47.
Makes 2 servings

1½ cups Beef Broth (see page 127) or beef bouillon
4 ounces uncooked green split peas
½ cup water
½ cup cut green beans, 1-inch pieces
¼ cup tomato paste
2 cups sliced mushrooms
Dash each salt and pepper
¼ teaspoon lemon juice
¼ teaspoon chili powder
⅛ teaspoon ground cumin
Few drops Worcestershire sauce
⅔ cup cooked enriched macaroni shells

Combine broth and peas in medium saucepan. Cover and bring to a boil. Reduce heat and simmer until peas are tender, about 20 minutes. Add water, green beans, and tomato paste; continue simmering for 5 minutes longer.

In medium skillet combine mushrooms, salt, and pepper. Cook over medium heat, stirring occasionally, until mushrooms are tender. Add mushrooms (plus any pan liquids), lemon juice, chili powder, cumin, and Worcestershire to peas. Simmer 10 minutes longer. Stir in macaroni shells and cook until heated.

Per serving: 323 calories; 20 g protein; 1 g fat; 60 g carbohydrate; 398 mg sodium

SPLIT PEA SOUP
See Menu Plan for Week 37.
Makes 2 servings

4 ounces uncooked green split peas
3 cups water
½ medium onion (about ¼ cup)
3 parsley stems
1 cup diced carrots, ¼-inch dice
½ cup diced celery, ¼-inch dice
⅛ teaspoon thyme leaves
⅛ teaspoon chervil leaves
Dash white pepper
2 teaspoons margarine

2 teaspoons enriched flour
½ cup skim milk
½ teaspoon salt

In medium saucepan combine peas, water, onion, and parsley stems. Cover and bring to a boil. Reduce heat and simmer until peas are soft, about 20 to 25 minutes. Remove and discard onion and parsley stems. Strain peas, returning liquid to saucepan. Set peas aside. Add carrots, celery, thyme, chervil, and pepper to saucepan. Cover and simmer until vegetables are tender, about 5 to 10 minutes. Stir in reserved peas and remove from heat.

In small saucepan melt margarine. Stirring constantly, add flour and cook 2 minutes. Add milk gradually, stirring briskly with a wire whisk until smooth. Cook over medium heat, stirring occasionally, until mixture comes just to a boil and thickens. Briskly stir milk mixture into soup; add salt and heat through, about 5 minutes. Serve at once.

Per serving: 298 calories; 17 g protein; 5 g fat; 49 g carbohydrate; 713 mg sodium

CREAMED CANNELLINI 'N' PASTA
See Menu Plan for Week 10.
Makes 2 servings

½ cup finely chopped mushrooms
Salt
2 teaspoons margarine
⅛ teaspoon minced fresh garlic
⅛ teaspoon oregano leaves
Dash pepper
2 teaspoons enriched flour
1 cup skim milk
6 ounces cooked cannellini beans (white kidney beans)
1⅓ cups cooked enriched spiral or elbow macaroni

Combine mushrooms and dash salt in small skillet. Cook over medium heat, stirring occasionally, until most of liquid is evaporated; set aside.

Melt margarine in small saucepan. Add garlic, oregano, and pepper; cook over medium heat until margarine begins to foam. Stirring constantly, add flour and cook 2 minutes. Remove from heat. Slowly pour in milk, stirring briskly with a wire whisk. Stir until margarine and flour are well blended with milk. Add ¼ teaspoon salt, return to heat, and slowly bring to a boil, stirring occasionally. Reduce heat to low. Add mushrooms, beans, and macaroni to sauce and stir to combine; cook 2 to 3 minutes or until thoroughly heated.

Per serving: 271 calories; 13 g protein; 5 g fat; 43 g carbohydrate; 474 mg sodium

CURRIED KIDNEY BEANS
See Menu Plan for Week 12.
Makes 2 servings

1 tablespoon vegetable oil
½ cup chopped onion
1 small apple, cored and diced
1 garlic clove, minced
1 tablespoon enriched flour
2 teaspoons curry powder
¾ cup Chicken Broth (see page 127)
12 ounces drained canned kidney beans
Dash each salt and pepper
2 tablespoons sliced scallion

Heat oil in saucepan; add onion, apple, and garlic and sauté until tender. Stir in flour and curry powder and cook over low heat, stirring constantly, for 2 minutes. Stirring with a wire whisk, gradually add broth; cook, stirring constantly, until sauce thickens. Add kidney beans and cook until heated. Add salt and pepper and garnish with scallion.

Per serving: 283 calories; 11 g protein; 9 g fat; 43 g carbohydrate; 632 mg sodium

"REFRIED" BEANS

Our version of the Mexican favorite, made typically spicy by the addition of chili powder and cumin.
See Menu Plan for Week 19.
Makes 2 servings

2 teaspoons vegetable oil
½ cup chopped onion
1 garlic clove, minced
6 ounces drained canned kidney beans
2 tablespoons tomato paste
2 teaspoons chili powder
⅛ teaspoon ground cumin
Dash salt
2 ounces grated Cheddar cheese

Heat oil in small skillet; add onion and garlic and sauté until tender. Add kidney beans, tomato paste, chili powder, cumin, and salt; cook, stirring often, for 5 minutes. Spray small casserole with nonstick cooking spray and add bean mixture. Top with Cheddar cheese and bake at 350°F. for 10 to 15 minutes or until cheese is melted.

Per serving: 266 calories; 13 g protein; 15 g fat; 21 g carbohydrate; 428 mg sodium

PINTO BEAN SALAD

See Menu Plans for Weeks 24 and 27.
Makes 2 servings

12 ounces cooked pinto beans
1 medium tomato, cut into 1-inch pieces
¼ cup diced green bell pepper
2 tablespoons diced red onion
2 tablespoons minced fresh parsley
3 tablespoons red wine vinegar
2 teaspoons vegetable oil
1 small garlic clove, minced
⅛ teaspoon powdered mustard
Dash each salt and pepper

In serving bowl combine beans, tomato, green pepper, onion, and parsley. Combine remaining ingredients in a small bowl; mix well. Pour over bean salad and toss. Cover and chill for 4 hours. Let stand at room temperature about ½ hour before serving.

Per serving: 192 calories; 9 g protein; 6 g fat; 29 g carbohydrate; 104 mg sodium

SAVORY PINTO BEANS

A hearty main dish that's easy on the budget.
See Menu Plan for Week 14.
Makes 2 servings

2 teaspoons vegetable oil
½ cup chopped onion
1 garlic clove, minced
1 cup canned tomatoes
1 tablespoon tomato paste
½ teaspoon each ground cumin and ground coriander
¼ teaspoon salt
⅛ teaspoon ground turmeric
½ cup water
12 ounces cooked pinto beans

Heat oil in saucepan; add onion and garlic and sauté until softened. Add tomatoes, tomato paste, cumin, coriander, salt, and turmeric; stir. Add water and bring to a boil; reduce heat and simmer 10 minutes. Add beans, cover, and simmer 5 minutes. Remove cover and simmer 5 minutes longer.

Per serving: 219 calories; 10 g protein; 6 g fat; 36 g carbohydrate; 519 mg sodium

BEAN AND SQUASH SOUP

This soup freezes well.
See Menu Plan for Week 2.
Makes 4 servings

2 tablespoons margarine
½ cup minced onion
1 small garlic clove, minced
1 quart water
1½ pounds cooked great northern beans
1½ cups pared and cubed butternut squash
2 packets instant chicken broth and seasoning mix
2 teaspoons minced fresh ginger root
Dash pepper

Melt margarine in saucepan; add onion and garlic and sauté until softened. Add water, beans, squash, broth mix, and ginger root. Cook mixture for 30 minutes or until beans and squash are very soft. Put mixture through a food mill or transfer to work bowl of food processor and process till pureed. Reheat; add pepper. Stir in a little more water if soup is too thick.

Per serving: 291 calories; 15 g protein; 7 g fat; 46 g carbohydrate; 455 mg sodium

LENTIL AND ESCAROLE SOUP
See Menu Plan for Week 8.
Makes 4 servings

4 ounces uncooked lentils
1½ quarts water
1 cup diced onions
1 cup diced carrots
1 cup diced celery
½ cup tomato juice
1 tablespoon plus 1 teaspoon olive oil
1 tablespoon minced fresh garlic
4 cups chopped escarole

Rinse lentils well. Place in large pot with water and bring to a boil; reduce heat, cover, and simmer about 40 minutes. Add remaining ingredients except escarole. Simmer until vegetables and lentils are just tender, about 20 minutes. Add escarole and simmer 15 minutes longer. Serve immediately.

Per serving: 201 calories; 10 g protein; 5 g fat; 31 g carbohydrate; 133 mg sodium

MEXICAN SOUP
See Menu Plan for Week 13.
Makes 4 servings

1 tablespoon vegetable oil
½ cup chopped onion
½ cup chopped celery
½ cup chopped green bell pepper
1 garlic clove, minced
12 ounces drained canned pink beans
¼ teaspoon each pepper and chili powder
Dash hot sauce
2 cups Beef Broth (see page 127)
4 corn tortillas, 6-inch diameter each, toasted
4 ounces shredded Cheddar cheese

Heat oil in medium saucepan; add onion, celery, green pepper, and garlic and sauté, stirring often, until vegetables are tender. Add beans, pepper, chili powder, and hot sauce; cook 5 minutes longer, stirring often. Add broth and bring to a boil. Reduce heat and simmer 10 minutes. Divide soup evenly into 4 ovenproof soup crocks. Break each tortilla into 10 pieces and place 1 broken tortilla on top of each portion of the soup. Top each with 1 ounce Cheddar cheese. Broil 3 to 5 minutes or until cheese melts.

Per serving: 273 calories; 13 g protein; 14 g fat; 26 g carbohydrate; 397 mg sodium

BEAN CURD SOUP
This recipe makes use of a variety of Chinese vegetables; most are readily available canned or frozen. Chinese cabbage and fresh snow peas can be purchased in Oriental food markets. Surprise your friends by telling them that you have used *Sui Choy* (Chinese cabbage) and *Sit Dow* (snow peas)!
See Menu Plan for Week 23.
Makes 4 servings

1½ quarts Chicken Broth (see page 127)
1 pound tofu (soybean curd), cut into cubes
1½ cups shredded Chinese cabbage
6 ounces boneless boiled ham, cut into thin strips
½ cup drained canned sliced bamboo shoots
¼ cup thinly sliced drained canned water chestnuts
1 to 2 tablespoons soy sauce
½ cup halved trimmed Chinese snow peas (strings and ends removed)

Combine all ingredients except snow peas in saucepan; bring to a boil. Reduce heat and simmer 15 minutes. Add snow peas and simmer 2 minutes longer.

Per serving: 215 calories; 23 g protein; 9 g fat; 11 g carbohydrate; 958 mg sodium

CHICKEN AND LEGUMES CASSEROLE

This dish is filling and easy on the budget.
See Menu Plans for Weeks 43 and 46.
Makes 2 servings

1½ pounds skinned chicken necks and
    backs
2 medium carrots, cut into chunks
1 large celery rib, cut into chunks
1 medium onion, cut in half
Salt, pepper, and thyme leaves
2 teaspoons margarine
2 teaspoons enriched flour
4 ounces tofu (soybean curd), diced
3 ounces cooked frozen lima beans

In medium saucepan combine chicken necks, carrots, celery, onion, and dash each salt, pepper, and thyme; add enough water to cover. Bring to a boil; reduce heat and simmer until necks are cooked, 1½ to 2 hours. Remove solids from broth, discarding vegetables. Pick 4 ounces meat from bones; refrigerate meat and discard bones. Refrigerate broth until fat congeals on top.

Remove and discard congealed fat. Strain broth through a cheesecloth; measure ¾ cup. Any remaining broth can be refrigerated or frozen for use at another time. Melt margarine in small saucepan; add flour and cook, stirring constantly, for 1 minute. Using a wire whisk briskly stir in broth, stirring until flour is absorbed. Add ¼ teaspoon salt and dash each thyme and pepper. Cook over medium heat, stirring constantly, until sauce begins to thicken.

Combine neck meat, tofu, lima beans, and sauce in 1½-quart casserole. Bake at 350°F. about 30 minutes or until heated through.

Per serving: 301 calories; 27 g protein; 11 g fat; 26 g carbohydrate; 459 mg sodium

STUFFED CHERRY TOMATOES

See Menu Plan for Week 20.
Makes 2 servings

4 ounces tofu (soybean curd)
2 tablespoons minced green bell pepper
1 tablespoon minced celery
2 teaspoons minced scallion
2 tablespoons reduced-calorie mayonnaise
½ teaspoon Dijon-style mustard
¼ teaspoon salt
Dash white pepper
10 cherry tomatoes, cut into halves

In a small bowl mash tofu. Add green pepper, celery, scallion, mayonnaise, mustard, salt, and pepper; stir to combine. Cut a small piece of skin from the bottom of each tomato half so that it will stand upright; reserve cut skin. Mound an equal amount of tofu mixture on each tomato half and garnish with reserved skin. Chill at least 1 hour.

Per serving: 92 calories; 5 g protein; 6 g fat; 7 g carbohydrate; 417 mg sodium

TOFU, BEANS, AND EGGPLANT

See Menu Plan for Week 6.
Makes 2 servings

4 cups pared and cubed eggplant, ½-inch
    cubes
½ teaspoon salt
1¼ cups canned whole tomatoes
1 cup tomato puree
1 teaspoon honey
½ teaspoon oregano leaves
¼ teaspoon thyme leaves
⅛ teaspoon ground allspice
Dash white pepper
8 ounces tofu (soybean curd), cubed
6 ounces drained canned red kidney beans

Place eggplant cubes on a rack over a pan and sprinkle with salt; let stand 30 minutes to release moisture. In saucepan combine tomatoes, tomato puree, honey, oregano, thyme, allspice, and white pepper. Add eggplant to tomato mixture; stir, cover, and cook over low heat 20 minutes or until eggplant is almost tender. Add tofu and beans and cook 5 to 10 minutes more.

Per serving: 323 calories; 21 g protein; 6 g fat; 53 g carbohydrate; 1,344 mg sodium

TOFU CASSEROLE

Tofu is the Japanese name for soybean curd. It has been popular throughout East Asia since ancient times. Although it has very

little flavor of its own, it absorbs the flavor of the food or seasoning with which it is combined. Tofu can be purchased in specialty food stores and in some supermarkets.
See Menu Plan for Week 19.
Makes 4 servings

2 teaspoons margarine
1 cup sliced mushrooms
½ cup chopped onion
1 garlic clove, minced
4 ounces uncooked brown rice
2 cups broccoli spears, blanched
1 pound tofu (soybean curd), cut into
    ½-inch dice
1 cup skim milk
2 tablespoons Worcestershire sauce
⅛ teaspoon ground nutmeg
⅛ teaspoon salt
Dash ground red pepper
4 ounces grated Cheddar cheese

Melt margarine in skillet; add mushrooms, onion, and garlic and sauté, stirring often, until vegetables are tender. Place rice in bottom of shallow 2-quart casserole; top with mushroom-onion mixture, broccoli, and tofu. In small bowl combine skim milk, Worcestershire sauce, nutmeg, salt, and ground red pepper; pour evenly over casserole. Top with Cheddar cheese. Cover with foil and bake at 350°F. for 1 hour or until rice is tender. Remove foil; bake 5 minutes longer.

Per serving: 390 calories; 25 g protein; 17 g fat; 37 g carbohydrate; 337 mg sodium

TOFU SALAD
See Menu Plan for Week 29.
Makes 2 servings

¼ cup diced green bell pepper
¼ cup diced tomato
¼ cup diced drained canned water
    chestnuts
¼ cup sliced celery
2 tablespoons sliced scallion
8 ounces tofu (soybean curd), cut into
    ½-inch cubes
1 tablespoon rice vinegar
1 teaspoon sesame oil
Dash pepper

Combine first 5 ingredients in a bowl; add tofu. In small bowl mix together vinegar and oil. Pour over tofu mixture and toss lightly. Sprinkle with pepper; cover and refrigerate 30 minutes. Toss lightly just before serving.

Per serving: 155 calories; 11 g protein; 7 g fat; 15 g carbohydrate; 34 mg sodium

TOFU SANDWICH SANS BREAD
See Menu Plan for Week 17.
Makes 2 servings

8 ounces tofu (soybean curd)
2 teaspoons margarine
2 tablespoons minced onion
2 tablespoons minced celery
⅓ cup plus 2 teaspoons plain dried bread
    crumbs
¼ teaspoon salt
Dash each pepper and thyme leaves
2 eggs, beaten with 1 tablespoon water
1 tablespoon prepared mustard
½ cup chopped romaine lettuce
½ medium tomato, cut into 4 thin slices

Preheat oven to 350°F. In a shallow pan mash tofu with fork into very small pieces. Bake for 30 minutes, stirring once after 15 minutes. Remove from oven and set aside.

Melt margarine in skillet. Add onion and celery. Cover and cook over low heat 5 minutes. Add bread crumbs, salt, pepper, and thyme. Sauté, stirring occasionally, 5 to 10 minutes or until bread crumbs are lightly toasted.

In bowl combine tofu, bread crumb mixture, beaten eggs, and mustard. Spray a 9-inch pie pan with nonstick cooking spray. Spread tofu mixture over bottom of pan; cover with foil and bake 20 minutes. Remove from oven, uncover, and let cool. Cut tofu into quarters and remove to serving plates. Arrange ¼ cup romaine and 2 tomato slices over surface of each of 2 quarters; top with remaining quarters.

Per serving: 277 calories; 18 g protein; 15 g fat; 19 g carbohydrate; 646 mg sodium

TOFU-VEGETABLE SALAD
See Menu Plan for Week 48.
Makes 2 servings

3 tablespoons red wine vinegar
1 tablespoon chopped fresh basil, or
    1 teaspoon dried
2 teaspoons olive oil
1 teaspoon salt
Dash freshly ground pepper
1 cup cooked broccoli florets
½ cup thinly sliced mushrooms
½ cup thinly sliced zucchini
6 cherry tomatoes, cut into quarters
¼ cup chopped scallions
¼ cup sliced red onion
4 ounces tofu (soybean curd), cut into
    cubes
4 black olives, pitted and sliced

Combine first 5 ingredients in salad bowl; add vegetables and toss to coat. Add tofu and stir gently. Cover and marinate in refrigerator for at least 2 hours. Garnish with olives just before serving.

Per serving: 156 calories; 9 g protein; 9 g fat;
13 g carbohydrate; 1,579 mg sodium

GREEN BEANS WITH PEANUT SAUCE
See Menu Plan for Week 16.
Makes 2 servings

3 tablespoons chunky-style peanut butter
3 tablespoons rice vinegar
1 garlic clove, minced
Dash salt
1 cup julienne green beans, blanched

In bowl combine peanut butter, vinegar, garlic, and salt. Add warm green beans and toss.

Per serving: 158 calories; 8 g protein; 12 g fat;
9 g carbohydrate; 242 mg sodium

PEANUT-CHEESE MUFFIN
See Menu Plan for Week 45.
Makes 2 servings

1 tablespoon peanut butter

1 English muffin, split and toasted
1 ounce sharp Cheddar cheese, sliced
¼ teaspoon caraway seeds

Spread 1½ teaspoons peanut butter over each muffin half; top each with ½ ounce cheese. Broil until cheese melts. Remove from broiler and sprinkle each half with ⅛ teaspoon caraway seeds.

Per serving: 170 calories; 8 g protein; 9 g fat;
15 g carbohydrate; 282 mg sodium

PEANUT SOUP
See Menu Plan for Week 42.
Makes 4 servings

1 tablespoon plus ¾ teaspoon enriched flour
2½ cups water
1½ cups chicken bouillon
¼ cup diced carrot
¼ cup diced celery
3 tablespoons chunky-style peanut butter
Dash white pepper
Chopped fresh parsley to garnish

In small saucepan "dry-toast" flour until lightly browned; set aside. In medium saucepan combine water, bouillon, carrot, and celery; bring to a boil. Reduce heat to medium and cook for 15 minutes; measure out about ¾ cup liquid and pour gradually into flour, stirring constantly until smooth. Pour dissolved flour into the medium saucepan and simmer 5 minutes. Measure another ½ cup bouillon; combine with peanut butter to thin. Add thinned peanut butter to saucepan and simmer about 5 minutes. Season with pepper and garnish with parsley. Serve immediately.

Per serving: 87 calories; 4 g protein; 6 g fat;
6 g carbohydrate; 467 mg sodium

FRUIT 'N' NUT CANDY
See Menu Plan for Week 22.
Makes 2 servings

4 medium dried apricot halves, chopped
3 tablespoons peanut butter
2 tablespoons raisins, chopped
2 teaspoons honey

1 teaspoon lemon juice
⅛ teaspoon cinnamon
⅔ cup nonfat dry milk powder
¼ cup water
2 graham crackers, 2½-inch squares, made
  into fine crumbs

In small bowl combine chopped apricot halves, peanut butter, raisins, honey, lemon juice, and cinnamon. Add milk powder and, using a spoon, combine ingredients. Then, using your fingers, knead ingredients until well blended. Add water and stir until thoroughly combined. Cover and refrigerate ½ hour.

Using a spoon, scoop mixture into 18 mounds. Roll each mound in cracker crumbs; then, using the palms of your hands, form into a smooth ball. Place candies on plate and refrigerate 1 hour.

Per serving: 315 calories; 16 g protein; 13 g fat;
41 g carbohydrate; 330 mg sodium

PEANUT BUTTER CUSTARD CUPS
See Menu Plan for Week 35.
Makes 2 servings

1 cup skim milk
¾ teaspoon unflavored gelatin
⅔ cup part-skim ricotta cheese
3 tablespoons smooth peanut butter
Artificial sweetener to equal 2 teaspoons
  sugar
1 teaspoon honey
⅛ teaspoon vanilla extract
1 small pear, pared, cored, and cut into
  small dice
Dash ground cinnamon

Pour milk into top half of double boiler; sprinkle gelatin over milk and let stand a few minutes to soften. Set over simmering water and stir until gelatin is fully dissolved. Cool until lukewarm.

In work bowl of food processor or blender container combine cheese, peanut butter, sweetener, honey, and vanilla; process until smooth. Transfer cheese mixture to medium bowl and, using a wire whisk, briskly stir in milk; cover and refrigerate 1 hour.

Remove from refrigerator and stir briskly again. Spoon ¼ of custard mixture into each of 2 bowls. Sprinkle ¼ of pear over each and top with an equal amount of remaining custard. Divide remaining pear evenly over each portion and garnish with cinnamon; cover and refrigerate at least 2 hours.

Per serving: 367 calories; 22 g protein; 19 g fat;
30 g carbohydrate; 318 mg sodium

PEANUT BUTTER FUDGE
See Menu Plan for Week 34.
Makes 4 servings

⅔ cup nonfat dry milk powder
⅓ cup plus 2 teaspoons chunky-style
  peanut butter
2 tablespoons raisins
2 teaspoons honey
¼ cup plus 1 tablespoon water
2 teaspoons sesame seeds, toasted

Combine first 4 ingredients in small bowl. Sprinkle with water and mix well. Press mixture into small nonstick loaf pan. Sprinkle with sesame seeds, pressing seeds into mixture. Chill until firm, approximately 1 hour. Cut into 1-inch squares.

Per serving: 216 calories; 11 g protein; 13 g fat;
17 g carbohydrate; 214 mg sodium

PEANUT BUTTER "ICE CREAM" SANDWICH
See Menu Plan for Week 44.
Makes 2 servings

6 ounces coffee- or vanilla-flavored dietary
  frozen dessert, softened
3 tablespoons chunky-style peanut butter
1 teaspoon vanilla extract
4 graham crackers, 2½-inch squares

In small bowl thoroughly combine frozen dessert, peanut butter, and vanilla. Spoon ½ of mixture onto each of 2 graham crackers; top each with 1 graham cracker. Seal each sandwich tightly in plastic wrap. Freeze until hardened.

Per serving: 300 calories; 12 g protein; 14 g fat;
33 g carbohydrate; 320 mg sodium

Vegetable Dishes

Vegetables are about the most versatile of all of nature's gifts.
Pureed, steamed, or spiced, baked, broiled, or diced—there are
almost as many ways to serve vegetables as there are vegetable
varieties. Discover new taste treats by adding unusual vegetables
to your standard repertoire. From crunchy crudites to substantial
casseroles, depend on vegetable dishes for color, texture,
and nutrition.

HEARTS OF ARTICHOKE ARREGANATA
See Menu Plan for Week 4.
Makes 2 servings

3 tablespoons plain dried bread crumbs
2 teaspoons grated Parmesan cheese
1 teaspoon finely chopped fresh parsley
Dash each oregano leaves, paprika, salt, and pepper
1 cup cooked artichoke hearts
2 tablespoons lemon juice

In small bowl combine bread crumbs, Parmesan cheese, parsley, oregano, paprika, salt, and pepper. Mound an equal amount of bread crumb mixture on each artichoke heart and place in small pan or casserole. Sprinkle with lemon juice and bake at 375°F. until brown, about 20 minutes.

Per serving: 83 calories; 6 g protein; 2 g fat;
17 g carbohydrate; 271 mg sodium

ASPARAGUS PIMIENTO
See Menu Plan for Week 47.
Makes 4 servings

24 medium frozen asparagus spears
3 tablespoons chopped pimiento
1 tablespoon chopped fresh parsley

Cook asparagus spears according to package directions. Arrange hot asparagus on serving dish. Sprinkle with pimiento and parsley.

Per serving: 21 calories; 2 g protein; 0.2 g fat;
4 g carbohydrate; 3 mg sodium

GINGER-SPICED BEAN SPROUTS AND ONIONS
See Menu Plan for Week 28.
Makes 2 servings

½-inch piece fresh ginger root, pared
½ garlic clove
¾ teaspoon salt, divided
2 teaspoons sesame oil
1 cup sliced red onion
3 cups bean sprouts

½ medium green bell pepper, seeded and cut into 1-inch squares
1 teaspoon lemon juice
1 teaspoon rice vinegar
⅛ teaspoon pepper

Mince ginger and garlic with ½ teaspoon salt; set aside. Heat oil in medium skillet. Add ginger-garlic mixture and onion and sauté over medium heat for 2 minutes. Add bean sprouts and green pepper. Cover and cook, tossing occasionally, about 5 minutes. Remove cover; add lemon juice, vinegar, remaining ¼ teaspoon salt, and pepper. Continue to cook until sprouts are limp and green pepper is tender.

Per serving: 128 calories; 7 g protein; 5 g fat;
18 g carbohydrate; 898 mg sodium

APPLE-BEET RELISH
See Menu Plan for Week 36.
Makes 2 servings

1 small apple, cored and cut into thin wedges
1 cup cooked julienne beets
½ cup diced celery
1 tablespoon plus 1½ teaspoons lemon juice
1 tablespoon plus 1 teaspoon reduced-calorie mayonnaise
1 tablespoon plus 1 teaspoon sweet pickle relish

Slice each apple wedge crosswise into small pieces. Combine all ingredients in a bowl; mix well. Chill.

Per serving: 102 calories; 1 g protein; 2 g fat;
21 g carbohydrate; 182 mg sodium

BAKED BROCCOLI WITH MUSTARD SAUCE
See Menu Plans for Weeks 25 and 36.
Makes 4 servings

Baked Broccoli
1 pound broccoli
1 medium carrot, scraped
1 celery rib
1 cup water
2 tablespoons lemon juice
¼ teaspoon salt

Mustard Sauce
2 teaspoons margarine
2 teaspoons enriched flour
1 cup skim milk
½ teaspoon salt
2 teaspoons prepared mustard
¼ teaspoon lemon juice
Dash white pepper

To Prepare Baked Broccoli: Preheat oven to 350°F. Trim leaves from broccoli and cut off 1 to 2 inches from bottom of stalks. Place broccoli, carrot, and celery in 8 x 8-inch baking pan. Combine water, lemon juice, and salt; pour over vegetables. Cover with foil and bake 1 to 1¼ hours or until broccoli stems can easily be pierced with a knife.

To Prepare Mustard Sauce: In a small saucepan melt margarine. Stirring constantly, add flour and cook 1 minute. Add milk gradually, stirring briskly with a wire whisk until well blended. Stir in salt and cook over medium heat, stirring constantly, until sauce starts to thicken. Stir in mustard, lemon juice, and pepper. Keep warm.

To Serve: Cut broccoli florets from stems. Slice stems, carrot, and celery on the diagonal into ¼-inch slices. Arrange vegetables on serving platter. Serve with Mustard Sauce.

Per serving: 92 calories; 7 g protein; 2 g fat; 14 g carbohydrate; 548 mg sodium

BROCCOLI MEDLEY
See Menu Plan for Week 20.
Makes 2 servings

1 teaspoon olive oil
½ cup diced onion
1 garlic clove, minced
3 cups broccoli florets
2 medium tomatoes, peeled and thickly sliced
⅓ cup water
½ teaspoon oregano leaves
¼ teaspoon salt
⅛ teaspoon pepper
4 black olives, pitted and quartered

Heat oil in skillet; add onion and garlic and sauté until softened. Add broccoli and sauté 2 minutes. Add tomatoes, water, and seasonings; bring to a boil. Reduce heat and simmer, covered, for 5 minutes. Add olives and simmer 2 minutes longer or until broccoli is tender.

Per serving: 162 calories; 11 g protein; 5 g fat; 25 g carbohydrate; 410 mg sodium

CREAMY BROCCOLI
See Menu Plan for Week 45.
Makes 2 servings

2 teaspoons margarine
1 garlic clove, minced
2 teaspoons enriched flour
½ cup skim milk
1 cup cooked broccoli, pureed or finely mashed
Dash each salt and freshly ground pepper

Melt margarine in small saucepan; add garlic and sauté over low heat. Add flour, stirring constantly until thoroughly combined. Gradually pour in milk and cook, stirring constantly, until mixture thickens. Add broccoli, salt, and pepper; cook until heated.

Per serving: 86 calories; 5 g protein; 4 g fat; 9 g carbohydrate; 182 mg sodium

ORANGE BROCCOLI
See Menu Plan for Week 3.
Makes 2 servings

½ cup orange juice
2 teaspoons grated orange rind
2 teaspoons lemon juice
1½ teaspoons vegetable oil
1 teaspoon soy sauce
⅛ teaspoon each salt and pepper
Dash artificial sweetener
3 cups broccoli florets, blanched

In a bowl combine orange juice, orange rind, lemon juice, vegetable oil, soy sauce, salt, pepper, and sweetener; stir well. Add broccoli; toss. Chill for at least 1 hour.

Per serving: 154 calories; 10 g protein; 5 g fat;
24 g carbohydrate; 387 mg sodium

PIMIENTO-TOPPED STEAMED BROCCOLI
See Menu Plan for Week 52.
Makes 6 servings

4 cups broccoli spears
2½ teaspoons lemon juice
Dash each salt and pepper
3 tablespoons diced pimientos

Pour about 1 inch of water into medium saucepan, or just enough to leave a ½-inch space between steamer insert and water. Bring water to a boil. Place broccoli in steamer insert and carefully place insert in saucepan. Cover tightly and reduce heat to medium; water should continue to bubble. Steam about 10 minutes or until tender. Transfer broccoli to serving dish; sprinkle with lemon juice, salt, and pepper. Garnish with pimientos.

Per serving: 43 calories; 5 g protein; 0.4 g fat;
8 g carbohydrate; 43 mg sodium

SAUTÉED CARAWAY CABBAGE
See Menu Plans for Weeks 34 and 47.
Makes 4 servings

1 head cabbage, about 2 pounds
1 quart water
1 teaspoon salt
1 bay leaf
2 whole cloves
1 tablespoon plus 1 teaspoon margarine
½ cup thinly sliced onion
⅓ cup plus 2 teaspoons Chicken Broth
  (see page 127)
Dash pepper
½ teaspoon caraway seeds

Wash and trim cabbage; cut into 4 wedges. In saucepan bring water to a boil; add salt, bay leaf, cloves, and cabbage. Boil for about 15 minutes or until tender; drain.

Melt margarine in nonstick skillet. Add onion slices and sauté briefly. Add cabbage, cut-side down, being careful not to break wedges. Sauté until lightly browned; turn and sauté other cut side. Add broth and simmer until most of the liquid has been absorbed. Season with pepper, then sprinkle with caraway seeds.

Per serving: 100 calories; 3 g protein; 4 g fat;
15 g carbohydrate; 679 mg sodium

STIR-FRIED CABBAGE 'N' SQUASH
See Menu Plan for Week 35.
Makes 2 servings

1 teaspoon olive oil
2 cups cut-up yellow straightneck squash,
    2 x ¼-inch strips
¼ teaspoon salt, divided
Dash each ground thyme and white and
    black pepper
1 cup thinly sliced red cabbage
4 black olives, pitted and chopped
¼ teaspoon lemon juice
¼ teaspoon chopped fresh parsley

Heat oil in large skillet; add squash, ⅛ teaspoon salt, thyme, and peppers. Sauté over high heat until squash is tender but not limp, 1 to 2 minutes. *Do not overcook.* Transfer squash to plate and set aside. Reduce heat to medium and combine cabbage, olives, and remaining salt in same skillet; stir-fry until cabbage is limp. Stir in lemon juice and parsley; add squash to cabbage mixture and heat thoroughly.

Per serving: 79 calories; 3 g protein; 4 g fat;
10 g carbohydrate; 367 mg sodium

SWEET AND SOUR CABBAGE
See Menu Plans for Weeks 43 and 52.
Makes 4 servings

2 to 3 tablespoons white wine vinegar
Artificial sweetener to equal 6 teaspoons
    sugar
1 teaspoon salt
4 whole cloves
4 peppercorns
2 bay leaves
Dash each ground coriander and freshly
    ground pepper
4 cups thinly sliced red cabbage
1 tablespoon plus 1 teaspoon margarine
1 cup chopped onions
2 small green apples, pared, cored, and
    sliced

Combine first 7 ingredients in bowl; add cabbage and toss well. Set aside and allow to marinate for 1 hour.

Melt margarine in medium skillet. Add onions and sauté until translucent. Add cabbage and marinade to skillet. Cover and simmer about 30 minutes. Stir in apples and simmer 10 minutes longer.

Per serving: 117 calories; 3 g protein; 4 g fat;
19 g carbohydrate; 630 mg sodium

CARDOONS MILANAISE
Cardoon is a long celerylike vegetable with green leaves. It can usually be found in stores in Italian neighborhoods and in recent years has become more readily available in supermarkets throughout the country.
See Menu Plan for Week 12.
Makes 2 servings

3 cups sliced pared cardoons, 2-inch pieces
3 tablespoons plain dried bread crumbs
1 tablespoon plus 1 teaspoon reduced-
    calorie margarine
2 teaspoons grated Parmesan cheese
1 teaspoon basil leaves
⅛ teaspoon garlic powder
Dash each salt and freshly ground pepper

In saucepan cook cardoons in 2 quarts boiling salted water for about 45 minutes or until tender; drain. In small bowl combine remaining ingredients. Transfer cardoons to shallow 1½-quart casserole. Top with bread crumb mixture. Bake at 350°F. for 20 minutes.

Per serving: 107 calories; 4 g protein; 6 g fat;
10 g carbohydrate; 622 mg sodium

MARINATED CARROTS
See Menu Plans for Weeks 2, 22, and 43.
Makes 8 servings

½ cup white wine vinegar
¼ cup water
½ teaspoon pickling spice, tied in
    cheesecloth
¼ teaspoon salt
1 garlic clove
1 pound carrots, about 8 medium, pared and
    cut into ¼-inch thick sticks

Dash artificial sweetener
1 teaspoon chopped fresh dill
1 teaspoon chopped fresh parsley
⅛ teaspoon pepper

In small saucepan combine vinegar, water, pickling spice, salt, and garlic; simmer 5 minutes. In another saucepan cook carrots in boiling water for 3 minutes. Drain and transfer to a shallow dish just large enough to hold carrots in 1 layer. Remove and discard pickling spice and garlic clove from vinegar mixture. Add sweetener to brine and pour over hot carrots; toss. Sprinkle with dill, parsley, and pepper. Cover tightly and chill at least 3 hours, turning every ½ hour.

Per serving: 27 calories; 1 g protein; 0.1 g fat; 7 g carbohydrate; 96 mg sodium

MINTED CARROTS

This dish may be kept refrigerated up to 1 week before serving.

See Menu Plans for Weeks 21 and 35.

Makes 4 servings

2 cups julienne carrots
1 cup orange juice
½ teaspoon grated fresh ginger root
Dash each salt and pepper
1 tablespoon chopped fresh mint

Combine all ingredients except mint in small saucepan. Cover and bring to a boil; reduce heat and simmer about 7 to 8 minutes or until fork-tender. Transfer carrots and liquid to bowl. Cover and chill overnight. Garnish with mint just before serving.

Per serving: 52 calories; 1 g protein; 0.2 g fat; 12 g carbohydrate; 72 mg sodium

SESAME AND GINGER CARROTS

See Menu Plan for Week 17.

Makes 2 servings

2 teaspoons sesame oil
2 cups thinly sliced carrots
1 teaspoon minced fresh ginger root
1 teaspoon sesame seeds, toasted and
  chopped

½ teaspoon salt
⅛ teaspoon minced fresh garlic

Heat oil in skillet. Add carrots and ginger; sauté over medium heat about 5 minutes. Add sesame seeds, salt, and garlic to carrots. Cover and sauté over low heat, stirring occasionally, until carrots are tender-crisp.

Per serving: 93 calories; 2 g protein; 5 g fat; 10 g carbohydrate; 662 mg sodium

CAULIFLOWER WITH MUSHROOM SAUCE

See Menu Plan for Week 30.

Makes 2 servings

2 cups cauliflower florets, cooked
2 teaspoons margarine
½ cup sliced mushrooms
1 tablespoon chopped scallion
2 teaspoons enriched flour
⅛ teaspoon salt
Dash white pepper
½ cup skim milk
2 teaspoons grated Parmesan cheese

Arrange cauliflower in small nonstick baking pan; set aside. Melt margarine in small saucepan; add mushrooms and scallion and sauté for 1 minute. Stir in flour, salt, and pepper; cook, stirring constantly, until flour is absorbed. Stirring continuously, pour in milk and cook until slightly thickened. Pour sauce over cauliflower and sprinkle evenly with cheese. Bake at 450°F. approximately 10 to 15 minutes or until top is lightly browned.

Per serving: 120 calories; 8 g protein; 6 g fat; 11 g carbohydrate; 331 mg sodium

CURRIED CAULIFLOWER
See Menu Plan for Week 11.
Makes 2 servings

2 cups cauliflower florets
2 teaspoons vegetable oil
½ cup chopped onion
1 garlic clove, chopped
½ teaspoon each curry powder and grated fresh ginger root
¼ teaspoon salt
½ cup canned tomatoes

Cook cauliflower in boiling water to cover for 3 minutes. With slotted spoon remove cauliflower and place in bowl. Reserve ½ cup cooking liquid. Heat oil in saucepan; add onion and garlic and sauté until softened. Stir in curry powder, ginger, and salt; add tomatoes. Bring mixture to a boil; add cauliflower and reserved liquid. Cover and simmer for 8 minutes. Remove cover and cook 3 to 5 minutes longer or until some of the liquid has evaporated and cauliflower is tender.

Per serving: 102 calories; 4 g protein; 5 g fat; 12 g carbohydrate; 415 mg sodium

SEASONED CUCUMBER BAKE
See Menu Plan for Week 40.
Makes 2 servings

2 medium cucumbers, pared
2 tablespoons wine vinegar
¼ teaspoon salt
½ cup green bell pepper strips
2 teaspoons margarine
¼ teaspoon chopped fresh parsley
¼ teaspoon minced fresh ginger root
⅛ teaspoon minced fresh garlic
Dash pepper

Halve cucumbers lengthwise; scoop out and discard seeds. Halve lengthwise again; then cut crosswise into 2-inch pieces. In bowl combine cucumbers, vinegar, and salt; allow to stand 1 to 2 hours, tossing lightly about every 20 minutes.

Preheat oven to 375°F. Drain cucumbers and combine with green pepper in glass or ceramic baking dish. Bake 15 minutes; remove from oven and stir. Return baking dish to oven and bake 10 to 15 minutes longer or until tender.

Melt margarine in small saucepan. Add parsley, ginger, garlic, and pepper and cook over low heat for 2 minutes; combine with cucumber mixture.

Per serving: 70 calories; 2 g protein; 4 g fat; 8 g carbohydrate; 355 mg sodium

BAKED EGGPLANT SLICES
See Menu Plans for Weeks 24, 43, 48, and 50.
Makes 2 servings

8 slices eggplant, ½-inch thick
¾ teaspoon salt, divided
2 small garlic cloves
½ teaspoon oregano leaves
⅛ teaspoon pepper

Place eggplant in colander; sprinkle with ½ teaspoon salt and top with heavy plate. Allow to drain for ½ hour. Pat slices dry with paper towels. In small bowl mash garlic with ¼ teaspoon salt until it forms a paste; add oregano and pepper. Arrange eggplant slices on nonstick baking sheet. Using ½ of the garlic mixture, season each slice equally; bake at 350°F. for 10 minutes. Turn slices and season with remaining garlic mixture; bake 10 minutes longer or until soft.

Per serving: 47 calories; 2 g protein; 0.4 g fat; 10 g carbohydrate; 855 mg sodium

Variations:
1. Prepare eggplant and bake for initial 10 minutes as directed above. Turn, season, and bake 5 minutes longer. Spread each slice with ½ teaspoon ketchup and bake 5 more minutes or until soft.

Per serving: 48 calories; 2 g protein; 0.4 g fat; 11 g carbohydrate; 869 mg sodium

2. Prepare eggplant and bake for initial 10 minutes as directed above. Turn and bake 5 minutes longer. Cut 1 medium tomato into 8 slices. Top each piece of eggplant with a tomato slice and season with re-

maining garlic mixture. Bake 5 more minutes or until tomato is cooked.

Per serving: 58 calories; 3 g protein; 1 g fat;
13 g carbohydrate; 856 mg sodium

EGGPLANT AND ZUCCHINI CASSEROLE
See Menu Plan for Week 22.
Makes 2 servings

¼ garlic clove
½ teaspoon each oregano leaves and salt
1 tablespoon plus 1 teaspoon chili sauce
1 teaspoon rice vinegar
½ teaspoon water
Dash pepper
1¼ cups sliced zucchini, ½-inch thick slices
1 cup sliced eggplant, ½-inch thick slices
2 teaspoons margarine
½ cup drained canned water chestnuts, slivered

Chop garlic with oregano and salt; using flat side of knife mash mixture to form a paste. Transfer paste to small bowl and combine with chili sauce, vinegar, water, and pepper.

Cover broiler pan with aluminum foil and arrange zucchini and eggplant slices in pan. Brush ½ of chili sauce mixture over vegetables; broil until well browned. Turn vegetables, brush with remaining chili mixture, and broil until other side is well browned. Layer vegetables in small casserole.

Melt margarine in small skillet. Add water chestnuts and sauté 2 minutes. Sprinkle water chestnuts over vegetables in casserole. Cover and bake at 350°F. for 25 minutes.

Per serving: 94 calories; 2 g protein; 4 g fat;
14 g carbohydrate; 790 mg sodium

FENNEL PARMESAN
Fennel is a bulbous white root that has the pleasant flavor of anise. It can be used raw in salads or cooked as a vegetable.
See Menu Plans for Weeks 8, 16, and 50.
Makes 2 servings

2 cups sliced fennel bulb, about ½ pound
¾ cup Chicken Broth (see page 127)
2 teaspoons grated Parmesan cheese
½ teaspoon minced fresh garlic
1 tablespoon minced fresh parsley

In saucepan combine fennel and broth; bring to a boil. Reduce heat and simmer approximately 15 minutes. Drain and transfer fennel to shallow 2-cup casserole; sprinkle with cheese and garlic. Bake at 375°F. for 10 minutes; then broil for 5 minutes. Sprinkle with parsley and serve immediately.

Per serving: 40 calories; 3 g protein; 2 g fat;
4 g carbohydrate; 96 mg sodium

GREEN BEANS AND TOMATOES HUNGARIAN STYLE
See Menu Plans for Weeks 5 and 41.
Makes 2 servings

2 cups cut green beans
2 teaspoons margarine
⅓ cup chopped onion
1 cup canned tomatoes, cut into pieces
¼ teaspoon paprika
Dash salt

Place green beans in saucepan with boiling salted water to cover and blanch 5 minutes. Drain in colander and refresh under cold running water; set aside. Melt margarine in saucepan; add onion and sauté until softened. Stir in tomatoes and paprika and simmer 5 to 8 minutes. Add beans and simmer, stirring occasionally, 5 minutes or until beans are tender-crisp; season and serve.

Per serving: 102 calories; 4 g protein; 4 g fat;
15 g carbohydrate; 304 mg sodium

CREAMED KALE AND ONIONS
See Menu Plan for Week 7.
Makes 2 servings

2 teaspoons margarine
2 teaspoons enriched flour
½ cup skim milk
Dash each ground nutmeg, salt, and pepper
2 cups cooked kale, warm
1 cup cooked small white onions, warm

Melt margarine in saucepan and stir in flour. Using a wire whisk, gradually stir in milk; cook, stirring constantly, until sauce thickens. Stir in seasonings. Add kale and onions and heat, stirring often.

Per serving: 139 calories; 9 g protein; 5 g fat; 19 g carbohydrate; 226 mg sodium

SAUTÉED MUSHROOMS AND ONIONS
Delicious with chicken, beef, or liver.
See Menu Plans for Weeks 39 and 49.
Makes 2 servings

1 teaspoon sesame or vegetable oil
½ cup sliced onion
1 cup sliced mushrooms
Dash each salt and pepper

Heat oil in skillet; add onion and sauté over medium heat until onion slices are translucent. Add mushrooms, salt, and pepper and sauté until mushrooms are cooked.

Per serving: 51 calories; 2 g protein; 2 g fat; 6 g carbohydrate; 106 mg sodium

STIR-FRY PEA PODS
See Menu Plan for Week 18.
Makes 4 servings

2 teaspoons walnut oil
2 cups trimmed Chinese pea pods (stem ends and strings removed)
2 garlic cloves, minced
1 packet instant beef broth and seasoning mix
½ to 1 cup water
1 tablespoon chopped fresh basil, or 1 teaspoon dried

Heat oil in skillet or wok. Add pea pods and garlic; sauté for 1 minute. Add broth mix and enough water to just cover bottom of pan. Cook, stirring constantly, until pods are tender-crisp and water is almost evaporated. Stir in basil and serve.

Per serving: 61 calories; 3 g protein; 2 g fat; 9 g carbohydrate; 170 mg sodium

CREAMED RUTABAGA
See Menu Plan for Week 37.
Makes 4 servings

2 cups pared and diced rutabaga
½ cup skim milk
2 teaspoons margarine
½ teaspoon salt
¼ teaspoon chopped fresh parsley
Dash each thyme leaves, ground nutmeg, and pepper
¼ cup diced and blanched green bell pepper

Steam rutabaga until very soft, about 8 to 10 minutes. Transfer to mixing bowl; add remaining ingredients except green pepper. Mash by hand or with electric mixer until smooth. Stir in green pepper.

Per serving: 63 calories; 2 g protein; 2 g fat; 10 g carbohydrate; 336 mg sodium

SAUTÉED SALSIFY
Salsify, a fleshy root native to southern Europe, is also known as oyster plant. Some people feel that its flavor is similar to that of the oyster. It is shaped like a carrot or parsnip, can be black or white, and is available canned and fresh.
See Menu Plan for Week 52.
Makes 2 servings

2 teaspoons margarine
¼ cup diced onion
¾ cup drained canned salsify
Dash each salt and pepper

Melt margarine in small skillet; add onion and sauté until onion starts to brown. Add salsify and seasonings; sauté, stirring occa-

Cream Puffs
with Strawberry Sauce

Orange Soufflé

From top: Swordfish Kebabs; Salmon-Zucchini Kebabs;
Bacon-Scallop Kebabs

Left: Fish and
Tomato Aspic

Right:
Macaroni-Cheese Mold

Clockwise: Chopped spinach; alfalfa sprouts on lettuce with lemon juice; Fennel Parmesan; Captain's Flounder; white wine

"Fallen" Strawberry Cheesecake; Fruited Custard Pie

Broccoli Quiche

Chick Pea Croquettes
(Falafel)
with pita bread

Skim milk; Granola

*Left to right:
Pineapple-Banana
Milk Shake;
Strawberry-Apple
Frost; Lime Cooler*

Shepherd's Beef Pie

Clockwise:
Lemony Brussels
Sprouts and
Carrots Salad;
Fruit Slaw;
Tofu-Vegetable Salad

*Clockwise: Cheese-Stuffed
Zucchini; Vegetable-Stuffed
Cabbage Leaves;
Seasoned Cucumber Bake*

*Clockwise:
Middle Eastern
Burgers;
Piquant Hamburgers;
Spicy Meat Turnovers*

Above:
Melon Mousse

Right:
Lady Fingers;
Pineapple-Coconut
Cookies

sionally, until onion is well browned and salsify is heated through.

Per serving: 78 calories; 2 g protein; 4 g fat; 10 g carbohydrate; 238 mg sodium

CREAMED SPINACH
See Menu Plan for Week 42.
Makes 2 servings

1 cup well-drained cooked chopped spinach
¼ cup evaporated skimmed milk
1 tablespoon plus 1 teaspoon grated
    Parmesan cheese
1 teaspoon margarine
¼ teaspoon salt
⅛ teaspoon white pepper

Combine all ingredients in small saucepan. Cook over medium heat, stirring constantly, until mixture becomes thick.

Per serving: 75 calories; 6 g protein; 3 g fat; 6 g carbohydrate; 397 mg sodium

BAKED SPICED ACORN SQUASH
A 12-ounce acorn squash will yield about 1 cup cooked squash.
See Menu Plan for Week 38.
Makes 2 servings

1 acorn squash, about 12 ounces
½ teaspoon honey
Dash each salt, ground cinnamon, and
    ground allspice

Bake squash on baking sheet at 375°F. about 1 hour or until very soft. Remove from oven and cut in half; scoop out and discard seeds. In bowl combine 1 cup squash, honey, salt, cinnamon, and allspice; mash by hand or beat with an electric mixer until smooth.

Per serving: 69 calories; 2 g protein; 0.4 g fat; 17 g carbohydrate; 95 mg sodium

SPAGHETTI SQUASH PESTO
Spaghetti squash is also known as cucuzzi, calabash, and suzza melon. It is actually not a true squash but an edible gourd. After cooking, the pulp assumes the appearance of spaghetti and is delicious in combination with various sauces. Here it is prepared with basil, which is why it is called Pesto.
See Menu Plan for Week 34.
Makes 4 servings

2½- to 3-pound spaghetti squash*
1 tablespoon plus 2 teaspoons olive oil
2 garlic cloves, minced
2 tablespoons chopped fresh basil, or
    2 teaspoons dried
1 teaspoon salt
Dash freshly ground pepper
1 tablespoon plus 1 teaspoon grated
    Parmesan cheese

Pierce squash in several places with prongs of fork. Place whole squash in baking pan; bake at 350°F. for 1 hour. Remove from oven and set aside.

Heat oil in small skillet; add garlic and sauté briefly. Remove from heat and add basil. Cut squash in half, discard seeds, and scoop out pulp. In bowl toss pulp with basil mixture. Season with salt and pepper and sprinkle with cheese.

Per serving: 102 calories; 3 g protein; 8 g fat; 7 g carbohydrate; 642 mg sodium

* A 2½- to 3-pound squash yields about 4 cups cooked squash.

SPAGHETTI SQUASH WITH TOMATO SAUCE

This recipe provides a quick and satisfying way to use up leftover squash.

See Menu Plan for Week 40.

Makes 2 servings

2 teaspoons olive oil
½ cup sliced onion
½ garlic clove, chopped with ½ teaspoon salt
2 cups canned whole tomatoes
½ teaspoon oregano leaves
½ teaspoon honey
Dash thyme leaves
3 cups cooked spaghetti squash,* heated

Heat oil in small skillet over medium heat. Add onion and garlic; sauté about 4 minutes or until onion is just tender. *Do not overcook.* Set aside.

In small saucepan combine tomatoes, oregano, honey, and thyme. Cook over medium heat 10 minutes, stirring occasionally; add onion mixture and cook an additional 5 minutes. Spoon sauce over warm spaghetti squash.

Per serving: 154 calories; 4 g protein; 6 g fat; 24 g carbohydrate; 870 mg sodium

* See Spaghetti Squash Pesto recipe (page 249) for cooking directions.

SQUASH PARMESAN

See Menu Plan for Week 41.

Makes 2 servings

2 cups sliced yellow summer squash, ¼-inch thick slices
2 cups sliced zucchini, ¼-inch thick slices
½ cup water
2 teaspoons margarine
⅛ teaspoon each salt and white pepper
2 teaspoons grated Parmesan cheese
Parsley sprigs to garnish

Combine yellow squash and zucchini slices with water in medium saucepan. Cover and cook over medium to high heat 3 to 5 minutes; drain well. Add margarine, salt, and pepper and toss to combine. Sprinkle with cheese and toss gently. Serve garnished with parsley.

Per serving: 108 calories; 5 g protein; 5 g fat; 12 g carbohydrate; 287 mg sodium

ZUCCHINI ITALIAN STYLE

This can be served hot or chilled, or can be frozen for use at a future date.

See Menu Plan for Week 4.

Makes 2 servings

2 medium zucchini, about 5 ounces each
1 medium tomato, seeded and chopped
1 garlic clove, minced
½ teaspoon basil leaves
½ teaspoon salt
Dash freshly ground pepper

Using a vegetable brush wash zucchini well. Cut off ends and cut into 1-inch thick slices; set aside.

Combine tomato, garlic, and basil in small saucepan; cook 5 minutes. Add zucchini, salt, and pepper and cook until zucchini is just tender, about 10 minutes. Serve immediately or refrigerate and serve chilled.

Per serving: 38 calories; 2 g protein; 0.3 g fat; 8 g carbohydrate; 589 mg sodium

ZUCCHINI SPAGHETTI

See Menu Plans for Weeks 13 and 35.

Makes 2 servings

1 tablespoon reduced-calorie margarine
2 medium zucchini, about 5 ounces each, cut into thin strips
1 tablespoon chopped fresh basil, or 1 teaspoon dried
Dash freshly ground pepper

Melt margarine in medium skillet; add zucchini and sauté, tossing constantly, for 5 minutes. Season with basil and pepper.

Per serving: 63 calories; 3 g protein; 3 g fat; 8 g carbohydrate; 75 mg sodium

ZUCCHINI STICKS
See Menu Plan for Week 33.
Makes 2 servings

2 medium zucchini, about 5 ounces each,
   pared
¼ teaspoon salt
3 tablespoons plain dried bread crumbs
1 teaspoon imitation bacon bits
½ teaspoon basil leaves
Dash ground red pepper

Cut each zucchini in half lengthwise and cut each half in half crosswise. Cut each quarter lengthwise into 3 strips. Place strips on paper towel; sprinkle with salt and let stand 30 minutes. Combine remaining ingredients in blender container; process until very fine. Transfer mixture to bowl. Dip each zucchini strip into crumb mixture, pressing crumbs to adhere. Place strips on a nonstick baking sheet that has been sprayed with nonstick cooking spray. Bake at 400°F., turning once, for 35 to 40 minutes, or until brown and crisp.

Per serving: 50 calories; 2 g protein; 1 g fat;
9 g carbohydrate; 360 mg sodium

BROILED TOMATO
See Menu Plan for Week 26 and various other weeks.
Makes 2 servings

1 medium tomato, cut in half
⅛ teaspoon soy sauce
Dash each white pepper, garlic powder,
   thyme leaves, and basil leaves

Place tomato in small broiling pan, cut-side up. Sprinkle with soy sauce and seasonings. Broil 4 to 6 inches from source of heat 6 to 8 minutes.

Per serving: 12 calories; 1 g protein; 0.1 g fat;
3 g carbohydrate; 26 mg sodium

BROILED ONION-TOPPED TOMATOES
See Menu Plan for Week 50.
Makes 2 servings

2 medium tomatoes, cut into halves
1 teaspoon Dijon-style mustard
½ cup sliced onion, separated into rings
1 teaspoon brown sugar

Place tomato halves, cut-side up, in broiler pan or on aluminum foil. Spread each with ¼ teaspoon mustard and top each with an equal amount of onion rings. Sprinkle each with ¼ teaspoon brown sugar. Broil for about 3 minutes.

Per serving: 51 calories; 2 g protein; 3 g fat;
11 g carbohydrate; 237 mg sodium

ESCAROLE AND TOMATO MEDLEY
See Menu Plan for Week 9.
Makes 2 servings

2 teaspoons olive oil
1 garlic clove, minced
2 cups chopped escarole
1 medium tomato, peeled, seeded, and
   chopped
Dash each salt and pepper

Heat oil in medium saucepan; add garlic and sauté, being careful not to brown. Add escarole, tomato, salt, and pepper. Cover and simmer approximately 15 minutes or until escarole is just tender.

Per serving: 76 calories; 2 g protein; 5 g fat;
7 g carbohydrate; 110 mg sodium

HERB-STUFFED TOMATOES

Standing the cherry tomatoes stem-side down will prevent them from rolling.
See Menu Plan for Week 42.
Makes 4 servings

20 cherry tomatoes
½ cup plain unflavored yogurt
2 teaspoons chopped chives
2 teaspoons chopped fresh parsley
½ teaspoon Dijon-style mustard
Dash each white pepper and
   Worcestershire sauce
Parsley sprigs to garnish

Place tomatoes on cutting board stem-side down; cut a thin slice off top of each. Using a small spoon scoop out and discard seeds and pulp, leaving a firm shell. In small bowl combine yogurt, chives, parsley, mustard, pepper, and Worcestershire. Stuff each tomato with an equal amount of yogurt mixture and garnish with a tiny parsley sprig; chill until ready to serve.

Per serving: 30 calories; 2 g protein; 2 g fat;
4 g carbohydrate; 34 mg sodium

COLACHE

This is a favorite Mexican vegetable dish that can be traced back to the Aztecs.
See Menu Plan for Week 7.
Makes 4 servings

1 tablespoon vegetable oil
1 cup chopped onions
2 cups diced zucchini
1 cup cut green beans
1 medium green bell pepper, seeded and
   diced
2 cups frozen or fresh whole-kernel corn
1 cup canned crushed tomatoes
½ cup water
½ teaspoon oregano leaves
Dash each salt and white pepper

Heat oil in large saucepan; add onions and sauté until softened. Add zucchini, green beans, and pepper; cook for 5 minutes, stirring often. Add remaining ingredients and simmer, stirring occasionally, for 10 minutes.

Per serving: 156 calories; 6 g protein; 4 g fat;
29 g carbohydrate; 122 mg sodium

HERBED VEGETABLES

See Menu Plan for Week 10.
Makes 2 servings

1 cup sliced mushrooms, ¼-inch thick slices
Dash salt
2 teaspoons margarine
Dash each thyme leaves, chervil leaves,
   and rosemary leaves
2 cups sliced zucchini, ¼-inch thick slices,
   blanched
2 cups broccoli florets, blanched
½ cup sliced red bell pepper, ¼-inch wide
   strips
1 teaspoon lemon juice

Heat large nonstick skillet; add mushrooms and salt. Cook over medium heat about 3 minutes to cook out moisture in mushrooms. They should be tender but not limp. Place mushroom slices on paper towels.

Wipe skillet dry with a paper towel. Melt margarine in skillet; add thyme, chervil, and rosemary and sauté 30 seconds. Stir in zucchini, broccoli, mushrooms, and red pepper. Cover and cook, stirring occasionally, about 2 to 3 minutes. Stir in lemon juice and serve.

Per serving: 143 calories; 10 g protein; 5 g fat;
19 g carbohydrate; 138 mg sodium

SLOW-COOKED VEGETABLE MEDLEY

A different method of preparing vegetables that concentrates their flavor by allowing them to cook slowly in their own juices.
See Menu Plan for Week 1.
Makes 2 servings

2 teaspoons olive oil
3 cups thinly sliced cabbage
1 cup julienne leeks
1 cup julienne carrots

1 teaspoon chopped fresh parsley
¼ teaspoon ground celery seed
½ garlic clove, finely chopped with
   1 teaspoon salt

Heat oil in large nonstick skillet. Add cabbage, leeks, and carrots. Toss to coat with oil. Cover and cook over low heat, tossing occasionally, about 45 minutes or until cabbage is soft and carrots tender. During last 15 minutes of cooking stir in parsley, celery seed, and chopped garlic.

Per serving: 141 calories; 4 g protein; 5 g fat;
22 g carbohydrate; 1,245 mg sodium

VEGETABLE MEDLEY
See Menu Plan for Week 15.
Makes 2 servings

2 cups torn iceberg lettuce leaves, large
   pieces
1 cup sliced onions
¾ cup finely chopped celery
¼ teaspoon salt
⅛ teaspoon thyme leaves
Dash each ground nutmeg and pepper
1½ cups sliced mushrooms, cooked
½ cup well-squeezed cooked chopped
   spinach

Heat nonstick skillet over medium-low heat. Add lettuce, onions, celery, and salt; stir to combine. Cover and cook until onions are almost tender. Add thyme, nutmeg, and pepper; cook 2 minutes longer. Add mushrooms and spinach. Cover and cook until heated through, stirring occasionally.

Per serving: 98 calories; 8 g protein; 1 g fat;
18 g carbohydrate; 374 mg sodium

VEGETABLE PILAF
See Menu Plan for Week 43.
Makes 2 servings

2 teaspoons reduced-calorie margarine
½ cup sliced onion
½ cup sliced celery
½ cup diced carrot
1 cup cooked enriched rice
1 teaspoon grated lemon rind

¼ teaspoon salt
Dash pepper
¼ cup raisins

Melt margarine over low heat in large nonstick skillet; add onion, celery, and carrot and sauté until tender. Add rice, lemon rind, and seasonings; toss lightly. Continue cooking until thoroughly heated, about 2 minutes, stirring occasionally. Stir in raisins.

Per serving: 200 calories; 3 g protein; 2 g fat;
44 g carbohydrate; 395 mg sodium

VEGETABLE-STUFFED CABBAGE LEAVES
See Menu Plan for Week 32.
Makes 2 servings

1 cup pared and diced eggplant, small dice
Salt
4 large cabbage leaves
2 cups sliced mushrooms
½ cup chopped broccoli florets
½ teaspoon chopped parsley stems
¼ teaspoon oregano leaves
Dash pepper
½ cup tomato sauce
¼ teaspoon dehydrated onion flakes

Sprinkle eggplant with dash salt and let stand on paper towels 1 hour.

Cook cabbage leaves in boiling salted water to cover until tender; rinse in cold water. Drain and set aside.

Heat nonstick skillet. Add eggplant, ½ teaspoon salt, mushrooms, broccoli, parsley stems, oregano, and pepper. Cover and cook over medium heat, stirring occasionally, until eggplant is soft and mushrooms are tender.

Preheat oven to 350°F. Remove about 1 inch from core end of each cabbage leaf. Place ¼ of vegetable mixture in center of each leaf. Roll tightly, tucking in sides to enclose filling. Place filled leaves seam-side down in baking dish. Combine tomato sauce and onion flakes; pour over leaves. Bake 15 minutes.

Per serving: 88 calories; 6 g protein; 1 g fat;
17 g carbohydrate; 941 mg sodium

VEGETABLE-STUFFED GRAPE LEAVES
See Menu Plans for Weeks 37 and 50.
Makes 4 servings

2 garlic cloves
1 teaspoon salt, divided
1½ cups tomato juice
½ bay leaf
Thyme leaves
Pepper
Dash ground thyme
2 cups sliced mushrooms
½ cup diced carrot
½ cup pared and diced celery*
1 teaspoon chopped fresh parsley
1 cup chopped and cooked spinach
12 grape leaves, packed in brine, rinsed well

Mince 1 garlic clove with ¾ teaspoon salt and set aside. Cut remaining garlic clove in half and combine in small saucepan with tomato juice, bay leaf, ⅛ teaspoon thyme leaves, and dash each pepper and ground thyme; simmer over low heat until liquid is reduced to 1 cup, about 30 minutes. Discard garlic and bay leaf. Stir in remaining ¼ teaspoon salt and set aside.

Heat large nonstick skillet; add minced garlic, mushrooms, carrot, celery, parsley, and dash each thyme leaves and pepper. Cover and cook over low heat, stirring occasionally, for 5 to 8 minutes; uncover, stir in spinach, and cook 5 minutes or until moisture evaporates.

Preheat oven to 350°F. Place an equal amount of vegetable mixture, about 1 tablespoon, in center of each grape leaf; fold leaf tightly around filling. Place filled leaves seam-side down into 1-quart baking pan; pour sauce over leaves. Cover and bake 20 to 25 minutes or until hot.

Per serving: 52 calories; 4 g protein; 0.4 g fat; 10 g carbohydrate; 819 mg sodium (These figures do not include grape leaves since nutrition analysis for this product is unavailable.)

* Use a vegetable peeler to remove stringy outer layer.

Grains, Pasta, and Potatoes

It's true that "man does not live by bread alone," but bread is still said to be the staff of life. Now you can enliven meals with some exciting new recipes featuring grains, pasta, and potatoes. Homemade White Bread, Linguine Primavera, and Potato-Pumpkin Puffs give old favorites a new twist—sense appeal. Aroma, appearance, taste, and texture are important aspects of your menu plan.

APPLESAUCE OATMEAL
See Menu Plans for Weeks 6, 22, 35, and 45.
Makes 2 servings

1 cup skim milk
1½ ounces uncooked old-fashioned oats
½ cup applesauce, no sugar added
Artificial sweetener to equal 4 teaspoons
   sugar
Few drops vanilla extract
Dash ground cloves

Heat milk in top of double boiler over boiling water. Add oats and stir. Cook, uncovered, until cereal begins to thicken. Add applesauce, sweetener, vanilla, and cloves. Cook, stirring occasionally, until cereal is desired consistency.

Per serving: 155 calories; 7 g protein; 2 g fat;
28 g carbohydrate; 66 mg sodium

CEREAL WITH SPICED FRUIT AMBROSIA
See Menu Plan for Week 1 and various other weeks.
Makes 2 servings

2 cups skim milk
1½ ounces uncooked cream of wheat cereal
1 cup canned fruit cocktail, no sugar added
Artificial sweetener to equal 2 teaspoons
   sugar
Dash each ground ginger and ground
   cinnamon
2 teaspoons shredded coconut, toasted

Pour milk into top of double boiler; place over boiling water and cook until hot. Slowly stir in cereal. Cook 3 to 5 minutes or until cereal is thickened. Remove from heat. Drain juice from fruit cocktail into cereal; add sweetener, ginger, and cinnamon. Stir to combine. Place ½ of fruit in bottom of each of 2 cereal bowls; spoon ½ of cereal over each. Garnish each with 1 teaspoon coconut.

Per serving: 218 calories; 11 g protein; 1 g fat;
41 g carbohydrate; 136 mg sodium

CREAMY APPLE-RAISIN OATMEAL
See Menu Plan for Week 47.
Makes 2 servings

2 cups skim milk
1½ ounces uncooked quick oats
1 small apple, pared, cored, and coarsely
   grated
2 tablespoons raisins
½ teaspoon ground cinnamon
¼ teaspoon salt
1 teaspoon honey

Combine first 6 ingredients in saucepan. Stirring constantly, bring to a boil and cook 1 minute or until thick and creamy. Stir in honey and serve in heated bowls.

Per serving: 198 calories; 8 g protein; 2 g fat;
39 g carbohydrate; 345 mg sodium

Variation:
Apple-Raisin Oatmeal—For a less creamy consistency, substitute 1½ cups water for the 2 cups skim milk. Proceed according to directions above and serve each portion with ½ cup skim milk.

Per serving: 154 calories; 4 g protein; 2 g fat;
33 g carbohydrate; 282 mg sodium

GRANOLA

This delicious dish can be made in advance and kept refrigerated in an airtight container for up to 1 week.
See Menu Plan for Week 10.
Makes 2 servings

½ small apple, pared and cored
¾ cup water
2 tablespoons lemon juice
2 ounces uncooked small pearl barley
1½ ounces uncooked old-fashioned oats
1 teaspoon ground cinnamon
¼ teaspoon ground nutmeg
⅛ teaspoon salt
1 tablespoon plus 1 teaspoon vegetable oil
1 teaspoon honey
⅔ cup nonfat dry milk powder
1 tablespoon raisins, chopped

Preheat oven to 300°F. Cut apple into small pieces. Combine water and lemon juice in small bowl; add apple and set aside.

Cook barley in boiling water to cover until just tender but not too soft, about 5 to 6 minutes (barley should have a chewy consistency); drain and transfer to medium bowl. Add oats, cinnamon, nutmeg, and salt and stir. Combine oil and honey in small metal measuring cup; heat until mixture begins to foam. Stir into barley mixture. Add dry milk and stir well. Spread mixture onto nonstick baking sheet.

Drain apple pieces and place on another baking sheet. Place both baking sheets in oven. Bake apples until dry and slightly browned, 20 to 30 minutes. Remove from oven and let cool. Bake barley mixture until it begins to brown, about 20 minutes. Remove from oven and break apart with wooden spoon, turning pieces over. Return to oven and bake until fully browned, about 20 minutes longer. Remove from oven and let cool. When cool, top with apple pieces and chopped raisins.

Per serving: 391 calories; 14 g protein; 12 g fat;
62 g carbohydrate; 278 mg sodium

HOMEMADE WHITE BREAD

See Menu Plans for Weeks 3 and 39.
Makes 2 loaves, about 20 ounces each

¼ cup water, warm or lukewarm
   (see method)
¼-ounce packet active dry or 0.6-ounce
   cake compressed yeast
2 tablespoons sugar
2 cups lukewarm skim milk
2 tablespoons margarine, melted
2 teaspoons salt
6 to 6½ cups sifted enriched all-purpose
   or bread flour, divided

Use warm water (105–115°F.) for dry yeast; use lukewarm water (80–90°F.) for compressed yeast. Pour water into 4-quart mixing bowl; add yeast, then sugar, and stir until dissolved. Stir in milk; add margarine and salt. Stir until well blended. Stir in 3 cups flour, 1 cup at a time. When adding first cup of flour, use a sturdy wooden spoon to remove lumps, then continue adding flour, beating vigorously with wooden spoon. Add 4th cup of flour and beat until dough is smooth and elastic. Add 5th cup of flour to make a stiff dough.

Measure 6th cup of flour; sprinkle about half of it on board or counter top. Turn out dough onto floured area of board. Keep coating of flour on the dough as you begin to knead. With floured hands, knead dough by pushing the heels of your hands down into the dough, away from you. Fold dough over, give it a quarter turn, and push again. Repeat for 5 to 10 minutes, adding more flour to board as necessary, until dough no longer sticks. Kneading is finished when dough is smooth and elastic (springs back when pressed lightly).

Put dough in greased bowl; turn dough to lightly coat. Cover bowl with clean towel and set in warm place to rise. Let dough rise until almost doubled in volume, about 1½ hours.

Test by inserting 2 fingers about ½ inch into risen dough. If indentations remain, the dough is ready to shape. Punch dough down; shape into a ball. Knead 2 to 3 minutes.

Reshape into ball. Grasp center of ball and squeeze dough; divide into 2 equal portions. Weigh dough so that each loaf will be the same size and weight. Shape each into an oval. Put each shaped loaf in greased 9 x 5 x 2½-inch pan, seam-side down. Cover; let rise in warm place until almost doubled in volume, about 45 minutes.

Preheat oven to 375°F. Bake loaves until nicely browned and just starting to pull away from sides of pan, about 45 minutes. Remove from oven; turn loaves out of pans onto wire racks to cool. Cut into 1-ounce slices.

Per slice: 76 calories; 2 g protein; 1 g fat; 15 g carbohydrate; 131 mg sodium

Variation:

Homemade Whole Wheat Bread—Use ½ cup light molasses or ½ cup firmly packed brown sugar and 1½ cups lukewarm skim milk instead of sugar and 2 cups milk. Use whole wheat flour instead of white. Follow directions for Homemade White Bread, adding molasses after yeast. Let dough rise about 2 hours instead of 1½, and about 1 hour instead of 45 minutes. Bake about 40 minutes instead of 45 minutes.

Per slice: 80 calories; 2 g protein; 1 g fat; 15 g carbohydrate; 130 mg sodium

GARLIC BREAD
See Menu Plan for Week 36 and various other weeks.
Makes 4 servings

1 tablespoon plus 1 teaspoon margarine
2 teaspoons chopped fresh parsley
1 garlic clove
8 slices enriched French bread, ½ ounce each

Preheat broiler. In small bowl combine margarine and parsley. Place garlic clove in garlic press and squeeze into margarine mixture; stir to combine. Spread each slice of French bread with an equal amount of margarine mixture. Place in broiler pan; broil for 1 minute.

Per serving: 117 calories; 3 g protein; 5 g fat; 16 g carbohydrate; 209 mg sodium

MELBA TOAST PARMESAN
See Menu Plan for Week 27.
Makes 1 serving

¾ teaspoon Dijon-style mustard
6 rye melba toast rounds
¾ teaspoon grated Parmesan cheese
1½ teaspoons chopped scallion

Spread ⅛ teaspoon mustard on each melba toast round. Sprinkle each with ⅛ teaspoon Parmesan cheese and top with ¼ teaspoon chopped scallion.

Per serving: 75 calories; 5 g protein; 1 g fat; 13 g carbohydrate; 178 mg sodium

MELBA TOAST PUFFS
See Menu Plan for Week 16.
Makes 2 servings

12 melba toast rounds
¼ cup sliced small white onions, separated into rings
1 tablespoon plus 1 teaspoon reduced-calorie mayonnaise
1 tablespoon plus 1 teaspoon nonfat dry milk powder
2 teaspoons grated Parmesan cheese
¼ teaspoon garlic powder
⅛ teaspoon oregano leaves
Dash each pepper and paprika

Place melba toast rounds on baking sheet. Lay an equal amount of onion rings on each round. In a bowl combine all remaining ingredients except paprika; mix to a thick paste. Mound an equal amount of mixture on each portion of onion rings. Sprinkle with paprika and bake at 475°F. for 8 to 10 minutes.

Per serving: 114 calories; 6 g protein; 3 g fat; 16 g carbohydrate; 157 mg sodium

CORN MUFFINS

See Menu Plan for Week 3.
Makes 2 servings, 3 muffins each

½ cup drained canned whole-kernel corn
¼ cup plus 1 tablespoon enriched flour
1 ounce uncooked enriched yellow cornmeal
2 teaspoons sugar
Artificial sweetener to equal 2 teaspoons
   sugar
¼ teaspoon salt
½ teaspoon baking powder
2 eggs, slightly beaten
¼ cup buttermilk
1 tablespoon margarine, melted

Preheat oven to 350°F. In bowl combine first 7 ingredients. In small bowl combine eggs, buttermilk, and margarine; slowly add to corn mixture, stirring until combined. Divide mixture evenly into a 6-cup nonstick muffin tin and bake for 30 minutes.

Per serving: 330 calories; 12 g protein; 12 g fat;
45 g carbohydrate; 749 mg sodium

HONEY-WHEAT MUFFINS

These muffins can be frozen and reheated.
See Menu Plan for Week 40.
Makes 6 servings

1½ cups buttermilk
3 ounces uncooked old-fashioned oats
2 tablespoons honey
2 tablespoons vegetable oil
1 cup less 1 tablespoon whole wheat
   flour
1 teaspoon baking powder
½ teaspoon baking soda
1 tablespoon reduced-calorie spread, any
   flavor (optional)

Combine buttermilk and oats in small mixing bowl. Set bowl in pan of hot water for 5 minutes; stir. Preheat oven to 350°F. Combine honey and vegetable oil with buttermilk mixture. In small bowl combine flour, baking powder, and baking soda; stir. Add to buttermilk mixture and mix thoroughly. Divide evenly into a 12-cup nonstick muffin tin. Bake about 30 minutes or until lightly browned and a cake tester, when inserted in center, comes out clean. Serve warm. If desired use ¼ teaspoon spread with each muffin.

Per serving: 207 calories; 7 g protein; 7 g fat;
32 g carbohydrate; 186 mg sodium
Add: 4 calories and 1 g carbohydrate if reduced-calorie spread is used.

BANANA BREAD PUDDING

See Menu Plan for Week 40.
Makes 2 servings

1 cup skim milk, scalded
1 medium banana, mashed
2 eggs
2 slices raisin bread, each cut into
   6 squares
1 teaspoon honey
1 teaspoon grated orange rind
¼ teaspoon salt

Preheat oven to 350°F. In mixing bowl blend together milk and banana. Add eggs, bread, honey, orange rind, and salt; stir to combine. Turn into 1-quart nonstick baking pan. Bake for 40 minutes or until toothpick, when inserted in pudding, comes out clean. Let stand 10 minutes before serving.

Per serving: 246 calories; 13 g protein; 7 g fat;
36 g carbohydrate; 511 mg sodium

BREAD PUDDING

See Menu Plan for Week 26 and various other weeks.
Makes 4 servings

4 eggs
⅔ cup nonfat dry milk powder, dissolved
   in 2 cups water
Artificial sweetener to equal 6 teaspoons
   sugar
1 teaspoon vanilla extract
½ teaspoon ground cinnamon
⅛ teaspoon ground nutmeg
⅛ teaspoon salt
4 slices raisin bread, toasted and cut into
   cubes

Preheat oven to 350°F. In bowl beat eggs until frothy. Add dissolved milk powder, sweetener, vanilla, cinnamon, nutmeg, and salt; stir to combine. Add bread cubes, pressing down with spatula so bread can absorb as much egg mixture as possible. Let stand 5 minutes. Spray an 8-inch square nonstick baking pan with nonstick cooking spray; pour in pudding mixture. Place pan in larger pan; pour hot water into larger pan to a depth of about 1 inch. Bake 35 to 40 minutes or until a knife, when inserted in center, comes out clean. Remove from oven and cool. May be served chilled or at room temperature.

Per serving: 193 calories; 12 g protein; 6 g fat;
20 g carbohydrate; 294 mg sodium

FRUITED BREAD PUDDING

May be served at room temperature or chilled.

See Menu Plan for Week 30.
Makes 4 servings

4 slices whole wheat bread, torn into pieces
2 cups evaporated skimmed milk
4 eggs
Artificial sweetener to equal 12 teaspoons
   sugar
Brown sugar substitute to equal 12
   teaspoons sugar
1 teaspoon ground cinnamon
¼ teaspoon salt
Dash ground nutmeg
1 medium banana, cut into small pieces
½ cup canned crushed pineapple, no sugar
   added
2 tablespoons raisins

Preheat oven to 375°F. Spray a round 8-inch nonstick cake pan with nonstick cooking spray. Combine first 8 ingredients in large bowl and let stand 15 minutes. Stir in fruit and turn into prepared pan. Bake until almost set, about 30 minutes; center should be soft. Serve at room temperature or refrigerate and serve chilled.

Per serving: 304 calories; 19 g protein; 7 g fat;
44 g carbohydrate; 486 mg sodium

BRAN WAFFLES

Serve with reduced-calorie spread or low-calorie maple syrup.

See Menu Plan for Week 18.
Makes 2 servings

¼ cup plus 1 tablespoon whole wheat flour
Artificial sweetener to equal 6 teaspoons
   sugar
1 teaspoon baking powder
½ teaspoon baking soda
¼ teaspoon salt
2 eggs, separated
¾ cup buttermilk
¾ ounce wheat bran ready-to-eat cereal
2 teaspoons margarine, melted
1 teaspoon grated lemon rind

Sift flour, sweetener, baking powder, baking soda, and salt into bowl. In another bowl beat egg yolks; add buttermilk, bran cereal, margarine, and lemon rind. Stir until cereal is moistened. Add to flour mixture and stir to combine. In separate bowl beat egg whites until stiff; fold into batter. Heat nonstick waffle iron. Pour batter into waffle iron; cook until browned.

Per serving: 248 calories; 13 g protein; 11 g fat;
29 g carbohydrate; 986 mg sodium

BUTTERMILK PANCAKES
See Menu Plan for Week 24.
Makes 2 servings

1 ounce uncooked enriched yellow
    cornmeal
2 tablespoons plus 1½ teaspoons enriched
    flour
1 teaspoon sugar
¼ teaspoon baking powder
¼ teaspoon baking soda
⅛ teaspoon salt
½ cup buttermilk
1 tablespoon plus 1 teaspoon reduced-
    calorie spread, any flavor

Sift first 6 ingredients into small bowl.
Gradually stir in milk; continue to stir until
batter is smooth. Spray a nonstick skillet
with nonstick cooking spray and heat. Drop
batter from a tablespoon onto skillet, making 8 pancakes. Brown pancakes on both
sides. Top each pancake with ½ teaspoon
spread.

Per serving: 133 calories; 4 g protein; 1 g fat;
27 g carbohydrate; 329 mg sodium

CORNMEAL PANCAKES
See Menu Plan for Week 14.
Makes 2 servings

2 ounces uncooked enriched yellow
    cornmeal
¼ cup plus 1 tablespoon enriched flour
¼ teaspoon baking soda
¼ teaspoon baking powder
⅛ teaspoon salt
2 teaspoons margarine, softened
1 cup buttermilk
1 tablespoon reduced-calorie strawberry
    spread

Combine cornmeal, flour, baking soda, baking powder, and salt; sift into a medium
bowl. Stir in margarine. Gradually add milk;
stir until just combined. Spray a 7-inch
skillet with nonstick cooking spray and heat.
Pour in ¼ cup of batter, spreading it with
a spatula. Cook until brown on bottom;
turn and brown other side. Remove to plate

and keep warm. Repeat with remaining batter, respraying pan if necessary. Makes 6
pancakes. Top each pancake with ½ teaspoon spread.

Per serving: 263 calories; 8 g protein; 5 g fat;
44 g carbohydrate; 439 mg sodium

FRUITED MATZO KUGEL
See Menu Plan for Week 15.
Makes 4 servings

1½ small apples, pared, cored, and coarsely
    grated
1 teaspoon lemon juice
4 eggs
2 tablespoons plus 2 teaspoons margarine,
    divided
Artificial sweetener to equal 4 teaspoons
    sugar
2 teaspoons sugar
¾ teaspoon cinnamon
½ cup plus 1 tablespoon matzo meal
3 tablespoons raisins
1 tablespoon plus 1 teaspoon potato starch
2 teaspoons honey
4 medium dried apricot halves, each cut
    into 3 strips
Dash salt

In small bowl toss grated apple with lemon
juice and set aside. Separate 2 of the eggs.
In a bowl combine yolks with 2 whole eggs,
2 tablespoons margarine, sweetener, sugar,
and cinnamon. Beat until mixture is light
and fluffy. Add matzo meal, raisins, potato
starch, and grated apple mixture; stir to
combine. Let stand 30 minutes.

Coat sides and bottom of a 7⅜ x 3⅝ x
2¼-inch loaf pan with 2 teaspoons margarine. Spread honey on bottom of pan.
Arrange apricot strips decoratively over
honey.

Preheat oven to 325°F. In a separate bowl
beat egg whites with salt until stiff peaks
form. Fold whites into matzo mixture. Carefully spoon batter into pan over fruit. Bake
for 1 hour. Remove from oven and place on
rack for 5 minutes. Using a small spatula

loosen edges of kugel and invert onto rack to cool.

Per serving: 282 calories; 8 g protein; 14 g fat; 33 g carbohydrate; 206 mg sodium

MOCK KISHKA

Try this as an appetizer or side dish.
See Menu Plan for Week 15.
Makes 4 servings, 2 slices each

½ cup coarsely chopped carrot
½ cup coarsely chopped celery
¼ cup coarsely chopped onion
2 matzo boards, broken into pieces
1 tablespoon margarine, softened
¼ teaspoon salt
⅛ teaspoon pepper
Parsley sprigs to garnish

In work bowl of food processor process carrot, celery, and onion until finely chopped. Add matzo, margarine, salt, and pepper, and process until the mixture holds together. Form into a small loaf about 5 inches long and 1½ inches wide. Place on nonstick baking sheet; bake at 400°F. for 20 to 25 minutes or until well browned. Let stand 10 minutes. Using a spatula, transfer to serving dish and allow to cool completely. Garnish with parsley. Cut into 8 equal slices.

Per serving: 107 calories; 3 g protein; 3 g fat; 17 g carbohydrate; 204 mg sodium

EGGPLANT STUFFING

See Menu Plan for Week 35.
Makes 2 servings

2 cups pared and cubed eggplant
½ teaspoon salt, divided
1½ cups sliced mushrooms
½ cup diced onion
½ cup cooked brown rice
½ English muffin, cut into cubes
½ teaspoon chopped fresh parsley
Dash each thyme leaves, sage leaves, and
    pepper

Place eggplant on paper towels and sprinkle with ¼ teaspoon salt; rub cubes together to distribute salt evenly and let stand 1 hour.

Preheat oven to 350°F. Spray baking sheet with nonstick cooking spray; place eggplant on sheet and bake for 15 minutes. Set aside.

Combine mushrooms, onion, and remaining ¼ teaspoon salt in medium nonstick skillet; cook over medium heat until mushrooms are tender but not limp, about 5 minutes. Combine eggplant, mushrooms, and remaining ingredients in 1-quart casserole, pressing mixture firmly into casserole. Cover and bake 25 to 30 minutes.

Per serving: 148 calories; 6 g protein; 1 g fat; 30 g carbohydrate; 677 mg sodium

MANDARIN RICE SALAD

See Menu Plan for Week 29.
Makes 2 servings

1 cup cooked enriched rice
½ cup diced celery
½ cup pared and diced cucumber
½ cup canned mandarin orange sections,
    no sugar added
2 tablespoons lemon juice
2 teaspoons olive oil
Dash each artificial sweetener, salt, and
    pepper

In serving bowl combine rice, celery, cucumber, and orange sections. In small bowl mix lemon juice with remaining ingredients. Pour over rice mixture and toss to combine. Cover and chill for 1 hour.

Per serving: 165 calories; 3 g protein; 5 g fat; 28 g carbohydrate; 129 mg sodium

RICE CRISPS
Delicious with salad or hot vegetables.
See Menu Plan for Week 31.
Makes 2 servings

1 corn tortilla, 6-inch diameter, crisped in
   oven
½ cup cooked brown rice
2 teaspoons grated Parmesan cheese
½ teaspoon salt
Dash white pepper

Break tortilla into small pieces; place between 2 sheets of wax paper and crush into
crumbs with rolling pin. Transfer crumbs to
bowl; add rice, cheese, salt, and pepper.
Mash rice mixture until it forms a paste.
Form mixture into 8 slightly flattened balls.
Place on nonstick baking sheet, leaving
enough space between balls for spreading.
Place sheet of wax paper over balls. Using
flat spatula or bottom of a glass, gently press
down and flatten each ball to about the
thickness of a rice grain. Carefully peel off
wax paper. Bake at 300°F. for 20 to 25 minutes or until lightly browned. Remove from
oven and cool.

Per serving: 95 calories; 4 g protein; 2 g fat;
16 g carbohydrate; 674 mg sodium

BULGUR PILAF
See Menu Plan for Week 52.
Makes 6 servings

1 cup diced onions
3 packets instant chicken broth and
   seasoning mix
6 ounces uncooked cracked wheat (Bulgur)
3 cups water
½ cup diced celery
½ teaspoon marjoram leaves
Dash each salt and pepper
Chopped fresh parsley to garnish

In saucepan combine onions and broth mix.
Cook, stirring frequently, until onions are
tender. Add cracked wheat. Gradually add
water and remaining ingredients except
parsley. Bring to a boil. Reduce heat; cover
and simmer, stirring occasionally, for 35

minutes or until cracked wheat is tender and
fluffy. Garnish with parsley.

Per serving: 120 calories; 4 g protein; 0.4 g fat;
27 g carbohydrate; 454 mg sodium

KASHA MIX
See Menu Plan for Week 37.
Makes 2 servings

¾ cup Chicken Broth (see page 127) or
   chicken bouillon
2 celery ribs, pared,* sliced lengthwise,
   and cut into 1½-inch sticks
Dash each salt and pepper
½ cup cooked short- or long-grain brown
   rice
½ cup cooked buckwheat groats (kasha)
½ teaspoon chopped fresh parsley

In small saucepan combine broth, celery,
salt, and pepper; cover and simmer about 10
minutes or until celery is tender. In medium
bowl combine rice, kasha, and parsley; pour
broth mixture over rice mixture and stir
gently to combine.

Per serving: 110 calories; 3 g protein; 1 g fat;
24 g carbohydrate; 148 mg sodium

* Use a vegetable peeler to remove stringy outer
layer.

MILLET WITH VEGETABLES
Millet, a grain that is a member of the grass
family, is grown as a staple for a third of the
world's population. It is extremely popular
in India, Egypt, and Africa. Uncooked millet
can be purchased in specialty and Oriental
food stores, as whole grain, grits, and ground.
Puffed millet is packaged and sold as a
ready-to-eat cereal.
See Menu Plan for Week 5.
Makes 2 servings

2 ounces uncooked hulled millet
2 teaspoons margarine
¼ cup chopped onion
1 packet instant chicken broth and
   seasoning mix

1 cup water
¾ cup pared and cubed butternut squash,
    1-inch cubes
½ cup sliced celery

Toast millet in nonstick skillet until lightly browned, stirring often. Melt margarine in saucepan; add onion and sauté until softened and lightly browned. Stir in broth mix; add water and bring to a boil. Reduce heat to low; add millet, cover, and cook 10 minutes. Add squash and celery; stir lightly and cook 20 minutes longer or until millet and vegetables are tender and water is absorbed.

Per serving: 173 calories; 5 g protein; 5 g fat;
32 g carbohydrate; 455 mg sodium

CURRIED PASTA WITH GINGERED PEAS
See Menu Plan for Week 22.
Makes 2 servings

2 teaspoons olive oil
1 teaspoon minced fresh ginger root
1 cup cooked peas
½ teaspoon salt
Dash pepper
1⅓ cups cooked enriched spaghetti
¼ teaspoon curry powder, dissolved in
    1 teaspoon lemon juice

Heat oil in 10-inch skillet; add ginger and sauté for 1 minute. Add peas, salt, and pepper; sauté 1 minute longer. Combine spaghetti and dissolved curry powder with peas and sauté, stirring occasionally, about 3 minutes longer or until thoroughly heated.

Per serving: 207 calories; 8 g protein; 5 g fat;
32 g carbohydrate; 684 mg sodium

LINGUINE PRIMAVERA
See Menu Plan for Week 27.
Makes 2 servings

2 teaspoons olive oil
2 teaspoons margarine
1 garlic clove, minced
1 cup broccoli florets, blanched

¼ cup thinly sliced carrot
½ medium tomato, seeded and diced
½ teaspoon basil leaves
1⅓ cups cooked enriched linguine
2 teaspoons grated Parmesan cheese
Dash each salt and freshly ground pepper

Heat oil and margarine in medium skillet; add garlic and sauté for 2 minutes. Add next 4 ingredients and cook, stirring often, for 5 minutes. Add linguine and cook, stirring often, 5 minutes longer or until hot. Sprinkle with Parmesan cheese, salt, and pepper.

Per serving: 245 calories; 9 g protein; 11 g fat;
30 g carbohydrate; 250 mg sodium

BASIL MACARONI
See Menu Plan for Week 51.
Makes 2 servings

2 ounces uncooked enriched elbow
    macaroni
¾ cup Chicken Broth (see page 127)
½ cup frozen peas
1 teaspoon chopped fresh basil, or
    ¼ teaspoon dried
Dash each salt and white pepper

Cook macaroni until al dente, about 7 minutes. In a saucepan bring broth to a boil; add peas. Cook for 3 minutes. Add macaroni, basil, salt, and pepper. Cook over medium-high heat, stirring occasionally, until most of the broth is absorbed.

Per serving: 141 calories; 6 g protein; 1 g fat;
28 g carbohydrate; 150 mg sodium

CHICK PEAS (GARBANZOS) WITH TINY SHELLS
See Menu Plan for Week 9.
Makes 2 servings

2 teaspoons olive oil
1 tablespoon minced scallion
1 garlic clove, mashed
3 ounces drained canned chick peas
    (garbanzos), reserve ½ cup liquid
Dash each salt and pepper
⅔ cup cooked enriched tiny macaroni shells

Heat oil in small saucepan; add scallion and garlic and sauté until translucent. Stir in chick peas, reserved liquid, salt, and pepper; bring to a boil. Add macaroni shells, heat through, and serve immediately.

Per serving: 116 calories; 4 g protein; 1 g fat;
23 g carbohydrate (sodium data
unavailable for chick peas)

PASTA KUGEL
See Menu Plan for Week 44.
Makes 2 servings

⅔ cup part-skim ricotta cheese
½ cup skim milk
2 eggs
Artificial sweetener to equal 4 teaspoons
    sugar
1 teaspoon honey
¼ teaspoon each apple pie spice and
    vanilla extract
Dash salt
1⅓ cups cooked enriched mafalde (mini-
    lasagna), cut into 1½-inch pieces
2 tablespoons raisins, chopped

Preheat oven to 350°F. In blender container combine all ingredients except mafalde and raisins; process until smooth. Transfer cheese mixture to medium bowl; stir in mafalde and raisins. Spoon ½ of mixture into each of two 1¾-cup casseroles* that have been sprayed with nonstick cooking spray. Bake until surface is firm and slightly browned, about 30 to 35 minutes.

Per serving: 395 calories; 22 g protein; 14 g fat;
45 g carbohydrate; 277 mg sodium

* A 1-quart casserole may be used instead of two 1¾-cup casseroles.

HOLIDAY NOODLE PUDDING
See Menu Plan for Week 38.
Makes 2 servings

2 teaspoons margarine
1 small McIntosh apple, pared, cored, and
    cut into quarters
2 tablespoons golden raisins
1 cup cooked enriched noodles
Dash salt
1 egg
Artificial sweetener to equal 2 teaspoons
    sugar
1 teaspoon sugar
⅛ teaspoon vanilla extract
Dash ground cinnamon

Melt margarine in small skillet. Cut each apple quarter crosswise into ¼-inch thick slices. Add apple slices and raisins to skillet; sauté over medium heat until apple slices are tender-crisp. Remove from heat and transfer apple-raisin mixture to medium bowl; add noodles and salt and stir to combine.

Preheat oven to 400°F. In mixing bowl combine egg, sweetener, sugar, vanilla, and cinnamon; beat with electric mixer at high speed for 2 minutes. Fold noodle mixture into egg mixture and transfer to 1-quart casserole that has been sprayed with nonstick cooking spray. Bake about 15 minutes or until a knife, when inserted in center, comes out clean. Remove from oven and serve.

Per serving: 244 calories; 7 g protein; 8 g fat;
37 g carbohydrate; 178 mg sodium

CANADIAN PARSLEY SOUP
See Menu Plan for Week 31.
Makes 4 servings

2¼ cups Chicken Broth (see page 127)
    or chicken bouillon
2 cups chopped romaine lettuce
1 cup water
8 ounces pared potatoes, diced
½ cup chopped fresh parsley
⅛ teaspoon white pepper

In saucepan combine broth, lettuce, water,

potatoes, and parsley. Bring to a boil; reduce heat, cover, and simmer 20 minutes. Add white pepper. In several batches, process mixture in blender container until pureed. Return soup to saucepan; heat and serve.

Per serving: 62 calories; 3 g protein; 0.2 g fat; 12 g carbohydrate; 6 mg sodium

POTATO SOUP
See Menu Plan for Week 45.
Makes 4 servings

1 pound pared and diced potatoes
1 tablespoon plus 1 teaspoon margarine
½ cup minced onion
¼ cup each minced carrot and celery
1½ cups Chicken Broth (see page 127)
1 cup evaporated skimmed milk
½ teaspoon salt
Dash pepper
Chopped chives to garnish

In medium saucepan place potatoes in just enough cold water to cover. Cover and bring to a boil; cook over moderate heat until tender. Puree potatoes with remaining cooking liquid, using a food mill or potato masher. Return potatoes to saucepan and set aside.

Melt margarine in nonstick skillet. Add onion and sauté over medium heat until translucent. Add carrot and celery and cook about 2 minutes. Add vegetable mixture to saucepan containing potatoes. Place over medium heat and stir in broth, milk, salt, and pepper. Simmer about 5 minutes or until thoroughly heated. Garnish with chives.

Per serving: 188 calories; 8 g protein; 4 g fat; 31 g carbohydrate; 431 mg sodium

BACON-FLAVORED POTATO SALAD
See Menu Plan for Week 14.
Makes 2 servings

8 ounces small potatoes
2 teaspoons sesame or vegetable oil
¼ cup diced onion

2 teaspoons imitation bacon bits
2 teaspoons red wine vinegar
⅛ teaspoon salt
Dash pepper

In medium saucepan combine potatoes with enough water to cover. Bring to a boil; cover, reduce heat to medium, and cook until just tender but not soft, about 10 minutes. Drain and allow to cool.

Heat oil in small skillet; add diced onion and sauté until tender. Add bacon bits and cook 2 minutes longer.

Peel potatoes and cut into cubes. In bowl gently toss potatoes with vinegar. Add onion mixture and seasonings; toss gently to combine.

Per serving: 145 calories; 3 g protein; 5 g fat; 22 g carbohydrate; 254 mg sodium

CREAMY POTATO SALAD
See Menu Plan for Week 11.
Makes 2 servings

8 ounces peeled cooked potatoes, cubed
3 tablespoons minced onion
1½ teaspoons white wine vinegar
¼ teaspoon salt
⅔ cup cottage cheese, sieved
1 tablespoon plus 1 teaspoon reduced-calorie mayonnaise
1 tablespoon chopped fresh parsley
½ teaspoon Dijon-style mustard
Dash hot sauce
2 eggs, hard-cooked and chopped
2 parsley sprigs

In bowl toss potatoes with onion, vinegar, and salt. In small bowl combine cottage cheese, mayonnaise, parsley, mustard, and hot sauce. Spoon cottage cheese mixture over potatoes; add eggs and toss to combine. Cover and refrigerate 1 hour. Garnish with parsley sprigs.

Per serving: 262 calories; 18 g protein; 11 g fat; 22 g carbohydrate; 756 mg sodium

POTATO AND GREEN BEAN SALAD
See Menu Plans for Weeks 34 and 41.
Makes 2 servings

8 ounces boiled and peeled small new
    potatoes, sliced
1 cup cooked cut green beans
1 cup cherry tomatoes, cut into halves
½ cup sliced red onion, separated into rings
2 tablespoons tarragon vinegar
2 teaspoons vegetable or olive oil
¾ teaspoon salt
Dash freshly ground pepper
Chopped fresh basil to garnish

Combine all ingredients except basil in a
medium bowl; toss. Sprinkle with basil.

Per serving: 163 calories; 5 g protein; 5 g fat;
28 g carbohydrate; 888 mg sodium

PARSLEY POTATOES
See Menu Plan for Week 52.
Makes 6 servings

1½ pounds new potatoes
½ teaspoon salt
2 tablespoons chopped fresh parsley

Place potatoes in a large saucepan with
enough water to cover; add salt. Cover and
boil about 20 minutes or until tender. Drain
and peel. Sprinkle with parsley.

Per serving: 74 calories; 2 g protein; 0.1 g fat;
17 g carbohydrate; 187 mg sodium

POTATO CRISPS
See Menu Plans for Weeks 6 and 30.
Makes 2 servings

8 ounces pared potatoes, sliced very thin
1 teaspoon salt
Dash pepper

Preheat oven to 250°F. Spray wire rack with
nonstick cooking spray. Arrange potato slices
on rack in a single layer. Sprinkle ½ of salt
over slices; turn and sprinkle with remaining
salt and pepper. Bake for 25 to 30 minutes.

Increase oven temperature to 350°F. and
bake 5 to 10 minutes longer or until slices
are browned and crisp. Carefully remove
from rack and serve.

Per serving: 86 calories; 2 g protein; 0.1 g fat;
19 g carbohydrate; 1,110 mg sodium

POTATO PANCAKES
See Menu Plan for Week 50.
Makes 1 serving

4 ounces pared potatoes, finely grated and
    drained
1 egg
2 tablespoons minced onion
1 tablespoon plus ¾ teaspoon enriched flour
¼ teaspoon salt
⅛ teaspoon white pepper
1 teaspoon vegetable oil

Combine all ingredients except oil in a bowl
and mix well. Heat oil in an 8-inch skillet.
Pour ½ of potato mixture into skillet and
cook over medium heat until bottom is
browned; turn and brown other side. Repeat
process with remaining mixture.

Per serving: 249 calories; 10 g protein; 11 g fat;
29 g carbohydrate; 628 mg sodium

POTATO PIE
See Menu Plan for Week 16.
Makes 2 servings

8 ounces grated pared potatoes
4 eggs, beaten slightly
½ cup minced scallions
¼ cup minced red bell pepper
½ teaspoon salt
Dash pepper
2 teaspoons grated Parmesan cheese
1 medium tomato, sliced
2 parsley sprigs

In bowl combine potatoes, eggs, scallions,
red pepper, salt, and pepper; mix thoroughly.
Pour into a nonstick pie pan that has been
sprayed with nonstick cooking spray. Bake
at 400°F. approximately 40 minutes or until

center is cooked. Sprinkle with Parmesan cheese and broil until lightly browned. Garnish with sliced tomato and parsley.

Per serving: 300 calories; 18 g protein; 13 g fat; 28 g carbohydrate; 822 mg sodium

POTATO-PUMPKIN PUFFS
See Menu Plan for Week 47.
Makes 4 servings

1 pound pared potatoes, cut into pieces
1 cup canned pumpkin
1 tablespoon plus 1 teaspoon margarine
¼ teaspoon pumpkin pie spice
¼ teaspoon salt

In saucepan boil potatoes in salted water to cover until soft. Drain well and transfer to a bowl. Preheat oven to 350°F. Mash potatoes until smooth. Add pumpkin, margarine, pumpkin pie spice, and salt; beat to combine. Fill a pastry bag, fitted with a pastry tube, with potato-pumpkin mixture. Make 8 puffs, each about 2 inches wide, on a baking sheet that has been sprayed with nonstick cooking spray; bake puffs 15 to 20 minutes or until lightly browned.

Per serving: 140 calories; 3 g protein; 4 g fat; 24 g carbohydrate; 323 mg sodium

POTATO-RICE CASSEROLE
See Menu Plan for Week 38.
Makes 2 servings

2 teaspoons margarine
2 teaspoons enriched flour
1 cup skim milk, heated
½ teaspoon salt
⅛ teaspoon tarragon leaves
Dash pepper
4 ounces cooked and peeled potatoes, diced
½ cup cooked brown rice
½ cup minced onion

Preheat oven to 350°F. In small saucepan melt margarine. Stirring constantly, add flour and cook over medium heat 1 minute. Add milk gradually, stirring briskly with a wire whisk. Add salt, tarragon, and pepper, and cook over low heat, stirring occasionally until thickened, about 5 minutes. Combine potatoes, rice, and onion with sauce and pour into 1-quart casserole. Bake for 25 minutes or until bubbly.

Per serving: 193 calories; 7 g protein; 4 g fat; 31 g carbohydrate; 701 mg sodium

POTATO-SPINACH COMBO
See Menu Plan for Week 48.
Makes 2 servings

8 ounces pared potatoes
½ cup frozen chopped spinach, thawed
1 tablespoon plus 1 teaspoon reduced-calorie margarine, divided
¾ teaspoon salt
Dash each pepper and paprika
2 eggs, separated

Cook potatoes in boiling water to cover until tender. Drain and transfer to mixing bowl. Preheat oven to 350°F. Whip potatoes until smooth and fluffy. Add spinach, 1 tablespoon margarine, salt, pepper, and paprika; mix well. Blend in egg yolks. In separate bowl beat whites until stiff peaks form; fold into potato mixture. Grease a 2-cup casserole with remaining margarine; spoon mixture into casserole. Bake for 40 minutes or until top is golden brown.

Per serving: 211 calories; 10 g protein; 10 g fat; 22 g carbohydrate; 961 mg sodium

VEGETABLE MOLD
See Menu Plan for Week 15.
Makes 4 servings

1 pound pared potatoes
½ teaspoon salt
Dash pepper
1¼ cups sliced zucchini, ¼-inch thick slices,
    steamed until tender-crisp
1 cup broccoli florets, steamed until
    tender-crisp
¼ cup sliced crookneck squash, ¼-inch
    thick slices, steamed until tender-crisp
30 green beans, about 2 cups, steamed until
    tender-crisp
3 medium carrots, cut into about 30 sticks
    (same length as beans), steamed until
    tender-crisp
4 cabbage leaves, steamed until tender-crisp

In saucepan boil potatoes until tender. Drain, reserving 3 tablespoons liquid. In bowl mash potatoes adding potato liquid, salt, and pepper; set aside.

Preheat oven to 350°F. Spray the bottom and sides of a 5-cup round soufflé dish, 5¾-inch diameter x 2¾ inches deep, with non-stick cooking spray. In bottom of dish, using some of the zucchini, make an outer circle of overlapping zucchini slices. Place a broccoli floret, flower-end down, in center. Arrange a circle of overlapping crookneck squash slices around floret, completely covering bottom of dish.

Stand green beans and carrot sticks upright, in an alternating pattern on top of zucchini, leaning against side of dish. As you arrange them, use 1 or 2 clean cloth towels, crumpled up and placed against beans and carrots to help support them. Trim beans and carrots flush with top rim of mold. Carefully remove towels and, using a spatula, spread ½ of potato mixture up sides of mold to support carrot sticks and beans, then over squash and broccoli on bottom.

Cover potatoes with 2 cabbage leaves. Press down. Arrange remaining broccoli over cabbage leaves. Place the remaining zucchini in overlapping circles over broccoli. Cover with last 2 cabbage leaves. Spread remaining potatoes over cabbage leaves.

Bake for 25 minutes. Remove from oven and let stand 15 minutes before unmolding onto serving platter.

Per serving: 150 calories; 6 g protein; 1 g fat;
33 g carbohydrate; 337 mg sodium

BAKED YAMS
This is so delicious you could use it for dessert. For something nice to have on hand, divide it into 4 individual portions and freeze them.
See Menu Plans for Weeks 4, 18, and the Last Day of the Year.
Makes 4 servings

4 medium yams
½ teaspoon freshly grated orange rind
Dash each ground allspice and salt

Place yams in 8-inch square baking pan. Cover with foil and bake at 350°F. about 1½ hours or until tender. Remove yams from oven and cut each in half; remove skin and weigh 12 ounces of yams into small bowl.* Add orange rind, allspice, and salt. Mash with potato masher or beat with electric mixer until smooth.

Per serving: 92 calories; 2 g protein; 0.2 g fat;
21 g carbohydrate; 88 mg sodium

* Remaining yams can be frozen in measured portions and used at a later date.

HONEY-GLAZED YAMS
Be sure to use an aluminum baking sheet or one with a shiny surface. The darker the surface, the more readily the yams will burn.
See Menu Plan for Week 42.
Makes 4 servings

2 large or 4 medium whole yams, unpeeled
2 teaspoons honey

Place yams in large saucepan with water to cover. Bring to a boil and cook until just tender (knife should insert with some ease). *Do not overcook.* Drain and rinse in cold water. Preheat oven to 400°F. Peel yams and weigh 12 ounces; any remaining can be frozen for use at a later date. Cut into ½-inch cubes. Arrange cubes in a single layer on aluminum baking sheet that has been sprayed with nonstick cooking spray; bake 15 minutes. Turn with spatula and bake until browned and a crisp crust forms, about 15 minutes longer. Warm honey in small custard or measuring cup placed in hot water and drizzle over yams.

Per serving: 101 calories; 2 g protein; 0.2 g fat; 23 g carbohydrate; 13 mg sodium

FRUIT AND YAM SALAD WITH HONEYED YOGURT DRESSING

For a taste treat try this unusual combination!

See Menu Plan for Week 51.

Makes 2 servings

¼ cup plain unflavored yogurt
1 teaspoon honey
⅛ teaspoon grated lemon rind
½ medium banana, cut into ¼-inch thick slices
1 tablespoon lemon juice
¼ small cantaloupe, pared and cut into ½-inch chunks
3 ounces cooked and peeled yam, chilled and cut into ½-inch chunks
6 large grapes, cut into halves

In small bowl combine yogurt, honey, and lemon rind; refrigerate 1 hour.

Combine banana slices and lemon juice in medium bowl; toss and let stand 1 minute. Drain off lemon juice. Add melon, yam, and grapes to banana and toss gently. Divide fruit mixture into 2 individual bowls. Serve each topped with ½ of the yogurt dressing or serve dressing on the side.

Per serving: 147 calories; 3 g protein; 1 g fat; 33 g carbohydrate; 47 mg sodium

MOCK HUMMUS WITH VEGETABLE DIPPERS

See Menu Plan for Week 28.

Makes 2 servings

1 teaspoon sesame seeds, toasted
¼ teaspoon salt
3 ounces drained canned chick peas (garbanzos)

3 ounces pared and cooked yam
½ teaspoon lemon juice
1 cup carrot sticks
1 cup zucchini sticks

Using a mortar and pestle or the flat side of a knife, pulverize sesame seeds with salt to form a dry paste. Transfer to work bowl of food processor or blender container. Add chick peas, yam, and lemon juice; process until smooth. Serve as a dip with carrot and zucchini sticks.

Per serving: 116 calories; 4 g protein; 1 g fat; 23 g carbohydrate; 307 mg sodium (sodium data unavailable for chick peas)

SPINACH-YAM LOAF

The process of baking food in a pan that has been placed in a larger pan containing hot water is called baking in a waterbath. This method is used to help control temperature and is particularly suited to egg cookery.

See Menu Plan for Week 6.

Makes 2 servings

⅔ cup cooked and well-squeezed chopped spinach
¼ cup diced red bell pepper, parboiled
2 eggs
¾ teaspoon salt, divided
Dash white pepper
6 ounces cooked, peeled, and mashed yams
Dash ground nutmeg

Preheat oven to 350°F. Combine spinach, red pepper, 1 egg, ¼ teaspoon salt, and white pepper in a bowl and set aside. In a separate bowl combine yams, remaining salt, nutmeg, and remaining egg. Spread ½ of yams over bottom of an 8 x 5 x 2½-inch loaf pan that has been sprayed with nonstick cooking spray. Carefully layer spinach mixture over yams. Spread remaining yams over spinach. Place loaf pan in a larger baking pan and pour in about 1 inch hot water. Bake 45 minutes. Remove from oven and cool 15 minutes. With sharp knife loosen edges of loaf and unmold onto serving platter.

Per serving: 199 calories; 11 g protein; 6 g fat; 27 g carbohydrate; 1,037 mg sodium

SWEET POTATO TZIMMES
See Menu Plan for Week 13.
Makes 2 servings

6 ounces peeled hot cooked sweet potatoes
1 cup hot cooked sliced carrots
½ cup canned crushed pineapple, no sugar
   added
1 tablespoon plus 1 teaspoon reduced-
   calorie orange marmalade
½ teaspoon grated orange rind
⅛ teaspoon ground cinnamon
Dash salt

In medium bowl mash together potatoes and
carrots. Add remaining ingredients; stir to
combine. Transfer to a 2-cup casserole and
bake at 375°F. for 30 minutes.

Per serving: 162 calories; 3 g protein; 0.4 g fat;
39 g carbohydrate; 159 mg sodium

Salads

Fresh crisp greens, bright flavorful vegetables,
aromatic herbs and spices—that's what
salads are made of. But don't stop there!
Try some of our salad specialties and your meal
is sure to be a delight. Braised Leek Salad,
Green Bean Confetti Salad, Curried Cole Slaw,
and Sunchoke and Kraut Salad are fresh and
unusual combinations of seasonal produce.
Make salads a year-round part of your menu plan.

BROCCOLI SALAD
See Menu Plan for Week 7.
Makes 4 servings

4 cups blanched broccoli florets
1 cup cherry tomatoes, cut into halves
4 black olives, pitted and sliced
3 tablespoons sliced scallion
2 tablespoons plus 2 teaspoons olive oil
2 tablespoons plus 2 teaspoons red wine
  vinegar
1 tablespoon water
1 teaspoon Dijon-style mustard
1 garlic clove, minced
Dash each salt and freshly ground pepper

In bowl combine broccoli, cherry tomatoes, olives, and scallion. Combine remaining ingredients in blender container; process for 30 seconds. Add to broccoli salad and toss to combine.

Per serving: 158 calories; 7 g protein; 12 g fat; 12 g carbohydrate; 136 mg sodium

LEMONY BRUSSELS SPROUTS AND CARROTS SALAD
See Menu Plan for Week 10.
Makes 2 servings

1 cup Brussels sprouts
2 teaspoons vegetable oil
3 medium carrots, pared and thinly sliced
  on the diagonal
Salt
2 teaspoons lemon juice
Dash white pepper
2 cups chopped lettuce
2 teaspoons diced red bell pepper

Steam Brussels sprouts until just tender, about 5 to 8 minutes. Cool under cold running water and set aside.

Heat oil in skillet. Add carrot slices in a layer. Sauté over medium heat until tender-crisp. Sprinkle with dash salt and turn slices over. Cover skillet, reduce heat to low, and cook an additional 3 minutes or until slices are just tender but not limp; set aside.

In bowl combine lemon juice, dash salt, and pepper. Slice each Brussels sprout in half lengthwise; combine with lemon juice and toss to coat.

Make a bed of 1 cup chopped lettuce on each of 2 salad plates. Top each portion of lettuce with ½ of the carrot slices, arranged in a circular pattern. Place ½ of the Brussels sprouts in center of each portion of carrots and sprinkle each salad with 1 teaspoon diced pepper. Serve well chilled.

Per serving: 119 calories; 4 g protein; 5 g fat; 18 g carbohydrate; 223 mg sodium

APPLE CIDER SLAW
See Menu Plan for Week 42.
Makes 4 servings

6 cups shredded cabbage
⅓ cup apple cider or juice, no sugar added
1 cup grated carrots
½ cup diced green bell pepper
½ cup diced celery
2 tablespoons minced onion
1 tablespoon plus 1 teaspoon mayonnaise
¼ teaspoon salt
⅛ teaspoon white pepper
Parsley sprigs to garnish

Combine cabbage and cider in large bowl, mixing well. Refrigerate for ½ hour.

In another bowl combine remaining ingredients except parsley; add to cabbage mixture. Refrigerate ½ hour longer. Just before serving toss well and garnish with parsley.

Per serving: 101 calories; 3 g protein; 4 g fat; 16 g carbohydrate; 237 mg sodium

COLE SLAW VINAIGRETTE

See Menu Plan for Week 31 and various other weeks.
Makes 4 servings

¼ cup cider vinegar
2 tablespoons plus 2 teaspoons vegetable oil
1 teaspoon celery seed
¼ teaspoon powdered mustard
Dash garlic powder
3 cups shredded cabbage
¼ cup grated carrot
¼ cup diced green bell pepper

In medium bowl, using a wire whisk, combine vinegar, oil, celery seed, mustard, and garlic powder. Add remaining ingredients; toss. Chill at least 1 hour.

Per serving: 112 calories; 1 g protein; 10 g fat; 7 g carbohydrate; 21 mg sodium

CURRIED COLE SLAW

See Menu Plan for Week 36 and various other weeks.
Makes 2 servings

2 cups shredded cabbage
¼ cup chopped green bell pepper
¼ cup chopped carrot
¼ teaspoon salt
⅛ teaspoon celery seed
Dash pepper
⅓ cup water
¼ cup cider vinegar
2 teaspoons dehydrated onion flakes
1 teaspoon lemon juice
⅛ teaspoon curry powder

Combine cabbage, green pepper, carrot, salt, celery seed, and pepper in medium bowl; set aside. Combine remaining ingredients in small bowl and let stand 5 minutes; add to cabbage mixture. Toss and refrigerate at least 2 hours. Toss again just before serving.

Per serving: 44 calories; 2 g protein; 0.3 g fat; 11 g carbohydrate; 324 mg sodium

FRUIT SLAW

See Menu Plan for Week 13.
Makes 4 servings

4 cups shredded cabbage
1 small apple, cored and cut into small pieces
1 tablespoon raisins
1 tablespoon sesame seeds, toasted, divided
½ cup plain unflavored yogurt
¼ cup canned crushed pineapple, no sugar added
2 tablespoons reduced-calorie mayonnaise
1 tablespoon lemon juice

In large bowl combine cabbage, apple, raisins, and 2 teaspoons sesame seeds. In small bowl combine remaining ingredients except sesame seeds. Add to cabbage mixture; toss to combine. Cover and chill overnight. Sprinkle with 1 teaspoon sesame seeds just before serving.

Per serving: 106 calories; 3 g protein; 4 g fat; 17 g carbohydrate; 73 mg sodium

CAULIFLOWER SALAD

See Menu Plan for Week 29.
Makes 2 servings

2 cups cauliflower florets
2 cups boiling water
½ teaspoon salt
1 tablespoon plus 1½ teaspoons white wine vinegar
4 black olives, pitted and diced
2 tablespoons pimiento strips
2 teaspoons olive oil
Dash each salt and pepper

Cook cauliflower in boiling salted water 6 minutes or until tender-crisp; drain and transfer to bowl. Add vinegar and toss to coat; chill 30 minutes. Add remaining ingredients and toss to combine.

Per serving: 87 calories; 3 g protein; 7 g fat; 6 g carbohydrate; 464 mg sodium

WHITE SALAD
See Menu Plan for Week 28.
Makes 2 servings

2 cups pared and thinly sliced cucumber
½ cup white vinegar
2 tablespoons pimiento strips
½ small garlic clove, minced with ¼ teaspoon salt
Dash pepper
2½ cups cooked cauliflower florets, seasoned with dash each salt and white pepper and chilled

In bowl combine cucumber, vinegar, pimiento, garlic, and pepper. Refrigerate 1 hour. Arrange cauliflower on serving platter. Drain cucumber mixture and spoon over cauliflower.

Per serving: 65 calories; 5 g protein; 1 g fat;
15 g carbohydrate; 412 mg sodium

CUCUMBER AND TOMATO SALAD
See Menu Plan for Week 26 and various other weeks.
Makes 1 serving

1 lettuce leaf
1 medium tomato, sliced
1 cup cucumber slices
1 tablespoon rice vinegar
1½ teaspoons olive oil
1 teaspoon imitation bacon bits

Line small plate with lettuce leaf. Arrange tomato and cucumber slices on lettuce. In small bowl combine remaining ingredients. When ready to serve, pour dressing over salad.

Per serving: 116 calories; 3 g protein; 8 g fat;
11 g carbohydrate; 107 mg sodium

TOMATO-CUCUMBER RAITO
Try this delicious salad from India, redolent with spices from the East.
See Menu Plan for Week 23.
Makes 2 servings

1 cup plain unflavored yogurt

1 medium cucumber, pared, cut in half lengthwise, seeded, and diced
1 medium tomato, peeled,* seeded, and diced
2 tablespoons drained and minced canned green chili peppers
1 tablespoon lemon juice
¼ teaspoon curry powder
Dash each ground cloves, ground ginger, coriander seed, ground cumin, and salt
2 large lettuce leaves

In bowl combine all ingredients except lettuce. Chill at least 2 hours. Line each of 2 salad plates with a lettuce leaf. Top each leaf with ½ of the chilled salad.

Per serving: 101 calories; 6 g protein; 4 g fat;
13 g carbohydrate; 154 mg sodium

* To peel tomato, scratch an X on the bottom, immerse in simmering water until the skin around the X begins to peel, remove from water and cool slightly. The skin should slip off easily.

CUCUMBER-RADISH SALAD
See Menu Plans for Weeks 12 and 50.
Makes 4 servings

2 medium cucumbers, pared, seeded, and cut into ⅛-inch thick slices
1½ cups quartered and thinly sliced zucchini
½ teaspoon salt
1 cup thinly sliced radishes
1 tablespoon plus 1½ teaspoons rice vinegar
1 teaspoon soy sauce
1 teaspoon sesame oil

In bowl combine cucumbers and zucchini with salt and let stand 15 minutes. Drain in colander and pat dry with paper towels. In salad bowl combine cucumbers, zucchini, and radishes. In small bowl mix vinegar with soy sauce and sesame oil; pour over vegetables and toss to coat. Chill about 1 hour. Toss again before serving.

Per serving: 39 calories; 2 g protein; 1 g fat;
6 g carbohydrate; 381 mg sodium

EGGPLANT AND PEPPER SALAD
See Menu Plan for Week 19.
Makes 4 servings

4 small eggplants, about ½ pound each
3 medium red bell peppers
3 tablespoons olive oil
2 tablespoons lemon juice
1 garlic clove, minced
Dash each salt and pepper
2 tablespoons chopped fresh parsley

Place eggplants and peppers on broiling pan. Broil for 5 to 7 minutes on all sides, or until slightly charred; cool. Remove skin from vegetables. Cut eggplants into 1-inch cubes; seed red peppers and cut into strips. In bowl combine olive oil, lemon juice, garlic, salt, and pepper. Add diced eggplants and pepper strips. Stir to thoroughly combine; sprinkle with parsley. Chill at least 2 hours.

Per serving: 177 calories; 4 g protein; 11 g fat; 19 g carbohydrate; 62 mg sodium

ENDIVE AND BEET SALAD
Endive and beets should be assembled just before serving, as beets will discolor the endive.
See Menu Plan for Week 9.
Makes 2 servings

½ teaspoon Dijon-style mustard
2 teaspoons olive oil
½ small garlic clove, mashed
2 teaspoons tarragon vinegar
Dash each salt and freshly ground pepper
2 cups sliced Belgian endives, ½-inch pieces
1 cup whole beets, cooked and shredded

In a small bowl whip mustard with oil and garlic. When mixture begins to thicken add vinegar, salt, and pepper. Just before serving, combine endives and beets in salad bowl; add dressing and toss.

Per serving: 93 calories; 3 g protein; 5 g fat; 11 g carbohydrate; 182 mg sodium

BEAN SALAD
See Menu Plans for Weeks 4, 21, and 35.
Makes 2 servings

2½ teaspoons lemon juice
½ teaspoon chopped fresh mint
2 teaspoons olive oil
½ teaspoon dill weed
2¼ cups green beans, blanched and cut into 2-inch pieces
1 cup diagonally sliced celery, ¼-inch thick slices
Dash each salt and pepper
2 teaspoons coarsely chopped fresh parsley
½ cup quartered peeled tomatoes

In small bowl combine lemon juice and mint. Set aside.

In skillet heat oil; add dill weed and sauté 20 seconds. Stir in beans, celery, salt, and pepper. Sauté about 2 minutes. Combine bean mixture with lemon juice mixture and parsley. Toss and refrigerate. Before serving toss salad again; then add tomatoes.

Per serving: 99 calories; 3 g protein; 5 g fat; 13 g carbohydrate; 163 mg sodium

GREEN BEAN CONFETTI SALAD
See Menu Plan for Week 11.
Makes 2 servings

2 cups French-style green beans
⅓ cup diced carrot
⅓ cup diced green bell pepper
1 tablespoon chopped scallion
3 tablespoons rice vinegar
2 teaspoons olive oil
1 small garlic clove, minced
⅛ teaspoon each salt and pepper

Cook green beans in boiling salted water to cover for 5 to 7 minutes or until tender-crisp. Drain in colander and refresh under cold running water. Transfer to salad bowl; add carrot, green pepper, and scallion. In small bowl combine vinegar, oil, garlic, salt, and pepper. Pour over vegetables and toss well. Cover and refrigerate at least 4 hours, tossing once or twice.

Per serving: 86 calories; 2 g protein; 5 g fat; 11 g carbohydrate; 166 mg sodium

BRAISED LEEK SALAD
See Menu Plan for Week 23.
Makes 2 servings

¾ cup Chicken Broth (see page 127)
½ cup water
1 cup cut-up leeks, white part only, 2-inch
    pieces
1 tablespoon olive oil
1 tablespoon red wine vinegar
1 teaspoon chopped fresh parsley
½ teaspoon drained capers, chopped
Dash each salt and freshly ground pepper
2 large lettuce leaves
1 medium tomato, sliced

In small saucepan combine broth and water;
bring to a boil. Add leeks; reduce heat, cover,
and simmer for 25 minutes. Remove from
heat and cool leeks in broth. When cooled,
remove leeks, using a slotted spoon, and
discard broth. In small bowl combine olive
oil, vinegar, parsley, capers, salt, and pepper. Line each of 2 small plates with a lettuce
leaf. Spoon an equal amount of leeks onto
each plate and garnish each portion with
½ of the tomato slices. Pour ½ of dressing
over each serving.

Per serving: 140 calories; 3 g protein; 8 g fat;
16 g carbohydrate; 107 mg sodium

RADISH SALAD
See Menu Plans for Weeks 5 and 29.
Makes 2 servings

2 cups sliced radishes
1 tablespoon plus 1 teaspoon chopped
    scallion
2 teaspoons chopped fresh parsley
¼ cup rice vinegar
1 teaspoon sesame oil
¼ teaspoon salt
Dash artificial sweetener (optional)

In a bowl combine radishes with scallion
and parsley. In a small bowl combine vinegar, sesame oil, salt, and sweetener if desired.
Toss with radish mixture.

Per serving: 50 calories; 2 g protein; 2 g fat;
7 g carbohydrate; 319 mg sodium

RED LEAF SALAD
See Menu Plan for Week 47.
Makes 4 servings

4 cups red leaf lettuce
3 tablespoons lemon juice
1 tablespoon vegetable oil
2 teaspoons minced fresh parsley
2 teaspoons chopped capers
⅛ teaspoon powdered mustard
Dash artificial sweetener

Place lettuce in salad bowl. In a small bowl
mix lemon juice with vegetable oil, parsley,
capers, mustard, and sweetener. Pour dressing over lettuce leaves and toss to combine.

Per serving: 43 calories; 1 g protein; 4 g fat;
3 g carbohydrate; 6 mg sodium

ORIENTAL-STYLE SPINACH SALAD
See Menu Plan for Week 20.
Makes 2 servings

2 cups spinach leaves
1 cup sliced mushrooms
½ cup sliced drained canned water
    chestnuts
2 tablespoons rice vinegar
2 teaspoons sesame oil
1½ teaspoons soy sauce
1 teaspoon sesame seeds, toasted

In large salad bowl combine spinach with
mushrooms and water chestnuts. In a small
bowl mix rice vinegar with sesame oil and
soy sauce. Pour dressing over salad and toss
to coat. Sprinkle with sesame seeds.

Per serving: 91 calories; 3 g protein; 6 g fat;
9 g carbohydrate; 307 mg sodium

SUNCHOKE AND KRAUT SALAD

The Jerusalem artichoke, also known as sunchoke, is a tuber and is actually native to America. It should not be confused with the globe artichoke, which is an edible thistle and native to France.

See Menu Plan for Week 32.

Makes 2 servings

1 cup pared and slivered Jerusalem
    artichokes, ¼ x ¼-inch slivers
1 cup drained canned sauerkraut, well rinsed
1 teaspoon chopped fresh parsley
½ teaspoon lemon juice
Dash each salt, white pepper, ground
    allspice, and ground ginger
1 medium tomato, sliced

Combine all ingredients except tomato in medium bowl; toss well. Arrange tomato slices in center of serving plate. Mound salad mixture around tomato. Chill and serve.

Per serving: 59 calories; 3 g protein; 0.4 g fat;
18 g carbohydrate; 962 mg sodium

CHILLED VEGETABLE SALAD

See Menu Plans for Weeks 17 and 37.

Makes 2 servings

¾ cup Brussels sprouts
¼ teaspoon salt, divided
Pepper
1 tablespoon plus 1 teaspoon reduced-
    calorie mayonnaise
½ teaspoon sesame seeds, toasted and
    chopped
¾ cup sliced celery, ¼-inch thick slices
¾ cup sliced zucchini, ¼-inch thick slices
¾ cup sliced mushrooms, ¼-inch thick
    slices
2 teaspoons lemon juice

Trim stems of Brussels sprouts; slice thinly crosswise from head to stem. Heat nonstick skillet. Add Brussels sprouts, ⅛ teaspoon salt, and dash pepper. Cover and cook over low heat 3 to 5 minutes or until tender-crisp; *do not overcook.* Transfer to bowl and cool.

Add mayonnaise and sesame seeds. Cover and refrigerate.

Heat nonstick skillet; add celery, zucchini, mushrooms, remaining ⅛ teaspoon salt, and dash pepper. Cover and cook over medium heat, stirring occasionally, until vegetables are tender, about 5 minutes. Remove from heat, drain, and transfer to a small bowl. Add lemon juice; cool. Cover and refrigerate until chilled.

Place half of vegetable mixture on each of 2 salad plates. Mound ½ of Brussels sprouts mixture over each portion of vegetables.

Per serving: 67 calories; 4 g protein; 3 g fat;
9 g carbohydrate; 484 mg sodium

CRISPY-CRUNCHY SALAD

See Menu Plans for Weeks 20, 25, and 43.

Makes 2 servings

1 cup pared and diced cucumber
1 cup diced zucchini
½ cup diced green bell pepper
1 tablespoon plus 1 teaspoon reduced-
    calorie mayonnaise
1 teaspoon chopped fresh parsley
½ teaspoon lemon juice
¼ teaspoon salt
Dash each thyme leaves and white pepper

In medium bowl combine all ingredients. Chill thoroughly.

Per serving: 57 calories; 2 g protein; 2 g fat;
9 g carbohydrate; 354 mg sodium

HOLIDAY SALAD

Any salad greens may be substituted for the endive—this will still be delicious!

See Menu Plan for Week 15.

Makes 4 servings

2 tablespoons tarragon vinegar
2 tablespoons lemon juice
1 teaspoon Dijon-style mustard
1 tablespoon plus 1 teaspoon vegetable oil
Dash white pepper

6 Belgian endives, about ¾ pound
10 cherry tomatoes, halved
1½ cups watercress

In a small bowl mix vinegar with lemon juice and mustard until smooth. Add oil and white pepper. Separate endive leaves. Arrange cherry tomato halves in center of round platter and surround with a ring of watercress and endive leaves. Serve with dressing.

Per serving: 72 calories; 2 g protein; 5 g fat;
6 g carbohydrate; 58 mg sodium

GREEN GODDESS SALAD
See Menu Plan for Week 21.
Makes 2 servings

2 cups torn mixed salad greens (romaine, Bibb, watercress)
½ cup sliced Bermuda onion
½ cup plain unflavored yogurt
1 tablespoon plus 1 teaspoon reduced-calorie mayonnaise
1 tablespoon chopped fresh parsley
1 garlic clove
1 teaspoon lemon juice
1 teaspoon tarragon vinegar
½ teaspoon prepared mustard
Dash each salt and pepper

Combine salad greens in bowl; top with sliced onion. Chill. Combine all remaining ingredients in blender container; process until well mixed. Pour dressing over salad just before serving.

Per serving: 89 calories; 4 g protein; 4 g fat;
11 g carbohydrate; 189 mg sodium

MIXED VEGETABLE SALAD
See Menu Plans for Weeks 2, 13, and 22.
Makes 2 servings

3 cups green beans
¾ cup frozen peas, blanched and chilled
½ cup shredded carrot
3 tablespoons chopped celery leaves, from heart
2 tablespoons lemon juice
2 teaspoons chopped chives
½ teaspoon salt
½ teaspoon chopped fresh parsley
Dash pepper

Place beans in steamer insert and set over boiling water. Steam until tender yet firm, about 4 to 5 minutes. Plunge into cold water to cool. In bowl combine beans, peas, carrot, and celery leaves. Add lemon juice, chives, salt, parsley, and pepper. Toss well and chill 1 hour.

Per serving: 108 calories; 7 g protein; 1 g fat;
22 g carbohydrate; 700 mg sodium

ORIENTAL SALAD

Lotus root and rice vinegar add touches of the Orient; both can be found in shops that specialize in Chinese foods.

See Menu Plan for Week 30.
Makes 4 servings

Salad

2 cups large cauliflower florets, blanched and cooled
2 cups green beans, blanched and cooled
2 cups sliced zucchini, ½-inch thick slices, blanched and cooled
1 cup thinly sliced drained canned lotus root

Sauce

1 tablespoon plus 1 teaspoon vegetable oil
1 tablespoon minced fresh garlic
3 tablespoons soy sauce
3 tablespoons rice or white vinegar
Artificial sweetener to equal 2 teaspoons sugar
Dash sherry extract

Garnish

2 teaspoons sesame seeds, toasted

To Prepare Salad: Arrange vegetables attractively on serving platter.

To Prepare Sauce: Heat oil in small saucepan; add garlic and sauté lightly, being careful not to burn. Remove from heat and stir in soy sauce, vinegar, sweetener, and extract.

To Serve: Drizzle sauce over vegetables and sprinkle evenly with sesame seeds.

Per serving: 119 calories; 5 g protein; 6 g fat;
15 g carbohydrate; 839 mg sodium

RELISH SALAD

See Menu Plan for Week 14.
Makes 2 servings

½ cup chopped tomato
½ cup sliced radishes
½ cup chopped red bell pepper
½ cup chopped green bell pepper
½ cup pared and diced cucumber
1 tablespoon plus 1½ teaspoons lemon juice
2 teaspoons olive oil
⅛ teaspoon salt
Dash pepper
1 tablespoon chopped fresh parsley

In bowl combine tomato, radishes, pepper, and cucumber. In a small bowl mix lemon juice with oil, salt, and pepper. Pour over vegetables and toss to coat. Cover and refrigerate at least 3 hours. Before serving toss again and sprinkle with parsley.

Per serving: 87 calories; 2 g protein; 5 g fat;
10 g carbohydrate; 173 mg sodium

VEGETABLE SALAD WITH RELISH DRESSING

See Menu Plan for Week 45.
Makes 2 servings

2 cups broccoli florets
½ cup cooked Brussels sprouts, cut lengthwise into halves
½ cup cooked small pearl onions
2 teaspoons olive oil
2 teaspoons sweet pickle relish
2 teaspoons lemon juice
Dash each salt and pepper

Combine vegetables in medium bowl. To prepare dressing, combine remaining ingredients in small bowl; using a wire whisk, whip dressing briskly for 1 minute. Pour over vegetables and toss.

Per serving: 131 calories; 8 g protein; 5 g fat;
17 g carbohydrate; 164 mg sodium

Sauces, Salad Dressings, and Dips

You mix and match parts of your wardrobe, adding different accessories for different occasions. You can do the same thing with the foods you eat, using sauces, dressings, and dips as flavor accents. Sweet or sour, spicy or bland, dress up your meals with the perfect accompaniment. The recipes in this section are designed to give a salad zing or make a main dish sing.

GARLIC "BUTTER"
See Menu Plan for Week 38.
Makes 2 servings

2 tablespoons reduced-calorie margarine
2 teaspoons chopped fresh parsley
1 garlic clove

In small bowl combine margarine and parsley. Place garlic clove in garlic press and squeeze into margarine mixture. Stir to combine.

Per serving: 53 calories; 0.2 g protein; 6 g fat;
1 g carbohydrate; 141 mg sodium

LEMON "BUTTER" SAUCE
See Menu Plan for Week 48 and various other weeks.
Makes 6 servings

¼ cup reduced-calorie margarine, melted
⅓ cup water
¼ cup white wine
2 teaspoons cornstarch
2 tablespoons lemon juice
2 tablespoons finely chopped fresh parsley

In saucepan melt margarine. Add water and white wine and bring to a boil. Combine cornstarch with lemon juice and add to wine mixture. Cook, stirring constantly, until thickened. Stir in parsley.

Per serving: 47 calories; 0.1 g protein; 4 g fat;
2 g carbohydrate; 94 mg sodium

GREEN CHILI SAUCE
This sauce may be prepared in advance and stored in the refrigerator until needed.
See Menu Plan for Week 18.
Yields 1 cup

1 cup chopped carrots
½ cup chopped scallions
⅓ cup well-packed fresh parsley leaves
⅓ cup white vinegar
2 tablespoons seeded and minced fresh or canned green chili pepper
2 teaspoons thyme leaves

2 garlic cloves, chopped
½ teaspoon salt

Combine all ingredients in blender container or work bowl of food processor; process until smooth. Use in Trinidad Snapper recipe (see page 211).

Per cup: 122 calories; 4 g protein; 1 g fat;
30 g carbohydrate; 1,242 mg sodium

HORSERADISH-CHILI SAUCE
Excellent with meat or fish.
See Menu Plans for Weeks 3 and 46.
Makes 2 servings

1 tablespoon plus 1 teaspoon prepared horseradish
1 tablespoon plus 1 teaspoon chili sauce

In small bowl combine horseradish and chili sauce; mix well.

Per serving: 15 calories; 0.4 g protein; 0.1 g fat;
4 g carbohydrate; 162 mg sodium

MARINARA SAUCE
This sauce can be prepared in advance, measured, and frozen for future use.
See Menu Plans for Weeks 21 and 50.
Yields 3 cups

1 tablespoon olive oil
2 tablespoons minced fresh garlic
4 cups canned plum tomatoes, crushed and strained
1 tablespoon chopped fresh basil, or 1 teaspoon dried basil leaves
½ teaspoon salt

Heat oil in medium saucepan; add garlic and sauté lightly. Add tomatoes and bring to a slow boil. Add basil and salt, reduce heat, and simmer for 20 minutes.

Per cup: 119 calories; 4 g protein; 5 g fat;
16 g carbohydrate; 844 mg sodium

MUSHROOM GRAVY
Serve with Roast Turkey (see page 167).
See Menu Plan for Week 47.
Makes 4 servings

2 cups sliced mushrooms
Dash each salt and pepper
2 tablespoons enriched flour
2 cups Turkey Broth (see page 128)
1 tablespoon minced fresh parsley

In small nonstick saucepan sprinkle mushrooms with salt and pepper and cook, stirring occasionally with wooden spoon, until tender; set aside. Brown flour in small nonstick saucepan, stirring constantly. Remove from heat. Using wire whisk, slowly stir in Turkey Broth. Return to heat and cook, stirring constantly, until thickened. Add cooked mushrooms and parsley; heat.

Per serving: 34 calories; 2 g protein; 0.2 g fat;
7 g carbohydrate; 425 mg sodium

ORANGE-APRICOT SAUCE
Serve with Roast Loin of Pork (see page 187).
See Menu Plan for Week 52.
Makes 6 servings

¼ cup reduced-calorie apricot spread
¼ cup dry white wine
1 teaspoon Dijon-style mustard
1 teaspoon teriyaki sauce
1½ teaspoons cornstarch
1 cup orange juice
½ cup orange sections

In a medium saucepan heat apricot spread until melted. Add wine, mustard, and teriyaki sauce. Dissolve cornstarch in orange juice; add to apricot mixture. Cook, stirring constantly, until thickened. Add orange sections and heat thoroughly.

Per serving: 55 calories; 0.4 g protein; 0.1 g fat;
12 g carbohydrate; 59 mg sodium

BASIC VINAIGRETTE
See Menu Plan for Week 1 and various other weeks.
Makes 4 servings

1 tablespoon plus 1 teaspoon olive or vegetable oil
1 tablespoon white wine vinegar
⅛ teaspoon each salt and prepared mustard

Combine all ingredients in small bowl; mix well.

Per serving: 42 calories; 0 g protein; 5 g fat;
0 g carbohydrate; 78 mg sodium

Variations:

Chili Vinaigrette (See Menu Plan for Week 49.)—Add 2 teaspoons chili sauce to Basic Vinaigrette.
Per serving: 45 calories; 0.1 g protein; 5 g fat;
1 g carbohydrate; 116 mg sodium

Cider Vinaigrette (See Menu Plan for Week 10 and various other weeks.)—Substitute cider vinegar for wine vinegar in Basic Vinaigrette.
Per serving: 42 calories; 0 g protein; 5 g fat;
0.2 g carbohydrate; 77 mg sodium

Garlic Vinaigrette (See Menu Plan for Week 5 and various other weeks.)—Prepare Basic Vinaigrette, omitting salt. With flat side of knife mash ¼ small garlic clove with ⅛ teaspoon salt to form a paste. Add paste to dressing.
Per serving: 43 calories; trace protein; 5 g fat;
0.1 g carbohydrate; 78 mg sodium

Gingered Vinaigrette (See Menu Plan for Week 3 and various other weeks.)—Add ¼ teaspoon minced fresh ginger root to Basic Vinaigrette.
Per serving: 42 calories; 0 g protein; 5 g fat;
trace carbohydrate; 78 mg sodium

Oregano Vinaigrette (See Menu Plan for Week 8 and various other weeks.)—Substitute oregano vinegar for wine vinegar in Basic Vinaigrette.
Per serving: 42 calories; trace protein; 5 g fat;
0.3 g carbohydrate; 77 mg sodium

Savory Vinaigrette (See Menu Plan for Week 9 and various other weeks.)—Add dash each thyme leaves and summer savory to Basic Vinaigrette.

Per serving: 42 calories; 0 g protein; 5 g fat; trace carbohydrate; 78 mg sodium

Tarragon Vinaigrette (See Menu Plan for Week 7 and various other weeks.)—Substitute tarragon vinegar for wine vinegar in Basic Vinaigrette.

Per serving: 42 calories; trace protein; 5 g fat; 0.3 g carbohydrate; 77 mg sodium

Vinaigrette Parmesan (See Menu Plan for Week 4 and various other weeks.)—Substitute 2 teaspoons grated Parmesan cheese for mustard in Basic Vinaigrette.

Per serving: 53 calories; 1 g protein; 5 g fat; 0.1 g carbohydrate; 86 mg sodium

Wine Vinaigrette (See Menu Plan for Week 14 and various other weeks.)—Substitute red wine vinegar for white wine vinegar in Basic Vinaigrette.

Per serving: 42 calories; 0 g protein; 5 g fat; 0 g carbohydrate; 78 mg sodium

DILL VINAIGRETTE
See Menu Plan for Week 38 and various other weeks.
Makes 2 servings

1 garlic clove
Dash salt
1 tablespoon red wine vinegar
1 tablespoon water
1 tablespoon olive oil
½ teaspoon chopped fresh dill
Freshly ground pepper to taste

Mash garlic with salt. In small bowl combine mashed garlic, vinegar, and water. Stirring with a small wire whisk, gradually add olive oil. Stir in dill and season with pepper.

Per serving: 66 calories; 0.2 g protein; 7 g fat; 1 g carbohydrate; 96 mg sodium

SESAME VINAIGRETTE
See Menu Plan for Week 33 and various other weeks.
Makes 4 servings

2 tablespoons rice vinegar

1 tablespoon water
2 teaspoons teriyaki sauce
1 teaspoon sesame oil
Pepper to taste

Combine all ingredients in small bowl; mix well.

Per serving: 14 calories; 0.1 g protein; 1 g fat; 1 g carbohydrate; 101 mg sodium

DIJON-HERB DRESSING
See Menu Plan for Week 39 and various other weeks.
Makes 2 servings

2 teaspoons red wine vinegar
½ teaspoon Dijon-style mustard
1 tablespoon water
1 teaspoon olive oil
½ teaspoon chopped fresh parsley
Dash freshly ground pepper

In small bowl combine red wine vinegar and mustard; add water. Stirring with a small wire whisk, gradually add olive oil. Stir in remaining ingredients.

Per serving: 23 calories; trace protein; 4 g fat; 0.1 g carbohydrate; 19 mg sodium

HERB DRESSING
See Menu Plan for Week 2 and various other weeks.
Makes 6 servings

3 tablespoons vegetable oil
2 tablespoons water
1 tablespoon wine vinegar
1 teaspoon basil leaves
½ teaspoon chopped fresh parsley
¼ teaspoon garlic powder
⅛ teaspoon oregano leaves

Place all ingredients in blender container; process until combined. Use immediately or store and shake well before serving.

Per serving: 64 calories; 0.1 g protein; 7 g fat; 0.3 g carbohydrate; 1 mg sodium

LEMON SALAD DRESSING
See Menu Plan for Week 36 and various other weeks.
Makes 4 servings

2 tablespoons lemon juice
2 tablespoons water
1 tablespoon olive oil
½ teaspoon prepared mustard
¼ teaspoon mashed fresh garlic
Dash each Worcestershire sauce, artificial sweetener, salt, freshly ground pepper, and crushed thyme leaves

Combine all ingredients in small bowl or jar with tight-fitting cover; mix well. Shake or stir well before serving.

Per serving: 34 calories; 0.1 g protein; 4 g fat; 1 g carbohydrate; 37 mg sodium

HOMEMADE MAYONNAISE
When about ½ the oil has been added, mayonnaise will thicken; you can actually hear this process taking place.
See Menu Plan for Week 49.
Makes 1¼ cups

1 egg, at room temperature
1 tablespoon lemon juice
2 teaspoons white vinegar
½ teaspoon salt
¼ teaspoon powdered mustard
1 cup vegetable oil

Place egg, lemon juice, vinegar, salt, and mustard in blender container; add ¼ cup oil. Cover blender and turn motor on low speed. While blender is running, remove insert from cover and pour in remaining oil in a *slow, steady stream.*

Per teaspoon: 33 calories; 0.1 g protein; 4 g fat; trace carbohydrate; 20 mg sodium

RUSSIAN DRESSING
See Menu Plan for Week 10 and various other weeks.
Makes 1 serving

2 teaspoons reduced-calorie mayonnaise
2 teaspoons chili sauce
½ teaspoon pickle relish

Combine all ingredients in small bowl; stir well.

Per serving: 38 calories; 0.3 g protein; 2 g fat; 5 g carbohydrate; 219 mg sodium

CREAMY ORIENTAL DRESSING
See Menu Plans for Weeks 40 and 52.
Makes 4 servings

1 cup plain unflavored yogurt
1 tablespoon plus 1 teaspoon chopped fresh parsley
1 tablespoon plus 1 teaspoon chopped chives
1 tablespoon mayonnaise
2 teaspoons Dijon-style mustard
2 teaspoons soy sauce
⅛ teaspoon ground ginger

Combine all ingredients in bowl; mix well. Chill.

Per serving: 67 calories; 2 g protein; 7 g fat; 4 g carbohydrate; 223 mg sodium

PESTO DRESSING
See Menu Plans for Weeks 13, 44, and 52.
Makes 4 servings

1 cup plain unflavored yogurt
¼ cup chopped fresh basil
1 tablespoon mayonnaise
2 teaspoons chopped fresh parsley
2 teaspoons lemon juice
½ teaspoon Dijon-style mustard
¼ teaspoon mashed fresh garlic
Dash each salt and pepper

Combine all ingredients in bowl; mix well. Chill.

Per serving: 65 calories; 2 g protein; 5 g fat; 4 g carbohydrate; 112 mg sodium

THOUSAND ISLAND DRESSING
See Menu Plans for Weeks 2, 6, and 16.
Makes 4 servings

1 cup plain unflavored yogurt
¼ cup reduced-calorie ketchup
1 tablespoon plus 1 teaspoon minced dill pickle
1 tablespoon mayonnaise

½ teaspoon prepared horseradish
¼ teaspoon Dijon-style mustard
Dash each salt and teriyaki sauce

Combine all ingredients in bowl; mix well. Chill.

Per serving: 68 calories; 2 g protein; 5 g fat;
5 g carbohydrate; 129 mg sodium

GREEN GODDESS SALAD DRESSING

Use over sliced tomatoes, eggs, seafood, or as a dip with vegetables.
See Menu Plans for Weeks 2, 22, 29, and 37.
Makes 1 serving

½ cup plain unflavored yogurt
1 tablespoon chopped fresh parsley
2 teaspoons chopped fresh dill
1 teaspoon Dijon-style mustard
½ teaspoon Worcestershire sauce
Dash each salt and white pepper

In bowl combine yogurt with parsley, dill, mustard, Worcestershire sauce, salt, and pepper; mix well. Serve immediately.

Per serving: 73 calories; 7 g protein; 1 g fat;
9 g carbohydrate; 320 mg sodium

CURRY DIP

Serve with crudités.
See Menu Plan for Week 43 and various other weeks.
Makes 4 servings

½ cup plain unflavored yogurt
¼ teaspoon curry powder
¼ teaspoon lemon juice
Dash each ground cumin, salt, and white pepper

Combine all ingredients in small bowl; mix well and chill.

Per serving: 18 calories; 1 g protein; 1 g fat;
1 g carbohydrate; 60 mg sodium

LIME YOGURT DIP WITH CRUDITÉS

See Menu Plans for Weeks 9 and 36.
Makes 2 servings

1 cup plain unflavored yogurt

2 teaspoons lime juice
1 teaspoon grated lime
1 teaspoon onion powder
½ teaspoon soy sauce
½ teaspoon salt
½ cup julienne carrot
½ cup mushroom caps
½ cup sliced cucumber
½ cup cauliflower florets

Mix together first 6 ingredients in bowl. Transfer to small serving bowl; place bowl in center of large serving platter and surround with raw vegetables (crudités).

Per serving: 105 calories; 6 g protein; 4 g fat;
13 g carbohydrate; 752 mg sodium

YOGURT-CHIVE DIP

Serve with crudités.
See Menu Plan for Week 51.
Makes 4 servings

½ cup plain unflavored yogurt
2 tablespoons minced green bell pepper
2 teaspoons chopped chives
⅛ teaspoon salt
⅛ teaspoon minced fresh garlic
⅛ teaspoon white pepper

Combine all ingredients in bowl; mix well and chill.

Per serving: 24 calories; 1 g protein; 1 g fat;
3 g carbohydrate; 162 mg sodium

YOGURT DIP OR DRESSING

See Menu Plan for Week 33 and various other weeks.
Makes 2 or 4 servings

½ cup plain unflavored yogurt
2 tablespoons Dijon-style mustard
2 tablespoons grated carrot
1 teaspoon chopped fresh parsley
1 garlic clove, minced

Combine all ingredients in small bowl; mix well. Chill.

Per ¼ recipe: 29 calories; 1 g protein; 9 g fat;
2 g carbohydrate; 239 mg sodium
Per ½ recipe: 58 calories; 2 g protein; 18 g fat;
4 g carbohydrate; 478 mg sodium

Desserts, Snacks, and Beverages

Desserts and snacks should be as nourishing as everything else you eat. But that doesn't mean they have to be boring. Blend good nutrition with creativity and stir up special treats like Frozen Mango Yogurt, Cherry Cobbler, and Pineapple Banana Milk Shake. They all make sensible eating fun. A glass of wine or beer now and then makes special occasions even more festive.

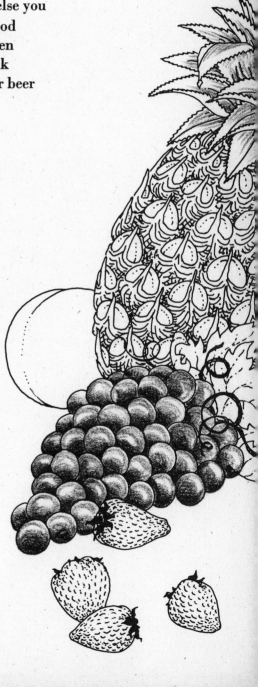

APPLE COMPOTE
See Menu Plans for Weeks 2 and 38.
Makes 2 servings

2 small apples, pared and cored
2 teaspoons lemon juice, divided
¾ cup water
2-inch strip lemon rind
1-inch piece vanilla bean
Artificial sweetener to equal 2 teaspoons
    sugar

Cut apples into sections and place in bowl
with enough water to cover; add 1 teaspoon
lemon juice to keep apples from discoloring.
In a saucepan combine ¾ cup water with
lemon rind and vanilla bean; boil for 5 minutes. Drain apples and add to saucepan along
with remaining lemon juice and sweetener;
simmer until apples are just tender, about
5 minutes. Cool. Remove and discard lemon
rind and vanilla bean.

Per serving: 61 calories; 0.2 g protein; 0.3 g fat;
16 g carbohydrate; 1 mg sodium

BAKED APPLE
*See Menu Plans for Week 4 and various other
weeks.*
Makes 2 servings

2 small apples
Artificial sweetener to equal 2 teaspoons
    sugar
Dash each ground cinnamon and ground
    nutmeg
¼ cup water
1 teaspoon lemon juice

Core apples; place in baking dish. Sprinkle
sweetener, cinnamon, and nutmeg into the
apples. Add water and lemon juice to baking dish and bake at 450°F. for 25 minutes
or until tender.

Per serving: 66 calories; 0.2 g protein; 1 g fat;
16 g carbohydrate; 1 mg sodium

STUFFED BAKED APPLE
Make one or more of these and put them
in the oven next time you have to use it for
a roast or casserole.
See Menu Plan for Week 13.
Makes 1 serving

1 small apple, cored
1 tablespoon raisins
1 teaspoon lemon juice
½ teaspoon shredded coconut
½ teaspoon honey
Dash ground cinnamon
1 teaspoon water

Pare apple ⅓ of the way down. In small
bowl combine remaining ingredients except
water. Stuff into cored apple. Place water in
bottom of an ovenproof custard cup; add
filled apple, cover with foil, and bake at
350°F. for 35 to 45 minutes.

Per serving: 114 calories; 0.1 g protein; 1 g fat;
29 g carbohydrate; 4 mg sodium

STEWED DRIED APRICOTS
See Menu Plans for Weeks 22 and 27.
Makes 2 servings

8 medium dried apricot halves
1 cup water
1 tablespoon lemon juice
1 cinnamon stick

Place apricots in small saucepan. Add remaining ingredients; simmer for 20 minutes.
Remove cinnamon stick.

Per serving: 39 calories; 1 g protein; 0.1 g fat;
10 g carbohydrate; 4 mg sodium

BERRIES WITH LEMON-CINNAMON YOGURT
See Menu Plan for Week 46.
Makes 1 serving

½ cup plain unflavored yogurt
1½ teaspoons grated lemon rind
½ teaspoon honey
⅛ teaspoon ground cinnamon
½ cup strawberries, sliced

In small mixing bowl combine yogurt, lemon rind, honey, and cinnamon; mix well. Chill for 2 hours. Place strawberries in dessert dish and top with yogurt mixture.

Per serving: 112 calories; 5 g protein; 4 g fat;
16 g carbohydrate; 53 mg sodium

FRUIT MÉLANGE
See Menu Plan for Week 43.
Makes 4 servings

1 cup melon chunks, 1 inch each, divided
1 cup strawberries, divided
1 medium kiwi fruit, pared and cut crosswise into 8 equal slices
4 lemon slices

Arrange ¼ cup melon chunks and ¼ cup strawberries in each of 4 dessert dishes. Top each with 2 kiwi fruit slices and a twisted lemon slice.

Per serving: 43 calories; 1 g protein; 0.1 g fat;
11 g carbohydrate; 11 mg sodium

RED, WHITE, AND BLUE PARFAIT
See Menu Plan for Week 24.
Makes 2 servings

½ cup blueberries, divided
½ cup plain unflavored yogurt, divided
½ cup raspberries, divided
¼ cup low-calorie whipped topping, divided

In each of 2 parfait glasses, make a layer of ¼ cup blueberries, then ¼ cup yogurt, then ¼ cup raspberries; top each with 2 tablespoons whipped topping. Serve immediately.

Per serving: 90 calories; 3 g protein; 4 g fat;
12 g carbohydrate; 26 mg sodium

RASPBERRY-GRAPE YOGURT
See Menu Plan for Week 50.
Makes 2 servings

24 large seedless grapes, cut into halves
1 cup plain unflavored yogurt
1 tablespoon plus 1 teaspoon reduced-calorie raspberry spread
1½ ounces crunchy nutlike cereal nuggets

Place grapes in small bowl; add yogurt and preserves and stir to combine. Chill. Sprinkle with cereal nuggets just before serving.

Per serving: 217 calories; 7 g protein; 4 g fat;
40 g carbohydrate; 237 mg sodium

BROILED GRAPEFRUIT
See Menu Plans for Weeks 2, 4, and 25.
Makes 2 servings

1 teaspoon vanilla or sherry extract, divided
1 medium grapefruit, cut in half

Pour ½ teaspoon vanilla or sherry extract over each grapefruit half. Place grapefruit in small broiling pan. Broil 6 to 8 inches from source of heat for 10 minutes.

Per serving: 49 calories; 1 g protein; 0.1 g fat;
10 g carbohydrate; 1 mg sodium

ORANGE AMBROSIA
See Menu Plans for Weeks 9, 23, and 41.
Makes 2 servings

2 small navel oranges, cut into wedges
Dash ground cinnamon
1 teaspoon honey, warmed
2 teaspoons shredded coconut

Sprinkle orange wedges with cinnamon. Dip into warmed honey and then into shredded coconut. Broil on rack until coconut is lightly toasted. Serve warm.

Per serving: 60 calories; 1 g protein; 1 g fat;
14 g carbohydrate; 1 mg sodium

ORANGE-STRAWBERRY CUPS
See Menu Plans for Weeks 24 and 41.
Makes 2 servings

1 cup strawberries, sliced
1 teaspoon honey
½ teaspoon curaçao extract
1 small orange
2 teaspoons shredded coconut

Combine first 3 ingredients in small bowl; let stand for 15 minutes. Cut orange in half; scoop out fruit, reserving shells. Cut orange segments into small pieces and combine with strawberry mixture. Spoon ½ of strawberry-orange mixture into each shell and sprinkle each with 1 teaspoon coconut. Chill for ½ hour.

Per serving: 80 calories; 1 g protein; 1 g fat;
17 g carbohydrate; 2 mg sodium

HONEY-GLAZED PEARS
See Menu Plans for Weeks 26, 43, and 46.
Makes 2 servings

1 tablespoon plus 1½ teaspoons lemon
   juice
Dash ground cinnamon
¼ cup water
2 small pears, with stems
1 teaspoon honey

Preheat oven to 350°F. Combine lemon juice and cinnamon in 9 x 5 x 2-inch glass loaf pan or 1½-quart casserole; add water. Stand pears upright in liquid. Cover pan with foil and bake about 45 minutes or until pears can easily be pierced with a fork. Remove pears; transfer cooking liquid to small saucepan. Add honey and bring mixture to a boil. Continue boiling until mixture reduces to a syruplike consistency. Using a pastry brush, brush ½ of glaze over each pear.

Per serving: 99 calories; 1 g protein; 1 g fat;
25 g carbohydrate; 3 mg sodium

HONEY-STEWED PRUNES
See Menu Plan for Week 31 and various other weeks.
Makes 4 servings

8 large or 12 medium prunes
1 teaspoon honey
¼ teaspoon ground cinnamon
Dash ground allspice

Place prunes in small saucepan and add water to cover. Bring to a boil; reduce heat and stir in honey, cinnamon, and allspice. Cover and simmer 20 to 30 minutes. Serve warm.

Per serving: 49 calories; 0.4 g protein; 0.1 g fat;
13 g carbohydrate; 1 mg sodium

OVEN-STEWED PRUNES
These will keep two weeks in the refrigerator.
See Menu Plans for Weeks 3, 6, and 14.
Makes 4 servings

12 medium or 8 large prunes
½ lemon, thinly sliced
Small piece cinnamon stick

Place all ingredients in 2-cup casserole; add just enough water to barely cover prunes. Bake at 350°F. for 1 hour or until prunes are tender.

Per serving: 46 calories; 1 g protein; 0.2 g fat;
12 g carbohydrate; 1 mg sodium

RAISIN-POPCORN SNACK
See Menu Plan for Week 18.
Makes 2 servings

4 cups plain prepared popcorn
¼ cup raisins
1 teaspoon honey, heated
2 teaspoons lemon juice

In medium bowl combine popcorn, raisins, honey, and lemon; toss and serve.

Per serving: 146 calories; 2 g protein; 4 g fat;
28 g carbohydrate; 4 mg sodium

COCONUT-COFFEE MOUNDS
See Menu Plans for Weeks 2, 8, 37, and 39.
Makes 4 servings

⅔ cup nonfat dry milk powder
Artificial sweetener to equal 6 teaspoons
    sugar
1 tablespoon plus 1 teaspoon instant coffee
    (not freeze-dried)
2 tablespoons water
1 teaspoon vanilla extract
2 teaspoons shredded coconut

Combine first 3 ingredients in a small bowl.
Sprinkle with water and vanilla. Stir until
mixture forms dry paste that holds together.
Wet hands and shape mixture into small
balls, ½ inch in diameter. Roll balls in
coconut to coat. Chill in freezer for at least
40 minutes. Serve or keep in refrigerator
until ready to use. Makes about 16 balls.

Per serving: 55 calories; 4 g protein; 0.4 g fat;
8 g carbohydrate; 66 mg sodium

PINEAPPLE-COCONUT COOKIES
See Menu Plan for Week 18.
Makes 2 servings

¼ cup plus 1 tablespoon enriched flour
Artificial sweetener to equal 2 teaspoons
    sugar
¼ teaspoon baking powder
⅔ cup nonfat dry milk powder
½ cup canned crushed pineapple, no sugar
    added
¼ teaspoon vanilla extract
2 teaspoons shredded coconut

Preheat oven to 350°F. Sift together first 3
ingredients; add remaining ingredients except coconut and mix well. Drop by tea-
spoonful onto nonstick baking sheet that
has been sprayed with nonstick cooking
spray, allowing room for cookies to spread.
Sprinkle cookies with coconut. Bake 15 minutes or until lightly browned. Remove from
pan; place cookies on rack and let cool until
they become crisp.

Per serving: 198 calories; 11 g protein; 1 g fat;
37 g carbohydrate; 200 mg sodium

BANANA AND RAISIN PUDDING CAKE
See Menu Plan for Week 25.
Makes 4 servings

1½ medium bananas
1 teaspoon lemon juice
2 eggs, beaten
½ cup plain unflavored yogurt
½ cup skim milk
1 hamburger roll, 2 ounces, made into
    crumbs
2 tablespoons raisins
Artificial sweetener to equal 4 teaspoons
    sugar
2 teaspoons sugar
½ teaspoon ground cinnamon
⅛ teaspoon salt
Dash each ground allspice and ground
    nutmeg

Preheat oven to 350°F. In a bowl, using a
fork, mash bananas with lemon juice into
a smooth pulp. Add eggs, yogurt, and milk,
mixing well to combine. Stir in remaining
ingredients until well blended. Pour mixture
into 7 x 5½ x 2-inch casserole that has been
sprayed with nonstick cooking spray. Bake
40 to 45 minutes. Serve warm or chilled.

Per serving: 179 calories; 7 g protein; 5 g fat;
28 g carbohydrate; 181 mg sodium

CREAM PUFFS WITH STRAWBERRY SAUCE
See Menu Plan for Week 52.
Makes 6 servings

Cream Puff Shells
¼ cup margarine
½ cup water
½ cup less 1½ teaspoons enriched flour
3 medium eggs

Strawberry Sauce
2¼ cups strawberries, cut into quarters
⅓ cup plus 2 teaspoons orange juice
1 to 1½ teaspoons freshly grated orange
    rind
Artificial sweetener to equal 6 teaspoons
    sugar

Filling
18 ounces vanilla-flavored dietary frozen dessert

To Prepare Cream Puffs: Preheat oven to 400°F. Place margarine in medium saucepan; add water and heat until boiling. Add flour all at once and stir vigorously until mixture leaves sides of pan. Remove from heat. Add eggs 1 at a time, beating well after each addition until mixture is smooth. Make 12 puff shells by dropping dough, by rounded teaspoonsful, onto a heavy aluminum baking sheet that has been sprayed with nonstick cooking spray, leaving a space of 3 inches between each. Bake 15 minutes; reduce oven temperature to 350°F. and bake an additional 15 minutes. Remove puff shells from oven; pierce side of each with the point of a sharp knife. Return to turned-off oven for 10 minutes, leaving oven door ajar. Transfer to racks away from drafts to cool.

To Prepare Sauce: Combine strawberries, orange juice, and rind in small bowl. Cover and refrigerate for at least 3 hours. Pour mixture into blender container; add sweetener and process until smooth.

To Serve: Slice off top of each puff shell and spoon 1½ ounces of frozen dessert into each. Replace top and spoon ¹⁄₁₂ of the sauce over each cream puff.

Per serving: 265 calories; 9 g protein; 11 g fat; 33 g carbohydrate; 207 mg sodium

½ cup evaporated skimmed milk
3 tablespoons enriched flour, sifted
1 teaspoon vanilla extract
1 teaspoon grated lemon rind
2 cups strawberries, cut into halves
2 tablespoons plus 2 teaspoons reduced-calorie strawberry spread

Preheat oven to 325°F. In a bowl blend cracker crumbs with 1 tablespoon melted margarine. With back of spoon press crumb mixture into bottom of an 8-inch springform pan. Brush sides of pan with remaining margarine. Using an electric mixer beat eggs until lemon-colored. Add sweetener and sugar and beat 5 minutes more. Add cheese and continue beating at low speed; then beat in ⅓ of the milk and 1 tablespoon flour. Repeat with remaining milk and flour. Add extract and lemon rind and stir to combine. Pour mixture into prepared pan and bake 1 hour. (Do not open oven door while cake is baking.) Turn off heat and leave cake in closed oven 1 hour longer. (Cake will sink.) Remove pan to a rack and cool. Carefully remove sides of springform pan and transfer cake to plate. Arrange strawberries decoratively on top of cake. In small saucepan melt strawberry spread; spoon over berries. Chill for 2 hours.

Per serving: 378 calories; 20 g protein; 18 g fat; 35 g carbohydrate; 348 mg sodium

"FALLEN" STRAWBERRY CHEESECAKE
See Menu Plan for Week 20.
Makes 4 servings

8 graham crackers (2½-inch squares), made into crumbs
1 tablespoon plus 1 teaspoon margarine, melted, divided
4 eggs
Artificial sweetener to equal 6 teaspoons sugar
2 teaspoons sugar
1⅓ cups part-skim ricotta cheese

LADY FINGERS
See Menu Plan for Week 10.
Makes 2 servings

1 very ripe medium banana
2 eggs, separated
½ teaspoon vanilla extract
¼ cup plus 1 tablespoon enriched flour
⅛ teaspoon salt
1 tablespoon sugar

Preheat oven to 375°F. Break banana into pieces and place in work bowl of food processor or blender container. Add egg yolks and vanilla; process until smooth. Sift flour and salt together 3 times and set aside. In separate bowl beat egg whites with sugar until stiff. Gently fold banana mixture into egg whites; then gradually fold in sifted flour. Spray a nonstick baking sheet with nonstick cooking spray. Spoon batter into pastry bag that has been fitted with a pastry tube. To form each lady finger squeeze out 4 inches of batter onto baking sheet, leaving a space of 2 inches between each. Bake about 12 minutes or until lightly browned. Transfer to wire rack and allow to cool slightly. Serve warm.

Per serving: 246 calories; 9 g protein; 6 g fat; 40 g carbohydrate; 223 mg sodium

OATMEAL-RAISIN LOAF
See Menu Plan for Week 35.
Makes 2 servings

1 cup skim milk
⅓ cup nonfat dry milk powder
1½ ounces uncooked quick oats
2 tablespoons raisins, chopped
2 eggs, separated
Artificial sweetener to equal 4 teaspoons sugar
1 teaspoon honey
¼ teaspoon lemon juice
¼ teaspoon ground cinnamon
⅛ teaspoon ground allspice
Dash salt
1 tablespoon reduced-calorie spread, any flavor (optional)

In top half of double boiler over simmering water combine skim and dry milks; using wire whisk, stir briskly to dissolve dry milk. Add oats and raisins and cook, stirring occasionally, until mixture thickens. Set aside.

In small bowl mix together egg yolks, sweetener, honey, lemon juice, cinnamon, allspice, and salt; stir yolk mixture into oatmeal.

Preheat oven to 350°F. In medium bowl beat egg whites until stiff peaks form; gently yet thoroughly fold oatmeal mixture into egg whites. Spray two 8 x 4 x 2½-inch loaf pans with nonstick cooking spray and spoon ½ of batter into each. Bake 20 to 25 minutes or until a knife, when inserted, comes out clean. Allow to cool 5 minutes; loosen edges with knife and turn out onto cooling rack. Serve with reduced-calorie spread, if desired.

Per serving: 292 calories; 18 g protein; 8 g fat; 40 g carbohydrate; 269 mg sodium
Add: 12 calories and 3 g carbohydrate if reduced-calorie spread is used.

SPICED PUMPKIN CAKE
See Menu Plan for Week 30.
Makes 4 servings

½ cup plus 2 tablespoons enriched flour
1½ teaspoons baking powder
½ teaspoon ground cinnamon
½ teaspoon ground nutmeg
Dash each ground cloves and salt
2 eggs, separated
¼ cup canned pumpkin
3 tablespoons water
Artificial sweetener to equal 6 teaspoons sugar
1 tablespoon plus 1 teaspoon vegetable oil
¼ teaspoon grated orange rind
Dash cream of tartar

Preheat oven to 325°F. Sift first 5 ingredients into medium bowl. Add egg yolks, pumpkin, water, sweetener, oil, and orange rind; beat until smooth. In separate medium bowl beat whites with cream of tartar until stiff peaks form; gently fold into pumpkin mixture. Transfer batter to a 7⅜ x 3⅝ x 2¼-

inch nonstick loaf pan that has been sprayed with nonstick cooking spray; bake for 40 minutes. Remove cake from pan and allow to cool.

Per serving: 157 calories; 5 g protein; 8 g fat; 16 g carbohydrate; 321 mg sodium

SWEDISH APPLE BAKE
See Menu Plan for Week 17.
Makes 2 servings

¼ cup plus 1 tablespoon enriched flour
Artificial sweetener to equal 2 teaspoons
    sugar
¾ teaspoon baking powder
¾ teaspoon ground cinnamon
Dash each ground allspice, ground nutmeg,
    and salt
2 small McIntosh apples, cored and diced
2 eggs, beaten with 3 tablespoons water
1 teaspoon honey
¼ teaspoon lemon juice
¼ teaspoon vanilla extract

Preheat oven to 350°F. Combine flour, artificial sweetener, baking powder, cinnamon, allspice, nutmeg, and salt; sift into a medium bowl. Add apples and stir to coat with dry ingredients. Add remaining ingredients and stir to combine. Spray an 8 x 5 x 2½-inch loaf pan with nonstick cooking spray. Spoon apple mixture into pan. Cover with foil and bake for 40 minutes. Let stand for 10 minutes. Sprinkle top of cake with cinnamon. Cut into slices and serve warm.

Per serving: 231 calories; 8 g protein; 7 g fat; 36 g carbohydrate; 370 mg sodium

CHERRY COBBLER
See Menu Plan for Week 28.
Makes 4 servings

1 English muffin, cut into ¼-inch dice
Artificial sweetener to equal 6 teaspoons
    sugar, divided
2 teaspoons sugar
¼ teaspoon ground cinnamon
⅛ teaspoon ground allspice
40 large cherries, pitted
1½ cups water
1 tablespoon plus 1 teaspoon cornstarch
½ teaspoon lemon juice

In a small bowl combine muffin pieces, sweetener to equal 2 teaspoons sugar, sugar, cinnamon, and allspice; set aside. In saucepan combine cherries and water. Cover and bring to a boil; reduce heat and simmer 3 minutes. Remove from heat and cool to room temperature. In small bowl dissolve cornstarch in 2 tablespoons cherry liquid. Stir dissolved cornstarch and lemon juice into saucepan containing cherries. Cook over medium heat, stirring constantly, until mixture begins to thicken. Stir in remaining sweetener. Divide evenly into 4 individual dessert dishes. Sprinkle each with an equal amount of muffin mixture. Refrigerate at least 2 hours.

Per serving: 101 calories; 2 g protein; 1 g fat; 24 g carbohydrate; 74 mg sodium

CHERRY TARTS

May be served at room temperature or chilled.

See Menu Plan for Week 8.
Makes 2 servings

Crust

4 graham crackers, 2½-inch squares, crushed
¼ teaspoon ground cinnamon
1 tablespoon plus 1 teaspoon reduced-calorie margarine

Filling

1 cup frozen dark sweet cherries, no sugar added
1 tablespoon plus 1 teaspoon lemon juice
2-inch cinnamon stick
Dash ground cloves
2 teaspoons arrowroot, dissolved in 1 tablespoon plus 1 teaspoon water

Topping

2 tablespoons low-calorie whipped topping (optional)

To Prepare Crust: In a small bowl combine graham cracker crumbs and cinnamon; add margarine and mix thoroughly. Divide mixture into two 5-inch aluminum tart pie pans, pressing mixture firmly with back of spoon onto bottom and up sides to form crust; refrigerate.

To Prepare Filling: In a small saucepan combine cherries, lemon juice, cinnamon, and cloves; cook until heated. Remove cinnamon stick. Add dissolved arrowroot to saucepan, stirring gently so as not to crush cherries. Remove from heat, cool 10 minutes, and pour into prepared crusts. Refrigerate until thickened. If desired, top each tart with 1 tablespoon whipped topping just before serving.

Per serving: 135 calories; 2 g protein; 4 g fat; 24 g carbohydrate; 189 mg sodium
Add: 3 calories and 1 g carbohydrate if low-calorie whipped topping is used.

FRUITED CUSTARD PIE

See Menu Plan for Week 21.
Makes 8 servings

½ cup plus 2 tablespoons enriched flour
¼ teaspoon salt
2 tablespoons plus 2 teaspoons margarine
¼ cup plain unflavored yogurt
1 envelope (4 servings) vanilla-flavored low-calorie milk pudding mix
2 cups skim milk
4 canned pineapple slices with ¼ cup juice, no sugar added
¼ cup reduced-calorie apricot spread
1 cup strawberries
½ medium banana, sliced

Combine flour and salt in mixing bowl. Cut in margarine until mixture resembles a coarse meal. Add yogurt and mix thoroughly; form into a ball. Roll dough out to approximately ⅛-inch thickness. Fit into a 9-inch pie pan; prick the dough generously with the prongs of a fork and flute edges. Bake at 400°F. for 15 to 20 minutes; cool. Prepare pudding mix according to package directions using 2 cups skim milk and ¼ cup juice from canned pineapple; chill. Spread pudding in prepared pie crust. In small pan melt apricot spread over low heat. Arrange fruit decoratively over top of pudding; brush with melted apricot spread. Chill.

Per serving: 148 calories; 4 g protein; 4 g fat; 24 g carbohydrate; 180 mg sodium

FRUIT "PIE"

See Menu Plans for Weeks 18, 20, and 47.
Makes 4 servings

1 canned peach half with 1 tablespoon juice, no sugar added
1 canned pineapple slice with 1 tablespoon juice, no sugar added
½ cup strawberries, cut into slices lengthwise
10 small grapes, halved
1½ teaspoons unflavored gelatin

Artificial sweetener to equal 2 teaspoons
sugar
¾ cup boiling water
2 tablespoons lemon juice

Combine peach and pineapple juices and set aside. Cut the peach half into 6 wedges. Cut the pineapple slice into 6 pieces. In the center of a 9-inch glass pie plate arrange 3 strawberry slices and 3 grape halves to form a flower. Alternate peach wedges and pineapple pieces to form a circle around the flower. Make an outer circle of remaining strawberry slices and grapes, alternating 2 strawberry slices with each grape half. In small bowl mix gelatin with sweetener. Add boiling water and stir until gelatin is completely dissolved. Stir in lemon juice and reserved fruit juice. Chill mixture until it is the consistency of unbeaten egg whites. Carefully pour about ⅓ of chilled gelatin mixture over fruit and chill in refrigerator until set. Gradually add remaining gelatin mixture and chill "pie" for 3 hours, or until set. Cut "pie" into 4 wedges.

Per serving: 38 calories; 2 g protein; 0.3 g fat;
8 g carbohydrate; 2 mg sodium

MANDARIN CHIFFON PIE
See Menu Plan for Week 16.
Makes 4 servings

Filling
1 envelope unflavored gelatin
1 cup orange juice, heated
¾ cup plain unflavored yogurt
Artificial sweetener to equal 6 teaspoons
sugar

Pie Crust
8 graham crackers, 2½-inch squares, crushed
½ teaspoon ground cinnamon
2 tablespoons plus 2 teaspoons reduced-
calorie margarine

Topping
½ cup canned mandarin orange sections,
no sugar added

To Prepare Filling: In bowl sprinkle gelatin over juice and stir until completely dissolved; chill until slightly thickened. Stir in yogurt and sweetener until well mixed.

To Prepare Crust: In small bowl combine graham cracker crumbs and cinnamon; add margarine and mix thoroughly. Divide mixture evenly into four 5-inch aluminum tart pie pans, pressing mixture firmly with back of a spoon onto bottom and up the sides to form pie crust.

To Serve: Divide filling into prepared crusts. Top each pie with an equal amount of orange sections; chill until set.

Per serving: 164 calories; 5 g protein; 7 g fat;
23 g carbohydrate; 210 mg sodium

BANANA "CREAM"
See Menu Plan for Week 32.
Makes 2 servings

1 cup skim milk, divided
⅓ cup nonfat dry milk powder
1 medium banana, divided
¼ teaspoon lemon juice
1 teaspoon honey
2 teaspoons cornstarch
Artificial sweetener to equal 2 teaspoons
sugar
⅛ teaspoon vanilla extract

In top half of double boiler thoroughly combine all but 2 tablespoons skim milk with milk powder. Using a fork mash ½ of the banana with lemon juice. Add mashed banana and honey to milk. Cook over boiling water until just heated through. Dissolve cornstarch in reserved 2 tablespoons milk. Using a wire whisk, briskly stir dissolved cornstarch into milk mixture. Cook, stirring occasionally, until mixture thickens, about 7 minutes. Remove from heat. Cut remaining banana in half lengthwise; slice halves crosswise into ¼-inch pieces. Stir sliced banana, sweetener, and vanilla into thickened "cream." Refrigerate 2 hours.

Per serving: 160 calories; 9 g protein; 0.4 g fat;
31 g carbohydrate; 130 mg sodium

BANANA-PRUNE PUDDING

Lemon-lime-flavored diet soda may be substituted for the grapefruit soda.
See Menu Plans for Weeks 11 and 30.
Makes 4 servings

4 large prunes, pitted
1½ teaspoons unflavored gelatin
½ cup plus 2 tablespoons grapefruit-
　flavored diet soda, divided
1 medium banana, cut into pieces
½ cup plain unflavored yogurt

In small saucepan cook prunes in water to cover until very soft. Drain and let cool. In a small heatproof cup sprinkle gelatin over 2 tablespoons soda to soften. Set cup in a pan containing enough hot water to reach halfway up side of cup. Stir until gelatin is dissolved. Place prunes, banana, dissolved gelatin, and remaining soda in blender container or work bowl of food processor; process until smooth. Add yogurt and process until just combined. Pour into 4 dessert dishes. Chill until set.

Per serving: 81 calories; 3 g protein; 1 g fat;
17 g carbohydrate; 15 mg sodium

BITTERSWEET CHOCOLATE "CREAM"

See Menu Plan for Week 29.
Makes 4 servings

1 envelope unflavored gelatin
2 cups skim milk, divided
3 tablespoons unsweetened cocoa
½ teaspoon instant coffee
Artificial sweetener to equal 6 teaspoons
　sugar
1 teaspoon vanilla extract

In small bowl sprinkle gelatin over ½ cup milk; let stand to soften. In saucepan combine remaining milk with cocoa and instant coffee; beat with a whisk and bring to a boil. Stir in softened gelatin mixture; cook over low heat, stirring constantly, until gelatin is dissolved. Remove from heat and stir in sweetener and vanilla. Transfer to a bowl and chill until thickened but not firm.

Whisk again until light and fluffy and pour into individual dessert dishes; cover lightly and chill until firm.

Per serving: 70 calories; 7 g protein; 1 g fat;
9 g carbohydrate; 67 mg sodium

CARROT-APPLE PUDDING

See Menu Plan for Week 43.
Makes 2 servings

½ cup grated carrot
½ small apple, pared, cored, and grated
2 eggs, separated
1 teaspoon grated lemon rind
½ teaspoon lemon juice
2 tablespoons plus 1½ teaspoons enriched
　flour
2 tablespoons raisins
Artificial sweetener to equal 2 teaspoons
　sugar
1 teaspoon margarine

Preheat oven to 350°F. In medium bowl combine carrot, apple, egg yolks, lemon rind, and juice. Stir in flour, raisins, and sweetener. In separate bowl beat egg whites until stiff peaks form; fold into carrot mixture. Grease a shallow 2-cup baking pan with margarine; transfer carrot pudding to pan. Bake for 30 minutes or until top is lightly browned.

Per serving: 187 calories; 8 g protein; 8 g fat;
22 g carbohydrate; 107 mg sodium

CARROT-PUMPKIN PUDDING

See Menu Plan for Week 1.
Makes 4 servings

1 tablespoon plus 1 teaspoon vegetable oil
3 cups thinly sliced carrots
1⅓ cups apple juice, no sugar added,
　divided
⅔ cup water
1 cup canned pumpkin
Artificial sweetener to equal 4 teaspoons
　sugar
½ teaspoon ground cinnamon
¼ teaspoon each ground nutmeg, ground
　allspice, and salt

1 tablespoon plus 1 teaspoon cornstarch

Heat oil in nonstick skillet. Stir in carrots; cover and cook over medium heat about 10 minutes. Add ⅔ cup apple juice and water; cover and simmer 30 minutes or until carrots are very tender. Drain off most of liquid in skillet and reserve. Transfer carrots and any remaining liquid to blender container or work bowl of food processor and process until pureed. In saucepan combine carrot puree, pumpkin, sweetener, cinnamon, nutmeg, allspice, and salt. Add reserved cooking liquid and stir well. Cook over medium heat 5 minutes, stirring constantly. Dissolve cornstarch in remaining apple juice; add to saucepan. Continue stirring over medium heat until pudding thickens and bubbles come to surface. Pour into 4 dessert dishes and chill.

Per serving: 144 calories; 2 g protein; 5 g fat; 25 g carbohydrate; 321 mg sodium

MELON MOUSSE
Do not keep any longer than one day or mousse will separate.
See Menu Plan for Week 19.
Makes 4 servings

2 cups honeydew chunks
¼ cup lemon juice
⅛ teaspoon salt
2 envelopes unflavored gelatin
¼ cup water
1 cup evaporated skimmed milk, chilled
Artificial sweetener to equal 10 teaspoons sugar
1 teaspoon vanilla extract
1 drop green food coloring (optional)
1 cup strawberries, thinly sliced, reserve 1 whole berry
1 medium kiwi fruit, pared and cut into 8 slices

Place honeydew chunks in blender container; puree until smooth. Transfer to bowl; add lemon juice and salt and macerate (let stand) at room temperature for several hours.
In small bowl sprinkle gelatin over water.

Let stand several minutes to soften. Set bowl in a larger pan that contains hot water; stir until gelatin is dissolved. Transfer to mixing bowl and chill until syrupy.
Add chilled evaporated skimmed milk, sweetener, and vanilla extract to gelatin; beat for 15 minutes or until stiff. Fold ¼ of the whipped milk into honeydew. Gently fold in remainder of milk, and food coloring if desired. Transfer to a 2-quart glass serving dish. Cover and chill for 6 hours. Decorate with strawberries and kiwi fruit.

Per serving: 138 calories; 10 g protein; 1 g fat; 23 g carbohydrate; 166 mg sodium

PINEAPPLE-ORANGE PUDDING
This pudding should be served on the same day that it is made.
See Menu Plan for Week 9.
Makes 4 servings

1 envelope unflavored gelatin
½ cup orange juice
½ cup canned crushed pineapple, no sugar added
½ cup water
Artificial sweetener to equal 6 teaspoons sugar
1 tablespoon lemon juice
1 cup plain unflavored yogurt

In saucepan sprinkle gelatin over orange juice and let stand a few minutes to soften; heat, stirring constantly, until gelatin is dissolved. In bowl combine pineapple, water, sweetener, and lemon juice; stir in gelatin mixture. Chill until almost set. Whip in yogurt. Pour into dessert cups and chill until set.

Per serving: 80 calories; 4 g protein; 2 g fat; 12 g carbohydrate; 29 mg sodium

PINEAPPLE-YOGURT PUDDING
See Menu Plan for Week 27.
Makes 4 servings

1 envelope unflavored gelatin
½ cup water
1 cup canned crushed pineapple, no sugar added
1 cup plain unflavored yogurt
Artificial sweetener to equal 4 teaspoons sugar
1 tablespoon vanilla extract
⅛ teaspoon ground cinnamon
4 graham crackers, 2½-inch squares, made into crumbs

In saucepan sprinkle gelatin over water; let stand 5 minutes to soften. Cook, stirring constantly, until gelatin is dissolved; cool. Add remaining ingredients except graham cracker crumbs and stir to combine. Divide evenly into four 6-ounce custard cups. Sprinkle each with ¼ of the graham cracker crumbs. Chill at least 4 hours.

Per serving: 121 calories; 5 g protein; 3 g fat;
18 g carbohydrate; 76 mg sodium

SPICED PINEAPPLE PUMPKIN
See Menu Plan for Week 36.
Makes 2 servings

¾ teaspoon unflavored gelatin
⅓ cup apple juice, no sugar added
1 cup canned pumpkin
Artificial sweetener to equal 2 teaspoons sugar
1 teaspoon honey
Dash each ground cinnamon and ground allspice
1 cup canned crushed pineapple, no sugar added

In small bowl sprinkle gelatin over apple juice and let stand to soften. Place bowl in pan containing hot water and stir constantly until gelatin is completely dissolved; remove bowl from water. In a larger bowl combine pumpkin, sweetener, honey, cinnamon, allspice, and gelatin mixture; mix well. Spread ¼ of mixture over bottom of each of 2 individual dishes; top each with ¼ cup pineapple. Repeat layers and chill at least 1 hour.

Per serving: 149 calories; 3 g protein; 1 g fat;
37 g carbohydrate; 277 mg sodium

AUTUMN TREAT
See Menu Plans for Weeks 44 and 50.
Makes 4 servings

1 envelope (4 servings) orange-flavored low-calorie gelatin
½ cup low-calorie whipped topping
1 tablespoon plus 1 teaspoon shredded coconut, toasted

Prepare gelatin according to package directions and pour into 4 dessert dishes; chill until set. Top each with 2 tablespoons whipped topping and sprinkle with 1 teaspoon shredded coconut.

Per serving: 20 calories; 2 g protein; 1 g fat;
1 g carbohydrate; 5 mg sodium

COCONUT-ORANGE GELATIN
See Menu Plans for Weeks 12 and 38.
Makes 2 servings

1 cup prepared orange-flavored low-calorie gelatin
½ cup canned pineapple chunks, no sugar added
2 teaspoons shredded coconut

Cut gelatin into cubes; combine with pineapple chunks in a serving dish and sprinkle with coconut.

Per serving: 20 calories; 2 g protein; 1 g fat;
10 g carbohydrate; 6 mg sodium

FRUITED YOGURT MOLD
Rinsing the mold in cold water will make unmolding easier.
See Menu Plans for Weeks 32 and 43.
Makes 4 servings

⅔ cup apple juice, no sugar added, divided
⅓ cup water
1 teaspoon honey

1 envelope unflavored gelatin
2 cups plain unflavored yogurt
Artificial sweetener to equal 4 teaspoons
    sugar
¼ teaspoon vanilla extract
1 cup strawberries, thinly sliced, divided
½ cup blueberries

In saucepan combine ⅓ cup apple juice, water, and honey. Sprinkle gelatin over liquid and allow to soften. Heat, stirring constantly, until gelatin is completely dissolved. Remove from heat and allow to cool slightly.

In medium bowl combine yogurt, remaining ⅓ cup apple juice, artificial sweetener, vanilla, and dissolved gelatin mixture. Blend thoroughly with wire whisk. Cover and refrigerate about 1 hour or until mixture reaches syrupy consistency. Stir in ½ cup strawberries and blueberries; reserve remaining strawberries.

Rinse stainless-steel or glass mold with cold water. Pour in fruited yogurt. Refrigerate 2 hours or until completely set. Unmold onto serving plate. Garnish with remaining strawberry slices.

Per serving: 130 calories; 6 g protein; 4 g fat;
18 g carbohydrate; 55 mg sodium

TROPICAL TREAT
See Menu Plans for Weeks 2, 14, and 26.
Makes 4 servings

1 cup flat lemon-lime flavored diet soda,
    divided
1½ teaspoons unflavored gelatin
2 medium bananas, mashed
2 tablespoons lemon juice
2 tablespoons lime juice
Artificial sweetener to equal 3 teaspoons
    sugar
1½ teaspoons grated lime rind, divided
¼ cup low-calorie whipped topping

Measure 2 tablespoons soda into a small bowl; sprinkle gelatin over soda and let stand 5 minutes to soften. Set bowl in saucepan of hot water; stir mixture until gelatin is completely dissolved. In another bowl combine bananas, lemon and lime juices, sweetener, 1 teaspoon lime rind, gelatin mixture, and remaining soda. Divide dessert into four 6-ounce custard cups. Cover and chill until set, about 6 hours. To unmold loosen edges of dessert with pointed knife; dip each cup into hot water for 1 minute and unmold onto individual dessert plate. Top each portion with 1 tablespoon whipped topping and sprinkle with ⅛ teaspoon lime rind.

Per serving: 63 calories; 1 g protein; 0.1 g fat;
16 g carbohydrate; 23 mg sodium

BANANA-APPLE SOFT "ICE CREAM"
See Menu Plan for Last Day of the Year.
Makes 4 servings

1 medium banana, broken into pieces
½ cup canned sliced apples, no sugar added
¾ cup buttermilk
⅓ cup nonfat dry milk powder
2 teaspoons honey
¾ teaspoon vanilla extract
¾ teaspoon lemon juice
Artificial sweetener to equal 4 teaspoons
    sugar
Dash each salt and ground cinnamon
1 cup plain unflavored yogurt

Combine all ingredients except yogurt in blender container; whip until smooth. Add yogurt and process briefly. Pour into 8-inch square pan or any shallow container (do not use aluminum). Cover and freeze until solid. Remove from freezer and allow to thaw just until mixture can be cut into chunks. Place chunks in blender container and whip until smooth. (Use an on-off motion and stir frequently.) Serve immediately.

Per serving: 134 calories; 6 g protein; 2 g fat;
23 g carbohydrate; 142 mg sodium

FROZEN APPLE-BANANA DESSERT
See Menu Plans for Weeks 6, 15, and 39.
Makes 2 servings

1 cup skim milk
1 small apple, pared, cored, and cut into
   pieces
½ medium banana, sliced
⅓ cup nonfat dry milk powder
Artificial sweetener to equal 4 teaspoons
   sugar
2 drops almond extract

Combine all ingredients in blender container; process until smooth. Pour into plastic container and freeze. Remove from freezer and thaw slightly. Transfer to blender container. Process until smooth. Pour into 2 dessert dishes and freeze. Serve frozen.

Per serving: 145 calories; 9 g protein; 1 g fat;
27 g carbohydrate; 131 mg sodium

FROZEN MANGO YOGURT
In this recipe, we recommend a shallow pan in order to hasten the freezing time.
See Menu Plans for Weeks 12 and 33.
Makes 2 servings

1 very ripe small mango, pared and pitted
½ cup plain unflavored yogurt
2 tablespoons lemon juice
Artificial sweetener to equal 2 teaspoons
   sugar

Combine all ingredients in blender container; process until smooth. Transfer to shallow 1½-quart pan; place in freezer. Stir every hour to break up ice crystals until mixture is solid. Thaw 10 minutes before serving.

Per serving: 73 calories; 2 g protein; 2 g fat;
13 g carbohydrate; 29 mg sodium

PINEAPPLE-MANGO "ICE CREAM"
See Menu Plan for Week 35.
Makes 2 servings

¾ cup buttermilk
½ small mango, pared and cut into pieces

½ cup canned crushed pineapple, no sugar
   added, drain and reserve juice
½ teaspoon fresh lime juice

In blender container combine buttermilk and mango; add reserved pineapple juice and lime juice and whip until smooth. Pour mixture into small pan and freeze until the consistency of soft ice cream. Remove from freezer and rewhip in blender container. Fold in crushed pineapple. Divide into 2 dessert dishes; freeze until firm but not solid.

Per serving: 99 calories; 4 g protein; 1 g fat;
21 g carbohydrate; 101 mg sodium

PIÑA FREEZE
See Menu Plans for Weeks 7 and 50.
Makes 4 servings

2 cups plain unflavored yogurt
2 cups canned crushed pineapple, no sugar
   added
Artificial sweetener to equal 6 teaspoons
   sugar
1 tablespoon lemon juice

Combine all ingredients in blender container; process until smooth. Transfer to a shallow 2½-quart casserole; place in freezer. Stir every hour to break up ice crystals until frozen, at least 3 or 4 hours. Thaw for 10 minutes before serving.

Per serving: 146 calories; 4 g protein; 4 g fat;
26 g carbohydrate; 53 mg sodium

PEAR FROZEN YOGURT
Frozen yogurt is a summertime favorite, and this version will help keep you slim as well as cool!
See Menu Plans for Weeks 3, 17, 23, and 31.
Makes 2 servings

4 canned pear halves with ¼ cup juice,
   no sugar added
1 cup plain unflavored yogurt
Artificial sweetener to equal 8 teaspoons
   sugar
2 tablespoons lemon juice

Combine all ingredients in blender container; process until smooth. Transfer to shallow 2½-quart casserole; place in freezer. Stir every hour to break up ice crystals until frozen, about 3 hours. Thaw for 10 minutes before serving.

Per serving: 120 calories; 4 g protein; 4 g fat; 19 g carbohydrate; 53 mg sodium

LIME-ORANGE ICE IN LIME CUPS
See Menu Plans for Weeks 15 and 50.
Makes 4 servings

4 small oranges, peeled, seeded, and cut into pieces
¾ cup water
½ cup lime juice, reserve lime shells*
Artificial sweetener to equal 8 teaspoons sugar
1 tablespoon grated lime rind
8 lime cups, made from 4 limes*
8 mint sprigs (optional)

Combine all ingredients except lime cups and mint sprigs in blender container. Process for 10 seconds. Pour into shallow dish. Freeze for 30 minutes. Stir with fork to break up ice particles. Return to freezer and stir every 15 minutes for about 2 hours or until frozen to desired consistency. Divide mixture evenly into 8 lime cups. Store in freezer until about 10 minutes before serving. Garnish, if desired, with mint sprigs.

Per serving: 62 calories; 1 g protein; 0.3 g fat; 16 g carbohydrate; 17 mg sodium

* Cut limes into halves. Cut a thin slice off bottom of each lime half so that it will stand upright. Carefully squeeze out juice. Scrape shells clean with spoon. Lime cups may be prepared ahead and frozen until ready to use.

MOCHA SUNDAE
See Menu Plans for Weeks 12, 28, 32, and 42.
Makes 4 servings

4 scoops coffee-flavored dietary frozen dessert, 3 ounces each
2 tablespoons low-calorie chocolate topping
2 teaspoons shredded coconut

Place 1 scoop frozen dessert in each of 4 dessert dishes. Spoon 1½ teaspoons low-calorie topping over each and sprinkle with ½ teaspoon coconut.

Per serving: 109 calories; 4 g protein; 1 g fat; 20 g carbohydrate; 79 mg sodium

OPEN-FACE "ICE CREAM" SANDWICH
See Menu Plan for Week 23.
Makes 2 servings

3 ounces vanilla-flavored dietary frozen dessert
2 graham crackers, 2½-inch squares
½ cup strawberries, cut into thick slices

Spread 1½ ounces frozen dessert on each graham cracker. Top each portion with ½ of the sliced strawberries.

Per serving: 89 calories; 3 g protein; 1 g fat; 18 g carbohydrate; 87 mg sodium

HOT COCOA
See Menu Plans for Weeks 2 and 39.
Makes 2 servings

⅔ cup nonfat dry milk powder
2 teaspoons unsweetened cocoa
1½ cups water
Artificial sweetener to equal 8 teaspoons sugar

Combine dry milk and cocoa in saucepan; gradually stir in water, blending thoroughly. Bring to a boil, stirring constantly; boil 2 minutes. Remove from heat, add sweetener, and serve.

Per serving: 98 calories; 9 g protein; 1 g fat; 16 g carbohydrate; 132 mg sodium

HOT MOCHA MILK

See Menu Plan for Week 1 and various other weeks.
Makes two 1-cup servings
or
four ½-cup servings

2 cups skim milk
2 teaspoons unsweetened cocoa
1 teaspoon instant coffee
Artificial sweetener to equal 4 teaspoons
    sugar
½ teaspoon vanilla extract

In small saucepan combine milk, cocoa, and coffee; bring to a boil. Remove from heat. Stir in sweetener and vanilla extract and serve.

Per ½ cup serving: 50 calories; 4 g protein; 0.4 g fat;
7 g carbohydrate; 65 mg sodium
Per 1 cup serving: 100 calories; 8 g protein; 0.8 g fat;
14 g carbohydrate; 130 mg sodium

HOT SPICED TEA

One can always buy spiced teas, but if you have the spices on hand, you can easily make your own—it's less expensive, too. Try this one to begin with, then start experimenting on your own.
See Menu Plan for Week 40 and various other weeks.
Makes 1 serving

1 tea bag
1 lemon slice
1½-inch piece cinnamon stick
1 whole clove
1 cup boiling water

Combine all ingredients except water in teapot. Add boiling water; let steep 3 to 5 minutes. Strain before serving.

Per serving: 3 calories; 0.1 g protein; 0 g fat;
1 g carbohydrate; 0 mg sodium

COCONUT-HONEY SHAKE

See Menu Plan for Week 45 and various other weeks.
Makes 2 servings

1 cup mineral water
½ cup plain unflavored yogurt
Artificial sweetener to equal 2 teaspoons
    sugar (optional)
2 teaspoons shredded coconut
1 teaspoon each honey and vanilla extract
Dash ground cinnamon
3 to 4 ice cubes

Combine all ingredients except ice cubes in blender container. Process until smooth, adding ice cubes 1 at a time. Serve immediately.

Per serving: 61 calories; 2 g protein; 2 g fat;
6 g carbohydrate; 26 mg sodium

COFFEE-YOGURT SHAKE

See Menu Plan for Week 44 and various other weeks.
Makes 2 servings

1 cup mineral water
½ cup plain unflavored yogurt
1 teaspoon instant coffee
Artificial sweetener to equal 1 teaspoon
    sugar
1 teaspoon sugar
⅛ teaspoon ground cinnamon
6 ice cubes

Combine all ingredients except ice cubes in blender container. Process, adding ice cubes 1 at a time, until smooth. Serve immediately.

Per serving: 44 calories; 2 g protein; 2 g fat;
5 g carbohydrate; 26 mg sodium

PINEAPPLE-BANANA MILK SHAKE

See Menu Plans for Weeks 24, 41, 42, and 50.
Makes 4 servings

1 cup canned crushed pineapple, no sugar
    added
1 medium banana, cut into chunks
1 cup ice water
⅔ cup nonfat dry milk powder
2 tablespoons lemon juice
¼ teaspoon vanilla extract
6 ice cubes

Combine all ingredients except ice cubes in blender container; add ice cubes 2 at a time, processing after each addition. Shake should be thick and smooth. Serve in tall glasses.

Per serving: 108 calories; 5 g protein; 0.2 g fat; 23 g carbohydrate; 66 mg sodium

PINEAPPLE-YOGURT SHAKE
See Menu Plan for Week 33.
Makes 2 servings

1 cup canned crushed pineapple, no sugar added
1 cup skim milk
½ cup plain unflavored yogurt
1 tablespoon lemon juice
1 teaspoon sugar

Combine all ingredients in blender container; process for 2 minutes. Chill; stir just before serving.

Per serving: 162 calories; 7 g protein; 2 g fat; 31 g carbohydrate; 92 mg sodium

STRAWBERRY SHAKE
See Menu Plan for Week 38 and various other weeks.
Makes 1 serving

1½ ounces vanilla-flavored dietary frozen dessert
½ cup strawberries
¼ cup skim milk
Artificial sweetener to equal 2 teaspoons sugar
½ teaspoon vanilla extract

Combine all ingredients in blender container; process until smooth. Chill 15 minutes in blender container. Process 2 minutes and serve.

Per serving: 110 calories; 5 g protein; 1 g fat; 20 g carbohydrate; 73 mg sodium

YOGURT-BANANA SHAKE
See Menu Plans for Weeks 28 and 41.
Makes 2 servings

⅔ cup skim milk
⅔ cup plain unflavored yogurt
1 medium banana, sliced
1 teaspoon honey
1 teaspoon lemon juice

Chill 2 glasses. Combine all ingredients in blender container; process until smooth and thick. Pour into chilled glasses.

Per serving: 136 calories; 6 g protein; 3 g fat; 24 g carbohydrate; 77 mg sodium

PINEAPPLE-STRAWBERRY WHIP
See Menu Plan for Week 51.
Makes 1 serving

⅓ cup chilled pineapple juice, no sugar added
½ cup chilled strawberries, reserve 1 strawberry
¼ cup chilled diet tonic water

In blender container or work bowl of food processor combine pineapple juice, strawberries, and tonic. Process until strawberries are pureed. Serve in 8-ounce glass. Garnish edge of glass with reserved strawberry.

Per serving: 71 calories; 1 g protein; 0.4 g fat; 17 g carbohydrate; 19 mg sodium

STRAWBERRY-APPLE FROST
See Menu Plans for Weeks 14 and 30.
Makes 2 servings

1 cup plain unflavored yogurt
1 cup very ripe strawberries, reserve 2 whole berries
⅓ cup apple juice, no sugar added
Artificial sweetener to equal 2 teaspoons sugar
1 teaspoon sugar
1 teaspoon vanilla extract
4 ice cubes

Combine all ingredients except reserved berries in blender container; process until frothy. Divide into 2 stemmed glasses; garnish each serving with a strawberry.

Per serving: 134 calories; 4 g protein; 4 g fat; 19 g carbohydrate; 53 mg sodium

ROOT BEER FROTH
See Menu Plan for Week 36 and various other weeks.
Makes 1 serving

1 cup diet root beer
½ cup skim milk
3 ice cubes

Combine root beer and milk in blender container; process until frothy. Add ice cubes, 1 at a time, and process until slightly thickened.

Per serving: 43 calories; 4 g protein; 0.2 g fat;
6 g carbohydrate; 128 mg sodium

LEMONADE
See Menu Plan for Week 48 and various other weeks.
Makes 2 servings

½ cup fresh lemon juice
Artificial sweetener to equal 6 teaspoons
    sugar
2 cups water
2 to 3 ice cubes

Combine lemon juice and sweetener in blender container; pour in water. Process, adding ice cubes 1 at a time.

Per serving: 20 calories; 0.3 g protein; 0.1 g fat;
6 g carbohydrate; 1 mg sodium

LIME COOLER
See Menu Plan for Week 46 and various other weeks.
Makes 1 serving

2 tablespoons fresh lime juice
Artificial sweetener to equal 4 teaspoons
    sugar
5 ice cubes
1 cup sparkling mineral water
Lime slice to garnish

Combine juice and sweetener in large goblet or tall glass; stir. Add ice and mineral water. Garnish with lime slice.

Per serving: 15 calories; 0 g protein; 0 g fat;
5 g carbohydrate; 32 mg sodium

Appendix

Weight Watchers Metric Conversion Table

WEIGHT

To Change	To	Multiply by
Ounces	Grams	30.0
Pounds	Kilograms	.48

VOLUME

To Change	To	Multiply by
Teaspoons	Milliliters	5.0
Tablespoons	Milliliters	15.0
Cups	Milliliters	250.0
Cups	Liters	.25
Pints	Liters	.5
Quarts	Liters	1.0
Gallons	Liters	4.0

LENGTH

To Change	To	Multiply by
Inches	Millimeters	25.0
Inches	Centimeters	2.5
Feet	Centimeters	30.0
Yards	Meters	.9

TEMPERATURE

To change degrees Fahrenheit to degrees Celsius subtract 32° and multiply by $\frac{5}{9}$.

Oven Temperatures

Degrees Fahrenheit =	Degrees Celsius	Degrees Fahrenheit =	Degrees Celsius
250	120	400	200
275	140	425	220
300	150	450	230
325	160	475	250
350	180	500	260
375	190	525	270

METRIC SYMBOLS

Symbol =	Metric Unit	Symbol =	Metric Unit
g	gram	°C	degrees Celsius
kg	kilogram	mm	millimeter
ml	milliliter	cm	centimeter
l	liter	m	meter

Midday Meal "Brown-Bag" Substitutions

GENERAL SUBSTITUTIONS

The following general suggestions apply to various menus throughout the book. Specific menu substitutions follow for meals that are not covered by these suggestions.

- *Juice* may be switched to the Evening Meal or used as a planned snack.
- *Soups* can be prepared in advance and carried in an insulated vacuum container.
- *Beef, Chicken,* and *Vegetable Broth* can be carried in an insulated vacuum container, consumed at the Evening Meal, used as a planned snack, or omitted from the menu.
- When *French* or *Mushroom Omelet* is indicated, substitute 2 hard-cooked eggs and add 1 teaspoon margarine (or 2 teaspoons reduced-calorie margarine) to daily bread serving, or 1 teaspoon vegetable oil or mayonnaise (or 2 teaspoons reduced-calorie mayonnaise) to salad at the Midday or Evening Meal.
- When *Open-Face Grilled Cheese Sandwich I* is indicated, substitute 1 ounce hard cheese and tomato slices on 1 slice bread; for *Open-Face Grilled Cheese Sandwich II* substitute 2 ounces hard cheese and tomato slices on 1 slice bread. Mustard may be used if desired.
- When *Reuben Sandwich* is indicated, substitute 2 ounces sliced cooked turkey or chicken and 1 ounce Swiss cheese on 1 slice rye bread. Mustard may be used if desired.
- When *Cheese Pizza Pocket* is indicated, substitute ⅔ cup cottage or part-skim ricotta cheese mixed with diced tomato and ½ teaspoon caraway seeds, and a 1-ounce pita bread.
- *Broiled, Steamed, Baked, Poached,* or *Roasted Poultry, Meat,* or *Fish* can be prepared in advance and taken chilled, or drained canned fish or chicken may be substituted.
- *Cooked Vegetables* can be prepared in advance and taken chilled, or raw vegetables may be substituted (e.g., cauliflower, broccoli, green beans, zucchini, green and red bell peppers, etc.).
- *Chilled Salads* and *Vegetables* can be transported in plastic containers. If salads contain perishable ingredients and/or unflavored gelatin, they should be packed in insulated vacuum containers.
- *Salad Dressing* should be packed in a separate container and added to salad at mealtime.
- *Margarine* and *Mayonnaise* at Midday Meal may be switched to another meal.
- *Fruit* may be switched to the Evening Meal, switched with the Evening Meal fruit, or used as a planned snack.
- *Flavored Gelatin* can be carried in a plastic container, consumed at the Evening Meal, used as a planned snack, or omitted from the menu.
- *Milk, Yogurt,* and *Milk Pudding* may be consumed at another meal, or as a planned snack.

• *Wine* and *Beer* may be consumed at the Evening Meal, used as a planned snack, or omitted from the menu.

SPECIFIC SUBSTITUTIONS

Week 1
Day 1—Switch Midday and Evening Meals, using Reuben Sandwich substitution noted above.
Day 2—Switch Midday and Evening Meals.
Day 4—Switch Midday and Evening Meal desserts.
Day 7—Substitute 3–4 ounces sliced cooked chicken or turkey for Sesame Chicken with Green Beans. Add 1 teaspoon vegetable oil to salad. Switch baked potato to Evening Meal.

Week 3
Day 3—Switch Midday and Evening Meal entrées.
Day 7—Omit butternut squash and add ¼ cup sliced water chestnuts to salad.

Week 4
Day 3—Substitute tomato slices for steamed spinach.
Day 4—Switch Liver Venetian, cauliflower, and romaine lettuce salad to Evening Meal, and Evening Meal entrée to Midday Meal.
Day 6—Switch Midday and Evening Meals.

Week 5
Day 2—Substitute 2 ounces sliced Cheddar cheese on 1 slice rye bread with 1 teaspoon margarine for Chili-Cheese Rarebit.
Day 7—Substitute 1 hard-cooked egg for scrambled egg.

Week 6
Day 1—Switch Midday and Evening Meal entrées.
Day 3—Substitute 3–4 ounces chilled cooked or drained canned fish for Scrod-Vegetable Bake.
Day 6—Substitute 3–4 ounces sliced cooked

chicken or turkey for Skewered Marinated Chicken. Add ¼ cup sliced onion and ¼ cup sliced water chestnuts to salad.

Week 7
Day 1—Switch Creamed Kale and Onions to Evening Meal and green beans to Midday Meal.
Day 5—Substitute 3 ounces (men: 4 ounces) boiled ham, bologna, or liverwurst for lamb chop.
Day 6—Omit Colache. Add 1 slice bread to Midday Meal and tomato slices, green bell pepper sticks, ¼ cup sliced onion, and ¾ teaspoon mayonnaise to salad.

Week 8
Day 1—Switch Fennel Parmesan to Evening Meal. Add tomato and cucumber slices to salad.
Day 7—Switch Midday and Evening Meals.

Week 9
Day 2—Switch Midday and Evening Meal desserts.
Day 4—Switch Midday and Evening Meals.
Day 6—Switch Midday and Evening Meals.
Day 7—Switch Midday and Evening Meal desserts.

Week 10
Day 4—Switch Midday and Evening Meal entrées.
Day 5—Switch Midday and Evening Meal entrées.
Day 6—Switch Midday and Evening Meals.
Day 7—Substitute tossed salad with tomato and cucumber slices for cooked okra with tomato sauce.

Week 11
Day 4—Substitute 2 hard-cooked eggs for scrambled eggs. Use 1 teaspoon margarine on squash at Evening Meal.

Week 12
Day 1—Substitute 2 hard-cooked eggs for

Egg Foo Yung. Add ½ cup cooked brown rice to Evening Meal. If desired, whole wheat roll may be switched to Midday Meal.

Day 2—Substitute ⅔ cup cottage or part-skim ricotta cheese and 1 ounce pita bread for "Calzone." Add 1 teaspoon vegetable oil to salad.

Day 3—Switch vegetables and dessert to Evening Meal and green bell pepper slices and pineapple chunks to Midday Meal.

Day 6—Switch Midday and Evening Meals, substituting 3–4 ounces sliced cooked chicken or turkey for veal chop.

Week 13

Day 1—Substitute ⅓ cup cottage or part-skim ricotta cheese, 1 hard-cooked egg, and 2 slices rye bread for Stuffed French Toast. If desired, 2 teaspoons reduced-calorie spread may be used. Add 1 tablespoon raisins to cereal at Morning Meal and ½ teaspoon margarine to Evening Meal.

Day 4—Switch Midday and Evening Meal entrées.

Day 5—Substitute 3–4 ounces chilled cooked or drained canned fish for Curried Scrod.

Day 6—Switch Midday and Evening Meal entrées, substituting 3–4 ounces sliced cooked chicken or turkey for baked veal cutlet.

Day 7—Omit Mexican Soup. Add 3 ounces drained canned chick peas and 1 ounce diced Cheddar cheese to salad. Add 4 melba toast slices to Midday Meal and 1½ teaspoons reduced-calorie margarine to Evening Meal.

Week 14

Day 3—Switch Midday and Evening Meal entrées.

Day 7—Substitute 3–4 ounces drained canned tuna or salmon mixed with 1 teaspoon mayonnaise (or 2 tea-spoons reduced-calorie mayonnaise) and 2 tablespoons chopped onion for Baked Striped Bass with Vegetables.

Week 16

Day 2—Switch Midday and Evening Meal entrées.

Day 7—Substitute ⅔ cup cottage or part-skim ricotta cheese mixed with ¾ teaspoon caraway seeds for Vegetable Lasagna.

Week 17

Day 1—Substitute 3–4 ounces drained canned tuna or salmon mixed with 1 teaspoon mayonnaise (or 2 tea-spoons reduced-calorie mayonnaise) for Pineapple Flounder. Add 2 medium dried apricot halves to Snacks, at Planned Times.

Day 5—Substitute 3–4 ounces drained canned tuna or salmon mixed with 1 teaspoon mayonnaise (or 2 tea-spoons reduced-calorie mayonnaise) and 2 tablespoons chopped onion for Poached Codfish with Asparagus and Tomatoes.

Day 6—Omit Red Chicken with Potatoes at Evening Meal. Switch broiled chicken livers to Evening Meal; serve with a 4-ounce baked potato or ½ cup cooked enriched rice, and 1 teaspoon margarine. Take 3–4 ounces sliced cooked chicken or turkey at Midday Meal.

Week 18

Day 5—Substitute 2 hard-cooked eggs for Egg Foo Yung. If desired, add 1–2 teaspoons imitation bacon bits to spinach salad. Add ½ cup cooked brown rice to Evening Meal. If desired, omit rye bread at Evening Meal and add 1 slice pumpernickel bread to Midday Meal.

Day 6—Substitute 3–4 ounces drained canned tuna or salmon mixed with 1 teaspoon mayonnaise (or 2 tea-spoons reduced-calorie mayonnaise) and 2 tablespoons chopped onion for Trinidad Snapper.

Week 19
Day 4—Substitute 3 ounces (men: 4 ounces) bologna, liverwurst, or boiled ham for knockwurst.
Day 5—Switch Midday and Evening Meals.
Day 6—Switch Midday and Evening Meals except desserts.
Day 7—Switch Midday and Evening Meal entrées.

Week 20
Day 3—Omit Shrimp on Toast. Add 2 ounces boiled shrimp to salad. Add 1 slice rye bread to Midday Meal, 1 teaspoon margarine to Evening Meal, and ½ cup skim milk to day's menu.
Day 4—Switch Midday and Evening Meal entrées.
Day 6—Omit Swordfish Kebabs. Switch Glazed Turkey Mold to Evening Meal. Take 3–4 ounces chilled cooked or drained canned fish at Midday Meal. Bread may be switched to Midday Meal if desired.
Day 7—If desired, Midday Meal may be switched with Evening Meal.

Week 21
Day 1—Substitute 2 hard-cooked eggs for Egg Foo Yung. Add ½ cup cooked brown rice to Evening Meal.
Day 2—Switch Midday and Evening Meal entrées.
Day 4—Substitute 3–4 ounces chilled cooked or drained canned fish for Layered Baked Flounder and ¼ cup sliced onion for Brussels sprouts. Add 1 slice bread to Midday Meal and 1¼ cups skim milk to day's menu.

Week 22
Day 2—Switch Midday and Evening Meal entrées.
Day 6—Switch Midday and Evening Meals

except beverages. Substitute ½ cup water chestnuts for acorn squash.

Week 23
Day 1—Switch Midday and Evening Meals except wine.
Day 2—Switch Midday and Evening Meals.
Day 4—Omit leg of lamb at Evening Meal. Switch liver to Evening Meal. Take 3 ounces (men: 4 ounces) bologna, liverwurst, or boiled ham at Midday Meal and omit spinach and mushrooms. Substitute 1 teaspoon reduced-calorie mayonnaise for margarine.
Day 7—Substitute 3–4 ounces drained canned tuna or salmon mixed with 1½ teaspoons mayonnaise (or 1 tablespoon reduced-calorie mayonnaise) and 1 slice bread for Sautéed Chick Peas Italian Style and ½ cup brown rice.

Week 24
Day 1—Substitute 2 ounces hard cheese for Layered Eggplant-Cheese Bake.
Day 3—If desired, Tofu-Sesame Appetizer may be switched to Evening Meal.
Day 4—Omit Chicken Indienne. Switch liver to Evening Meal. Add ¼ cup steamed sliced onion and a 4-ounce baked potato with ½ teaspoon margarine (or 1 teaspoon reduced-calorie margarine) to Evening Meal. Take 3–4 ounces sliced cooked chicken or turkey at Midday Meal. Substitute lettuce and sliced tomato for onions and mushrooms and 1 teaspoon mayonnaise for margarine. If desired, omit roll from Evening Meal and add 1 slice enriched bread to Midday Meal. Add ½ cup cooked rhubarb to Snacks, at Planned Times.

Week 25
Day 1—Switch margarine to Morning Meal.
Day 2—Substitute 1½ ounces (men: 2 ounces) bologna, liverwurst, or

boiled ham and 1 hard-cooked egg for Canadian bacon and scrambled egg. Switch Baked Broccoli with Mustard Sauce and 1 teaspoon margarine (or 2 teaspoons reduced-calorie margarine) to Evening Meal.

Day 3—Substitute ⅔ cup cottage or part-skim ricotta cheese mixed with diced tomato and a 1-ounce pita bread for Tomato–Cheese-Stuffed Pitas.

Day 5—If desired, Banana and Raisin Pudding Cake may be switched to Evening Meal.

Week 26
Day 4—Switch Midday and Evening Meal entrées.

Week 27
Day 2—Substitute 3–4 ounces sliced cooked turkey or chicken for Turkey Kiev. Omit melba toast at Evening Meal and add 1 slice bread and 2 teaspoons mayonnaise to Midday Meal. Add ½ cup cooked brown rice and 1 teaspoon margarine to Evening Meal. If desired, ½ teaspoon imitation bacon bits may be added to salad at Midday or Evening Meal.

Day 3—Substitute 3–4 ounces chopped boiled shrimp mixed with 1 teaspoon mayonnaise (or 2 teaspoons reduced-calorie mayonnaise) for Shrimp Scampi. Add 3 melba toast rounds to Midday Meal.

Day 4—Switch Midday and Evening Meal entrées.

Day 5—Switch Midday and Evening Meals.

Day 6—Switch Midday and Evening Meals.

Week 28
Day 1—Omit Lemon "Butter" Sauce at Midday Meal. Add 1 teaspoon margarine to Morning or Evening Meal.

Day 5—Substitute 3–4 ounces sliced cooked chicken or turkey or drained canned fish for veal chop. Switch Ginger-Spiced Bean Sprouts and Onions to Evening Meal.

Day 6—Substitute 2 ounces Cheddar cheese for Potato-Cheddar Broil. Add a 4-ounce baked potato to Evening Meal.

Week 30
Day 1—Switch Midday and Evening Meal entrées.

Day 2—Substitute 3–4 ounces sliced cooked chicken or turkey or drained canned fish and tomato and cucumber slices for Polynesian Chicken. Omit reduced-calorie margarine and add 1½ teaspoons mayonnaise to Midday Meal. Add ½ cup steamed onion slices to Evening Meal. Add ¼ small pineapple to day's menu.

Day 4—Substitute 2 ounces hard cheese for Cheese-Stuffed Zucchini. Add 1 teaspoon margarine to Midday Meal. If desired, 1 teaspoon imitation bacon bits may be added to tossed salad.

Week 31
Day 4—Switch Midday and Evening Meals, substituting 3–4 ounces sliced cooked chicken or turkey for veal chop.

Week 32
Day 5—Omit Two-Cheese Herbed Pasta. Add 1½–2 ounces diced cooked chicken and 1 teaspoon vegetable oil to tossed salad. Add a 4-ounce baked potato to Evening Meal. If desired, melba toast may be switched to Midday Meal.

Week 33
Day 3—Substitute 1 hard-cooked egg, 1½ ounces (men: 2 ounces) boiled ham and 2 slices bread for Egg and Prosciutto Melt. Add ½ teaspoon vegetable oil to green salad.

Day 4—Switch Midday and Evening Meals.

Day 7—Substitute 2 hard-cooked eggs for Mediterranean Eggs in Nest. Add ¼ cup sliced water chestnuts to tossed salad. If desired, 2 olives and 1 teaspoon grated Parmesan cheese may be added to tossed salad. Add a 4-ounce baked potato and 1 teaspoon margarine to Evening Meal.

Week 34
Day 2—Substitute 3–4 ounces chilled cooked or drained canned fish for Baked Red Snapper. Add 1 teaspoon vegetable oil to green salad at Evening Meal.

Day 4—Switch Midday and Evening Meals.

Day 7—Keep Peanut Butter Fudge chilled or switch to Evening Meal.

Week 35
Day 1—Switch Midday and Evening Meal entrées.

Day 2—Substitute 3–4 ounces chilled cooked or drained canned fish for Pan-Broiled Snappers. Add 3 melba toast rounds to Midday Meal. Switch baked potato to Evening Meal.

Day 3—Substitute 2 hard-cooked eggs for scrambled eggs. Add 1 teaspoon margarine to Evening Meal.

Day 4—Switch Midday and Evening Meal entrées, substituting 3–4 ounces cooked sliced chicken or turkey for roast veal. Switch onion to Evening Meal.

Day 5—Switch Stir-Fried Cabbage 'n' Squash to Evening Meal and escarole salad to Midday Meal.

Day 6—Omit Chili-Cheese Rarebit. Switch Creamed Shrimp Pasta to Evening Meal. Take 2 ounces hard cheese with 1 teaspoon margarine on 1 slice bread at Midday Meal. If desired, 1 olive may be added to Midday Meal.

Week 37
Day 1—Omit Papaya Shrimp. Switch Crêpes Divan to Evening Meal. Take 3–4 ounces boiled shrimp or drained canned fish at Midday Meal. Add ¼ small cantaloupe to Midday Meal.

Day 2—Omit Turkey-Cheese Strata. Switch Liver Venetian to Evening Meal. Take 2 ounces sliced cooked chicken or turkey and 1 ounce hard cheese at Midday Meal. Add 1 cup Plain Popcorn to Snacks, at Planned Times.

Day 5—Substitute 3 ounces (men: 4 ounces) bologna, liverwurst, or boiled ham for Curried Meat Hash. Add 1 teaspoon reduced-calorie margarine to Evening Meal and increase pineapple at Midday Meal to ½ cup. If desired, ¼ cup onion slices may be added to Midday Meal.

Day 6—Substitute 3–4 ounces cooked sliced chicken or turkey, or drained canned fish for veal cutlet. Switch Kasha Mix to Evening Meal.

Week 38
Day 4—Switch Midday and Evening Meal entrées.

Day 7—Substitute 3–4 ounces chilled cooked or drained canned fish for Baked Codfish with Lemon. Add 1 teaspoon vegetable oil to salad at Evening Meal.

Week 39
Day 2—Switch Midday and Evening Meal entrées.

Week 40
Day 1—Switch Midday and Evening Meal entrées.

Day 5—Substitute 3–4 ounces chilled cooked or drained canned fish for Mustard-Broiled Flounder.

Day 7—Switch Midday and Evening Meal entrées, substituting 3–4 ounces sliced cooked chicken or turkey for veal chop.

Week 41
Day 2—Substitute ⅔ cup cottage or part-skim ricotta cheese mixed with diced tomato and a 1-ounce pita bread for Tomato–Cheese-Stuffed Pitas.

Day 4—Switch Midday and Evening Meal

entrées, substituting 3–4 ounces sliced cooked chicken or turkey for veal chop. Switch sliced onion to Evening Meal.

Day 6—Switch Midday and Evening Meals.

Week 42
Day 1—Switch Honey-Glazed Yams to Evening Meal. If desired, crispbread may be switched to Midday Meal.

Day 6—Substitute 3–4 ounces sliced cooked chicken or turkey for veal chop.

Week 43
Day 1—Omit Salmon-Zucchini Kebabs. Switch Chicken and Legumes Casserole to Evening Meal. Take 3–4 ounces chilled cooked or drained canned fish at Midday Meal. If desired, 2 olives may be added to Midday Meal.

Day 4—Switch Midday and Evening Meals.

Day 6—Substitute ⅓ cup cottage or part-skim ricotta cheese, 1 hard-cooked egg, and 2 slices rye bread for Stuffed French Toast. If desired, 2 teaspoons reduced-calorie spread may be used. Add 1 tablespoon raisins to cereal at Morning Meal and 1 teaspoon reduced-calorie margarine to Evening Meal.

Day 7—Omit broiled steak at Evening Meal. Switch Flounder Italiano to Evening Meal. Take 3 ounces (men: 4 ounces) bologna, liverwurst, or boiled ham at Midday Meal.

Week 44
Day 3—Switch Midday and Evening Meals.

Day 4—Switch Midday and Evening Meals except Evening Meal appetizer.

Day 5—Switch Midday and Evening Meals.

Week 45
Day 3—Substitute 3–4 ounces sliced cooked chicken or turkey for Sesame Chicken with Green Beans. Add 1 teaspoon vegetable oil to salad. If desired, 2 olives may be added to Midday or Evening Meal.

Day 4—Switch Midday and Evening Meals substituting 3–4 ounces sliced cooked chicken or turkey for Veal Patties and Mushrooms. If desired, add ¼ cup onion to Evening Meal and 1 teaspoon shredded coconut to cherry-flavored gelatin.

Day 6—Switch Midday and Evening Meals. Omit acorn squash.

Week 46
Day 7—Substitute 1 hard-cooked egg and 1 ounce Swiss cheese for Cheese Omelet I. Add 1 teaspoon margarine to Midday or Evening Meal.

Week 48
Day 3—Substitute 1 hard-cooked egg and 1 slice bread for Potato-Spinach Combo. Add 1 teaspoon mayonnaise to Midday Meal.

Day 4—Switch Midday and Evening Meals, substituting 3–4 ounces sliced cooked chicken or turkey for veal chop.

Day 5—Omit Lemon "Butter" Sauce. Add 1 teaspoon margarine or mayonnaise to Morning, Midday, or Evening Meal. If desired, 2 teaspoons ketchup or 1 teaspoon imitation bacon bits may be added to Evening Meal.

Week 49
Day 2—Switch Midday and Evening Meal desserts.

Day 4—Switch Midday and Evening Meals.

Day 6—Substitute 3–4 ounces sliced cooked chicken or turkey and 1 slice bread for Stir-Cooked Turkey. Switch baked potato to Evening Meal.

Day 7—Substitute 1½ ounces bologna, 1 ounce Swiss cheese, 1 slice bread, and ½ teaspoon mayonnaise (or 1 teaspoon reduced-calorie mayonnaise) for Broiled Bologna-Cheese Muffin.

Week 50
Day 1—Switch Midday and Evening Meals, substituting 3–4 ounces drained

canned tuna or salmon mixed with 1½ teaspoons reduced-calorie mayonnaise and 2 tablespoons chopped onion for Flounder in Orange Sauce. Add ¾ cup strawberries to Snacks, at Planned Times.

Day 2—Switch Midday and Evening Meals except desserts.

Day 3—Switch Broiled Onion-Topped Tomatoes to Evening Meal.

Day 4—Substitute 1 hard-cooked egg and 1 ounce Swiss cheese for Cheese Soufflé. If desired, whole wheat bread or enriched roll may be switched to Midday Meal. Add 1½ teaspoons margarine or mayonnaise to Morning, Midday, or Evening Meal. Add ½ cup skim milk to day's menu. If desired, 1 teaspoon each grated Parmesan cheese and imitation bacon bits may be added to salad.

Week 51

Day 4—Switch Midday and Evening Meals, substituting 3–4 ounces sliced cooked chicken or turkey for Sautéed Curried Veal and Eggplant. Add 2 teaspoons reduced-calorie margarine or mayonnaise to Midday or Evening Meal. If desired, spaghetti squash may be omitted.

Week 52

Day 3—Switch Midday and Evening Meal entrées.

Day 4—Switch Sautéed Salsify to Evening Meal.

Day 5—Switch Midday and Evening Meals.

Day 6—Substitute ⅓ cup part-skim ricotta cheese and 1 slice bread for Cauliflower-Cheese Crisp. Omit melba toast from Evening Meal.

Day 7—Switch Midday and Evening Meal entrées, substituting 3–4 ounces sliced cooked chicken or turkey for roast veal.

Food Plan Information per Serving

Some of the information below indicates Protein additions for Men's portions; if additions are made as indicated, do not make the Protein additions for Men that are specified on the Menu Plan.

STARTERS

Artichoke and Eggplant Appetizer—
page 121
2 tablespoons plus 2 teaspoons Limited Vegetables; 1¼ servings Vegetables

Artichoke Hearts Español—page 121
¼ cup Limited Vegetables; ½ serving Extras (olives)

Asparagus Soup—page 128
1¼ servings Vegetables; 1½ servings Fats; 1½ servings Extras (flour)

Beef Broth—page 127
¾ cup broth = 1 serving Extras

Blueberry Soup—page 125
1 serving Fruits; 1 serving Extras (cornstarch and honey)

Broccoli-Shoot Appetizer—page 121
4 servings Vegetables; ½ serving Fats

Cauliflower and Zucchini Soup—page 129
4½ servings Vegetables

Chicken Broth—page 127
¾ cup broth = 1 serving Extras

Chilled Cucumber Soup—page 126
1 teaspoon Limited Vegetables; 3 servings Vegetables; 1 serving Milk

Chilled Tomato Appetizer—page 121
1 serving Vegetables; 1 serving Bonus (tomato juice)

Creamed Turnip and Cauliflower Soup—
page 131
1 serving Vegetables; ½ serving Fats; ⅛ serving Milk; 1½ servings Extras (broth and flour)

Cream of Asparagus and Leek Soup—
page 130
⅓ cup Limited Vegetables; ⅙ serving Vegetables; 1 serving Fats; ¼ serving Milk; 1 serving Extras (broth and flour)

Cream of Broccoli Soup—page 130
1 tablespoon plus 1 teaspoon Limited Vegetables; 1 serving Vegetables; 1 serving Fats; ⅓ serving Milk; 1½ servings Extras (broth and flour)

Cream of Cauliflower Soup—page 131
2 servings Vegetables; ⅛ serving Milk; ¾ serving Extras (arrowroot and broth mix)

Danish Apple Soup—page 126
1 serving Fruits; 1¾ servings Extras (cornstarch, sugar, and wine)

Fresh Mushroom Soup—page 129
3 tablespoons Limited Vegetables; 2 servings Vegetables; 2½ servings Extras (broth mix and flour)

Fruited Yogurt Soup—page 126
1 serving Fruits; 1 serving Milk; 1 serving Extras (honey)

Gazpacho—page 126
1 tablespoon Limited Vegetables; ¾ serving Vegetables; 1½ servings Fats; ½ serving Bonus (tomato juice)

Green Bean and Red Cabbage Appetizer—
page 122
2½ servings Vegetables; 1 serving Fats
Herbed Beef Broth—page 127
1 serving Extras (broth)
Hot Mushroom Turnovers—page 122
½ serving Bread (flour); ⅓ serving
Vegetables; 1 serving Fats; 1½ teaspoons
Yogurt (serving Milk)
Marinated Broccoli Appetizer—page 122
1½ teaspoons Limited Vegetables;
1¼ servings Vegetables; 1 serving Fats;
¼ serving Fruits
Marinated Mushroom Appetizer—page 123
1½ teaspoons Limited Vegetables;
2¼ servings Vegetables; 1 serving Fats
Onion Soup—page 129
¼ cup plus 2 tablespoons Limited
Vegetables; 1 serving Fats; 1 serving Extras
(broth)
Variation—Onion Soup Gratinée—
Midday or Evening Meal
Add 1 serving Protein (2 ounces Hard
Cheese) and 1 serving Bread to Onion
Soup equivalents
Radish Pinwheels—page 123
⅜ serving Bread; ¼ serving Vegetables;
½ serving Fats
Rutabaga Appetizer—page 123
¼ cup Limited Vegetables; 1   servings
Vegetables; 1 serving Fats; 1 serving
Extras (sugar)
Spiced Tomato Appetizer—page 124
1½ teaspoons Limited Vegetables;
2 servings Vegetables; 1 serving Fats;
1 serving Extras (sugar)
Steak Tartare—page 124—½ Midday or
Evening Meal
½ serving Protein (2 ounces Meat
Group); 1 serving Bread; 1 teaspoon
Limited Vegetables
Stuffed Mushroom Appetizer—page 124
⅛ cup Limited Vegetables; 2½ servings
Vegetables; 1 serving Extras (broth and
Parmesan cheese)
Tofu-Sesame Appetizer—page 125—
¼ Midday or Evening Meal
(Men—⅕ meal)
¼ (or ⅕) serving Protein (2 ounces

Tofu); 2½ servings Extras (cornstarch,
honey, sesame seed, and wine)
Tomato Soup—page 130
¼ cup Limited Vegetables; 5 servings
Vegetables; 1 serving Extras (honey)
Turkey Broth—page 128
¾ cup broth = 1 serving Extras
Vegetable Broth—page 128
¾ cup broth = 1 serving Extras
Vegetable Chowder—page 131
¼ cup Limited Vegetables; 3¼ servings
Vegetables; 1 serving Fats; ¼ serving
Milk; ½ serving Bonus (tomato sauce);
⅔ serving Extras (broth)
Vegetable Soup—page 130
⅛ cup Limited Vegetables; 1¼ servings
Vegetables; 1 serving Fats; 2 servings
Extras (broth mix and flour)
Yogurt-Mushroom Appetizer—page 125
¼ cup Limited Vegetables; 4½ servings
Vegetables; 1½ servings Fats; ¼ serving
Milk

EGGS AND CHEESE

Baked Corn and Tomato Omelet—
page 135—1 Morning or ½ Midday or
Evening Meal
1 or ½ serving Protein (1 Egg); ½ serving
Bread Substitutes (corn); ¾ serving
Vegetables; ½ serving Bonus (tomato
sauce)
Bean Sprouts with Muenster Julienne—
page 151—Midday or Evening Meal
1 serving Protein (2 ounces Hard Cheese);
2½ servings Vegetables
Broccoli "Meatballs"—page 152—¼ Midday
or Evening Meal
¼ serving Protein (½ Egg); 1 serving
Bread (bread crumbs and cornflakes);
½ serving Vegetables; 1 serving Extras
(Parmesan cheese)
Broccoli Quiche—page 145—¾ Midday or
Evening Meal
¾ serving Protein (½ Egg and 1 ounce
Hard Cheese); ½ serving Bread (flour);
1½ teaspoons Limited Vegetables;
¼ serving Vegetables; 1 serving Fats;
serving Milk (1½ teaspoons yogurt

and ⅛ cup evaporated skimmed milk);
½ serving Extras (bacon bits)
"Calzone"—page 149—Midday or Evening
Meal
1 serving Protein (⅓ cup Soft Cheese
and 1 ounce Hard Cheese); 1 serving
Bread; 2 servings Vegetables; 1 serving
Fats
Caraway-Cheese Toast—page 142—
1 Morning or ½ Midday or Evening Meal
1 or ½ serving Protein (1 ounce Hard
Cheese); 1 serving Bread; ½ serving
Extras (caraway seed)
Carob Soufflé—page 137—½ Midday or
Evening Meal
½ serving Protein (1 Egg); 1 serving
Bread; 1 serving Fats; 3 servings Extras
(carob powder and sugar)
Cauliflower-Cheese Crisp—page 152—
½ Midday or Evening Meal
½ serving Protein (1 ounce Hard Cheese);
¼ serving Bread (bread crumbs);
1 serving Vegetables
Celery-Ricotta Bake—page 145—½ Midday
or Evening Meal
½ serving Protein (⅓ cup Soft Cheese);
1½ servings Vegetables; ½ serving Extras
(broth)
Cheese and Rice-Stuffed Mushrooms—
page 152—Midday or Evening Meal
1 serving Protein (2 ounces Hard Cheese);
1 serving Bread Substitutes (rice);
5⅔ servings Vegetables
Cheese Omelet I—page 135—Midday or
Evening Meal
1 serving Protein (1 Egg and 1 ounce Hard
Cheese); 1 serving Fats
Variation—Cheese Omelet II—
omit 1 serving Fats from equivalent listing
Cheese Pizza Pocket—page 149—Midday or
Evening Meal
1 serving Protein (⅔ cup Soft Cheese);
1 serving Bread; ½ serving Vegetables;
1 serving Extras (Parmesan cheese)
Cheese-Salad Sandwich—page 150—Midday
or Evening Meal
1 serving Protein (2 ounces Hard Cheese);
1 serving Bread; 1½ teaspoons Limited

Vegetables; ¾ serving Vegetables;
1½ servings Fats
Cheese Soufflé—page 138—Midday or
Evening Meal
1 serving Protein (1 Egg and 1 ounce Hard
Cheese); 1½ teaspoons Limited
Vegetables; 1½ servings Fats; ½ serving
Milk; 3 servings Extras (flour)
Cheese-Stuffed Zucchini—page 146—
Midday or Evening Meal
1 serving Protein (2 ounces Hard Cheese);
3 servings Vegetables; 1 serving Fats;
1 serving Extras (Parmesan cheese)
Chili-Cheese Rarebit—page 148—Midday or
Evening Meal
1 serving Protein (2 ounces Hard Cheese);
1 serving Bread; 1½ teaspoons Limited
Vegetables; 1⅛ servings Vegetables;
1 serving Fats; ½ serving Extras
(cornstarch)
Cinnamon-Cheese Toast—page 142—
1 Morning or ½ Midday or Evening Meal
1 or ½ serving Protein (⅓ cup Soft
Cheese); 1 serving Bread; 1 serving Extras
(coconut)
Coffee Cheese Delight—page 142—
1 Morning or ½ Midday or Evening Meal
1 or ½ serving Protein (⅓ cup Soft
Cheese); 1 serving Bread; 1 serving Fruits
Cornmeal-Swiss Bake—page 146—
½ Midday or Evening Meal
½ serving Protein (1 ounce Hard Cheese);
1 serving Bread Substitutes (cornmeal);
2 servings Vegetables
Creamed Egg 'n' Muffin—page 148—
1 Morning or ½ Midday or Evening Meal
1 or ½ serving Protein (1 Egg);
2 servings Bread; 1 serving Fats; ½ serving
Milk; ¾ serving Extras (flour)
Crêpes à l'Orange—page 153—½ Midday or
Evening Meal
½ serving Protein (1 Egg); 1 serving
Bread (flour); 1 serving Fruits; ¼ serving
Milk; 1 serving Extras (flour);
16 calories Specialty Foods (marmalade)
Crêpes Divan—page 154—Midday or
Evening Meal
1 serving Protein (1 Egg and 2 ounces
Poultry); 1 serving Bread (flour);

1 serving Vegetables; 1 serving Fats; ¼ serving Milk; 1½ servings Extras (bouillon and flour)

Egg and Green Goddess Platter (includes equivalents for Green Goddess Dressing)—page 140—Midday or Evening Meal
1 serving Protein (2 Eggs); 3 servings Vegetables; 1 serving Milk

Egg and Prosciutto Melt—page 149— Midday or Evening Meal (Men—add ¼ ounce prosciutto)
1 serving Protein (1 Egg, ½ ounce Hard Cheese, and ¾ ounce Meat Group-cured—Men, 1 ounce Meat Group-cured); 2 servings Bread; 1 serving Vegetables

Egg Foo Yung—page 136—Midday or Evening Meal
1 serving Protein (2 Eggs); 1 serving Bread Substitutes (rice); ¼ cup Limited Vegetables; 2 servings Vegetables; 2½ servings Extras (broth, cornstarch, and sesame seed)

Egg Salad—page 140—Midday or Evening Meal
1 serving Protein (2 Eggs); ½ serving Vegetables; 2 servings Fats

Feta Cheese Salad—page 140—Midday or Evening Meal
1 serving Protein (2 ounces Hard Cheese); 7½ servings Vegetables; 1 serving Extras (olives)

French Omelet—page 136—Midday or Evening Meal
1 serving Protein (2 Eggs); 1 serving Fats

Fruited Cheese Delight—page 154—Midday or Evening Meal
1 serving Protein (⅔ cup Soft Cheese); ¼ serving Vegetables; 1 serving Fruits; 1¼ servings Extras (gelatin and honey)

Greek Salad—page 140—Midday or Evening Meal
1 serving Protein (2 ounces Hard Cheese); ¼ cup Limited Vegetables; 5½ servings Vegetables; 1 serving Fats; 1 serving Extras (olives)

Grilled Cheese Soufflé—page 138—Midday or Evening Meal
1 serving Protein (1 Egg and 1 ounce Hard Cheese); 1 serving Bread; ½ serving Vegetables; 1 serving Fats; ½ serving Extras (Parmesan cheese)

Grilled Tortillas—page 142—1 Morning or ½ Midday or Evening Meal
1 or ½ serving Protein (1 ounce Hard Cheese); 1 serving Bread (tortilla); 1½ to 3 teaspoons Vegetables; 1 serving Extras (bacon bits)

Gypsy Cheese Salad—page 141—Midday or Evening Meal
1 serving Protein (⅔ cup Soft Cheese); 3 servings Vegetables; ¼ serving Fruits

Hominy Grits Soufflé—page 138—Midday or Evening Meal
1 serving Protein (1 Egg and 1 ounce Hard Cheese); 1 serving Bread Substitutes (hominy grits); ⅛ cup Limited Vegetables; serving Vegetables; 1 serving Fats

Honey-Coconut Toast—page 142— 1 Morning or ½ Midday or Evening Meal
1 or ½ serving Protein (1 Egg); 1 serving Bread; 1 serving Fats; 1 tablespoon Buttermilk (serving Milk); 2 servings Extras (coconut and honey)

Layered Eggplant-Cheese Bake—page 146— Midday or Evening Meal
1 serving Protein (2 ounces Hard Cheese); 1¾ servings Vegetables

Macaroni-Cheese Mold—page 150—Midday or Evening Meal
1 serving Protein (2 ounces Hard Cheese); 1 serving Bread Substitutes (macaroni); ½ serving Vegetables; 1 serving Fats; ¼ serving Milk

Matzo Brei—page 136—1 Morning or ½ Midday or Evening Meal
1 or ½ serving Protein (1 Egg); 1 serving Bread (matzo); 1 serving Fats

Mediterranean Eggs in Nest—page 149— Midday or Evening Meal
1 serving Protein (2 Eggs); 1 serving Bread Substitutes (potatoes); ¼ cup Limited Vegetables; 1 serving Vegetables; 1 serving Fats; 2 servings Extras (olives and Parmesan cheese)

Mushroom Caps Soufflé—page 139— ½ Midday or Evening Meal

½ serving Protein (1 Egg); ⅛ cup Limited Vegetables; 3¾ servings Vegetables; 1 serving Fats; ¼ serving Milk; 2 servings Extras (flour)

Mushroom Loaf—page 147—Midday or Evening Meal
1 serving Protein (1 Egg and ⅓ cup Soft Cheese); 1 serving Bread (bread crumbs); 6 servings Vegetables

Mushroom Omelet—page 136—Midday or Evening Meal
1 serving Protein (2 Eggs); 4½ servings Vegetables; 1 serving Fats

Mushroom Pizza—page 143—Midday or Evening Meal
1 serving Protein (1 Egg and 1 ounce Hard Cheese); 1 serving Bread Substitutes (rice); 2 servings Vegetables; 1 serving Fats; 1 serving Bonus (tomato sauce); 1 serving Extras (Parmesan cheese)

Mushroom-Stuffed Eggs—page 144—Midday or Evening Meal
1 serving Protein (2 Eggs); 2 teaspoons Limited Vegetables; 1 serving Vegetables; 2 servings Fats

Open-Face Grilled Cheese Sandwich I—page 143—1 Morning or ½ Midday or Evening Meal
1 or ½ serving Protein (1 ounce Hard Cheese); 1 serving Bread; ½ serving Vegetables (optional)

Open-Face Grilled Cheese Sandwich II—page 143—Midday or Evening Meal
1 serving Protein (2 ounces Hard Cheese); 1 serving Bread; ½ serving Vegetables (optional)

Orange Soufflé—page 139—½ Midday or Evening Meal
½ serving Protein (1 Egg); ¼ serving Bread (flour); ¼ serving Milk; 1 serving Extras (sugar); 16 calories Specialty Foods (marmalade)

Pancakes—page 144—1 Morning or ½ Midday or Evening Meal
1 serving Protein (1 Egg); ½ serving Bread (flour); 1½ servings Fats; ½ serving Milk; 2 servings Extras (sugar)

Peach and Cottage Cheese Mold—page 155—Midday or Evening Meal
1 serving Protein (⅔ cup Soft Cheese); 1 serving Fruits; ¼ serving Milk; 3 servings Extras (gelatin and honey)

Peaches and Cheese Breakfast—page 155—Morning Meal
1 serving Protein (⅓ cup Soft Cheese); 1 serving Fruits; 2 servings Extras (gelatin and honey)

Potato-Cheddar Broil—page 153—Midday or Evening Meal
1 serving Protein (2 ounces Hard Cheese); 1 serving Bread Substitutes (potato); 2 servings Vegetables

Potato, Eggs, and Cheese Salad—page 141—Midday or Evening Meal
1 serving Protein (1 Egg and 1 ounce Hard Cheese); 1 serving Bread Substitutes (potato); 1 serving Fats

Reuben Sandwich—page 143—Midday or Evening Meal
1 serving Protein (1 ounce Hard Cheese and 2 ounces Poultry); 1 serving Bread; 1 serving Vegetables

Salad with Sliced Egg (includes equivalents for Basic Vinaigrette Dressing)—page 141—¼ Midday or Evening Meal
¼ serving Protein (½ Egg); 1 serving Fats; 3 servings Vegetables

Scramble 'n' Spinach—page 135—1 Morning or ½ Midday or Evening Meal
1 or ½ serving Protein (1 Egg); 1½ teaspoons Limited Vegetables; 1 serving Vegetables

Spinach-Cucumber Egg Salad—page 141—Midday or Evening Meal
1 serving Protein (2 Eggs); 1 serving Vegetables; 1 serving Extras (pickle relish)

Spinach Frittata—page 137—Midday or Evening Meal
1 serving Protein (2 Eggs); ⅛ cup Limited Vegetables; ¾ serving Vegetables; 1½ servings Fats; 1 serving Extras (sesame seed)

Stuffed Eggs—page 144—Midday or Evening Meal
1 serving Protein (2 Eggs); ¼ serving Vegetables; 1 serving Fats

Stuffed French Toast—page 144—Midday or Evening Meal

1 serving Protein (1 Egg and ⅓ cup Soft Cheese); 2 servings Bread; ½ serving Fats; ½ serving Fruits; ½ serving Extras (sugar); 16 calories Specialty Foods (strawberry spread)

Stuffed Rigatoni (includes equivalents for Marinara Sauce)—page 147—Midday or Evening Meal
1 serving Protein (⅔ cup Soft Cheese); 1 serving Bread Substitutes (macaroni); 1⅓ servings Vegetables; ½ serving Fats; 1 serving Extras (Parmesan cheese)

Swiss-Stuffed Pears—page 156—1 Morning or ½ Midday or Evening Meal
1 or ½ serving Protein (1 ounce Hard Cheese); 1 serving Fruits

Tomato-Cheese-Stuffed Pitas—page 150— Midday or Evening Meal
1 serving Protein (⅓ cup Soft Cheese and 1 ounce Hard Cheese); 1 serving Bread; ⅛ serving Vegetables

Tomato Stuffed with Herb Cheese— page 150—Midday or Evening Meal
1 serving Protein (⅔ cup Soft Cheese); 1 tablespoon Limited Vegetables; 2 servings Vegetables

Tortilla Bake—page 147—Midday or Evening Meal
1 serving Protein (1 Egg and 1 ounce Hard Cheese); 1 serving Bread (tortilla); 1 teaspoon Limited Vegetables; ½ serving Vegetables; ¼ serving Fats; ¼ serving Milk; ¼ serving Bonus (tomato sauce)

Two-Cheese Herbed Pasta—page 153— ½ Midday or Evening Meal
½ serving Protein (cup Soft Cheese and ½ ounce Hard Cheese); 1 serving Bread Substitutes (spaghetti); 1 serving Fats

Vegetable-Cheese Platter—page 151— Midday or Evening Meal
1 serving Protein (1 Egg and ⅓ cup Soft Cheese); 4 servings Vegetables; ¼ serving Milk

Vegetable Cottage Cheese—page 151— 1 Morning or ½ Midday or Evening Meal
1 or ½ serving Protein (⅓ cup Soft Cheese); 1 tablespoon Limited

Vegetables; ⅔ serving Vegetables; ¼ serving Milk

Vegetable Lasagna—page 148—Midday or Evening Meal
1 serving Protein (⅓ cup Soft Cheese and 1 ounce Hard Cheese); 2½ servings Vegetables; ½ serving Extras (Parmesan cheese)

POULTRY, VEAL, AND WILD GAME

Apricot Chicken—page 165—Midday or Evening Meal
1 serving Protein (4 ounces Poultry); 1 serving Fats; 1 serving Fruits; 1 serving Extras (cornstarch)

Baked Veal Loaves—page 172—Midday or Evening Meal
1 serving Protein (4 ounces Veal); ½ serving Bread; ⅛ cup Limited Vegetables; ½ serving Vegetables; 1 serving Fats; ¼ serving Extras (arrowroot)

Braised Chicken with Vegetables— page 163—Midday or Evening Meal
1 serving Protein (4 ounces Poultry); ¼ cup Limited Vegetables; 2 servings Vegetables; 1½ servings Fats

Chicken and Cannellini Casserole— page 161—Midday or Evening Meal (Men—add 1 ounce cannellini beans)
1 serving Protein (2 ounces Poultry and 3 ounces Legumes—Men, 4 ounces Legumes); 1½ teaspoons Limited Vegetables; ⅔ serving Vegetables; ⅛ serving Bonus (tomato paste)

Chicken and Eggplant Bake—page 162— Midday or Evening Meal
1 serving Protein (½ Egg and 3 ounces Poultry); ¼ cup Limited Vegetables; 2 servings Vegetables; 1 serving Fats; ¼ serving Bonus (tomato sauce)

Chicken and Peppers—page 164—Midday or Evening Meal
1 serving Protein (4 ounces Poultry); ½ cup Limited Vegetables; 2 servings Vegetables; 1 serving Fats

Chicken Breasts with Raisin Sauce— page 165—Midday or Evening Meal
1 serving Protein (4 ounces Poultry);

1 serving Fats; ¼ serving Fruits;
1¼ servings Extras (broth and flour)
Chicken Cavalfiore—page 159—Midday or
Evening Meal
1 serving Protein (4 ounces Poultry);
2 servings Vegetables; 1 serving Fats;
2 servings Extras (broth, flour, and wine)
Chicken Donna—page 159—Midday or
Evening Meal
1 serving Protein (4 ounces Poultry);
¼ cup Limited Vegetables; 4 servings
Vegetables; 1 serving Fats; 2 servings
Extras (broth, flour, and wine)
Chicken Greek Style—page 159—Midday or
Evening Meal
1 serving Protein (4 ounces Poultry);
1 serving Fats; ½ serving Extras (broth)
Chicken Indienne—page 160—Midday or
Evening Meal
1 serving Protein (4 ounces Poultry);
1 serving Bread Substitutes (rice);
¼ cup Limited Vegetables; ½ serving
Fats; ½ serving Fruits; 1⅔ servings Extras
(broth and coconut)
Chicken Provençale—page 160—Midday or
Evening Meal
1 serving Protein (4 ounces Poultry);
½ cup Limited Vegetables; 5 servings
Vegetables; 1 serving Fats; 2 servings
Extras (olives and wine)
Chicken Salad Oriental—page 166—Midday
or Evening Meal
1 serving Protein (4 ounces Poultry);
¼ cup plus 2 tablespoons Limited Vegetables; ⅓ serving Vegetables; 1 serving
Fats
Chicken Sorrentino (includes equivalents for
Marinara Sauce)—page 160—Midday or
Evening Meal
1 serving Protein (1 ounce Hard Cheese
and 2 ounces Poultry); 1 serving Bread
(bread crumbs); 2⅓ servings Vegetables;
½ serving Fats; 1¼ servings Extras
(broth or bouillon and Parmesan cheese)
Chicken Teriyaki—page 161—Midday or
Evening Meal
1 serving Protein (4 ounces Poultry);
½ serving Fats; ½ serving Fruits; 1 serving
Extras (honey)

Cold Chicken Platter—page 166—Midday
or Evening Meal
1 serving Protein (4 ounces Poultry);
1½ teaspoons Limited Vegetables;
2½ servings Vegetables; 1½ servings Fats;
½ serving Milk; 1 serving Extras
(ketchup)
Crisp "Oven-Fried" Chicken—page 163—
Midday or Evening Meal
1 serving Protein (4 ounces Poultry);
1 serving Bread (cornflakes)
Curried Chicken Salad—page 166—Midday
or Evening Meal
1 serving Protein (4 ounces Poultry);
2½ servings Vegetables; 1 serving Fats;
½ serving Fruits
Fruited Chicken—page 166—Midday or
Evening Meal
1 serving Protein (4 ounces Poultry);
1 serving Fats; 1 serving Fruits;
1½ servings Extras (flour and wine)
Ginger-Broiled Chicken—page 164—Midday
or Evening Meal
1 serving Protein (4 ounces Poultry)
Glazed Turkey Mold—page 168—Midday or
Evening Meal
1 serving Protein (4 ounces Poultry);
1 serving Bread Substitutes (potato);
1 tablespoon Limited Vegetables;
¾ serving Vegetables; 3 servings Fats;
¼ serving Milk; 1 serving Extras (gelatin
and olive)
Honeyed Turkey with Broccoli—page 168—
Midday or Evening Meal
1 serving Protein (4 ounces Poultry);
2 servings Vegetables; 1 serving Fats;
½ serving Fruits; 1 serving Extras (honey)
Japanese Chicken Salad—page 167—Midday
or Evening Meal
1 serving Protein (4 ounces Poultry);
2 teaspoons Limited Vegetables; 1 serving
Fats
Jellied Veal Mold—page 172—Midday or
Evening Meal
1 serving Protein (4 ounces Veal);
½ serving Vegetables; 1   servings Extras
(broth and gelatin)
Lunch Box Veal—page 175—Midday or
Evening Meal

1 serving Protein (4 ounces Veal); ¼ cup Limited Vegetables; 1 serving Fats; ½ serving Milk

Polynesian Chicken—page 161—Midday or Evening Meal
1 serving Protein (4 ounces Poultry); ½ cup Limited Vegetables; 1½ servings Vegetables; 1 serving Fats; 1 serving Fruits; 1½ servings Extras (broth or bouillon and cornstarch)

Rabbit Bourguignon—page 176—Midday or Evening Meal
1 serving Protein (4 ounces Game); ¼ cup Limited Vegetables; 4 servings Vegetables; 1½ servings Fats; 1 serving Extras (wine)

Red Chicken with Potatoes—page 162— Midday or Evening Meal
1 serving Protein (4 ounces Poultry); 1 serving Bread Substitutes (potato); ½ serving Vegetables; 1 serving Fats; 1 serving Bonus (tomato puree)

Roast Shoulder of Veal—page 172—Midday or Evening Meal
1 serving Protein (4 ounces Veal); ⅛ cup Limited Vegetables;   serving Vegetables; ¾ serving Extras (broth and wine)

Roast Turkey—page 167—Midday or Evening Meal
1 serving Protein (4 ounces Poultry);   serving Extras (broth)

Sautéed Chicken and Vegetables— page 164—Midday or Evening Meal
1 serving Protein (4 ounces Poultry); 3   servings Vegetables; 1 serving Fats

Sautéed Curried Veal and Eggplant— page 174—Midday or Evening Meal
1 serving Protein (4 ounces Veal); ¼ cup Limited Vegetables; 2 servings Vegetables; 1 serving Fats

Sesame Chicken with Green Beans— page 164—Midday or Evening Meal
1 serving Protein (4 ounces Poultry); 2 servings Vegetables; 1 serving Fats; 1½ servings Extras (coconut and sesame seed)

Skewered Marinated Chicken—page 164— Midday or Evening Meal
1 serving Protein (4 ounces Poultry);

½ cup Limited Vegetables; 1½ servings Vegetables

Stir-Cooked Turkey—page 168—Midday or Evening Meal
1 serving Protein (4 ounces Poultry); 1 serving Bread (bread crumbs)

Turkey-Barley Soup—page 167—¾ Midday or Evening Meal
¾ serving Protein (3 ounces Poultry); 1 serving Bread Substitutes (barley); ¼ cup Limited Vegetables; 1¾ servings Vegetables; 1 serving Extras (broth)

Turkey Breast with Cream of Corn Sauce— page 169—Midday or Evening Meal
1 serving Protein (4 ounces Poultry); 1 serving Bread Substitutes (corn); 1⅔ servings Vegetables

Turkey-Cheese Strata—page 170—Midday or Evening Meal
1 serving Protein (1 ounce Hard Cheese and 2 ounces Poultry); ½ serving Bread Substitutes (potato); 2¼ servings Vegetables

Turkey Florentine—page 170—Midday or Evening Meal
1 serving Protein (4 ounces Poultry); 4 servings Vegetables; 2 servings Fats; ¼ serving Milk; 2½ servings Extras (flour, Parmesan cheese, and wine)

Turkey Island Style—page 169—Midday or Evening Meal
1 serving Protein (4 ounces Poultry); ½ cup Limited Vegetables; 1⅔ servings Vegetables; 1 serving Fruits; ¼ serving Bonus (tomato juice); 1½ servings Extras (cornstarch)

Turkey Kiev—page 171—Midday or Evening Meal
1 serving Protein (4 ounces Poultry); 1 serving Bread Substitutes (rice); ½ serving Bread (cornflakes); 3 servings Fats; ½ serving Extras (bacon bits)

Turkey Piccata—page 170—Midday or Evening Meal
1 serving Protein (4 ounces Poultry); ¼ serving Bread (flour); 1½ servings Fats; ¼ serving Extras (broth)

Turkey Pockets—page 171—Midday or Evening Meal

1 serving Protein (4 ounces Poultry);
1 serving Bread; ⅛ cup Limited Vegetables; ½ serving Vegetables; 1 serving
Fats

Veal à la Fontina—page 174—Midday or
Evening Meal
1 serving Protein (1 ounce Hard Cheese
and 2 ounces Veal); ¾ teaspoon Limited
Vegetables; ½ serving Vegetables;
1 serving Fats; 2 servings Extras (broth,
flour, tomato paste, and wine)

Veal Medley—page 175—Midday or
Evening Meal
1 serving Protein (4 ounces Veal);
1 serving Bread Substitutes (noodles);
3 servings Vegetables; 2½ servings Fats;
3 servings Extras (broth, flour, and
Parmesan cheese)

Veal Patties and Mushrooms—page 173—
Midday or Evening Meal
1 serving Protein (4 ounces Veal); ¼ cup
plus 2 tablespoons Limited Vegetables;
2 servings Vegetables; 1¼ servings Extras
(broth mix and cornstarch)

Veal Ragout—page 174—Midday or
Evening Meal
1 serving Protein (4 ounces Veal);
1½ servings Vegetables; 2 servings Fats;
3 servings Extras (broth and flour)

Veal Soup—page 171—Midday or Evening
Meal
1 serving Protein (4 ounces Veal);
1 tablespoon Limited Vegetables;
2½ servings Vegetables; ¼ serving Bonus
(tomato paste); 2 servings Extras (broth)

Vegetable-Stuffed Chicken Breasts—
page 162—Midday or Evening Meal
1 serving Protein (4 ounces Poultry);
4½ servings Vegetables; ½ serving Fats;
½ serving Extras (sesame seed)

MEATS

Armenian Lamb Casserole—page 186—
Midday or Evening Meal
1 serving Protein (4 ounces Meat Group);
⅛ cup Limited Vegetables; 5½ servings
Vegetables; ¾ serving Fats

Bacon-Scallop Kebabs—page 193—Midday
or Evening Meal
(Men—add ½ ounce Canadian bacon)
1 serving Protein (1½ ounces Meat
Group-cured and 2 ounces Fish—Men,
2 ounces Meat Group-cured); ¼ cup
Limited Vegetables

Baked Oat Burgers—page 179—Midday or
Evening Meal
1 serving Protein (4 ounces Meat Group);
½ serving Bread (quick oats); ¼ cup
Limited Vegetables; ½ serving Vegetables

Beef and Corn Casserole—page 181—
Midday or Evening Meal
1 serving Protein (4 ounces Meat Group);
1 serving Bread Substitutes (corn);
3 servings Vegetables

Beef Liver Creole—page 197—Midday or
Evening Meal
1 serving Protein (4 ounces Liver); ¼ cup
plus 2 tablespoons Limited Vegetables;
2 servings Vegetables

Broiled Bologna-Cheese Muffin—page 192—
Midday or Evening Meal
(Men—add ½ ounce bologna)
1 serving Protein (1 ounce Hard Cheese
and 1½ ounces Meat Group-cured—
Men, 2 ounces Meat Group-cured);
1 serving Bread; ½ serving Fats

Calf Liver with Tomato—page 198—
Midday or Evening Meal
1 serving Protein (4 ounces Liver);
1 serving Vegetables; 1 serving Fats;
1½ servings Extras (broth and wine)

Chicken and Pork Meatballs—page 188—
Midday or Evening Meal
1 serving Protein (2 ounces each Poultry
and Meat Group); ½ serving Bread
Substitutes (potato); ½ serving Fats

Chicken Liver Pilaf—page 196—Midday or
Evening Meal
1 serving Protein (4 ounces Liver);
1 serving Bread Substitutes (rice); ½ cup
Limited Vegetables; 3 servings Vegetables;
1½ servings Fats

Chicken Livers Florentine—page 195—
Midday or Evening Meal
1 serving Protein (4 ounces Liver); ½ cup

Limited Vegetables; 1½ servings
Vegetables; 1 serving Fats

Chicken Livers Sautéed in Wine—
page 194—Midday or Evening Meal
1 serving Protein (4 ounces Liver); ¼ cup
Limited Vegetables; ¾ serving Fats;
¾ serving Extras (wine)

Chicken Livers "Stroganoff"—page 195—
Midday or Evening Meal
1 serving Protein (4 ounces Liver); ¼ cup
Limited Vegetables; 1 serving Vegetables;
1 serving Fats; ½ serving Milk; 2 servings
Extras (chili sauce and flour)

Chili-Burgers—page 179—Midday or
Evening Meal
1 serving Protein (4 ounces Meat Group);
¼ cup Limited Vegetables; ½ serving
Vegetables; ½ serving Milk; 1 serving
Extras (ketchup)

Coffee-Roasted Leg of Lamb—page 185—
Midday or Evening Meal
1 serving Protein (4 ounces Meat Group)

Creamed Cabbage and Ham—page 190—
Midday or Evening Meal (Men—¾ meal)
1 (or ¾) serving Protein (3 ounces Meat
Group-cured); ½ serving Bread (flour);
½ cup Limited Vegetables; 4 servings
Vegetables; 1 serving Fats; ¼ serving
Milk; ½ serving Extras (broth)

Cucumber-Ham Bake—page 190—Midday
or Evening Meal (Men—add ½ ounce
ham)
1 serving Protein (1 ounce Hard Cheese
and 1½ ounces Meat Group-cured—
Men, 2 ounces Meat Group-cured);
1 tablespoon Limited Vegetables;
1⅛ servings Vegetables; ½ serving Fats;
⅛ serving Milk; ½ serving Extras (flour)

Cucumber-Liverwurst Sandwich—
page 192—Midday or Evening Meal
(Men—¾ meal)
1 (or ¾) serving Protein (3 ounces Meat
Group-cured); 2 servings Bread; ½ serving
Vegetables; 1 serving Extras (bacon bits)

Curried Meat Hash—page 181—Midday or
Evening Meal
1 serving Protein (4 ounces Meat Group);
¼ cup Limited Vegetables; ½ serving

Fats; ¾ serving Fruits; ½ serving Extras
(arrowroot)

Easy Beef Soup—page 179—Midday or
Evening Meal
1 serving Protein (4 ounces Meat Group);
1½ servings Vegetables; 1 serving Extras
(broth)

Fennel Pork—page 187—Midday or Evening
Meal
1 serving Protein (4 ounces Meat Group);
¾ serving Fats; 2 servings Extras
(bouillon and flour)

Frankfurter Stir-Fry—page 193—Midday or
Evening Meal (Men—¾ meal)
1 (or ¾) serving Protein (3 ounces Meat
Group-cured); ½ cup Limited Vegetables; ¾ serving Vegetables; ½ serving
Fats; 1 serving Fruits; ½ serving Extras
(cornstarch)

Grilled Ham Steak with Pineapple—
page 189—Midday or Evening Meal
(Men—¾ meal)
1 (or ¾) serving Protein (3 ounces Meat
Group-cured); ½ serving Fruits; 1 serving
Extras (honey)

Ham and Rutabaga Dice—page 190—
Midday or Evening Meal (Men—¾ meal)
1 (or ¾) serving Protein (3 ounces Meat
Group-cured); ½ cup Limited Vegetables;
3 servings Vegetables; 1 serving Fats

Ham and Vegetables with Paprika Yogurt—
page 191—Midday or Evening Meal
(Men—¾ meal)
1 (or ¾) serving Protein (3 ounces Meat
Group-cured); 1 serving Bread Substitutes
(potato); 2¼ servings Vegetables;
1 serving Milk; 1 serving Extras
(cornstarch)

Ham 'n' Turkey Casserole—page 191—
Midday or Evening Meal (Men—⅞ meal)
1 (or ⅞) serving Protein (2 ounces
Poultry and 1½ ounces Meat Group-
cured); 1 serving Bread Substitutes
(noodles); ½ serving Vegetables;
½ serving Milk; 1 serving Extras
(Parmesan cheese)

Ham 'n' Vegetable Burgers—page 191—
Midday or Evening Meal (Men—⅞ meal)
1 (or ⅞) serving Protein (1 Egg and

1½ ounces Meat Group-cured); ½ serving
Bread (quick oats); ¾ serving Vegetables

Ham Strips with Rice and Water
Chestnuts—page 192—Midday or
Evening Meal (Men—¾ meal)
1 (or ¾) serving Protein (3 ounces Meat
Group-cured); 1 serving Bread Substitutes
(rice); ¼ cup Limited Vegetables;
1 serving Fats

Knockwurst Breakfast—page 192—Morning
Meal
1 serving Protein (1 ounce Meat Group-
cured); ¾ serving Vegetables; 1 serving
Fats

Lamb Rosé—page 186—Midday or Evening
Meal
1 serving Protein (4 ounces Meat Group);
½ cup Limited Vegetables; 1 serving
Vegetables; 1 serving Fats; 2 servings
Extras (broth, tomato paste, and wine)

Lemon-Minted Lamb—page 186—Midday
or Evening Meal
1 serving Protein (4 ounces Meat Group);
1 serving Fats

Liver Loaf Pâté—page 196—Midday or
Evening Meal
1 serving Protein (4 ounces Liver);
1 serving Bread Substitutes (potato);
⅛ cup Limited Vegetables; 1 serving Fats;
¼ serving Milk; 1½ servings Extras
(broth mix and sherry)

Liver Manfredi—page 198—Midday or
Evening Meal
1 serving Protein (4 ounces Liver);
1 serving Bread (bread crumbs); 2 servings
Extras (bacon bits and sesame seed)

Liver-Noodle Casserole—page 197—Midday
or Evening Meal
1 serving Protein (4 ounces Liver);
1 serving Bread Substitutes (noodles);
⅛ cup Limited Vegetables; 1½ servings
Fats; 1 serving Bonus (tomato sauce);
½ serving Extras (Parmesan cheese)

Liver Venetian—page 198—Midday or
Evening Meal
1 serving Protein (4 ounces Liver); ¼ cup
Limited Vegetables; 1 serving Vegetables;
½ serving Fats; ½ serving Extras (wine
or vermouth)

Liver-Yam Pâté—page 196—Midday or
Evening Meal
1 serving Protein (4 ounces Liver);
½ serving Bread Substitutes (yams);
1 serving Bread (saltines); 1 serving
Extras (Parmesan cheese)

Marinated Chuck Steak—page 183—Midday
or Evening Meal
1 serving Protein (4 ounces Meat Group);
½ teaspoon Limited Vegetables;
1¼ servings Extras (honey and wine)

Marinated Julienne Beef—page 183—
Midday or Evening Meal
1 serving Protein (4 ounces Meat Group);
¼ cup Limited Vegetables; 1 serving Fats

Mediterranean Stew—page 182—Midday or
Evening Meal
1 serving Protein (4 ounces Meat Group);
¼ cup Limited Vegetables; ¾ serving
Fats; ¼ serving Fruits; ½ serving Bonus
(tomato paste); ¾ serving Extras (honey
and wine)

Mexican Beef Patty—page 180—Midday or
Evening Meal
1 serving Protein (1 ounce Hard Cheese
and 2 ounces Meat Group); ½ teaspoon
Limited Vegetables; 1 serving Vegetables

Middle Eastern Burgers—page 180—Midday
or Evening Meal
1 serving Protein (4 ounces Meat Group);
1 serving Bread; ¼ cup Limited Vegetables; 2 servings Vegetables; 1 serving
Fats

Mushroom-Beef Hash—page 182—Midday
or Evening Meal
1 serving Protein (4 ounces Meat Group);
1 serving Bread; ¼ cup Limited Vegetables; 1 serving Vegetables; 1 serving Fats;
1 serving Extras (broth and flour)

Oriental Steak Salad—page 184—Midday or
Evening Meal
1 serving Protein (4 ounces Meat Group);
⅛ cup Limited Vegetables; 5 servings
Vegetables; 1 serving Fats

Pepper Steak—page 184—Midday or
Evening Meal
1 serving Protein (4 ounces Meat Group);
1 serving Vegetables; 1½ servings Fats;
1½ servings Extras (broth and cornstarch)

Piquant Hamburgers—page 180—Midday or Evening Meal
1 serving Protein (4 ounces Meat Group); ⅛ cup plus 1½ teaspoons Limited Vegetables; 1 serving Vegetables; ½ serving Fats; 1 serving Extras (olives)

Pork and Vegetable Medley—page 188—Midday or Evening Meal
1 serving Protein (4 ounces Meat Group); ½ cup Limited Vegetables; 1½ servings Vegetables; 1½ servings Fats; ⅓ serving Extras (broth)

Potato-Beef Hash—page 182—Midday or Evening Meal
1 serving Protein (4 ounces Meat Group); 1 serving Bread Substitutes (potato); ¼ cup Limited Vegetables; 1¼ servings Vegetables; 1½ servings Fats

Potted Shoulder Lamb Chops—page 186—Midday or Evening Meal
1 serving Protein (4 ounces Meat Group); ¼ cup plus 2 tablespoons Limited Vegetables; 1½ servings Vegetables; 1 serving Fats

Roast Fillet of Beef with Green Peppercorns—page 185—Midday or Evening Meal
1 serving Protein (4 ounces Meat Group)

Roast Loin of Pork—page 187—Midday or Evening Meal
1 serving Protein (4 ounces Meat Group)

Roast Pork Tenderloin—page 187—Midday or Evening Meal
1 serving Protein (4 ounces Meat Group); 1 serving Fruits

Sautéed Liver with Mustard Cauliflower—page 199—Midday or Evening Meal
1 serving Protein (4 ounces Liver); 2 servings Vegetables; 1 serving Fats

Shepherd's Beef Pie—page 182—Midday or Evening Meal
1 serving Protein (1 ounce Hard Cheese and 2 ounces Meat Group); 1 serving Bread Substitutes (potato); ¼ cup Limited Vegetables; 1½ servings Vegetables; 1 serving Fats; ⅛ serving Milk; 1½ servings Extras (broth and flour)

Spaghetti with Chicken Liver Sauce—page 196—Midday or Evening Meal
1 serving Protein (4 ounces Liver); 1 serving Bread Substitutes (spaghetti); cup Limited Vegetables; 2 servings Vegetables; 1 serving Fats; 1 serving Extras (broth mix and tomato paste)

Spicy Meat Turnovers—page 181—Midday or Evening Meal
1 serving Protein (4 ounces Meat Group); ¼ cup Limited Vegetables; 1 serving Fats; ½ serving Occasional Substitutes (beer)

Steak au Poivre (Peppered Steak) with "Garlic-Butter"—page 184—Midday or Evening Meal
1 serving Protein (4 ounces Meat Group); 1 serving Fats

Steak Pizzaiola—page 184—Midday or Evening Meal
1 serving Protein (4 ounces Meat Group); ⅛ cup Limited Vegetables; 1 serving Vegetables; 1 serving Fats; 1 serving Extras (olives)

Stewed Tripe—page 194—Midday or Evening Meal
1 serving Protein (4 ounces Meat Group); ½ cup Limited Vegetables; 1½ servings Vegetables; 1 serving Fats; 1 serving Bonus (tomato puree); 1 serving Extras (wine)

Stuffed Cucumber—page 192—Midday or Evening Meal (Men—¾ meal)
1 (or ¾) serving Protein (3 ounces Meat Group-cured); 1½ teaspoons Limited Vegetables; 1 serving Vegetables; 1 serving Fats; 1 serving Extras (bacon bits)

Sweet 'n' Sour Liver—page 198—Midday or Evening Meal
1 serving Protein (4 ounces Liver); 1 tablespoon Limited Vegetables; ½ serving Fruits; ½ serving Extras (cornstarch)

Swiss Steak—page 185—Midday or Evening Meal
1 serving Protein (4 ounces Meat Group); ¼ cup Limited Vegetables; 2 servings Vegetables; 1½ servings Fats; 1 serving Extras (flour)

Székely Goulash—page 188—Midday or Evening Meal
1 serving Protein (4 ounces Meat Group);

½ cup Limited Vegetables; 1 serving
Vegetables; ¼ serving Milk; 2¼ teaspoons
Tomato Puree (serving Bonus);
¾ serving Extras (flour)

Tangy Pork and Rice—page 189—Midday or
Evening Meal
1 serving Protein (4 ounces Meat Group);
1 serving Bread Substitutes (rice);
¼ cup Limited Vegetables; ½ serving
Fats; 1 serving Bonus (mixed vegetable
juice and tomato puree); ½ serving Extras
(wine)

Tarragon Chicken Livers—page 195—
Midday or Evening Meal
1 serving Protein (4 ounces Liver);
1 serving Bread; ¼ cup plus 2 tablespoons
Limited Vegetables; 1 serving Fats;
½ serving Extras (wine)

Texas Barbecued Pork Chops—page 188—
Midday or Evening Meal
1 serving Protein (4 ounces Meat Group);
½ serving Bonus (tomato sauce);
1 serving Extras (chili sauce)

Veal Tongue with Onion Sauce—page 194—
Midday or Evening Meal
1 serving Protein (4 ounces Meat Group);
½ cup Limited Vegetables; 1 serving
Fats; 1½ servings Extras (broth and flour)

FISH

Baked Codfish with Lemon—page 203—
Midday or Evening Meal
1 serving Protein (4 ounces Fish);
1 serving Fats

Baked Fish Casserole—page 208—Midday
or Evening Meal
1 serving Protein (½ ounce Hard Cheese
and 3 ounces Fish); ¼ cup Limited
Vegetables; 2¼ servings Vegetables;
1½ servings Fats; ¼ serving Milk;
1½ servings Extras (flour)

Baked Red Snapper—page 211—Midday or
Evening Meal
1 serving Protein (4 ounces Fish);
1 serving Fats; 1 serving Extras (Parmesan
cheese)

Baked Striped Bass with Vegetables—

page 212—Midday or Evening Meal
1 serving Protein (4 ounces Fish); ¼ cup
Limited Vegetables; 3 servings Vegetables;
1 serving Fats; 1 serving Extras (wine)

Broiled Soft-Shell Crabs—page 218—
Midday or Evening Meal
1 serving Protein (4 ounces Fish);
1 serving Fats

Calamari with Spaghetti—page 214—
Midday or Evening Meal
1 serving Protein (4 ounces Fish);
1 serving Bread Substitutes (spaghetti);
¼ cup Limited Vegetables; 1 serving
Vegetables; 1 serving Fats

Captain's Flounder—page 204—Midday or
Evening Meal
1 serving Protein (4 ounces Fish);
½ serving Bread; ¼ cup Limited Vegetables; 1¾ servings Vegetables; 1 serving
Fats; 1 serving Extras (broth and wine)

Chilled Fish and Rice Salad—page 208—
Midday or Evening Meal
1 serving Protein (4 ounces Fish);
1 serving Bread Substitutes (rice);
¼ serving Vegetables; 1 serving Fats

Chilled Fish Salad—page 205—Midday or
Evening Meal
1 serving Protein (4 ounces Fish);
1 tablespoon Limited Vegetables;
½ serving Vegetables; 1 serving Fats;
1 serving Extras (pickle relish)

Crab Meat Mold—page 218—Midday or
Evening Meal
1 serving Protein (4 ounces Fish);
⅛ cup Limited Vegetables; 1½ servings
Vegetables; 2 servings Fats; ½ serving
Milk; 1 serving Extras (gelatin)

Crab Meat Salad in Pita Bread—page 219—
Midday or Evening Meal
1 serving Protein (4 ounces Fish);
1 serving Bread; 1 tablespoon Limited
Vegetables; ½ serving Vegetables;
1½ servings Fats; 1 serving Extras (chili
sauce)

Creamed Shrimp Pasta—page 223—Midday
or Evening Meal
1 serving Protein (4 ounces Fish);
1 serving Bread Substitutes (margherite or
spaghetti); 2 servings Vegetables;

1 serving Fats; ½ serving Milk;
1½ servings Extras (flour)

Creamy Tuna Salad—page 215—Midday or
Evening Meal
1 serving Protein (⅓ cup Soft Cheese and
2 ounces Fish); ¼ serving Vegetables

Curried Scrod—page 209—Midday or
Evening Meal
1 serving Protein (4 ounces Fish);
2 servings Extras (honey)

Curried Seafood Salad—page 220—Midday
or Evening Meal
1 serving Protein (4 ounces Fish);
2¼ servings Vegetables; 1 serving Fats;
¼ serving Milk

Far East Scallops—page 222—Midday or
Evening Meal
1 serving Protein (4 ounces Fish);
¼ cup Limited Vegetables; 2½ servings
Vegetables; 1 serving Fats; 1½ servings
Extras (broth mix and cornstarch)

Fillet of Sole Florentine—page 212—
Midday or Evening Meal
1 serving Protein (4 ounces Fish);
¾ serving Vegetables; 1 serving Fats;
¼ serving Extras (cornstarch)

Fish and Tomato Aspic—page 203—Midday
or Evening Meal
1 serving Protein (4 ounces Fish);
1⅓ servings Vegetables; 1 serving Bonus
(tomato juice); 1 serving Extras (gelatin)

Fish Balls with Herb Sauce—page 203—
Midday or Evening Meal
1 serving Protein (1 Egg and 2 ounces
Fish); 1 serving Bread (saltines);
1½ servings Fats; ½ serving Milk;
1½ servings Extras (flour)

Flounder Fillet Rolls with Vegetables—
page 205—Midday or Evening Meal
1 serving Protein (4 ounces Fish);
1 tablespoon Limited Vegetables;
½ serving Vegetables; 1 serving Fats;
½ serving Fruits; ½ serving Extras
(cornstarch)

Flounder in Orange Sauce—page 206—
Midday or Evening Meal
1 serving Protein (4 ounces Fish);
⅛ cup Limited Vegetables; ½ serving

Vegetables; ¾ serving Fats; ¾ serving
Fruits; ¾ serving Extras (flour)

Flounder Italiano—page 206—Midday or
Evening Meal
1 serving Protein (4 ounces Fish);
½ serving Bread (flour); ⅛ cup Limited
Vegetables; ½ serving Vegetables;
1 serving Fats; 3 servings Extras (wine)

Flounder Meunière—page 206—Midday or
Evening Meal
1 serving Protein (4 ounces Fish);
1 serving Fats; 2 servings Extras (broth,
flour, and wine)

Flounder Véronique—page 206—Midday or
Evening Meal
1 serving Protein (4 ounces Fish);
1½ servings Fats; ½ serving Fruits;
⅛ serving Milk; 2¾ servings Extras
(broth, flour, and wine)

Frogs Legs Meunière—page 214—Midday or
Evening Meal
1 serving Protein (4 ounces Fish);
½ serving Bread (flour); 1 serving Fats;
½ serving Extras (broth)

Iceberg-Tomato Ring—page 216—Midday
or Evening Meal
1 serving Protein (4 ounces Fish);
1 tablespoon Limited Vegetables; 1 serving
Vegetables; 1½ servings Fats; ½ serving
Bonus (tomato juice); ½ serving Extras
(gelatin)

Layered Baked Flounder—page 207—
Midday or Evening Meal
1 serving Protein (4 ounces Fish);
1 serving Bread (bread crumbs);
1¼ servings Vegetables; 1¼ servings Milk

Lemon-Broiled Snappers (Baby Blue
Fish)—page 210—Midday or Evening
Meal
1 serving Protein (4 ounces Fish);
1 tablespoon Limited Vegetables; 1 serving
Fats

Lobster in Creamy Sauce—page 220—
Midday or Evening Meal
1 serving Protein (4 ounces Fish);
¾ serving Bread (bread and flour);
¼ cup Limited Vegetables; 1 serving
Fats; ½ serving Milk; ⅛ serving Bonus
(tomato paste); 1 serving Extras (wine)

Lunch Box Fish 'n' Cheese—page 204—
Midday or Evening Meal
1 serving Protein (1 ounce Hard Cheese
and 2 ounces Fish); 1 serving Bread;
1 serving Vegetables

Mackerel Patties—page 213—Midday or
Evening Meal
1 serving Protein (4 ounces Fish);
½ serving Bread Substitutes (potato);
½ serving Bread; 1 tablespoon Limited
Vegetables; ¼ serving Vegetables;
1½ servings Fats

Mussel-Rice Casserole—page 220—Midday
or Evening Meal
1 serving Protein (4 ounces Fish);
1 serving Bread Substitutes (rice); ¼ cup
Limited Vegetables; 1½ servings
Vegetables; 1 serving Fats; 1 serving Fruits;
1½ servings Extras (broth and cornstarch)

Mussel Stew—page 221—Midday or
Evening Meal
1 serving Protein (4 ounces Fish);
½ cup Limited Vegetables; 2 servings
Vegetables; 1 serving Fats; 1⅔ servings
Extras (broth and wine)

Mustard-Broiled Flounder—page 207—
Midday or Evening Meal
1 serving Protein (4 ounces Fish)

Oyster Stew—page 221—Midday or Evening
Meal
1 serving Protein (4 ounces Fish);
2 servings Fats; ½ serving Milk; 2 servings
Extras (flour)

Pan-Broiled Snappers—page 210—Midday
or Evening Meal
1 serving Protein (4 ounces Fish);
½ serving Bread (flour)

Papaya Shrimp—page 224—Midday or
Evening Meal
1 serving Protein (4 ounces Fish);
1 serving Vegetables; ½ serving Fruits;
½ serving Extras (broth)

Pineapple Flounder—page 208—Midday or
Evening Meal
1 serving Protein (4 ounces Fish);
1 serving Fats; ½ serving Fruits

Poached Codfish with Asparagus and
Tomatoes—page 204—Midday or Evening
Meal

1 serving Protein (4 ounces Fish); ¼ cup
Limited Vegetables; 1½ servings Vegetables; 1 serving Fats

Poached Halibut Parmesan—page 208—
Midday or Evening Meal
1 serving Protein (4 ounces Fish);
1½ servings Fats; 1 serving Extras
(Parmesan cheese)

Poached Swordfish—page 211—Midday or
Evening Meal
1 serving Protein (4 ounces Fish);
2 servings Vegetables

Salmon Chowder—page 214—Midday or
Evening Meal
1 serving Protein (4 ounces Fish);
1 serving Bread Substitutes (corn);
¼ serving Bread (flour); ¼ cup Limited
Vegetables; 1½ servings Vegetables;
1 serving Fats

Salmon Mousse—page 215—Midday or
Evening Meal
1 serving Protein (4 ounces Fish);
1½ teaspoons Limited Vegetables;
1½ servings Fats; ⅜ serving Milk (¼ cup
skim milk and 1 tablespoon yogurt);
½ serving Extras (gelatin)

Salmon Salad—page 215—Midday or
Evening Meal
1 serving Protein (4 ounces Fish);
¾ serving Vegetables; 1 serving Fats

Salmon-Zucchini Kebabs—page 213—
Midday or Evening Meal
1 serving Protein (4 ounces Fish);
½ teaspoon Limited Vegetables;
3½ servings Vegetables; 1 serving Extras
(wine)

Sardine Salad—page 215—Midday or
Evening Meal
1 serving Protein (4 ounces Fish);
1 tablespoon Limited Vegetables;
1½ servings Fats

Sautéed Shrimp and Corn—page 224—
Midday or Evening Meal
1 serving Protein (4 ounces Fish);
1 serving Bread Substitutes (corn); ½ cup
Limited Vegetables; 1 serving Fats;
2 servings Extras (cornstarch and sugar)

Scallop Bisque—page 222—½ Midday or
Evening Meal

½ serving Protein (2 ounces Fish);
½ serving Bread Substitutes (potato);
¼ cup plus 2 tablespoons Limited
Vegetables; 2 servings Vegetables;
1 serving Fats; ¼ serving Milk; ¼ serving
Bonus (clam juice); 1 serving Extras
(flour)

Scrod Greek Style—page 209—Midday or
Evening Meal
1 serving Protein (4 ounces Fish);
½ cup Limited Vegetables; 2 servings
Vegetables; 1 serving Fats; 2½ servings
Extras (broth, olives, and wine)

Scrod-Vegetable Bake—page 209—Midday
or Evening Meal
1 serving Protein (4 ounces Fish);
2 servings Vegetables; 1 serving Vegetables
(optional); 1 serving Bonus (tomato
sauce)

Seafood Garden Salad (includes equivalents
for Thousand Island Dressing)—
page 219—Midday or Evening Meal
1 serving Protein (4 ounces Fish); ⅛ cup
Limited Vegetables; 4½ servings
Vegetables; 1½ servings Fats; ½ serving
Milk; 8 calories Specialty Foods
(reduced-calorie ketchup)

Sea Trout with Mushroom Stuffing—
page 213—Midday or Evening Meal
1 serving Protein (4 ounces Fish);
1½ teaspoons Limited Vegetables;
⅔ serving Vegetables; 1 serving Fats

Seviche—page 223—Midday or Evening
Meal
1 serving Protein (4 ounces Fish);
1 tablespoon Limited Vegetables;
⅛ serving Vegetables; ¾ serving Fats

Shrimp on Toast—page 224—½ Midday or
Evening Meal
½ serving Protein (2 ounces Fish);
1 serving Bread; 1 serving Fats; ½ serving
Milk; 1¾ servings Extras (flour and
tomato paste)

Shrimp Oregano—page 225—Midday or
Evening Meal
1 serving Protein (4 ounces Fish);
1 serving Fats; 1 serving Extras (flour)

Shrimp Scampi—page 225—Midday or
Evening Meal

1 serving Protein (4 ounces Fish);
½ serving Bread (bread crumbs);
⅛ serving Vegetables; 1 serving Fats

Sweet and Tangy Scrod—page 210—Midday
or Evening Meal
1 serving Protein (4 ounces Fish); ⅛ cup
Limited Vegetables; 1 serving Vegetables;
1 serving Fats; ¼ serving Fruits; 2 servings
Extras (cornstarch and sugar)

Swordfish Kebabs—page 212—Midday or
Evening Meal
1 serving Protein (4 ounces Fish);
2¾ servings Vegetables; ¼ serving Extras
(steak sauce)

Tangy Oyster-Vegetable Medley—
page 222—Midday or Evening Meal
1 serving Protein (4 ounces Fish);
2¾ servings Vegetables; ½ serving Bonus
(clam juice); 1 serving Extras (chili sauce)

Trinidad Snapper (includes equivalents for
Green Chili Sauce)—page 211—Midday
or Evening Meal
1 serving Protein (4 ounces Fish); ¼ cup
plus 2 tablespoons Limited Vegetables;
1½ servings Vegetables; 1 serving Fats

Tuna Boats—page 216—Midday or Evening
Meal
1 serving Protein (4 ounces Fish);
⅔ serving Vegetables; 2 servings Fats;
1½ servings Extras (olives and pickle
relish)

Tuna Casserole Parmesan—page 216—
Midday or Evening Meal
1 serving Protein (4 ounces Fish);
3 servings Vegetables; 1½ servings Fats;
½ serving Milk; 2 servings Extras (flour
and Parmesan cheese)

Tuna-Cheese Burgers—page 216—Midday
or Evening Meal
1 serving Protein (1 ounce Hard Cheese
and 2 ounces Fish); 1 serving Bread
(matzo); ⅛ cup Limited Vegetables;
1⅛ servings Vegetables; 2 servings Extras
(broth mix and ketchup)

Tuna "Newburg"—page 217—Midday or
Evening Meal
1 serving Protein (4 ounces Fish);
1 serving Bread; 1 tablespoon Limited
Vegetables; 1 serving Vegetables;

½ serving Fats; ¾ serving Milk;
1½ servings Extras (flour)

Tuna-Potato Cakes—page 217—Midday or
Evening Meal
1 serving Protein (1 Egg and 2 ounces
Fish); 1 serving Bread Substitutes
(potato); ¼ cup Limited Vegetables;
1 serving Extras (flour); 1 serving Extras
(honey)—optional

Tuna Ratatouille—page 218—Midday or
Evening Meal
1 serving Protein (4 ounces Fish); ½ cup
Limited Vegetables; 6¾ servings Vegetables; 1 serving Fats

Tuna Tomato Flowers—page 218—Midday
or Evening Meal
1 serving Protein (4 ounces Fish);
3 servings Vegetables; 1 serving Fats

LEGUMES AND PEANUT BUTTER

Bean and Squash Soup—page 232—Midday
or Evening Meal (Men—¾ meal)
1 (or ¾) serving Protein (6 ounces
Legumes); ½ cup Limited Vegetables;
1½ servings Fats; ½ serving Extras (broth
mix)

Bean Curd Soup—page 233—Midday or
Evening Meal (Men—add 1 ounce tofu
and ½ ounce boiled ham)
1 serving Protein (4 ounces Tofu and
1½ ounces Meat Group-cured—
Men, 5 ounces and 2 ounces);
3 tablespoons Limited Vegetables;
1 serving Vegetables; 2 servings Extras
(broth)

Chicken and Legumes Casserole—
page 234—Midday or Evening Meal
(Men—add ½ ounce each tofu and lima
beans)
1 serving Protein (2 ounces Poultry,
1½ ounces Legumes, and 2 ounces Tofu—
Men, 2 ounces Legumes and 2½ ounces
Tofu); 1 serving Fats; 1½ servings Extras
(broth and flour)

Chick Pea Croquettes (Falafel)—
page 229—Midday or Evening Meal
(Men—¾ meal)
1 (or ¾) serving Protein (6 ounces

Legumes); ½ serving Bread (bread
crumbs); 1 serving Milk

Chilled Squash and Chick Pea Salad—
page 229—½ Midday or Evening Meal
(Men—add 1 ounce chick peas)
½ serving Protein (3 ounces Legumes—
Men, 4 ounces); 3¼ servings Vegetables;
1 serving Fats

Creamed Cannellini 'n' Pasta—page 231—
½ Midday or Evening Meal (Men—add
1 ounce cannellini beans)
½ serving Protein (3 ounces Legumes—
Men, 4 ounces); 1 serving Bread
Substitutes (macaroni); ½ serving
Vegetables; 1 serving Fats; ½ serving
Milk; 1 serving Extras (flour)

Curried Kidney Beans—page 231—Midday
or Evening Meal (Men—¾ meal)
1 (or ¾) serving Protein (6 ounces
Legumes); ¼ cup plus 1 tablespoon
Limited Vegetables; 1½ servings Fats;
½ serving Fruits; 2 servings Extras (broth
and flour)

Fruit 'n' Nut Candy—page 236—½ Midday
or Evening Meal
½ serving Protein (1 tablespoon plus
1½ teaspoons Peanut Butter); ½ serving
Bread (graham crackers); 1 serving Fats
(Peanut Butter); 1 serving Fruits;
1 serving Milk; 2 servings Extras (honey)

Garbanzo-Stuffed Peppers—page 229—
½ Midday or Evening Meal (Men—add
1 ounce chick peas)
½ serving Protein (3 ounces Legumes—
Men, 4 ounces); ⅛ cup Limited
Vegetables; 3 servings Vegetables

Green Beans with Peanut Sauce—page 236—
½ Midday or Evening Meal
½ serving Protein (1 tablespoon plus
1½ teaspoons Peanut Butter); 1 serving
Vegetables; 1 serving Fats (Peanut
Butter)

Lentil and Escarole Soup—page 233—
½ Midday or Evening Meal (Men—add
1 ounce lentils)
½ serving Protein (3 ounces Legumes—
Men, 4 ounces); ¼ cup Limited Vegetables; 3 servings Vegetables; 1 serving
Fats; ⅛ serving Bonus (tomato juice)

Lunch Box Chick Pea Sandwich—
page 230—Midday or Evening Meal
(Men—add 1 ounce chick peas)
1 serving Protein (2 ounces Poultry and
3 ounces Legumes—Men, 4 ounces
Legumes); 2 servings Bread; ½ serving
Vegetables; 1 serving Fats; 1 serving
Extras (sesame seed)

Mexican Soup—page 233—Midday or
Evening Meal (Men—add 1 ounce pink
beans)
1 serving Protein (1 ounce Hard Cheese
and 3 ounces Legumes—Men, 4 ounces
Legumes); 1 serving Bread (tortilla);
⅛ cup Limited Vegetables; ½ serving
Vegetables; ¾ serving Fats; ⅔ serving
Extras (broth)

Peanut Butter Custard Cups—page 237—
Midday or Evening Meal
1 serving Protein (⅓ cup Soft Cheese and
1 tablespoon plus 1½ teaspoons Peanut
Butter); 1 serving Fats (Peanut Butter);
½ serving Fruits; ½ serving Milk;
1¼ servings Extras (gelatin and honey)

Peanut Butter Fudge—page 237—½ Midday
or Evening Meal
½ serving Protein (1 tablespoon plus
1½ teaspoons Peanut Butter); 1 serving
Fats (Peanut Butter); ¼ serving Fruits;
½ serving Milk; 2 servings Extras (honey
and sesame seed)

Peanut Butter "Ice Cream" Sandwich—
page 237—½ Midday or Evening Meal
½ serving Protein (1 tablespoon plus
1½ teaspoons Peanut Butter); 1 serving
Bread (graham crackers); 1 serving Fats
(Peanut Butter); 1 serving Fruits;
½ serving Milk

Peanut-Cheese Muffin—page 236—Morning
Meal
1 serving Protein (½ ounce Hard Cheese
and 1½ teaspoons Peanut Butter);
1 serving Bread; ½ serving Fats (Peanut
Butter); ¼ serving Extras (caraway seed)

Peanut Soup—page 236—¼ Midday or
Evening Meal
¼ serving Protein (2¼ teaspoons Peanut
Butter); ⅛ serving Bread; ¼ serving
Vegetables; ½ serving Fats (Peanut
Butter); ½ serving Extras (bouillon)

Pinto Bean Salad—page 232—Midday or
Evening Meal (Men—¾ meal)
1 (or ¾) serving Protein (6 ounces
Legumes); 1 tablespoon Limited
Vegetables; 1¼ servings Vegetables;
1 serving Fats

"Refried" Beans—page 232—Midday or
Evening Meal (Men—⅞ meal)
1 (or ⅞) serving Protein (1 ounce Hard
Cheese and 3 ounces Legumes); ¼ cup
Limited Vegetables; 1 serving Fats;
¼ serving Bonus (tomato paste)

Sautéed Chick Peas Italian Style—
page 230—Midday or Evening Meal
(Men—¾ meal)
1 (or ¾) serving Protein (6 ounces
Legumes); 1½ servings Fats; ½ serving
Bonus (tomato sauce); ½ serving Extras
(Parmesan cheese)

Savory Pinto Beans—page 232—Midday or
Evening Meal (Men—¾ meal)
1 (or ¾) serving Protein (6 ounces
Legumes); ¼ cup Limited Vegetables;
1 serving Vegetables; 1 serving Fats;
¾ serving Extras (tomato paste)

Split Pea-Mushroom Stew—page 230—
Midday or Evening Meal (Men—¾ meal)
1 (or ¾) serving Protein (6 ounces
Legumes); ½ serving Bread Substitutes
(macaroni); 2½ servings Vegetables;
½ serving Bonus (tomato paste);
1 serving Extras (broth or bouillon)

Split Pea Soup—page 230—Midday or
Evening Meal (Men—¾ meal)
1 (or ¾) serving Protein (6 ounces
Legumes); ⅛ cup Limited Vegetables;
1½ servings Vegetables; 1 serving Fats;
¼ serving Milk; 1 serving Extras (flour)

Stuffed Cherry Tomatoes—page 234—
¼ Midday or Evening Meal
(Men—⅕ meal)
¼ (or ⅕) serving Protein (2 ounces
Tofu); 1 teaspoon Limited Vegetables;
1 serving Vegetables; 1½ servings Fats

Tofu, Beans, and Eggplant—page 234—
Midday or Evening Meal (Men—add

1 ounce each kidney beans and tofu)
1 serving Protein (3 ounces Legumes and 4 ounces Tofu—Men, 4 ounces and 5 ounces); 5¼ servings Vegetables; 1 serving Bonus (tomato puree); 1 serving Extras (honey)

Tofu Casserole—page 234—Midday or Evening Meal (Men—   meal)
1 (or   ) serving Protein (1 ounce Hard Cheese and 4 ounces Tofu); 1 serving Bread Substitutes (rice); ⅛ cup Limited Vegetables; 1½ servings Vegetables; ½ serving Fats; ¼ serving Milk

Tofu Salad—page 235—½ Midday or Evening Meal (Men—add 1 ounce Tofu)
½ serving Protein (4 ounces Tofu—Men, 5 ounces); 3 tablespoons Limited Vegetables; ¾ serving Vegetables; ½ serving Fats

Tofu Sandwich sans Bread—page 235—Midday or Evening Meal (Men—   meal)
1 (or   ) serving Protein (1 Egg and 4 ounces Tofu); 1 serving Bread (bread crumbs); 1 tablespoon Limited Vegetables; 1⅛ servings Vegetables; 1 serving Fats

Tofu Vegetable Salad—page 236—¼ Midday or Evening Meal (Men—add ½ ounce tofu)
¼ serving Protein (2 ounces Tofu—Men, 2½ ounces); ¼ cup Limited Vegetables; 2½ servings Vegetables; 1 serving Fats; 1 serving Extras (olives)

Vegetable Dishes

Apple-Beet Relish—page 241
½ cup Limited Vegetables; ½ serving Vegetables; 1 serving Fats; ½ serving Fruits; 2 servings Extras (pickle relish)

Asparagus Pimiento—page 241
1 serving Vegetables

Baked Broccoli with Mustard Sauce—page 242
2⅔ servings Vegetables; ½ serving Fats; ¼ serving Milk; ½ serving Extras (flour)

Baked Eggplant Slices—page 246
2 servings Vegetables
Variation I—Add ½ serving Extras (ketchup) to Baked Eggplant Slices
Variation II—Add 1 serving Vegetables to Baked Eggplant Slices

Baked Spiced Acorn Squash—page 249
½ cup Limited Vegetables; ½ serving Extras (honey)

Broccoli Medley—page 242
¼ cup Limited Vegetables; 5 servings Vegetables; ½ serving Fats; 1 serving Extras (olives)

Broiled Onion-Topped Tomatoes—page 251
¼ cup Limited Vegetables; 2 servings Vegetables; 1 serving Extras (sugar)

Broiled Tomato—page 251
1 serving Vegetables

Cauliflower with Mushroom Sauce—page 245
1½ teaspoons Limited Vegetables; 2½ servings Vegetables; 1 serving Fats; ¼ serving Milk; 2 servings Extras (flour and Parmesan cheese)

Cardoons Milanaise—page 244
½ serving Bread (bread crumbs); 3 servings Vegetables; 1 serving Fats; 1 serving Extras (Parmesan cheese)

Colache—page 252
1 serving Bread Substitutes (corn); ¼ cup Limited Vegetables; 2½ servings Vegetables; ¾ serving Fats

Creamed Kale and Onions—page 248
½ cup Limited Vegetables; 2 servings Vegetables; 1 serving Fats; ¼ serving Milk; 1 serving Extras (flour)

Creamed Rutabaga—page 248
½ cup Limited Vegetables; ⅛ serving Vegetables; ½ serving Fats; ⅛ serving Milk

Creamed Spinach—page 249
1 serving Vegetables; ½ serving Fats; ¼ serving Milk; 2 servings Extras (Parmesan cheese)

Creamy Broccoli—page 242
1 serving Vegetables; 1 serving Fats; ¼ serving Milk; 1 serving Extras (flour)

Curried Cauliflower—page 246

¼ cup Limited Vegetables; 2½ servings
Vegetables; 1 serving Fats
Eggplant and Zucchini Casserole—page 247
¼ cup Limited Vegetables; 2¼ servings
Vegetables; 1 serving Fats; 1 serving
Extras (chili sauce)
Escarole and Tomato Medley—page 251
3 servings Vegetables; 1 serving Fats
Fennel Parmesan—page 247
2 servings Vegetables; 1½ servings Extras
(broth and Parmesan cheese)
Ginger-Spiced Bean Sprouts and Onions—
page 241
½ cup Limited Vegetables; 3½ servings
Vegetables; 1 serving Fats
Green Beans and Tomatoes Hungarian
Style—page 247
cup Limited Vegetables; 3 servings
Vegetables; 1 serving Fats
Hearts of Artichoke Arreganata—page 241
½ serving Bread (bread crumbs); ½ cup
Limited Vegetables; 1 serving Extras
(Parmesan cheese)
Herbed Vegetables—page 252
5½ servings Vegetables; 1 serving Fats
Herb-Stuffed Tomatoes—page 252
¼ serving Vegetables; ¼ serving Milk
Marinated Carrots—page 244
2 servings Vegetables
Minted Carrots—page 245
1 serving Vegetables; ½ serving Fruits
Orange Broccoli—page 243
3 servings Vegetables; ¾ serving Fats;
½ serving Fruits
Pimiento-Topped Steamed Broccoli—
page 243
1⅓ servings Vegetables
Sautéed Caraway Cabbage—page 243
⅛ cup Limited Vegetables; 6 servings
Vegetables; 1 serving Fats; ½ serving
Extras (broth and caraway seed)
Sautéed Mushrooms and Onions—page 248
¼ cup Limited Vegetables; 1 serving
Vegetables; ½ serving Fats
Sautéed Salsify—page 248
½ cup Limited Vegetables; 1 serving Fats
Seasoned Cucumber Bake—page 246
2½ servings Vegetables; 1 serving Fats
Sesame and Ginger Carrots—page 245

2 servings Vegetables; 1 serving Fats;
1 serving Extras (sesame seed)
Slow-Cooked Vegetable Medley—page 252
½ cup Limited Vegetables; 4 servings
Vegetables; 1 serving Fats
Spaghetti Squash Pesto—page 249
2 servings Vegetables; 1¼ servings Fats;
1 serving Extras (Parmesan cheese)
Spaghetti Squash with Tomato Sauce—
page 250
¼ cup Limited Vegetables; 5 servings
Vegetables; 1 serving Fats; ½ serving
Extras (honey)
Squash Parmesan—page 250
4 servings Vegetables; 1 serving Fats;
1 serving Extras (Parmesan cheese)
Stir-Fried Cabbage 'N' Squash—page 244
3 servings Vegetables; ½ serving Fats;
1 serving Extras (olives)
Stir-Fry Pea Pods—page 248
½ cup Limited Vegetables; ½ serving
Fats; ¼ serving Extras (broth mix)
Sweet and Sour Cabbage—page 244
¼ cup Limited Vegetables; 2 servings
Vegetables; 1 serving Fats; ½ serving
Fruits
Vegetable Medley—page 253
½ cup Limited Vegetables; 4¾ servings
Vegetables
Vegetable Pilaf—page 253
1 serving Bread Substitutes (rice); ¼ cup
Limited Vegetables; 1 serving Vegetables; ½ serving Fats; 1 serving Fruits
Vegetable-Stuffed Cabbage Leaves—
page 253
4½ servings Vegetables; ½ serving Bonus
(tomato sauce)
Vegetable-Stuffed Grape Leaves—
page 254
2¼ servings Vegetables; ⅜ serving Bonus
(tomato juice)
Zucchini Italian Style—page 250
3 servings Vegetables
Zucchini Spaghetti—page 250
2 servings Vegetables; ¾ serving Fats
Zucchini Sticks—page 251
½ serving Bread (bread crumbs);
2 servings Vegetables; ½ serving Extras
(bacon bits)

GRAINS, PASTA, AND POTATOES

Applesauce Oatmeal—page 257—Morning Meal
1 serving Protein (¾ ounce Cereal with milk); ½ serving Fruits; ½ serving Milk

Bacon-Flavored Potato Salad—page 267
1 serving Bread Substitutes (potato); ⅛ cup Limited Vegetables; 1 serving Fats; 1 serving Extras (bacon bits)

Baked Yams—page 270
1 serving Bread Substitutes (yam)

Banana Bread Pudding—page 260—
1 Morning or ½ Midday or Evening Meal
1 or ½ serving Protein (1 Egg); 1 serving Bread; 1 serving Fruits; ½ serving Milk; 1 serving Extras (honey)

Basil Macaroni—page 265
1 serving Bread Substitutes (macaroni); ¼ cup Limited Vegetables; ½ serving Extras (broth)

Bran Waffles—page 261—1 Morning or ½ Midday or Evening Meal
1 or ½ serving Protein (1 Egg); 1½ servings Bread (cereal and flour); 1 serving Fats; ½ serving Milk

Bread Pudding—page 260—1 Morning or ½ Midday or Evening Meal
1 or ½ serving Protein (1 Egg); 1 serving Bread; ½ serving Milk

Bulgur Pilaf—page 264
1 serving Bread Substitutes (cracked wheat); cup Limited Vegetables; serving Vegetables; ½ serving Extras (broth mix)

Buttermilk Pancakes—page 262
½ serving Bread Substitutes (cornmeal); ½ serving Bread (flour); ⅓ serving Milk; 1 serving Extras (sugar); 16 calories Specialty Foods (fruit-flavored spread)

Canadian Parsley Soup—page 266
½ serving Bread Substitutes (potato); 1 serving Vegetables; ¾ serving Extras (broth)

Cereal with Spiced Fruit Ambrosia—
page 257—Morning Meal
1 serving Protein (¾ ounce Cereal with milk); 1 serving Fruits; 1 serving Milk; 1 serving Extras (coconut)

Chick Peas (Garbanzos) with Tiny Shells—page 266
1 serving Bread Substitutes (chick peas and macaroni); 1½ teaspoons Limited Vegetables; 1 serving Fats

Cornmeal Pancakes—page 262
1 serving Bread Substitutes (cornmeal); 1 serving Bread (flour); 1 serving Fats; ⅔ serving Milk; 12 calories Specialty Foods (strawberry spread)

Corn Muffins—page 260—1 Morning or ½ Midday or Evening Meal
1 or ½ serving Protein (1 Egg); 1 serving Bread Substitutes (corn); 1 serving Bread (flour); 1½ servings Fats; serving Milk; 2 servings Extras (sugar)

Creamy Apple-Raisin Oatmeal—page 257—Morning Meal
1 serving Protein (¾ ounce Cereal with milk); 1 serving Fruits; 1 serving Milk; 1 serving Extras (honey)
Variation—Apple-Raisin Oatmeal—
Reduce Milk equivalent to ½ serving.

Creamy Potato Salad—page 267—Midday or Evening Meal
1 serving Protein (1 Egg and ⅓ cup Soft Cheese); 1 serving Bread Substitutes (potato); 1 tablespoon plus 1½ teaspoons Limited Vegetables; 1 serving Fats

Curried Pasta with Gingered Peas—page 265
1 serving Bread Substitutes (spaghetti); ½ cup Limited Vegetables; 1 serving Fats

Eggplant Stuffing—page 263
½ serving Bread Substitutes (rice); ½ serving Bread; ¼ cup Limited Vegetables; 3½ servings Vegetables

Fruit and Yam Salad with Honeyed Yogurt Dressing—page 271
½ serving Bread Substitutes (yam); 1 serving Fruits; ¼ serving Milk; 1 serving Extras (honey)

Fruited Bread Pudding—page 261—
1 Morning or ½ Midday or Evening Meal
1 or ½ serving Protein (1 Egg); 1 serving Bread; 1 serving Fruits; 1 serving Milk

Fruited Matzo Kugel—page 262—
1 Morning or ½ Midday or Evening Meal
1 or ½ serving Protein (1 Egg); ¾ serving Bread (matzo meal); 2 servings Fats;

1 serving Fruits; 3 servings Extras (honey, potato starch, and sugar)

Garlic Bread—page 259
1 serving Bread; 1 serving Fats

Granola—page 258—Morning Meal
1 serving Protein (¾ ounce Cereal with milk); 1 serving Bread Substitutes (barley); 2 servings Fats; ½ serving Fruits; 1 serving Milk; 1 serving Extras (honey)

Holiday Noodle Pudding—page 266—¼ Midday or Evening Meal
¼ serving Protein (½ Egg); 1 serving Bread Substitutes (noodles); 1 serving Fats; 1 serving Fruits; 1 serving Extras (sugar)

Homemade White Bread—page 258
1-ounce slice = 1 serving Bread
Variation—Homemade Whole Wheat Bread—1-ounce slice = 1 serving Bread

Honey-Glazed Yams—page 270
1 serving Bread Substitutes (yam); 1 serving Extras (honey)

Honey-Wheat Muffins—page 260
1⅔ servings Bread (cereal and flour); 1 serving Fats; ⅓ serving Milk; 2 servings Extras (honey); 4 calories Specialty Foods (fruit-flavored spread)—optional

Kasha Mix—page 264
1 serving Bread Substitutes (buckwheat groats and rice); ½ serving Vegetables; ½ serving Extras (broth)

Linguine Primavera—page 265
1 serving Bread Substitutes (linguine); 1¾ servings Vegetables; 2 servings Fats; 1 serving Extras (Parmesan cheese)

Mandarin Rice Salad—page 263
1 serving Bread Substitutes (rice); 1 serving Vegetables; 1 serving Fats; ½ serving Fruits

Melba Toast Parmesan—page 259
1 serving Bread (melba toast); 1½ teaspoons Limited Vegetables; ¾ serving Extras (Parmesan cheese)

Melba Toast Puffs—page 259
1 serving Bread (melba toast); ⅛ cup Limited Vegetables; 1 serving Fats; ⅛ serving Milk; 1 serving Extras (Parmesan cheese)

Millet with Vegetables—page 264
1 serving Bread Substitutes (millet); ½ cup Limited Vegetables; ½ serving Vegetables; 1 serving Fats; ½ serving Extras (broth mix)

Mock Hummus with Vegetable Dippers—page 271
1 serving Bread Substitutes (chick-peas and yam); 2 servings Vegetables; 1 serving Extras (sesame seed)

Mock Kishka—page 263
1 serving Bread (matzo); 1 tablespoon Limited Vegetables; ½ serving Vegetables; ¾ serving Fats

Parsley Potatoes—page 268
1 serving Bread Substitutes (potato)

Pasta Kugel—page 266—Midday or Evening Meal
1 serving Protein (1 Egg and ⅓ cup Soft Cheese); 1 serving Bread Substitutes (mafalde); ½ serving Fruits; ¼ serving Milk; 1 serving Extras (honey)

Potato and Green Bean Salad—page 268
1 serving Bread Substitutes (potato); ¼ cup Limited Vegetables; 2 servings Vegetables; 1 serving Fats

Potato Crisps—page 268
1 serving Bread Substitutes (potato)

Potato Pancakes—page 268—½ Midday or Evening Meal
½ serving Protein (1 Egg); 1 serving Bread Substitutes (potato); ½ serving Bread (flour); ⅛ cup Limited Vegetables; 1 serving Fats

Potato Pie—page 268—Midday or Evening Meal
1 serving Protein (2 Eggs); 1 serving Bread Substitutes (potato); ¼ cup Limited Vegetables; 1¼ servings Vegetables; 1 serving Extras (Parmesan cheese)

Potato-Pumpkin Puffs—page 269
1 serving Bread Substitutes (potato); ¼ cup Limited Vegetables; 1 serving Fats

Potato-Rice Casserole—page 269
1 serving Bread Substitutes (potato and rice); ¼ cup Limited Vegetables; 1 serving Fats; ½ serving Milk; 1 serving Extras (flour)

Potato Soup—page 267
1 serving Bread Substitutes (potato);
⅛ cup Limited Vegetables; ¼ serving
Vegetables; 1 serving Fats; ½ serving
Milk; ½ serving Extras (broth)

Potato-Spinach Combo—page 269—
½ Midday or Evening Meal
½ serving Protein (1 Egg); 1 serving
Bread Substitutes (potato); ½ serving
Vegetables; 1 serving Fats

Rice Crisps—page 264
½ serving Bread Substitutes (rice);
½ serving Bread (tortilla); 1 serving
Extras (Parmesan cheese)

Spinach-Yam Loaf—page 271—½ Midday
or Evening Meal
½ serving Protein (1 Egg); 1 serving
Bread Substitutes (yam); 1 serving
Vegetables

Sweet Potato Tzimmes—page 272
1 serving Bread Substitutes (sweet
potato); 1 serving Vegetables; ½ serving
Fruits; 16 calories Specialty Foods
(marmalade)

Vegetable Mold—page 270
1 serving Bread Substitutes (potato);
4¼ servings Vegetablts

SALADS

Apple Cider Slaw—page 275
1½ teaspoons Limited Vegetables;
4 servings Vegetables; 1 serving Fats;
¼ serving Fruits

Bean Salad—page 278
3¾ servings Vegetables; 1 serving Fats

Braised Leek Salad—page 279
½ cup Limited Vegetables; 1¼ servings
Vegetables; 1½ servings Fats; ½ serving
Extras (broth)

Broccoli Salad—page 275
2¼ teaspoons Limited Vegetables;
2½ servings Vegetables; 2 servings Fats;
½ serving Extras (olive)

Cauliflower Salad—page 276
2⅛ servings Vegetables; 1 serving Fats;
1 serving Extras (olives)

Chilled Vegetable Salad—page 280
¼ cup plus 2 tablespoons Limited
Vegetables; 2¼ servings Vegetables;
1 serving Fats; ½ serving Extras (sesame
seed)

Cole Slaw Vinaigrette—page 276
1¾ servings Vegetables; 2 servings Fats

Crispy-Crunchy Salad—page 280
2½ servings Vegetables; 1 serving Fats

Cucumber and Tomato Salad—page 277
4¼ servings Vegetables; 1½ servings Fats;
1 serving Extras (bacon bits)

Cucumber-Radish Salad—page 277
2¼ servings Vegetables; ¼ serving Fats

Curried Cole Slaw—page 276
2½ servings Vegetables

Eggplant and Pepper Salad—page 278
4½ servings Vegetables; 2¼ servings Fats

Endive and Beet Salad—page 278
½ cup Limited Vegetables; 2 servings
Vegetables; 1 serving Fats

Fruit Slaw—page 276
2 servings Vegetables; ¾ serving Fats;
½ serving Fruits; ¼ serving Milk;
1½ servings Extras (sesame seed)

Green Bean Confetti Salad—page 278
1½ teaspoons Limited Vegetables;
2⅔ servings Vegetables; 1 serving Fats

Green Goddess Salad—page 281
¼ cup Limited Vegetables; 2 servings
Vegetables; 1 serving Fats; ½ serving Milk

Holiday Salad—page 280
2⅔ servings Vegetables; 1 serving Fats

Lemony Brussels Sprouts and Carrots
Salad—page 275
½ cup Limited Vegetables; 5 servings
Vegetables; 1 serving Fats

Mixed Vegetable Salad—page 281
¼ cup plus 2 tablespoons Limited
Vegetables; 3⅔ servings Vegetables

Oriental Salad—page 282
¼ cup Limited Vegetables; 3 servings
Vegetables; 1 serving Fats; 1 serving Extras
(sesame seed)

Oriental-Style Spinach Salad—page 279
¼ cup Limited Vegetables; 3 servings
Vegetables; 1 serving Fats; 1 serving
Extras (sesame seed)

Radish Salad—page 279
2 teaspoons Limited Vegetables; 2 servings
Vegetables; ½ serving Fats

Red Leaf Salad—page 279
  2 servings Vegetables; ¾ serving Fats
Relish Salad—page 282
  2½ servings Vegetables; 1 serving Fats
Sunchoke and Kraut Salad—page 280
  ½ cup Limited Vegetables; 2 servings
  Vegetables
Tomato-Cucumber Raito—page 277
  2⅓ servings Vegetables; 1 serving Milk
Vegetable Salad with Relish Dressing—
  page 282
  ½ cup Limited Vegetables; 2 servings
  Vegetables; 1 serving Fats; 1 serving
  Extras (pickle relish)
White Salad—page 277
  4⅔ servings Vegetables

SAUCES, SALAD DRESSINGS, AND DIPS

Basic Vinaigrette—page 286
  1 serving Fats
  Variations
  Chili Vinaigrette
    1 serving Fats; ¼ serving Extras (chili
    sauce)
  Cider Vinaigrette
    1 serving Fats
  Garlic Vinaigrette
    1 serving Fats
  Gingered Vinaigrette
    1 serving Fats
  Oregano Vinaigrette
    1 serving Fats
  Savory Vinaigrette
    1 serving Fats
  Tarragon Vinaigrette
    1 serving Fats
  Vinaigrette Parmesan
    1 serving Fats; ½ serving Extras
    (Parmesan cheese)
  Wine Vinaigrette
    1 serving Fats
Creamy Oriental Dressing—page 288
  ¾ serving Fats; ½ serving Milk
Curry Dip—page 289
  ¼ serving Milk
Dijon-Herb Dressing—page 287
  ½ serving Fats

Dill Vinaigrette—page 287
  1½ servings Fats
Garlic "Butter"—page 285
  1½ servings Fats
Green Chili Sauce—page 285
  ¼ cup Limited Vegetables; 1⅛ servings
  Vegetables
Green Goddess Salad Dressing—page 282
  1 serving Milk
Herb Dressing—page 287
  1½ servings Fats
Homemade Mayonnaise—page 288
  1 teaspoon = 1 serving Fats
Horseradish-Chili Sauce—page 285
  1 serving Extras (chili sauce)
Lemon "Butter" Sauce—page 285
  1 serving Fats; 1⅓ servings Extras
  (cornstarch and wine)
Lemon Salad Dressing—page 288
  ¾ serving Fats
Lime Yogurt Dip with Crudités—page 289
  2 servings Vegetables; 1 serving Milk
Marinara Sauce—page 285
  ½ cup = 1⅓ servings Vegetables;
  ½ serving Fats
  1 cup = 2⅔ servings Vegetables; 1 serving
  Fats
Mushroom Gravy—page 286
  1 serving Vegetables; 2   servings Extras
  (broth and flour)
Orange-Apricot Sauce—page 286
  ½ serving Fruits; 1¼ servings Extras
  (cornstarch and wine); 16 calories
  Specialty Foods (apricot spread)
Pesto Dressing—page 288
  ¾ serving Fats; ½ serving Milk
Russian Dressing—page 288
  1 serving Fats; 1½ servings Extras (chili
  sauce and pickle relish)
Sesame Vinaigrette—page 287
  ¼ serving Fats
Thousand Island Dressing—page 288
  1 teaspoon Vegetables; ¾ serving Fats;
  ½ serving Milk; 8 calories Specialty Foods
  (reduced-calorie ketchup)
Yogurt-Chive Dip—page 289
  ⅛ serving Vegetables; ¼ serving Milk
Yogurt Dip or Dressing—page 289
  ¼ recipe = 1½ teaspoons Vegetables;

¼ serving Milk
½ recipe = ⅛ serving Vegetables;
½ serving Milk

Desserts, Snacks, and Beverages

Apple Compote—page 293
1 serving Fruits
Autumn Treat—page 304
1 serving Extras (coconut); 14 calories
Specialty Foods (low-calorie gelatin and
whipped topping)
Baked Apple—page 293
1 serving Fruits
Banana and Raisin Pudding Cake—
page 296—¼ Midday or Evening Meal
¼ serving Protein (½ Egg); ½ serving
Bread; 1 serving Fruits; ⅜ serving Milk
(⅛ cup each skim milk and yogurt);
1 serving Extras (sugar)
Banana-Apple Soft "Ice Cream"—page 305
¾ serving Fruits; 1 serving Milk; 1 serving
Extras (honey)
Banana "Cream"—page 301
1 serving Fruits; 1 serving Milk; 2 servings
Extras (cornstarch and honey)
Banana-Prune Pudding—page 302
1 serving Fruits; ¼ serving Milk;
¼ serving Extras (gelatin); 1 calorie
Specialty Foods (diet soda)
Berries with Lemon-Cinnamon Yogurt—
page 294
½ serving Fruits; 1 serving Milk; 1 serving
Extras (honey)
Bittersweet Chocolate "Cream"—page 302
½ serving Milk; 2¾ servings Extras
(cocoa and gelatin)
Broiled Grapefruit—page 294
1 serving Fruits
Carrot-Apple Pudding—page 302—
½ Midday or Evening Meal
½ serving Protein (1 Egg); ½ serving
Bread (flour); ½ serving Vegetables;
½ serving Fats; ¾ serving Fruits
Carrot-Pumpkin Pudding—page 302
¼ cup Limited Vegetables; 1½ servings
Vegetables; 1 serving Fats; 1 serving
Fruits; 1 serving Extras (cornstarch)

Cherry Cobbler—page 299
½ serving Bread; 1 serving Fruits;
2 servings Extras (cornstarch and sugar)
Cherry Tarts—page 300
1 serving Bread (graham crackers);
1 serving Fats; 1 serving Fruits; 1 serving
Extras (arrowroot); 3 calories Specialty
Foods (whipped topping)—optional
Coconut-Coffee Mounds—page 296
½ serving Milk; ½ serving Extras
(coconut)
Coconut-Honey Shake—page 308
½ serving Milk; 2 servings Extras
(coconut and honey)
Coconut-Orange Gelatin—page 304
½ serving Fruits; 1 serving Extras
(coconut); 8 calories Specialty Foods
(low-calorie gelatin)
Coffee-Yogurt Shake—page 308
½ serving Milk; 1 serving Extras (sugar)
Cream Puffs with Strawberry Sauce—
page 296—¼ Midday or Evening Meal
¼ serving Protein (½ Egg); ½ serving
Bread (flour); 2 servings Fats; 1½ servings
Fruits; ½ serving Milk
"Fallen" Strawberry Cheesecake—
page 297—Midday or Evening Meal
1 serving Protein (1 Egg and ⅓ cup Soft
Cheese); 1¼ servings Bread (flour and
graham crackers); 1 serving Fats;
½ serving Fruits; ¼ serving Milk;
1½ servings Extras (flour and sugar);
16 calories Specialty Foods (strawberry
spread)
Frozen Apple-Banana Dessert—page 306
1 serving Fruits; 1 serving Milk
Frozen Mango Yogurt—page 306
1 serving Fruits; ½ serving Milk
Fruited Custard Pie—page 300
½ serving Bread (flour); 1 serving Fats;
½ serving Fruits; 1½ teaspoons Yogurt
(serving Milk); ½ serving Milk
Substitutes; 12 calories Specialty Foods
(apricot spread)
Fruited Yogurt Mold—page 304
1 serving Fruits; 1 serving Milk; 1 serving
Extras (gelatin and honey)
Fruit Mélange—page 294
¾ serving Fruits

Fruit "Pie"—page 300
½ serving Fruits; ¼ serving Extras
(gelatin)
Honey-Glazed Pears—page 295
1 serving Fruits; 1 serving Extras (honey)
Honey-Stewed Prunes—page 295
1 serving Fruits; ½ serving Extras (honey)
Hot Cocoa—page 307
1 serving Milk; 1 serving Extras (cocoa)
Hot Mocha Milk—page 308
½ cup = ½ serving Milk; ½ serving
Extras (cocoa)
1 cup = 1 serving Milk; 1 serving Extras
(cocoa)
Hot Spiced Tea—page 308
Use in reasonable amounts
Lady Fingers—page 298—½ Midday or
Evening Meal
½ serving Protein (1 Egg); 1 serving
Bread (flour); 1 serving Fruits; 3 servings
Extras (sugar)
Lemonade—page 310
Use in reasonable amounts
Lime Cooler—page 310
Use in reasonable amounts
Lime-Orange Ice in Lime Cups—page 307
1 serving Fruits
Mandarin Chiffon Pie—page 301
1 serving Bread (graham crackers);
1 serving Fats; ¾ serving Fruits;
⅜ serving Milk (3 tablespoons yogurt);
½ serving Extras (gelatin)
Melon Mousse—page 303
1 serving Fruits; ½ serving Milk; 1 serving
Extras (gelatin)
Mocha Sundae—page 307
1 serving Fruits; ½ serving Milk;
½ serving Extras (coconut); 8 calories
Specialty Foods (chocolate topping)
Oatmeal-Raisin Loaf—page 298—½ Midday
or Evening Meal
½ serving Protein (1 Egg); 1 serving
Bread (quick oats); ½ serving Fruits;
1 serving Milk; 1 serving Extras (honey);
12 calories Specialty Foods (fruit-flavored
spread)—optional
Open-Face "Ice Cream" Sandwich—
page 307

½ serving Bread (graham cracker);
¾ serving Fruits; ¼ serving Milk
Orange Ambrosia—page 294
1 serving Fruits; 2 servings Extras (coconut
and honey)
Orange-Strawberry Cups—page 295
1 serving Fruits; 2 servings Extras (coconut
and honey)
Oven-Stewed Prunes—page 295
1 serving Fruits
Pear Frozen Yogurt—page 306
1 serving Fruits; 1 serving Milk
Piña Freeze—page 306
1 serving Fruits; 1 serving Milk
Pineapple-Banana Milk Shake—page 308
1 serving Fruits; ½ serving Milk
Pineapple-Coconut Cookies—page 296
1 serving Bread (flour); ½ serving Fruits;
1 serving Milk; 1 serving Extras (coconut)
Pineapple-Mango "Ice Cream"—page 306
1 serving Fruits; ½ serving Milk
Pineapple-Orange Pudding—page 303
½ serving Fruits; ½ serving Milk;
½ serving Extras (gelatin)
Pineapple-Strawberry Whip—page 309
1½ servings Fruits
Pineapple-Yogurt Pudding—page 304
½ serving Bread (graham cracker);
½ serving Fruits; ½ serving Milk;
½ serving Extras (gelatin)
Pineapple-Yogurt Shake—page 309
1 serving Fruits; 1 serving Milk; 1 serving
Extras (sugar)
Raisin-Popcorn Snack—page 295
1 serving Bread Substitutes (popcorn);
1 serving Fruits; 1 serving Extras (honey)
Raspberry-Grape Yogurt—page 294
1 serving Bread (cereal nuggets); 1 serving
Fruits; 1 serving Milk; 16 calories
Specialty Foods (raspberry spread)
Red, White, and Blue Parfait—page 294
1 serving Fruits; ½ serving Milk; 6 calories
Specialty Foods (whipped topping)
Root Beer Froth—page 310
½ serving Milk; 1 calorie Specialty Foods
(diet soda)
Spiced Pineapple Pumpkin—page 304
½ cup Limited Vegetables; 1½ servings

Fruits; 1¼ servings Extras (gelatin and honey)

Spiced Pumpkin Cake—page 298—
¼ Midday or Evening Meal
¼ serving Protein (½ Egg); 1 serving Bread (flour); 1 tablespoon Limited Vegetables; 1 serving Fats

Stewed Dried Apricots—page 293
1 serving Fruits

Strawberry-Apple Frost—page 309
1 serving Fruits; 1 serving Milk; 1 serving Extras (sugar)

Strawberry Shake—page 309
1 serving Fruits; ½ serving Milk

Swedish Apple Bake—page 299—1 Morning or ½ Midday or Evening Meal
1 or ½ serving Protein (1 Egg); 1 serving Bread (flour); 1 serving Fruits; 1 serving Extras (honey)

Stuffed Baked Apple—page 293
1½ servings Fruits; 1½ servings Extras (coconut and honey)

Tropical Treat—page 305
1 serving Fruits; ¼ serving Extras (gelatin); 4 calories Specialty Foods (diet soda and whipped topping)

Yogurt-Banana Shake—page 309
1 serving Fruits; 1 serving Milk; 1 serving Extras (honey)

Index

Photographs of recipes are indicated by page numbers in italics.

Notes

WEIGHT WATCHERS®
International Cookbook

*More than 750 recipe adaptations from
around the world including
Appetizers, Soups, Meats, Poultry, Fish, Eggs,
Cheese Dishes, Breads, Pastas, Vegetables, Salads,
Fruits, Pastries, Desserts, and Beverages from:*

*FRANCE • ITALY • AUSTRIA AND HUNGARY •
GERMANY • SPAIN • GREECE • CHINA •
JAPAN • THE UNITED STATES • AND 15
OTHER PARTS OF THE WORLD*

Introduction by
JEAN NIDETCH

Plume Softcover Edition: $7.95 U.S., $9.95 Canada (0-452-25416-7)
NAL Hardcover: $11.95 U.S., $12.95 Canada (0-453-01004-0)

To order, use the convenient coupon on the last page.

Everyone knows that the hardest time
to stay on a diet is when you're entertaining,
especially around the holidays . . .

WEIGHT WATCHERS®

PARTY & HOLIDAY COOKBOOK

Over 400 recipes for every season and occasion
including: Appetizers, Soups, Meats, Poultry,
Fish, Eggs, Cheese Dishes, Breads, Pastas, Salads,
Vegetables, Fruits, Desserts, and Beverages.

With a Foreword by Jean Nidetch

Plume Softcover Edition: $7.95 U.S., $8.95 Canada (0-452-25324-1)
NAL Hardcover: $12.95 U.S., $13.95 Canada (0-453-01005-9)

To order, use the convenient coupon on the last page.

WEIGHT WATCHERS®
FOOD PLAN DIET COOKBOOK

NEARLY 600 SAVORY RECIPES
THE COMPLETE UP-TO-DATE FOOD PLAN
USED BY THE WORLD'S MOST SUCCESSFUL
WEIGHT-CONTROL ORGANIZATION

---

by

JEAN NIDETCH

The first cookbook based on Weight Watchers Full Choice, Limited Choice, and No Choice food plans, with almost 600 delectable new recipes created specifically for these plans.

This revised Weight Watchers program and the recipes included here allow you to indulge in foods such as peanut butter, popcorn, coconut, honey, and sugar, to cook with and drink beer and wine, and to relish both stir-fried and sautéed foods.

NAL Hardcover $13.95 U.S., $16.95 Canada (0-453-01007-5)

To order, use the convenient coupon on the last page.

WEIGHT WATCHERS® COOKBOOKS for Your Enjoyment
(0452—0453)

WEIGHT WATCHERS®
International Cookbook

☐ NAL Hardcover Edition (010040—$11.95 U.S., $12.95 Canada)
☐ PLUME Softcover Edition (254167—$7.95 U.S., $9.95 Canada)

WEIGHT WATCHERS®
PARTY & HOLIDAY COOKBOOK

☐ NAL Hardcover Edition (010059—$12.95 U.S., $13.95 Canada)
☐ PLUME Softcover Edition (253241—$7.95 U.S., $8.95 Canada)

WEIGHT WATCHERS®
FOOD PLAN DIET COOKBOOK

☐ NAL Hardcover Edition (010075—$13.95 U.S., $16.95 Canada)
